PSYCHOLOGY IN CONTEXT

PSYCHOLOGY IN CONTEXT

Voices and Perspectives

David N. Sattler

College of Charleston

Virginia Shabatay

Palomar College

HOUGHTON MIFFLIN COMPANY   Boston   New York

Sponsoring Editor: David C. Lee
Editorial Assistant: Gwen Fairweather
Senior Project Editor: Carol Newman
Production/Design Coordinator: Jennifer Meyer
Senior Manufacturing Coordinator: Priscilla Bailey
Marketing Manager: David Lenehan

Cover Design: Harold Burch, Harold Burch Design, NYC
Cover Photographs: Eric Perry-Photonica (upper left); © 1995 Neo Vision-Photonica (upper right);
Y. Hirota-Photonica (lower left); © 1993 Allan Montaine-Photonica (lower right).

Printed in the U.S.A.

Library of Congress Catalog Card Number: 96-76957

ISBN: 0-395-75749-5

1 2 3 4 5 6 7 8 9-DH-00 99 98 97 96

To my father, Jerome M. Sattler
with deep respect and love
to Alden "Doc" Holmes and Clyde L. Glasson
for friendship, and for passing along their love of nature
and long walks in the High Sierra
and
to my wife, Sudie Back Sattler
for sharing poetry and beauty, joy and love

DAVID N. SATTLER

To Heidi Sattler Philips
with love, and for all that binds us as mother and daughter
and
to Yehuda Shabatay, husband and friend
for his stories and songs, laughter and love

VIRGINIA SHABATAY

Brief Contents

Contents

1

PHYSIOLOGICAL BASES OF BEHAVIOR   1

Carnal Acts   3

Nancy Mairs

> **Psychological Concepts:** multiple sclerosis, myelin, axon, cell body, dendrite, synapse
>
> A gifted writer duels with the progression of multiple sclerosis, a slowly debilitating disease that has conquered neither her spirit nor her talent.

Journey with Grandpa: Our Family's Struggle with Alzheimer's Disease   7

Rosalie Walsh Honel

> **Psychological Concepts:** Alzheimer's disease, hippocampus, limbic system
>
> A family portrays the pain of living with a relative who has Alzheimer's disease and who deals with his increasing memory losses with anger and resistance.

Newton's Madness: Further Tales of Clinical Neurology   12

Harold L. Klawans

> **Psychological Concepts:** Parkinson's disease, substantia nigra, striatum, dopamine
>
> A successful businessman who develops Parkinson's disease is "not ready to be a shaky old man" and wants to try an experimental drug whose safety and effectiveness are unknown.

2

SENSATION AND PERCEPTION   27

3

CONSCIOUSNESS   47

4

LEARNING   70

5

MEMORY 89

6

THOUGHT AND LANGUAGE 113

7

HUMAN DEVELOPMENT   137

8

MENTAL ABILITIES   162

10

PERSONALITY   199

11

PSYCHOLOGICAL DISORDERS 221

12

HEALTH, STRESS, AND COPING   250

13

SOCIAL THOUGHT AND SOCIAL BEHAVIOR   277

Preface

Our experience in teaching introduction to psychology has convinced us that students are enriched by reading personal narratives and essays written by people whose experiences are at the core of what we study in the classroom. This book presents a collection of essays by individuals who write about their personal experience with autism, consciousness, memory loss, learning, posttraumatic stress disorder, development, language, prejudice, and giftedness, to name just a few. Such themes are the substance of psychology, and students respond with enthusiasm whenever we use these works in class.

Our goals for *Psychology in Context: Voices and Perspectives* are the following:

- To promote students' retention of psychological concepts and to spark their interest in the subject matter by presenting key psychological concepts in the context of personal narratives and essays.

- To promote active learning by challenging students to consider, think critically about, and discuss narratives and essays as they relate to the psychological principles and concepts presented in the course textbook.

- To broaden students' perspectives on human behavior and mental processes by including selections that explore multicultural, cross-cultural, and gender issues.

Personal-Academic Approach to Teaching Psychology

We constantly encourage students to question and to see another's perspective. We can define an issue and examine its causes and effects, but not until we feel it "on the pulse," to use a phrase of John Keats, will we know something of the inner experience of another person. Students respond positively to personal accounts because something of themselves is called forth. Consider the following:

An African-American man, a graduate student at the University of Chicago, walks at night. Women run, car doors click. Others run from him; suspect, he runs from them. What is it like to be pursued by stereotypes and prejudice? Sociology tells us, history tells us, poets tell us, biology tells us, psychology tells us. But here, Brent Staples, now an editor on the *New York Times*, tells us, "My first victim was a woman," and we are hooked by the intrigue.

When we get students interested, then we and they have begun our work together. Being interested means being responsive, which leads to bringing forth ideas, thinking critically, seeing linkages, making hypothesis, and embarking on research. The personal narratives and essays in this book will excite, anger, and inspire readers.

Criteria for Selecting the Readings

We used several criteria for selecting the narratives and essays. First, each piece had to be provocative: it had to arouse us, send us into discussion, and stir us with questions. Second, the material had to place important psychological concepts in a context. Third, each narrative had to be short, timely, and so well presented that it could serve as an effective stimulus for thinking critically about psychological concepts and research issues. Fourth, the selection had to illustrate psychological concepts that are covered in most introduction to psychology textbooks. We carefully examined more than twenty-five of the current best-selling introduction to psychology textbooks to select these concepts.

Chapter Organization

The order of the chapters corresponds to most introduction to psychology textbooks. Each chapter contains an average of five selections that are between two to six pages in length.

The chapter introduction presents an overview of each narrative and essay. The introductions to each selection present the psychological concepts that are illustrated and prepare the reader for the material. Three types of questions (Response and Analysis, Personal Experience and Application, and Research) follow each selection:

- *Response and Analysis* questions ask students to react to the material and to investigate psychological concepts in each selection.

- *Personal Experience and Application* questions ask students to examine and evaluate their reactions and experiences to the issues, and to explore how the issues may affect the community.

- *Research* questions present methodological issues appropriate for students at the introductory level. The questions allow students to begin thinking about research methodology. They cover basic concepts and principles of research design, including idea generation, hypothesis testing, independent and dependent variables, random selection, random assignment, ethical treatment of subjects and participants, and a variety of procedural issues. The research questions show students that (a) methodology and statistics are important for all areas of psychology; and that (b) psychologists studying diverse areas of behavior (such as physiology, child development, memory, and interpersonal behavior) rely on a common set of scientific methods to conduct investigations in their areas of special interest.

Suggestions for the Instructor: How to Use This Book

This book is designed for introduction to psychology courses, although it also may be relevant for psychology of adjustment courses. It can be used in a variety of ways for either small or large classes. Instructors may assign the readings and refer briefly to them in their lectures and class discussions. Some may wish to use the readings for tests and grading purposes. Items for multiple-choice, short answer, and essay tests are provided in the *Instructor's Resource Manual.* The book also works well to stimulate class discussion, research projects, group activities, and writing assignments.

Class Discussion

Students enjoy discussing their reactions to the readings in class.

1. The questions that follow each selection (i.e., Response and Analysis, Personal Experience and Application, and Research) stimulate good class discussion and reinforce students' understanding of key psychological concepts. Students could be asked to share their responses to the assigned readings and to the questions that follow during an allotted period of time after a lecture.

   The research questions serve as a good foundation for discussing research methodology. The questions teach basic concepts and principles and also show students the importance of methodology and statistics to all areas of psychology.

2. Students often enjoy a class debate. Many of the issues raised by the readings and the questions serve well for critical thinking and examination of opposing views. For example, Richard Vigil's essay, *I Don't Get Lost Very Often*, in the Mental Abilities chapter, raises the issue of what factors should be considered when someone who has mental retardation wishes to marry and have children. Rosalie Walsh Honel's essay, *Journey with Grandpa: Our Family's Struggle with Alzheimer's Disease*, in the Physiological Bases of Behavior chapter, raises the issue of what factors may be involved in deciding whether a family member suffering from Alzheimer's disease should be placed in a care facility or remain at home. Students could debate various sides of the same issue in class.

Group Activities

Students can be divided into groups for various activities.

1. Each group could answer either one, several, or all of the questions that follow every selection. After an allotted time for discussion (e.g., five to fifteen minutes), a representative from the group could present her or his group's responses to the class.

   More than one group could respond to the same question. This can be beneficial because it allows students to see different perspectives on the same issue. If all of the group representatives cannot present their answers because of time constraints or class size, then the group representatives could take turns and present their answers to different chapters on different days.

2. Each group could identify linkages between concepts in other selections in the same chapter or in different chapters. For example, in the Human Development chapter, Dick Gregory tells how poverty had a negative effect on his ability to learn in school. Students could use this essay to explore not only development and learning but also prejudice and stereotypes.

Research Projects

The readings can be used to generate interesting research projects.

1. Students could work alone or in groups to design a research proposal based on an idea raised by a research question. The proposal might include (a) a statement of the problem or question and why it is interesting or important; (b) a brief reference to previous research about the problem or question; (c) a statement indicating the hypothesis, independent variable(s), and dependent variable(s); and (d) a description of the method (e.g., the participants, materials, and procedures).

2. Students could work alone or in small groups and select a topic or research idea illustrated in this book. They could read journal articles or books on their selected topic and summarize the literature. They could then submit a review paper or present their work to the class during a ten- to fifteen-minute group presentation.

   This project could also be modified in several ways. Each student or group could answer the research questions that follow the narratives and essays. At the end of the term, the students could submit an individual or group report that presents their responses. Alternatively, they could write an individual or group report exploring several methodological issues raised by the research questions (e.g., random assignment, counterbalancing, ethical treatment of subjects and participants).

3. In honors classes or advanced general psychology courses, the students could learn more about the political, social, and economic forces that might have affected the author and/or had a bearing on the issue illustrated in the reading.

Journals and Response Papers

Journals and response papers are a valuable way for students to focus on academic material, to engage in critical thinking, and to analyze, question, and give personal responses to what they have read. Students could write short response papers in class or as a weekly written assignment out of class and submit their papers several times during the term.

   Students could receive grades, credit, or extra credit depending on the class size and the time available to read and grade the journals and papers.

Instructor's Resource Manual

We have written an *Instructor's Resource Manual* to accompany the book. The manual serves as a resource for examinations and provides questions and answers for multiple-choice, short answer, and essay tests. Instructors may wish to quiz students over the readings, psychological concepts, and issues surrounding the research questions. The resource manual is available from Houghton Mifflin Company.

Extending the Borders: A Final Note

In his remarkable book, *An Anthropologist from Mars*, Oliver Sacks reports that what he has found most effective in understanding both his patients and their illnesses is to get out of his office and into their lives, making "house calls at the far borders of human experience." In this way he comes to know them and their conditions from within, as persons, and not merely as patients who have been handed a diagnosis. It is our conviction that students, too, will better understand the issues in psychology whenever they extend the borders of the theoretical into the world of human experience. Such is the aim of this book.

Acknowledgments

It is a special pleasure to express our appreciation to the many talented and dedicated people who provided suggestions and creative ideas for this book. We have been extremely fortunate in having Douglas A. Bernstein of the University of Illinois collaborate with us on this project. Doug's enthusiasm for our idea prompted him to put us in contact with Houghton Mifflin Company. His ongoing support, guidance, and contributions have played a significant role in shaping the book. Whenever we had a question regarding the structure of the book, pedagogical features, or choice of material, Doug readily offered his expertise and invaluable suggestions. It has been a privilege working with him both professionally and as a friend.

We would also like to express our gratitude to the colleagues listed below, who read various portions of the manuscript and offered constructive criticism to improve the book.

Ruth L. Ault, Davidson College
Peter K. Ballantyne, San Diego State University
Wendy J. Beller, Quincy University
Winfield Brown, Florence Darlington Technical College
Thomas Lee Budesheim, Creighton University
Jack Demick, Suffolk University
Kathleen A. Flannery, Saint Anselm College
E. Keith Gerritz, Wilmington College of Ohio
Janet M. Gibson, Grinnell College
Ronald W. Jacques, Ricks College
Sally Holland Kline, Henderson Community College
Geoffrey P. Kramer, Indiana University at Kokomo

Dorothy Ledbetter, Grossmont College
Don Marguilis, Middlesex Community College
Gail Martino, Colgate University
Douglas W. Matheson, University of the Pacific
David G. McDonald, University of Missouri
Joseph L. Miele, East Stroudsburg University
Richard L. Robbins, Washburn University
Connie Schick, Bloomsburg University
Toni Spinelli-Nannen, American International College
Lori Van Wallendael, University of North Carolina at Charlotte

We have enjoyed working with the outstanding staff at Houghton Mifflin Company and appreciate their professionalism, support, and encouragement. David Lee, Sponsoring Editor, has been a strong advocate for the book and provided invaluable advice. Jane Knetzger, Senior Associate Editor, offered many perceptive and helpful suggestions on the structure of the book and on pedagogy. Gwen Fairweather, Editorial Assistant, provided insightful suggestions on all aspects of the book, including structure and pedagogy. We very much appreciate her synthesis of reviewer comments and enthusiasm for the project. Carol Newman, Senior Project Editor, is a dedicated professional who oversaw the production of the book. Aimee Bedo, Permissions Editor, provided advice on securing permissions and helped us locate copyright holders. Senior Sales Representative Karen Pund-Hutto has been very supportive. We would also like to acknowledge Becky Dudley, who originally signed the book.

We are indebted to Alis Whitt and the staff at the College of Charleston Interlibrary Loan department for helping us obtain books and other materials. We thank David Gentry, Stacy Clark, and the College of Charleston Psychology Department faculty for their support. We would especially like to thank the College of Charleston introduction to psychology students who critiqued portions of the book.

We wish to thank Judy Barkley, good friend and colleague at Grossmont College, for her continual enthusiasm for this project and for her critical reading of the entire manuscript. Her responses to the selections and her many helpful suggestions gave good direction. We also wish to thank Maurice Friedman, scholar, mentor, and long-time friend, for his encouragement and helpful counsel. Our appreciation extends to Yehuda Shabatay for his ardent support from the inception of this project, for his thorough reading of the manuscript, and for his always valuable suggestions. We are indebted to Sudie Back Sattler for her thorough reading of the manuscript, insightful suggestions, and enthusiastic support. We extend our appreciation to Jerome M. Sattler for his wise counsel and unwavering support. Finally, we would like to thank other family members for their support: Walter, Nicole, and Justin Philips; Bonnie and Keith Sattler; Debbie Hendrix; Elizabeth, Tom, and Phoenix Voorhies; Deborah and Eli Knaan; and Michael Shabatay.

It has been a delight working on this project together. In many ways the book grew out of our wonderful discussions about education and society that we have had over the years. To work together as colleagues while being mother and son is a pleasure twice over.

David N. Sattler
College of Charleston
Department of Psychology
Charleston, South Carolina 29424
E-mail: sattlerd@cofc.edu

Virginia Shabatay
Palomar College
Department of English
1140 W. Mission Road
San Marcos, California 920069

About the Authors

David N. Sattler received his B.A. in psychology with a minor in Spanish from San Diego State University and his M.A. and Ph.D. in social psychology from Michigan State University. He teaches at the College of Charleston, a four-year, medium-sized liberal arts college. David Sattler has held academic positions at the University of California at San Diego, San Diego State University, and Scripps College. He enjoys teaching introduction to psychology, statistics, research methods, social psychology, organizational psychology, and environmental psychology. His research examines behavior in social dilemmas and behavior following natural disasters. He has published in numerous journals, including *Teaching of Psychology* and *Journal of Personality and Social Psychology*. He is an avid photographer and backpacker.

Virginia Shabatay has a Ph.D. in humanities. She teaches at Palomar College and Grossmont College in San Diego, California, and has held academic positions at San Diego State University, Portland State University, and Lewis and Clark College. She has served as editorial consultant on numerous books, including *Martin Buber's Life and Work* by Maurice Friedman, and has contributed essays to several books. Her most recent publications are "Martin Buber and Sisela Bok: Against the Generation of the Lie," in *Martin Buber and the Human Sciences*, and "The Stranger: Who Calls? Who Answers?" in *Stories Lives Tell: Narrative and Dialogue in Education*. In her leisure time, she likes to read, travel, swim, and take long walks on the beach.

chapter 1

PHYSIOLOGICAL BASES OF BEHAVIOR

*What a piece of work is a man! how noble
in reason! how infinite in faculty!
in form and moving how express and
admirable!*

WILLIAM SHAKESPEARE, *Hamlet*

The intricacy and detail of human physiology astound us. The human body delights us in its form and in the way it allows us to move and to perceive. Not only are we amazed by how our senses respond to the world, but we marvel at the genius of human creativity: from developing the alphabet to carving the lute to inventing computers. Out of the wonders of physical being come science, art, literature.

But sometimes part of the body goes awry because of genetics, illness, or accident. In this chapter we read about people who struggle with various conditions that have physiological bases: neurological disorders, such as epilepsy, multiple sclerosis, and Parkinson's disease; strokes; and Alzheimer's disease. These readings underscore, however, the wisdom that a particular condition does not define the person.

Nancy Mairs has multiple sclerosis, yet she is a successful writer, college professor, lecturer, wife, mother, and political activist. A few years ago, wheelchair bound, she was on the front line with others who risked arrest as they protested further nuclear testing in Nevada. Mairs writes candidly about the demands of her daily life and her ability to recognize humorous situations brought on by her illness.

In the second selection, a sympathetic granddaughter helps us understand what it is like for her grandfather to suffer from Alzheimer's disease. Frustrated, forgetful, and sometimes angry, Grandfather has lost much of his life. His granddaughter understands his pain and the difficulties his family encounter as they take care of him at home.

Roberto Garcia d'Orta, a man in his sixties, was a successful businessman with a young family living in Madrid, Spain. Suffering from Parkinson's disease, and finding that his medication did not give him the relief he needed, d'Orta flew to Chicago to consult with specialist Dr. Harold L. Klawans. Dr. Klawans told him about an experimental drug that had helped some patients; however, its effectiveness and safety were unknown. Mr. d'Orta had no qualms: he wanted to try it. Klawans graphically depicts the physical sensations associated with Parkinson's and the desperate attempts of his patient to find relief.

When Katherine Lipsitz was a sophomore in college, she was diagnosed with epilepsy. She tried to refuse the diagnosis, but her body wouldn't let her. Lipsitz details the process of her denial, resignation, and eventual recognition that with medicine, she could live a reasonably normal life.

Rod McLean describes what it was like to have suffered a ruptured aneurysm in the brain (a stroke) that nearly caused his death. What was unusual was that he was barely twenty years old at the time. He recalls the pain, the lack of control, and the rage he experienced. After surgery, McLean was in a coma for three weeks, and his doctors did not think he would be able to communicate again. This selection is testimony to McLean's resilience.

CARNAL ACTS

Nancy Mairs

Psychological Concepts
multiple sclerosis, myelin, axon, cell body, dendrite,
synapse

Nancy Mairs was a young housewife and mother when she developed multiple
sclerosis, or MS. Multiple sclerosis is a serious neurological disease that involves a
progressive breakdown of myelin sheaths around nerves. In this process, certain
axons that have lost myelin may lose insulation from other axons. As a result, signals
in the nervous system may scramble and short-circuit, and the transmission of signals
from the brain to the muscles of the arms or legs may be delayed.

MS is a slowly debilitating disease that may result in paralysis. Those afflicted
may experience a lack of energy and eventually need to use a cane or wheelchair.
Others remain in remission for years and work and live productively.

Mairs, who has talent and grit, speaks of the effects her illness has had on her
family, work, and self-image. She credits MS for sparking her sense of humor. How
does Mairs describe the progression of her illness? What strategies does she use to
cope with her disability?

The beginning of MS wasn't too bad. The first symptom, besides the pernicious
fatigue that had begun to devour me, was "foot drop," the inability to raise my left
foot at the ankle. As a consequence, I'd started to limp, but I could still wear high
heels, and a bit of a limp might seem more intriguing than repulsive. After a few
months, when the doctor suggested a cane, a crippled friend gave me quite an elegant wood-and-silver one, which I carried with a fair amount of panache. The real
blow to my self-image came when I had to get a brace. As braces go, it's not bad:
lightweight plastic molded to my foot and leg, fitting down into an ordinary shoe
and secured around my calf by a Velcro strap. It reduces my limp and, more important, the danger of tripping and falling. But it meant the end of high heels. And it's
ugly. Not as ugly as I think it is, I gather, but still pretty ugly. It signified for me,
and perhaps still does, the permanence and irreversibility of my condition. The
brace makes my MS concrete and forces me to wear it on the outside. As soon as I
strapped the brace on, I climbed into trousers and stayed there (though not in the
same trousers, of course). The idea of going around with my bare brace hanging
out seemed almost as indecent as exposing my breasts. Not until 1984, soon after I
won the Western States Book Award for poetry, did I put on a skirt short enough to

reveal my plasticized leg. The connection between winning a writing award and baring my brace is not merely fortuitous; being affirmed as a writer really did embolden me. Since then, I've grown so accustomed to wearing skirts that I don't think about my brace any more than I think about my cane. I've incorporated them, I suppose: made them, in their necessity, insensate but fundamental parts of my body.

Meanwhile, I had to adjust to the most outward and visible sign of all, a three-wheeled electric scooter called an Amigo. This lessens my fatigue and increases my range terrifically, but it also shouts out to the world, "Here is a woman who can't stand on her own two feet." At the same time, paradoxically, it renders me invisible, reducing me to the height of a seven-year-old, with a child's attendant low status. "Would she like smoking or nonsmoking?" the gate agent assigning me a seat asks the friend traveling with me. In crowds I see nothing but buttocks. I can tell you the name of every type of designer jeans ever sold. The wearers, eyes front, trip over me and fall across my handlebars into my lap. "Hey!" I want to shout to the lofty world. "Down here! There's a person down here!" But I'm not, by their standards, quite a person anymore.

My self-esteem diminishes further as age and illness strip from me the features that made me, for a brief while anyway, a good-looking, even sexy, young woman. No more long, bounding strides: I shuffle along with the timid gait I remember observing, with pity and impatience, in the little old ladies at Boston's Symphony Hall on Friday afternoons. No more lithe, girlish figure: my belly sags from the loss of muscle tone, which also creates all kinds of intestinal disruptions, hopelessly humiliating in a society in which excretory functions remain strictly unspeakable. No more sex, either, if society had its way. The sexuality of the disabled so repulses most people that you can hardly get a doctor, let alone a member of the general population, to consider the issues it raises. Cripples simply aren't supposed to Want It, much less Do It. Fortunately, I've got a husband with a strong libido and a weak sense of social propriety, or else I'd find myself perforce practicing a vow of chastity I never cared to take.

Afflicted by the general shame of having a body at all, and the specific shame of having one weakened and misshapen by disease, I ought not to be able to hold my head up in public. And yet I've gotten into the habit of holding my head up in public, sometimes under excruciating circumstances. Recently, for instance, I had to give a reading at the University of Arizona. Having smashed three of my front teeth in a fall onto the concrete floor of my screened porch, I was in the process of getting them crowned, and the temporary crowns flew out during dinner right before the reading. What to do? I wanted, of course, to rush home and hide till the dental office opened the next morning. But I couldn't very well break my word at this last moment. So, looking like Hansel and Gretel's witch, and lisping worse than the Wife of Bath, I got up on stage and read. Somehow, over the years, I've learned how to set shame aside and do what I have to do. . . .

One may cry harder in the clutches of a troubled existence, but one may laugh harder as well. I had almost no sense of humor at all, particularly with regard to myself; before I started really experiencing difficulties, in the form of depression and MS, I was as sour as a pickle. Now, my life seems full of merriment. Imagine me, for instance, coming home from a shopping trip one winter evening. As I enter the screened porch, Pinto, my little terrier puppy, bounces forward to greet me, throwing my precarious balance off. I spin around and fall over backward, whacking my head on the sliding glass door to the house, but a quick check (I'm getting good at those) suggests no serious damage this time. This is called a pratfall, a burlesque device used in plays and films for a surefire laugh. In keeping with this spirit, I start to giggle at the image of this woman sprawled flat on her back, helpless under the ecstatic kisses of a spotted mongrel with a comic grin who is thrilled to have some-one at last get right down to his own level. The night is chilly. George isn't due home for an hour. Pinto's kisses are unpleasantly damp. "Oh Lord," I think, "if I'm too weak to get up this time, it's going to be a long night." Spurred by the cold and the kisses, I get up.

In addition to making me more humorous, I think the difficult life has made me more attentive. In part, this trait is self-defensive: I *have* to watch out for all kinds of potential threats—bumps and cracks, for instance, and small comic dogs lurking in doorways—that others might ignore without courting disaster. But this is only a drill for a more valuable attentiveness to the objects and people around me. I notice more details. I take more delight in them. I feel much more connected to others than I used to, more aware of their troubles, more tolerant of their short-comings. Hardship can be terrifically humanizing.

The most valuable response I've developed, I think, is gratitude. I don't mean that I'm grateful for having MS. I'm not, not in the least, and I don't see why I should be. What I'm grateful for is that, in spite of having MS, I've fulfilled ambi-tions I never dreamed I would. When I was first diagnosed, I didn't think I'd see my children grow up, and now I have a foster son in the navy, a daughter in the Peace Corps, and a son in college. I was sure my illness would drive George and me apart, and now we've celebrated our twenty-fifth wedding anniversary. I couldn't imagine that I'd make it through graduate school, but I did—twice. I thought I'd have to give up on being a writer, but here I am, writing for my life. I might have managed all these things—maybe even managed them better—without having MS. Who can tell? But through having MS, I've learned to cherish them as I don't think I could have otherwise. . . .

And so I say, *I'm afraid of having MS: of the almost daily deterioration of my strength; of the loss of control over my own body; of my increasing dependence on others to help me with the simplest personal tasks—tying my shoes, getting out of bed. Where will it all end? I'm afraid. I'm afraid. I'm afraid.* But like other MS people (and on the whole we're not very different from people in general, except perhaps that our fears are more focused and therefore easier to get at if we try), I don't give in to my fears. *If I weren't scared of this catastrophic disease,* I remind myself, *I'd have at least one screw loose somewhere.* So I put my fears to the best use I can, analyzing them to discover how to live carefully and choose my actions wisely. I'm nourished by the encourage-ment of others, like George, who believe that what's important is not that I'm scared but that I do what I need to do whether I'm scared or not. By speaking my fear aloud, I've reduced it from a giant trampling my interior landscape to an ordinary imp, the kind who dances through everybody's inner house from time to time, curdling the milk and smashing the crockery but leaving the structure basically intact. Surveying the damage, I get out my mop and broom. *This is my life*, I say to myself, *fear and all. I'm responsible for it. And I'd better get on with it, because it matters.*

Response and Analysis

1. What is Nancy Mairs's attitude toward having MS? Briefly describe her psychological responses to living with MS, including laughing harder and being grateful. Why does she believe these are valuable responses? How has living with MS affected her view of herself and her self-esteem?

2. The progressive breakdown of myelin sheaths plays a critical role in the development of MS. What are myelin sheaths? Define dendrite, cell body, axon, and synapse. How do myelin sheaths influence the transmission of signals along the axon?

Personal Experience and Application

1. Mairs writes that although her electric scooter significantly increases her mobility, paradoxically it renders her invisible. Briefly describe how she is "invisible" when riding the scooter. What are your first impressions when you see someone riding an electric scooter or a wheelchair? Do you behave differently than you do with an able-bodied person?

2. Briefly describe the daily difficulties that may be associated with living with MS.

Research

Researchers in the field of neuroscience use a variety of methodological approaches. Suppose you are interested in using the case study approach to understand how MS affects physical functioning. Assume that you have scheduled an appointment to interview someone with MS. Make a list of topics that you would want to discuss with the participant.

Briefly discuss two advantages and two disadvantages of the case study approach. What types of questions or issues cannot be answered with this approach?

JOURNEY WITH GRANDPA: OUR FAMILY'S STRUGGLE WITH ALZHEIMER'S DISEASE

Rosalie Walsh Honel

Psychological Concepts
Alzheimer's disease, hippocampus, limbic system

Alzheimer's disease is a progressive neurological disease that damages brain cells and causes serious cognitive impairment. It seldom affects people before age sixty-five. Rosalie Honel's father-in-law, Grandpa Frank, was diagnosed with Alzheimer's when he was in his seventies. Grandpa Frank's memory began to fail; he no longer knew where he was or whom he was with. He dealt with his confusion and suffering with anger and resistance.

When Grandpa could no longer take care of himself, his son's family insisted that he move in with them. Grandpa was often difficult to manage, and friction became a part of the family's daily life. The following account includes a story written by the granddaughter, Cindy, that shows her understanding of her grandfather's condition.

Frank was seventy-five years old, widowed, and had been living alone for several years when he started getting forgetful. He couldn't remember what he had eaten the day before. He kept misplacing his glasses and his money. Sometimes he was hungry and couldn't find anything to eat. He had been shopping and cooking for himself, since his wife had died, but now he was finding it hard to do these things. He was aware that there was food inside the cans in his pantry, but he couldn't remember how to open the cans. He used to know how. Why couldn't he remember?
. . .

Frank began to worry about his forgetfulness, although he made light of it. "I'll soon be pushing up daisies," he said, but he was afraid that something was wrong with him and that he might have to go to an "old people's home" because of it. A hateful thought. . . .

One day Frank had a terrible pain in his stomach, and he started vomiting. He tried to call his son but couldn't find the number, though he knew it was there somewhere. He went outside and saw a young man on the street, washing his car. "Doctor! Get a doctor!" he said. "I'm so sick!"

The next thing Frank knew, he was in an unfamiliar place and there were a lot of strangers around. They wanted him to stay in bed, but he got out anyway, and then they tied him up. He could scarcely move. As he lay there, Frank felt tired. He remembered the factory where he had worked for so many years, and it seemed that his tiredness was caused by his hard work.

From the place they claimed was a hospital, Frank was taken to his son's home. Everything was confusing there, too. The bathroom was always someplace other than where he thought it would be. When he was hungry, people were always telling him he had already eaten. If he had something in his hand, someone would say, "No, don't take that, it's mine." He couldn't understand. He wanted to go back home, but his son and daughter-in-law wouldn't let him. They said he had to live with them now; they claimed it was better for him.

He didn't believe them, and he didn't trust them, either. Where were all his things? Where was his money? They took everything. They had a lot of nerve keeping him here. Didn't they know that he had to go home? Who were they, anyway? Dammit, he had always done what he wanted, gone where he wanted to go! They had no business bossing him. He'd get out somehow. He'd show them. He pounded on the door with his fist, shouting angry words, calling them names. Everyone was against him. No one understood that he had to go home. Now! . . .

For an assignment in her junior English class, Cindy chose to write about Grandpa. She wrote the following story in which she describes a typical event from his point of view.

Cindy's Story: Prisoner of the Mind

"I hate you! I hate you!" I screamed at them, daring them to challenge me. Those people, they take everything I have. It's getting late and I have to be home. I go to the door, but it is locked. I can't get out. The panic rises within me as I turn to a man standing there. "I gotta go home," I tell him. He shrugs his shoulders. I try again. "It's locked. I can't get out. I have to go. It's late. I have to go home."

"I'm sorry," he says, "but you can't leave now. You can stay here. This is your home."

"Open the door!" I scream at him.

"No. I can't. You can stay here."

"I hate you!" I say again. I know he locked the door just so I couldn't get out. I can see it in his eyes. I feel my face burning with hatred, and I try the door again. It doesn't open. Maybe there's another door. I walk through the hall to look for another door. There are some papers on the table, all messed up. I have to straighten them. I put them together in neat piles. Someone comes into the room and tells me to leave his things alone. He takes the papers away from me. I try to grab them back, but I am too tired. It's late. I have to go home. I find some other papers, a spoon, and a small saucer. I will need them later. I carefully pack them up and walk to the door. I try not to let anyone see what I'm carrying. I try the door. It opens easily and I walk out. I walk to the end of the driveway and turn towards home. I have to go west. That's where my home is—west. After I have walked a short distance, there is a woman with me.

"Hello, Frank," she says.

"Go away!" I snap back. "I'm going home."

"But your home is over there." She points. I don't even bother looking. I just keep walking.

"Where are you going?" she asks.

"Home!"

"See that house over there?" she points again. I stop and look back. "The Honels live there. Is your name Honel? My name is Honel; we should stay together. Let's go this way."

She leads me back to the house, pulling my arms so that I have no choice but to go with her. I'm too tired anyway. But then I remember my wife will be waiting for me. She will get mad at me if I'm not home.

"But my wife . . ." I start to say.

"Grandpa, your wife died years ago. You live here now, with your son and his family. You stay here now."

"No," I say. My voice sounds funny, but I can't help it. My wife, dead? Years ago? "No," I say again. "She was a good woman, my wife," I tell the woman next to me. She nods her head.

"You live here now. Come on, I'll show you."

"Thank you," I say, and kiss her hand. "Thank you."

"Mom, telephone."

"Okay—you want to take Grandpa in the house?"

"Sure. Come this way, Grandpa, over here. Look! There's your room, see?"

The epilogue to Cindy's story read, "I watch as his face lights up with recognition and wonder what exactly goes on in his mind and why he thinks he must go home even though he is at home with his family. Well, at least he's not mad anymore."

It pleased me to know that Cindy was concerned enough about Grandpa to want to write about him and to try to understand why he did some of the things he did. I could see that this experience was making a deep impression on her.

During one of my early-morning writing periods, my own thoughts turned to Grandpa's habit of talking constantly: how it had revealed his feelings to us over the years, particularly now that his mind was less rational. In a study of his various moods, I wrote his words as I recalled hearing them, a kind of poetic, rhythmic flow ranging from contentment to anger and back again. As the disease progressed, this habit had become a compulsion. With each breath he would say something, usually two or three words that expressed his thoughts or feelings at that moment. If there was no particular feeling he would keep repeating "My, my." This was very annoying, but it was something we had to get used to.

Moods of Alzheimer's: Speech Patterns of a Victim

Morning

> Good morning! It's nice. Very nice. I like it.
> What shall I do? What shall I do? What shall I do?
> Thank you. It's good. You're so good. You want to eat, too.
> You take half. You have to take half! Lady, where are you?
> Come here! I want to give you. Where are they? Nobody.
> Nobody comes. What shall I do? I don't like it. What's this?

> Oh, oohh—I feel bad. Toilet! Oh, I feel bad.
> It hurts. Oohh. It hurts. Here. Something wrong.
> Wait, what are you doing? What's that for?
> Sit down? No, I'm afraid. Water. I don't want it.
> I don't like it. I'm afraid. It's going. It's going.
> It's going.

(Arranging newspapers)

> What's this? My, my. My, my. My, my. My, my. My, my.
> Ninety. Very nice. It'll be good. How nice. I make it.
> Very nice. That's nice. For us. It be nice. Very nice . . .

Late Afternoon

> Nothing. I ain't got nothing. No good. They take it.
> They take everything. I'm going home. Where is it?
> I don't know. I'm going. Out. I have to get out.
> Let me out. God dammit. Let me out. I want out.
> Bastar'! Bastar'! That's what you are. You're no good.
> Let me out. I want to get out.

Evening

> My, my. My, my. My, my. Come with you?
> Now? Okay. My, my. My, my. My, my. My, my.
> Down? Here? Lay down? Me?
> My, my. My, my. My, my. My, my . . .

As each day progressed, there was a pattern of behavior that ranged from passive and contented to agitated and angry, with the agitation occurring anywhere from midafternoon through evening and sometimes into the night. At these times, nothing could satisfy Grandpa. He became so "hyper" that it was as if he were wired for electricity and the switch was on. He was on his feet constantly, moving from room to room, picking things up, tearing at them, going to the door, and going outside regardless of the weather or his state of dress; if he tried to go outside and the door wouldn't open, he would hammer on it furiously with his fist, all the while fuming and repeating "I want to go out!" and more colorful expressions.

As caretakers, each of us in the family had strong feelings of our own, running the gamut from positive to negative. Unfortunately, it was much easier to talk about the negative. It was good for us to acknowledge those feelings, yet the negatives often led to positives that we might never have experienced but for this situation.

Response and Analysis

1. What cognitive difficulties did Grandpa Frank experience as a result of Alzheimer's disease? Briefly describe his moods and his ability to communicate.

2. Research suggests that Alzheimer's disease is associated with degeneration of the hippocampus and other limbic structures. Briefly describe the functions of the hippocampus and the limbic system. What structures are associated with the limbic system? What structures in the limbic system are associated with emotion?

Personal Experience and Application

1. Do you know or have you seen someone who is a victim of Alzheimer's disease? Describe his or her cognitive abilities. What short-term and long-term memory difficulties do you notice?

2. How has reading about Grandpa Frank affected your view of the elderly? Do you have a new understanding of the elderly or more compassion toward them? Briefly discuss the difficulties that may be involved with taking care of a person suffering from Alzheimer's.

Research

Suppose you are part of a research team that is testing a new drug designed to reduce cognitive difficulties due to Alzheimer's disease. Assume that your participants are thirty people diagnosed with the disease. You plan to give fifteen people the new drug for six weeks and fifteen people a placebo for six weeks. After six weeks, you will assess cognitive functioning.

What is the independent variable? What is the dependent variable? What is your hypothesis? Be sure to discuss the levels or conditions of the independent variable in your hypothesis.

NEWTON'S MADNESS: FURTHER TALES OF CLINICAL NEUROLOGY

Harold L. Klawans

Psychological Concepts
Parkinson's disease, substantia nigra, striatum, dopamine

Roberto d'Orta was in the prime of life. He was successful, was married to a woman twenty-three years younger than he, and had two small children. One day he began to have tremors, had difficulty getting out of chairs, and felt cold much of the time. He was suffering from Parkinson's, a progressive neurological disease in which cells in the substantia nigra that produce the neurotransmitter dopamine degenerate.

Mr. d'Orta grappled with issues central to his life: What would happen to his marriage? How could he provide for his family? What treatment could bring him relief? After having had Parkinson's for more than ten years, d'Orta's medication was no longer effective, and he became desperate. The following is the physician's account of Mr. d'Orta's attempts to regain his life.

Mr. d'Orta's problem had begun over a decade earlier. He'd been in his early fifties then, what he had considered to be the prime of his life. Perhaps that was what had caused it; perhaps his hubris had angered the gods. No matter. He took a deep breath, sighed, and started again. His voice became a level softer. I had to concentrate to hear his words. The tone never varied—no highs, no lows, no emotional inflections. Flat, soft, hushed, and, at times, halting.

He'd married late in life. His wife was twenty-three years younger. He repeated that figure several times, not in the repetitive rambling of a confused mind but with the genuine concern of a man whose body was failing him far too soon. They had two young children, a boy and a girl. His leather-goods business had been flourishing. Life had been good to him. He'd always worked hard for what he got from life, but still life had been good to him.

Then it happened—not all at once, not suddenly, but slowly, subtly, insidiously, yet perniciously. And inexorably.

What had he first noticed? What had been his first symptom?

A tremor.

Had his tremor been disabling?

He hesitated and thought for a moment. It was a question he had never considered before. "No," he said. "I think not. My hands shake worse when they are doing nothing at all. But," he added, "it was most embarrassing. Even then. I was not ready to be a shaky old man. I still would prefer not to be."

The other problems that make up parkinsonism are not quite so benign and are not as obvious to the patient as is the tremor. They are difficult to perceive and hard to quantify, but they can change a vigorous man into a lizard. Many of these symptoms are collectively called *akinesia* or *bradykinesia*, terms that refer to a number of related symptoms: a marked poverty of spontaneous movements, hesitation in starting to move, and slowness in the execution of voluntary movements. The poverty of movement includes such traits as the frozen or "masked" parkinsonian face. The patient's face lacks both voluntary and emotionally motivated movements. Its features are flattened, and the face itself becomes smoother than normal, so that a frozen or wooden "masked" expression results. Whatever emotional responses occur are slow in developing but can become prolonged, resulting, for example, in a frozen smile. The term "reptilian stare" is often used to describe the characteristic lack of blinking and widely opened eyes gazing out of the motionless facial background, a set of features that truly seems more reptilian than human. A lizard in the eyes of the world.

Mr. d'Orta had gone one step further than the classic "reptilian stare." He described his entire body as being that of a reptile, and he was accurate; it is not just the face that becomes akinetic in parkinsonism. The entire body shares the same fate. The patient often sits immobile, seldom crossing his legs, folding his arms or displaying any of the wide variety of spontaneous movements seen in normal individuals at rest. The spontaneous movements that we all make constantly but of which we are hardly conscious are no longer made. Patients are rarely aware of this and never complain of it. Their friends and families notice that something is wrong, but what? It is hard to define, hard to describe. The patient looks different—less human, less warm. Perhaps he's merely depressed.

Unfortunately, looking not quite right is one of the minor components of akinesia. Far worse is the fact that the patient has a great deal of difficulty initiating whatever movements he wants to make. The simple task of rising from a chair becomes a trial. The patient has to rock back and forth several times to gain momentum and then push down with his arms merely to get up and walk.

Mr. d'Orta had long had that problem. He had first noticed it about the time his tremor had spread to his left hand. He would drive home from his office, feeling more tired than usual. Perhaps he was working harder. He would finally arrive home, only to discover that he could hardly get out of his car. His body seemed to be frozen into his Alfa Romeo Julietta. He would rock back and forth, slowly at first, until he finally gained enough speed and momentum to be able to swing his legs out of the car. A few more swings, and he could ease the rest of his body through the door.

The next morning when he drove to work, it was better. Not normal, but better. A couple of rocks back and forth, and he was on his way.

His problems did not stop with getting out of the car. Getting up from chairs at home, in restaurants, and at the office, and rolling over in bed at night. It was not merely overwork, exhaustion, or fatigue. And he could no longer ignore it.

It was time to see his doctor. That was nine years before he saw me. His doctor sent him to a neurologist. The neurologist talked to him, examined him, and did something James Parkinson had never done; he touched his patient, and in so doing documented the third component of Roberto d'Orta's Parkinson's disease: the rigidity of his muscles. Rigidity is a type of resistance to passive movement. It is felt by a doctor when he or she moves the patient's arm. Normally, there is virtually no resistance to such a maneuver. In Parkinson's disease, the rigid muscle exhibits an irregular jerkiness, as if it were being pulled out over a ratchet or cogwheel. The result is an alternating series of jerks, referred to as *cogwheel rigidity.*

Mr. d'Orta still remembered that examination. The neurologist had moved his arm back and forth several times. Mr. d'Orta himself could see the intermittent jerking or wheeling. "Rigidity," the neurologist had said solemnly. "Cogwheel rigidity."

Mr. d'Orta had never heard that term before, but somehow he knew what it meant. It meant he had a disease, a disease that would affect him for the rest of his life.

The doctor also pushed him suddenly, and he almost fell down.

The story was complete. He had all four of the cardinal problems of Parkinson's disease: tremor, akinesia, rigidity, and abnormal postural fixation. The term *postural fixation* describes the unconscious mechanisms whereby the body maintains its posture. As you walk or sit, your head is held erect not by any conscious willed action but by an unconscious postural control mechanism. In patients with Parkinson's disease, postural fixation of the head is often abnormal. A patient's head tends to fall slowly forward from an upright position, reminiscent of the way a normal person's head falls when he becomes drowsy. So the parkinsonian begins to walk with his head bent forward and his body flexed, more like a monkey than erect human.

Patients with Parkinson's disease are frequently able to walk quite well and support their bodies against the normal forces of gravity; however, if other forces are added, they may not be able to adjust. A single shove on the chest—which the Spanish neurologist had given Mr. d'Orta—may produce a series of backward steps or retropulsion that the patients cannot prevent. In more severely involved individuals, a similar push may result in the patients falling because of a complete lack of response. This may occur whether or not the patient is expecting to be pushed.

What was happening in Mr. d'Orta's brain? A small group of nerve cells, called the *substantia nigra* or black substance, were unaccountably dying. In fact, most of them had already died. These neurons make a particular chemical called dopamine, which they deliver to another part of the brain, known as the striatum. As the cells of the substantia nigra die, the amount of dopamine they can deliver goes down; it is this deficiency that causes parkinsonism. The striatum helps control movement, and to do that normally, it needs dopamine. Deprived of dopamine, the patient develops tremor, rigidity, slowness, imbalance. In essence—Parkinson's disease.

Mr. d'Orta's neurologist started him on L-dopa. And it worked. He was a new man, almost the same man he had been two years earlier. He still had some tremor at times, and his arms still did not swing normally, but he could get out of a chair, even out of his Alfa Romeo. When his voice became stronger, he discovered that he hadn't realized that it had grown softer. And he could do things more quickly, even those things he had not been aware had slowed down: shaving, buttoning clothes, writing, walking, eating, and one he had never even mentioned to his doctor—making love to his wife. . . .

Mr. d'Orta began taking bromocriptine, and again improved. Not 100 percent, but he was better for a few more years. Each year, there was progressive disability, with corresponding changes in his medications, balancing the needed improvements with the unwanted side effects. And now he was a slow, frozen lizard searching for the sun. Could I supply the warmth he so desperately needed?

Perhaps; I would make no promises. And what was that ray of light called? Pergolide. It was, I explained, a cousin of bromocriptine. Similar yet different. Some patients who no longer benefit from bromocriptine get better on pergolide. Was he willing to try it? It was still experimental. Its safety was not proved, nor was its value.

He had come to me to seek a new solution; he would try it.

His willingness to take an experimental medication was not the sole criterion for accepting him into our study. The presence of other diseases would exclude him. I ran all the appropriate tests, and aside from Parkinson's disease, he was healthy.

He lived too far away for our usual study, so follow-up would have to be less frequent than usual. Fortunately, we'd already treated over one hundred patients, so we knew what to expect.

Still, his case was unique. I called the chairman of the hospital's Committee on Human Experimentation. Could I treat someone who lived that far away? We negotiated the conditions. Mr. d'Orta had to stay in Chicago until he was on a stable dose of the medication. He had to be seen once every three months by one of the investigators. He had to have a local neurologist I knew and trusted. He had to read and sign the informed-consent form and understand the entire process just as every other patient placed on an experimental drug did.

I told all this to Mr. d'Orta. He, of course, still wanted to try the pergolide. I could not dissuade him, for he had come all that way for something new.

So try it we did.

And it worked. Spring arrived on schedule in Chicago, bringing with it another spring for Roberto Garcia d'Orta. His sun returned from behind the clouds and he could again live the life of a new man. He stayed in Chicago a total of six weeks and then returned to Spain. After that, I saw him once every three months. Sometimes he came to Chicago, sometimes I flew to Madrid, and occasionally we met somewhere in Europe, if I had a meeting to attend.

The pergolide did wonders for the first year. It did fairly well during the second year, and less well the third. Mr. d'Orta had been on it for almost four years when I saw him in Barcelona. I had flown there to participate in a meeting on recent advances in the treatment of Parkinson's disease. He came up from Madrid to see me, and we met in my hotel room.

He had once again become a lizard, and the world was an even colder place than it had been when we had first met. We talked at length. His speech was so quiet I had to strain to hear him. Its slow, monotonous pace was interrupted by brief spurts of words crowded together in a forceful yet soft, cascade.

He continued to ask the same questions. Was there anything more I could do? Did I have any new drugs?

I asked him question after question, trying to ferret out some factor that might be contributing to his decline other than the natural progression of his disease. That was undoubtedly the major issue, but it offered little hope to either of us. Before the use of L-dopa, Parkinson's disease decreased the life expectancy by an average of seven years. Today life expectancy is pretty much back to normal, and one can certainly not expect much more from any medication.

Quantity of life, however, is only one factor, for it is the quality of life that must be faced day by day. After many years, Parkinsonian patients begin to develop increased disability, with more rigidity, more akinesia, and worse postural reflexes. Have the treatments for some reason lost their effectiveness? Is the "progression" due to the imperfect nature of our pharmacology? Or is it due to the disease and its inexorable progression?

Probably the latter. L-dopa and the other medications do nothing to combat the advance of the disease. The brain cells, including those that manufacture dopamine, continue to die. Each year, drugs are asked to do more and more. When Roberto first started taking L-dopa, he'd still been working, and it almost turned him back into the vigorous businessman he had once been. He had expected similar results from his medications for the rest of his life, and the medicines had failed him. Or had they? He'd been on L-dopa for fourteen years now, fourteen years of dying brain cells, fourteen years of the progression of his disease.

When he took his first dose of L-dopa, he was far from normal, but he could get out of bed in the morning, brush his teeth, get dressed, eat breakfast, drive to work, work all day, and so on. Now, without L-dopa, he would be not a lizard but a slab of marble—totally immobile and incapable of movement. In fact, had it not been for the very same medications he was certain had failed him, he would probably have died of severe Parkinson's disease several years earlier. I did not tell him any of this. What good would it have done? It would not have changed his needs any and could have served only to decrease his hope, a situation we did not need. And he had such enormous needs.

Response and Analysis

1. What were Mr. d'Orta's physical symptoms of Parkinson's disease? Mr. d'Orta told the doctor that he felt like a lizard. What did he mean by that? Describe the lizardlike qualities that d'Orta complained about.

2. According to Dr. Klawans, what are the substantia nigra, the striatum, and dopamine? What is the main drug that is used to offset the symptoms of Parkinson's disease? How does the drug work?

Personal Experience and Application

1. Imagine that you suffer from hand tremors. What daily activities might be difficult or embarrassing?

2. Briefly describe a few of the daily difficulties that people with Parkinson's disease may experience.

Research

Neuroscientists have learned a great deal about the relationship between the brain and behavior by studying people who have suffered damage in specific areas of the brain. However, this research approach has drawbacks. First, the location and severity of brain damage cannot be controlled. Second, there are not many human participants available for study.

Because of these problems, neuroscientists often use animals to study more precisely the relationship between the brain and behavior. They purposely damage portions of animal brains and then study the resulting behavior. Do you think it is necessary to use animals to study brain functioning? Why or why not? Is it ethical to use animals in this way? Why or why not? How do you think a researcher should care for and handle animals that are serving as research subjects?

I REFUSED TO BE SICK . . . AND IT ALMOST KILLED ME

Katherine H. Lipsitz

Psychological Concepts
epilepsy, grand mal seizure

Katherine Lipsitz was a successful college student "struggling hard for perfection." She had the usual concerns of most young women her age: a desire to be attractive, to enjoy good times with friends, and to succeed in school. But she suffered from muscle spasms and seizures, which she kept secret from others as long as possible. When she was told she had epilepsy, she ignored her doctor's treatment program.

Epilepsy is a serious neurological disorder caused by continual firing of neurons in one area of the brain. This firing rapidly spreads to other areas of the brain; as a result, those with this illness not only have seizures but may speak incoherently and even lose consciousness. Medication is available to control the disease, and most people with epilepsy are able to live reasonably normal lives.

But what might happen when a person receives a diagnosis of such an illness? At one point Lipsitz decided "not to be an epileptic." What motivated this decision? What stages of acceptance did she experience?

This is what they say I do: First I lose consciousness. Then my knees buckle and I collapse. Where I am is important when I collapse: I've tumbled down a flight of stairs, fallen on the sidewalk and slipped under the water in a bath. Many times I go into convulsions. For me, convulsions last three to five minutes and cause a complete loss of muscle control, so that I writhe and shake and sometimes hurt my head. Occasionally, I'm told, I have vomited and lost continence. Afterward, I breathe heavily or snore; it takes a while until I know where I am.

I have never seen another person go through a grand mal epileptic seizure, and I don't remember my own: I black out. But my college roommate and others have described my seizures to me, and I know that they're not pretty.

I must have understood that epilepsy isn't pretty, because the first time a doctor told me I had it, during the summer after my sophomore year at Vassar College, I immediately and passionately denied the diagnosis. I couldn't have epilepsy, I told myself; epileptics are flawed, and I was struggling hard for perfection.

By the time I entered Vassar, I thought I had finally overcome a lifetime of imperfections. I grew up in New York City with a beautiful mother, a successful father—a music producer—and two very intelligent older brothers. For 12 years, I attended an Upper East Side private school. My childhood was privileged; but I was the youngest in my family, the tallest in class—and always overweight. This last flaw was unacceptable. When I was young, classmates called me names. Adults would murmur: "What a shame! She has such a pretty face."

At age 15 I became thin—by force of will combined with bouts of anorexia and bulimia. I started hanging out with a fast, popular crowd at Studio 54, Area and Xenon. Yet I continued to feel awkward and out of place—like the fat, ugly kid I thought I'd been.

About this time, I also became dimly aware that something else was bothering me. I began to have muscle spasms, which I later learned were called myocolonus, a pre-epileptic condition. These spasms would happen in the early morning or in moments of stress. I hid them from family and friends. I spent a lot of time alone, dreaming of the day when some man who was smart, kind and funny would come along and carry me away to happiness.

That first year at Vassar, I began to have full-fledged seizures, though I still didn't know what they were. Amazingly, nobody found out. I was very pleased about that. I also met and began to date a boy who wore a Rolex watch and Bally loafers and was strong-minded, quick-witted and smart. I was not about to tell him of my seizures or my growing fears. I know I was afraid that he'd leave me, but I think I was even more afraid of admitting to myself that something was very wrong.

I spent the summer after my sophomore year in Spain. I had one seizure before I left home and another after I returned—the latter one I couldn't hide from my parents, who took me to a doctor. The doctor, a neurologist, ruled out a brain tumor and then, describing epilepsy as a mysterious disorder whose causes he couldn't be sure of, cautioned that I'd have to rest every day, abstain from alcohol and take medicine that would prevent seizures but might also cause weight gain, raise my testosterone level and promote growth of body hair.

That's when I decided not to be an epileptic. I had worked so hard to be like everybody else; I wasn't about to become the overweight male ape the doctor seemed to be describing. My attitude was: I would drink when I felt like it and sleep only if it didn't interfere with my social life; what the doctor didn't know wouldn't hurt him. I left his office. I never took the pills, and went on with my life as though nothing had changed.

When I returned to school junior year, things were different. The guy I dated had graduated from Vassar and from me. I stopped wearing makeup and caring how I dressed. As I revealed my condition to a few friends, I grew self-conscious about being the only kid I knew who spent quality time with her neurologist. Mostly, I was afraid—not so much of the seizures themselves as of hitting my head during convulsions. I was sure epilepsy would kill me. I believed I should make a will. I didn't think about getting better.

I woke up early one morning junior year facing three men I'd never seen before. "I don't know you," I said. My roommate, stepping forward, explained, "Kate, these men are paramedics. You had a seizure, and you have to go with them." The men took me to the emergency room of the county hospital, where I saw people in real pain, shouting for help. This scared me, but not enough to change. I told myself that all I wanted was to be a normal college kid and I would do it with willpower.

The second semester of my junior year, I met a different kind of guy—no Bally loafers or Rolexes, but I liked him—partly because he liked me. By now I'd gained 20 pounds; whenever I felt sorry for myself I ate, and I'd been feeling very sorry for myself. I was amazed that this boy found me attractive.

Then early one morning, after he and I had gone out drinking and fallen asleep in his dorm room, I woke up feeling strange. I tried to go back to sleep. When I awoke again, my friends the Emergency Medical Technicians were there. The boy had called them. They took me to the Vassar health clinic, where the boy sat with me for hours and held my hand—teaching me a lesson I've never forgotten in how to treat people. Later, he told me how scared he'd been that I would die. I didn't know how to reassure him, because his fears were exactly like my own. So I stopped dating him—stopped dating anyone for the next five years.

Now I know that people experience epilepsy at different times of life and for different reasons, and that it can be controlled. Some people are born with epilepsy; others have their first attack after a blow to the head or similar trauma. I seem to have what's called "idiopathic" epilepsy—literally meaning "cause unknown," but in my case associated with a genetic susceptibility. At the end of my junior year in college, however, I felt as though I were the only person on earth who had this illness, that nothing could be done to stop it and that no one could accept me with it. The truth is, I couldn't accept myself.

I hit a low point: I wasn't like other college kids. They were experimenting with alcohol while I was experimenting with different combinations of medication. Hard alcohol was poison. And every time I drank, trying to prove I couldn't be something I knew I was, I had a seizure. My friends drove back and forth to New York City; I couldn't even apply for a driver's license until I could prove I'd been seizure free for 18 months. So I went to classes, watched TV and ate anything I could get my hands on. I became more isolated. Food took the place of a best friend. Then a new neurologist finally convinced me to give up drinking.

This doctor, whom I still see, saved my life. Highly regarded in his field, and also kind and gentle, he was the first person I met whom I couldn't manipulate or make feel sorry for me. By taking a firm stand, he showed me that the only thing keeping me from getting my epilepsy under control was me.

Under his care, I began to take all my medicine. I graduated from Vassar—60 pounds heavier than when I'd entered, but also changed in other, more positive ways. I wasn't so arrogant or insistent on perfection; I'd stopped being a spoiled brat. I moved back to New York City and gathered a group of close friends whose idea of a wild night was dinner out. I didn't drink. I rested. And, for the first time since I was 15, my seizures stopped.

I got a job as a secretary in a large advertising agency—where I wanted to be. Six months later, two weeks before my 23rd birthday, I was promoted to junior copywriter. I had lost a few pounds in spite of my medication, and hadn't had a seizure in a year. I felt I had epilepsy beaten.

To prove it, I went to a party on my birthday and drank everything in sight—margaritas, alcohol punch, beer. The next morning I woke early and took my dog for a walk. Out on the street, I suddenly didn't feel well. My knees buckled and I fell to the ground. As in previous days, I woke up in the hospital. I had a blood-stained face, and a doctor was putting stitches in my chin. My mother was there, crying, and my roommate from Vassar, with whom I now shared an apartment, was there asking me if I was okay. That's when it hit me—I wasn't okay, and I knew it. Both these women had always been there for me, putting my welfare above their own concerns, never blaming me or losing patience. And how had I repaid them? By being selfish—never once thinking what effect my careless behavior had on them. For the first time, it was clear to me that I'd have to change—not for a month or a year but for life.

That's how I arrived where I am today—26 years old and free of seizures for the last two years. Some days I still feel shaky, but I take my medicine and know how to manage my illness. I eat fruits and vegetables and brown rice instead of junk food, and I work out five days a week. I've lost 45 of the 60 pounds I gained in college. I have a driver's license that I don't use much but that makes me feel free. For a year, I went out with a guy who loved me as I am; now I believe that's in the cards for me.

I have joined the Epilepsy Society of New York City, where I do volunteer work. I've learned a lot there. For one thing, many people find the hardest part of epilepsy is living not with the illness but with the stigma attached to it. This was true of me, and has been true through the ages. In medieval Portugal, epilepsy was considered divine punishment for acts of bestiality committed by a person's ancestors. The Catholic Church once prohibited epileptics from becoming priests, fearing they were possessed by the devil. Until the 1980s, a law barred epileptics from marrying in Missouri. Other myths hold epilepsy a mark of genius. I am neither a possessed person nor a genius, but I am better for having learned to live with epilepsy. It's taught me to be kinder and more empathetic. A few months ago at the Epilepsy Society I met a beautiful, blonde-haired 15-year-old girl. We were talking about her boyfriend. "Does he know you have epilepsy?" I asked. "Oh, no. I could never tell him *that*," she said. So I asked her how she would feel if *he* were the one with epilepsy. "I'd keep dating him and love him anyway," she said, a slow smile spreading across her lovely face.

It was the right answer. Though the road is rocky, I hope she learns to love herself as well.

Response and Analysis

1. Why did Katherine Lipsitz deny having epilepsy? What stages of acceptance did she experience? Briefly describe her physical symptoms during a grand mal epileptic seizure, including changes in consciousness.

2. According to Lipsitz, why might people develop epilepsy? How does Lipsitz control her epilepsy?

Personal Experience and Application

1. Lipsitz writes that "many people find the hardest part of epilepsy is living not with the illness but with the stigma attached to it." What stigmas do you believe are associated with epilepsy? If you were at a party and saw a friend having an epileptic seizure, how do you think you would act toward him or her the next day?

2. Why do you think living with epilepsy has taught Lipsitz to be "kinder and more empathetic"?

Research

Most seizure disorders like epilepsy are caused by one or more regions of scar tissue—seizure foci—that irritate the brain tissue surrounding them. Suppose you are part of a research team that is testing a new drug designed to reduce seizures. Like other research groups, your team is using rats to evaluate the effectiveness of the new drug. Assume that you are using twenty rats and create seizure foci in each rat. You give ten rats the new drug and ten rats the standard drug. You record the number of seizures each rat experiences over a thirty-day period.

Is it important that the rats in both groups live in the same physical environment? Is it important that both groups of rats be fed the same amount of food at the same time? Why or why not? What other factors should you control?

STROKE SURVIVORS

William H. Bergquist, Rod McLean, and Barbara A. Kobylinski

Psychological Concepts
stroke, lobes (parietal, frontal, occipital, temporal)

Rod McLean was an active, involved college student on his way to a fast-food restaurant with a friend. Suddenly he had difficulty walking. He couldn't see or speak clearly, and he began to fall. Several of his friends took him to the hospital. McLean had suffered a stroke, which is rare for someone is his twenties.

A stroke, or cerebrovascular accident, occurs when the blood supply to the brain is cut off. When that happens brain cells are damaged because the brain does not receive the oxygen it needs. The location and severity of the stroke largely determine which functions are affected. Some people may have permanent brain damage; others may suffer paralysis in various parts of the body. Rehabilitation is often lengthy. The resulting physical handicaps also may affect stroke victims' psychological well-being and their interpersonal relationships.

Particularly impressive is McLean's memory of his stroke. He recalls the intense headache that came on suddenly, his inability to make his friends understand him, and his frustration with losing his balance. What reasons does he give for his survival and recovery?

I'm Rod McLean. I'm a stroke survivor. As a matter of fact, a neurologist described my stroke as a "spontaneous hemorrhage from an angioma or arteriovenous malformation in the left parietal area." In other words, a blood vessel in the left side of my brain had a weak point and burst. And it hurt! I was told later that I was within seconds or minutes of dying. But I guess I was as lucky as I could be, for it just happened that one of the best neurosurgeons in the region was right there when I was carried into the emergency room. He jumped into action to open my cranium and halted the rupture within moments.

The big one! It sure was. I think it was a Wednesday, late afternoon. Patty— a friend of mine—and I decided to walk four or five blocks to the fast-food restaurant. About halfway back, something started happening. It was really strange! I was invaded by an instant and massive headache. Everything started to become different—I didn't know what it was. I looked at my feet, but they didn't seem as though they were mine. I had to concentrate to make sure they would do what they were supposed to, because I noticed that I was having a harder and harder time walking.

At the same time, Patty became aware that something was going on. When she asked me questions, I heard and understood everything, but then I couldn't understand that I was forgetting whatever it was she had said. Not only that, her voice sounded like an echo. I had no reference point and quickly became afraid; I was scared of the unknown. I noticed the sun was too bright and that I was seeing things surrealistically. My walking became wobbly, but Patty helped me get home.

Gary and Rolf, close friends and roommates, were out in the front yard; they saw something was wrong. In a way, I guess I was relieved to see my friends because it gave me a sense of security. They could see that I was afraid and that I appeared disoriented. They asked what was wrong and, to no avail, tried to figure out something to relieve the situation. Meanwhile, I was staggering and falling around. I struggled to answer their questions and pleaded for help and solutions. Looking at Patty, I tried to reach into my right front pocket to get some money to give her so she could go get me some aspirin. But somehow I couldn't find the right words to convey my needs.

I was trying to do all these simple things at the same time, and nothing was working right! My friends didn't know what to do. They carried me upstairs and laid me down on my bed, saying that I would be all right. They left! I was in pain. Everything was so hot; my entire body was drenched with sweat. I tried to sit up to take my shirt off over my head. I had no balance; every time I fought to sit up, I kept falling back down. The last time I hadn't been able to sit up was when I was a baby! Inside I was screaming, but on the outside I had somehow forgotten how to do that. Next, I tried again and again to take my shoes and socks off—that was practically impossible, too. I'd reach for the laces, but my fingers would totally miss them and I'd fall over sideways. Eventually, my friends came back and saw that I was in worse shape than a few minutes ago. They both stared at me in the realization of my anguish, glanced at each other, and agreed that they should take me to the hospital right away.

Lying on my side, I was starting to completely lose it; I was not really in control of anything. About all I could do was force myself to remain conscious—not really alert, but only distortedly aware that something was happening. Gary and Rolf carried me, limp, to the car and poured me in. Gary raced to the emergency room as Rolf held on to me. My body was still sweating and I was so hot that I had to hang my head out the window. It was odd. All the sounds—my friends' voices echoing and the outside sounds, such as the rush of traffic, cars honking, the wind, and everything else—angered me to the point of extreme hatred. I felt like lashing out to destroy and eliminate the grating noises that became an overwhelming irritation. My brain was throbbing, exploding with pain. Everything around me was aggravating the problem. I wanted it all to stop!

When we got to the hospital, they carried me into the Emergency Room and put me on a gurney. I was in tremendous pain. I was lying on the bed—out of control. I wanted out! As I internally screamed to escape, my brain continued to grasp for explanations or solutions. At the same time, I had no control of my body; my limbs and torso were writhing back and forth. My instinctual body was trying to get away from this unbelievable pain, too. But since the brain didn't have control, the body was just fighting it all. A nurse came in and looked at me rolling around, obviously in outrageous pain. She held up two fingers and asked me how many I saw. Remember, I was still in a pure rage. When she made that request, my wrath exploded and destroyed my image of her.

I noticed my vision was warped and distorted, and the colors were skyrocketing and forming different patterns; it was like the grand finale of a fireworks extravaganza, and it was all happening in my mind. When I blinked my eyes again and again, I discovered that what I saw was the same whether my eyes were open or closed. Either way, I was *not* seeing things as they were in reality. "Oh my God, I'm blind!" I thought.

Then, for some reason the writhing and internal chaos seemed to cease. I didn't hurt, feel, or hear anything anymore, though I was still scared. I realized that up to that moment, I had been totally exuding anger and hatred. While I was consumed with this hatred, I felt that if I were physically able, I would have flailed about and crushed anything in front of me.

My thought process shut down. My mind's eye rapidly flashed before me scenes from my entire life—from birth to the present. I was floating away into another dimension as if I were watching myself; maybe my spirit was separating from my body. In retrospect, it all seems so strange. Earlier, my body and mind had been working on instinct as I writhed and contorted, attempting to get rid of the horrendous anguish and all-encompassing pain. I had been fighting against death with ultimate fear. But all of a sudden, my entire being succumbed and then accepted what was happening. At that point, I felt I was floating in the "right" direction; I didn't resist anymore. The battle was over and I comfortably accepted my approaching death. I was exiting. I anticipated a new future in a new dimension. Then, I believe I was brought back to life by the brain surgeon. I was redirected into a deep sleep (or coma) and did not regain consciousness until twenty-one days later, when I awoke into the so-called reality of Tacoma General Hospital's Intensive Care Unit.

Let me explain a bit of what had happened. I had had what's commonly called an *aneurysm*, or ruptured blood vessel in the brain. The brain has many different sections, each with different functions in the overall "system." When the blood vessel exploded in the left hemisphere, a major "glitch" occurred in the communication area—the area that controls our abstract thinking processes as well as our physical movements, fine motor control, sense of balance, and other functions. My aneurysm caused the loss of at least three of the five senses: touch, hearing, and vision. I don't know if I lost smell or taste.

When my stroke happened, it was as if the system shut down. All of the physical components of my body transferred energy to where the emergency was. Unfortunately, this is the sequence that one's body follows, not only when it is reacting to a crisis, but also when it is about to die. I was told later that I had been in critical condition. My parents and friends were informed that I would be dead within ten to fifteen minutes if the brain surgeon didn't operate and snip the area of my brain where the bleeding occurred. The doctors anticipated that I would be confined to a wheelchair and unable to communicate for the rest of my life—a vegetable, a ruta-baga. But I turned out to be an artichoke—"prickly on the outside, with a wonder-ful heart on the inside" (to quote an extraordinary man and advocate for the disabled, Ed Roberts)!

One thing that was so odd was that the brain attack happened when I was only twenty years old. (The stroke definitely sped up my maturation process!) At that time, I admittedly had no knowledge of what a stroke was; as a matter of fact, I didn't even know what a disability was. At that age, I had no conception of disabili-ties or fatal traumas—I still had a young adult mind-set and thought I was invinci-ble. I was only beginning to mature.

Response and Analysis

1. What cognitive and physical difficulties did Rod McLean experience before he went to the emergency room? How did the stroke affect McLean physically and emo-tionally?

2. According to McLean, his stroke occurred in the parietal lobe. What are the functions of the parietal lobe? What if McLean's stroke had occurred in the frontal lobe? What changes in behavior or types of problems might you expect? What if in the occipital lobe or the temporal lobe?

Personal Experience and Application

1. What thoughts and feelings do you have after reading McLean's account of his stroke?

Research

Strokes, heart disease, and cancer are associated with lifestyle behaviors, such as using alcohol, smoking, and diet. Researchers examining the relationship between lifestyle behaviors and dis-ease in humans typically use correlational designs. Why? What is the primary drawback to using a correlational design?

chapter 2

SENSATION AND PERCEPTION

*A man may see how this world goes
with no eyes. Look with thine ears.*

WILLIAM SHAKESPEARE, *King Lear*

Our senses let us enter the world, and we perceive what comes to us in complex ways. This chapter focuses on issues concerning sensation and perception: physical characteristics of sound; auditory transduction; touch and pain sensation; olfaction; aromatic memory; and theories of color vision.

Diane Ackerman celebrates the meeting of our senses with the world. Sight, touch, taste, smell, hearing—we use them all for pleasure, warning, survival. Here Ackerman observes our sense of smell. How does it serve us? Do humans and animals use the sense of smell in different ways?

John Hockenberry's senses are all intact except in the area below his lower chest. Hockenberry was injured in an automobile accident when he was nineteen years old. He writes, often in explicit detail and sometimes with anger, about how his paralysis affects his life. Particularly impressive is the strength he has developed in the rest of his body, and the tenacity and stamina he has developed to pursue his career as an international reporter. In this selection, Hockenberry recalls preparing stuffing for a Thanksgiving turkey and placing a hot pan on his lap. Because he had no sensation of pain, he burned one leg badly. He and his doctors did not realize the seriousness of the burn until several months later. That burn nearly cost him his life.

David Wright is deaf. Yet he states that "there is no such thing as absolute deafness." What does he "hear"? Interestingly, Wright says that the world seldom *appears* silent because "silence is not absence of sound but of movement." Therefore, at a time when not a leaf stirs, he sees the silence; when the wind stirs, he sees and "hears" the motion.

Oliver Sacks worked with a man named Virgil whose vision was partially restored after some forty years. Virgil and his fiancée, Amy, consulted an ophthalmologist, who agreed that there was a possibility that surgery might restore Virgil's sight. The surgery was at least partially successful, and Virgil was able to see about 20/80 and to discern very large letters. Unfortunately, the restoration of his eyesight proved a mixed blessing. He had difficulty seeing objects in their wholeness and difficulty with depth perception. How difficult might it be to adjust to some renewed vision after having adapted so well without it?

A NATURAL HISTORY OF THE SENSES

Diane Ackerman

Psychological Concepts
olfaction, aromatic memory, pheromones

Does scent have a memory? What fragrances bring to your mind a specific time or place? The salt air of the sea? A pine forest? A cologne?

Our olfactory sense bears a mysterious quality. We can't paint it or touch it; we can't see it or hear it. Yet it is as strong and important as any of our other senses. Odors affect every part of our lives, warning us of dangerous gases, driving us away from rot, and increasing our appetite for fragrant foods or our pleasure in delectable aromas.

How do we describe these scents? "Smell," writes Ackerman, "is the mute sense, the one without words" (p. 6).* Although we can describe smells as floral, musky, resinous, ethereal, foul, or acrid, this cataloging does not convey what the smell of a gardenia is like. Nevertheless, being an astute observer and gifted writer, Ackerman manages to write about this powerful sense and makes us more aware of its importance.

We each have our own aromatic memories. One of my most vivid involves an odor that was as much vapor as scent. One Christmas, I traveled along the coast of California with the Los Angeles Museum's Monarch Project, locating and tagging great numbers of overwintering monarch butterflies. They prefer to winter in eucalyptus groves, which are deeply fragrant. The first time I stepped into one, and every time thereafter, they filled me with sudden tender memories of mentholated rub and childhood colds. First we reached high into the trees, where the butterflies hung in fluttering gold garlands, and caught a group of them with telescoping nets. Then we sat on the ground, which was densely covered with the South African ice plant, a type of succulent, and one of the very few plants that can tolerate the heavy oils that drop from the trees. The oils kept crawling insects away, too, and, except for the occasional Pacific tree frog croaking like someone working the tumblers of a

---

*In this and all subsequent introductions, any quotations that are not in the excerpt can be found in the unabridged version of the selection.

safe, or a foolish blue jay trying to feed on the butterflies (whose wings contain a digitalis-like poison), the sunlit forests were serene, otherworldly, and immense with quiet. Because of the eucalyptus vapor, I not only smelled the scent, I felt it in my nose and throat. The loudest noise was the occasional sound of a door creaking open, the sound of eucalyptus bark peeling off the trees and falling to the ground, where it would soon roll up like papyrus. Everywhere I looked, there seemed to be proclamations left by some ancient scribe. Yet, to my nose, it was Illinois in the 1950s. It was a school day; I was tucked in bed, safe and cosseted, feeling my mother massage my chest with Vicks VapoRub. That scent and memory brought an added serenity to the hours of sitting quietly in the forest and handling the exquisite butterflies, gentle creatures full of life and beauty who stalk nothing and live on nectar, like the gods of old. What made this recall doubly sweet was the way it became layered in my senses. Though at first tagging butterflies triggered memories of childhood, afterward the butterfly-tagging *itself* became a scent-triggerable memory, and, what's more, it replaced the original one: In Manhattan one day, I stopped at a flower-seller's on the street, as I always do when I travel, to choose a few flowers for the hotel room. Two tubs held branches of round, silver-dollar-shaped eucalyptus, the leaves of which were still fresh—bluish-green with a chalky surface; a few of them had broken, and released their thick, pungent vapor into the air. Despite the noise of Third Avenue traffic, the drilling of the City Works Department, the dust blowing up off the streets and the clotted gray of the sky, I was instantly transported to a particularly beautiful eucalyptus grove near Santa Barbara. A cloud of butterflies flew along a dried-up riverbed. I sat serenely on the ground, lifting yet another gold-and-black monarch butterfly from my net, carefully tagging it and tossing it back into the air, then watching for a moment to make sure it flew safely away with its new tag pasted like a tiny epaulet on one wing. The peace of that moment crested over me like a breaking wave and saturated my senses. A young Vietnamese man arranging his stock looked hard at me, and I realized that my eyes had suddenly teared. The whole episode could not have taken more than a few seconds, but the combined scent memories endowed eucalyptus with an almost savage power to move me. That afternoon, I went to one of my favorite shops, a boutique in the Village, where they will compound a bath oil for you, using a base of sweet almond oil, or make up shampoos or body lotions from other fragrant ingredients. Hanging from my bathtub's shower attachment is a blue net bag of the sort Frenchwomen use when they do their daily grocery shopping; I keep in it a wide variety of bath potions, and eucalyptus is one of the most calming. How is it possible that Dickens's chance encounter with a few molecules of glue, or mine with eucalyptus, can transport us back to an otherwise inaccessible world? . . .

Smells spur memories, but they also rouse our dozy senses, pamper and indulge us, help define our self-image, stir the cauldron of our seductiveness, warn us of danger, lead us into temptation, fan our religious fervor, accompany us to heaven, wed us to fashion, steep us in luxury. Yet, over time, smell has become the least necessary of our senses, "the fallen angel," as Helen Keller dramatically calls it. Some researchers believe that we do indeed perceive, through smell, much of the same information lower animals do. In a room full of businesspeople, one would get information about which individuals were important, which were confident, which were sexually receptive, which in conflict, all through smell. The difference is that we don't have a trigger response. We're aware of smell, but we don't automatically react in certain ways because of it, as most animals would.

One morning I took a train to Philadelphia to visit the Monell Chemical Senses Center near the campus of Drexel University. Laid out like a vertical neighborhood, Monell's building houses hundreds of researchers who study the chemistry, psychology, healing properties, and odd characteristics of smell. Many of the news-making pheromone studies have taken place at Monell, or at similar institutions. In one experiment, rooms full of housewives were paid to sniff anonymous underarms; in another study, funded by a feminine hygiene spray manufacturer, the scene was even more bizarre. Among Monell's concerns: how we recognize smells; what happens when someone loses their sense of smell; how smell varies as one grows older; ingenious ways to control wildlife pests through smell; the way body odors can be used to help diagnose diseases (the sweat of schizophrenics smells different from that of normal people, for example); how body scents influence our social and sexual behavior. Monell researchers have discovered, in one of the most fascinating smell experiments of our time, that mice can discriminate genetic differences among potential mates by smell alone; they read the details of other animals' immune systems. If you want to create the strongest offspring, it's best to mate with someone whose strengths are different from yours, so that you can create the maximum defenses against any intruder, bacteria, viruses, and so on. And the best way to do that is to produce an omnicompetent immune system. Nature thrives in mongrels. *Mix well* is life's motto. Monell scientists have been able to raise special mice that differ from one another in only a single gene, and observe their mating preferences. They all chose mates whose immune systems would combine with theirs to produce the hardiest litters. Furthermore, they did not base their choices on their perception of their own smell, but on the remembered smell of their parents. None of this was reasoned, of course; the mice just mated according to their drive, unaware of the subliminal fiats.

Can it be possible that human beings do this, too, without realizing it? We don't require smell to mark territories, establish hierarchies, recognize individuals or, especially, know when a female is in heat. And yet one look at the obsessive use of perfume and its psychological effect on us makes it clear that smell is an old warhorse of evolution we groom and feed and just can't let go of. We don't need it to survive, but we crave it beyond all reason, maybe, in part, out of a nostalgia for a time when we were creatureal, a deeply connected part of Nature. As evolution has phased out our sense of smell, chemists have labored to restore it. Nor is it something we do casually; we drench ourselves in smells, we wallow in them. Not only do we perfume our bodies and homes, we perfume almost every object that enters our lives, from our cars to our toilet paper. Used-car dealers have a "new-car" spray, guaranteed to make a buyer feel good about the oldest tin warthog. Real estate dealers sometimes spray "cake-baking" aromas around the kitchen of a house before showing it to a client. Shopping malls add "pizza smell" to their air-conditioning system to put shoppers in the mood to visit their restaurants. Clothing, tires, magic markers, and toys all reek with scent. One can even buy perfume discs that play like records, except that they exude scent. As has been proven in many experiments, if you hand people two cans of identical furniture polish, one of which has a pleasant odor, they will swear that the pleasantly scented one works better. Odor greatly affects our evaluation of things, and our evaluation of people. Even so-called unscented products are, in fact, scented to mask the chemical odors of their ingredients, usually with a light musk. In fact, only 20 percent of the perfume industry's income comes from making perfumes to wear; the other 80 percent comes from perfuming the objects in our lives. Nationality influences fragrances, as many companies have discovered. Germans like pine, French prefer flowery scents, Japanese like more delicate odors, North Americans insist on bold smells, and South Americans want even stronger ones. In Venezuela, floor-cleaning products contain ten times as much pine fragrance as those in the United States. What almost all nationalities share is the need to coat our floors and walls with pleasant odors, especially with the smell of a pine forest or lemon orchard, to nest in smells.

Response and Analysis

1. What does Diane Ackerman mean when she writes that "we each have our own aromatic memories"? Briefly describe one of Ackerman's aromatic memories. What anatomical features in humans might account for the relationship between olfaction and memory?

2. Briefly describe the experiments being conducted at the Monell Chemical Senses Center that investigate the relationship between smell and mood. Why might smell influence mood and the way we evaluate objects? Why might it influence social behavior and mate selection in animals?

Personal Experience and Application

1. Think about an experience in which a smell triggered a distant memory. Briefly describe the scent and the memory that you associated with it. How did you feel when you recollected the memory? Why?

2. Many industries, such as wineries, perfumeries, and food manufacturers, need expert smellers. Suppose the Human Resources Department at a perfumery asks you to make a few recommendations for teaching newly hired employees to detect and identify various smells. What recommendations might you offer?

Research

Suppose you want to conduct an experiment to explore whether people in certain cultures can detect and identify odors better than people in other cultures. You decide to use a scratch-and-sniff test with various odors, and you ask the participants (a) if they can smell the scent; and (b) to identify the scent. You plan to administer the scratch-and-sniff test in four countries: England, Singapore, Japan, and Kenya. The participants will be second-year male and female college students who were born in their countries. How might their experiences with the odors in your study influence their ability to detect and identity those odors?

MOVING VIOLATIONS

John Hockenberry

Psychological Concepts
touch, pain sensation and perception, paraplegia

John Hockenberry, former correspondent for National Public Radio and currently with NBC-TV's news magazine program *Dateline,* suffered a spinal cord injury at the age of nineteen from an automobile accident. That injury left him a paraplegic without sensation in his legs or abdomen and little in his chest.

Hockenberry is reporter *extraordinaire.* He has ridden a mule up a hillside in Iraq, maneuvered his wheelchair through almost intractable stretches of Middle Eastern sand, and applied to be the first journalist in space. There are few places Hockenberry has not gone with his wheelchair. When riding a New York subway, he has climbed up and down the often filthy stairs, lugging his wheelchair as he crawled where he could not ride.

Along with frank details about how others sometimes perceive and treat him, Hockenberry writes of the frustrations of limited sensation. In the following selection, he tells of how he nearly lost his life because of a burn he suffered on his leg when he placed a hot pan on his lap. Unable to feel any pain from the heat, Hockenberry was unaware of the burn that was taking place.

Numbness is a distinct feeling. Just as zero gives meaning to all numbers, numbness is a placeholder of the flesh, the boundary where consciousness and body divide, where life becomes the inanimate vessel we live in. Our lives are played out under an inanimate universe. Sensation is the sideshow, a spotlight inside a tent of darkness. We step in and out of the white circle. It blinds us if we look directly at it. We are just as sightless in the dark.

We worship sensation, longing to make its impressions real. We endow our awareness with the divinity of the creator. We scour our pleasures for a sign that good feelings mean that the universe actually likes us. We make excuses for our pain, insisting that others acknowledge its seriousness. Or we push into our pain, seeking the actual mechanical limits of our bodies. We yearn to equate sense with reality. We discover, every time, that sensation is just the playpen where we have been put. The odd toys handed down to us are all we have to work with. Like a baby, we can throw toys away, but we cannot get any more.

To honor sensation is to honor an illusion. To honor what has none is humanity's original act of faith. My legs have no sensation. Neither does my abdomen or much of my chest. With heart and lungs inside, my chest and abdomen retain their function despite numbness. My legs have lost even that. They are culs-de-sac of blood and bone that carry no weight, must themselves be carried, and justify their existence on the slimmest of pretexts: that regardless of all that, they are still my legs.

Occasionally they will jerk with a spastic, repeating rhythm. The accidental poke of a pen point, the drops of scalding water dribbled from a teapot, an ice cube landing in my lap are sometimes answered by a muscle's spastic movement. Their connection to the spinal cord, if not to the brain above it, is still intact. My legs move by themselves. I feel nothing, but my legs must still feel something akin to pain or pleasure. They remain connected; their nerves do what they have always done. They call home. The phone has been ringing off the hook for nineteen years.

The loss of sensation takes some getting used to. On my left thigh, midway between my knee and my hip, is a scar about six inches long and two to three inches wide. It looks like Madagascar. It also precisely resembles the shape that the bottom of a large Corning Ware baking dish makes when pressed into soft dough, or the soft spongy tissue that used to lie between my lap and my left femur. In 1977 I was cooking stuffing for a Thanksgiving turkey on an electric stove in an apartment in Springfield, Oregon. The Corning Ware dish was taken from the refrigerator first. Its ceramic handles were quite cold, a sensation they conveyed even after several minutes on the hot burner of an electric range.

If this had been a metal pot, a few minutes on the burner would have conducted heat all over its surface and into the air around it. A metal pot would have broadcast its temperature, conveying immediately that it was an object to keep well away from the skin. On any other body but mine, if the pot had made accidental contact, pain would have made sure the pot was swiftly moved. But ceramic is not a conductor of heat. Just a few minutes out of the refrigerator, the dish was cold to the touch everywhere but underneath, where the burner of the stove was beginning to cook the bread cubes, spices, and melting butter. On the bottom of the dish, next to the burner, it was probably three hundred degrees. It was certainly close to that temperature when I picked up the dish, and holding its still-cold handles set it down absently and squarely on my lap.

With a wooden spoon, I mixed the crumbs and spices and butter while I held the dish steady. The aroma of cooking rose from inside the dish. I felt nothing. With no saucepan resting on its element, the electric burner I had taken the dish from moments before began to glow red. Its heat hit my face. I continued to stir. I added a little milk and heard a sizzling sound as the liquid contacted the hot bottom of the plate. I still felt nothing and continued stirring and adding spices, and talking to whoever else was in the room.

When I removed the dish, my left leg trembled. The spasticity was odd. Normally my legs had coarse, slow movements when they were spastic. This time their motions were tiny and very fast. There was no sensation, but a slight queasiness passed over me. Something was wrong, but the idea that I had actually set a hot pan on my lap and had been calmly stirring its contents for several minutes was so absurd that even then I did not think I had burned my leg severely. It seemed impossible that such a thing could have happened.

It was only after I could see a slight outline of fluid on my pants leg that I suspected something terrible might have happened. I looked at the leg. Its motions now were more pronounced, erratic, and unknown to me. I had not seen this kind of motion before. From my detached position, looking down, it was as though I was watching a horror movie. My legs appeared to be in agony. It was clear even without sensation that the legs were now trying to account for an act of the creator above that seemed senseless and cruel. I felt embarrassed and foolish. Then, as the stain on my thigh became more apparent, I felt scared.

Removing my trousers revealed the place where the hot dish had sat for perhaps two full minutes. It was something to see, and even more shocking to watch, without feeling the slightest pain. The skin was gathered into a leathery, shrunken depression on the top of my thigh. The hairs had all been cooked into a blistered white wound. The root of each hair was a raised dot where the glands beneath the skin had simply exploded from the heat. There was no blood, for reasons that would become apparent later. The wound looked unearthly. It was just as unusual to the doctors at the local hospital who examined it and concluded that it was only a second-degree burn.

If I had any sensation about this whole affair, it was embarrassment. To go to the hospital over something that didn't hurt at all seemed like complaining. I laughed about it with the doctors. I was ashamed to have done such a stupid thing. I was trying to be a good paraplegic and not make silly mistakes. I felt sorry for wasting the doctors' time. That I felt nothing, and was so apologetic about what appeared to be a pretty serious burn, made the doctors suspicious. They began to ask about my life at home. Perhaps there was some more sinister explanation for the burn. "Did anyone get mad at you this morning?" a nurse asked. They asked about drugs or some angry relative who might have wanted to punish me. I told them I lived alone. They called my house to make sure it was so. One of the doctors asked if this burn might have been self-inflicted. "Yes," I said, "I told you it was." He looked at me again. "Is there anything you want to tell me?"

The burn no longer scared me. This emergency room intern who thought I might have tried to kill myself with a Corning Ware dish filled with bread cubes and butter pats was suddenly making me very nervous. He was so convinced that this was a plausible explanation for my leg burn that for a moment I thought I might be in shock, and that someone had actually tried to cook me that morning but that I was just blocking it out. "Look, I just made a stupid mistake with the dish. It felt cold on the top. I couldn't feel that it was hot on the bottom. I set it on my lap for a minute. I won't do it again. Can I go now?"

In their haste to establish some explanation for the burn other than that I had accidentally cooked my thigh while preparing a turkey, they missed just how serious a burn it was. The numbness in my legs threw them off. A third-degree burn is rarely the result of a moderate amount of heat applied over a period of minutes. More commonly, it is an extremely high temperature contacting the skin for a short period of time. A slowly cooked leg is not a textbook injury. It suggests torture, an unusual malady in Springfield, Oregon, in 1977. The doctors did what they normally would for a second-degree burn—they gave me a large bandage, some iodine, and sent me home.

The wound did not heal for months. For a while it shed large chunks of dead tissue and a brown fluid totally unlike anything I had ever seen emerge from my body. I tried to get it to scab over, or heal under a bandage. It simply got worse. Each morning and night I would look at a wound that, if I could feel it, would have been infinitely more painful than anything that had happened in my accident. I stared down at it from above as though I were on some leisurely balloon ride. I had no sensation, yet I worried about the leg. I felt sorry for its pain. It could not tell me how it felt, it could not do anything for me. I became sentimental about all of the times my legs had helped me. I wanted to help them. But I was also fascinated by the invulnerability of numbness. There was no urgency about this wound because I felt no pain. I slept normally. I ate normally. I had to bandage the leg before going out to prevent it from staining my pants, but otherwise I could go about my life without much concern that my thigh was dangerously infected.

This was still the case three months later, so I went to the only doctor I knew by name in Oregon. Dr. Ellison was a urologist who handled all of the local crips' catheter problems and said he would be glad to look at this burn trouble I was having. He told me to remove my pants. He eyed the size of the bandage as I started to untape it from the skin around the wound. When he saw the wound, he stopped cold. He told his nurses to shut all of the doors to the examination rooms and to scrub him for surgery. He declared the room I was in in quarantine and began spraying the air with antiseptic. When the nurse asked if he needed anesthetic, he nodded and then caught himself. "No, I guess I won't be needing it this time."

Without anesthesia, and for nearly an hour while I calmly watched, Dr. Ellison poked and scrubbed and pulled away dead skin. For the first time since Thanksgiving, my leg began to bleed profusely. When he was finished, he wrapped my leg in gauze and removed a surgical mask he had put on. "You would have lost your leg if you had waited much longer." He shook his head as he took my temperature. "If you had started to run a fever, you could have died."

All of this had happened with me as a spectator feeling no pain. I did feel guilty that I might have put my legs through a nearly fatal ordeal. With the wound cleaned and its dead tissue removed, my leg began to heal. The circulation came back. My thigh returned to its normal pink color. In a matter of weeks, the wound was fully closed. All that remained of the trauma was a spectacular scar. On my last visit to the doctor he noted that while the wound had healed well, the nerves in the thigh were probably damaged beyond repair. "There will be no feeling here ever again," he said gravely as he probed the scar with his finger.

It was odd to think that my legs and I shared numbness now. Two degrees of sensation: my own loss of feeling in the parts of me below the break in my spinal cord, and the loss of nerves in the skin on my thigh. With my fingers I could feel the cold, leathery numbness of the scar surrounded by warm, healthy skin. Numbness has a feeling and a texture. Doctor Ellison suddenly realized his mistake. "I'm sorry, I forgot for a moment that you can't feel anyway. I guess it doesn't really matter," he said.

Response and Analysis

1. John Hockenberry raises an important issue regarding sensation: "We yearn to equate sense with reality." How do sensation and numbness affect Hockenberry's perceptions of reality and self-identity? Give examples from his narrative to support your ideas.

2. Briefly describe John Hockenberry's limits to feeling pain below his chest. Briefly discuss one theory that explains how the spinal cord influences the amount of pain that reaches the brain. What factors may influence the amount of pain we experience?

Personal Experience and Application

1. Briefly describe the daily difficulties that may be associated with being unable to walk and not having sensation below the waist. Do you think people behave differently when they interact with someone in a wheelchair than with an able-bodied person? Why or why not?

2. People use different techniques to relieve pain. Suppose you are babysitting a six-year-old boy. You are watching him ride his bicycle on the sidewalk in front of his house. Suddenly the tire hits a rock and he falls off the bike, scrapes his elbow on the pavement, and begins to cry. You want to calm the child. Briefly discuss two approaches you might take to help relieve his pain. How might your words help reduce his pain?

Research

The procedures of an experiment must be ethical and must protect the rights and dignity of the participants. One of the challenges to conducting research on pain is designing a procedure that does not harm the participants, since most people do not enjoy pain. How might you ethically examine how we perceive pain?

DEAFNESS:
AN AUTOBIOGRAPHY

David Wright

Psychological Concepts
hearing, physical characteristics of sound

What might it be like to suddenly be cut off from the world of sound? Do the other senses compensate for the loss? In what way?

Poet David Wright, born in 1920 in Johannesburg, South Africa, became deaf from scarlet fever when he was seven years old. At the age of fourteen he went to England, where he attended a school for the deaf, and in 1942 he graduated from Oxford University. If deafness was to be his "destiny," Wright observes, he was fortunate that he had already developed language skills. He could speak and had a vocabulary that could easily be developed further by reading. These advantages helped him personally and professionally.

In this selection Wright points out what might at first seem a contradiction: he can't hear, yet he doesn't live in complete silence. His explanation helps us understand what kinds of sounds break up his silent world.

About deafness I know everything and nothing. Everything, if forty years' first-hand experience is to count. Nothing, when I realize the little I have to do with the converse aspects of deafness—the other half of the dialogue. Of that side my wife knows more than I. So do teachers of the deaf and those who work among them; not least, people involuntarily but intensely involved—ordinary men and women who find themselves, from one cause or another, parents of a deaf child. For it is the non-deaf who absorb a large part of the impact of the disability. The limitations imposed by deafness are often less noticed by its victims than by those with whom they have to do.

Deafness is a disability without pathos. Dr. Johnson called it "the most desperate of human calamities." Yet its effects are slapstick:

"Where's the baby?"

"I put it in the dustbin."*

There is a buffoonery about deafness which is liable to rub off on anybody who comes into contact with it. Having to shout at the hard of hearing is not ele-

---

*To a lipreader the words *baby* and *paper* are almost indistinguishable.

gant, nor is finger-spelling or the mouthing of words to magnify lip movements for those whose eyes are their ears. . . .

Very few are absolutely deaf. Their experience must necessarily be different from that of the severely deaf, the partially deaf, and the merely hard of hearing. The partially deaf, it seems to me, have the worst of both worlds. They hear enough to be distracted by noise yet not enough for it to be meaningful. For the merely hard of hearing there is the strain of extracting significance from sounds that may be as loud as life yet out of focus; what comes through is an auditory fuzz. Of course there are hearing-aids, but not everybody can profit from these.

Yet what is crucial is the age at which hearing is lost. Those who have been born deaf, whether completely or partially, must always be at a disadvantage compared with those who lose hearing later in life. The deaf-born cannot pick up speech and language naturally like ordinary children. They have to be taught, a difficult and slow process, the slower and more difficult the later the teaching begins. For the most intense activity of the brain takes place in the first few years of one's life, and thereafter—from the age of about three—gradually decreases. That is why small children quickly and easily pick up foreign languages while older children and adults find it an effort. But the born deaf and those who become deaf in early childhood have the compensation that they do not feel the loss of a faculty they never had or cannot remember. They are at least spared the painful effort of adjustment. The later in life one loses hearing, the sharper the test of character and fortitude: because adaptability lessens with age. On the other hand the years of hearing are so much money in the bank. Those to whom deafness comes late do not have to acquire with pain and struggle the elements of language, vocabulary, speech. These assets—pure gold—are theirs already. . . .

I do not live in a world of complete silence. There is no such thing as absolute deafness. Coming from one whose aural nerve is extinct, this statement may be taken as authoritative.

Let me attempt to define the auditory limits of the world I inhabit. They are perhaps less restricted than may be imagined. Without entering into technicalities about sones, decibels, and so on, it may be said that all sound is vibration and that the ear, roughly speaking, is a highly specialized organ for the reception of air-vibrations or sound-waves. But other things beside air conduct vibration and therefore sound—wood for instance. If I stand on a wooden floor I can "hear" footsteps behind me, but not when standing on a floor made of some less resonant substance—for example stone or concrete. I can even partially "hear" my own voice. This is not surprising, for people hear themselves talk mainly by bone-conduction inside their heads (but other persons by air-conduction; that is why people find their own voices sounding surprisingly different when thrown back at them by a tape recorder). Yet like nearly all deaf people I cannot judge the loudness or quality of my own voice. To some extent I can do so by putting a finger against my Adam's apple or voicebox. This is well known as one of the ways in which the deaf can be made to "hear" something of a speech-instructor's voice. Likewise I "hear" a piano if I place a finger on it while it is being played; a radio and gramophone too, when touching the sound box or amplifier. (The gramophone needle gives best results, but this isn't good for the record.) Such "hearing" is selective; I receive only the low notes of the scale, the high ones elude me. No matter how loud the volume is turned on what comes through is a bent or incomplete version of actual sound. In "touch-hearing" most music, and all speech, comes across as a blurry bumble of noise.

Nevertheless there is some music that I enjoy after a fashion. But it has to be produced by stringed instruments (harp, guitar, piano, double-bass, and so on) as I cannot hear wind-instruments (flute, bagpipes, oboe). Percussive instruments like drums are naturally well inside my range. I have a passion for military bands, though hearing little except the drumtaps, a sad boom-thud from the big drum and a clattering exhilaration from the kettledrums. . . .

To get on with the list of things audible, or at least interfering with the silence that might be expected to compensate a totally occluded ear, let me tabulate the following: gunfire, detonation of high-explosive, low-flying aeroplanes, cars backfiring, motor-bicycles, heavy lorries, carts clattering over cobblestones, wurlitzers, pneumatic drills. There can't be much that I miss of the normal orchestration of urban existence. I should add that I also once heard the human voice. One day in 1963 I was at Lord's cricket ground; Ted Dexter had just come in to bat against the West Indies. He put a couple of runs on the board with the air of a man who means to get another ninety-eight before lunch. Suddenly he was bowled. While the bails were still flying, coats, hats, cushions, umbrellas, sandwiches, for all I know babies even, were hurled into the air by some nine or ten thousand West Indians in the free seats where I was watching. Up went a simultaneous roar of delight. Hearing that sound, for me not very loud but like a croaking bark, was a queer and spooky experience. I have never forgotten it.

It will be seen that the world a deaf man inhabits is not one of complete silence, which is perhaps the chief complaint he has to make about it. There is another point. Though noise, as such, does not obtrude to the extent that the above catalogue would seem to imply, the world in which I live seldom *appears* silent. Let me try to explain what I mean. In my case, silence is not absence of sound but of movement.

Suppose it is a calm day, absolutely still, not a twig or leaf stirring. To me it will seem quiet as a tomb though hedgerows are full of noisy but invisible birds. Then comes a breath of air, enough to unsettle a leaf; I will see and hear that movement like an exclamation. The illusory soundlessness has been interrupted. I see, as if I heard, a visionary noise of wind in a disturbance of foliage. Wordsworth in a late poem exactly caught the phenomenon in a remarkable line:

> *A soft eye-music of slow-waving boughs*

which may have subconsciously derived from an equally cogent line in Coleridge's *The Eolian Harp:*

> *A light in sound, a sound-like power of light.*

The "sound" seen by me is not necessarily equivalent to the real one. It must often be close enough, in my case helped by a subliminal memory of things once heard. I cannot watch a gale without "hearing" an uproar of violent movement: trees thrashing, grassblades battling and flattened; or, at sea, waves locked and staggering like all-in wrestlers—this kind of thing comes through as hubbub enough. On the other hand I also live in a world of sounds which are, as I know quite well, imaginary because non-existent. Yet for me they are part of reality. I have sometimes to make a deliberate effort to remember I am not "hearing" anything, because there is nothing to hear. Such non-sounds include the flight and movement of birds, even fish swimming in clear water or the tank of an aquarium. I take it that the flight of most birds, at least at a distance, must be silent—bar the creaking noise made by the wings of swans and some kinds of wild geese. Yet it *appears* audible, each species creating a different "eye-music," from the nonchalant melancholy of seagulls to the staccato flitting of tits.

This is not to subscribe to the irritating theory that the loss of one sense is compensated for by the quickening of another. There are no compensations, life is not like that. At best we are offered alternatives. We have no choice but to take them.

This is by no means a complete picture of the world I live in, or of any other deaf person's, come to that. Almost nothing has been said about the major hurdle of deafness, the problem of communication. It is simply an attempt to convey what deafness is like physically, or at least what it's like so far as one deaf man is concerned, before I go on to tell the story of how I lost my hearing, how I reacted, how I was educated, and the various stratagems necessity forced me to adopt to get on and get by in a non-deaf world.

For I am now, after forty years of what we will term silence, so accommodated to it (like a hermit-crab to its shell) that were the faculty of hearing restored to me tomorrow it would appear an affliction rather than a benefit. I do not mean that I find deafness desirable but that in the course of time the disability has been assimilated to the extent that it is now an integral condition of existence, like the use of a hand. By the same token the restoration of my hearing, or the loss of my deafness, whichever is the right way of putting it, would be like having that hand cut off.

Response and Analysis

1. Briefly discuss the types of sounds that David Wright can hear. How can Wright "hear" footsteps and his own voice? Then describe the physical characteristics of sound (e.g., amplitude, wavelength, and frequency).

2. Why does Wright believe that the age at which hearing is lost is crucial to language acquisition and speech?

Personal Experience and Application

1. Do you or does someone you know have a hearing impairment? At what age did the hearing difficulties begin? What speech and communication difficulties do you observe?

2. Research indicates that excessive exposure to sounds that are 85 decibels and louder can cause hearing loss. Here is a brief list of

common sounds and their approximate intensities: normal conversation: 60 decibels; vacuum cleaner: 70 decibels; city traffic: 80 decibels; power lawn mower: 90 decibels; subway train from a distance of 20 feet: 100 decibels; jackhammer: 110 decibels; amplified rock music: 120 decibels. One study found that the average intensity of music that college students play over headphones is 88 decibels (Brody, 1982). List the sounds you hear every day that may be 85 decibels or louder.

Research

Suppose you conduct a longitudinal study to investigate the impact of repeated exposure to loud music on hearing ability. You conduct your project for one year. The participants are thirty 18-year-old rock musicians who practice with their band at least twice a week and play at a music club at least twice a month. You measure their hearing ability on the first day of each month. Unfortunately, during the year half of the musicians move out of the area and discontinue their participation in your study. At the end of the year, you have complete data for only fifteen musicians. Might the loss of the fifteen musicians affect your conclusions? Why or why not?

TO SEE AND NOT SEE

Oliver Sacks

Psychological Concepts
top-down processing, trichromatic theory of color vision, opponent process theory of color vision

What if, after some forty years of blindness, you were to have your sight restored? How would you feel? Would you expect to have any difficulties, and if so, what might they be?

Oliver Sacks tells the story of a man who regained partial eyesight in midlife. Virgil was a fifty-year-old man who had been blind since early childhood. He was soon to be married, and his fiancée, Amy, had taken him to her ophthalmologist for an examination. The couple learned that through a relatively simple operation

Virgil might be able to see again. Virgil consented to the surgery, and when the bandages were removed, some of his sight was restored.

However, Virgil faced many difficulties: shadows confused him, and stairways became a hazard because of problems with depth perception. When Tibbles, his cat, came to him, Virgil struggled to see the ears and head, body and tail, as all of a piece so that he could see Cat. "Now, five weeks after surgery," Oliver Sacks writes, "he often felt more disabled than he had felt when he was blind" (p. 121). Virgil's story illustrates the difficulties that may occur when one's sight is restored after so long a time.

When we arrived at the house, Virgil, caneless, walked by himself up the path to the front door, pulled out his key, grasped the doorknob, unlocked the door, and opened it. This was impressive—he could never have done it at first, he said, and it was something he had been practicing since the day after surgery. It was his show-piece. But he said that in general he found walking "scary" and "confusing" without touch, without his cane, with his uncertain, unstable judgment of space and distance. Sometimes surfaces or objects would seem to loom, to be on top of him, when they were still quite a distance away; sometimes he would get confused by his own shadow (the whole concept of shadows, of objects blocking light, was puzzling to him) and would come to a stop, or trip, or try to step over it. Steps, in particular, posed a special hazard, because all he could see was a confusion, a flat surface, of parallel and crisscrossing lines; he could not see them (although he knew them) as solid objects going up or coming down in three-dimensional space. Now, five weeks after surgery, he often felt more disabled than he had felt when he was blind, and he had lost the confidence, the ease of moving, that he had possessed then. But he hoped all this would sort itself out with time.

I was not so sure; every patient described in the literature had faced great difficulties after surgery in the apprehension of space and distance—for months, even years. This was the case even in Valvo's highly intelligent patient H.S., who had been normally sighted until, at fifteen, his eyes were scarred by a chemical explosion. He had become totally blind until a corneal transplant was done twenty-two years later. But following this, he encountered grave difficulties of every kind, which he recorded, minutely, on tape:

> During these first weeks [after surgery] I had no appreciation of depth or distance; street lights were luminous stains stuck to the window panes, and the corridors of the hospital were black holes. When I crossed the road the traffic terrified me, even when I was accompanied. I am very insecure while walking; indeed I am more afraid now than before the operation.

We gathered in the kitchen at the back of the house, which had a large white deal table. Bob [an ophthalmologist] and I laid out all our test objects—color charts, letter charts, pictures, illusions—on it and set up a video camera to record the testing. As we settled down, Virgil's cat and dog bounded in to greet and check us—and Virgil, we noted, had some difficulty telling which was which. This comic and embarrassing problem had persisted since he returned home from surgery: both animals, as it happened, were black and white, and he kept confusing them—to their annoyance—until he could touch them, too. Sometimes, Amy said, she would see him examining the cat carefully, looking at its head, its ears, its paws, its tail, and touching each part gently as he did so. I observed this myself the next day—Virgil feeling and looking at Tibbles with extraordinary intentness, correlating the cat. He would keep doing this, Amy remarked ("You'd think once was enough"), but the new ideas, the visual recognitions, kept slipping from his mind.

Cheselden described a strikingly similar scene with his young patient in the 1720s:

> One particular only, though it might appear trifling, I will relate: Having often forgot which was the cat, and which the dog, he was ashamed to ask; but catching the cat, which he knew by feeling, he was observed to look at her steadfastly, and then, setting her down, said, So, puss, I shall know you another time. . . . Upon being told what things were . . . he would carefully observe that he might know them again; and (as he said) at first learned to know, and again forgot, a thousand things in a day.

Virgil's first formal recognitions when the bandages were taken off had been of letters on the ophthalmologist's eye chart, and we decided to test him, first, on letter recognition. He could not see ordinary newsprint clearly—his acuity was still only about 20/80—but he readily perceived letters that were more than a third of an inch high. Here he did rather well, for the most part, and recognized all the commoner letters (at least, capital letters) easily—as he had been able to do from the moment the bandages were removed. How was it that he had so much difficulty recognizing faces, or the cat, and so much difficulty with shapes generally, and with size and distance, and yet so little difficulty, relatively, recognizing letters? When I asked Virgil about this, he told me that he had learned the alphabet by touch at school, where they had used letter blocks, or cutout letters, for teaching the blind. I was struck by this and reminded of Gregory's patient S.B.: "much to our surprise, he could even tell the time by means of a large clock on the wall. We were so surprised at this that we did not at first believe that he could have been in any sense blind before the operation." But in his blind days S.B. had used a large hunter watch with no glass, telling the time by touching the hands, and he had apparently made an instant "crossmodal" transfer, to use Gregory's term, from touch to vision. Virgil too, it seemed, must have been making just such a transfer.

But while Virgil could recognize individual letters easily, he could not string them together—could not read or even see words. I found this puzzling, for he said that they used not only Braille but English in raised or inscribed letters at school—and that he had learned to read fairly fluently. Indeed, he could still easily read the inscriptions on war memorials and tombstones by touch. But his eyes seemed to fix on particular letters and to be incapable of the easy movement, the scanning, that is needed to read. This was also the case with the literate H.S.:

My first attempts at reading were painful. I could make out single letters, but it was impossible for me to make out whole words; I managed to do so only after weeks of exhausting attempts. In fact, it was impossible for me to remember all the letters together after having read them one by one. Nor was it possible for me, during the first weeks, to count my own five fingers: I had the feeling that they were all there, but . . . it was not possible for me to pass from one to the other while counting.

Further problems became apparent as we spent the day with Virgil. He would pick up details incessantly—an angle, an edge, a color, a movement—but would not be able to synthesize them, to form a complex perception at a glance. This was one reason the cat, visually, was so puzzling: he would see a paw, the nose, the tail, an ear, but could not see all of them together, see the cat as a whole.

Amy had commented in her journal on how even the most "obvious" connections—visually and logically obvious—had to be learned. Thus, she told us, a few days after the operation, "he said that trees didn't look like anything on earth," but in her entry for October 21, a month after the operation, she noted, "Virgil finally put a tree together—he now knows that the trunk and leaves go together to form a complete unit." And on another occasion: "Skyscrapers strange, cannot understand how they stay up without collapsing." . . .

Although Virgil could recognize letters and numbers, and could write them, too, he mixed up some rather similar ones ("A" and "H," for example) and on occasion, wrote some backward. (Hull describes how, after only five years of blindness in his forties, his own visual memories had become so uncertain that he was not sure which way around a "3" went and had to trace it in the air with his fingers. Thus the numeral was retained as a tactile-motor concept, but no longer as a visual concept.) Still, Virgil's performance was an impressive one for a man who had not seen for forty-five years. But the world does not consist of letters and numbers. How would he do with objects and pictures? How would he do with the real world?

His first impressions when the bandages were removed were especially of color, and it seemed to be color, which has no analogue in the world of touch, that excited and delighted him—this was very clear from the way he spoke and from Amy's journal. (The recognition of colors and movement seems to be innate.) It was colors to which Virgil continually alluded, the chromatic unexpectedness of new sights. He had had Greek salad and spaghetti the night before, he told us, and the spaghetti startled him: "White round strings, like fishing line," he said. "I thought it'd be brown."

Seeing light and shape and movements, seeing colors above all, had been completely unexpected and had had a physical and emotional impact almost shocking, explosive. ("I felt the violence of these sensations," wrote Valvo's patient H.S., "like a blow on the head. The violence of the emotion . . . was akin to the very strong emotion I felt on seeing my wife for the first time, and when out in a car, I saw the huge monuments of Rome.")

We found that Virgil easily distinguished a great array of colors and matched them without difficulty. But, confusingly, or confusedly, he sometimes gave colors the wrong names: yellow, for example, he called pink, but he knew that it was the same color as a banana. We wondered at first whether he could have a color agnosia or color anomia—defects of color association and color naming that are due to damage in specific areas of the brain. But his difficulties, it seemed to us, came simply from lack of learning (or from forgetting)—from the fact that early and long blindness had sometimes prevented his associating colors with their names or had caused him to forget some of the associations he had made. Such associations and the neural connections that underlay them, feeble in the first place, had become disestablished in his brain, not through any damage or disease, but simply from disuse.

Response and Analysis

1. Briefly describe Virgil's ability to identify objects on the day his bandages were removed. Which objects were easy and which were difficult for him to identify? How might Virgil's expectations influence his perception of objects, including the physical appearance of a cat or a dog?

2. What were Virgil's impressions of color? Briefly describe his difficulty in naming colors. Why might he have had this difficulty? What are the main features of the trichromatic theory of color vision and the opponent process theory of color vision? Why are both theories useful?

Personal Experience and Application

1. Imagine that glasses and contact lenses are not available. What visual, cognitive, and emotional difficulties might someone who needs corrective lenses experience? How might life change for this person?

2. Suppose you were blindfolded and walked through your house or neighborhood. How would you orient yourself? What senses might you rely upon, and for what purpose? How might life change for you if you were blind?

Research

Suppose you want to examine how experience with visual stimuli may modify the visual system that detects movement. You train your participants to detect extremely small movements by having them look at very small dots on one of five computer screens. Four screens present dots that make extremely small movements in the same direction: up, down, left, or right. The fifth screen presents stationary dots. The participants watch only one screen for thirty minutes each day for four days. On the fifth day, you measure their ability to detect movements by showing dots that move in all four directions. You find that the participants are better at detecting movement only in the direction in which they were trained; the training did not affect their ability to detect movement in the other three directions. Eight weeks later, you retest the participants and find the same effect.

Why was it necessary to have the participants look at only one screen rather than at all five screens? What might happen if the participants watched more than one screen? On the basis of your findings, what might you conclude about how our experiences influence our perception of the world?

chapter 3

CONSCIOUSNESS

*Octavio Paz cites the example of
Saint-PolRoux, who used to hang the
inscription "The poet is working" from his
door while he slept.*

ANNIE DILLARD, *The Writing Life*

What is consciousness? Can our minds be at work while we sleep, as Saint-PolRoux suggests? This chapter presents narratives about consciousness: sleep deprivation; visions; the influence of drugs and alcohol; and hypnosis.

Does sleep deprivation affect our consciousness? Lydia Dotto tells of the difficulties she had concentrating on various tasks when she went for long periods without sleep. The findings of the study in which she took part may have important implications for those who work long hours.

Mary Crow Dog and Richard Erdoes write about an ancient Sioux Indian ceremony, the yuwipi, during which a medicine man leads members of the tribe to a different state of consciousness. The purpose is to help someone find something he or she has lost, like an object or a thought. Crow Dog recalls the visions and sensations she had during her first yuwipi.

Luis Rodriguez remembers being a gang member in Los Angeles. As a teenager, he wanted to escape the misery of poverty by changing his state of consciousness with drugs and chemicals. Not until drugs almost killed him was he able to quit using them and leave the gang.

When Bob Welch, a pitcher for the Los Angeles Dodgers, used alcohol, his perceptions of the world changed. He believed that alcohol liberated his inhibitions and subdued his anxieties. Though Welch was rich and successful, he still felt he needed alcohol. Under pressure from his team, he sought help and eventually was able to admit that he had become an alcoholic.

The case of Julie demonstrates how hypnosis can be used to relieve pain. Julie lost a leg in an accident and suffered from phantom limb syndrome. With the help of hypnotherapists who used visualization, direct suggestion, and posthypnotic suggestion, she was able to lessen and eventually eliminate her pain.

ASLEEP IN THE FAST LANE

Lydia Dotto

Psychological Concepts
sleep deprivation, functions of sleep, REM sleep

Could you easily go a day without sleep? Two days? What abilities would fail first if you had to stay awake for twenty-four hours? Could you manage a cognitive task like balancing your checkbook? Would your reaction time be slower?

Researchers at the Defence and Civil Institute of Environmental Medicine in Toronto, Canada, conducted experiments to examine how sleep deprivation affects task performance. Their findings may have important implications for doctors, air traffic controllers, and others who must be alert for long periods of time. Lydia Dotto tells us of the difficulties she and others had concentrating on various tasks when she participated in one of the experiments and went for long periods without sleep. What states of consciousness does she experience as she goes without sleep? What enables her to be more successful in performing the assigned tasks?

I t has taken just two days and two nights to reduce me to this sorry state—a fact that annoys me no end, because I'd started the experiment determined not to let it get the better of me. How difficult can it be to last two days without sleep, I'd asked myself as I checked in at the Defence and Civil Institute of Environmental Medicine (DCIEM) in Toronto shortly before noon on a Tuesday in early April. At that point, it was not hard to feel self-confident. I'd been awake only four hours, having awakened at 8:00 a.m. after sleeping a full eight hours the night before. I felt alert and mentally geared up for the challenge ahead.

The researchers are rather bemused by my enthusiasm for this project. Most of their subjects are paid volunteers recruited from the ranks of the Canadian Forces. "We don't usually get subjects who are looking forward to the experience," Bob Angus, Head of Applied Psychology at DCIEM, comments wryly.

He takes me down to the sleep lab, located in the basement off a drab, narrow hallway barricaded at both ends with Do Not Disturb signs. The lab consists of a suite of four small rooms in which the subjects work and a control room filled with computer equipment as well as a bank of small closed-circuit TV monitors lining one wall. Here the researchers, working in shifts, maintain an around-the-clock watch on the subjects. Drooping eyelids and nodding heads are picked up by wall-mounted TV cameras in each room, and within moments, one of the researchers is headed down the hall to nudge the subject awake. As the hours wear on, these trips become more frequent. "I just kind of scratch on the door before I go in, to give them a chance to fool me," says Bob. . . .

It's about 8:00 p.m. on Tuesday night, and I have now been awake for 12 hours.

During the first 90-minute session, I feel very alert—quite hyped up, in fact, and ready to face whatever challenges the computer throws my way. At the first break, between 9:30 and 10:00 p.m., I'm still feeling pretty good, and I note into the tape recorder that my motivation remains strong: "I really want to keep things under control and to keep myself awake and alert." But by the time the second break rolls around, just before midnight, I'm beginning to feel fatigued and my concentration is slipping: I become annoyed and frustrated if I can't understand something right away. The repetitive tasks are becoming both boring and irritating, eliciting a reaction of "Oh, Lord, not this one again." Being confronted with a test that I don't like to do provokes a few episodes of fist-waving at the terminal. Ross later observes that the frequency of these displays of temper, which have been duly witnessed on the closed-circuit TV, seems to be increasing.

Periodically during sessions, the computer instructs me to sit with my eyes closed for 4 minutes. Now, as I enter the wee hours of the first night of sleep loss, I find myself drifting toward sleep during these closed-eyes sessions and I comment that although "I still feel I'm on top of the tasks, I'm glad when the breaks come." The computer also inquires solicitously from time to time about my mood and the degree of sleepiness and fatigue I feel. The sleepiness scale contains seven statements, starting with *alert, wide awake* through *foggy, slowed down, beginning to lose interest in remaining awake* to *fighting sleep, losing the struggle to remain awake.* The fatigue checklist asks me to record whether I am *better than, the same as* or *worse than* a series of statements ranging from *very lively* and *extremely peppy* to *slightly pooped* and *ready to drop.* And the mood scale asks me to describe my feelings in terms such as *carefree, cheerful* and *full of pep* or *dull, drowsy* and *defiant.*

By 7:00 a.m. on Wednesday, *dull, drowsy* and *defiant* don't even come close to describing how I feel. Now approaching 24 hours without sleep, I am not in a happy frame of mind. My subjective feelings of sleepiness and fatigue have increased sharply, and my mood, along with my performance, has begun to deteriorate badly. The words *cheerful* and *peppy* are no longer in my vocabulary. Although I can still remain reasonably alert during the war game exercises, I'm beginning to struggle against falling asleep during the more boring tasks. "Sleep is starting to ambush me," I report into the tape recorder. "I find myself staring into space. I just kind of blank out; it's like I vanish, disappear."

I know that sometime during this experiment, I'll be allowed to have a nap. Periodically, the computer taunts me with questions like "If you could sleep now, would you do so?" For the first time, I start hinting that I wouldn't turn down a nap if it were to be offered. It isn't. The computer, it seems, is only interested in knowing if I'd *like* a nap, not in actually satisfying my wish.

During the next break, which I have calculated occurs during early morning, Ross appears looking suspiciously well scrubbed and wearing a cheerful grin. He does not look like a sleep-deprived person and this makes me feel distinctly grumpy. I find that I'm also depressed. I "hit the wall" during the last work session, and as a result, I've broken my rule not to think too far ahead. The certain knowledge that there's at least another full day and night of this to get through induces a state of mild despair, and for the first time I wonder if I'm going to make it. Julia is also beginning to despair about her ability to carry on, reflecting, "It's this rough now and I have to make it through another night." Ours is a typical response to "the first-night effect." Subjects hit a low point between about 4:00 and 6:00 a.m. after the first night of lost sleep, says Ross. "They feel very depressed because they think, 'If I'm feeling this tired and it's only the first night, I'll never make it. I'm going to die.'"

Certainly, I'm beginning to wonder how I'm going to marshal the resources needed to go back into that room. As it happens, however, I don't have to. At the end of the break period, about 10:00 a.m. on Wednesday, Ross announces that it's nap time. When I was six years old, these were dreaded words; now they couldn't have been more welcome.

Julia and I bed down on cots in two of the unused rooms. We're allowed to remove the belts of tape recorders, which are laid beside the beds trailing their wires. The electrodes have to stay on, of course, but it hardly matters; I've reached the stage where nothing's going to keep me awake, not even the sensation of having my head in a vise.

The nap occurs between 10:00 a.m. and noon on Wednesday. For me, it comes at just the right time, rescuing me as I'm about to hit rock bottom. As I settle gratefully into the bed and close my eyes, I experience a momentary anxiety that I won't be able to sleep on demand, even though—or perhaps because—I desperately want to. But, given my advanced state of exhaustion, and perhaps the fact that I am used to napping in my "regular" life, I manage to fall asleep very quickly, even under these unusual circumstances.

Julia, though also highly fatigued, is less happy than I about the timing of the nap. She's a morning person and by midmorning is usually at the height of alertness. Even though she's in a sleep-deprived state, her biological rhythms had begun to climb by 10:00 a.m. and she had trouble falling asleep. "I'd have preferred the nap earlier on, say at 4:00 a.m., because that was my really low point," she commented later. But she began to pick up after the early-morning break during which we had breakfast: "I was awake by the time the nap came along because that's my high point of the day. It wasn't when I craved sleep. I hadn't geared up to having a nap; I was not thinking, 'I've just got to last till the nap.' I think that's why I had such difficulty getting to sleep." She too put psychological pressure on herself, knowing the nap would be her only opportunity to sleep until the end of the experiment. "I knew the nap was two hours long and I was saying, 'C'mon, got to get to sleep, got to make the most of this two hours of sleep.'" In the end, she managed about 1½ hours of sleep.

The nap helped both of us tremendously. I woke up feeling completely refreshed and in a greatly improved frame of mind—feeling, in fact, pretty much as I had when the experiment began. Even though she did not sleep for the full 2 hours,

Julia felt the nap helped her too. "If I hadn't had it, I'd be dead by now," she said during the last break before the end of the experiment. Ross asked her if she felt the nap had allowed her to do better on the computer tasks. "I felt better, yes, but whether I did better or not, I don't know."

In fact, the nap had a significant impact on our performance of the tasks. Our scores on the logical reasoning and serial reaction time tasks improved by more than 40 percent after the nap, and in one case, Julia's score almost doubled. Equally important, for a period of more than 12 hours after the nap, our performance was maintained well above the levels to which they'd dropped before the nap. At times, our performance after the nap was nearly equal to—and occasionally even better than—our performance when we first started the experiment. In some cases, our scores did not fall below their prenap lows until about 5:30 a.m. on the second night of lost sleep, some 17½ hours after the nap.

Studying the effect of napping on performance was the whole point of this experiment, one of a series of such studies conducted by Angus and his group in recent years. They're focusing on factors that affect the performance of military personnel under battle conditions (referred to as "sustained operations"), when they might have to function for days on end with only brief snatches of sleep. However, these studies on napping—currently one of the hottest new fields of sleep research—have much wider implications. The knowledge gained about human sleep/wake patterns may someday help others—doctors, pilots, athletes, air traffic controllers, firefighters, nuclear plant operators and astronauts, to name just a few—whose jobs demand high levels of alertness over long periods of time and/or sustained high-quality performance under extremely demanding conditions. These studies may also help people with more normal but still stressful jobs, such as executives who work long hours or travel a lot, and millions of people trying to cope, often unsuccessfully, with shift work.

Reviewing the data from my experiment, Angus noted with satisfaction that "the nap seemed to give you almost a whole day. It really helped." But it couldn't sustain me indefinitely. Both Julia and I began to disintegrate during the early-morning hours after the second night of sleep loss, and toward the end, we both exhibited a sharp roller-coaster pattern on the tests, performing moderately well—though with ever-diminishing accuracy—immediately after a break but falling apart rapidly in the middle of the 90-minute work sessions. These extreme swings are a striking feature of work sessions during the second day or so without sleep. Ross commented that when subjects are well rested, breaks don't make much difference in their performance because they're already very alert. But as time wears on and fatigue starts to build, the breaks do have a brief noticeable effect, causing the roller-coaster performance pattern. Ultimately, however, they lose their effectiveness and "after you've been awake two or three days, they don't make much difference."

There were many similarities in the way Julia and I reacted to extreme sleep deprivation, but there were also some intriguing differences. While I experienced sensations of blanking out and "disappearing," Julia felt that her thoughts were wandering aimlessly. "My mind would shoot off and I had no control over it," she said. "My thought patterns were going off in different directions." Often, she could not comprehend words printed on the screen because they seemed to be spelled wrong. "They looked totally weird and I thought, 'What is this word?' When you look at a word for a long time, it just appears to be odd. That kept capturing my attention, rather than what I was supposed to be doing." She also had some mild hallucinatory experiences; sometimes she was uncertain whether she was actually doing a task or merely dreaming that she was doing it, and at times she felt as though there was someone in the room. "I got quite worried about the shadows around me. I kept on thinking that somebody's in the room with me because I see shadows on the walls. My vision's a bit iffy."

Like me, she was easily annoyed by the computer's "damn fool questions," but, she added, "I was less grouchy than I thought I was going to be."

Response and Analysis

1. Briefly describe Lydia Dotto's mood, cognitive abilities, and task performance at the beginning of the study and after being awake for twenty-four hours. How did a nap affect these same factors? How might sleep during a nap differ from a normal night's sleep?

2. What are the main functions of sleep? What is REM sleep? What are its possible functions?

Personal Experience and Application

1. What is the longest amount of time you have gone without sleeping? What changes in mood and cognitive ability did you notice?

2. Automobile accidents and injuries on the job are often related to lack of sleep. What practical benefits might result from the study of sleep deprivation?

Research

Sleep studies have implications for people whose "jobs demand high levels of alertness over long periods of time and/or sustained high-quality performance under extremely demanding conditions." Would the study in which Lydia Dotto participated be considered applied or basic research? Why? What are the main goals of applied research and basic research? Name a few similarities and differences between the two.

LAKOTA WOMAN

Mary Crow Dog and Richard Erdoes

Psychological Concepts
altered state of consciousness, hallucinations

Mary Crow Dog, wife of civil rights leader and chief medicine man Leonard Crow Dog, tells how hard it is to be a Sioux woman. In South Dakota, in 1973, she participated in the Battle of Wounded Knee, a conflict which she believes resulted from long-standing tensions between the whites of the community and the American Indians, the impossible living conditions of her people, and the mismanagement of tribal affairs. Crow Dog wants to live in peace according to traditional Indian customs and to observe ancient ceremonies. She does not want to become "whitemanized," which she believes would be equivalent to trading in her birthright.

Central to the Sioux's religion and culture are the Ghost Dance, sweat baths, the Sun Dance, and the yuwipi ceremony. Each of these ceremonies has a spiritual dimension and affects the consciousness of the participants. Here is Mary Crow Dog's account of her first yuwipi ceremony, during which she saw gourds flying around the room and lights dancing, and felt the wings of birds on her face. What contributed to Crow Dog's change of consciousness during this ceremony?

Leonard is also a yuwipi man. Yuwipi is one of our oldest, and also strangest, ceremonies. I had never been to a yuwipi until I met Leonard. It is an unexplainable experience. How can you explain the supernatural for which there is no rationalization? When the first yuwipi ceremony that I took part in was being prepared, I became apprehensive, and once it was in progress, I was even scared. I was still reacting like a white woman.

A yuwipi is put in motion when a man or woman sends a sacred pipe and tobacco to a medicine man. That is the right way to ask for a ceremony. Some person wants to find something—something that can be touched, or something that exists only in the mind. Maybe a missing child or the cause of an illness. The yuwipi man is a finder. He is the go-between, a bridge between the people and the spirits. Through him people ask questions of the supernaturals, and through him the spirits answer back. The person who sent the pipe is the sponsor. Yuwipi men do not get paid for their services, but the sponsor has to feed all comers who want to participate and take advantage of the ritual.

A dog feast is part of the yuwipi ritual, and dog meat is the holy food that is served at the end of the ceremony. This did not bother me. I had eaten dog many times as a child—not in a sacred way, but simply because we were so poor that we ate any kind of meat we could get our hands on—dog, gopher, prairie dog, jackrabbits—just about anything that walked on four legs. The dog feast is an almost human sacrifice. In the old days, young men from the warrior societies would go through the camp selecting dogs for a dog feast. Sometimes they would pick the dog of a great chief or famous hunter. It would have been very bad manners for the owner to object or let his face betray his feelings. It was an honor bestowed upon the owner as well as the dog. Whether they always appreciated the honor is another matter. It is because we are so fond of our dogs that the feast takes on the character of a sacrifice. They scent the dog, paint a red stripe on its back, and strangle it so that its neck is broken and it dies instantly. . . .

While the girls made tobacco ties, others prepared the biggest room in the house for the ceremony. All furniture was removed, the floors swept and covered with sage. All pictures were taken from the walls. Mirrors were turned around because nothing that reflects light is allowed to remain during the ceremony. For this reason participants must remove jewelry, wristwatches, even eyeglasses before entering. All windows were covered with blankets because the ritual takes place in total darkness. Blankets and bedrolls were placed all along the four walls for everybody to sit on.

The string of tobacco ties was laid out in a square within the room. Nobody was allowed in this sacred square except the yuwipi man. All others remained outside. At the head of the square, where the sponsor and singer with his drum had taken their seats, were put a large can filled with earth and two smaller cans on each side. Planted into the big can was the sacred staff. It was half red and half black, the colors separated by a thin yellow stripe. To the top half of the staff was fastened an eagle feather and to the lower half, the tail of a black-tailed deer. The red of the staff stands for the day; the black, for the night. The eagle feather represents wisdom because the eagle is the wisest of all birds. An eagle's center feather will make the spirits come into the ceremony.

The deer is very sacred. Each morning, before any other creature, the deer comes to the creek to drink and bless the water. The deer is medicine. It is a healer. It can see in the dark. If any doctoring is to be done, the deer's spirit will enter. Leonard uses a certain kind of medicine from behind the animal's ears to cure certain diseases. It is very powerful. So that is what the deer tail stands for.

In the smaller, earth-filled tin cans were planted sticks with colored strips of cloth, like flags, attached to them. These represent the sacred four directions, red for the west, white for the north, yellow for the east, and black for the south. In front of the staff was put the buffalo skull, serving as an altar. There was also a small earth altar, representing Grandmother Earth. On it was placed a circle of tobacco ties. Inside this circle, with his finger, Leonard traced a lightning design, because on this occasion he also wanted to use lightning medicine. It is believed that if a spirit comes in and then backs away from a person, that person cannot be cured.

Against the horns of the buffalo skull rested the sacred pipe. Also used were two special, round finding stones and three gourd rattles. Out of the tiny rocks inside the gourds come the spirit voices. These rocks, not much bigger than grains of sand, come from ant heaps. They are crystals, agates, and tiny fossils. They sparkle in the sunlight. Ants are believed to have power because they work together in tribes and don't have hearts but live by the universe.

Everybody then received a twig of sage to put behind their ears or into their hair. This is supposed to make the spirits come to you and to enable you to hear their voices. Then the yuwipi man was brought into the center of the square. His helpers first put his arms behind his back and tied all his fingers together. Then they wrapped him up in a star blanket, covering him completely. A rawhide thong, the kind once used to make bowstrings, was then wound tightly around the blanket and secured with knots. Then the yuwipi man was placed face down on the sage-covered floor. On this occasion it was Leonard who had been tied up. He lay there like a mummy. I could not imagine how he could breathe. Then the kerosene lamps with the big reflectors were extinguished, leaving us sitting in absolute, total darkness. For a short while we sat in utter silence. Then, with a tremendous roar, the drum started to pound, filling the room with its reverberations as the singers began their yuwipi songs. It sent shivers down my spine.

Almost at once the spirits entered. First I heard tiny voices whispering, speaking fast in a ghostly language. Then the gourds began to fly through the air, rattling, bumping into walls, touching our bodies. Little sparks of light danced through the room, wandered over the ceiling, circled my head. I felt the wing beats of a big bird flitting here and there through the darkness with a whoosh, the feathers lightly brushing my face. At one time the whole house shook as if torn by an earthquake. One woman told me later that in one of the flashes of light she had seen the sacred pipe dancing. I was scared until I remembered that the spirits were friends. The meeting lasted almost until the morning. Finally they sang a farewell song for the spirits who were going home to the place from which they had come.

The lamp was lit and revealed Leonard sitting in the middle of the sacred square—unwrapped and untied. He was weeping from emotion and exhaustion. He then told us what the spirits had told him. Then we ate the dog, and afterward wojapi, a kind of berry pudding, drank mint tea and coffee, and of course smoked the pipe, which went around clockwise from one person to the next.

Response and Analysis

1. Briefly describe the preparations for the Sioux Indian yuwipi ceremony. What did Mary Crow Dog see and hear when the spirits entered the room? How might the preparations for the ceremony and the participants' expectations about what might happen have influenced their state of consciousness?

2. What is an altered state of consciousness? Do you believe that Mary Crow Dog was in such a state during the ceremony? Why? What is the difference between an altered state of consciousness and the pre-

conscious, the subconscious, and the unconscious?

Personal Experience and Application

1. Briefly describe an experience in which you were in an altered state of consciousness. Why do you believe you were in that state? Did you enjoy the experience? Why or why not?

2. Some cultures view any change from waking consciousness as abnormal, whereas other cultures promote such a change in order to alter perceptions and decrease inhibitions. List two cultures whose rituals involve altering the participants' state of consciousness. Briefly discuss what the participants do during the ceremony or ritual. Do you believe this experience is normal or helpful? Why or why not?

Research

One way to study a state of consciousness is to experience it oneself. For example, on several occasions, Harvard researcher Andrew Wiel participated in a Sioux Indian sweat lodge religious ceremony. He reported feeling an increased awareness of his strength and well-being after participating in the ceremony. List a few of the advantages and disadvantages of the self-experience approach to understanding states of consciousness. When might the risks of using this approach outweigh the potential benefits?

ALWAYS RUNNING: LA VIDA LOCA: GANG DAYS IN L.A.

Luis J. Rodriguez

Psychological Concepts
psychoactive drugs, drug dependence

Luis Rodriguez gives a piercing account of "the crazy life" of gangs with which some American youth are involved. Rodriguez believes that poverty and racism are the chief reasons for violence and despair. Gangs are held together by their members, who desire to belong, and by the power held by adolescents over younger children.

How does a child join a group that organizes criminal activity? *De volada*—on impulse, without thinking. How does a child take drugs or sniff chemicals that can destroy the brain? *De volada.*

Rodriguez, also known as Chin, remembers wanting to run from being "this thing of bone and skin." When Chin sniffed spray to escape, "the world became like jello, like clay, something which could be molded and shaped. Sounds became louder, clearer. . . ." What other changes in consciousness did Chin experience? What physical and psychological effects did the drugs have on him? Why might a thirteen-year-old boy want to alter so severely his state of consciousness?

Some readers may find portions of Rodriguez's account disturbing because of the behavior and language in which these young people engage.

Not going to school meant a lot of free time. Sniffing became my favorite way to waste it. I stole cans of anything that could give a buzz: carbono, clear plastic, paint or gasoline. Sometimes I'd mix it up in a concoction and pour it on a rag or in a paper bag we sniffed from.

Behind the school, on the fields, inside the tunnel, at Marrano Beach and alongside the concrete banks of the San Gabriel River: I sniffed. Once I even climbed on top of a back hoe at a construction site, removed the lid off the gas tank and inhaled until somebody checked out the noise and chased me away.

Spray was dangerous; it literally ate your brain. But it was also a great escape. The world became like jello, like clay, something which could be molded and shaped. Sounds became louder, clearer—pulsating. Bodies removed themselves from bodies, floating with the sun. I sought it so desperately. I didn't want to be this thing of bone and skin. With spray I became water.

Once I sniffed with Chicharrón and Yuk Yuk behind the "Boys" Market in San Gabriel. I don't remember the trip, but they told me I suddenly stood up and proceeded to repeatedly bang my head against a wall. Pieces of hair and skin scraped on the brick. Chicharrón walked me home; refused to give me any more spray.

While on spray I yelled. I laughed. I clawed at the evening sky. I felt like a cracked egg. But I wouldn't stop.

Then another time Baba, Wilo and I gathered in the makeshift hideout we had alongside the Alhambra Wash, next to the drive-in. We sat ourselves down on the dirt, some blankets and rags nearby to lie on. We covered the entrance with banana leaves and wood planks. There were several cans of clear plastic—what we called *la ce pe*—around us. We each had paper bags and sprayed into them—and I had already dropped some pills and downed a fifth of Wild Turkey. I then placed the bag over my mouth and nose, sealed it tightly with both hands, and breathed deeply.

A radio nearby played some Led Zeppelin or Cream or some other guitar-ripping licks. Soon the sounds rose in pitch. The thumping of bass felt like a heartbeat in the sky, followed by an echo of metal-grating tones. I became flesh with a dream. The infested walls of the wash turned to mud; the trickle of water a vast river. The homeboys and I looked like something out of Huckleberry Finn or Tom Sawyer.

With stick fishing poles. The sparkle of water below us. Fish fidgeting below the sheen.

Dew fell off low branches as if it were breast milk. Birds shot out of the tropical trees which appeared across from us. Perhaps this trip had been the pages of a book, something I read as a child. Or saw on TV. Regardless, I was transported away from what was really there—yet it felt soothing. Not like the oil stains we sat in. Not like the factory air that surrounded us. Not this plastic death in a can.

I didn't want it to end. As the effect wore thin, I grabbed the spray and bag, and resumed the ritual. Baba and Wilo weren't far behind me.

Then everything faded away—the dew, the water, the birds. I became a cartoon, twirling through a tunnel, womb-like and satiated with sounds and lines and darkness. I found myself drifting toward a glare of lights. My family called me over: Seni, Mama, Papa, Tía Chucha, Tío Kiko, Pancho—everybody. I wanted to be there, to know this perpetual dreaming, this din of exquisite screams—to have this mother comfort surging through me.

The world fell into dust piles around me. Images of the past pitched by: my brother tossing me off rooftops, my mother's hearty laughter, my father's thin and tired face, the homeboys with scarred smiles and the women with exotic eyes and cunts which were the churches I worshipped in. Everything crashed. Everything throbbed. I only knew: I had to get to the light, that wondrous beacon stuffed with sweet promise: Of peace. Untroubled. The end of fear. *Don't close the door, Mama. I'm scared. It's okay, m'ijo.* * *There's no monsters. We'll be here. Don't be scared.*

No more monsters. Come to the light. I felt I would be safe there—finally. To the light. The light.

Suddenly everything around me exploded. An intense blackness enveloped me. A deep stillness. Nothing. Absolute. No thinking. No feeling. A hole.

Then an electrified hum sank its teeth into my brain. Hands surrounded me, pulled at me, back to the dust of our makeshift hideaway.

A face appeared above me. It leaned down and breathed into me. Images of leaves, crates, stained blankets came into view. Wilo pulled back and looked into my eyes. A haze covered everything. I felt dizzy. And pissed off.

"Give me the bag, man."

"No way," Baba said. "You died, Chin—you stopped breathing and died."

I tried to get up, but fell back to the ground. A kind of grief overwhelmed me. I was no longer this dream. I was me again. I wished I did die.

"You don't understand," I yelled to the homeboys. "I have to go back."

I crept toward a paper bag but Baba kicked it out of my reach. Later I found myself stepping down a street. Baba and Wilo had pointed me in the direction of home and I kept going. I hated being there. I didn't know what to do. God, I wanted that light, this whore of a sun to blind me, to entice me to burn—to be sculptured marble in craftier hands.

---

*m'ijo: my son

Wilo's sister Payasa liked me and told him. She was okay, I guess, a real *loca* * when it came to the 'hood. She had the high teased hair, the short tight skirts, the "raccoon" style makeup and boisterous presence. I ended up going with her. Mostly for Wilo's sake at first.

After I got expelled from school, Payasa and I spent time together during the day since she refused to go to classes herself. We'd walk to Garvey Park. She would hand me some *colies* which I'd drop and soon start to sway, talk incoherently and act stupid.

"Oh, you'll get over it," Payasa said. "Eventually."

She always said that.

After a time, whenever a car crashed, a couple argued or somebody tripped and fell, we'd look at each other and say at the same time: "Oh, you'll get over it . . . eventually."

When Wilo and I sniffed aerosol spray, sometimes Payasa joined us.

"Why do you let your sister do this?" I asked.

"That's her," Wilo shrugged. "I can't stop her."

Payasa was always high. The higher she got, the more bold she became. One time we were sniffing in the tunnel beneath the freeway. I started tripping: Snakes crawled from the sides, as well as melted faces and bolts of lights and a shower of shapes. She brushed up to me and pulled off her blouse. Erect nipples confronted me on firm breasts. I kissed them. She laughed and pulled me away.

"Oh, you'll get over it," she said. "Eventually."

I was too fucked up to care.

One time in the park she said she wanted to take her pants and underwear off.

"Right here? Right now? . . . in front of everybody?"

"Yeah, why not?" she responded. "You dare me."

"Sure—I dare you."

She did.

Sniffing took the best out of her. Sometimes I'd walk through the tunnel and she would be there, alone, with a bag of spray, all scuffed up, her eyes glassy.

Payasa became a *loca* because of her older brothers. They were Lomas *veteranos*, older gangsters. Because Wilo and Payasa were younger, they picked on them a lot; beating them to make them stronger.

Payasa fought all the time at school. Whenever she lost, her older brothers would slice her tongue with a razor. She wasn't ever supposed to lose. This made her meaner, crazier—unpredictable.

As a girlfriend Payasa was fun, but she couldn't be intimate unless she was on reds, spray or snort.

I had to break with her. I loved the spray and shit but Payasa became too much like the walking dead. So I told her I didn't want to see her anymore. She didn't say

---

*loca: crazy girl

anything, just turned around and left. I faintly said to myself, "Oh, you'll get over it
. . . eventually."

   She was later found in a daze, her arms with numerous deep cuts all the way to
her elbows. Nobody would let me see her after she was taken to a rehabilitation
hospital for teenage addicts. Wilo suggested I let it go.

   "That's Payasa, man," Wilo said, and shrugged his shoulders.

Response and Analysis

1. Briefly describe one of Chin's hallucinations
after he sniffed clear plastic, paint, or gasoline. What changes in consciousness did
Chin experience? What are hallucinogens
(also known as psychedelic drugs)? How do
hallucinogens alter brain chemistry?

2. Do you think that Chin was psychologically
or physically dependent on drugs, or both?
Why or why not? What is the difference
between psychological and physical dependence? Why did Chin conclude that "spray
was dangerous"?

Personal Experience and Application

1. Do you know someone who decided to drink
a large quantity of alcohol or take illegal
drugs? How might psychological and social
factors have influenced that decision?

2. Suppose you are a member of a committee
whose mission is to reduce drug abuse
among students on your college or university
campus. The committee chairperson asks
you to help design a program to decrease
drug abuse on campus. Briefly discuss a few
of your recommendations.

Research

Suppose a committee whose mission is to reduce
drug abuse among students asks you to conduct a
study to determine the percentage of students on
campus who are abusing drugs. Because you do
not have the time to interview every student, you
ask a small group of students to participate. How
would you select the students to participate? How
can you be fairly sure that the information you
gather will generalize to the entire student body?

THE COURAGE TO CHANGE

Dennis Wholey

Psychological Concepts
alcohol abuse, expectations and drug effects

Baseball star Bob Welch began drinking in his early teens and always chose friends who were heavy drinkers. What Welch wanted from the alcohol was instant transformation as he "guzzled the thing, looking for the effect." He didn't worry about becoming an alcoholic, for he thought alcoholics were failures or were people passed out on the street. They were not celebrated ball players or his friends.

In this interview with Dennis Wholey, Welch tells how he used emotion, thinking, and social influence to justify his drinking. How did he use these same forces to help him quit?

I thought an individual who had a problem with alcohol could not be successful, especially as a major league pitcher who could purchase anything he wanted at a very young age, as I could. I thought an alcoholic had to be lying on a street corner on skid row. That was my definition of an alcoholic. I didn't believe I was one. When someone would raise the question and say, "Well, I think you're an alcoholic," he'd grab my attention, but he'd pissed me off more than anything. "Maybe I have a little problem with drinking," I said to myself many times, but there was no way I could be an alcoholic. I didn't believe it until I got over to the treatment center and saw what it was like for someone at my young age to have the characteristics of an alcoholic. By the time I got there, I was well on my way to drinking a fifth or a quart a day. That was three or four years ago.

My girlfriend, Mary Ellen, had no idea. She wasn't knowledgeable. She didn't know about the disease, what an alcoholic was. And I never paid attention to the fact that I might be causing my mother and father and my girlfriend some pain.

When I was fifteen years old some friends and I went out to a park, and I drank a bottle of Mogen David blackberry wine. I liked it. I liked what it did for me because I was able to speak with girls a lot more easily. That was important to me at that time. After the first time, I didn't need anyone to pull on me and say, "Hey, let's go have a beer." It just snowballed.

I was shy. I was scared to death of girls. But when I got drunk I could tell a girl I liked her. I couldn't wait for the weekend because I thought maybe I'd get a chance to talk to a girl and even kiss her. I also thought that if you didn't like a girl and she didn't like you, you could drink to cover it up. Very early on, I started run-

ning from my feelings, hiding instead of talking. I covered up my feelings by
drinking.

As I look back now, I see that the friends with whom I first started drinking at
fifteen were heavy drinkers. I started choosing such friends even before I started going to college. They had to be people who drank and acted and talked the same way
I did. But whether it was in class or on a baseball team, if my friends didn't want to
go get drunk with me, I'd go to a bar alone. I did that from the time I started drinking. I didn't go out to drink socially. I went out to drink for the effect, for what it
gave me. I knew what I was going to be able to do after I drank—go to the football
games, be able to talk a lot more, maybe even go to a party and dance with a girl.

I built up a reputation as both a great baseball player and a very good drinker
at a young age.

In college I wanted to prove to people that I was the best baseball player, and
when I was done playing, I wanted to show them that I was the best drinker. My
mother told me at the treatment center that when I left to go to college the one
thing she was worried about was that I was going to turn into an alcoholic. She had
this insight when I was seventeen.

When I got to college, I was away from my mother and father and didn't have
to worry about coming home, sneaking in the back room, or driving their car. It
was a perfect setup for someone who enjoyed drinking. I had some friends there
with whom I played baseball in the summertime, and I knew exactly which ones
would drink like I did. Then I started finding people over at my dormitory. When
I wanted to get away from baseball players, I'd go to these individuals. At seventeen
I knew exactly what I was doing. I knew the people who lived in certain bars. There
is a bar up in Ypsilanti where the gentlemen are full-fledged practicing alcoholics.
I knew that I could go over there and fit right in with those guys. They liked me.
I used to go in there and talk about playing baseball. They're probably still sitting
there. I didn't associate with people who didn't drink and I didn't want anybody to
look at me and question me about how much I drank.

I didn't drink and sip it. I didn't want to see what happened. It was boom! I
guzzled the thing, looking for the effect. You like it or dislike it. I happened to
like it.

If I pitched a game and lost, I went out and got drunk. I drowned my sorrows
or my aggravation or my anger in drinking. If we won, I could celebrate. On both
ends, I always had it covered.

I got to the majors by the time I was twenty-one. I'd go out and get drunk
whenever I wanted to. In baseball, you don't even have to go anywhere. They have
the beer in the clubhouse. It was a perfect setup. I started pitching once every five
days. You start mapping out your strategy. You know exactly when you can get
drunk, and you know how much time it takes you to recover. The thing that was
difficult about baseball for me was that it gave me an opportunity to drink just
about every day. I could stay out until three o'clock and sleep until three o'clock. I
had plenty of time to rest. There were many times I said, "I'm not going out drinking tonight," but I was right back out there.

Everybody wants to be associated with a professional baseball player. They all want to party with you and buy you drinks, and they all want to push other types of drugs on you. In Los Angeles, where I was living, I knew who was going to get drunk, just like in college.

I'd get drunk four out of five days, get sober the night before pitching, and go back out drinking that night. I didn't wake up in the morning and have a drink or drink at a definite time daily, and I didn't drink every day, but 85 to 95 percent of the times that I started to drink, I couldn't stop. I'd drink until I was drunk or passed out or there was nothing left.

I had pitched in 1978 and done very well. I played in the World Series. In 1979 I participated for about two months and hurt my arm. I knew I wasn't going to play, and I was traveling to all these towns, so I'd get drunk during the games. I'm not going to play, I thought, so let's pop a few cans of beer. Not just one or two, but three or four or five or six. I justified sitting on the bench by saying, "Hell, I'm going to have a few beers and root and at least enjoy myself." I was terribly hurt that I wasn't playing, and feeling bad because one part of the team wasn't doing so well. I wanted to put myself in there and I just couldn't. I covered that up by drinking all the time.

On the way to the park, I'd know I wasn't going to pitch, so I'd say to myself, Why not have a nice little drink on my way there? I'm going to sit in traffic and I'm going to be itchy and edgy. I've got to have a drink. I'm going to have one on the way. Toward the end of the season, I really was not taking care of myself and not being concerned too much with my occupation because I was drinking so heavily. My girlfriend was beginning to hear some whispers. Friends and family members and wives of other baseball players were saying, "Hey, do you hear what your boyfriend does?" I could barely speak to her. My family was beginning to be concerned, too. I could tell not so much by what they were saying, but when I got around them they would look at me when I was drinking. They were concerned about how much I was drinking and where I was going. My health really wasn't affected too much. Basically, I took care of myself, but my ability to prepare myself to play baseball was starting to go downhill.

There was one time in San Francisco, after I was injured, that I had a chance to pitch. They wanted me to start a couple of games at the end of the season. I went out there and my elbow was feeling terrible. It was cold and windy in San Francisco. I gave up a home run. My pitching was a disaster. I went out that night and had a few drinks, went home, and went to bed. I really didn't get drunk. I woke up the next morning and I, another player, and a gentleman we knew in San Francisco went out to this place and had lunch. I started drinking, and I must have drunk three bottles of wine at lunch. The guy on our team went home. I stayed out there and drank ten more Seven and Seven's and a few more beers. I went back to the hotel about a quarter to five. Our bus was leaving about five o'clock. I went upstairs, drank a bottle of wine, guzzled it in about five minutes, then went down and got on the bus. There were a lot of reporters. I just started raising hell. I was screaming and hollering at the manager, making an ass out of myself, embarrassing everybody.

I got to the ball park and fell asleep by the stall. One of my teammates woke me up and started helping me get dressed and tried to hide it from my manager. Everybody knew I was drunk. I thought it was funny. A couple of my teammates helped me out. I went out on the field and started a few fights with the guys on the Giants. I got out there in center field and then started a couple of fights with my own teammates. My manager called me in and said, "Hey, you've got to take off your uniform and stay inside." I was never so embarrassed in my life.

Before I went home to Michigan that winter, the Dodgers called me into their office and said, "We fine you for being drunk at the park. We want you to know that we want you to be a part of this club next year, and we're not going to finish last or next to last. We want you to be ready. We want you to take a look at your drinking." I told them all to go shit in their hats and leave me alone. I told them it was their fault, anyway, that if I didn't pitch in the bullpen, I wouldn't be getting drunk, I would have been healthy. "It's your fault," I said, "so why don't you get out of my life and leave me alone? If I don't pitch here, I'll pitch somewhere else."

I came home that winter and tried to quit drinking, but couldn't do it. I stopped for about two to three weeks, until Thanksgiving. That was a deadly time, because I liked to drink and there were a lot of parties in our family. I had my first drink and then I think I was drunk until after Christmas.

A telephone call came from the Dodgers on about January tenth. "We want you to come out here and speak to some people and meet with us." I knew exactly what it was all about. They didn't have to say anything about drinking. I knew what the hell was going on. I knew what was going to happen the next day. I flew out to L.A., and when I arrived I smoked a couple of joints, then stopped at a place and grabbed a six-pack. I went to the Biltmore, went to sleep, woke up the next morning, and met with a gentleman who was a recovering alcoholic.

It was really the first time that someone knew exactly how to handle me, knew exactly what to say. It wasn't "Hey, you have a problem." It was "I have a problem." He sat down and shared his story with me, the story of what it was like when he was young, how his drinking had caused great pain to his family, how he had made an ass out of himself and embarrassed himself many, many times. Boy, I could see myself in that same category. I knew this was my time. I really wanted to do something about my drinking, and this gentleman helped me out by sharing his own story, not by saying, "You have a problem. What are you going to do about it?" It was more or less, "I care. There are things you can do." . . .

I was in treatment for thirty-six days. When I first came out, I had the idea that just because I didn't drink, it was O.K. to smoke a joint or pop a few pills. I almost killed myself running into the back end of someone's car. I was on Valium. Until I eliminated everything, I really didn't get a good foundation. What helped was being in the AA program, and wanting to stay sober. I'm really just now getting to the point where I can finally give in. I don't care if I never take a drink again. I don't care if I don't get high again. It's O.K. to be right here, to be sober, not get high; that's fine. I've struggled for quite a while now. It doesn't seem hard not to drink.

Response and Analysis

1. The introduction mentions that Bob Welch used emotion, thinking, and social influences to justify drinking and then to break his addiction. Give some examples of this statement. Briefly discuss Welch's description of the physical and psychological effects of abusing alcohol.

2. How do alcohol and other depressant drugs affect the nervous system and the brain? How can expectations about the effects of alcohol influence behavior?

Personal Experience and Application

1. Have you ever been in a situation in which you drank alcohol but did not want to? Why then did you drink? If you had a friend who was going to a party where alcohol would be present and who did not want to drink, what advice would you offer so that he or she might feel less pressure to drink?

2. Do you think alcohol use on your campus is a problem? Why or why not? When do the students usually drink alcohol? List the reasons why you believe they drink alcohol.

Research

Suppose you want to replicate a study examining how expectations about alcohol influence aggressive behavior. You decide that all participants will be given the same amount of a beverage. Half will drink tonic water and half will drink alcohol that does not taste when it is mixed with tonic water. Participants drinking alcohol will receive enough alcohol to become legally intoxicated. Before you hand out the beverage, you tell half of the participants who receive both tonic water and half who receive tonic water and alcohol that they are drinking tonic water; you tell the other half that they are drinking alcohol. That is, one quarter of the participants will:

*   expect alcohol and drink alcohol, or
*   expect alcohol but drink tonic water only, or
*   expect tonic water but drink alcohol, or
*   expect tonic water and drink tonic water.

After the participants drink the beverage, your research assistant will pretend to be a participant and irritate and annoy the real participants. Then you will give the participants an opportunity to deliver electric shocks to your research assistant. The degree of electric shock delivered will be your measure of aggression. In fact, no shocks will be delivered to the assistant; the participants do not know that the shock-generating machine is not operational.

Is it ethical to have people drink alcohol without their foreknowledge? If not, how can a researcher inform potential participants without creating expectations about how they should behave? Is it ethical to tell participants that they have delivered electric shocks to someone when no shocks will be delivered? How might a researcher debrief his or her participants regarding these issues? Do you think that the human subjects Institutional Review Board at your college or university would approve this study? Why or why not?

PRACTICAL
CLINICAL HYPNOSIS

Robert G. Meyer

Psychological Concepts
hypnosis, pain control

Can hypnotherapy help reduce pain? Julie, a twenty-seven-year old nurse, lost her leg in an accident and suffered from phantom limb syndrome, a response that occurs because the brain attempts "to seek the stimulation of the (now-departed) nerves that had been sending information from the limb." As a result, Julie was depressed and anxious and no longer saw herself as attractive or desirable.

The hypnotherapists whom Julie consulted treated her for pain in her absent leg by using several techniques, including self-hypnosis. What techniques did they teach to control, alleviate, and eliminate the pain? What guided imagery did they suggest?

We had occasion recently to treat a woman who had lost her left leg in an auto-mobile accident. Julie, a twenty-seven-year-old nurse, came seeking hypnotherapy to deal with a condition referred to as phantom limb. This often occurs when a limb is amputated and is due to the brain's attempting to seek the stimulation of the (now-departed) nerves that had been sending information from the limb. This condition can last for some time, even years, and it can be uncomfortable or even painful. Julie had been without her leg for almost nine months at the time she [came] for her first session.

We first got a history of her symptom and the factors surrounding it. She was experiencing a lot of anticipatory anxiety because she did not know when the pain would begin, but she usually felt it each day for a few hours. If it happened at work, it could be incapacitating. In the middle of the night, it was simply painful and frightening. There was also the issue of Julie's self-esteem and self-image, which were severely damaged by her accident. She had lost confidence in her ability to do the things she had loved to do, although her doctors assured her that with the new prosthetics available, she could jog, ride a bicycle, and even play tennis. Depression was thus part of the picture.

We decided together that we would work on the anxiety and pain first and then deal with the depression, trying to get Julie back into the swing of her life. Julie was an excellent hypnotic subject, as is often the case with pain clients. She achieved a deep trance during our first session, using the eye fixation method* and testing the depth via glove anesthesia.**

We had agreed that she should have an imaginal refuge she could retreat to when she was feeling anxious or if the pain was beginning. Julie would use this "safe place" only when she was not at work, not driving, and not in other situations where she needed to be alert. The safe place served two functions. First, she had an autohypnotic technique† she could use to relax and avoid pain, and second, it gave her confidence in her ability to cope with her condition.

Julie had grown up in the state of Washington and fondly recalled walks on the beach as a youngster. Therefore, we set her safe place on a beach she loved, on a warm, summer day, with a cool breeze blowing the salt smell of the ocean on her face. Direct suggestions were used to set the imagery.

Guided imagery:

"Julie, you are feeling warm and comfortable. It is a summer day, and you can feel the sun on your face. You are sitting on a picnic table near the sandy beach, and you decide you want to go for a walk down that favorite path. You stand up, and as you do, you feel the breeze blowing across your face; you smell the salt spray from the sea, the scent of the kelp, and the mustiness of the warm sand. What do you smell?" [At this point, it is a good idea to check for the sensory hallucinations. If the client is not smelling and experiencing the hallucination, deepening through more progressive relaxation or another technique will help.]

"Good. Now you are proceeding down the beach to your safe place, the cove on the west side of the inlet. You see the cove. You feel relaxed and comfortable. Proceed to your favorite spot, and indicate to me when you are there by raising your finger. [Once we established that she was there, we could proceed with one of the pain reduction techniques we used.]

"Julie, I want you to look around you on the beach. You will see a bottle half buried in the sand. Pick it up. There is a piece of paper in your pocket, as well as a pencil. Take them out. Write 'my pain' on the paper. Now roll the paper up and put it in the bottle. Now stand up and throw the bottle as far out to sea as you can. You will count to ten as you see the bottle get farther and farther away. With each count, your pain becomes less and less, until at the count of ten you feel no pain from your leg. You will realize that the bottle is likely to come back in. The tide and waves will bring it back. All you have to do is pick up the bottle and throw it back out to sea, and count from one to ten."

---

*eye fixation method: a method of inducing hypnosis by having the client focus on an object, such as a spot on the wall or a pendulum.

**glove anesthesia: a process in which the therapist makes a suggestion to the client that his or her hand is becoming numb and insensitive, and transfers this new perception of numbness to a part of the body that is experiencing discomfort.

†autohypnotic technique: also known as self-hypnosis, when an individual induces hypnosis in himself or herself.

It is important to note that the dialogue did not follow this straight-through pace. Throughout the process, we were making sure she was experiencing the imagery and feeling the sensation by asking simple questions and looking for a finger movement in response.

This technique was very successful for Julie; however, we needed to deal with her pain in a less complex manner for those times when she could not go into autohypnosis and retreat to her safe place, where she could throw the pain away. We did this by transferring a glove anesthesia to her missing leg—not to the missing leg, obviously, but to a spot on her thigh that, when numb, would not allow any pain messages from the phantom limb. This was the suggestion we gave:

Direct suggestion:

"Julie, I want you to notice that your hand is getting numb. As I touch it, you notice that you are feeling less and less sensation from it, as though it is covered in a protective covering. I could be touching the chair, and you would not know the difference. I want you to be aware of the fact that you are controlling the feeling in this hand. You are making it numb. Now I want you to use that power to make another spot numb. I am going to touch you on the left thigh, and on that spot you will notice you will lose sensation. I am touching your thigh with one finger, and I want you to take that numbness and extend it around your thigh in a band, just as if you have a tourniquet around your thigh that is cutting off the feeling instead of the blood supply. Now that loss of feeling means that no sensation below it will get by; no loss of sensation will occur above the ring of numbness."

Two approaches were used in posthypnotic suggestions. To alleviate the pain directly and indirectly, Julie was given posthypnotic suggestions that she would be able to control the pain and that if she experienced pain it would be tolerable.

Therapist:

Julie, you have indicated to me that you experience pain at certain times during the day, such as in the morning, late in the afternoon, and in the evening just before you retire. In the morning after you rise, you will feel refreshed and invigorated. You will be aware of the fact that you often have felt the pain of your leg at these times, but you will feel no apprehension about it. If you begin to feel pain, you will use the anesthetic technique you have learned to eliminate the pain. You will feel the pain and make it go away by using the band of numbness you have control over. The pain will never be so severe that you will not be able to tolerate it.

The direct techniques that we used with Julie were successful in helping her to deal with her loss. In addition to hypnosis, we used interpersonal process techniques* to help Julie regain her lost self-esteem and deal with her depression. But

---

*interpersonal process techniques: a general term for pyschotherapy.

direct suggestions were used throughout the therapy to reinforce and enhance the psychotherapy.

Direct suggestions have an important place in hypnotherapy, especially since cognitive-behavioral and behavioral therapies have been shown to be so effective in treatment of specific disorders. The extent to which direct suggestions and post-hypnotic techniques may be used in hypnotherapy is bounded only by the imagination of the therapist. Entering into a therapeutic alliance in which the input and motivation of the client is encouraged and supported is fertile ground for a direct approach. Direct suggestions and posthypnotic techniques benefit motivated clients by giving them the tools they need to change and by showing them that change occurs through efforts they ultimately have control over. In medical and dental applications, direct suggestions and posthypnotic techniques work not only to alleviate the pain of the procedures but also to reduce the associated anxiety, and thus they may make it more likely that the patient will comply with the treatment.

Response and Analysis

1. How did the hypnotists help Julie create a "safe place" to cope with pain? Where was the safe place? What is a posthypnotic suggestion? Briefly describe the posthypnotic suggestion that the hypnotists gave to Julie to help her relieve her pain.

2. Briefly discuss one theory that supports and one theory that does not support the belief that hypnosis represents an altered state of consciousness. Do you believe that people who are hypnotized experience an altered state of consciousness? Why or why not?

Personal Experience and Application

1. Have you seen someone hypnotized or know someone who was hypnotized? Briefly describe the hypnotist's instructions. What behaviors did the hypnotist have the person perform? How did the person describe the experience? Did the person believe he or she was in an altered state of consciousness?

Research

Suppose you want to use the case study approach to examine the effectiveness of a new hypnotheraputic technique to relieve pain. You work with one client continuously for six months and find that the new technique effectively diminishes the client's perceptions of pain. How could you determine if your findings would be equally effective for people with similar problems?

chapter *4*

LEARNING

*There is only one thing more powerful than
learning from experience and that is not
learning from experience.*

Archibald MacLeish, in Marian Wright Edelman,
The Measure of Our Success

What makes us want to learn, and how do we learn most effectively? Psychologists have made valuable contributions to our understanding of learning principles. This chapter illuminates learning principles and concepts at work: classical conditioning; operant conditioning; positive and negative reinforcement; observational (social) learning; role models; and cooperative learning.

Various disadvantages, whether physical, emotional, or environmental, make constructive learning onerous. Our first selection is about an individual who surmounted her handicaps with the personal involvement of an extraordinarily devoted teacher. Helen Keller, who was blind and deaf since she was eighteen months old, says she would never have been able to know the world she lived in so fully without the superb instruction of her beloved teacher, Anne Sullivan.

Positive reinforcement also serves as an effective learning tool. We present a fascinating interview with an expert who describes how animal trainers work and play with killer whales. Chuck Tompkins of Sea World explains how important it is for trainers to develop positive relationships with whales when teaching them to perform.

Susan Goodwillie gathered interviews by teenagers of other teenagers who come from families and neighborhoods of poverty and violence. Their powerful stories tell of inadequate role models, of learning not to learn, and of gaining the wrong sort of knowledge. In our selection a young man from Brooklyn tells how he was able to turn away from drugs and gangs. He would like to get a high school diploma, but he believes he has little chance because of his unstable life.

Jaime Escalante well deserves the awards he has received as an outstanding teacher. What Escalante accomplished teaching advanced mathematics to students in East Los Angeles is exemplary of the finest educator; his approach is richly portrayed in the film *Stand and Deliver.* Here he discusses how he uses passion, devotion, and cooperative learning to inspire students to become excited about learning.

EVERYTHING HAD A NAME

Helen Keller

Psychological Concepts
association, repetition

How does a person who is deprived of sound and sight learn language? This was the challenge for Helen Keller. Blind and deaf from an illness she contracted at the age of eighteen months, Keller was cut off from the knowledge that language brings until Anne Sullivan, a great teacher, came into her life.

Until she was almost seven years old, Keller lived "in the still, dark world" where "there was no strong sentiment or tenderness." Neither had she yet conceived of thought. By being patient and gentle, intuitive and understanding, Sullivan was able to show Keller how to give shape to thought, how to name and identify. Here Keller tells of how Sullivan taught her sign language that enabled her to understand concepts and labels. Gradually, she was able to join in conversations with people beyond her immediate family.

The most important day I remember in all my life is the one on which my teacher, Anne Mansfield Sullivan, came to me. I am filled with wonder when I consider the immeasurable contrasts between the two lives which it connects. It was the third of March, 1887, three months before I was seven years old.

On the afternoon of that eventful day, I stood on the porch, dumb, expectant. I guessed vaguely from my mother's signs and from the hurrying to and fro in the house that something unusual was about to happen, so I went to the door and waited on the steps. The afternoon sun penetrated the mass of honeysuckle that covered the porch, and fell on my upturned face. My fingers lingered almost unconsciously on the familiar leaves and blossoms which had just come forth to greet the sweet southern spring. I did not know what the future held of marvel or surprise for me. Anger and bitterness had preyed upon me continually for weeks and a deep languor had succeeded this passionate struggle.

Have you ever been at sea in a dense fog, when it seemed as if a tangible white darkness shut you in, and the great ship, tense and anxious, groped her way toward the shore with plummet and sounding-line, and you waited with beating heart for something to happen? I was like that ship before my education began, only I was without compass or sounding-line, and had no way of knowing how near the harbour was. "Light! give me light!" was the wordless cry of my soul, and the light of love shone on me in that very hour.

I felt approaching footsteps. I stretched out my hand as I supposed to my mother. Some one took it, and I was caught up and held close in the arms of her who had come to reveal all things to me, and, more than all things else, to love me.

The morning after my teacher came she led me into her room and gave me a doll. The little blind children at the Perkins Institution had sent it and Laura Bridgman had dressed it; but I did not know this until afterward. When I had played with it a little while, Miss Sullivan slowly spelled into my hand the word "d-o-l-l." I was at once interested in this finger play and tried to imitate it. When I finally succeeded in making the letters correctly I was flushed with childish pleasure and pride. Running downstairs to my mother I held up my hand and made the letters for doll. I did not know that I was spelling a word or even that words existed; I was simply making my fingers go in monkey-like imitation. In the days that followed I learned to spell in this uncomprehending way a great many words, among them *pin*, *hat*, *cup* and a few verbs like *sit*, *stand* and *walk*. But my teacher had been with me several weeks before I understood that everything has a name.

One day, while I was playing with my new doll, Miss Sullivan put my big rag doll into my lap also, spelled "d-o-l-l" and tried to make me understand that "d-o-l-l" applied to both. Earlier in the day we had had a tussle over the words "m-u-g" and "w-a-t-e-r." Miss Sullivan had tried to impress it upon me that "m-u-g" is *mug* and that "w-a-t-e-r" is *water*, but I persisted in confounding the two. In despair she had dropped the subject for the time, only to renew it at the first opportunity. I became impatient at her repeated attempts and, seizing the new doll, I dashed it upon the floor. I was keenly delighted when I felt the fragments of the broken doll at my feet. Neither sorrow nor regret followed my passionate outburst. I had not loved the doll. In the still, dark world in which I lived there was no strong sentiment or tenderness. I felt my teacher sweep the fragments to one side of the hearth, and I had a sense of satisfaction that the cause of my discomfort was removed. She brought me my hat, and I knew I was going out into the warm sunshine. This thought, if a wordless sensation may be called a thought, made me hop and skip with pleasure.

We walked down the path to the well-house, attracted by the fragrance of the honeysuckle with which it was covered. Some one was drawing water and my teacher placed my hand under the spout. As the cool stream gushed over one hand she spelled into the other the word *water*, first slowly, then rapidly. I stood still, my whole attention fixed upon the motions of her fingers. Suddenly I felt a misty consciousness as of something forgotten—a thrill of returning thought; and somehow the mystery of language was revealed to me. I knew then that "w-a-t-e-r" meant the wonderful cool something that was flowing over my hand. That living word awakened my soul, gave it light, hope, joy, set it free! There were barriers still, it is true, but barriers that could in time be swept away.

I left the well-house eager to learn. Everything had a name and each name gave birth to a new thought. As we returned to the house every object which I touched seemed to quiver with life. That was because I saw everything with the strange, new sight that had come to me. On entering the door I remembered the doll I had broken. I felt my way to the hearth and picked up the pieces. I tried vainly to put them together. Then my eyes filled with tears; for I realized what I had done, and for the first time I felt repentance and sorrow.

I learned a great many new words that day. I do not remember what they all were; but I do know that *mother, father, sister, teacher* were among them—words that were to make the world blossom for me, "like Aaron's rod, with flowers." It would have been difficult to find a happier child than I was as I lay in my crib at the close of that eventful day and lived over the joys it had brought me, and for the first time longed for a new day to come. I had now the key to all language, and I was eager to learn to use it. Children who hear acquire language without any particular effort; the words that fall from others' lips they catch on the wing, as it were, delightedly, while the little deaf child must trap them by a slow and often painful process. But whatever the process, the result is wonderful. Gradually, from naming an object we advance step by step until we have traversed the vast distance between our first stammered syllable and the sweep of thought in a line of Shakespeare.

At first, when my teacher told me about a new thing I asked very few questions. My ideas were vague, and my vocabulary was inadequate; but as my knowledge of things grew, and I learned more and more words, my field of inquiry broadened, and I would return again and again to the same subject, eager for further information. Sometimes a new word revived an image that some earlier experience had engraved on my brain.

I remember the morning that I first asked the meaning of the word "love." This was before I knew many words. I had found a few early violets in the garden and brought them to my teacher. She tried to kiss me; but at that time I did not like to have any one kiss me except my mother. Miss Sullivan put her arm gently round me and spelled into my hand, "I love Helen."

"What is love?" I asked.

She drew me closer to her and said, "It is here," pointing to my heart, whose beats I was conscious of for the first time. Her words puzzled me very much because I did not then understand anything unless I touched it.

I smelt the violets in her hand and asked, half in words, half in signs, a question which meant, "Is love the sweetness of flowers?"

"No," said my teacher.

Again I thought. The warm sun was shining on us.

"Is this not love?" I asked, pointing in the direction from which the heat came, "Is this not love?"

It seemed to me that there could be nothing more beautiful than the sun, whose warmth makes all things grow. But Miss Sullivan shook her head, and I was greatly puzzled and disappointed. I thought it strange that my teacher could not show me love.

A day or two afterward I was stringing beads of different sizes in symmetrical groups—two large beads, three small ones, and so on. I had made many mistakes, and Miss Sullivan had pointed them out again and again with gentle patience. Finally I noticed a very obvious error in the sequence and for an instant I concentrated my attention on the lesson and tried to think how I should have arranged the beads. Miss Sullivan touched my forehead and spelled with decided emphasis, "Think."

In a flash I knew that the word was the name of the process that was going on in my head. This was my first conscious perception of an abstract idea.

For a long time I was still—I was not thinking of the beads in my lap, but trying to find a meaning for "love" in the light of this new idea. The sun had been under a cloud all day, and there had been brief showers; but suddenly the sun broke forth in all its southern splendour.

Again I asked my teacher, "Is this not love?"

"Love is something like the clouds that were in the sky before the sun came out," she replied. Then in simpler words than these, which at that time I could not have understood, she explained: "You cannot touch the clouds, you know; but you feel the rain and know how glad the flowers and the thirsty earth are to have it after a hot day. You cannot touch love either; but you feel the sweetness that it pours into everything. Without love you would not be happy or want to play."

The beautiful truth burst upon my mind—I felt that there were invisible lines stretched between my spirit and the spirits of others.

From the beginning of my education Miss Sullivan made it a practice to speak to me as she would speak to any hearing child; the only difference was that she spelled the sentences into my hand instead of speaking them. If I did not know the words and idioms necessary to express my thoughts she supplied them, even suggesting conversation when I was unable to keep up my end of the dialogue.

This process was continued for several years; for the deaf child does not learn in a month, or even in two or three years, the numberless idioms and expressions used in the simplest daily intercourse. The little hearing child learns these from constant repetition and imitation. The conversation he hears in his home stimulates his mind and suggests topics and calls forth the spontaneous expression of his own thoughts. This natural exchange of ideas is denied to the deaf child. My teacher, realizing this, determined to supply the kinds of stimulus I lacked. This she did by repeating to me as far as possible, verbatim, what she heard, and by showing me how I could take part in the conversation. But it was a long time before I ventured to take the initiative, and still longer before I could find something appropriate to say at the right time.

The deaf and the blind find it very difficult to acquire the amenities of conversation. How much more this difficulty must be augmented in the case of those who are both deaf and blind! They cannot distinguish the tone of the voice or, without assistance, go up and down the gamut of tones that give significance to words; nor can they watch the expression of the speaker's face, and a look is often the very soul of what one says.

Response and Analysis

1. How did Anne Sullivan use association and repetition to teach Helen Keller sign language? What other lessons did Sullivan teach Keller?

2. Do you think that classical conditioning was at work when Helen Keller learned to finger-spell the word *water*? Why or why not? What processes may have been involved in her learning to finger-spell *water*?

Personal Experience and Application

1. Think of a time when you learned something through classical conditioning, such as a fear or food aversion. Briefly describe the situation and what you learned.

2. What difficulties may be involved in teaching language to someone who is deaf and blind?

Research

Suppose you want to investigate how advertisers use classical conditioning to form positive associations with their products. How might you determine (a) what types of positive images are associated with various products, and (b) the degree to which advertisers use classical conditioning on television?

POSITIVE REINFORCEMENT IN ANIMAL TRAINING

David N. Sattler and Chuck Tompkins

Psychological Concepts
operant conditioning, reinforcement, shaping, reinforcers, successive approximation

Chuck Tompkins, vice-president of animal training at Sea World of Florida, began working with animals as a child. Whenever somebody had an injured animal, Tompkins says that he was the kid on the block to whom everyone turned because he always found the right person or the right way to get the animal back on its feet. Training animals didn't become a serious love for Tompkins until he began working at Disneyworld. Soon thereafter, he joined Sea World as an apprentice trainer and has been there ever since.

In this interview Tompkins answers a few intriguing questions. How are trainers able to get close enough to a 6,000-pound killer whale to scratch its belly and live to tell about it? His answer is very clear: by using learning principles and developing a strong, ongoing relationship between the trainer and the whale. For Tompkins, the way to achieve this is through positive reinforcement at every step.

Working with killer whales is one of the most rewarding experiences I've ever had. I came to Sea World eighteen years ago, and my work is as exciting as it was when I first began. When I'm in the water interacting with the whales and we are working together as a team, it as absolutely exhilarating.

Before we begin training a new whale, we make sure that the animal is in good physical condition and is adapting well to its new environment. Then we immediately start working on our relationship. We start by asking the animal to come over to us, and we begin giving the animal things we know it will like. We make certain that we pair ourselves with the positive things that the animal wants in its environment, such as food, attention, body rubs, and play toys. Every killer whale likes a particular part of its body scratched. We use these body rubs as reinforcement. For killer whales a play toy could be a 55-gallon barrel; a 100-foot-long, 6-inch rope, with which we play tug-of-war; mirrors we bring to the side of the pool so they can look at themselves; or a water jet. The whales love to be sprayed on the body, and they associate these reinforcers with the trainer who is giving them. In a very short time, interacting with a trainer becomes a positive event.

By developing a strong relationship, we provide more reinforcements than just food. With some animals this relationship develops quickly; with those who may not be comfortable around humans or who may have had a negative experience with humans, this relationship may take longer to develop.

We only use positive reinforcement to train our killer whales. We know that the behavior we want to increase needs to be immediately reinforced, so during the training process we teach the whales a signal we call a "bridging stimulus" to bridge the time gap between when the animals have performed correctly and when we are able to deliver a reinforcement. Many times we can reach out and give immediate reinforcement when an animal performs the correct behavior. But when we're working in a pool as large as our Shamu performing pool we use the sound of a dog whistle to let the whale know immediately that it has performed the correct behavior. Then when the animal returns to the trainer, a reinforcement is given. The sound of the whistle is always paired with positive reinforcement and therefore becomes a secondary reinforcer.

After we establish the bridging stimulus, we bring out the tools of training. One of the main tools is a long white pole with a ball at the end. We call this the target. We teach the whales to touch their rostrum (an area of the whale's nose) to the end of the pole. By teaching the animals to follow the white ball, we can use the movement of the target to manipulate the whales' body movements. Through posi-tive reinforcement and successive approximation training—reinforcing small steps—we get a whale to understand that he or she should turn when the ball turns or that he or she should jump out of the water if the ball rises up out of the water. We ma-nipulate the whale's body posture, its position in the pool, and its swimming speed by moving the target and having the whale follow it very closely. We then pair a hand signal with the behavior we're trying to train. Eventually, we fade out the tar-get, and the hand signal becomes the stimulus to perform the behavior. This proc-ess, depending on the complexity of the behavior and the experience of the trainer, can take months.

We don't rely just on food and other primary reinforcers to reinforce behavior. An experienced trainer also uses secondary reinforcers effectively. He or she might be able to do an entire interaction without feeding food and by using the relation-ship as the reinforcement. A trainer who has developed a strong relationship with an animal doesn't need to use many primary reinforcers because the animal enjoys interacting with the trainer. If I took that experienced animal and I put it with a less experienced trainer, I would expect the trainer to use more primary reinforcers be-cause he or she has not developed a strong relationship with the whale. A strong re-lationship with a killer whale takes anywhere from two to five years to develop.

At Sea World, we feel strongly about not using negatives in our animals' envi-ronments. Unfortunately, some facilities and trainers around the world still use negative reinforcement and food deprivation to modify behavior. When I first started training eighteen years ago, we used negatives to some degree to modify be-havior, but we learned quickly that negatives create frustrated animals and have the potential of getting people hurt. We then decided to use only positive reinforce-ment. As most people have probably experienced, behavior can be quickly modified by using negatives, but most people also don't realize the long-term effects that they have on behavior. By using negatives, people can lose the trust and respect they have developed with their animals. When working with a 6,000-pound killer whale, a trainer has to develop a strong positive relationship before he or she can enter that animal's environment. Without this trust and respect, a trainer entering the water with an animal like a killer whale could be in an extremely dangerous situation.

The way we handle incorrect behavior at Sea World is very simple and brings the least amount of attention to incorrect behavior. When an animal does some-thing incorrectly, we apply a least reinforcing stimulus. This simply means that when the animal returns to the trainer after performing, the trainer doesn't change the environment for three seconds. After the three seconds we have the option of repeating the behavior or going to the next behavior. We have found that by not changing the environment or bringing attention to incorrect behavior and by pro-viding environmental change and reinforcement to correct behavior, we teach the animals to make the choice of performing correctly.

People ask us when training begins with our baby killer whales. The training process begins within the first few days after birth. We begin reinforcing the baby by touching it and swimming with it. Obviously, the baby is still nursing, but by playing with it on stage or in the water, our attention becomes a reinforcer. The mother allows us to interact with her and the newborn in the water because of the strong trust we have developed with her. As the baby matures it will begin to mimic the mother. The trainers will reinforce this mimicry and eventually the young animal will acquire its own behavioral repertoire.

One of the greatest rewards of working with animals is developing a relationship with them. There are times when we put on the scuba gear and enter the pool with our killer whales and simply play with them. I can't explain in words what it feels like to play with a killer whale under water. We rub their bellies and scratch them. They pull us around the pool while we hold on to their dorsal fin and pectoral flippers. It's a fantastic experience.

Response and Analysis

1. According to Chuck Tompkins, why do the animal trainers pair themselves with positive items? Why is it important for a trainer to effectively use secondary reinforcers? How do the trainers use successive approximation to shape behavior?

2. Take the whale's point of view. In what ways have the whales "shaped" the trainers to treat them as they want to be treated? What punishing consequences do the whales have at their disposal? What reinforcements can they supply to the humans?

Personal Experience and Application

1. Suppose you want to train a puppy to sit. How might you use shaping, secondary reinforcement, and a schedule of reinforcement?

2. Do you believe trainers should use negative reinforcement when working with animals? What are the advantages and disadvantages of negative reinforcement compared to positive reinforcement? Do you think parents should use negative reinforcement with their children? Why or why not?

Research

Suppose you want to determine whether pigeons learn to walk in a circle faster when they are on a variable ratio schedule or a variable interval schedule of reinforcement. You train five birds under each schedule of reinforcement. What is the independent variable? What are the levels or conditions of the independent variable? What is the dependent variable?

VOICES FROM THE FUTURE

Susan Goodwillie (Editor)

Psychological Concepts
observational (social) learning, role models, violence

How can the environment in which we live affect how well we do in school? Consider the story of Manny, a twenty-year-old who lives in Brooklyn. Seventeen-year-old Shane Tilston, who interviewed Manny, writes that even though Manny had "been through hell and back," he still had "the most phenomenally wonderful, positive attitude." Manny learned to be violent from the time he was five, when his stepfather began beating him and his mother remained indifferent. He turned to the streets, became involved with gangs, and served time in jail.

Although he often did well in school, Manny says that he received no praise, and he began to doubt whether an education could help him. Because he was always getting into fights, he was kicked out of school when he was in the ninth grade. He is trying to survive in his environment and would like to improve his chances for a better life. However, he is not optimistic about his future. After Manny's story, we include a brief discussion among other teenage interviewers on what hope they see for teenagers in America.

I guess I've known violence all my life, since I was about five or six when my step-father started brutalizing me. I guess I did violence because that's all I knew. And drugs somehow seemed to make it better.

I grew up in Brooklyn. It's tough in Brooklyn. You have to be dressed hip and be down with everybody else, and if they get into a fight with a bunch of white kids, you have to get involved in it. You have to do stupid things like steal, rob, you know, all that crap, take drugs and things like that. I do admit it, when I was younger, I took drugs and hung out in a gang.

But then, as I grew older, I started learning that drugs and hanging out and being in gangs, it's not going to help me in life. It's not even gonna save my ass, 'cause in the streets, it's like . . . it's hectic. You know, the only way you could survive is to be yourself. Avoid problems. Avoid certain kinds of people you know that's gonna cause problems. Like if you see a certain group of kids hanging out, go around them. Don't go through them, 'cause if you go through them, you're going to get into serious trouble.

Right now, I'm trying to sell my Rollerblades for fifty bucks 'cause, well, it's hard to find a job. It's not easy finding jobs, especially if you ain't got a high-school diploma. I got kicked out of school in ninth grade—you know, too much fighting, carrying knives and guns and things like that to school. And I would pick fights to get kicked out of certain schools. I didn't want to be in that school. I even fought teachers. I fought a principal. I punched the principal in the mouth when I was young.

If I didn't fight, I wasn't satisfied. It was like a daily habit for me. And then I hit seventeen and I got locked up for a year because of fighting and assault charges and things like that. Came out, started learning, you know, jail is not the place, streets is not the place. The only place that it can be is through yourself, in your heart.

Now I'm drug-free. I just did it with willpower because I was realizing it was killing me and I was wasting too much money on drugs. I would spend two to three hundred dollars a day taking cocaine and smoking pot. That shit almost killed me. The only drug I take now is smoking cigarettes and drinking coffee. That's caffeine and nicotine. It's still bad, but it's a slow death.

I basically raised myself in the streets 'cause my mother wasn't there for me. She was home, but she wasn't there. She could be in the living room, I could walk into the house, and she wasn't there. She would not treat me like I was there, you know? She literally threw me out when I was younger so her boyfriend could live there.

And my stepfather, he used to beat me. He used to make me bend over the bed, naked, and beat me with a leather belt until I bled. Now, that's kinda crazy, you know what I mean? He used to do that to me and my brother, and then he would tell us if we did good in school he would buy us something, like clothes. We'd do good in school, and he wouldn't buy us shit. He'd leave us without buying anything. We were kids with no clothes, nothing.

So me and my brother started doing stuff to make money and live. We started stealing, 'cause that was the only way of survival. And then my mom and my stepfather would say that we were no good and all this and that and I said, If you would have helped us when we was younger, we wouldn't have been in this area where we are now.

They said, Oh, we did everything for you, we did this and we did that, and then they would send me to a psychiatrist. I tell the psychiatrist what they did to me and he would ask my parents if it was true and they would deny it and then when I got home I'd get beat again. Then I would go to school with beat marks and my parents would say I fell down the stairs—you know, that old line—so in other words, I was child-abused.

I turned rebellious against them at the age of fourteen and that's when I started hanging out in the streets and doing all this other shit because nobody will help me. I would do good in school, hoping I'd get something. But I would never get anything, so I said, Fuck it. I'm not going to go to school if I'm not gonna get nothin' for it, you know what I mean? I didn't realize how much I needed school.

I was living in the streets for a while, but then I said, That's not gonna help me. I said, Let me go home. 'Cause I was hungry, I'd go into the house when my mother wasn't there and steal food and take my bath, wash myself, change, and then go back in the streets. Every day I would do that and then I started stealing money from them. I stole two hundred dollars from my grandmother 'cause nobody would buy me toys, and I played with the money, but then I gave it all away to my friends because I couldn't take it home.

You know, a lot of these kids have broken lives. They don't have nobody to take care of them. They don't have nobody helping them. They have to do it all their life, practically helping themselves. Some of them came from good families and they're still fucked up. Me, I came from a bad family and I'm fucked up, anyway.

Now, basically, I'm a collector. I collect comics, I buy things and then sell them. Just to survive, I sell my comics. I keep them or make trade-offs. Like I give someone a bunch of comics that's worth three dollars and they'll give me a comic that's worth twenty dollars and I'll sell it for fifteen or ten dollars, and that way I can get a profit. That's a way of living, you know, you gotta survive that way.

You come out here every day, you're going to see how crazy it is. And how hard these people work just to survive. In a way it's good, 'cause we learn, we learn experience 'cause we're in the street and you learn from the streets, you learn to survive. Like some homebound kids, they're in the house, they don't know much about the streets. If you left them out in the streets for about a week without a place to live, they'd probably go crazy. They wouldn't know how to survive.

You know, you tell somebody something, they don't learn their lesson until they see it happen to themselves. Like when my big brother used to tell me, Don't take drugs anymore, man. Chill out with it, don't do this shit anymore. I didn't want to listen to him, I was like, You did it for so many years, man, you're gonna tell me now not to do it? But then I started getting locked up, getting beat up, getting robbed, and I started realizing, Now I know how those people that I beat up feel, because I got beat up. I started realizing a lot of shit because what I did to people, they did to me. They say what goes around comes around and, I might say, it came around to me.

So, right at this moment, I just try to survive. Later on in the future, I don't know what's going to happen to me. For what I know, I could be dead tomorrow. But I'm really going to try to straighten out my life, try to make it somewhere. I'd like to get a high-school diploma, but I can't right now because I really don't have a stable environment. I have a permanent address but not a permanent residence.

I try to live day by day now. Buy my comics, read my comics, then sell them. If I die, at least I died reading my comics, you know, I did something I enjoy. . . .

Reporters from *Children's Express*—A Discussion

Do you think there's any hope for kids and teenagers in America in the future?

Amy: When I talked to those kids, they didn't know that they could do things with their lives. No one ever told them, You can make good grades, you can go to college, or you can *be* anything. Their parents could care less that they quit school or that they come home and smoke pot, or not go to school at all. It is so sad, all those parents who just don't care.

Sarah: Without parents to support kids, they have no one to go to. So they look up at the people who are in gangs, and then they get in the gang and then they have to sell drugs because that's their job in the gang, and they have to steal cars and they have to do all this stuff. It takes like ten years and then they wonder, Why am I doing this? I did it because I needed someone to help me. I needed friends. And then they realize, by the time they're twenty-five, I want to go back. I want to get my GED. I want to get a job. But there are no jobs for people who haven't been in high school because that's just the way our country is. It's all really bad.

There really aren't very many role models anymore. I think the most important role model for someone is their parents, and I know there are tons of kids who live in foster homes, or nowhere, who don't have any parents to look up to. If you don't have someone to guide you and tell you what's right and wrong, then how are you going to find out? You're going to find out on the streets, or from your friends in school who are in the same situation as you are.

If your parents aren't serious, if you're doing bad in school and the teacher calls your parents and they don't do anything, they don't care, why should you care? You're a kid. You don't know what to do.

We need to reevaluate what we feel is important in society. Right now violence is a very important thing in our society. For some reason, everyone loves it. People go to the movies to see people get shot and killed. They like to see blood. That's what sells. Violence and sex and all that stuff. It sells. If that's the way our society is going to continue to go, we're just not going to make it.

Amy: Every time I'd interview someone, I'd ask, Who's your role model, who do you look up to? And usually they'd say, My big brother, he's in a gang, he beats up people every day. And I was like, Don't you look up to your parents? And they'd say stuff like, My mom sleeps all day or my dad sells drugs. I just can't imagine not having *any*one to look up to who's a positive influence in your life.

TJ: I think that's why gangs are formed, because there's nobody to look up to. Gangs are a substitute when families aren't there. If there could be somebody in the community they could go to and look up to, instead of gangs, maybe it could start to change things.

Hector: You have to live a positive life, don't always think that everything is going to turn on negative. If you live a negative life, you're never going to get anywhere. How do you expect to become something in life if you're saying, Oh, I'm not going to make it, I'm not going to do this and I'm not going to do that? . . .

Sarah: I think violence relates to poverty because if you don't have any money, you have to steal things so that you can have them. Or you can sell drugs. So we need to help people who are poor, more than we're doing now. I'm really glad we have a new President, because the other two weren't doing anything except making it a lot worse.

Kids shouldn't have to grow up with violence in their homes or on their streets or in their schools or anywhere. It's ridiculous that you need a metal detector to get into school. A school is a place where kids are supposed to learn and then go to the next school. It's not a place for drugs and guns and knives and things like that. It just really angers me that our world has come to this.

Hector: I think television is also a big problem. When you see this family, like on "Beverly Hills, 90210," living this good life and all their problems get solved and they have a car and people say, Why should I not have a life like that? I'll do anything to get that way, and that's like another way to promote violence. I'm never going to be like those people, so I'll just push my way through. And if you have this mentality, that you're harder than everyone else, you're definitely not going to do it by education. You're going to do it by force. You're going to fight your way up there, use your hands, kill people, deal drugs.

Sarah: I have hope for a lot of kids in America but not for all. I'm really upset about all the crack babies that are born. When they're born they already have something against them. They're already addicted to a drug. And no one wants them. Their mothers, their fathers, no one wants them. No one wants to adopt babies with AIDS, either.

I don't know what we can do, but every person that wants to help makes it better. I think we have to work together and figure out something to do. Bill Clinton cannot make our country not violent. He's one person. Even his administration is just going to be a bureaucratic organization. What are they going to do? Write laws. But laws obviously haven't gotten us anywhere. It's the law that you can't steal. You can't kill. You can't rape. You can't do all these things. But it doesn't matter. It's against the law to sell drugs, but that doesn't help.

I don't think putting people in jail is the answer to all our problems, either. A lot of the violence is happening inside jails. I think we all need to find out our values again. I'm not saying I want it to be like the fifties with the mom and the dad and the mom stays home all day and bakes cookies and they have a little dog and a picket fence. That's not what I want. I just want everyone to be a little kinder instead of trying to be against everybody else who you don't even know.

Response and Analysis

1. Manny says that he has known violence since the age of five or six. What were his experiences with violence at home? Who were Manny's role models? What did he learn from them?

2. According to the reporters of *Children's Express*, who were the role models for the young people they interviewed? What effects do the reporters believe the role models had on the children? How can observational, or social, learning influence socialization and violent behavior?

Personal Experience and Application

1. Who are your role models? Do you think they have a positive or negative influence on

your life? Why? List a few public figures who may be role models for children. Do you believe they have a positive or negative influence? Why?

2. Suppose the principal at a local elementary school in your community invites you to help develop a program to provide positive role models for the children. Whom might you choose? Why? Briefly discuss two activities in which the students and the role models might participate.

Research

Suppose you want to interview students at your college or university about their experiences with violence. What types of demographic information might you ask the participants to report? Write ten questions you would ask the students.

THE JAIME ESCALANTE MATH PROGRAM

Jaime Escalante and Jack Dirmann

Psychological Concepts
goals, cooperative learning

What excites us and makes us willing to work hard to learn? What student or teacher does not ask this question? As a graduate student in La Paz, Bolivia, Jaime Escalante discovered that "children learn faster when learning is fun, when it is a game and a challenge." Now, a highly successful high school teacher in California, Escalante often recruits students for his math program who are known for causing problems on campus. All he asks of those who join his class is an eagerness to succeed. He provides them with the concern and support that enable them to discover the pleasure of learning.

In 1952, while still an undergraduate in La Paz, Bolivia, I began teaching mathematics and physics—first at one high school, then a second, and finally a third. I found early in my career that children learn faster when learning is fun, when it is a game and a challenge. From the beginning, I cast the teacher in the role of the "coach" and the students in the role of the "team." I made sure they knew that we were all working together. . . .

Few students today have not been lectured on the necessity and importance of a good education; but the dictum "get a good education" may be too nebulous a message for easily distracted young minds. Their focus easily shifts to other more pressing problems, particularly when they are living in poverty. The AP test provides the formidable outside "opponent" that galvanizes the students and teacher in a united charge toward a tangible and inexorable deadline—the second week of May. Over the years I have found it easy to focus student attention on this challenge and its very real rewards of possible college credit and advanced placement in college mathematics courses.

Not all students who take the test score a "three" or better, which enables them to receive college credit at over 2,000 colleges and universities, but those who sit for the exam have already won the real game being played. They are winners because they have met a larger challenge than any single examination could present. They have attained a solid academic background in basic skills, especially math and science, and are prepared to move on and compete well against the challenges of both higher education and life. Many of my former students who have gone on to college mathematics or calculus courses often call me. "Kimo," they say ("Kimo" is the shortened, student-preferred spelling of "Kemo Sabe," the nickname I was given by one of my gang kids in the 1970s), "this was easy after your course."

As the number of students enrolled in my program has grown to between 140 and 200 studying calculus alone, Advanced Placement at Garfield High School has also exploded in other technical subjects such as physics, chemistry, biology, and computers. Many of my students now take two, three, and sometimes even four AP tests in various subjects. In 1989 the school set a record with over 450 AP tests administered in 16 different subjects. By comparison, in 1978, the year before I started my AP program, only 10 tests were administered for the entire school and not one student sat for the calculus examination.

A growing number of junior high school students who wish to be part of the program enroll early and participate in their first math class during the summer program at East Los Angeles College (ELAC) between their ninth grade year (last year of junior high school) and their tenth grade year. Thus, by the time these students enter the tenth grade they are prepared to take geometry. Currently, six Escalante program students are studying math analysis at a local junior high school. By the time they reach the twelfth grade, they will be ready for third-year college math.

I have been able to reach down into the three feeder junior high schools and establish an unofficial recruiting network within their math departments. We are constantly trying to pick out promising kids with *ganas* (*ganas* translates loosely from Spanish as "desire," or the "wish to succeed") while they are yet junior high school students, so that they can enter the program before or just as they arrive at Garfield.

I do not recruit these students by reviewing test scores or grades, nor are they necessarily among the "gifted" or on some kind of "high IQ track," because I believe that tracking is unworkable and unproven as a guarantee that students will be channeled into the program of classes best suited to them. My sole criterion for acceptance in this program is that the student wants to be a part of it and sincerely wants to learn math. I tell my students, "The only thing you need to have for my program—and you must bring it every day—is *ganas*." If motivated properly, any student can learn mathematics. Kids are not born as bad students; however, the school and the student's home and community environment can combine to produce a bad student. The teacher is the crucial point in this equation. It is up to the teacher to bring out the *ganas* in each student.

Today, the junior high school teachers in our locale have a much better idea of what we need for our program. I often tell the following story to show the difference between the attitude of junior high school math teachers when I first started teaching at Garfield ten years ago and their attitude today. In 1979, when junior high school teachers would tell me, "Take Johnny, he's gifted in math," I would almost always ignore them. Such a recommendation was almost a guarantee that I would pass that child over. If the child was in fact gifted, I figured he or she would need less help from the teacher. Secondly, few of the "gifted" were appreciably different from the "average"—except in their ability to score high on tracking tests. Instead, I often chose the rascals and kids who were "discipline problems," as well as those who simply liked math. I found that the "class cut-ups" were often the most intelligent, but were extremely bored by poor teaching and disillusioned by the perceived dead-end that school represented for them. Sometimes they showed themselves to have the most *ganas* when their "learning light" finally switched on. . . .

I exhibit deep love and caring for my students. I have no exclusive claim to these attributes; they are as natural as breathing to most parents and teachers. The power of love and concern in changing young lives should not be overlooked.

A few months ago I surveyed a large number of students in each of my six classes. I asked them, "What do you want from your parents?" There was a variety of answers, but those that appeared most often really surprised me and made me think twice. They were:

(1)   unconditional love; that is, with no strings attached;
(2)   peace at home;
(3)   to be understood;
(4)   trust, and the freedom of choice that such trust implies.

I believe that unconditional love must be extended to each student. This happens when a teacher loves to motivate and teach the difficult students as well as the good ones. I make sure that my students know that I believe in them. I know that the strong intention I communicate to them to succeed must be great enough to overcome the combined negativity of their previous failures, the prejudices of others who predict their likely future failures, and the lack of preparation in mathematics with which they are burdened after nine years in our education system.

Response and Analysis

1. Why does Jaime Escalante believe that students of any race or economic status will work to their potential when they have teachers who challenge them and believe in them? Why does he believe that exhibiting love for students is important to learning? How might cooperative learning (i.e., a team approach) facilitate learning?

2. What is *ganas*? Why does Escalante believe that he is responsible, in part, for generating *ganas* in his students?

Personal Experience and Application

1. Think about one or two of your teachers who motivated or inspired you to learn. What did they do to inspire or motivate you? How did your inspiration or motivation influence your performance in other courses?

2. Suppose a teacher at a high school in your community invites you to give a lecture to her class. She asks you to present the information on operant conditioning that is in your psychology textbook. There will be twenty-five sophomore students in the class. How might you create interest in the topic and generate *ganas* among the students?

Research

Suppose you want to identify teaching techniques that motivate junior high school students to excel in their studies. You decide to ask high school teachers in your community to provide you with a list of their successful techniques. Is it important to randomly select teachers from your community to participate in your study? Why or why not?

chapter 5

MEMORY

My forgetter works very well.

NELLYE LEWIS, age 92,
personal communication

How much can we rely on our own memory or on the memories of others? In this chapter we examine the following concepts: acquisition, retention, and retrieval; short- and long-term memory; memory contamination; eyewitness testimony; amnesia; and exceptional memory.

In the first two selections, psychologist Elizabeth Loftus describes fascinating accounts of trials for which she served as an expert in eyewitness testimony. One is the case of Tyrone Briggs, a man accused of assault and rape in Seattle. Loftus demonstrates how memory can be subject to suggestibility, how it can vacillate under stress, and how, in the case of Briggs, numerous errors in recall can work to bring a conviction against an innocent man.

The other case involves serial murderer Ted Bundy, who was eventually executed in Florida. A woman who survived his abduction remembered his face and certain other details, yet there were inconsistences and gaps in her testimony. Loftus illustrates the problems that can be associated with short- and long-term memory. However, the witness was correct: it was Bundy who had abducted her.

Very different from having inaccurate memory is having little or no memory at all. Dr. Tony Dajer tells of a woman who lost her memory for only twenty-four hours. Dajer describes his patient's sudden confusion and the various conditions that might have caused her attack. What caused her memory loss and how did she recover?

In Russia in the first half of the twentieth century, A. R. Luria worked for several years with a young man of unusual memory whom he called "S." S. was able to remember long series of words and numbers and seemed to have no limit to how much or how long he was able to retain what he had learned. He was equally gifted in his ability to recall extensive details about minutiae, events, conversations, and scenes. Could such a memory pose problems as well as offer benefits?

WITNESS FOR THE DEFENSE:
A MOLE AND A STUTTER:
TYRONE BRIGGS

Elizabeth Loftus and Katherine Ketcham

Psychological Concepts
eyewitness memory, memory contamination

In November 1986 a series of assaults, robberies, and attempted rapes began near the Yesler Terrace Housing Project in Seattle, Washington. The public demanded that the perpetrator be found and convicted. One victim worked with a police artist until a sketch of the suspect took form. This drawing was published in local papers and shown on television. In January 1987, a woman who lived in the housing project said that the sketch looked like a boy who lived nearby. Thus was Tyrone Briggs, a nineteen-year-old high school basketball star, targeted and evidence gathered against him.

By March 1987, defense attorney Richard Hansen had phoned Elizabeth Loftus, a psychologist and an expert in the fallibility of eyewitness testimony, to appear as an expert witness. The case ended in mistrial, only to be opened again. In December 1987, the second jury declared Briggs guilty, and he was sentenced to sixteen years three months in prison. But in July 1989, Briggs's conviction was reversed on the basis of a juror misconduct issue. When the case went to trial again, the jury ended in deadlock. The charges were dropped and the case was not retried.

In looking at the details that Hansen and Loftus gathered for the first trial, what impresses you the most about the findings, the effects of suggestibility on witnesses' memory, and the reliability of memory?

"The police have made a grievous error," Richard said. "They were under intense pressure to find someone—a black man was out there attacking white and Asian professional women—and Tyrone happened to look something like the man in the artist's sketch. From that point on, it's been a tragedy of errors."

Tragedy of errors. I liked that.

"Tyrone is nineteen years old, a high school basketball star, living in an apartment in the Yesler Terrace Housing Project with his family. He's the sweetest kid you could imagine. And he's got a terrible stutter. It's the worst stutter I've ever heard."

Richard wouldn't be relating that little fact without a reason. I waited, enjoying the suspense.

"Not one of the victims mentioned a stutter," he continued. "Not one. In fact, from the victims' initial descriptions, it would appear that the attacker couldn't stop talking. He was calm, he didn't whisper or shout but spoke in a 'normal conversational tone.' If you could hear Tyrone speak, you would know that this could not be the same man—he's had a severe stutter ever since his parents can remember. I'm talking severe—it takes him nearly a minute to say his name and address."

Stutter, I wrote on a piece of note paper.

"But that's not the only problem with the prosecution's case. The victims' initial descriptions of the attacker are so far off the mark it's like the proverbial shotgun that can't hit the side of a barn. One victim described a man with a receding hairline, a short Afro, about 190 pounds; another described a full-grown man in his mid-twenties, between five eight and five nine. The most detailed description was given by the last victim, who described her attacker as twenty-two to twenty-five years old, five nine to five ten, with yellow crooked teeth, a space between the two front teeth, a bushy Afro tinted red, and a ski-jump nose. At the time of the attacks, Tyrone Briggs was barely nineteen years old, wore his hair in jeri curls—the Michael Jackson look—weighed about 155 pounds, had straight, white teeth, a very large nose, very large lips, and a prominent mole above his right lip. Not one of the eyewitnesses mentioned a mole. In fact, the only detail that consistently fits is the fact that Tyrone is black. I'll send this stuff to you by messenger, and we can discuss it after you've had a chance to review it. I've got to be in court in"—a slight pause while Richard cupped the receiver against his shoulder and looked at his wristwatch—"ye gods, in five minutes. Gotta run. Call me."

I spent that evening in my office going through the Briggs file, making my little checkmarks in the margins, scribbling my notes, sifting, sorting, and separating the facts into the relevant categories. Right away three things bothered me about the case. First and most obvious, five women victims and a male eyewitness had identified Tyrone Briggs as the Harborview attacker. Eyewitness testimony is problematic, but when you have six positive witnesses pointing their fingers at the same man, even a skeptic like me begins to believe there might be something to it.

The second problem had to do with the available lighting conditions when the attacks took place. In daylight or artificial lighting conditions, we process more information into memory and thus have more information to pull out of memory later, when we are asked to recall an event. Even though it was gray and rainy in Seattle and close to the shortest day of the year when these attacks took place, there was, theoretically at least, enough light available for the victims to see their attacker.

The third problem concerned the duration of the attacks. The longer a person has to look at something, the better his or her memory will be, and only one of the attacks could be considered "fleeting"; several of the women were with the attacker for at least a minute or two.

I sipped my coffee and stared at the sheets of paper covering my desk. This just wasn't one of those cases that came hurtling at me, screaming of injustice. It didn't hit me, for example, like the recent case I'd worked on in Florida, where a teenager was accused of attempted rape and attempted murder after stabbing a twenty-four-year-old woman in the stomach with an eight-inch butcher knife. On the night she was attacked, the victim told a detective that her assailant was a teen-ager who wore braces; later she identified eighteen-year-old Todd Neely, who had never worn braces and who had an ironclad alibi confirmed by credit card receipts that showed that he was eating dinner at a restaurant with his family when the crime occurred. Police claimed Neely left the restaurant early, although they had no proof; moreover, the victim changed her testimony about her assailant's braces. In court she said she might have seen a reflection of the indoor light off his teeth and mistaken that for braces. Neely was convicted in a nonjury trial and sentenced to fifteen years.*

When the Florida lawyer sent me the police reports and preliminary hearing transcripts, I became convinced that Todd Neely was a victim of mistaken identifi-cation. But with Tyrone Briggs I wasn't so sure. I kept thinking—six eyewitnesses. *Six.* I knew of cases where five, six, seven, even as many as fourteen eyewitnesses were wrong, but these were the unusual, highly publicized cases that occurred once in a blue moon. Most of the cases I work on involve just one or two eyewitnesses.

But, I reminded myself, if one person can make a mistaken identification, so can five. The odds may go up, but it can happen. It had happened before.

I began a more careful reading of the police reports, incident reports, and lineup statements, looking specifically for contamination. Our memories are not, as so many people believe, perfectly preserved in our brains, frozen in time. Like other organic substances, memories can go "bad" when exposed to polluting influences.

I put on my glasses and went to work.

On January 20 Tyrone Briggs was tentatively identified from the police artist's sketch by a Yesler Terrace resident. "That looks something like him," she told De-tective Clark. Briggs was arrested on an outstanding traffic ticket, his picture was taken and included in a stack of twenty-one photographs that was then shown to Karl Vance, the man who held the gun on the attacker in the December 18 attack. Vance positively identified Briggs, signing this statement:

> Today Detective Clark showed me a photo montage of twenty-one pictures. I positively picked picture numbered four as the person I saw dragging a lady into an apartment and I stopped him as he was trying to rape her. As soon as I saw the picture, I picked it up and knew it was the same person. I am absolutely positive that that is the person.

A lineup was scheduled for the morning of January 23; but newspaper and TV reporters discovered that the police had arrested a suspect in the Harborview at-tacks and arrived en masse at the Public Safety Building, cameras loaded and ready

---

[1]On August 24, 1990 charges against Todd Neely were dropped and he was cleared after an appeals court ruled that prosecutors withheld crucial evidence in the case. "We can't get it through our heads that it's over," Neely's stepfather told the *Palm Beach Post.* "It's sort of like being on a battlefield when the shell-ing stops. The silence is deafening." The four-and-a-half-year ordeal cost the Neely family approxi-mately $300,000.

to shoot, a hastily assembled, celluloid firing squad. Four of the five victims were brought into the lineup room, a small auditorium on the fifth floor of the building. At that time, Richard wrote in his notes, a police sergeant prepared the women for the shock of seeing their attacker in person. "It is not uncommon for a person to have an emotional reaction upon seeing a suspect again for the first time," he said. "Those feelings manifest themselves in a lot of different ways. Some people get a chill down the spine, a rumbling in the stomach, palpitations, some people sweat, some people get frightened all over again."

This was already a kind of memory contamination. The police sergeant had, in effect, told the victims that they were about to see the man who attacked them. He had set them up, communicating to them that the police had a definite suspect.

The sergeant left the room, then, and returned some time later to apologize for the delay. He explained to the victims that they couldn't get enough people together to make sure that the person they had in custody—another not-so-subtle clue that the police had a definite suspect waiting in the wings—would get a fair lineup. They would have to do a photo montage instead.

The witnesses were kept waiting while a photo montage was hastily assembled. Robin Clark, the detective in charge of the investigation, took a ball-point pen and marked a mole on every photograph, being careful to make it match in size and shape the mole above Tyrone Briggs's right lip.

Now this was tricky. It's a well-established psychological finding that unusual features or objects draw our attention. When people try to recall the details of Mikhail Gorbachev's face, for example, they might first mention the prominent birth mark on his forehead. In a photo lineup, it's standard police practice to either cover up an unusual facial feature or to make sure that everyone has it. If a suspect has a strange hairdo, the police will cover the "distractors'" heads with a hat; if the suspect wears braces, the police would ask the suspect and others in the lineup to keep their mouths closed; if the suspect has a deep scar on his face, the scar should be concealed or the distractors should have a similar scar.

When Detective Clark drew a mole on the other five faces in the montage she was actually following standard police procedure designed to protect the suspect from bias or prejudice. Nevertheless, there were two significant, potentially serious problems stemming from this act. First, not one victim ever mentioned a mole on the attacker, but since every face in the photo montage had a mole, it would not take great powers of deduction to conclude that the police had a suspect who had a mole. The eyewitnesses' original memories, exposed to this potent source of postevent information, might then undergo change and contamination. Their minds would simply use their own mental pen to draw a mole on the face in their memory. Just like that, with little or no conscious thought, the memory would change to incorporate the new information.

The second problem would come later, in the actual in-person lineup. If Tyrone Briggs was the only person in that lineup with a mole, then the whole identification procedure would be tainted. After the photo identification, the eyewitnesses would be left with the impression that the suspect had a mole. When they viewed the in-person lineup, they would notice the man with the mole. They might, then, pick him out as the attacker not necessarily because he *was* the attacker, but because he was the man with the mole.

I wanted to jump ahead and look through the in-person lineup statements and photographs, but I forced myself to proceed slowly, going step by step, inch by inch through the evidence, sifting through the facts.

I found the Xerox copies of the victims' "montage identification statements." All five victims identified Tyrone Briggs as their attacker, but in every case the victims expressed reservations and uncertainty; in their written statements, they indicated that they arrived at their choice through the process of elimination.

The Seattle University student who had been assaulted on November 28 wrote: "I picked picture number 4 as the person who looks like and could be the person that assaulted me. His lips in the front view look thick but I don't really remember the lips. Everything else about his face looks right. It is definitely not any of the other five photographs."

The victim of the December 3 robbery wrote: "I am not positive it is number 4, he could be the person. It is definitely not numbers 1, 2, 3, 5, or 6."

According to the December 4 victim: "It seems more like number 4 because number 1 is not heavy enough, and number four is lighter complected and has smoother features. However, I am not positive that it is number 4."

The December 15 assault victim wrote: "I feel that it is number 4. I don't remember a mole being there, but I don't remember it not being there."

According to the December 18 assault victim: "It is definitely not numbers 1, 2, 3, 5, and 6. I am sure that it is number 4, but I don't remember the mole on his face, but I do remember a spot on his face."

Every one of these statements reflected a response that was closer to a guess than a positive statement. Guessing can be extremely dangerous, because when a witness is uncertain, guessing may actually fill the gaps in the initial skeletal representation of the event, causing an actual change in the underlying memory. Later, when searching her memory, the witness may incorrectly recall something that had earlier been merely a guess as an entrenched part of memory. Furthermore, while an initial guess may be offered with low confidence, later, when the witness mistakes the guess for a real memory, the confidence level can rise. The witness is no longer able to distinguish the original facts from the subsequent guesses, and in her mind she "sees" the entire construction as the truth. The facts have been cemented together through guesswork.

Imagine a memory as a pile of assorted bricks (details, facts, observations, and perceptions) piled up in a big mound. Guessing is the cement slapped on the bricks, allowing them to become a solid, cohesive structure. In the beginning, the guesswork may be liquid and malleable, but it can harden over time, becoming firm and resistant to change. Each time the memory is recalled, it becomes more vivid, more colorful, more *real*, and the witness becomes more confident that this is, indeed, the way things were.

In an actual criminal identification procedure, police and prosecutors often exert a subtle but profound pressure on their witnesses to be complete and accurate; under such pressure, a guess can quickly solidify into a certainty. Witnesses will also put pressure on themselves, for it is a general characteristic of human nature that we will try to avoid looking uncertain or confused. Once we have offered a response, we tend to stick by it, becoming increasingly more confident as time goes by. Any attempt to get us to rethink or question a statement that we have offered as fact may be perceived as an assault on our honor and integrity.

One other factor may have affected the witnesses' identifications of Tyrone Briggs. Three of the victims were Caucasians, two were Asians, and the assailant was black. It's a well-established fact that people are better at recognizing faces of people of their own race than they are at recognizing people from different races. This phenomenon, known as cross-racial identification, has been observed in numerous psychological experiments, yet many people remain unaware of its effects.

Response and Analysis

1. Briefly describe the three features of the Tyrone Briggs case that bothered Elizabeth Loftus. Why did they concern her? What does Loftus mean when she writes that our "memories can go 'bad' when exposed to polluting influences"?

2. How might the instructions during the lineup and the unusual face mole have influenced the memory of the eyewitnesses? How can guessing about a memory or feeling pressure to give complete and accurate details influence memory?

Personal Experience and Application

1. Have you ever thought about a past event over and over, trying to remember details? What was the event? Do you believe that in doing so your memory of the event became more accurate or less accurate? Why?

2. Suppose the local police department in your community asks you to offer two recommendations to minimize the contamination of eyewitness memories during an interview. Briefly discuss each recommendation and why it would be effective.

Research

Suppose you want to examine how cultural experiences influence memory. You expect that people will most accurately remember information that is consistent with their own cultural experiences. You need to identify two cultures that have very different approaches to the same event, and you discover that Americans and Nigerians have markedly different experiences with funerals (see Nsedu Onyile's description of funerals in Chapter 7, "Human Development"). You speculate that Americans and Nigerians will be more familiar with funerals in their own country than with funerals in the other country.

You decide to recruit participants from a university in Nigeria and from your own institution. A professor at the Nigerian university will help you recruit participants from his or her university. The participants will read a description of either a traditional American funeral or a traditional Nigerian funeral. After reading the description, you will ask them to write an essay describing what they remember.

Suppose you suspect that the participants know a great deal about how funerals in the other country are conducted. How might this knowledge influence their memory of the essay? What could you do to be sure that the participants did not know very much about how funerals in the other country are conducted?

WITNESS FOR THE DEFENSE:
THE ALL-AMERICAN BOY:
TED BUNDY

Elizabeth Loftus and Katherine Ketcham

Psychological Concepts
stages of memory (acquisition, retention, retrieval),
eyewitness memory, experiences and memory

Is eyewitness testimony reliable? Can leading questions alter our memory? Psychologist Elizabeth Loftus points out that our memories are vulnerable to suggestibility and suffer from the effects of time. In addition, what we originally perceive may be influenced by the amount of stress we are under, by conditions of weather and light, and by our own selectivity.

In 1975, Dr. Loftus received a call from John O'Connell, a defense attorney in Salt Lake City, who wanted her to work as an expert in eyewitness testimony in the case of Ted Bundy. In the early 1970s the "Ted cases" had become well known in the Northwest, which had been beset with the murders of several young women.

Loftus and O'Connell examined the way memory, bias, and perception influence a witness's allegations. Although there were conflicting statements about the accused in the testimony of the woman who survived Bundy's attack, the judge did not believe Bundy and sent him to prison. He was later transferred to a jail in Colorado, from which he escaped, and eventually he was arrested in Florida for the murders of two women at Florida State University. Bundy was indeed the serial killer who had murdered several women in the Northwest and elsewhere.

Loftus had many qualms about having worked for Bundy's defense. But her devotion to being a social scientist who carefully analyzes testimony in order to aid justice and to keep innocent people from being convicted prompted her to become involved with the case.

Now that I think back on it, I don't remember John O'Connell ever telling me that his client, twenty-three-year-old law student Ted Bundy, was innocent. I have a letter from O'Connell in which he refers to the kidnapping charge against Bundy as "one of the more interesting cases involving eyewitness identification." I remember a phone conversation in which he talked about the "extremely weak case" against his client. He often stressed the confusion and uncertainty of the kidnapping victim—the only eyewitness, it would turn out, who lived to tell about her few moments of terror with Ted Bundy.

But when I dredge up the strange and painful memories of my involvement with Ted Bundy, I have no recollection of John O'Connell insisting with his characteristic passion and intensity that his client was innocent. Maybe that particular silence should have given me a clue.

The name Ted Bundy meant nothing to me back in December 1975 when John O'Connell first contacted me about the kidnapping charge against his client. The name might as well have been anyone's. But one comment in O'Connell's letter did set off an alarm system in my memory. It was the second line of his five-page, single-spaced letter.

> Dear Dr. Loftus,
> I am representing Ted Bundy on a charge of aggravated kidnapping here in Salt Lake. Mr. Bundy is a law student from the Seattle area and has achieved a great deal of notoriety there because this case has made him a prime suspect in the "Ted cases." . . .

I knew all about the "Ted cases": I'd be willing to bet that every woman living in the state of Washington knew about the "Ted cases." Beginning in January 1974, young women in their late teens and early twenties, all pretty, all with long brown hair parted down the middle, began to disappear. Every month another woman would vanish. The media, in a hideous display of insensitivity, began referring to the missing women as "Miss February," "Miss March," "Miss April," and "Miss May."

In June 1974 the pace speeded up as two more women disappeared, and in July two women vanished on the same day from the same park at Lake Sammamish, twelve miles east of Seattle. But now, finally, there were witnesses who told police that an attractive, polite young man calling himself "Ted" and wearing his left arm in a sling approached several women and asked for their help in lifting a sailboat onto his car. He couldn't do it himself, he explained with a shy grin, because of his sprained arm.

The disappearances seemed to stop then, but the grisly discoveries began. In September the remains of three women were discovered by a grouse hunter near an abandoned logging road twenty miles east of Seattle. The next spring another "dumping site"—a favorite media expression—was discovered by two forestry students hiking on the lower slopes of Taylor Mountain near the town of North Bend. Four skulls and assorted bones would eventually be unearthed there, each cranium fractured by a heavy blunt instrument wielded with tremendous force and fury.

I turned to page 2 of O'Connell's letter, where he described the kidnapping incident, and continued on to page 3 where he discussed Bundy's arrest on a traffic charge almost ten months after the kidnapping.

> There is no other evidence whatsoever connecting the defendant to this crime except that he has type O blood and some type O blood was found sometime later on the victim's clothing. All this, despite the fact that Ted Bundy has been subjected to the most

thorough police investigation that I have ever seen. Due to the great time lapse, we are unable to establish an alibi for the time concerned.

O'Connell included with his letter a twenty-page police report and typed transcript of a taped statement the victim made the night of the incident. Throughout both the police report and the transcript, O'Connell used a thick black pen to underline certain words and phrases and scrawl notes in the margins. I began reading.

OFFENSE: Abduction
DATE OF OCCURRENCE: 11-8-74
SUSPECT: Male, white, American, 25–30 years, brown hair, medium length, approximately six feet tall, thin to medium build, moustache neatly trimmed. Wearing green pants and sports jacket, color unknown. Patent leather, shiny black shoes.

An arrow led from the underlined word to the left-hand margin where O'Connell had scrawled, "See taped statement—reddish brown shoes."

I leafed through the remaining pages of the police report, noting the other underlined parts.

Victim believed that she scratched suspect, probably on either the hands or arms, that she did note some blood on her hands that must have come from the suspect, that she was not injured herself. However, does not remember actually hurting the suspect.

In talking to victim, she states she believes she could identify suspect if she saw him again, that she spent approximately 20–30 minutes with him in the mall and walking through the parking lot and in the vehicle. Victim taped a report which will be included as a supplement of this report.

The supplementary report contained the transcript of a conversation between the victim, Carol DaRonch, and Detective Riet. . . .

"Let's review the major eyewitness issues in this case," I said.

O'Connell searched through some papers on his desk and handed me a lined, legal-size piece of paper with "Loftus—Main Points" handwritten at the top of the page. "I took notes from our telephone conversations," he explained, grinning at me.

I read the first point.

Perception and memory do not function like T.V. camera and videotape. Only that which was perceived can be remembered—i.e., memory cannot be "replayed" to get details which were not noted in original perception. Analogy to watching football play. If observer did not notice great block because concentrating on runner, cannot replay and recall from memory the block as one could do with the videotape of the same play.

"Nice analogy," I said.

"I'm a great football fan," O'Connell said, puffing on his pipe. "Why don't you explain this videotape concept to me again."

I'd given this particular lecture dozens of times to college students; I was on automatic pilot. "Most theoretical analyses of memory divide the process into three separate stages," I began. "First, the acquisition stage, in which the perception of the original event is put into the memory system; second, the retention stage, the period of time that passes between the event and the recollection of a particular piece of information; and third, the retrieval stage, in which a person recalls stored information.

"Contrary to popular belief," I continued, "facts don't come into our memory and passively reside there untouched and unscathed by future events. Instead, we pick up fragments and features from our environment and these go into memory where they interact with our prior knowledge and expectations—information that is already stored in our memory. Thus experimental psychologists think of memory as being an integrative process—a constructive and creative process—rather than a passive recording process such as a videotape."

I switched from the general to the specific. "All the 'I don't knows' and 'I don't remembers' in Carol DaRonch's testimony could mean that the information was never stored in the first place—there was a failure, in other words, in the acquisition stage. Or it could mean that the information was stored but then forgotten—a failure in either the retention stage or the retrieval stage. There's really no way of telling exactly what happened."

I looked at O'Connell's list and read number 2: Memory deteriorates at an exponential rate.

"The accumulation of research shows that memory decays or deteriorates as time goes by," I explained. "After a week, memory is less accurate than after a day. After a month, memory is less accurate than after a week. And after a year, memory will be less accurate than after a month."

"Eleven months is presumably one hell of a long time for Carol DaRonch to hold a memory of Ted Bundy's face in her mind," O'Connell observed.

"That's right," I agreed, "although many people are under the mistaken impression that memory for faces lasts a lifetime. The distinction—and it's an important one—must be made between memory for faces of people we've known for years and memory for the face of a stranger whom we see once, for a short period of time. Many people do remember the faces of friends whom they haven't seen for years or even decades. We graduate from high school, go off on our own, and twenty years later come back to a reunion where we immediately recognize the faces of our former friends.

"But this is not the same thing as remembering the face of a stranger. When it comes to strangers—people seen only briefly and only once—the overwhelming trend is that memory deteriorates as time passes. Most of the studies have used periods of time much shorter than eleven months and have shown great deterioration of memory for faces."

O'Connell nodded his head and looked at the paper, reading over my shoulder. "Some stimulation improves perception and memory, but great stress interferes. Fear to the point of hysteria has a negative effect on memory."

"This third point refers to the relationship between stress and memory," I said, "which is explained by the Yerkes-Dodson law, named after the two men who first noted the relationship back in 1908. At very low levels of arousal—for example, when a person is just waking up in the morning—the nervous system may not be fully functioning and sensory messages may not get through. Memory is not functioning very well. At moderate levels—say if you were slightly nervous about an upcoming trial or anxious about a confrontation with your teenage son—memory performance will be optimal. But with high levels of arousal, the ability to remember begins to decline and deteriorate."

"Tell me, Elizabeth," O'Connell said. "If you were in a car with a man who had identified himself as a police officer but who was driving the wrong way to the police station in a rundown Volkswagen, who then ran the car up onto the curb, snapped handcuffs on your wrist, brandished a gun, and raised a crowbar in an effort to hit you over the head—would you rate that as a high level of stress?"

"Yes, I would," I said. "But I should warn you about a potential problem."

O'Connell raised his eyebrows at me.

"Carol DaRonch wasn't under great emotional stress for the first five or ten minutes that she was with 'Officer Roseland,' " I said. "Part of that time she walked around with him in a well-lighted mall. It could be argued that she was under a moderate level of emotional arousal, which tends to produce alertness and fairly good recall."

"The prosecutor will be sure to pick up on that," O'Connell said. "Still, if you put all the facts together, we've got a good case for reduced accuracy of memory." He pointed to number 4 on the list. "Difficult to maintain separate visual images without transference and merging."

"This point refers to a process known as unconscious transference," I said, "a phenomenon in which a person seen in one situation is confused with or recalled as a person seen in a second situation. Again, with reference to this particular case, when the police showed Carol DaRonch two different photos of Ted Bundy—a mug shot and then, within a few days, a driver's license photo—they could have created a memory for her. 'Planted it in her brain,' as you once said."

O'Connell nodded his head. He understood that point well enough.

"Point 5," I said, reading the last paragraph on the list. "Effect of interviewer bias—particularly unintentional cueing and reinforcing. Support proposition that increasing excitement and activity of peace officers from September 1 (original photo selection) to October 2 (lineup) had effect of changing weak identification to positive identification."

"Do you always refer to the police as peace officers?" I asked.

"Yup," he said. "That's what I call them, because that's what they're supposed to be." But in this case O'Connell believed that the "peace officers" had gone too far and biased their witness, transmitting through words, gestures, or other "cues" their belief that Ted Bundy was, in fact, the kidnapper. After DaRonch tentatively identified Bundy's photo on September 1, 1975, and then more firmly identified him a few days later from a different photograph, the police may have communicated to her, intentionally or unintentionally, the feeling that they had "a live one." In her desire to help the police and finally put an end to her ordeal, DaRonch might have picked up on the signals and decided in her own mind that Bundy was, in fact, her abductor. Questions suggested answers that encouraged more sharply detailed questions until the whole thing picked up speed, steamrolling neatly ahead, with Bundy—guilty or innocent?—trapped beneath the wheels. . . .

In the beginning had I been fooled, as so many others were fooled, by the all-American boy with the polite manner and the deep smile lines? Unaccustomed to evil, could I not recognize it when it stared me in the face?

Response and Analysis

1. Elizabeth Loftus provides examples from Carol DaRonch's testimony to illustrate how perceptions of the environment interact with prior knowledge. How can expectations influence memory? According to Loftus, what are the main features of the acquisition, retention, and retrieval stages of memory?

2. According to Loftus, how might an interviewer's questions affect memory? What theoretical model might best explain how this happens? How can stress affect memory?

Personal Experience and Application

1. Suppose you are asked to remember the face of a newscaster who works for a national television station. Describe in as much detail as possible the face of the anchorman or anchorwoman. Then watch the news program. Which of the features that you listed were accurate? Which features did you omit?

2. Suppose you are a member of a jury. The case involves a convenience store robbery that occurred in the middle of the night. What factors might influence the degree to which you believe the testimony of the witness? Why?

Research

Suppose you want to replicate an experiment examining how memory can be altered (Loftus & Palmer, 1974). You show a videotape of a car accident to students in an introduction to psychology class. You then ask the participants what they saw in the videotape. You ask half of the students, "About how fast were the cars going when they *hit* each other?" You ask the other half, "About how fast were the cars going when they *smashed* into each other?" Then you dismiss the participants. Seven days later, you ask the participants whether they remember seeing broken glass in the accident. In fact, there was no broken glass. Which group do you think would "recall" seeing more broken glass—the participants hearing the word *hit* or those hearing the word *smashed*? Why might one group recall seeing more broken glass than another group? Do you think this study adequately illustrates how memories can be distorted? Why or why not?

THE LOST 24 HOURS

Tony Dajer

Psychological Concepts
amnesia (retrograde, anterograde), hippocampus

Imagine that one day you suddenly lose your memory. You don't remember what day it is, whether it is time for lunch, or why groceries are sitting on the table. That is what happened to Mrs. Duke, a woman in her mid-sixties, whose story is told by Dr. Dajer, her physician. In the thirty minutes it took her husband to go shopping one morning, Mrs. Duke became confused and unable to recall important details. The next twenty-four hours became "lost." While she was in the hospital and the doctors looked for the source of her amnesia, Mrs. Duke's spirits remained positive. Note the characteristics of her conversations, and Dr. Dajer's reactions to her. How would you describe the interaction between them during that twenty-four-hour period? Does Mrs. Duke show signs of reconnecting to the life she had before her memory loss?

For an emergency room, the scene seemed almost too tranquil: a couple in their mid-sixties were chatting quietly in a small exam cubicle. The man had his right elbow perched atop a cabinet; the woman sat on the stretcher, still wearing her street clothes.

"Hello, I'm Dr. Dajer," I said, walking in. "How can I help you?"

Mr. Duke spoke first. "My wife is confused."

While his wife paid close attention—as if hearing a recap of the first half of a movie she'd missed—he very precisely recounted the events of the previous two hours: He had left the house for 30 minutes to buy groceries; his wife had taken a bath. When he'd returned, she had seemed fine, but then she had started asking odd questions.

"What day is it?" for instance. Or, "Is it time for lunch yet?" (She'd already had lunch.) Then, "What are the groceries for?"

She should have known: it was her favorite niece's birthday, and they'd been planning the party for weeks. When he answered her, she didn't seem to know what to do next. A few minutes later she began asking the same questions all over again.

"So I called my daughter—she's a nurse—and she told me to bring my wife to the emergency room right away," Mr. Duke concluded.

"Sounds like your daughter was right," I replied, trying to look more intrigued than concerned.

I turned to Mrs. Duke. She was a silver-haired 66-year-old but seemed ten years younger. We chatted a bit about her daughter, whom I happened to know. While she spoke—coherently and easily—I scrutinized her face for the telltale drooping eyelid or asymmetrical smile of a transient ischemic attack, or TIA, sometimes called a ministroke, that might have accounted for her mental lapse. She appeared perfectly normal, though.

"Okay with you if we do a once-over-lightly?" I asked her. I quickly listened to the heart and lungs, palpated the abdomen, then zeroed in on the neurological exam. I tested the cranial nerves, the ones controlling the facial muscles we use to move our eyes and smile, which are typically affected in TIAs. Then I checked the muscle strength in her arms and legs, examined her reflexes and ability to feel a sensation like a pinprick, and tested her coordination. But I couldn't find the slightest abnormality.

Last came the mental-status exam, which measures cognitive functions like reasoning and memory.

"Mrs. Duke," I began, "do you know where you are right now?"

She took a look around and replied, "Why, in the hospital, I think."

"Do you know what day it is?"

"Of course." She opened her mouth to answer, but then she stopped. "Well, isn't that strange? I don't know."

I kept an encouraging note in my voice: "Sometimes I don't even know myself. How about the month?"

"July?" she answered, tentatively.

"September, actually."

"Oh dear." She pressed three fingers to her forehead, as if urging herself to concentrate a bit more.

"Do you know who the president is?" (She didn't.) "Is there some trouble with a country in the Middle East right now?" (The Iraqi invasion of Kuwait had been in the headlines for a month.)

She didn't know. Each time she would start to answer the question as if she were opening a familiar cupboard, only to find it unexpectedly bare. With every miss her husband's lips pressed tighter together.

"Let's try this," I ventured. "I'm going to name three objects. In five minutes I'll ask you to repeat them back to me, all right?"

She smiled bravely. "I'll do my best."

I glanced around the room: "Bed, chair, sink. Got it?"

"Bed, chair, sink. Yes."

"Okay, I'll be back in a few minutes and ask you to repeat those objects."

"Bed, chair, sink," she intoned as I left the room.

"Bed, chair, sink," I whispered to myself as I went to examine another patient. Then I walked back in.

"Well, Mrs. Duke," I boomed heartily, "what were the three objects?"

She peered at me for a second, then in a bewildered tone asked, "Who are you?"

I stopped in my tracks. "I'm the emergency room doctor. I was here just five minutes ago. Don't you remember?"

"Oh dear. I'm sorry. Should I?"

Her husband took her hand. "That's how she's been since I came home from shopping," he told me. "It's as if nothing sticks."

Amnesia. Absence of memory. Few medical phenomena have so intrigued the imagination or shaped so many plots as the idea that we can forget our past, even forget who we are. Most fictional cases, of course, don't fit medical fact (for example, the spy in Robert Ludlum's thriller *The Bourne Identity* couldn't possibly forget his entire life history and still fully assimilate new information). But there are enough holes in our knowledge of how the brain processes and stores memories—and how it loses them—to leave room for poetic license.

Imagine if the brain remembered absolutely everything, if every thought, impression, and sensation, no matter how trivial, was indelibly recorded. Then imagine that a past event could be recalled only by sorting through each and every event that came after it. Retrieving a childhood memory would take hours. Clearly, the brain must edit and file memories to make them retrievable and useful.

Crucial to this complicated process is the hippocampus, a curled, sea-horse-shaped structure that is tucked inside the brain's temporal lobes. First it appears to gather new information and store it as a short-term memory. Then it edits, or consolidates, the short-term memory and after a while files the boiled-down product permanently in other parts of the brain. Finally, it helps retrieve those files when needed later. Thus the hippocampus acts both as a way station for recent memories—a monkey whose hippocampus has been destroyed can't remember tasks learned two weeks earlier—and as a retrieval system for old memories.

Although Mrs. Duke could speak and reason normally, her memory acted like a faulty computer in which each new entry erased the one ahead of it—before it could be stored. In short, her hippocampus could construct no new memories. Nor could it recall the events in the recent past, such as the invasion of Kuwait. Finally, her inability to recollect long-established facts such as the president's name suggested her file-retrieval system was jumbled.

The question we needed to answer was whether the amnesia was permanent—the result of a tumor in the hippocampus or of a large blood clot causing a major stroke. The other, much more hopeful possibility was transient global amnesia, a rare condition that is probably caused by a small clot passing through the arteries that feed the hippocampus. Like any other TIA, this disturbance usually resolves itself within 24 hours. Only time and the CT scan could reveal what was the matter with Mrs. Duke. And neither verdict would be in till morning.

I arranged for Mrs. Duke's admission into the intensive care unit. With child-like trust, she agreed to be hospitalized when her husband suggested it, though she herself felt nothing was wrong: she literally couldn't remember that she kept forgetting. Every time I reentered the room, to her it was the first time. All she knew was that she could rely on her husband to decide what was best, even if she couldn't remember why or how or even what he had decided.

That night, Mrs. Duke kept asking the nurses the same questions: "Why am I here?" And, most disconcerting of all, "Who are you?" It was as if she kept waking up in an unfamiliar room.

When I got off my emergency room shift at 7 A.M., I went up to see her. She seemed more alert than 12 hours before. Tentatively, I asked the questions she should have been sick of hearing by now.

"Do you know where you are?"

She smiled. "Why, in the hospital."

"Do you remember coming into the hospital yesterday?"

A small frown. "No."

"What's the last thing you do remember?"

"Breakfast, I think. We were getting ready for my niece's birthday." (She had clearly made progress—though the 24 hours after that would remain a permanent blank to her.)

"Do you think you could remember three objects if I listed them for you?"

"I'll try."

We repeated yesterday's exercise. I went into the hall for five minutes, then returned. "Well?" I prompted.

"Bed, chair, sink," she replied.

Her hippocampus, apparently, had clicked back on. That meant she'd almost certainly had transient global amnesia, not a massive clot or a tumor. Her prognosis was excellent: unlike other TIAs, this temporary condition is not a harbinger of strokes to come, and better yet, it rarely repeats itself.

"We still need to do that CT scan, just to be sure," I told her. "But I think you're going to do just fine."

"Well, that's nice of you to say so," she replied, as if I had paid her a compliment.

As I took my leave, though, it struck me that maybe her recovery was too good to be true, that by repeating the same list, I'd "primed" her too well. I stopped and retraced my steps. Would she remember me if I took her by surprise?

I poked my head back into the room.

"Hello, Mrs. Duke."

"Oh, hello, Dr. Dajer." She smiled solicitously. "Is there something you've forgotten?"

Response and Analysis

1. What problem did Dr. Dajer suspect caused Mrs. Duke's amnesia? Did Mrs. Duke's experience resemble retrograde amnesia or anterograde amnesia? Why?

2. Briefly describe Mrs. Duke's difficulty recalling short-term and long-term memories. What is the role of the hippocampus in short-term and long-term memory? Briefly describe two other brain structures involved in memory.

Personal Experience and Application

1. Do you know someone who has experienced temporary or long-term memory loss, such as from an automobile accident or stroke? Briefly describe his or her ability to recall events that occurred within a few minutes and from many years in the past. What difficulties did this person experience because of his or her memory impairment? What was done to help the person remember?

2. Imagine that you are a victim of amnesia. How might anterograde amnesia affect your life? How might retrograde amnesia affect your day-to-day activities?

Research

Suppose you design a study to examine how anxiety (low, medium, high) and noise (soft, loud) affect the ability to retrieve and remember information. In this study, what are the independent variables? What are the levels or conditions of each independent variable? What is the dependent variable?

THE MIND OF A MNEMONIST

A. R. Luria

Psychological Concepts
exceptional memory, mental imagery, mnemonist

What advantages or disadvantages might there be in not forgetting anything you have learned? Might people who remember nearly everything one day find their "memory disk" overloaded? Indeed, are there people haunted by thorough and accurate memories?

The distinguished Soviet psychologist A. R. Luria presents the famous case of S., a man who had unusual mnemonic and perceptual abilities. When S. was a journalist and was given instructions by his editor, he was able to remember everything he had been told without taking notes. He assumed that everyone had that ability.

S. was also able to repeat a list of numbers or words of any length that Dr. Luria presented to him—even when the sessions were days, weeks, and even years apart. More fascinating were S.'s responses to sounds, decibels, words, and scenes. Upon hearing one particular individual speak, S. said, "What a crumbly, yellow voice you have."

After you read Dr. Luria's portrayal of S., imagine that you are S. and then listen to numbers or voices. Do any colors or images come to you?

When I began my study of S. it was with much the same degree of curiosity psychologists generally have at the outset of research, hardly with the hope that the experiments would offer anything of particular note. However, the results of the first tests were enough to change my attitude and to leave me, the experimenter, rather than my subject, both embarrassed and perplexed.

I gave S. a series of words, then numbers, then letters, reading them to him slowly or presenting them in written form. He read or listened attentively and then repeated the material exactly as it had been presented. I increased the number of elements in each series, giving him as many as thirty, fifty, or even seventy words or numbers, but this, too, presented no problem for him. He did not need to commit any of the material to memory; if I gave him a series of words or numbers, which I read slowly and distinctly, he would listen attentively, sometimes ask me to stop and enunciate a word more clearly, or, if in doubt whether he had heard a word correctly, would ask me to repeat it. Usually during an experiment he would close his eyes or stare into space, fixing his gaze on one point; when the experiment was over, he would ask that we pause while he went over the material in his mind to see if he had retained it. Thereupon, without another moment's pause, he would reproduce the series that had been read to him.

The experiment indicated that he could reproduce a series in reverse order—from the end to the beginning—just as simply as from start to finish; that he could readily tell me which word followed another in a series, or reproduce the word which happened to precede the one I'd name. He would pause for a minute, as though searching for the word, but immediately after would be able to answer my questions and generally made no mistakes.

It was of no consequence to him whether the series I gave him contained meaningful words or nonsense syllables, numbers or sounds; whether they were presented orally or in writing. All he required was that there be a 3–4 second pause between each element in the series, and he had no difficulty reproducing whatever I gave him.

As the experimenter, I soon found myself in a state verging on utter confusion. An increase in the length of a series led to no noticeable increase in difficulty for S., and I simply had to admit that the capacity of his memory *had no distinct limits;* that I had been unable to perform what one would think was the simplest task a psychologist can do: measure the capacity of an individual's memory. I arranged a second and then a third session with S.; these were followed by a series of sessions, some of them days and weeks apart, others separated by a period of several years.

But these later sessions only further complicated my position as experimenter, for it appeared that there was no limit either to the *capacity* of S.'s memory or to the *durability of the traces he retained.* Experiments indicated that he had no difficulty reproducing any lengthy series of words whatever, even though these had originally been presented to him a week, a month, a year, or even many years earlier. In fact, some of these experiments designed to test his retention were performed (without his being given any warning) 15 or 16 years after the session in which he had originally recalled the words. Yet invariably they were successful. During these test sessions S. would sit with his eyes closed, pause, then comment: "Yes, yes. . . . This was a series you gave me once when we were in your apartment. . . . You were sitting at the table and I in the rocking chair. . . . You were wearing a gray suit and you looked at me like this. . . . Now, then, I can see you saying . . ." And with that he would reel off the series precisely as I had given it to him at the earlier session. If one takes into account that S. had by then become a well-known mnemonist, who had to remember hundreds and thousands of series, the feat seems even more remarkable. . . .

Our curiosity had been aroused by a small and seemingly unimportant observation. S. had remarked on a number of occasions that if the examiner said something during the experiment—if, for example, he said "yes" to confirm that S. had reproduced the material correctly or "no" to indicate he had made a mistake—a blur would appear on the table and would spread and block off the numbers, so that S. in his mind would be forced to "shift" the table over, away from the blurred section that was covering it. The same thing happened if he heard noise in the auditorium; this was immediately converted into "puffs of steam" or "splashes" which made it more difficult for him to read the table.

This led us to believe that the process by which he retained material did not consist merely of his having preserved spontaneous traces of visual impressions; there were certain additional elements at work. I suggested that S. possessed a marked degree of *synesthesia.* * If we can trust S.'s recollections of his early childhood (which we will deal with in a special section later in this account), these synesthetic reactions could be traced back to a very early age. As he described it:

> When I was about two or three years old I was taught the words of a Hebrew prayer. I didn't understand them, and what happened was that the words settled in my mind as

---

*synesthesia: the stimulation of one sense evokes another sense, as in visualizing a color when hearing a particular sound.

puffs of steam or splashes. . . . Even now I *see* these puffs or splashes when I hear certain sounds.

Synesthetic reactions of this type occurred whenever S. was asked to listen to *tones*. The same reactions, though somewhat more complicated, occurred with his perception of *voices* and with speech sounds.

The following is the record of experiments that were carried out with S. in the Laboratory on the Physiology of Hearing at the Neurological Institute, Academy of Medical Sciences.

Presented with a tone pitched at 30 cycles per second and having an amplitude of 100 decibels, S. stated that at first he saw a strip 12–15 cm. in width the color of old, tarnished silver. Gradually this strip narrowed and seemed to recede; then it was converted into an object that glistened like steel. Then the tone gradually took on a color one associates with twilight, the sound continuing to dazzle because of the silvery gleam it shed.

Presented with a tone pitched at 50 cycles per second and an amplitude of 100 decibels, S. saw a brown strip against a dark background that had red, tongue-like edges. The sense of taste he experienced was like that of sweet and sour borscht, a sensation that gripped his entire tongue.

Presented with a tone pitched at 100 cycles per second and having an amplitude of 86 decibels, he saw a wide strip that appeared to have a reddish-orange hue in the center; from the center outwards the brightness faded with light gradations so that the edges of the strip appeared pink.

Presented with a tone pitched at 250 cycles per second and having an amplitude of 64 decibels, S. saw a velvet cord with fibers jutting out on all sides. The cord was tinged with a delicate, pleasant pink-orange hue.

Presented with a tone pitched at 500 cycles per second and having an amplitude of 100 decibels, he saw a streak of lightning splitting the heavens in two. When the intensity of the sound was lowered to 74 decibels, he saw a dense orange color which made him feel as though a needle had been thrust into his spine. Gradually this sensation diminished.

Presented with a tone pitched at 2,000 cycles per second and having an amplitude of 113 decibels, S. said: "It looks something like fireworks tinged with a pink-red hue. The strip of color feels rough and unpleasant, and it has an ugly taste—rather like that of a briny pickle. . . . You could hurt your hand on this."

Presented with a tone pitched at 3,000 cycles per second and having an amplitude of 128 decibels, he saw a whisk broom that was of a fiery color, while the rod attached to the whisks seemed to be scattering off into fiery points.

The experiments were repeated during several days and invariably the same stimuli produced identical experiences.

What this meant was that S. was one of a remarkable group of people, among them the composer Scriabin, who have retained in an especially vivid form a "complex" synesthetic type of sensitivity. In S.'s case every sound he heard immediately produced an experience of light and color and, as we shall see later in this account, a sense of taste and touch as well.

S. also experienced synesthetic reactions when he listened to someone's *voice.* "What a crumbly, yellow voice you have," he once told L. S. Vygotsky while conversing with him. At a later date he elaborated on the subject of voices as follows:

> You know there are people who seem to have many voices, whose voices seem to be an entire composition, a bouquet. The late S. M. Eisenstein had just such a voice: Listening to him, it was as though a flame with fibers protruding from it was advancing right toward me. I got so interested in his voice, I couldn't follow what he was saying. . . .
>
> But there are people whose voices change constantly. I frequently have trouble recognizing someone's voice over the phone, and it isn't merely because of a bad connection. It's because the person happens to be someone whose voice changes twenty to thirty times in the course of a day. Other people don't notice this, but I do. (Record of November 1951.)
>
> To this day I can't escape from seeing colors when I hear sounds. What first strikes me is the color of someone's voice. Then it fades off . . . for it does interfere. If, say, a person says something, I see the word; but should another person's voice break in, blurs appear. These creep into the syllables of the words and I can't make out what is being said. (Record of June 1953.)

"Lines," "blurs," and "splashes" would emerge not only when he heard tones, noises, or voices. Every speech sound immediately summoned up for S. a striking visual image, for it had its own distinct form, color, and taste. Vowels appeared to him as simple figures, consonants as splashes, some of them solid configurations, others more scattered—but all of them retained some distinct form.

When S. read through a long series of words, each word would elicit a graphic image. And since the series was fairly long, he had to find some way of distributing these images of his in a mental row or sequence. Most often (and this habit persisted throughout his life), he would "distribute" them along some roadway or street he visualized in his mind. Sometimes this was a street in his home town, which would also include the yard attached to the house he had lived in as a child and which he recalled vividly. On the other hand, he might also select a street in Moscow. Frequently he would take a mental walk along that street—Gorky Street in Moscow—beginning at Mayakovsky Square, and slowly make his way down, "distributing" his images at houses, gates, and store windows. At times, without realizing how it had happened, he would suddenly find himself back in his home town (Torzhok), where he would wind up his trip in the house he had lived in as a child. The setting he chose for his "mental walks" approximates that of dreams, the difference being that the setting in his walks would immediately vanish once his attention was distracted but would reappear just as suddenly when he was obliged to recall a series he had "recorded" this way.

This technique of converting a series of words into a series of graphic images explains why S. could so readily reproduce a series from start to finish or in reverse order; how he could rapidly name the word that preceded or followed one I'd select from the series. To do this, he would simply begin his walk, either from the beginning or from the end of the street, find the image of the object I had named, and "take a look at" whatever happened to be situated on either side of it. S.'s visual patterns of memory differed from the more commonplace type of figurative memory by virtue of the fact that his images were exceptionally vivid and stable; he was also able to "turn away" from them, as it were, and "return" to them whenever it was necessary.

When S. read a passage from a text, each word produced an image. As he put it: "Other people *think* as they read, but I *see* it all." As soon as he began a phrase, images would appear; as he read further, still more images were evoked, and so on.

As we mentioned earlier, if a passage were read to him quickly, one image would collide with another in his mind; images would begin to crowd in upon one another and would become contorted. How then was he to understand anything in this chaos of images? If a text were read slowly, this, too, presented problems for him. Note the difficulties he experienced:

> . . . I was read this phrase: "N. was leaning up against a tree. . . ." I saw a slim young man dressed in a dark blue suit (N., you know, is so elegant). He was standing near a big linden tree with grass and woods all around. . . . But then the sentence went on: "and was peering into a shop window." Now how do you like that! It means the scene isn't set in the woods, or in a garden, but he's standing on the street. And I have to start the whole sentence over from the beginning. . . . (Record of March 1937.)

Thus, trying to understand a passage, to grasp the information it contains (which other people accomplish by singling out what is most important), became a tortuous procedure for S., a struggle against images that kept rising to the surface in his mind. Images, then, proved an obstacle as well as an aid to learning in that they prevented S. from concentrating on what was essential. Moreover, since these images tended to jam together, producing still more images, he was carried so far adrift that he was forced to go back and rethink the entire passage. Consequently a simple passage—a phrase, for that matter—would turn out to be a Sisyphean task. These vivid, palpable images were not always helpful to S. in understanding a passage; they could just as easily lead him astray.

Response and Analysis

1. Why did A. R. Luria believe that there was no limit to S.'s memory? What were S.'s short-term and long-term memory capabilities? Briefly describe one of S.'s reactions in which he saw colors when listening to someone's voice.

2. Briefly describe how S. would "elicit a graphic image" when he "read through a long series of words." What images did he create? How does his use of mental imagery explain, in part, his exceptional memory?

Personal Experience and Application

1. Do you know someone with an exceptional memory? What types of special techniques does he or she use to remember? What kinds of information is he or she able to remember?

2. Suppose the psychology club at your college or university asks you to give a five-minute presentation on improving memory and study skills. Write a brief talk that addresses the following questions: Should a student study in the same location for an exam? Should the study area be quiet rather than noisy? Should a student study for an exam over a period of several days or "cram" for an exam?

Research

Luria's case study revealed that S. was an unusual person, both for his ability to remember and for his synesthesia. Can psychologists generalize what they learn about extraordinary people to normal people? What are the advantages and disadvantages of doing research on extraordinary people?

chapter 6

THOUGHT AND
LANGUAGE

_But if thought corrupts language, language
also corrupts thought._

GEORGE ORWELL,
Politics and the English Language

How does language draw us together? How do the words we use and the manner in which we speak contribute to misunderstandings we may have with one another? This chapter explores several key issues that pertain to language and thought: conflict between the sexes; cultural misunderstandings; some effects of bilingualism; and the power of thought.

Linguist Deborah Tannen suggests that men are more comfortable speaking in public whereas women prefer the privacy of intimate conversations. These preferences may be learned in childhood, when boys talk for attention and girls criticize those who try to impress others. For these reasons, women may feel left out in conversations with men: in the public arena men appear to speak out readily, leaving less opportunity for women to do so, and in private, where some men may not feel comfortable discussing personal matters, women may feel isolated. Tannen suggests that these tensions may result from different styles and that understanding gender language may prevent conflict.

Nancy Masterson Sakamoto experiences another form of miscommunication because she married a man from Japan and moved to Tokyo. Sakamoto, an American who knows Japanese, was puzzled why her in-laws often became silent whenever she spoke with them. She discovered that they were not personally affronted but were confused by the different conversational style of Americans. Such differences can affect social interaction for those who don't know the "rules."

Although being bilingual can have great advantages, Richard Rodriguez describes how it can also be problematic. For Rodriguez, Spanish was the "family language," a language of intimacy, whereas English was a public language, the primary language of the country. As Rodriguez became more proficient in English, he entered a world less accessible to his parents. He thus discovered that language can both join and separate people.

Psychologist Daniel Wegner examines the power that thoughts can have over us. When thoughts trap us, how do we escape? Through distraction? Suppression? Where do our thoughts go when we send them packing? Wegner observes how people deal with unwanted thoughts and speculates about effective and ineffective ways of controlling our thoughts.

Two years before she became the 1984 Olympic silver medalist, Michele Mitchell was "almost paralyzed" each time she had to dive off a three-story high diving board. Either she would have to give up a sport she loved, or she would have to overcome her fears. Mitchell recognized that her "complex reactions to fear" were connected to her "skewed attentional focus." After some self-analysis, she decided upon several ways to deal with her reactions to fear. Mitchell details the stages she went through in making this decision, including the techniques she uses when she is practicing and competing, and reflects on how her decisions have enabled her to succeed.

"PUT DOWN THAT PAPER AND TALK TO ME!": RAPPORT-TALK AND REPORT-TALK

Deborah Tannen

Psychological Concepts
communication, gender socialization

Do the different conversational styles of men and women contribute to misunderstandings between the sexes? Deborah Tannen bases much of her work on that premise. What are those styles? We know some of the complaints men and women level against one another: women talk too much; men are too bossy; women's talk is emotional; men clam up and are poor listeners.

Tannen explains these differences by saying that for most women, conversation is primarily a way of establishing rapport, whereas for men it is primarily a way of preserving independence and status. She traces these differences to the ways boys and girls are raised and says that often misunderstandings are based on these different styles. Knowing this, each group has an opportunity to change in a constructive way.

I was sitting in a suburban living room, speaking to a women's group that had invited men to join them for the occasion of my talk about communication between women and men. During the discussion, one man was particularly talkative, full of lengthy comments and explanations. When I made the observation that women often complain that their husbands don't talk to them enough, this man volunteered that he heartily agreed. He gestured toward his wife, who had sat silently beside him on the couch throughout the evening, and said, "She's the talker in our family."

Everyone in the room burst into laughter. The man looked puzzled and hurt. "It's true," he explained. "When I come home from work, I usually have nothing to say, but she never runs out. If it weren't for her, we'd spend the whole evening in silence." Another woman expressed a similar paradox about her husband: "When we go out, he's the life of the party. If I happen to be in another room, I can always hear his voice above the others. But when we're home, he doesn't have that much to say. I do most of the talking."

Who talks more, women or men? According to the stereotype, women talk too much. Linguist Jennifer Coates notes some proverbs:

A woman's tongue wags like a lamb's tail.

Foxes are all tail and women are all tongue.

The North Sea will sooner be found wanting in water than a woman be at a loss for a word.

Throughout history, women have been punished for talking too much or in the wrong way. Linguist Connie Eble lists a variety of physical punishments used in Colonial America: Women were strapped to ducking stools and held underwater until they nearly drowned, put into the stocks with signs pinned to them, gagged, and silenced by a cleft stick applied to their tongues.

Though such institutionalized corporal punishments have given way to informal, often psychological ones, modern stereotypes are not much different from those expressed in the old proverbs. Women are believed to talk too much. Yet study after study finds that it is men who talk more—at meetings, in mixed-group discussions, and in classrooms where girls or young women sit next to boys or young men. For example, communications researchers Barbara and Gene Eakins tape-recorded and studied seven university faculty meetings. They found that, with one exception, men spoke more often and, without exception, spoke for a longer time. The men's turns ranged from 10.66 to 17.07 seconds, while the women's turns ranged from 3 to 10 seconds. In other words, the women's longest turns were still shorter than the men's shortest turns.

When a public lecture is followed by questions from the floor, or a talk show host opens the phones, the first voice to be heard asking a question is almost always a man's. And when they ask questions or offer comments from the audience, men tend to talk longer. Linguist Marjorie Swacker recorded question-and-answer sessions at academic conferences. Women were highly visible as speakers at the conferences studied; they presented 40.7 percent of the papers at the conferences studied and made up 42 percent of the audiences. But when it came to volunteering and being called on to ask questions, women contributed only 27.4 percent. Furthermore, the women's questions, on the average, took less than half as much time as the men's. (The mean was 23.1 seconds for women, 52.7 for men.) This happened, Swacker shows, because men (but not women) tended to preface their questions with statements, ask more than one question, and follow up the speaker's answer with another question or comment.

I have observed this pattern at my own lectures, which concern issues of direct relevance to women. Regardless of the proportion of women and men in the audience, men almost invariably ask the first question, more questions, and longer questions. In these situations, women often feel that men are talking too much. I recall one discussion period following a lecture I gave to a group assembled in a bookstore. The group was composed mostly of women, but most of the discussion was being conducted by men in the audience. At one point, a man sitting in the middle was talking at such great length that several women in the front rows began shifting in their seats and rolling their eyes at me. Ironically, what he was going on about was how frustrated he feels when he has to listen to women going on and on about topics he finds boring and unimportant.

Who talks more, then, women or men? The seemingly contradictory evidence is reconciled by the difference between what I call *public* and *private speaking*. More men feel comfortable doing "public speaking," while more women feel comfortable doing "private" speaking. Another way of capturing these differences is by using the terms *report-talk* and *rapport-talk*.

For most women, the language of conversation is primarily a language of rapport: a way of establishing connections and negotiating relationships. Emphasis is placed on displaying similarities and matching experiences. From childhood, girls criticize peers who try to stand out or appear better than others. People feel their closest connections at home, or in settings where they *feel* at home—with one or a few people they feel close to and comfortable with—in other words, during private speaking. But even the most public situations can be approached like private speaking.

For most men, talk is primarily a means to preserve independence and negotiate and maintain status in a hierarchical social order. This is done by exhibiting knowledge and skill, and by holding center stage through verbal performance such as storytelling, joking, or imparting information. From childhood, men learn to use talking as a way to get and keep attention. So they are more comfortable speaking in larger groups made up of people they know less well—in the broadest sense, "public speaking." But even the most private situations can be approached like public speaking, more like giving a report than establishing rapport. . . .

The difference between public and private speaking, or report-talk and rapport-talk, can be understood in terms of status and connection. It is not surprising that women are most comfortable talking when they feel safe and close, among friends and equals, whereas men feel comfortable talking when there is a need to establish and maintain their status in a group. But the situation is complex, because status and connection are bought with the same currency. What seems like a bid for status could be intended as a display of closeness, and what seems like distancing may have been intended to avoid the appearance of pulling rank. Hurtful and unjustified misinterpretations can be avoided by understanding the conversational styles of the other gender.

When men do all the talking at meetings, many women—including researchers—see them as "dominating" the meeting, intentionally preventing women from participating, publicly flexing their higher-status muscles. But the *result* that men do most of the talking does not necessarily mean that men *intend* to prevent women from speaking. Those who readily speak up assume that others are as free as they are to take the floor. In this sense, men's speaking out freely can be seen as evidence that they assume women are at the same level of status: "We are all equals," the metamessage of their behavior could be, "competing for the floor." If this is indeed the intention (and I believe it often, though not always, is), a woman can recognize women's lack of participation at meetings and take measures to redress the imbalance, without blaming men for intentionally locking them out.

The culprit, then, is not an individual man or even men's styles alone, but the difference between women's and men's styles. If that is the case, then both can make adjustments. A woman can push herself to speak up without being invited, or begin to speak without waiting for what seems a polite pause. But the adjustment should not be one-sided. A man can learn that a women who is not accustomed to speaking up in groups is *not* as free as he is to do so. Someone who is waiting for a nice long pause before asking her question does not find the stage set for her appearance, as do those who are not awaiting a pause, the moment after (or before) another speaker stops talking. Someone who expects to be invited to speak ("You haven't said much, Millie. What do you think?") is not accustomed to leaping in and claiming the floor for herself. As in so many areas, being admitted as an equal is not in itself assurance of equal opportunity, if one is not accustomed to playing the game in the way it is being played. Being admitted to a dance does not ensure the participation of someone who has learned to dance to a different rhythm.

Response and Analysis

1. According to Deborah Tannen, what are the main similarities and differences between the communication styles of men and women?

2. Briefly discuss two communication problems that occur between women and men. What remedies might Tannen suggest?

Personal Experience and Application

1. Think about two of your close friends—a male and a female. Make a short list of the main topics that you talk about with them. Are they similar? Why or why not?

2. Suppose you are invited to give a five-minute presentation on improving communication in intimate relationships to an introduction to psychology class. List three recommendations you would offer. How might each recommendation improve communication?

Research

Suppose you want to examine the communication styles of boys and girls. You are interested in whether three- to five-year-old boys and girls include others in the decision-making process when they play doctor. You hypothesize that boys will issue orders such as "Give me your arm" and "Sit down," whereas girls will propose activities such as "Let's do this. . . ." After the Institutional Review Board at your college or university approves your study and the parents agree to let their children participate, you have one boy and one girl of the same age come to your lab, which is a small room with a two-way mirror. In the room is a doctor's toy medical kit, a variety of toy medical instruments, and a doctor's smock. When the children come into the room, you tell them that you would like them to play doctor. You randomly select one of the children to be the doctor and one to be the patient. You tell the "doctor" that she or he can wear the doctor's smock and can use the toy medical instruments. You then tell the children that they may begin playing and that you will return in a few minutes. You observe the children through the two-way mirror.

After observing thirty boys and thirty girls, you tabulate the data. The results suggest that boys issued more orders than girls, and girls proposed activities more than boys. Would you conclude that the findings support your hypothesis? Why or why not? If you were to repeat the study, what would you do differently? Why?

CONVERSATIONAL BALLGAMES

Nancy Masterson Sakamoto

Psychological Concepts
cross-cultural communication, miscommunication

As infants we receive cues about how others respond to our sounds and how long they will tolerate our cries. As we get older, we learn how to carry on a conversation and to pick up the rhythms of give and take. How do we know whose turn it is to talk and how much time we have to speak? Do conversational styles vary from group to group even within a country?

What seldom occurs to us is that there are acceptable and unacceptable styles of engaging in conversation in different parts of the world. Israelis, for example, may expect everyone to speak up; they may look for an active exchange, as do most Americans. Nancy Masterson Sakamoto, however, often shocked her Japanese in-laws into silence when she visited with them. Here Sakamoto explains why she needed to learn more than the Japanese language to be comfortable speaking in her second homeland.

After I was married and had lived in Japan for a while, my Japanese gradually improved to the point where I could take part in simple conversations with my husband and his friends and family. And I began to notice that often, when I joined in, the others would look startled, and the conversational topic would come to a halt. After this happened several times, it became clear to me that I was doing something wrong. But for a long time, I didn't know what it was.

Finally, after listening carefully to many Japanese conversations, I discovered what my problem was. Even though I was speaking Japanese, I was handling the conversation in a western way.

Japanese-style conversations develop quite differently from western-style conversations. And the difference isn't only in the languages. I realized that just as I kept trying to hold western-style conversations even when I was speaking Japanese, so my English students kept trying to hold Japanese-style conversations even when they were speaking English. We were unconsciously playing entirely different conversational ballgames.

A western-style conversation between two people is like a game of tennis. If I introduce a topic, a conversational ball, I expect you to hit it back. If you agree with me, I don't expect you simply to agree and do nothing more. I expect you to add something—a reason for agreeing, another example, or an elaboration to carry the idea further. But I don't expect you always to agree. I am just as happy if you question me or challenge me, or completely disagree with me. Whether you agree or disagree, your response will return the ball to me.

And then it is my turn again. I don't serve a new ball from my original starting line. I hit your ball back again from where it has bounced. I carry your idea further, or answer your questions or objections, or challenge or question you. And so the ball goes back and forth, with each of us doing our best to give it a new twist, an original spin, or a powerful smash.

And the more vigorous the action, the more interesting and exciting the game. Of course, if one of us gets angry, it spoils the conversation, just as it spoils a tennis game. But getting excited is not at all the same as getting angry. After all, we are not trying to hit each other. We are trying to hit the ball. So long as we attack only each other's opinions, and do not attack each other personally, we don't expect anyone to get hurt. A good conversation is supposed to be interesting and exciting.

If there are more than two people in the conversation, then it is like doubles in tennis, or like volleyball. There's no waiting in line. Whoever is nearest and quickest hits the ball, and if you step back, someone else will hit it. No one stops the game to give you a turn. You're responsible for taking your own turn.

But whether it's two players or a group, everyone does his best to keep the ball going, and no one person has the ball for very long.

A Japanese-style conversation, however, is not at all like tennis or volleyball. It's like bowling. You wait for your turn. And you always know your place in line. It depends on such things as whether you are older or younger, a close friend or a relative stranger to the previous speaker, in a senior or junior position, and so on.

When your turn comes, you step up to the starting line with your bowling ball, and carefully bowl it. Everyone else stands back and watches politely, murmuring encouragement. Everyone waits until the ball has reached the end of the alley, and watches to see if it knocks down all the pins, or only some of them, or none of them. There is a pause, while everyone registers your score.

Then, after everyone is sure that you have completely finished your turn, the next person in line steps up to the same starting line, with a different ball. He doesn't return your ball, and he does not begin from where your ball stopped. There is no back and forth at all. All the balls run parallel. And there is always a suitable pause between turns. There is no rush, no excitement, no scramble for the ball.

No wonder everyone looked startled when I took part in Japanese conversations. I paid no attention to whose turn it was, and kept snatching the ball halfway down the alley and throwing it back at the bowler. Of course the conversation died. I was playing the wrong game.

This explains why it is almost impossible to get a western-style conversation or discussion going with English students in Japan. I used to think that the problem was their lack of English language ability. But I finally came to realize that the biggest problem is that they, too, are playing the wrong game.

Whenever I serve a volleyball, everyone just stands back and watches it fall, with occasional murmurs of encouragement. No one hits it back. Everyone waits until I call on someone to take a turn. And when that person speaks, he doesn't hit my ball back. He serves a new ball. Again, everyone just watches it fall.

So I call on someone else. This person does not refer to what the previous speaker has said. He also serves a new ball. Nobody seems to have paid any attention to what anyone else has said. Everyone begins again from the same starting line, and all the balls run parallel. There is never any back and forth. Everyone is trying to bowl with a volleyball.

And if I try a simpler conversation, with only two of us, then the other person tries to bowl with my tennis ball. No wonder foreign English teachers in Japan get discouraged.

Now that you know about the difference in the conversational ballgames, you may think that all your troubles are over. But if you have been trained all your life to play one game, it is no simple matter to switch to another, even if you know the rules. Knowing the rules is not at all the same thing as playing the game.

Even now, during a conversation in Japanese I will notice a startled reaction, and belatedly realize that once again I have rudely interrupted by instinctively trying to hit back the other person's bowling ball. It is no easier for me to "just listen" during a conversation than it is for my Japanese students to "just relax" when speaking with foreigners. Now I can truly sympathize with how hard they must find it to try to carry on a western-style conversation.

If I have not yet learned to do conversational bowling in Japanese, at least I have figured out one thing that puzzled me for a long time. After his first trip to America, my husband complained that Americans asked him so many questions and made him talk so much at the dinner table that he never had a chance to eat. When I asked him why he couldn't talk and eat at the same time, he said that Japanese do not customarily think that dinner, especially on fairly formal occasions, is a suitable time for extended conversation.

Since westerners think that conversation is an indispensable part of dining, and indeed would consider it impolite not to converse with one's dinner partner, I found this Japanese custom rather strange. Still, I could accept it as a cultural difference even though I didn't really understand it. But when my husband added, in explanation, that Japanese consider it extremely rude to talk with one's mouth full, I got confused. Talking with one's mouth full is certainly not an American custom. We think it very rude, too. Yet we still manage to talk a lot and eat at the same time. How do we do it?

For a long time, I couldn't explain it, and it bothered me. But after I discovered the conversational ballgames, I finally found the answer. Of course! In a western-style conversation, you hit the ball, and while someone else is hitting it back, you take a bite, chew, and swallow. Then you hit the ball again, and then eat some more. The more people there are in the conversation, the more chances you have to eat. But even with only two of you talking, you still have plenty of chances to eat.

Maybe that's why polite conversation at the dinner table has never been a traditional part of Japanese etiquette. Your turn to talk would last so long without interruption that you'd never get a chance to eat.

Response and Analysis

1. According to Nancy Masterson Sakamoto, what are the main differences between American-style and Japanese-style conversations? Why does Sakamoto believe that it is "almost impossible to get a western-style conversation or discussion going" with Japanese students who are taking an English class?

2. What types of misunderstandings might occur when people of different cultures converse?

Personal Experience and Application

1. Have you tried to communicate with someone who did not speak your language? What difficulties did you experience? Did you or the other person understand the context in which all of the words were spoken—the idiomatic expressions and the way a word was used in a sentence? What nonverbal behaviors helped you communicate?

2. Suppose the outings club on your campus asks you to be one of five guides on a ten-day tour of the Grand Canyon. The tour group will consist of a total of twenty German and Chinese college exchange students who have had three English classes. What communication difficulties might you expect? What might you do to facilitate communication? What nonverbal cues could you use to convey important information?

Research

Sakamoto suggests that certain customs within our culture influence how we talk with and understand others. Suppose you want to replicate a study examining how our experiences influence how we understand and interpret new events. You wonder whether college students with different interests and experiences might perceive the same situation differently, so you recruit fifty music majors and fifty business majors at your college or university to participate in your study. You have the participants read a paragraph containing ambiguous words. Here is a brief excerpt from the paragraph:

Every Saturday night, four good friends got together. When Jerry, Mike, and Pat arrived, Karen was sitting in her living room writing some notes. She quickly gathered the cards and stood up to greet her friends at the door. They followed her into the living room but as usual they couldn't agree on exactly what to play. Jerry eventually took a stand and set things up. Finally, they began to play. Karen's recorder filled the room with soft and pleasant music (Anderson et al., 1977).

After the participants read the paragraph, you ask them to tell you how they interpreted the paragraph. Write three questions that you might ask to determine if the students' majors affected how they interpreted the information.

Which words do you believe are ambiguous? Why? Why might a student's major influence how she or he interprets the information?

ARIA: A MEMOIR OF A BILINGUAL CHILDHOOD

Richard Rodriguez

Psychological Concept
bilingualism

Richard Rodriguez learned the power of language early in his life. Growing up in a Spanish-speaking section of Sacramento, California, Rodriguez recognized two separate cultures: that of the Chicanos and that of "los gringos." Pressured by the nuns who taught him and by his parents who wanted him to do well, Rodriguez took on the language of "los gringos." But once he began using English and moved into the public domain, his life with his parents and his intimate, protected world of home and barrio changed.

I remember, to start with, that day in Sacramento, in a California now nearly thirty years past, when I first entered a classroom—able to understand about fifty stray English words. The third of four children, I had been preceded by my older brother and sister to a neighborhood Roman Catholic school. But neither of them had revealed very much about their classroom experiences. . . .

Because I wrongly imagined that English was intrinsically a public language and Spanish was intrinsically private, I easily noted the difference between classroom language and the language at home. At school, words were directed to a general audience of listeners. ("Boys and girls . . .") Words were meaningfully ordered. And the point was not self-expression alone, but to make oneself understood by many others. The teacher quizzed: "Boys and girls, why do we use that word in this sentence? Could we think of a better word to use there? Would the sentence change its meaning if the words were differently arranged? Isn't there a better way of saying much the same thing?" (I couldn't say. I wouldn't try to say.)

Three months passed. Five. A half year. Unsmiling, ever watchful, my teachers noted my silence. They began to connect my behavior with the slow progress my brother and sisters were making. Until, one Saturday morning, three nuns arrived at the house to talk to our parents. Stiffly they sat on the blue living room sofa. From the doorway of another room, spying on the visitors, I noted the incongruity, the clash of two worlds, the faces and voices of school intruding upon the familiar setting of home. I overheard one voice gently wondering, "Do your children speak only Spanish at home, Mrs. Rodriguez?" While an other voice added, "That Richard especially seems so timid and shy."

That Rich-heard!

With great tact, the visitors continued, "Is it possible for you and your husband to encourage your children to practice their English when they are home?" Of course my parents complied. What would they not do for their children's well-being? And how could they question the Church's authority which those women represented? In an instant they agreed to give up the language (the sounds) which had revealed and accentuated our family's closeness. The moment after the visitors left, the change was observed. "*Ahora*, speak to us only *en inglés*," my father and mother told us.

At first, it seemed a kind of game. After dinner each night, the family gathered together to practice "our" English. It was still then *inglés*, a language foreign to us, so we felt drawn to it as strangers. Laughing, we would try to define words we could not pronounce. We played with strange English sounds, often overanglicizing our pronunciations. And we filled the smiling gaps of our sentences with familiar Spanish sounds. But that was cheating, somebody shouted, and everyone laughed.

In school, meanwhile, like my brother and sisters, I was required to attend a daily tutoring session. I needed a full year of this special work. I also needed my teachers to keep my attention from straying in class by calling out, "*Rich-heard*"— their English voices slowly loosening the ties to my other name, with its three notes, *Ri-car-do.* Most of all, I needed to hear my mother and father speak to me in a moment of seriousness in "broken"—suddenly heartbreaking—English. This scene was inevitable. One Saturday morning I entered the kitchen where my parents were talking, but I did not realize that they were talking in Spanish until, the moment they saw me, their voices changed and they began speaking English. The gringo sounds they uttered startled me. Pushed me away. In that moment of trivial misunderstanding and profound insight, I felt my throat twisted by unsounded grief. I simply turned and left the room. But I had no place to escape to where I could grieve in Spanish. My brother and sisters were speaking English in another part of the house.

Again and again in the days following, as I grew increasingly angry, I was obliged to hear my mother and father encouraging me: "Speak to us *en inglés*." Only then did I determine to learn classroom English. Thus, sometime afterward it happened: One day in school, I raised my hand to volunteer an answer to a question. I spoke out in a loud voice and I did not think it remarkable when the entire class understood. That day I moved very far from being the disadvantaged child I had been only days earlier. Taken hold at last was the belief, the calming assurance, that I *belonged* in public.

Shortly after, I stopped hearing the high, troubling sounds of *los gringos*. A more and more confident speaker of English, I didn't listen to how strangers sounded when they talked to me. With so many English-speaking people around me, I no longer heard American accents. Conversations quickened. Listening to persons whose voices sounded eccentrically pitched, I might note their sounds for a few seconds, but then I'd concentrate on what they were saying. Now when I heard someone's tone of voice—angry or questioning or sarcastic or happy or sad—I didn't distinguish it from the words it expressed. Sound and word were thus tightly wedded. At the end of each day I was often bemused, and always relieved, to realize how "soundless," though crowded with words, my day in public had been. An eight-year-old boy, I finally came to accept what had been technically true since my birth: I was an American citizen.

But diminished by then was the special feeling of closeness at home. Gone was the desperate, urgent, intense feeling of being at home among those with whom I felt intimate. Our family remained a loving family, but one greatly changed. We were no longer so close, no longer bound tightly together by the knowledge of our separateness from *los gringos*. Neither my older brother nor my sisters rushed home after school any more. Nor did I. When I arrived home, often there would be neighborhood kids in the house. Or the house would be empty of sounds.

Following the dramatic Americanization of their children, even my parents grew more publicly confident—especially my mother. First she learned the names of all the people on the block. Then she decided we needed to have a telephone in our house. My father, for his part, continued to use the word gringo, but it was no longer charged with bitterness or distrust. Stripped of any emotional content, the word simply became a name for those Americans not of Hispanic descent. Hearing him, sometimes, I wasn't sure if he was pronouncing the Spanish word *gringo*, or saying gringo in English.

There was a new silence at home. As we children learned more and more English, we shared fewer and fewer words with our parents. Sentences needed to be spoken slowly when one of us addressed our mother or father. Often the parent wouldn't understand. The child would need to repeat himself. Still the parent misunderstood. The young voice, frustrated, would end up saying, "Never mind"—the subject was closed. Dinners would be noisy with the clinking of knives and forks against dishes. My mother would smile softly between her remarks; my father, at the other end of the table, would chew and chew his food while he stared over the heads of his children.

My mother! My father! After English became my primary language, I no longer knew what words to use in addressing my parents. The old Spanish words (those tender accents of sound) I had earlier used—*mamá* and *papá*—I couldn't use any more. They would have been all-too-painful reminders of how much had changed in my life. On the other hand, the words I heard neighborhood kids call their parents seemed equally unsatisfactory. "Mother" and "father," "ma," "papa," "pa," "dad," "pop" (how I hated the all-American sound of that last word)—all these I felt were unsuitable terms of address for *my* parents. As a result, I never used them at home. Whenever I'd speak to my parents, I would try to get their attention by looking at them. In public conversations, I'd refer to them as my "parents" or my "mother" and "father."

My mother and father, for their part, responded differently, as their children spoke to them less. My mother grew restless, seemed troubled and anxious at the scarceness of words exchanged in the house. She would question me about my day when I came home from school. She smiled at my small talk. She pried at the edges of my sentences to get me to say something more. ("What . . . ?") She'd join conversations she overheard, but her intrusions often stopped her children's talking. By contrast, my father seemed to grow reconciled to the new quiet. Though his English somewhat improved, he tended more and more to retire into silence. At dinner he spoke very little. One night his children and even his wife helplessly giggled at his garbled English pronunciation of the Catholic "Grace Before Meals." Thereafter he made his wife recite the prayer at the start of each meal, even on formal occasions when there were guests in the house.

Hers became the public voice of the family. On official business it was she, not my father, who would usually talk to strangers on the phone or in stores. We children grew so accustomed to his silence that years later we would routinely refer to his "shyness." (My mother often tried to explain: Both of his parents died when he was eight. He was raised by an uncle who treated him as little more than a menial servant. He was never encouraged to speak. He grew up alone—a man of few words.) But I realized my father was not shy whenever I'd watch him speaking Spanish with relatives. Using Spanish, he was quickly effusive. Especially when talking with other men, his voice would spark, flicker, flare alive with varied sounds. In Spanish he expressed ideas and feelings he rarely revealed when speaking English. With firm Spanish sounds he conveyed a confidence and authority that English would never allow him.

The silence at home, however, was not simply the result of fewer words passing between parents and children. More profound for me was the silence created by my inattention to sounds. At about the time I no longer bothered to listen with care to the sounds of English in public, I grew careless about listening to the sounds made by the family when they spoke. Most of the time I would hear someone speaking at home and didn't distinguish his sounds from the words people uttered in public. I didn't even pay much attention to my parents' accented and un-grammatical speech—at least not at home. Only when I was with them in public would I become alert to their accents. But even then their sounds caused me less and less concern. For I was growing increasingly confident of my own public identity.

I would have been happier about my public success had I not recalled, sometimes, what it had been like earlier, when my family conveyed its intimacy through a set of conveniently private sounds. Sometimes in public, hearing a stranger, I'd hark back to my lost past. A Mexican farm worker approached me one day downtown. He wanted directions to some place. "*Hijito, . . .*" he said. And his voice stirred old longings. Another time I was standing beside my mother in the visiting room of a Carmelite convent, before the dense screen which rendered the nuns shadowy figures. I heard several of them speaking Spanish in their busy, singsong, overlapping voices, assuring my mother that, yes, yes, we were remembered, all our family was remembered, in their prayers. Those voices echoed faraway family sounds. Another day a dark-faced old woman touched my shoulder lightly to steady herself as she boarded a bus. She murmured something to me I couldn't quite comprehend. Her Spanish voice came near, like the face of a never-before-seen relative in the instant before I was kissed. That voice, like so many of the Spanish voices I'd hear in public, recalled the golden age of my childhood.

Response and Analysis

1. Why did Richard Rodriguez believe that he was at a disadvantage by not knowing English? How did not knowing English affect his social life? What prompted Rodriguez to learn English?

2. Psychologist Walter Lambert distinguishes between additive and subtractive bilingualism. In additive bilingualism, an individual respects both languages and is proficient in both his or her first language and the new second language. In subtractive bilingualism, an individual becomes proficient in the new second language but loses proficiency in the first language. Eventually, the new second language replaces the first language. Do you believe Rodriguez became more or less proficient in Spanish as his proficiency in English increased? Why?

Personal Experience and Application

1. More than six million children in the United States come from homes in which English is not the primary language. Some experts predict that the number of bilingual children will triple in the twenty-first century. Do you believe that children who are not proficient in English should be taught in their native (first) language? Why or why not? Suppose your local school board asks you to offer a few recommendations on how to instruct elementary school children who are not proficient in English. List three recommendations.

2. Suppose when you were six years old your family moved to a country in which your native language was not spoken. What difficulties at school might you have experi-

enced? How difficult might it have been to make friends? Why?

Research

Suppose you are interested in whether bilingualism is harmful or beneficial to children. You want to determine if bilingual children have different intelligence test scores than monolingual children. When choosing children to participate in your study, you make sure that you have a similar number of bilingual and monolingual boys and girls of the same age, that they have a similar number of brothers and sisters, and that they have lived in the United States for a similar number of years. Unfortunately, you have difficulty matching the participants on socioeconomic status: the bilingual children live in an upper-class neighborhood and the monolingual children live in a lower-class neighborhood. After securing the approval of the Institutional Review Board at your college or university and permission from the children's parents, you administer an intelligence test to each student. You find that bilingual children have higher intelligence test scores than monolingual children. Can you conclude that bilingualism is beneficial? What other factors may have influenced the relationship between bilingualism and the intelligence test score? If you were to repeat this study, what changes would you make to minimize these problems?

WHITE BEARS AND OTHER UNWANTED THOUGHTS

Daniel M. Wegner

Psychological Concepts
mental image, elements of thought, distraction

Are we able to control our thoughts? Do we want to? Psychologist Daniel Wegner demonstrates how difficult it can be to keep some thoughts at bay. He tells of the time he and his wife were going on vacation to Florida to "soak up some sun." The day they were leaving, Wegner says, "a good friend came back from a dermatology appointment sporting several scars where minor skin cancers had been removed. He casually pointed to a spot on my arm and said, 'Hey, that's just like one of them.' This totally ruined my vacation." Wegner's mind had been "high-jacked" for ten days!

If someone says to us, "Don't think of a white bear," what do we think of? How can we get rid of that bear? Wegner suggests that we do have some options. In varying ways, suppression, self-distraction, and absorption may turn our attention away from disturbing or unwanted thoughts.

When I first learned there was such a thing as an indelible pencil (I think it was in third grade) I was overwhelmed. Its purplish marks could *never be erased.* This finality was too much for my young sensibilities. Erasing was my life, the center of a daily eternity of smudges, errors, and regret played out under the eye of my teacher, a universal master of human penmanship. As it happened, of course, I learned that many things are as good as indelible, from bounced checks to auto wrecks, and I have come to accept this as a necessary part of life on earth.

There is still one slight problem. Although reality can't be erased, it seems only fair that our *thoughts* about things might be erasable. We can change our mind, get new ideas, see things in different ways, and easily move our attention from one thing to another. In other words, it usually seems that we can control what we think. When we try not to think about something, though, our thoughts can be as indelible as the marks made by that purple pencil. Unwanted thoughts—about food when we're on a diet, about that little lump that could be cancer, about a lost love whose absence we grieve, even about the mutton-headed thing we said to the boss yesterday—often seem etched permanently in our mind. The silliest little thought can be this way. Try right now, for instance, not to think of a white bear. Really. Put down the book and look away and stop thinking of a white bear. I'm serious. Try it.

The White Bear   Welcome back. How successful were you? Did you avoid a white bear for a few seconds or a minute? Did it return to your mind even once after you had wished it away? Most people report one or more returns, and some of them also stop at this point and remark that it is a cute trick, maybe good for a full minute of entertainment at children's birthday parties. There may be something to learn, however, on taking seriously the observation that people do not do a good job of avoiding an unwanted thought, even a warm fuzzy one like a white bear. . . .

Why *shouldn't* we be able to suppress a thought? Suppression seems like a simple, obvious, and important ability, as basic as thinking itself, and we don't seem to have it. Imagine—we are drawn to the very item we are attempting to avoid, clambering desperately away from the thought only to stumble back upon it again and again. Like a moth drawn to a flame, or a chicken entranced by a line drawn in the dirt, the person attempting to avoid an unwanted thought doesn't seem very smart. We can do so much—our minds so flexible and imaginative and complex—but all the IQ points in the world don't keep us from puzzling repeatedly over one thought. . . .

Distracting oneself seems easy enough. In fact, this is what I've been doing all day prior to writing this chapter. First I dawdled over coffee, read the newspaper, and became involved in an unusually thorough tooth-flossing project. I used my own teeth, so this didn't cause nearly the uproar or delay that it could have. Then, I went to the office, read my mail, made a phone call, and . . . hard to believe but it's three in the afternoon and I have to quit soon to get the baby from the sitter's. Procrastination is a kind of self-distraction, an engagement in trivial activities when we wish to avoid a more important task that looks too much like work.

Now that I've gotten myself started, I can point out that the kind of self-distraction I did this morning was the easy kind. I slipped into it without any planning or effort. When we wish to avoid a disturbing unwanted thought, however, self-distraction is not something we can do so naturally or effectively, and it can escalate into a major chore. Try distracting yourself, for instance, when you are looking down from a great height, or when the itch of an insect bite is begging for a nice rough scratching. Self-distraction is one of the key strategies we use to keep our mind away from our fears, worries, secrets, forbidden ideas, and even itches, and for this reason it is important that we understand how to do it well.

Children are not very skilled at self-distraction, so they become quick victims to whatever grabs their attention. They can cry interminably as the result of a broken dolly, or become overwrought with a "boo boo" on their finger. They seem to be able to whine for hours about one thing, and always tend to become interested in what will soon spill or explode. Parents must learn, then, to supply distracters on a regular basis, helping the child to redirect attention away from things that can cause grief and toward more benign points of interest. After flying cross-country in a crowded plane with my toddler on my lap, I was convinced that the ability to distract is one of the great skills of parenting. All the passengers nearby agreed. The most effective parents I know are able to guide their children from the brink of hell to a state of bemused puttering in a matter of moments. Eventually, of course, the child must learn to do this for himself or herself, and self-distraction becomes one of the key abilities we have that gets us through adulthood—and through flights crowded with other people's children. . . .

A Change of Plans   We have learned that "naked" suppression is not possible. Our mental apparatus is not built to clear itself, to think "I will not think of X" and then in fact immediately stop thinking of X forever. Indeed, it seems that the more energy we invest in the attempt to suppress, the more likely is the attempt to fail, landing us directly in that untidy spot in the road we were trying to step over. If all we ever did on encountering an unwanted thought, then, was to try direct suppression, we would make no progress at all. Trying not to think of X makes us think of X, as vividly, frequently, and efficiently as if we had decided to think of X from the start.

Suppression thus requires a mental transformation of the task. We move from "I will not think of X" to "I will think of Y." This is the basic form of self-distraction. It is a metacognitive strategy, a move from one way of metathinking about a thought to another. Admittedly, this mental transformation is a precarious one, in that trying to think of Y can remind us of why we undertook this task, and so bring us back to "avoid X." However, the movement to "think of Y" has a number of benefits that can make it a useful first step in shaking loose the unwanted thought of X. In particular, the self-distractive thought does not automatically bring us back to X. Back when we were thinking "avoid X," the more effort we expended on our thought, the more it all backfired. But now in the "think Y" mode, the more cognitive effort we expend, the more we will focus on Y—and thus actually stay away from X.

This is a critical feature of self-distraction. As long as we attempt suppression only, then the harder we try, the deeper we get ourselves into the soup. When we attempt self-distraction, in contrast, our efforts can get us somewhere. Although we may still be reminded of the unwanted thought from time to time, there is at least some room in self-distraction for a brief respite, a time during which we can focus on something other than the unwanted idea. At least now, when we try harder to think, we do not find our thoughts defeating their own purposes. And it is in this time that our automatic perception and memory processes may edge the conscious window away from the whole mess, toward a more pleasing view that can hold our attention.

This way of understanding self-distraction helps us get a grip on the effects of stress and activity on unwanted thoughts. It helps us to understand why being busy (because of stress or just plain activity) can sometimes increase the occurrence of unwanted thoughts and at other times will seem to push them away. I've wondered about this a lot because of the odd things that vacations can do to my mental state. Sometimes going away and relaxing clears my mind wonderfully, whereas other times leaving the activities and stresses of my usual routine produces a unique sensitivity to worry and makes me wish I were home. The difference between these effects seems to hinge on whether one is trying to suppress or trying to self-distract.

Consider what happens when you go on vacation right after you have a major argument with your boss. With this nasty incident fresh in your mind, you set off to the beach. An argument like this has not happened before, so you probably have not had the occasion to try to distract yourself from such problems. In all likelihood, then, you will simply try to suppress the thought when you're on the vacation. And if so, you will find that you are refreshingly distracted by the water, the beach, and the surroundings. These things keep you from even trying to suppress the thought, and as a result the thought is swept away and you are left in peace. You wonder at this time how a vacation could ever *promote* an unwanted thought, and you scoff at the idea.

The next year, though, you go to the mountains. This time, the boss has been after you for some time to straighten up your act, and things at work are very unpleasant. To deal with this, you have taken to watching TV a lot at home and following the programs very carefully. Sure, it is not very exciting—but it keeps your mind off the mess at work and also keeps you up to date on all the fine bargains that your local retailers have to offer. In the cabin in the mountains, there is also a TV. But you don't watch it very much and instead you hike, take pictures, and enjoy the breathtaking views. Amidst all this, you find that the turmoil at work keeps coming to mind. You see a DON'T FEED THE BEARS sign and imagine your boss mauling a tourist. The vacation, rather than taking your mind off your worries, has taken your mind off your distractions—and so leaves you oddly worried even though you have come to "relax."

An important mental transition occurs when we change strategies—from the strategy of suppressing a thought to the strategy of distracting ourselves from that thought. This changes the rules by which external distractions influence the occurrence of unwanted thoughts. Such a rule change must be common, however, because when people are asked what they do to avoid unwanted thoughts, they mention self-distraction nearly every time. And when people who identify themselves as chronic worriers are asked what they're doing wrong, they blame their inability to distract themselves from the targets of their worry. The change from suppression to self-distraction is natural, the path we follow away from the thoughts we desire to avoid, but it also changes the way our mental efforts influence our thoughts. When we are suppressing, attention to what we are doing is injurious to our plan; when we are self-distracting, attention to what we are doing is exactly what we need.

Can Distraction Work?   Most of what we currently know about the effectiveness of distraction comes from experiments on pain. Dentists and physicians would love it if their patients would just stop whining, not to mention that the patients might be pleased as well, so pain control is an issue that has received a fair amount of scientific attention. In these studies, people are exposed to something painful—a real dental or surgical procedure, or a somewhat analogous discomfort such as keeping a hand in ice water for several minutes. They are asked to report when they begin to feel pain, how strong it is, whether they can continue, or the like, and these judgments are taken as measures of the degree of pain they are feeling. This is really all we have to go on, as there is no special "pain behavior" in the body that we can monitor to see how much discomfort the person is feeling. Wiggling and hopping and saying "Yipes!" are signs, but even they are unreliable at times.

If there is a general rule that emerges from pain studies, it is that distracters work best when they are absorbing. For instance, music piped in during a dental procedure doesn't seem to make that much difference, whereas allowing the patient to play a video game reduces pain reports quite a bit. You might argue that the kind of Muzak most dentists play can cause minor pain before you even sit in the chair. And it is true that a rendition of one's favorite music on a good stereo system might turn out to be more engaging than even a video game. These seemingly minor variations in the quality of the distracter could have a critical influence on the degree to which the distraction can hold one's attention away from the unwanted thought.

Response and Analysis

1. When Daniel Wegner asks you not to think of a white bear, what do you think about? Do you have a mental image of a white bear? If so, briefly describe that image. Mental images are one of several elements that make up thought. Discuss two other elements.

2. According to Wegner, what is distraction? Briefly describe a few techniques that Wegner offers for controlling unwanted thoughts. Why might distraction "suppress" unwanted thoughts?

Personal Experience and Application

1. Are you sometimes bothered by thoughts that will not go away? What do you do to get rid of them? When you are trying to get to sleep, how do you get rid of distracting thoughts that keep you awake?

2. Often people use the same solution to solve different problems, even if there is an easier solution. This is referred to as a "mental set." Briefly describe a situation in which you or someone you know used a familiar but less effective solution to solve a problem. Were you or the person aware of the simpler solution? If so, why didn't you or the person you know use it?

Research

Suppose you want to investigate how often people use mental imagery. You decide to have one hundred students at your institution record their mental images every day for one month. The participants will list their mental images for each of the five senses—hearing, taste, vision, smell, and touch. Which of the five senses do you believe will be reported most frequently? Why? Does this study have an independent variable or a dependent variable? Why or why not?

FEAR

Michele Mitchell

Psychological Concepts
decision making, thinking strategies

Michele Mitchell, who won the 1984 Olympic silver medal for the 10-meter platform dive, was terrified of diving from great heights. Driven to succeed at a skill she was good at, yet terrified of jumping off the diving board, Mitchell had to make a choice. She did not want to give up diving. Neither did she want fear to affect her physically, make her unable to concentrate, or deprive her of enjoying the camaraderie of her fellow athletes. Mitchell analyzed her anxieties and developed several methods to overcome them. The strategies she uses to overcome her fear show courage and determination.

Diving off a platform the height of a three-story building and falling at speeds of up to 33 miles per hour requires me to work through my fears every day. I'm afraid every time I go up there, but getting through the fear makes me feel stronger; it makes me feel that I can achieve any goal I put my mind to.

But that realization didn't come naturally. Two years before the Olympic Games I was almost paralyzed every time I climbed up to the 10-meter platform. There were days, after years of practice from that height, when I couldn't even look over the edge. And there were times that I couldn't go off the tower. It was as if all of my potential had been sealed in a jar by my own subconscious fears of the "what if."

Finally one day after I had climbed down the tower in disgust, I decided that if I was going to continue diving, I would have to study my complex reactions to fear and find ways to conquer it.

I realized that stress evoked three changes in me: physical, mental, and attentional. Physically, my heart would pound, my respiratory rate would increase, my stomach would hurt, I would feel shaky and weak, and my adrenalin levels would rise. Worst of all, my muscles would become so tight that I could hardly move, let alone attain the flowing style required in diving.

Mentally, too, I would become very rigid. I felt shaky, unable to control my thoughts. I'd see visions of landing incorrectly in the water or hitting my hand on the edge of the board. The more I tried to shut out those thoughts, the more severe they became.

Later I realized that this thinking was a result of my skewed attentional focus. Instead of relaxing and enjoying the circumstantial rewards of training, such as the social life or the humor, I'd be focusing on my pounding heart and my shaking hands. I became a victim of my own tunnel vision. At other times, instead of concentrating on one or two important parts of a dive, I would be paying attention to occurrences that I had no control over. I'd watch cars passing on the street or people walking under the tower even as I stood, ready to launch myself into the air.

After a few weeks of self-analysis I began some deep contemplation of how I could deal with my responses to fear. The techniques I started then are the ones I am still using in every practice session and every competition I'm in, even today.

I always begin by writing my short, intermediate, and long-term goals on a piece of paper. On one side of each goal I list the fears I will have to overcome to achieve that goal. On the other side I write down the rewards I'll receive at the completion of each goal. Obviously the harder the goal, the higher the reward I place next to it. The rewards can be anything from a dinner out on the town to a gold medal. This makes a systematic method of achieving those things I set out to do.

Next I force myself toward the positive. The first step is to remember that I am not unique in this situation. When I begin getting mentally and physically tense, I start a conversation about it with my teammates who experience the same fears.

Putting my ego to work also helps. If I want to impress someone who is watching me, I acknowledge that to myself and use it to fuel the fires to burn up my fears. A bet with a teammate can do the trick as well. Last fall two of us had to learn a new dive on the same day and both of us were nervous. So, at the beginning of practice we each put a $100 bill on the deck. If each of us did our new dive we would take back our money; however, if only one of us did the dive, she would be $100 richer. Guess what? The bet worked. Neither of us lost the bet, and both of us got through the fear to gain a new dive.

Defining positively reinforcing words also works for me. For instance, Webster defines courage as "the attitude of facing and dealing with anything recognized as dangerous." Being able to repeat that definition when I am trying to summon up my courage is reassuring. I also have other standard comments such as, "Yes, I'm nervous, but it's okay; I've felt this way before and I'm still alive," or "I may be scared but I *am* going to do it!"

Time for general relaxation is crucial. On competition days or tough training days I always try to walk slowly rather than hurrying, talk calmly rather than chattering, and focus my eyes rather than allowing them to dart from object to object.

As I am actually walking or driving to the pool I always make sure to have a relaxing radio station or tape playing. After awhile it gets to the point that even humming a tune actually calms me down. Finally, I always try to shake the last little bit of tension out of my arms and legs. Some slow stretching and deep breathing never hurt, either. These activities coupled with positive statements and a quick review of previous successful experiences always prepare me mentally, physically, and attentionally. From that feeling on, I'm set. All I have to do is launch myself into the air and go for it, because at that point, I *know* I can do it.

Response and Analysis

1. Briefly describe Michele Mitchell's strategy for understanding her fear of diving into a swimming pool from a three-story-tall platform. What positive and negative attributes of diving affect her decision to dive? How does "tunnel vision" affect her thoughts about diving?

2. What techniques and thinking strategies does Mitchell use to control her fear? Why might these techniques reduce her fear?

Personal Experience and Application

1. Do you know someone who has a fear that is difficult to overcome? How does the fear inhibit the person? Does the fear serve a useful purpose? If so, what is it? What thinking strategies might the person use to control or overcome the fear?

2. Suppose the director of the Learning Skills Center at your college or university asks you to give a five-minute talk on reducing test anxiety. The director tells you that some students become anxious when taking an exam and may experience a racing heart and perspire. They may attribute these physiological reactions to their anxiety about taking the exam. Offer two recommendations that students might use to reduce test anxiety.

Research

Suppose the swimming coach at your college or university asks you to design a program to help a few team members overcome their fear of diving into a swimming pool from a three-story-tall platform. Before making any recommendations, you decide to interview team members to understand how they attempt to control their fears. Make a list of questions that you would ask the swimmers.

chapter 7

HUMAN DEVELOPMENT

_A few nights in your life, you know this
like the taste of lightning in your teeth:
Tomorrow I will be changed. Somehow
in the next passage of light, I will shed
reptilian skin and feel the wind's friction
again. Sparks will fly. It's a hope for the
right kind of fear, the kind that does not
turn away._

KIM R. STAFFORD, _Having Everything Right_

What physical, emotional, and cognitive changes can we expect as we grow from one stage to another? This chapter highlights the experiences of people who are at different stages in life: preschool; childhood; early adolescence; midlife; and old age.

Vivian Gussin Paley, a nursery school teacher, records the stories and conversations that take place among three- and four-year-old children. The youngsters charm us with their imaginative play and symbolic thinking and show us how they begin to think intuitively.

Dick Gregory writes of how a physically, socially, and economically impoverished environment can affect development. Because he came from a poor family, he often went to school without breakfast. His inability to concentrate contributed to his poor work, and he was typecast by his teacher as a boy who was always fooling around and getting into trouble.

Growing up in relative comfort, Annie Dillard was free to investigate her world and to know the spontaneity of creative play. She describes the excitement of exploration and the exhilaration and freedom that many of us can recall about our childhood. Dillard wonders how it would feel to fly like a bird. How close can she come, she wonders, as she gears up speed and runs through the streets.

Adults in midlife are sometimes called the "sandwich generation." H. Michael Zal shows how parents in this middle-aged group are often caught between their children, who may be young adults and may still need some kind of parental support, and their elderly parents, who also may need care.

Malcolm Cowley shares his view on living in his eightieth year. "The year from 79 to 80," he writes, "is like a week" of time when he was a boy. His body, too, sends messages. It often can't or won't do what Cowley would like. Yet there are rewards. Simple needs "become a pleasure to satisfy."

After the death of her grandmother in Nigeria, Nsedu Onyile has decisions to make about the time and place of her grandmother's burial. She decides that the grandmother will be buried in two months in a bedroom of the family home, and Onyile has to choose who will have the honor of sleeping in that room. Onyile, who lives in America, alludes to different approaches that some Nigerians and some Americans have toward death.

MOLLIE IS THREE

Vivian Gussin Paley

Psychological Concepts
Piaget's theory, preoperational period,
accommodation, assimilation

Vivian Gussin Paley, a talented teacher at the University of Chicago's nursery school, brings us into her classroom to observe the cognitive and social development of Mollie and her classmates. Using a tape recorder, Paley kept track of her students' stories and conversations for a year.

The three-year-old children are representative of Piaget's preoperational period, and they are beginning to understand, create, and use symbols. They like to set up "scary" situations, and when one group pretends to be monsters or witches, another group tries various means of defense, such as hiding in a house or holding pretend guns. Mollie, however, is especially creative. When another child announces that a monster is on the way and offers Mollie a gun, Mollies refuses it. "I'm a statue," she says.

How do the children use toys to interact with one another and to develop friendships? How do they explore gender roles in their play? Whatever they do, they are inventive. In Paley's words, the children are involved in "experimental theater."

Learning is a reciprocal process; Mollie is as much teacher as student. She tells Christopher that he, like Peter Rabbit, will have blackberries and milk if he is good, and warns Margaret not to dial the fire department because Curious George "false alarmed them." She urges Erik to plant the seeds he finds in the playground so he can climb up the beanstalk "when the giant is not there," and asks Emily to help her build a brick house "so the wolf doesn't huff us."

Mollie at three displays a natural affinity for life as art. Such is the instinct of all children, of course, but in Mollie the impulse finds clear expression in words. She knows how to bring book characters into conversation, play, and stories, and the new stories she creates out of old ones produce an exciting sense of continuity.

Today, for example, she puts "Mushroom in the Rain," "The Three Pigs," and "Hansel and Gretel" into a Wonderwoman story. In the original "Mushroom in the Rain," a butterfly, a mouse, and a sparrow are drenched in a heavy downpour, then sheltered under a mushroom by a kindly ant. A frightened rabbit and a hungry fox also enter the story, but Mollie gives star billing to the wet butterfly.

"I want to be the wet butterfly and Wonderwoman. First he goes under the mushroom. Now we got to do the big, bad wolf and the three pigs and the fox is going to catch the butterfly and put it in the cage, that one from Hansel. Then Wonderwoman comes. Then I open the cage and the wet butterfly goes under the mushroom because the ant says to come in."

How has Mollie learned to integrate these bits and pieces into a sensible whole? No one else offers Christopher blackberries and milk if he is good or unites the big, bad wolf with a fox to make trouble for a butterfly. However, it is the sort of storytelling that is heard every day during play: Cinderella and Darth Vader put the baby to bed while Superman serves tea and saves the baby from the witch just as Daddy comes home from work and sits down to eat a birthday cake.

If Mollie is quicker than most to transfer the process into her stories it is because, more than most children, she sees life as a unified whole. To her, fantasy characters and real people all communicate in the same language. . . .

It is especially easy to witness in the doll corner, where family matters dominate. Samantha and Amelia are there now, covered with veils and shawls, chanting, "We're getting married." Libby enters, frowning; she senses she is being left out of an important ceremony.

"What are you doing, Samantha?"

"Watch out, Libby. We're getting married."

"Can I get married with you?"

"Hurry up, Amelia. Put on the lace, honey."

"Just us, Libby."

"I'm getting married too," Libby says. "By myself."

"Not with us, Libby, 'cause you didn't see my flower girl dress and only Amelia saw it."

"I saw my own flower girl dress and *I'm* going to the ballet."

"So am I," Samantha counters.

"I'm going to *be* the ballet."

"Well, I know how to dance and you don't."

"Yes I do!" Libby begins to cry. "Teacher, Samantha says I can't dance."

"I'm sure you can, Libby."

"She's stupid! She's a liar."

Mollie has been watching the scene from the telephone table. She walks over to the two angry girls and smiles. "Guess what! Margaret's coming to my house today. She's my friend."

Her declaration is not out of context. The argument she interrupts is not about marriage or the ballet, but concerns who is playing with whom. This is the proper time to announce that she will play with Margaret, all by herself, at her house today.

The girls look at Mollie and Margaret and remember that they too are friends. Samantha dials the telephone. "Hello, Libby? Call the police. There's a noise. I think it's a lion."

"Yeah. I hear roaring. Turn off the light. Pretend we're not home."

Margaret takes Mollie's hand as they leave. Neither one is comfortable in the doll corner when the lion is at the door.

A few minutes later Mollie returns, uncertainly. She knows the girls are only pretending something bad is about to happen; but what if the bad thing doesn't know it's pretend? Nonetheless, Mollie decides to stay, keeping one foot outside the drama.

"Go to sleep, Mollie," Libby orders. "There might be something dangerous. You won't like it."

"I know it," Mollie says. "But I got a bunk bed at home and I sleep there."

"Bunk beds are too scary," Amelia says.

"Why are they?" Mollie looks worried.

"It's a monster, Mollie. Hide!"

"I know. But there's no monsters in my house today."

"You have to hide, Mollie. It's a real monster."

"I'm going to hide by the teacher."

"No, Mollie, stay here. Under here. Under the cover."

"I'm going to be a statue," Mollie whispers. "So he won't see me."

"He won't get me," Libby says, "because I've got a real gun. You want one?"

Mollie shakes her head. "I'm a statue."

"No, Mollie, hide. Come here. I'll hide you. The boys are going to scare us." Libby looks around for an available boy and catches sight of Fredrick at the painting table. "Watch out!" she shouts. "Fredrick is coming! He's a monster! Hide!"

Fredrick drops his brushes and rushes into the doll corner on all fours. "Roar!" He arches his back and claws the air. "G-r-r!"

"Teacher! Fredrick's scaring Mollie!"

"I'm a lion. I'm roaring."

"Is he scaring you, Mollie?"

"No."

"Is anyone scaring you?"

"The bunk bed," she answers solemnly. . . .

My games consistently miss the point of *their* games: the recognition and repetition of what is obvious to all. The threes have been demonstrating these facts to me for months, but I keep adding complications. A few days later the unadorned simplicity of it all comes across to me.

We are playing an invention of mine called "Who's missing, who's missing, guess who's not here," in which one child hides behind a screen while another child tries to guess his identity. The fours play the game easily, giving appropriate hints and not peeking. I cannot, however, convince the threes to observe two important rules: do not reveal the hidden person's name and, if you are the one who is hiding, do not come out before your name is guessed.

Suddenly I see the game through younger eyes. "Let's play a different way," I tell the children. "We'll all watch the hider, we'll pretend we don't know who it is, and then we'll all say who it is."

We sing the original refrain, changing the last line to suit the new rules: "Who's missing, who's missing, guess who's not here. It's Mollie, it's Mollie, now she is here."

Together we watch Mollie hide and after a moment of closing our eyes we call out her name. Mollie jumps out laughing. "It's me!"

The new game is a splendid success, not unlike the three-year-olds' hide-and-seek, in which they pretend to hide and pretend to seek. Carrie has her own version: she hides a favorite possession, then asks a teacher to help her find it. She pretends to look for it as she takes the teacher directly to the missing item. "Oh, here's my dolly's brush!" she squeals delightedly. All these games resist the unknown and the possibility of loss. They are designed to give the child control in the most direct way.

Sometimes, however, the child has no control; something is really missing. Then the threes are likely to approach the problem as if the question is "What is *not* missing?" This is exactly what happens when I try to direct the children's attention to an empty space in the playground. Over the weekend, an unsafe climbing structure has been removed. The doll corner window overlooks the area that housed the rickety old frame.

"See if you can tell what's missing from our playground?" I ask.

"The sandbox."

"The squirrely tree."

"The slide."

"But I can *see* all those things. They're still in the playground. Something else was there, something very big, and now it's gone."

"The boat."

"Mollie, look. There's the boat. I'm talking about a big, brown, wooden thing that was right there where my finger is pointing."

"Because there's too much dirt."

"But what was on top of the place where there's too much dirt?"

"It could be grass. You could plant grass."

Libby and Samantha see us crowded around the window and walk over to investigate. "Where's the climbing house?" Libby asks. "Someone stoled the climbing house."

"No one stole the house, Libby. We asked some men to take it down for us. Remember how shaky it was? We were afraid somebody would fall."

The threes continue staring, confused. I should have anticipated their response and urged that the structure be dismantled during school hours. After all, these are the children who scrub a clean table because it had playdough on it the day before, and worry about birds coming in to bother the blocks.

"Does everyone remember the climbing house? Here, I'll draw a picture. Let's see, it went up this high and here were some steps . . ."

"Where are the steps?" Mollie asks.

"The men chopped everything up and took it all away in a truck."

"Where are they stepping to?"

"The steps are not steps any more. I'll bet they're using all the old wood for firewood."

"They use them to step out of the fire," Mollie says.

"Like the D!" Barney exclaims. There is a moment of recognition and smiles all around. With Barney's symbol of change, the children can avoid the disturbing image of a missing stairway and think instead of magical escapes they have acted out many times.

Response and Analysis

1. How do Mollie and her schoolmates play hide-and-seek? Why do you think that the children do not hide out of sight? How do the children react when something is missing? Why is the sense of control important for preschool children?

2. What cognitive abilities do you see in Mollie and her schoolmates that represent Piaget's preoperational period? Briefly describe two examples of assimilation and/or accommodation that Mollie and her schoolmates display.

Personal Experience and Application

1. Suppose you volunteer to be a teacher's aide at a preschool in your community. The teacher asks you to create a new game or activity that the children can play on rainy days. Describe the main features of the game. Why is it appropriate for the cognitive and social abilities of three-year-old children?

2. Suppose you observe a child for thirty minutes at a public place such as a playground, park, or nursery school (with the permission of the nursery school and the human subjects Institutional Review Board at your college or university). What behaviors may reveal whether the child is physically, socially, or intellectually advanced? How could you determine if the child gets along with the other children?

Research

Vivian Paley's work may be considered participant-observation research because she interacts with the children and observes their behavior. List two advantages and two disadvantages of this approach. Do you believe that the advantages outweigh the disadvantages, or vice versa? Why or why not? Briefly describe another way Paley could study the cognitive and social development of preschool children.

SHAME

Dick Gregory

Psychological Concepts
cognitive development, emotional development, environmental influences

How do impoverished surroundings and humiliating experiences affect a child's cognitive and emotional development? Comedian and civil rights activist Dick Gregory remembers that without a father or financial security he and his family lived in hunger and crowded living conditions. Handouts and pity embarrassed him. The identical coats given to poor children became badges of poverty for all to see. The insensitive treatment Gregory received in school added to his growing sense of shame. How might these conditions affect his ability to learn in school? How do his experiences impede his developing self-respect?

I have never learned hate at home, or shame. I had to go to school for that. I was about seven years old when I got my first big lesson. I was in love with a little girl named Helene Tucker, a light-complected little girl with pigtails and nice manners. She was always clean and she was smart in school. I think I went to school then mostly to look at her. I brushed my hair and even got me a little old handkerchief. It was a lady's handkerchief, but I didn't want Helene to see me wipe my nose on my hand. The pipes were frozen again, there was no water in the house, but I washed my socks and shirt every night. I'd get a pot, and go over to Mister Ben's grocery store, and stick my pot down into his soda machine. Scoop out some chopped ice. By evening the ice melted to water for washing. I got sick a lot that winter because the fire would go out at night before the clothes were dry. In the morning I'd put them on, wet or dry, because they were the only clothes I had.

Everybody's got a Helene Tucker, a symbol of everything you want. I loved her for her goodness, her cleanness, her popularity. She'd walk down my street and my brothers and sisters would yell, "Here comes Helene," and I'd rub my tennis sneakers on the back of my pants and wish my hair wasn't so nappy and the white folks' shirt fit me better. I'd run out on the street. If I knew my place and didn't come too close, she'd wink at me and say hello. That was a good feeling. Sometimes I'd follow her all the way home, and shovel the snow off her walk and try to make friends with her Momma and her aunts. I'd drop money on her stoop late at night on my way back from shining shoes in the taverns. And she had a Daddy, and he had a good job. He was a paper hanger.

I guess I would have gotten over Helene by summertime, but something happened in that classroom that made her face hang in front of me for the next twenty-two years. When I played the drums in high school it was for Helene and when I broke track records in college it was for Helene and when I started standing behind microphones and heard applause I wished Helene would hear it, too. It wasn't until I was twenty-nine years old and married and making money that I finally got her out of my system. Helene was sitting in that classroom when I learned to be ashamed of myself.

It was on a Thursday. I was sitting in back of the room, in a seat with a chalk circle drawn around it. The idiot's seat, the troublemaker's seat.

The teacher thought I was stupid. Couldn't spell, couldn't read, couldn't do arithmetic. Just stupid. Teachers were never interested in finding out that you couldn't concentrate because you were so hungry, because you hadn't had any breakfast. All you could think about was noontime, would it ever come? Maybe you could sneak into the cloakroom and steal a bite of some kid's lunch out of a coat pocket. A bit of something. Paste. You can't really make a meal of paste, or put it on bread for a sandwich, but sometimes I'd scoop a few spoonfuls out of the paste jar in the back of the room. Pregnant people get strange tastes. I was pregnant with poverty. Pregnant with dirt and pregnant with smells that made people turn away, pregnant with cold and pregnant with shoes that were never bought for me, pregnant with five other people in my bed and no Daddy in the next room, and pregnant with hunger. Paste doesn't taste too bad when you're hungry.

The teacher thought I was a troublemaker. All she saw from the front of the room was a little black boy who squirmed in his idiot's seat and made noises and poked the kids around him. I guess she couldn't see a kid who made noises because he wanted someone to know he was there.

It was a Thursday, the day before the Negro payday. The Eagle always flew on Friday. The teacher was asking each student how much his father would give to the community chest. On Friday night, each kid would get the money from his father, and on Monday he would bring it to school. I decided I was going to buy me a Daddy right then. I had money in my pocket from shining shoes and selling papers, and whatever Helene Tucker pledged for her Daddy I was going to top it. And I'd hand the money right in. I wasn't going to wait until Monday to buy me a Daddy.

I was shaking, scared to death. The teacher opened her book and started calling out names alphabetically.

"Helene Tucker?"

"My Daddy said he'd give two dollars and fifty cents."

"That's very nice, Helene. Very, very nice indeed."

That made me feel pretty good. It wouldn't take too much to top that. I had almost three dollars in dimes and quarters in my pocket. I stuck my hand in my pocket and held onto the money, waiting for her to call my name. But the teacher closed her book after she called everybody else in the class.

I stood up and raised my hand.

"What is it now?"

"You forgot me."

She turned toward the blackboard. "I don't have time to be playing with you, Richard."

"My Daddy said he'd . . ."

"Sit down, Richard, you're disturbing the class."

"My Daddy said he'd give . . . fifteen dollars."

She turned around and looked mad. "We are collecting this money for you and your kind, Richard Gregory. If your Daddy can give fifteen dollars you have no business being on relief."

"I got it right now, I got it right now, my Daddy gave it to me to turn in today, my Daddy said . . ."

"And furthermore," she said, looking right at me, her nostrils getting big and her lips getting thin and her eyes opening wide, "we know you don't have a Daddy."

Helene Tucker turned around, her eyes full of tears. She felt sorry for me. Then I couldn't see her too well because I was crying too.

"Sit down, Richard."

And I always thought the teacher kind of liked me. She always picked me to wash the blackboard on Friday, after school. That was a big thrill, it made me feel important. If I didn't wash it, come Monday the school might not function right.

"Where are you going, Richard?"

I walked out of school that day and for a long time I didn't go back very often. There was shame there.

Now there was shame everywhere. It seemed like the whole world had been inside that classroom, everyone had heard what the teacher had said, everyone had turned around and felt sorry for me. There was shame in going to the Worthy Boys Annual Christmas Dinner for you and your kind because everybody knew what a worthy boy was. Why couldn't they just call it the Boys Annual Dinner, why'd they have to give it a name? There was shame in wearing the brown and orange and white plaid mackinaw the welfare gave to 3,000 boys. Why'd it have to be the same for everybody so when you walked down the street the people could see you were on relief? It was a nice warm mackinaw and it had a hood, and my Momma beat me and called me a little rat when she found out I stuffed it in the bottom of a pail full of garbage way over on Cottage Street. There was shame in running over to Mister Ben's at the end of the day and asking for his rotten peaches, there was shame in asking Mr. Simmons for a spoon full of sugar, there was shame in running out to meet the relief truck. I hated that truck, full of food for you and your kind. I ran into the house and hid when it came. And then I started to sneak through alleys, to take the long way home so the people going into White's Eat Stop wouldn't see me. Yeah, the whole world heard the teacher that day, we all know you don't have a Daddy.

Response and Analysis

1. Dick Gregory writes that "shame was every-where." Where did Gregory find shame? Why? What messages discouraged him from developing self-respect?

2. What does Gregory mean when he says he was "pregnant with poverty"? Briefly describe the physical and economic conditions that may have limited Gregory's ability to learn in school.

Personal Experience and Application

1. Briefly describe two characteristics of the physical, social, or cultural environment in which you grew up. How do you think those characteristics positively or negatively influenced your cognitive or emotional development?

2. Suppose that a parent group at a local elementary school asks you to help develop a day-care program for economically disadvantaged children between the ages of two and four. What types of activities might you suggest to promote cognitive development?

Research

Suppose you have used a correlational design to examine the relationship between the economic conditions in which children are raised and the academic abilities of seven-year-old children. Assume that you have conducted the study and have analyzed the data. Your analysis shows a correlation coefficient of +0.85 between economic conditions and academic ability. Does this indicate that the relationship is (a) positive or negative; and (b) strong or weak? Because you used a correlational design, why can't you conclude that the economic conditions caused the children's abilities? What other variables may influence the relationship between economic conditions and academic ability?

FLYING

Annie Dillard

Psychological Concepts
Erikson's stages of psychosocial development, Piaget's
concrete operational stage

Annie Dillard remembers when she was a young girl filled with restless, joyful energy.
She wanted to find a challenge that would release her youthful exuberance. What
better way than trying to fly, not in an airplane but by her own force. How close
could she come? As she runs through the streets of Pittsburgh, flapping her arms
wide, she startles one pedestrian and delights another. What does her "flight" reveal
about her and about this stage in her life?

I was running down the Penn Avenue sidewalk, revving up for an act of faith. I
was conscious and self-conscious. I knew well that people could not fly—as well as
anyone knows it—but I also knew the kicker: that, as the books put it, with faith all
things are possible.

Just once I wanted a task that required all the joy I had. Day after day I had noticed that if I waited long enough, my strong unexpressed joy would dwindle and
dissipate inside me, over many hours, like a fire subsiding, and I would at last calm
down. Just this once I wanted to let it rip. Flying rather famously required the extra
energy of belief, and this, too, I had in superabundance.

There were boxy yellow thirties apartment buildings on those Penn Avenue
blocks, and the Evergreen Café, and Miss Frick's house set back behind a wrought-
iron fence. There were some side yards of big houses, some side yards of little
houses, some streetcar stops, and a drugstore from which I had once tried to heist a
five-pound box of chocolates, a Whitman sampler, confusing "sampler" with "free
sample." It was past all this that I ran that late fall afternoon, up old Penn Avenue
on the cracking cement sidewalks—past the drugstore and bar, past the old and new
apartment buildings and the long dry lawn behind Miss Frick's fence.

I ran the sidewalk full tilt. I waved my arms ever higher and faster; blood
balled in my fingertips. I knew I was foolish. I knew I was too old really to believe
in this as a child would, out of ignorance; instead I was experimenting as a scientist
would, testing both the thing itself and the limits of my own courage in trying it
miserably self-conscious in full view of the whole world. You can't test courage cautiously, so I ran hard and waved my arms hard, happy.

Up ahead I saw a business-suited pedestrian. He was coming stiffly toward me down the walk. Who could ever forget this first test, this stranger, this thin young man appalled? I banished the temptation to straighten up and walk right. He flattened himself against a brick wall as I passed flailing—although I had left him plenty of room. He had refused to meet my exultant eye. He looked away, evidently embarrassed. How surprisingly easy it was to ignore him! What I was letting rip, in fact, was my willingness to look foolish, in his eyes and in my own. Having chosen this foolishness, I was a free being. How could the world ever stop me, how could I betray myself, if I was not afraid?

I was flying. My shoulders loosened, my stride opened, my heart banged the base of my throat. I crossed Carnegie and ran up the block waving my arms. I crossed Lexington and ran up the block waving my arms.

A linen-suited woman in her fifties did meet my exultant eye. She looked exultant herself, seeing me from far up the block. Her face was thin and tanned. We converged. Her warm, intelligent glance said she knew what I was doing—not because she herself had been a child but because she herself took a few loose aerial turns around her apartment every night for the hell of it, and by day played along with the rest of the world and took the streetcar. So Teresa of Avila checked her unseemly joy and hung on to the altar rail to hold herself down. The woman's smiling, deep glance seemed to read my own awareness from my face, so we passed on the sidewalk—a beautifully upright woman walking in her tan linen suit, a kid running and flapping her arms—we passed on the sidewalk with a look of accomplices who share a humor just beyond irony. What's a heart for?

I crossed Homewood and ran up the block. The joy multiplied as I ran—I ran never actually quite leaving the ground—and multiplied still as I felt my stride begin to fumble and my knees begin to quiver and stall. The joy multiplied even as I slowed bumping to a walk. I was all but splitting, all but shooting sparks. Blood coursed free inside my lungs and bones, a light-shot stream like air. I couldn't feel the pavement at all.

I was too aware to do this, and had done it anyway. What could touch me now? For what were the people on Penn Avenue to me, or what was I to myself, really, but a witness to any boldness I could muster, or any cowardice if it came to that, any giving up on heaven for the sake of dignity on earth? I had not seen a great deal accomplished in the name of dignity, ever.

Response and Analysis

1. Annie Dillard writes that her joy would dwindle and dissipate if it was unexpressed. "Just this once I wanted to let it rip." What did the child Annie gain from her attempt to fly? How would you describe her sense of curiosity and eagerness to learn? At which stage was Dillard in Erikson's psychosocial development model? Why?

2. Annie most likely is at Piaget's concrete operational stage. What characteristics of this stage does she show?

Personal Experience and Application

1. At which stage do you believe you are in Erikson's psychosocial development model? Why? What is the main issue or crisis that you need to resolve before moving to the next stage? How do you think you will resolve it?

2. Suppose you are the parent of an eight-year-old child. Can you think of an activity that might promote your child's sense of industry, curiosity, and eagerness to learn? Why might it do that?

Research

Suppose you want to replicate Piaget's research examining conservation among seven- to eleven-year-old children. After securing approval from the human subjects Institutional Review Board at your college or university, you have a group of parents escort their children to your lab. You seat one child at a time and place two pieces of clay of equal size and shape at the table in front of the child. You allow the child to look at both pieces of clay for one minute. Then, keeping both pieces on the table, with your hand you roll one piece of clay into a tube. You do not touch the other piece of clay. Once again, you allow the child to look at both pieces of clay for one minute. You then ask the child to tell you if the piece of clay you did not touch or the tube of clay weighs more. Which age group will tell you that one shape weighs more than the other? Why? Which shape will be perceived as weighing more? Why?

THE SQUEEZED GENERATION

H. Michael Zal

Psychological Concepts
midlife transition, Erikson's generativity versus
stagnation stage, midlife crisis, social clock

Many people reappraise their lives and relationships around the age of forty. During the midlife transition, they may feel caught between the younger and the older generations.

What do people hope for when they become forty or fifty years old? What is unique about that stage? People have honed their careers and talents and hope to have some status and respect on the job and in the community. If they have families, their children are close to being independent. So, what now? H. Michael Zal tells us that "What now?" does not always bring what this group anticipated.

People in midlife transition may feel pressured to assist their children financially or to take care of their elderly parents. In addition, they may worry about their own health or job security. Husbands and wives may reflect on what they have not yet achieved and begin to feel a kind of desperation. Their marriages may be "old hat," and they may wonder how to rekindle love. Yet most people find solutions to these issues and find that this stage, like all the others, has great rewards. What suggestions does Zal offer this "sandwich generation"?

Nora was 49. Something was wrong. It felt physical. She often had pressure in her chest and felt faint and short of breath. It felt emotional. She was often tense and moody. At times she thought that she would lose control and burst apart. She visited her family doctor. Except for moderate hypertension, the results of her physical exam were normal. All the lab test findings were within normal limits. Maybe it was menopause? A psychiatric opinion was sought. The clinical diagnosis was depression and anxiety. The real issue was the dilemma of middle age.

Nora's worries and complaints were not unique. As with many people in the sandwich generation she felt caught in the middle between generations, responsibilities, needs, and expectations. "I'm trying to sort out my obligations to my children, to my husband, to our aging parents, to my career, and to myself," she said. Nora felt stressed and driven by an intense emotional pressure which she did not fully understand.

"At this point in my life, I expected that I would be growing old gracefully and that everything would be O.K. I always assumed that as I got older I would get wiser, mellow, and have the answers to some questions. I thought that I would know what to expect and what others expected of me. I felt that I would be a calm and cool person. Instead, I feel terrible inside. I'm not who I should be. I'm not in control." Her turmoil and confusion were influencing her work and her relationship with her husband, Don. Let's look at some of the people in her life and some of the problems fueling her anxiety and discontent.

The Children Jose was 19 and a college student living out of town. She called several times a week and dumped her problems concerning her boyfriend, school, and girlfriends on her parents. Nora worried for days only to find out when she called back that Jose had already forgotten the crisis and gone on to a new day and new issues.

Ben was 23, married, and had two beautiful twin daughters. He and his wife, Dianne, had lived with Nora and Don for 10 months after they married. They then moved to North Carolina. Ben was now unemployed and had gotten into a fight in a bar and been arrested. He and Dianne had separated three months ago, and Dianne and the babies were living with her mother. Nora worried about them all.

Henrietta, 25, planned to marry in October. Fiancé Bob was a carpenter and worked sporadically. They had a 14-week-old baby son, Matthew. Henrietta, Bob, and Matthew all lived with Nora and Don, while they saved to buy a house of their own. At a time when she expected her life to be her own, Nora was cooking and cleaning for five all over again. "The only comfort is that all my friends are going through the same thing. When I was young, you moved out and didn't go back. Things are different with the kids today."

The Parent Nora was concerned about her mother, Ethel, who was 72 and lived many miles away. She had had a mild stroke last year. She had been recently hospitalized due to lack of appetite, fatigue, and insomnia. No new physical diagnosis was made. She was told to seek counseling for depression. Nora described her mother as a wise, productive, intelligent, and religious woman who allowed no disagreement. Nora's father also had had a history of depression and hypertension. He had been a heavy drinker. Since her husband died 10 years ago, Ethel had been self-sufficient and independent. When Nora visited her in the hospital, she could see a change. For the first time, Ethel looked frail and older. Uncharacteristically, she cried in her daughter's arms and shared her fear that she would have another stroke alone in her apartment and die. Nora realized that she too was aging. She began to think about her own health, her own future, and her own mortality.

Nora found it hard to be a caregiver at a distance. Her first instinct was to ask her mother to move to her home in Philadelphia. Somehow she knew that the offer would be rejected. She did talk to her brother and was very firm about what she felt her mother needed. She also called a local agency and was able to get someone to stay with her mother in the evenings several days a week.

The Spouse Don had taken a new hobby. He was fixing up the house and adding a new porch. Nora complained that it had become an obsession. "He spends 85 percent of his spare time on the house. I want to go out dancing. By the time we're done with the house, I'll be too old to enjoy myself. I'm getting older. I want to do some of the things that I want to do." In quiet moments, she wondered if Don still found her attractive and worried about gaining weight. His business commitments were also very time consuming. In spite of her resentment, she worried about his health. He smoked one-and-a-half packs of cigarettes a day and had had a heart attack four years ago. She wondered what would happen if he had another health crisis and what life would be like without him. "It seems that he and I are always faced with something. We don't have time for each other."

The Inlaw Don's father, Joseph, age 78, had been retired for many years. His wife, Camille, had died four years earlier after a long illness. Initially, Joe seemed to be making a good adjustment. Unlike many men his age, he had some hobbies and interests and played cards once a week. During the last year, his memory had been declining. Twice he had left the oven on overnight. His prostate had been removed, leaving him incontinent, and his vision was failing. Nora and Don constantly talked about the options that were available for Joe, including placement in a nursing home. They could never seem to make a decision.

The Job Nora was well respected at the office. She had worked hard for many years and was now a manager supervising 12 employees. She was taken aback at times when they called her "Mame" and complained that the "kids" were not as diligent about their work as she and her contemporaries were at their age. There had been some recent administrative changes which added to the turmoil at work. There was talk of further changes and possible layoffs. Nora handled the pressure by working harder and taking on more responsibility. She felt tense, insecure, and irritable. When told that she had high blood pressure, she responded that she had no time to be sick.

Job security was important to Nora. She had heard many stories about her parents suffering during the Depression. The recent upheaval at work also created tension for her because it threatened a hidden agenda in her life. "When I took this job, I thought that I had finally reached a pinnacle in my career. I've been in a fast track mode. I thought that this might finally be the end of the line employment-wise. I could stay here. It would be a nice way to end my career and eventually retire. I wanted to stop work at 55. I would still have energy and still be young enough to enjoy the things we postponed all these years. They're messing up my life. If I have to start a new job at my age, it will shatter my plans." Even more confusing to her was the fact that she sometimes woke up at night and thought, "Maybe I'll give up my career and do some other kind of work."

As you can see, it is not surprising that Nora felt stressed and out of control. Her frustration was further fueled by her unfulfilled expectations. After early financial and marital struggles, the trials and tribulations of caring for children and attending to career goals, Nora, at 49, expected to be able to coast for awhile. Instead, she was caught between demanding children, a frightened parent, a needy father-in-law, and her own needs and desires. Her marriage was drifting. At this stage in life, she expected that she would feel mellow and content. Instead, she felt conflicted and needy. Instead of a rest, she had new problems to solve. No wonder she was angry inside.

More traditionally oriented, like her mother, it had been difficult for Nora to cope with a grandchild born out of wedlock and a son who was not particularly goal-directed. She joked and called him a "free spirit," but was really quite disappointed in him. Prior to therapy, Nora had assumed that at her age she was done learning and changing. However, life is synonymous with change. This too was part of her frustration. Change was difficult for her. Middle age is a developmental stage where we can resolve old issues and continue to mature and grow. She had to accept these truths. Nora found that even in middle age she had conflicts to resolve, new feelings to understand, and new problems to solve. She started to see middle age as a challenge. She did well.

Medication helped improve her mood and calm her anxieties. In therapy, she became a little more introspective and gained new insight through her reflections. She was able to ventilate some of her anger and understand some of her other feelings. She got her younger brother to spend more time with Ethel. She started to set some limits on Henrietta and Bob and asked for more help around the house. The "kids" moved to their own house in November. Nora expressed some of her pent-up anger and disappointment at Ben and told me how she felt that he had let her down. She tried hard to encourage Jose to solve some of her own problems and to be more independent. Most of all, she tried not to feel guilty if she could not be everything to everyone. At work, she started to see herself in a new role as a consultant who had much experience and expertise to share but who no longer had to do it all herself. She started to delegate more.

Seventeen years earlier, she and Don had gone for marriage counseling. At the time, Nora had been depressed and unhappy. In a short course of outpatient therapy, she was able to come out of her depression and better communicate her needs. At this stage of her life, she again felt suddenly insecure and alone. She very much needed Don and felt resentful that he could not see this on his own and pay more attention to her instead of the house. Now, after 28 years of marriage, she could be more insightful. "It's happening again," she said. Fortunately, with a little therapeutic encouragement, she was able to talk to Don. She told him what she wanted from him and how much she cared. They started to take walks together and even went dancing one Saturday night. Their relationship started to improve again.

In therapy, Nora reminisced about her father's love of music. He had often sung and played the guitar for his children. She remembered how relaxing it had been in her childhood home when her father played operatic music on their Victrola. She bought a compact disc player and started to enjoy music again. As she relaxed, a more creative side emerged. She worked in the garden more and talked about taking a course in flower arranging. She started to see the big picture and put things in perspective. "I can't get so crazy. I have to take one day at a time. I'll do what I can for others and take better care of me." Although still uptight at times, Nora started to feel more content and more in control. She even took her antihypertensive medication regularly. Life was not perfect but it was much improved.

Nora is representative of many of you in the sandwich generation. The fabric of her life is made up of relationships. Her children and the other members of her family are important to her. She also has her own needs and priorities and wants to continue to grow. Her worries about her health and her future are universal. She has certain expectations about life in middle age. Her dilemma is not unique. In spite of the current turmoil and the angry feelings, a special bond of love exists between Nora and her family which will endure forever.

Response and Analysis

1. Nora "felt caught in the middle between generations, responsibilities, needs, and expectations." Briefly describe the problems or issues that contributed to Nora's anxiety: her children, parents, spouse, in-laws, and job. How did she resolve her marital difficulties?

2. What are the characteristics of a midlife crisis? Who is most likely to experience such a crisis? Why? What are the main issues facing someone who is at Erikson's generativity ver-

sus stagnation stage of psychosocial development?

Personal Experience and Application

1. Most cultures have a social clock that prescribes when certain social events and major life events should occur, such as marriage, children, and retirement. Think of someone you know who has felt pressured by a social clock. What did he or she feel pressured to do? Briefly discuss any pressures you have felt because of a social clock.

2. List at least five characteristics of a satisfying marriage. What factors lead people to divorce?

Research

Suppose you want to conduct a cross-cultural study to examine the social clock phenomenon. You want to know if college students in the United States, Brazil, South Africa, and Holland have similar expectations about when major life events like marriage should occur. Write three questions that you might ask your participants. Will the questions be short answer or use a fixed-response scale (e.g., strongly disagree, disagree, neither disagree nor agree, agree, strongly agree)? Why?

THE VIEW FROM 80

Malcolm Cowley

Psychological Concept
late adulthood

Martin Buber writes that "to be old is a glorious thing when one has not unlearned what it means to begin" (p. 6). Malcolm Cowley surely knew how to begin again: he published five books after he turned seventy. He died at the age of ninety-one. Cowley valued ceremonies, and when his friends and family celebrated his eightieth birthday with a party, he knew it was a rite of passage.

Aging, he said, is different from what any of us expect. When he discovers that other people see him as old, he is forced to redefine himself. He becomes aware of various messages he receives from his body that tell him he is aging.

Here Cowley shares his experiences, some challenging, some delightful, of becoming older. What he enjoys are moments of "simply sitting still, like a snake on a sun-warmed stone."

They gave me a party on my 80th birthday in August 1978. First there were cards, letters, telegrams, even a cable of congratulation or condolence; then there were gifts, mostly bottles; there was catered food and finally a big cake with, for some reason, two candles (had I gone back to very early childhood?). I blew the candles out a little unsteadily. Amid the applause and clatter I thought about a former custom of the Northern Ojibwas when they lived on the shore of Lake Winnipeg. They were kind to their old people, who remembered and enforced the ancient customs of the tribe, but when an old person became decrepit, it was time for him to go. Sometimes he was simply abandoned, with a little food, on an island in the lake. If he deserved special honor, they held a tribal feast for him. The old man sang a death song and danced, if he could. While he was still singing, his son came from behind and brained him with a tomahawk.

That was quick, it was dignified, and I wonder whether it was any more cruel, essentially, than some of our civilized customs or inadvertencies in disposing of the aged. I believe in rites and ceremonies. I believe in big parties for special occasions such as an 80th birthday. It is a sort of belated bar mitzvah, since the 80-year-old, like a Jewish adolescent, is entering a new stage of life; let him (or her) undergo a *rite de passage*, with toasts and a cantor. Seventy-year-olds, or septuas, have the illusion of being middle-aged, even if they have been pushed back on a shelf. The 80-year-old, the octo, looks at the double-dumpling figure and admits that he is old. That last act has begun, and it will be the test of the play.

He has joined a select minority that numbers, in this country, 4,842,000 persons (according to Census Bureau estimates for 1977), or about two percent of the American population. Two-thirds of the octos are women, who have retained the good habit of living longer than men. Someday you, the reader, will join that minority, if you escape hypertension and cancer, the two killers, and if you survive the dangerous years 75 to 79, when half the survivors till then are lost. With advances in medicine, the living space taken over by octos is growing larger year by year.

To enter the country of age is a new experience, different from what you supposed it to be. Nobody, man or woman, knows the country until he has lived in it and has taken out his citizenship papers. Here is my own report, submitted as a road map and guide to some of the principal monuments.

The new octogenarian feels as strong as ever when he is sitting back in a comfortable chair. He ruminates, he dreams, he remembers. He doesn't want to be disturbed by others. It seems to him that old age is only a costume assumed for those others; the true, the essential self is ageless. In a moment he will rise and go for a ramble in the woods, taking a gun along, or a fishing rod, if it is spring. Then he creaks to his feet, bending forward to keep his balance, and realizes that he will do nothing of the sort. The body and its surroundings have their messages for him, or only one message: "You are old." Here are some of the occasions on which he receives the message:

- when it becomes an achievement to do thoughtfully, step by step, what he once did instinctively
- when his bones ache
- when there are more and more little bottles in the medicine cabinet, with instructions for taking four times a day
- when he fumbles and drops his toothbrush (butterfingers)
- when his face has bumps and wrinkles, so that he cuts himself while shaving (blood on the towel)
- when year by year his feet seem farther from his hands
- when he can't stand on one leg and has trouble pulling on his pants
- when he hesitates on the landing before walking down a flight of stairs
- when he spends more time looking for things misplaced than he spends using them after he (or more often his wife) has found them
- when he falls asleep in the afternoon
- when it becomes harder to bear in mind two things at once
- when a pretty girl passes him in the street and he doesn't turn his head
- when he forgets names, even of people he saw last month ("Now I'm beginning to forget nouns," the poet Conrad Aiken said at 80)
- when he listens hard to jokes and catches everything but the snapper
- when he decides not to drive at night anymore
- when everything takes longer to do—bathing, shaving, getting dressed or undressed—but when time passes quickly, as if he were gathering speed while coasting downhill. The year from 79 to 80 is like a week when he was a boy.

Those are some of the intimate messages. "Put cotton in your ears and pebbles in your shoes," said a gerontologist, a member of that new profession dedicated to alleviating all maladies of old people except the passage of years. "Pull on rubber gloves. Smear Vaseline over your glasses, and there you have it: instant aging." Not quite. His formula omits the messages from the social world, which are louder, in most cases, than those from within. We start by growing old in other people's eyes, then slowly we come to share their judgment.

I remember a morning many years ago when I was backing out of the parking lot near the railroad station in Brewster, New York. There was a near collision. The driver of the other car jumped out and started to abuse me; he had his fists ready. Then he looked hard at me and said, "Why, you're an old man." He got back into his car, slammed the door, and drove away, while I stood there fuming. "I'm only 65," I thought. "He wasn't driving carefully. I can still take care of myself in a car, or in a fight, for that matter." . . .

But there are also pleasures of the body, or the mind, that are enjoyed by a greater number of older persons.

Those pleasures include some that younger people find hard to appreciate. One of them is simply sitting still, like a snake on a sun-warmed stone, with a delicious feeling of indolence that was seldom attained in earlier years. A leaf flutters down; a cloud moves by inches across the horizon. At such moments the older person, completely relaxed, has become a part of nature—and a living part, with blood coursing through his veins. The future does not exist for him. He thinks, if he thinks at all, that life for younger persons is still a battle royal of each against each, but that now he has nothing more to win or lose. He is not so much above as outside the battle, as if he had assumed the uniform of some small neutral country, perhaps Liechtenstein or Andorra. From a distance he notes that some of the combatants, men or women, are jostling ahead—but why do they fight so hard when the most they can hope for is a longer obituary? He can watch the scrounging and gouging, he can hear the shouts of exultation, the moans of the gravely wounded, and meanwhile he feels secure; nobody will attack him from ambush.

Response and Analysis

1. What pleasures does Malcolm Cowley associate with old age? What messages about old age does he receive from society? Cowley suggests that "the aging person may undergo another identity crisis like that of adolescence." Briefly discuss the crisis.

2. Briefly summarize the physical, cognitive, social, and intellectual changes about which Cowley writes.

Personal Experience and Application

1. How do you feel when you are around senior citizens? What do you think is remarkable about senior citizens and people who are in their eighties? What do you think may be rewarding and satisfying and what may be difficult for people in this age group?

2. Suppose a local organization of retired people asks you to design a program to enhance the intellectual life of senior citizens. What types of activities might you suggest?

Research

Suppose you wish to conduct an experiment to examine how senior citizens describe their personal identity. You decide to ask a random sample of senior citizens to participate. You have to decide which of two assessment procedures to use. One procedure involves asking the participants to list as many words as they can that describe themselves. The other procedure involves presenting a list of one hundred traits to the participants and asking them to place a check next to each trait that describes themselves. List two advantages and two disadvantages of each approach. Which approach would you use? Why?

CELEBRATING DEATH—AND LIFE

Nsedu Onyile

Psychological Concepts
death and dying, Erikson's integrity versus despair
stage

The way we confront the death of a loved one varies from culture to culture. Nsedu Onyile's presentation of the way Nigerians honor their dead is striking in its contrast with the burial customs of North Americans.

When Onyile's grandmother died, Onyile and her mother agreed to bury her within two months. Onyile's mother embalmed the body, which was kept in the grandmother's bedroom "with no air conditioning in tropical Nigeria." The grandmother would be buried according to custom: in a vault in her bedroom. While some North Americans would be uncomfortable living in a home where someone is buried, in Nigeria it is an honor to have the body of a loved one entombed in a vault at home.

What conclusions can you draw about the different attitudes of Westerners and Nigerians toward death and dying?

I received a phone call from my mother in Nigeria on May 10 telling me that my grandmother died at 3 that morning. I asked her when we were having the funeral, and she said, "Whenever you are ready."

What an honor! I was spiritually and emotionally very close to my grandmother. I was named after her; she is the only other Nsedu that I know and that uniqueness means a lot to me. Our first name was all we had in common. She was very kind, could never hold a grudge, was always positive and just plain simple. I turned out to be her exact opposite.

In awe of this last humane being on earth, I spent my life taking up arms against anybody whose treatment of her was not up to par. My grandmother was a person whom you could not do a lot for when she was alive because of her simplicity. The opportunity to be responsible for her funeral made me feel blessed. We agreed on burying her within two months.

A Nigerian in America, my family at home is as important to me as my family here. I am a hard-working wife and mother whose fantasy in America is owning as much real estate as possible. We were working toward investing in a third house when the phone call about my grandmother came. I told my husband that her timing was rotten but, in all honesty, there is no perfect time to die.

Immediately, I started planning a funeral in Nigeria. The reaction of my American colleagues to the two-month wait reminded me that I am in a society where every aspect of death is generically regulated by law. After answering questions like, "How can you do that?" "Is it not illegal to keep a body at home for that long?" "Is she in a freezer?" I acquired a new level of respect for my mother's art of embalming.

I remember following my mother from house to house while she embalmed bodies that were awaiting family funeral plans. It was no big deal.

My dead grandmother at this moment is lying on her brass bed decorated with a lot of lace. She is in her bedroom with no air conditioning in tropical Nigeria. She will lie there until her burial on June 23. Her daughter, my mother, is responsible for the embalmment. I think one has to have a healthy view of death to keep one's mother embalmed for months.

I made numerous phone calls to Nigeria for three to four hours daily. We have all the details in place for a funeral befitting a 97-year-old mother, grandmother, great-grandmother and great-great-grandmother.

In my culture, we bury people on their private property. So we need to knock down the walls of her bedroom and expand it. A concrete vault will be built in the room.

We consider it a privilege to occupy a room where an important or beloved family member is buried. After the funeral, I will lock up the room and decide who will get the honor of occupying it when I am not there.

Some traditions I had forgotten: hiring professional mourners and feeding everybody who shows up—friends, family, enemies, whoever. Some traditions I had not learned before my departure 13 years ago, like notifying the local chief of the funeral plans with a basket full of presents.

We have reserved a big band and the church band. I ordered holographic pens in memory of grandmother. I would have liked bigger items, but two days ago when I was placing my order, my suitcases were filled.

All this planning has been emotionally satisfying. This is one of the few times I have truly enjoyed spending money despite our modest financial status. Other family members are contributing, too, which is appreciated but not necessary, as I feel a great sense of satisfaction pulling this one through financially.

When I was in graduate school, my favorite and most memorable course was "Death, Dying and Bereavement." We watched many tapes and studied numerous cultures on the subject. I really admired the cultures that celebrated the death of the aged person. I am convinced that those who accept the idea of death and dying as a natural phase of life possess a deeper appreciation for life and living.

I know of a culture in Africa that burns the bodies of its dead elders and mixes the ashes in a drink that is consumed by the living family members. That might be considered an extreme display of comfort with death by some. But so too might Western society's habit of establishing homes for the aged, and funeral homes that rush the bodies of the dead into the ground in a matter of days be considered a display of extreme discomfort with the issue of death and dying.

So while my American friends have questions about leaving my dead grandmother lying beautifully on her bed till June 23, I am wondering why families in America do not individualize funerals.

Meanwhile, I have my bags packed and can hardly wait for the day I leave for Nigeria to bury my grandmother.

Response and Analysis

1. According to Nsedu Onyile, what are the different attitudes toward death and dying among Westerners and Nigerians? What are the characteristics of Erikson's integrity versus despair stage of psychosocial development? Do you think this stage applies equally well to Westerners and Nigerians? Why or why not?

Personal Experience and Application

1. Are you more comfortable with the Western or Nigerian attitudes as presented in Onyile's essay? Why?

Research

Suppose you are interested in investigating attitudes toward burial practices in the United States. You decide to randomly select 1,500 Americans and ask them to complete your survey. First, define the following terms: sample, random selection, population. Second, who makes up the sample and population? How might you choose your participants?

chapter 8

MENTAL ABILITIES

*As I began to explain my ideas, [Einstein]
asked me to write the equations on the
blackboard so he could see how they
developed. Then came the staggering—and
altogether endearing—request: "Please go
slowly. I do not understand things quickly."
This from Einstein! He said it gently, and
I laughed. From then on, all vestiges of
fear were gone.*

BANESH HOFFMAN, "My Friend, Albert Einstein"

What is intelligence, and how do we work with the faculties we have been given?
This chapter looks at the following concepts: giftedness; mental retardation; theories
of intelligence; and the role intelligence tests may play in the year 2000.

Josh is a talented teenager who excels in all his subjects but whose passion is
math. A concern for many bright adolescents is that their giftedness may make them
seem like "completely weird" people. By participating in athletics and choosing
friends unlike himself, Josh works at keeping others from thinking him strange. He
also faces the dilemma of whether to choose a high-paying career or a less-well-
paying field but one that will benefit humankind.

S. I. Hayakawa writes about his son Mark, who was born with Down syndrome.
Hayakawa presents some of the challenges of raising his child at home, the
relationship between Mark and his brother and sister, and the activities the family
shares. He concludes: "It's a strange thing to say, and I am a little startled to find
myself saying it, but often I feel that I wouldn't have had Mark any different."

Richard Vigil, a mentally challenged individual, tells of his pain at being
institutionalized as a child, of missing his family, and of his hopes to have a job and
to marry. When he lived in institutions, Vigil would often run away; now at age
twenty-nine he lives in a group home and likes it. Vigil shares how he feels about
himself and what he would like in his future.

Many people excel in certain areas like math but struggle with verbal skills. John Philo Dixon describes how his varied talents posed a problem not only for himself but also for his teachers and family. It was not until he was in the ninth grade that "the long depression of elementary school ended." Then he found his forte with algebra, higher mathematics, and later with physics. Dixon says that when he was a child he thought his problem was "personal" and "endured it in silence." Now he knows that children who have a special ability should not be made to feel inadequate just because they can't do everything.

Will measurements of intelligence change much by the year 2000? Jerome M. Sattler offers the thoughts of several experts in the field, who note that intelligence tests are alive and well and that not only will computerized testing come into use, but the testing of different types of abilities may become commonplace.

TALENTED TEENAGERS

Mihaly Csikszentmihalyi, Kevin Rathunde, and Samuel Whalen

Psychological Concepts
giftedness, environmental influences on intelligence

How do talented teenagers spend their time? What attitudes do they have toward being talented? Josh, a bright high school student who loves math, does not want "to come across as brainy, or anything other than an average teenager." Josh experiences the conflict of many gifted teenagers. He wants to join his peers with their "'normal' interests and values"; yet he also wants to meet his parents' expectations that he develop his talents. In spite of his desire to be a typical teen, he spends a great deal of time with computers, in playing chess, and in solving math problems alone and with others. What are Josh's dreams? Do they differ from his parents' aspirations?

In most respects Josh's preferences and interests resemble those of other males his age. A freshman at his school, he participates in a broad range of sports and looks forward to his first taste of high school athletic competition. His conversation turns easily to cars, rock groups, and his favorite foods. He can't wait until he is old enough to get a driver's license. But in at least one way Josh is quite an extraordinary 14-year-old. For Josh possesses a truly exceptional gift for mathematics. He combines this gift with formidable abilities in language and science as well as in most other academic subjects he has attempted thus far.

Meeting Josh in person, one would not suspect him of being a gifted type, an impression that would please him. Describing himself as shy and easygoing, Josh seems determined not to come across as brainy, or anything other than an average teenager. Like most adolescents, he does not want to be recognized as outstanding by adult standards, lest he alienate his peers. "I try not to let things like school take over my whole life," he says, adding that in general he tries "not to take everything too seriously."

Math, he admits, has always been easy and natural for him and has never demanded much hard work. Accelerated into advanced mathematics classes since the second grade, he was more than a year ahead of his peers by sixth grade and successfully competed in regional math tournaments. He began freshman year in high school in an advanced junior section, studying college algebra and trigonometry. By sophomore year he had exhausted the school's considerable offerings in mathematics.

Although he is aware of the magnitude of his talent, Josh's goals reflect a conventional pattern of "good grades, college, preferably in California, and a high-paying job." Asked why he wants a good job, he replies, "I want not to have to worry about where everything is coming from—have enough to be comfortable." When confronted with a hypothetical choice between a job that was enjoyable, and one that paid a lot of money, Josh answered, "I'd like to think I'd choose to do what I'd like to do, but you never know."

He knows that in these plans for a comfortable future, math figures as his "strongest suit." But rarely does Josh show enthusiasm for mathematics in itself. In his interview answers, math is a part of the generally uninteresting province of school, a typically boring place that nonetheless provides occasional opportunities for recognition and display. Of the things he admits enjoying about math, competition with the school's math team stands out because it provides a sense that he "knows what he is doing," that he is in control of a problem. He especially enjoys the satisfaction of cracking a problem for the first time, particularly one that is complex and interesting.

Compared with the guarded enthusiasm of the interview, the record of responses to the Experience Sampling Method (ESM)* shows a different picture. Despite his blasé protestations, there is no question that mathematics takes up a great deal of Josh's attention and that it provides some of the most rewarding experiences of his young life. Over 25% of his pager responses during the week of ESM experimentation involve mathematics in some form. Most of these instances involve computers: playing chess against a PC, reading an article about computer poetry, trying to write a program that will play a rock song, watching a program "completely blow up." The highest moods he reported all week were on a Monday afternoon working hard on a problem with the math team. It was a session that combined enjoyment of the company of his friends with real interest in the elusive solution to the problem. When he is thinking about math Josh always reports a level of skills above the average, sometimes much above. He also tends to report high challenges when working with math, and these are usually matched to the level of reported skills. Generally his moods when working with the computer are also appreciably above the mean—in other words, for Josh doing mathematics is usually a flow experience.

So even though Josh wishes to appear "cool" about his talent and does not want to seem too serious about it, the domain of mathematics has succeeded in providing sufficient intrinsic reward to sustain his investing attention over extended periods of time. This exclusive investment of psychic energy, which is very rare in adolescence—or, for that matter, in adulthood—is necessary to reach the higher levels of proficiency in any domain. As Newton replied when asked how he developed

*Experience Sampling Method: a technique that allows researchers to associate daily events with moods and behaviors. Participants carry a pager; when it sounds (at predetermined intervals), the participants record their activities and complete a questionnaire.

the universal theory of gravitation, he did it "by thinking about it constantly." One cannot think all the time productively about something one does not enjoy.

But the task of cultivating talent does not rest on Josh's shoulders alone. As is the case with most of the other teenagers we studied, Josh's entire family acts as a support system to help him concentrate. His mother, especially, clearly expresses high hopes for her gifted son. Seeing him as a potential "astronaut, physicist, or astronomer," she is emphatic that he "should use his extraordinary gifts . . . to make the world a better place." She expects that he will earn a "doctorate in something that interests him" and hopes that "he'll be driven more by his interests than by large amounts of money."

The only cloud on the horizon, as far as Josh's mother is concerned, is the potentially harmful effect of peers. She worries that Josh is too sensitive and therefore emotionally fragile, and that his friends are more callous and superficial. On this issue Josh disagrees. Intent on becoming more friendly and outgoing, he has chosen these friends precisely because they "aren't really the smart, smart type," thus helping him avoid acting like "a complete weird person." Recently he joined one of these friends on the water polo team, a sport he finds enjoyable but that conflicts with the practice schedule of the math team.

Josh's case illustrates several of the dilemmas confronting young people with exceptional intellectual gifts. On the one hand, there is the attraction of the peer group with its "normal" interests and values; on the other hand, there are parents who expect ascetic dedication to the cultivation of talent. There is the attraction of making a lot of money in the future, counterbalanced by the possibility of helping make the world a better place. There is the enjoyment of being with friends and of doing sports, counterbalanced by the solitary enjoyment of solving difficult problems on the computer. To a certain extent these options are not mutually exclusive, and Josh does a good job of trying to do justice to them all. But attention is a limited resource, and in a 24-hour day he can concentrate on only so many things. How Josh allocates his attention in the 4 years of high school will determine to a large extent whether his outstanding mathematical talent will be realized or not.

Response and Analysis

1. Describe Josh's mathematical abilities. Briefly describe one of the challenges that face Josh and other intellectually gifted youth. Why is Josh's mother concerned that he might not use his intellectual gifts in the future?

2. How does Josh's home environment support the development of his academic abilities? Briefly discuss three environmental conditions that may be associated with high intelligence test scores.

Personal Experience and Application

1. Why might some teenagers make fun of other teenagers who have a passion for a scholarly subject and devote much time to the subject, but admire someone who works hard at being a guitar player or a football

player? Do you think that girls and boys hide their academic talents in order to be accepted by other teenagers? Why or why not?

2. Do you believe that schools may unknowingly discourage academically talented teenagers from using their talents? Why? How might the school staff and school policy motivate a student to use and enhance his or her academic gifts?

Research

Suppose you want to identify variables that promote cognitive development in children. List the environmental conditions that you believe may promote cognitive development. Choose one of the variables on your list. Briefly discuss one way to determine whether this variable promotes cognitive development.

OUR SON MARK

S. I. Hayakawa

and

I DON'T GET LOST VERY OFTEN

Richard Vigil

Psychological Concepts
Down syndrome, mental retardation

In the following two selections, S. I. Hayakawa and Richard Vigil write about mental retardation from two different perspectives. Hayakawa presents the view of a parent whose son has Down syndrome; Richard Vigil tells about his own life as a person with mental retardation. One striking difference is that Mark's family decided to keep him at home, whereas Richard's family placed him in an institution. Severity of retardation, family resources, and community pressures may all affect the decision of whether to keep a child at home.

What are Mark and Richard capable of learning? What do others teach them by their attitudes and care? Hayakawa says his son responds to how others measure him, and that because he has been loved and accepted by his family, he has learned to feel good about himself and is a pleasure to live with.

Can either Mark or Richard hold jobs? What chores are they able to do? Both are impressive in what they have learned and are capable of doing, and both are able to hold deep affection for others.

It was a terrible blow for us to discover that we had brought a retarded child into the world. My wife and I had had no previous acquaintance with the problems of retardation—not even with the words to discuss it. Only such words as imbecile, idiot, and moron came to mind. And the prevailing opinion was that such a child must be "put away," to live out his life in an institution.

Mark was born with Down's syndrome, popularly known as mongolism. The prognosis for his ever reaching anything approaching normality was hopeless. Medical authorities advised us that he would show some mental development, but the progress would be painfully slow and he would never reach an adolescent's mental age. We could do nothing about it, they said. They sympathetically but firmly advised us to find a private institution that would take him. To get him into a public institution, they said, would require a waiting period of five years. To keep him at home for this length of time, they warned, would have a disastrous effect on our family.

That was twenty-seven years ago. In that time, Mark has never been "put away." He has lived at home. The only institution he sees regularly is the workshop he attends, a special workshop for retarded adults. He is as much a part of the family as his mother, his older brother, his younger sister, his father, or our longtime housekeeper and friend, Daisy Rosebourgh.

Mark has contributed to our stability and serenity. His retardation has brought us grief, but we did not go on dwelling on what might have been, and we have been rewarded by finding much good in things the way they are. From the beginning, we have enjoyed Mark for his delightful self. He has never seemed like a burden. He was an "easy" baby, quiet, friendly, and passive; but he needed a baby's care for a long time. It was easy to be patient with him, although I must say that some of his stages, such as his love of making chaos, as we called it, by pulling all the books he could reach off the shelves, lasted much longer than normal children's.

Mark seems more capable of accepting things as they are than his immediate relatives; his mental limitation has given him a capacity for contentment, a focus on the present moment, which is often enviable. His world may be circumscribed, but it is a happy and bright one. His enjoyment of simple experiences—swimming, food, birthday candles, sports-car rides, and cuddly cats—has that directness and intensity so many philosophers recommend to all of us.

Mark's contentment has been a happy contribution to our family, and the challenge of communicating with him, of doing things we can all enjoy, has drawn the family together. And seeing Mark's communicative processes develop in slow motion has taught me much about the process in all children.

Fortunately Mark was born at a time when a whole generation of parents of retarded children had begun to question the accepted dogmas about retardation. Whatever they were told by their physicians about their children, parents began to ask: "Is that so? Let's see." For what is meant by "retarded child"? There are different kinds of retardation. Retarded child No. 1 is not retarded child No. 2, or 3, or 4. Down's syndrome is one condition, while brain damage is something else. There are different degrees of retardation, just as there are different kinds of brain damage. No two retarded children are exactly alike in all respects. Institutional care *does* turn out to be the best answer for some kinds of retarded children or some family situations. The point is that one observes and reacts to the *specific* case and circumstances rather than to the generalization.

This sort of attitude has helped public understanding of the nature and problems of retardation to become much deeper and more widespread. It's hard to believe now that it was "definitely known" twenty years ago that institutionalization was the "only way." We were told that a retarded child could not be kept at home because "it would not be fair to the other children." The family would not be able to stand the stress. "Everybody" believed these things and repeated them, to comfort and guide the parents of the retarded.

We did not, of course, lightly disregard the well-meant advice of university neurologists and their social-worker teams, for they had had much experience and we were new at this shattering experience. But our general semantics, or our parental feelings, made us aware that their reaction to Mark was to a generalization, while to us he was an individual. They might have a valid generalization about statistical stresses on statistical families, but they knew virtually nothing about our particular family and its evaluative processes.

Mark was eight months old before we were told he was retarded. Of course we had known that he was slower than the average child in smiling, in sitting up, in responding to others around him. Having had one child who was extraordinarily ahead of such schedules, we simply thought that Mark was at the other end of the average range. . . .

It was parents who led the way: They organized into parents' groups; they pointed out the need for preschools, schools, diagnostic centers, work-training centers, and sheltered workshops to serve the children who were being cared for at home; they worked to get these services, which are now being provided in increasing numbers. But the needs are a long way from being fully met.

Yet even now the cost in money—not to mention the cost in human terms—is much less if the child is kept at home than if he is sent to the institutions in which children are put away. And many of the retarded are living useful and independent lives, which would never have been thought possible for them.

But for us at that time, as for other parents who were unknowingly pioneering new ways for the retarded, it was a matter of going along from day to day, learning, observing, and saying, "Let's see." . . .

Our daughter, Wynne, is now twenty-five. She started as Mark's baby sister, passed him in every way, and really helped bring him up. The fact that she had a retarded brother must have contributed at least something to the fact that she is at once delightfully playful and mature, observant, and understanding. She has a fine relationship with her two brothers.

Both Wynne and Alan, Mark's older brother, have participated, with patience and delight, in Mark's development. They have shown remarkable ingenuity in instructing and amusing him. On one occasion, when Mark was not drinking his milk, Alan called him to his place at the table and said, "I'm a service station. What kind of car are you?" Mark, quickly entering into the make-believe, said, "Pord."

Alan: "Shall I fill her up?"

Mark: "Yes."

Alan: "Ethyl or regular?"

Mark: "Reg'lar."

Alan (bringing the glass to Mark's mouth): "Here you are."

When Mark finished his glass of milk, Alan asked him, "Do you want your windshield cleaned?" Then, taking a napkin, he rubbed it briskly across Mark's face, while Mark grinned with delight. This routine became a regular game for many weeks.

Alan and Wynne interpret and explain Mark to their friends, but never once have I heard them apologize for him or deprecate him. It is almost as if they judge the quality of other people by how they react to Mark. They think he is "great," and expect their friends to think so too. . . .

What does [the] future hold for Mark?

He will never be able to be independent; he will always have to live in a protected environment. His below-50 IQ reflects the fact that he cannot cope with unfamiliar situations.

Like most parents of the retarded, we are concentrating on providing financial security for Mark in the future, and fortunately we expect to be able to achieve this. Alan and his wife and Wynne have all offered to be guardians for Mark. It is wonderful to know they feel this way. But we hope that Mark can find a happy place in one of the new residence homes for the retarded.

The residence home is something new and promising and it fills an enormous need. It is somewhat like a club, or a family, with a house-mother or manager. The residents share the work around the house, go out to work if they can, share in recreation and companionship. Away from their families, who may be overprotective and not aware of how much the retarded can do for themselves (are we not guilty of this, too!), they are able to live more fully as adults.

An indication that there is still much need for public education about the retarded here in California is that there has been difficulty in renting decent houses for this kind of home. Prospective neighbors have objected. In some ways the Dark Ages are still with us; there are still fear and hostility where the retarded are concerned.

Is Mark able to work? Perhaps. He thrives on routine and enjoys things others despise, like clearing the table and loading the dishwasher. To Mark, it's fun. It has been hard to develop in him the idea of work, which to so many of us is "doing what you don't want to do because you have to." We don't know yet if he could work in a restaurant loading a dishwasher. In school, he learned jobs like sorting and stacking scrap wood and operating a delightful machine that swoops the string around and ties up a bundle of wood to be sold in the supermarket. That's fun, too.

He is now in a sheltered workshop where he can get the kind—the one kind—of pleasure he doesn't have much chance for. That's the pleasure of contributing something productive and useful to the outside world. He does various kinds of assembling jobs, packaging, sorting, and simple machine operations. He enjoys getting a paycheck and cashing it at the bank. He cannot count, but he takes pride in reaching for the check in a restaurant and pulling out his wallet. And when we thank him for dinner, he glows with pleasure.

It's a strange thing to say, and I am a little startled to find myself saying it, but often I feel that I wouldn't have had Mark any different.

I'm twenty-nine years old now, and I like the place I live and I like my job. I have a girlfriend, and I love her very much. I hope that we can get married someday, but we have a lot of work to do first, mostly work about how to handle money and take care of an apartment.

I live in a group home, and I am learning a lot about those things now. I have to try things over and over and over again, but I don't remember ever trying to learn something and finding out that I couldn't learn it. Except playing the piano. I just couldn't do it, but I am going to try again someday. It takes a long time for me to learn something, but I just keep on trying.

When I was a little kid I lived in an institution. I hated it. I especially hated this one teacher in the school there who told me that I couldn't learn. I thought I was in the school to learn, and I thought the teacher should help me instead of telling me that I couldn't do it. I told my parents when they came to visit me, and they got angry with the teacher. After that I got a chance to show her that I could learn things.

But I hated living there, and I ran away when I was older. I ran away more than once. They can't make me stay there. I won't live there because I don't like it and I don't think I have to.

---

*Note: This second selection is written by Richard Vigil.

I feel free the way I live now. I go to work, I come back to the group home. I can go to see my girlfriend. Or I can go out to the movies. I get all around on the bus. I learned to ride the buses when I was in a sheltered workshop. They taught me. If I want to go someplace I've never been before I call the bus company offices and ask how to get there. Then I just try it out. Or I ask the bus drivers. Some are nice and some aren't. I don't get lost very often.

One of my favorite things to do is to go downtown at Christmas and see the parade and all the Christmas decorations. I know that they're for little kids, but I see a lot of grownups down there too. I really love Christmas. That was the happiest time I remember with my family. I don't see my family anymore. I miss them. I know that my mother didn't want to send me away, but I think that my brothers and sisters didn't want me around because they thought I couldn't learn anything.

I don't like to be called "retarded" because it means something bad to most people. I know it just means "slow-learning," but it doesn't mean anything to me in my own situation. What is M.R. anyway? It's just another word. We might be slow learners, but we're just as good as anybody.

I hope I have a kid someday. I really love kids, and I'd do anything to help them. If I had a retarded kid I'd love him and help him to learn things because I'd do anything in the world to help little kids. I think I would be a good father because I'd love my kid.

Response and Analysis

1. In what ways has Mark positively contributed to his family? How do Mark's siblings treat him? S. I. Hayakawa suggests that the public has had misconceptions about mental retardation. What are some of them?

2. People with IQ scores between 50 and 70 are considered mildly retarded, and those with scores between 35 and 49 are considered moderately retarded. People with IQ scores less than 70 may have difficulty communicating and performing tasks that are expected of people their age. Mark's IQ score is less than 50. Briefly discuss Mark's ability to perform tasks, communicate, and live on his own.

Personal Experience and Application

1. Were you ever chided or laughed at if you did not learn something fast enough to suit someone else? If so, how did that make you feel? Why do you think children, and even adults, sometimes make fun of people or deride them if they do not learn quickly?

2. Richard dreams of getting married and having a child of his own. What factors are important to consider in deciding about marriage? About having a child?

Research

Suppose you develop a test to assess verbal skills (e.g., the ability to define words, the ability to understand and answer questions). You want to know if the test is reliable. You individually test twenty children who are six years old. Two weeks later, you readminister the same test to the same children. You find that the scores were higher for all of the children on the second test than on the first test. Why might this have occurred?

THE SPATIAL CHILD

John Philo Dixon

Psychological Concepts
theories of intelligence, verbal and quantitative ability

What happens to children when they have slower learning skills in some areas? How do they feel about themselves? John Philo Dixon, now the research director for the American Shakespeare Theater, had to wait until he was in the ninth grade before he dared believe that he wasn't inferior is some way. He recalls how not being a good reader in the first grade made him feel "defective." He had become a "problem child" to his teacher, then his parents, and finally to himself. Would he make it into or out of second grade? These are heavy burdens for a child, burdens that left him with fears that still affect him.

Most impressive, however, are the talents which Dixon does have and which for too long went unrecognized. To what extent did motivation and desire influence Dixon's ultimate achievements in school?

I t was a combination of mystification and depression that set in when Mrs. Wilson struggled at introducing me to reading in the first grade. As I looked around at my classmates, their ease at turning written words into the correct spoken words seemed to make them coconspirators. They possessed a secret wisdom to which I was not privy. Mrs. Wilson looked upon them with eyes of pleasure. They were her teacher's delight, her measure of success. She looked upon me with eyes of forlorn patience. I was the stumbling block in her attempt to deliver a class full of readers to the second grade teachers. I remember sitting bent low at my school desk, eyes downward, hoping not to be noticed as I bumbled over *Dick and Jane*.

Panic struck me when my mother had to visit school to talk about my difficulties. My mother had never had doubts about me. I could run, I could talk, I could play games, I could build things, I could sing—all those things that mark normalcy to a hopeful mother. Mrs. Wilson had found me defective, and I had become a problem child, even to those who were most dear to me. My mother's visit to Mrs. Wilson also caused terror in the confusion of my child's mind. I feared that my unused schemes to cheat on spelling tests—a strategic planning undertaken in the desire to avoid being lowest in the class—might have been found out. Perhaps Mrs. Wilson in her infinite wisdom could even read into the hearts of little boys. However, the conference had only to do with my incompetence. My mother sat beside

Mrs. Wilson, and I sat at my desk across the otherwise empty room. My ears strained to hear bits and pieces of the litany of my problems. Mrs. Wilson concluded that I wasn't prepared to go on to second grade. Flunking was the ultimate stigma for a school child in rural Nebraska. It would have put my self-regard at the lowest of levels. To my everlasting gratitude, things weren't left at that. A deal was struck between Mrs. Wilson and my mother. I would only be allowed to enter second grade in the fall if my mother gave me special instruction in reading for the whole summer vacation. My mother's reading lessons had little more effect than those of Mrs. Wilson. I tried, but reading wasn't yet in me.

I entered second grade as much a nonreader as before, but thanked my lucky stars that I had made it, and braced for another year of being the uninformed outsider in a society of secret code decipherers. Sometime during the second grade I began to catch on to reading, and I don't remember being in serious threat of flunking after that. My school performance settled into the slow-poke category for most of elementary school. There were a few breaks in this eight-year stint of questionable reputation. There was the day the second grade teacher asked several students to make a line a yard long on the chalkboard without looking at the yard stick. Mine came closest to being the right length. The teacher hardly noticed this insignificant victory of one of her more unpromising students, but for me it was one of those rare triumphs that stands etched in my mind.

My third grade teacher told my mother there was a lot going on in my mind. How did she guess? In the small town in which I grew up, the "farmerish" wisdom of silence would occasionally be applied to me; more than a few times people would take note of my basically unspoken character and say, "Still water runs deep." I never did know how to take that. Was deep good or bad?

There was the week in Miss Reine's fourth grade class. I was allowed to help construct a model colonial village. I made houses, a stockade, and an intricate little spinning wheel. It was the most glorious week in elementary school. As far as I was concerned, it could have gone on forever. However, then it was necessary to move on to the "real" work of school. Miss Reine told me that I couldn't work on the model any more because I had spent too much time and gotten behind in my school work.

Throughout these eight years there was an interesting discrepancy. Although my reading never changed from a slow to halting pace, I nevertheless loved reading. Sometimes I would spend every minute possible devouring whole sets of books from the library bookcase in the back of the classroom; slowly, ruminatingly, but devouring. There was no way my reading could be rushed. Deep twinges of anguish accompanied speed reading drills. I would pretend to be reading faster than I could because I didn't want to be the last student to raise his hand to indicate being finished. Most of all I hated reading tests. If I didn't rush through tests much faster than I could possibly comprehend the material, I would find myself far from the end of the test when the time was called. Yet there were times when I spent all the time I could reading. Books were the entry way to the larger world. The ideas in books were marvelous even if my reading mechanics were tortuous. The ideas in books came to be an important focus of my life, and I would learn to put up with the difficulty for the sake of learning.

Crude drawing was something I did through my childhood, even though I don't remember ever having an art class or being encouraged in any way. In the early grades I would draw what I thought of as the structures of buildings; the beam patterns of skyscrapers and things like that. I was sort of embarrassed for doing these sketches because I didn't know why I wanted to. . . . I just did. Later I took up making crude architectural plans for buildings. I enjoyed music, sang in the chorus, and played different instruments in the band. Music was in me, and if I weren't so shy, I might have been a good musical performer, although I never learned to read music very well.

When I entered algebra class in the ninth grade, the long depression of elementary school ended. Algebra was fascinating to me from the moment I encountered it. In algebra I was the best in my class, and it wasn't just a momentary triumph like when I drew the most accurate length of a yard stick in second grade. My triumph in algebra stuck. In geometry and physics, I was even better. For the physics class in eleventh grade my school was participating in a statewide experiment to see whether instruction through a set of movies was better than regular instruction. My school had regular instruction and my teacher, Mr. Kasle, was good. As a part of the experiment, every other week we would take a special test, which would be sent to a university for scoring. When the scores came back, I would be several points above anyone else in the class. Having lived through the nightmare of the elementary school, I savored every moment of these victories, but savored them in trepidation that they were somehow a fluke, in fear that my incompetencies would descend upon me and I would once again fail. I live in fear of that to this day. It is not easy to free oneself of eight years of degradation when it is experienced at an age too young to have had a chance to know that success is also possible.

Sometime in the ninth grade my class was given a nonverbal IQ test. I don't know exactly how I scored on this test, but there were hints that I had done very well, and after the testing, I was accorded much more respect by my school teachers than before. Had the IQ test been a verbal one, the results, of course, would have been entirely opposite and I would have been seen as anything but brilliant.

There was no program for gifted children in the high school, but the teachers seemed to sense my need and arranged for me to take a correspondence course in advanced algebra. I received a text book in the mail along with my first assignment. I would do my assignments, send them off to the university, and receive them back corrected along with the next assignment. This solitary exercise in doing lists of algebra problems for a disembodied tutor did little to spark my imagination. Though I appreciate the good intention on my behalf in making this arrangement, I would most likely have been better off spending some extra time with Mr. Kasle, the local science teacher who seemed to have a good scientific mind.

The discrepancies in my abilities have persisted. When I took the Graduate Record Exams (GRE) at the completion of undergraduate school, my mathematics score was in the top 2 percent, while my verbal score was just barely in the top quarter. This difference has continually resulted in what to others may seem like an uneven performance. To the extent that tasks depend on a careful understanding of the spatial-mechanical world around me, I usually do quite well. To the extent that it depends on quick verbal analysis, my performance can seem debilitated.

As a child I thought of my problem as personal, and I endured it in silence. Now I cannot be so generous. I see no reason that children who have considerable ability of a distinct kind should be taught that they are inadequate, if not stupid.

Response and Analysis

1. Briefly describe John Dixon's reading difficulties and his mathematical and spatial ability. What did the Graduate Record Exam suggest about his verbal and quantitative ability? Why does Dixon fear that his success with mathematics and physics may be due to chance?

2. Which theoretical approach to intelligence argues for the presence of spatial intelligence? Briefly summarize this theoretical perspective.

Personal Experience and Application

1. What types of academic experiences in elementary or secondary school might cause some children to develop low self-esteem? How might these experiences affect an individual's sense of self when he or she becomes an adult?

2. What environmental factors do you think nourish or hinder intellectual development? Why?

Research

Suppose you want to investigate whether the gender of a test administrator influences a child's performance on an intelligence test. You hypothesize that children will receive higher IQ scores when the test is administered by someone of the same gender than by someone of the opposite gender. What is the research, or alternative, hypothesis? What is the null hypothesis? Imagine that you conduct the study and find that the children's scores are the same regardless of the test administrator's gender. Would you accept or reject the research hypothesis? Would you accept or reject the null hypothesis?

INTELLIGENCE TESTS IN THE FUTURE

Jerome M. Sattler

Psychological Concept
intelligence tests

Will intelligence tests change by the turn of the century? What new tests might evolve and for what purposes? Jerome M. Sattler offers the opinions of several experts in the field. John Horn hopes that the tests will "provide for measurements of many separate abilities." Lauren B. Resnick points to the continuing need for assessment of the mentally handicapped, and Ann L. Brown and Lucia A. French hope to predict school failure before it occurs. Other experts agree that computer-controlled testing will continue to evolve.

John Horn   Realistic appraisal, based on historical analysis, suggests that in the year 2000 the tests used to measure intellectual abilities in applied settings will be very similar to the tests used today and 40 years ago. However, if the technology of measurement for applied purposes follows advancements in scientific understanding of human intelligence, then we can expect that intelligence tests of the future:

1. will be architectonically structured* to provide for measurements of many separate abilities, ranging from very elementary processes to broad but distinct dimensions of intelligence;
2. will involve, perhaps be focused on, abilities to comprehend and assimilate information that comes to one via the continuous flow of TV-like presentations;
3. will contain subtests designed to indicate features of temporal integration of information, auditory organization, and elementary cognitive processing of information;
4. will derive more from the study of adulthood development than from the study of childhood development.

The mainstreams of cognitive psychology will be diverted more and more into the study of intelligence and thus will influence the shape of practical tests. Tests

---

*Architectonically structured: a systematic, scientific measurement.

will be used less and less to measure global intelligence just for the sake of measuring it, or to make invidious distinctions, but more testing will be done to help identify particular ability strengths and weaknesses. Theory about intelligence will improve and more test construction will be based on sound theory.

Lauren B. Resnick   What is the likelihood that IQ tests as we currently know them will still be in use in the schools at the turn of the century? . . . What new kinds of tests of aptitude and intelligence can we reasonably look for? . . . IQ tests, or some very similar kind of assessment instrument, are likely to be functionally necessary in the schools as long as the present form of special education for the mentally handicapped remains with us—or until we are prepared to spend substantially more public resources on education for all children than we are now doing. Further, I have suggested that there is a very real possibility of a *revival* of interest in IQ tests in the educational mainstream as a protective response by school people threatened with legal responsibility for ensuring that all children, even the very hard-to-teach, learn. I believe these two areas—special education and the school's legal responsibility—are the things to watch over the next twenty years for new developments in global IQ measurement. . . .

What new kinds of tests can we expect? I have suggested the possibility of a serious shift in the science and therefore the technology of intelligence testing. Aptitude tests useful for monitoring instruction and adapting it to individual differences are essentially nonexistent today. Current work on the cognitive analysis of intelligence and aptitude tests may be able to provide the basis for much more systematic and refined matching of instructional treatments to aptitudes within two decades. We can particularly look forward to this development as work on the cognitive components of intelligence shifts attention from performance on the tests themselves to the *learning* processes that underlie both skillful test performance and skillful performance in school subject matters.

Ann L. Brown and Lucia A. French   By the year 2000 we would like to see an extension of the predictive power of intelligence tests so that we are able to (a) predict school failure prior to its occurrence and (b) predict potential adult competence by a consideration of performance on tests of everyday reasoning. To achieve these ends we will need to invest considerable energy in ethnographic surveys and experimental testing programs directed at improving our scanty knowledge in two main areas. First we need sensitive indices of early cognitive (in)competence that are related to subsequent academic intelligence. Secondly we need theories and measures of functional literacy, minimal competence, and mundane cognition, so that we can begin to predict life adaptation as well as academic success.

We would also like to see an increased emphasis on the diagnosis and remediation of cognitive deficits, of both the academic and everyday variety.

William W. Turnbull   My view . . . is that over the next 20 years or so we are likely to see evolutionary rather than quantum changes in intelligence tests, at least as they are used in academic settings. We are likely to see tests that provide separate scores on a variety of abilities. They are likely to be standard scores. The ratio defining the IQ may by then have been abandoned everywhere and the term IQ may have disappeared into psychological and educational history.

Norman Frederiksen   Realistic simulations of real-life problem situations might be used to supplement the usual psychological tests and thus to contribute to the database needed to develop a broader conception of intelligence. It is possible to develop scoring systems that describe intelligent behavior in ways that go far beyond the *number right* score, that make possible the measurement of qualitative variables, such as problem-solving strategies and styles, and that may even provide information about some of the information-processing components of intelligent behavior. Many of the scores based on simulations are reliable, their interrelationships are consistent across different groups of subjects, and some of them predict real-life criteria that are not well predicted by conventional tests. . . .

Our glimpse of a broader picture of human intelligence suggests that the structure of intellect of the future will include a much broader spectrum of intelligent behaviors. Furthermore, it will not be a static model but will be one that recognizes the interactions involving test formats, subject characteristics, and the settings in which the problems are encountered. The structure of intelligence is not necessarily a fixed structure but one that may vary as the subjects learn and as the circumstances are altered.

Earl Hunt and James Pellegrino   Microcomputers can serve as automated testing stations for use in psychometric assessment. There are economic advantages in conducting aptitude and intelligence testing with such stations. Is it possible to improve the quality of cognitive assessment by extending the range of cognitive abilities to be assessed? Two types of extension are considered: modifying and expanding testing procedures for psychological functions that are components of conventional tests, and the extension of testing to psychological functions not generally assessed by conventional intelligence or aptitude tests. Computerized presentations will make relatively little difference in our ways of testing verbal comprehension. Computer-controlled testing could well extend the ways in which we evaluate spatial-visual reasoning and memory. The impact of testing on the evaluation of reasoning is unclear. Computer-controlled item presentation makes it possible to conceive of tests of learning and attention, neither of which is evaluated in most psychometric programs today.

Response and Analysis

1. How might the concept and measurement of intelligence change in the future? How might the use of intelligence tests change?

2. Why are intelligence tests currently used? The most widely used intelligence tests in schools today are the Wechsler test and the Stanford-Binet. What aspects of mental ability do they measure?

Personal Experience and Application

1. Have you taken an intelligence test? Briefly describe your experience. Do you think your

performance on the test was a fair reflection of your intelligence? Why or why not?

2. Do you believe that intelligence tests are culturally biased? Why or why not? What measures should be taken to protect tests against cultural bias?

Research

Suppose you conduct a study to examine the relationship between intelligence test score and high school grade point average. You find a correlation coefficient of +0.50. Could you conclude that IQ score *leads* to high school grade point average? What factors other than IQ score may influence students' performance in high school?

chapter *9*

MOTIVATION AND
EMOTION

*Itzaak Perlman, born to an unmusical
family in Israel, is said to have heard, at
age three, a broadcast of a concerto being
played by Jascha Heifetz. He kept pointing
to the radio when the violin was heard,
saying "I want that!" until his parents
understood; they enrolled him with a
private tutor to learn to play the
instrument. Despite having become partly
paralyzed, Perlman is considered one of the
great virtuosi of his time.*

MIHALY CSIKSZENTMIHALYI, *Talented Teenagers*

What motivates us? What is the connection between emotion and motivation? Several key concepts help us understand this connection: the effect of hormones; hierarchy of needs; eating disorders; intrinsic and extrinsic motivation; and need for achievement.

Although D. H. was a good football player, he was not as muscular as some of the other players and so was eager to take steroids to increase his size. He describes his desires and discloses the negative effects steroids had on him both psychologically and physically.

Miguel Torres repeatedly crosses illegally into the United States from Mexico. He explains his reasons and hopes of becoming a United States citizen. What drives Torres, in the face of continual deportation and fines, to keep returning?

Sally, an attractive and successful businesswoman, tells her story of obsession with food and with being thin. She develops bulimia and tries to hide her condition from family and friends. Eventually, she is caught between her desire to be thin and her desire to restore her health.

When Annie Dillard receives her first microscope, she is eager to see wildlife. What she wants most is to see the amoeba, but it does not turn up readily. When she finally gets puddle water and finds the amoeba under the microscope, she is elated. Dillard wants to share her discovery with her parents, but they decide not to join her. How does Dillard feel when she is left alone with no one to share her excitement? Does she lose interest and become less motivated?

DYING TO BE BIGGER

D. H.

Psychological Concepts
hormones, testosterone

What motivates a person to achieve a goal even at the risk of endangering his or her health? At age fifteen, D. H. is so determined to be a football star that he uses steroids to increase his size and prowess. Ignoring the prescribed dosage, he swallows five pills a day. Within weeks D. H. notices unpleasant physical and emotional changes; he eventually becomes overly aggressive and, as his condition worsens, almost sterile. With the help of his parents, D. H. quits using steroids for a year. But what happens when he enters college and has as his roommate a six-foot-three, 250-pound linebacker? What adjustment problems does he experience after he quits taking steroids?

I was only fifteen years old when I first started maiming my body with the abuse of anabolic steroids. I was always trying to fit in with the "cool" crowd in junior high and high school. Willingly smoking or buying pot when offered, socially drinking in excess, displaying a macho image—and, of course, the infamous "kiss and tell" were essentials in completing my insecure mentality.

Being an immature, cocky kid from a somewhat wealthy family, I wasn't very well liked in general. In light of this, I got beat up a lot, especially in my first year of public high school.

I was one of only three sophomores to get a varsity letter in football. At five-foot-nine and 174 pounds, I was muscularly inferior to the guys on the same athletic level and quite conscious of the fact. So when I heard about this wonderful drug called steroids from a teammate, I didn't think twice about asking to buy some. I could hardly wait to take them and start getting bigger.

I bought three months' worth of Dianobol (an oral form of steroids and one of the most harmful). I paid fifty-five dollars. I was told to take maybe two or three per day. I totally ignored the directions and warnings and immediately started taking five per day. This is how eager I was to be bigger and possibly "cooler."

Within only a week, everything about me started to change. I was transforming mentally and physically. My attention span became almost nonexistent. Along with becoming extremely aggressive, I began to abandon nearly all academic and family responsibilities. In almost no time, I became flustered and agitated with simple everyday activities. My narcissistic ways brought me to engage in verbal as well as physical fights with family, friends, teachers, but mostly strangers.

My bodily transformations were clearly visible. In less than a month, I took the entire three-month supply. I gained nearly thirty pounds. Most of my weight was from water retention, although at the time I believed it to be muscle. Instead of having pimples like the average teenager, my acne took the form of grotesque, cystlike blood clots that would occasionally burst while I was lifting weights. My nipples became the size of grapes and hurt severely, which is common among male steroid users. My hormonal level was completely out of whack.

At first I had such an overload of testosterone that I would have to masturbate daily, at minimum, in order to prevent having "wet dreams." Obviously these factors enhanced my lust, which eventually led to acute perversion. My then almost-horrifying physique prevented me from having any sexual encounters.

All of these factors led to my classification as a wretched menace. My parents grew sick and tired of all the trouble I began to get in. They were scared of me, it seemed. They cared so much about my welfare, education, and state of mind that they sent me to a boarding school that summer.

I could not obtain any more steroids there, and for a couple of months it seemed I had subtle withdrawal symptoms and severe side effects. Most of the time that summer I was either depressed or filled with intense anger, both of which were uncontrollable unless I was in a state of intoxication from any mind-altering drug.

After a year of being steroid-free, things started to look promising for me, and I eventually gained control over myself. Just when I started getting letters from big-name colleges to play football for them, I suffered a herniated disc. I was unable to participate in any form of physical activity the entire school year.

In the fall, I attended a university in the Northeast, where I was on the football team but did not play due to my injury. I lifted weights with the team every day. I wasn't very big at the time, even after many weeks of working out. Once again I found myself to be physically inferior and insecure about my physique. And again came into contact with many teammates using steroids.

My roommate was a six-foot-three, 250-pound linebacker who played on the varsity squad as a freshman. As the weeks passed, I learned of my roommate's heavy steroid use. I was exposed to dozens of different steroids I had never even heard of. Living in the same room with him, I watched his almost daily injections. After months of enduring his drug offerings, I gave in.

By the spring of my freshman year, I had become drastically far from normal in every way. My body had stopped producing hormones due to the amount of synthetic testosterone I injected into my system. At five-foot-eleven, 225 pounds, disproportionately huge, acne-infested, outrageously aggressive, and nearing complete sterility, I was in a terrible state of body and mind. Normal thoughts of my future (not pertaining to football), friends, family, reputation, moral status, etc., were entirely beyond me. My whole entire essence had become one of a primitive barbarian. This was when I was taking something called Sustunon (prepackaged in a syringe labeled "For equine use only") containing four types of testosterone. I was "stacking" (a term used by steroid users which means mixing different types) to get well-cut definition along with mass.

It was around this time when I was arrested for threatening a security guard. When the campus police came to arrest me, they saw how aggressive and large my roommate and I were. So they searched our room and found dozens of bottles and hundreds of dollars' worth of steroids and syringes. We had a trial, and the outcome was that I could only return the next year if I got drug-tested on a monthly basis. I certainly had no will power or desire to quit my steroid abuse, so I transferred schools.

After a summer of even more heavy-duty abuse, I decided to attend a school that would cater to my instinctively backward ways. That fall I entered a large university in the South. Once again I simply lifted weights without being involved in competition or football. It was there that I finally realized how out of hand I'd become with my steroid problem.

Gradually I started to taper down my dosages. Accompanying my reduction, I began to drink more and more. My grades plummeted again. I began going to bars and keg parties on a nightly basis.

My celibacy, mental state, aggressiveness, lack of athletic competition, and alcohol problem brought me to enjoy passing my pain onto others by means of physical aggression. I got into a fight almost every time I drank. In the midst of my insane state, I was arrested for assault. I was in really deep this time. Finally I realized how different from everybody else I'd become, and I decided not to taper off but to quit completely.

The average person seems to think that steroids just make you bigger. But they are a drug, and an addictive one at that. This drug does not put you in a stupor or in a hallucinogenic state but rather gives you an up, all-around "bad-ass" mentality that far exceeds that of either normal life or any other narcotic I've tried when not taking steroids. Only lately are scientists and researchers discovering how addictive steroids are—only now, after hundreds of thousands may have done such extreme damage to their lives, bodies, and minds.

One of the main components of steroid addiction is how unsatisfied the user is with his overall appearance. Although I was massive and had dramatic muscular definition, I was never content with my body, despite frequent compliments. I was always changing types of steroids, places of injection, workouts, diet, etc. I always found myself saying, "This one oughta do it" or "I'll quit when I hit 230 pounds."

When someone is using steroids, he has psychological disorders that increase when usage stops. One disorder is anxiety from the loss of the superior feeling you get from the drug. Losing the muscle mass, high energy level, and superhuman sensation that you're so accustomed to is terrifying.

Another ramification of taking artificial testosterone over time is the effect on the natural testosterone level (thus the male sex drive). As a result of my steroid use, my natural testosterone level was ultimately depleted to the point where my sex drive was drastically reduced in comparison to the average twenty-one-year-old male. My testicles shriveled up, causing physical pain as well as extreme mental anguish. Thus I desired girls less. This however did lead me to treat them as people, not as objects of my desires. It was a beginning step on the way to a more sane and civil mentality.

The worst symptoms of my withdrawal after many months of drug abuse were emotional. My emotions fluctuated dramatically, and I rapidly became more sensitive. My hope is that this feeling of being trailed by isolation and aloneness will diminish and leave me free of its constant haunting.

Response and Analysis

1. Why did D. H. continue using anabolic steroids even when he knew they were harmful for him? D. H. writes that he was in a "terrible state of mind and body" when using steroids. What physical problems did he experience? What psychological problems?

2. How did excessive use of steroids affect D. H.'s sexual interest and behavior? Why? How do masculine and feminine sex hormones (androgens and estrogens) affect sexual behavior after puberty? How can lack of testosterone production influence sexual interest and behavior in males?

Personal Experience and Application

1. What pressures to conform to a particular group's style of appearance and behavior did you feel in high school? Did you give in to any of these pressures? Why? When might conformity be harmful? When might conformity be helpful?

2. D. H. reported that his school would only let him return if he had a drug test every month. What penalties do you believe should be brought against athletes at your school who use steroids? Do you think penalties can deter the use of steroids?

Research

Suppose you want to know if people who use steroids have low self-esteem and tend to be depressed. You must decide whether you want to develop a questionnaire to assess self-esteem and depression or to use existing questionnaires whose reliability and validity are known. What are the advantages and disadvantages of using existing questionnaires or developing your own questionnaire?

FROM MEXICO, 1977

Miguel Torres

Psychological Concepts
Maslow's hierarchy of needs, self-actualization

Miguel Torres represents countless immigrants who cross over illegally into America from Mexico. Some have been given amnesty under a government provision; others have married Americans and have thereby been granted citizenship. Neither of these opportunities has come to Torres. He explains why he is determined to return each time he is sent back to Mexico: the promise of work and of wages higher than he might be able to earn in Mexico. What is particularly striking is his willingness to endure great difficulties to improve his life. What is your reaction to Torres's predicament and to his dreams?

I was born in a small town in the state of Michoacán in Mexico. When I was fifteen, I went to Mexico City with my grandmother and my mother. I worked in a parking lot, a big car lot. People would come in and they'd say, "Well, park my car." And I'd give them a ticket and I'd park the car and I'd be there, you know, watching the cars. I got paid in tips.

But I wanted to come to the United States to work and to earn more money. My uncle was here, and I thought if I could come to him, I could live with him and work and he would help me.

It's not possible to get papers to come over now. So when I decided to come, I went to Tijuana in Mexico. There's a person there that will get in contact with you. They call him the Coyote. He walks around town, and if he sees someone wandering around alone, he says, "Hello, do you have relatives in the United States?" And if you say yes, he says, "Do you want to visit them?" And if you say yes, he says he can arrange it through a friend. It costs $250 or $300.

The Coyote rounded up me and five other guys, and then he got in contact with a guide to take us across the border. We had to go through the hills and the desert, and we had to swim through a river. I was a little scared. Then we came to a highway and a man was there with a van, pretending to fix his motor. Our guide said hello, and the man jumped into the car and we ran and jumped in, too. He began to drive down the highway fast and we knew we were safe in the United States. He took us to San Ysidro that night, and the next day he took us all the way here to Watsonville. I had to pay him $250 and then, after I'd been here a month, he came back and I had to give him $50 more. He said I owed him that.

I was here for two months before I started working, and then my uncle got me a job, first in the celery fields picking celery, washing it, packing it, and later picking prunes. Then, all of a sudden, one day the Immigration showed up, and I ran and I hid in a river that was next to the orchard. The man saw me and he questioned me, and he saw I didn't have any papers. So they put me in a van and took me to Salinas, and there was some more illegals there and they put us in buses and took us all the way to Mexicali near the border. We were under guard; the driver and another one that sleeps while one drives. The seats are like hard boards. We'd get up from one side and rub, you know, that side a little bit and then sit on the other side for a while and then rub that side because it's so hard. It was a long trip.

When we arrived in Mexicali, they let us go. We caught a bus to Tijuana, and then at Tijuana, that night, we found the Coyote again and we paid him and we came back the next day. I had to pay $250 again, but this time he knew me and he let me pay $30 then and $30 each week. Because he knew me, you know. He trusted me.

We came through the mountains that time. We had to walk through a train tunnel. It all lasted maybe about three hours, through the tunnel. It was short; for me it was short. We're used to walking, you know. Over in Mexico we have to walk like ten miles to go to work or to go home or to go to school, so we're used to walking. To me it was a short distance to walk for three hours. And after we got out of the tunnel, we got into a car; and from there, from the tunnel, we came all the way into Los Angeles. That was the second time. We didn't see any border patrol either time.

The second time I was here for three months. My uncle managed to get me a job in the mushroom plant. I was working there when the Immigration came. There's this place where they blow air between the walls to make it cool and I hid there. And I was watching. The Immigration was looking around the plant everywhere. There was another illegal there, and he just kept on picking the mushrooms. He'd only been back a couple of days himself. The Immigration walked over there, and that kid turned around and looked at the Immigration and said, "What's the matter? What happened?" And the Immigration looked at him and said, "Oh, nothing," and the kid kept right on picking mushrooms. Yet he was an illegal! He knew how to act, play it cool. If you just sit tight they don't know you're illegal.

Well, the Immigration looked between the walls then and he caught me again. That was the second time. They put handcuffs on me with another guy and we were handcuffed together all the way from California to Mexicali.

Altogether I've been caught three times this year and made the trip over here four times. It's cost me one thousand dollars but it's still better than what I was making in Mexico City.

It's the money. When you come back here you get more money here than you do over there. Right now, the most that I'd be getting in Mexico would be from 25 to 30 pesos a day, which is maybe $2.00 to $2.50. And here, with overtime, sometimes I make a $150 a week. Things are expensive here, but it's expensive over there, too. And I like the way people live here. All the—what do you call it—all the facilities that you have here, all the things you can get and everything.

The boss at the mushroom factory doesn't ask for papers. He doesn't say anything about it. The last time, he hired me back as soon as I got back here, without any questions.

I learned to hide my money when the Immigration catch me. You know, if you have a lot on you, they take you fifteen or twenty miles from the border in Mexico. But if you have just two dollars or so, they let you go right in Tijuana. Then it's easier to come back. You can just walk right down the street and find the Coyote or someone like him. A man I know was hitchhiking along the road near San Diego and someone picked him up and it was the Immigration man who had just brought him back to Mexico! The Immigration laughed and said, "You got back faster than I did." Of course, he took him back to Mexico again then. But that man is back in Watsonville now, working in the brussels sprouts. It takes a longer time for the Immigration to catch us than it does for us to come back. [*Laughs.*]

I'd like to be able to stay here, to live here and work; but the only way now is to find someone that'll say, "Well, I'll marry you, I'll fix your papers for you." There's a lot of them who do that. I'd be willing to if I could find someone that would do it for me. You pay them, you know. You don't sleep together or even live in the same house, but they marry you. A long time ago you could fix up papers for your nephew or brother, a friend, a cousin. It was real easy then. But now it has to be close relations: mother, father, wife, son, or daughter. My uncle can't do it for me. The only way I could do it would be if I could marry an American citizen.

I'd like to learn English because it would be easier for me. There is a night school here, but I don't like to go because after work I like to go out and mess around and goof off. [*Laughs.*] Maybe I'll go later. If I could just learn a tiny bit of English, you know, I could turn around and tell the Immigration, "What's the matter with you? What do you want?" and I wouldn't be recognized as an illegal.

Response and Analysis

1. Abraham Maslow proposed that basic human needs, such as food, water, and safety, must be satisfied before higher-level needs, such as respect and realization of potential, can be fulfilled. Which needs do you believe are motivating Miguel Torres to illegally cross the border and work in the United States? Why? To what degree is Torres's desire to live in the United States influenced by his physical needs, by social influences, or by the opportunities provided him by his uncle who lives in the United States? Explain.

2. The highest need in Maslow's motivational hierarchy is the need for self-actualization. What is self-actualization? Briefly discuss the conditions that Maslow believes must be met before someone can fulfill her or his potential. If Torres's living conditions do not change, might he have difficulty realizing his full potential? Why or why not?

Personal Experience and Application

1. What personal, professional, economic, social, and familial difficulties might immigrants have when they arrive in the United States? Are you sympathetic to Torres's plight, or do his actions anger and upset you? Why? Do you know someone who immigrated to the United States? Why did he or she immigrate?

2. Describe a situation in which you were motivated to achieve a goal. What did you want to achieve? Why? What did you do to achieve the goal? What is your attitude toward people who do not give up easily?

Research

Suppose you want to investigate how goal setting affects task performance. You will have female and male psychology students participate in your study. Half will be asked to set clear and specific performance goals for the task. The other group will participate in the control condition and will not set performance goals.

Suppose that you do not randomly assign the participants to the goal-setting or control condition. Is it possible that all of the men might participate in one condition, and all of the women in the other condition? If so, how might this influence your results?

NEW HOPE FOR BINGE EATERS

Harrison G. Pope, Jr. and James I. Hudson

Psychological Concepts
eating disorders, anorexia nervosa, bulimia nervosa

Why would an attractive, young woman go on food binges, gain weight, vomit to lose the weight, and then repeat the cycle? Does she suffer from a chemical imbalance? Is she a victim of a "Barbie and Ken" culture that worships thinness?

Sally's story is representative of others, often women, who suffer from bulimia. Sally graduated from college, was hired as a public relations consultant, dated, and had friends. However, as her bulimia progressed, she began to withdraw from social life. The lifestyle she developed had an addictive quality to it: she had little choice in how she reacted to food. How does Sally attempt to reverse this process?

Her story was familiar. As far back as her sophomore year, while a student at a prestigious women's college in Massachusetts, she had already noticed that she seemed unusually preoccupied with food. In the cafeteria line, she often stopped to study the labels on bottles of salad dressing, cans of juice, and containers of yogurt, to see how many calories each contained, often calculating and recalculating the total number of calories that she had consumed during the day. She was not at all overweight then—although at times, in the privacy of her room, she critically examined herself in the mirror and wished that she had the self-discipline to be thinner. But these feelings seemed little different from those of her friends. Perhaps, during those early years, she had been a bit more depressed than average—particularly so, she remembered, during the days just prior to her menstrual periods—but on the whole her life in the dormitory, her dates with the boys from a nearby college, her grades, her summers in Maine with her family, seemed much the same as those of everyone else.

It was in her senior year that the eating binges began. During the early fall of that year, she felt despondent and unhappy with herself. With this depression came a rise in her preoccupation with food and her thoughts about wanting to lose weight. She paid more attention to her diet. But then one night, alone in her room, she suddenly found herself compulsively devouring chocolate cookies until the entire package of sixty cookies was gone. But the craving for food continued. She rushed to the corner store to buy more supplies. Minutes later, back in her room with an entire gallon of chocolate chip ice cream, abandoning any last pretense of restraint, Sally began eating it with a tablespoon, straight from the carton. Incredibly, it was gone in twenty minutes. Feeling sick, sedated, and disgusted with herself, she collapsed into her bed and slept for twelve hours.

The next morning she discovered to her horror that she had gained seven pounds. Only a strict diet, if not an outright fast, could erase what she had done. Slowly, painstakingly, over the next eight days she lost all of the dreadful weight. But toward the end of that time a strange, uneasy feeling built up inside her—and on the eighth night, it all happened again.

The second binge started a new cycle of fasting, but this time, before she had quite lost all the weight she had gained, a third binge erupted. Soon the binges settled down into a regular pattern, occurring every fourth or fifth night, with rigorous diets in between. Sally quickly learned to recognize the vague tension that heralded the approach of the next episode; she found herself making elaborate plans to be alone on that evening, to stockpile the food in advance in her room, and to guard against any possible interruption.

The cycle of binging and fasting developed its own inexorable momentum. Whatever her attempts to control it, whatever schemes she tried to interrupt it, it continued. She did not dare to confide in other girls at the school or in her boyfriend, although she was convinced that he must have guessed her secret from watching her sharp fluctuations of weight. When he broke up with her that winter, it seemed to confirm that he knew.

Her depression mounted. Within six months she had gained thirteen pounds; each new binge left guilt and hopelessness in its wake. She recalled a dark morning in February, when she awakened in her room after a binge the previous night, overcome with shame and loneliness, and thought seriously, for the first time, of suicide. She even fumbled through the medicines on her bureau—aspirin, decongestants, cough medicine—wondering if enough of them could be painlessly fatal. The feeling dissipated within a few hours, but it was to return many times in the following years.

That spring came a blessing and a curse: Sally discovered how to use laxatives. At first they were an immense relief; she could purge some of the food that she ate, and no longer was forced to fast between binges. She even managed to lose ten pounds before her graduation. But before long, she had to take twenty, then fifty, and sometimes even a hundred times the usual dose to achieve an effect—and felt wasted and drained for the next twenty-four hours.

After graduating, she began her first job as a public relations consultant for a firm in Boston, and found an apartment of her own in a quiet suburb west of the city. Even though her job proved rewarding, the work atmosphere inviting, and her associates friendly, her work offered only scant relief from the tyranny of her chronic preoccupation with food. The binges occurred almost nightly, as soon as she got home from work. Soon she found herself spending eighty to a hundred dollars a week on food, and another twenty or thirty on laxatives. Her social life dissolved. She no longer had a boyfriend, but it didn't matter; food seemed to occupy all of her thoughts. She developed a repertoire of excuses to extricate herself from evening social obligations so as to be free to go home and binge. Arriving at her local supermarket, she often felt compelled to explain as she was checking out that she was throwing a party, in order to justify a shopping cart filled with ice cream, cookies, and other carbohydrate-rich foods. Then she usually drove several miles to a large pharmacy in a neighboring town; the clerk in the local drugstore had noticed her too many times buying laxatives.

"There was no one to whom I could talk about it," she said. "I didn't know anyone else who ever had these experiences, or at least admitted to them. I thought I must just be weird; I'd never heard the word *bulimia*. There wasn't any publicity about it in those days."

From time to time, Sally resolved to fight her affliction, forcing herself to go without binging. But within two or three days, intolerable tension and anxiety would begin to build, her resolve would collapse, and the cycle would begin again.

After countless attempts, Sally eventually learned to make herself vomit. Vomiting was difficult at first, but it liberated her from her dependence on laxatives, and made it easier for her to lose weight. In fact, she soon lost another fifteen pounds, to the point where she dipped several pounds below the lowest weight she had attained in college. Even then, she still found herself wondering, many times a day, if she looked fat. Often she would forgo breakfast and eat only sparingly at lunch—but this only increased the ferocity of the nightly binges. Recognizing this, she tried deliberately to eat more during the day, but could not bring herself to do so; the thought of consuming even a few hundred calories, without the option of vomiting, aroused too much anxiety.

Despite this, she managed to advance at work, fulfill her few social obligations, and maintain an unblemished exterior. She even began dating, but her sexual drive, she recalled, was almost nil; ninety-nine percent of her thoughts revolved around food.

It was nearly five years after the onset of the bulimic symptoms that Sally finally sought out counseling.

"I would have seen someone sooner," she said, "but I didn't know where I could find someone who could possibly understand my problem. Then I learned the name of a psychologist who had seen a friend of mine at work, and I decided to give it a try.

"At first, I was embarrassed even to describe my problem to him. But he proved to be a very warm and understanding person, and he quickly put me at ease. After I had seen him only a few times, I learned a number of things about myself— that I had constantly tried to be perfect in my family, in my schoolwork, and in my appearance. It seemed to make a lot of sense. But I still binged. The therapist tried hard to work with me, but I was never able to gain much control. I felt like a failure."

Sally continued seeing him once a week, sometimes twice, for more than a year. Finally she stopped, not because she questioned the value of the sessions, but because the expense seemed too great for her to manage. Little did she realize the new expense that awaited her: a dentist discovered that the enamel on her teeth was seriously eroded as a result of her vomiting. He estimated that the work required would cost a minimum of two thousand dollars. The news stunned her, but it did not stop the binges.

A few months later, she experienced a period of new and unfamiliar symptoms: strange attacks of anxiety began to strike her, seemingly at random, several times a week. She described one such episode that occurred while she was riding to work on the train: A sudden feeling of dread came over her; her heart raced, her hands tingled, and she gasped for air. Something horrible seemed about to happen—as if she were about to have a heart attack, or suddenly go crazy. Her only thought was to find some escape, someplace to hide. The attack faded over the course of half an hour; she hastily got off the train in Boston, shaken but able to get to work. For months afterward she drove her car to work, fearing that another trip on the train might trigger a similar experience. But the attacks continued; more and more she sought the safety of her apartment when not at work. Finally, she decided to consult a psychiatrist.

"I never got the feeling that he really understood my problems. After only two sessions, he prescribed some large orange pills that made me feel like a zombie even when I took only half the prescribed amount. He called them 'major tranquilizers.' I could barely get out of bed in the morning, and I walked around feeling dazed and uninterested in everything going on around me."

"The pills did nothing for the anxiety attacks, and they seemed to make the eating binges worse. I complained to the doctor, but he felt that I should continue to take them, even though I could not understand his explanation of what they were supposed to do. I finally stopped taking them on my own, and stopped seeing him soon afterward."

Sally's medication had probably been one of the phenothiazines—a family of drugs designed to treat psychotic symptoms such as delusions and hallucinations. Although Sally had displayed none of these symptoms, it was not surprising to hear that someone had prescribed a phenothiazine for her; these powerful drugs, with numerous side effects, are sometimes prescribed for syndromes in which they are valueless, based on the questionable assumption that they are effective for ordinary anxiety or depression.

But after her unfortunate encounter with the psychiatrist something good finally happened. Sally heard of a self-help organization dedicated to the problem of eating disorders. She found the organization filled with women who told stories very much like her own. Soon she joined a group workshop. Talking with the other group members gave her immense relief and new resolve, for the first time in years. Her self-esteem improved; no longer did she feel quite so ashamed. In a bold move, she even described the binges—at least in part—to her boyfriend. He seemed to understand, and, contrary to her fears, did not seem alienated by her confession. In fact, they grew closer, and six months later they became engaged.

But despite her release from shame and isolation, Sally found that the binges stubbornly persisted—and the morning depressions that followed them remained devastating. Most of the other women in her group admitted that they still binged as well; only one seemed to have freed herself from the symptoms. Like Sally, some wondered aloud if they would ever be liberated from their compulsion; they spoke of successive experiences with three, four, or five different courses of treatment, with many different sorts of therapists. Several of the group members described positive and rewarding experiences in therapy—but they were still binging.

Sally concluded her story:

"I've got to keep trying. Cliff and I plan to get married in September. It's been nine years now, and I'm still binging three or four times a week—never less than once a week even during the best periods. I can't stand it anymore; I'm tired of spending my life constantly obsessed with food; I'm tired of making myself throw up; I'm tired of wrecking my body."

With each passing month, more and more patients like Sally come to our offices, and to the offices of other professionals around the country. They tell stories of years of uncontrollable binge eating—sometimes unknown to even their closest friends—accompanied by depression, anxiety, and suicidal feelings. Often their occupational, social, and sexual lives have been eroded as a result of their all-consuming preoccupation with food. With growing desperation, as one treatment after another has failed, they come, as Sally did, torn between hope and skepticism, afraid to believe that any treatment could possibly be successful. Some are well informed about bulimia; others are the victims of fanciful ideas or frank misinformation. Many never reach the offices at all. For every Sally who seeks professional help, there may be five, ten, or even twenty others who covertly suffer from uncontrollable eating binges—perhaps not even knowing that their syndrome is a recognized illness, for which effective treatments are now being developed. It appears that bulimia is reaching epidemic proportions in this country, and probably around the world. But it is a secret epidemic, and we in our offices see only a tiny portion of those who suffer from it.

Fortunately, new research suggests that bulimia, unlike some other epidemic illnesses, can now often be treated rapidly. Thus, it becomes all the more tragic that so many people—numbering into the millions in the United States alone—may suffer unnecessarily, unaware that improved treatment is available.

Response and Analysis

1. What factors may have influenced Sally to develop an eating disorder? How did Sally attempt to control her weight? Briefly describe her "binge-purge" cycle. What physical and psychological problems did she experience as a result of binging and purging?

2. What are anorexia nervosa and bulimia nervosa? What are the typical characteristics—such as age, gender, and personality characteristics—of people who suffer from an eating disorder, such as anorexia nervosa or bulimia nervosa? Briefly discuss one biological factor and one nonbiological factor that regulates or influences eating.

Personal Experience and Application

1. Do you believe that American society places too much emphasis on physical appearance and thinness? Why or why not? How are these values conveyed to children, adolescents, and adults? What pressures might young men and women experience if they do not conform with the idealized image? What pressures do you feel to conform to the idealized image? How do these pressures affect your self-esteem?

2. Do you know someone who has an eating disorder? How has the disorder affected his or her life, including self-esteem and relationships? How has it affected your relationship with the person? Has the person overcome the problem? If so, how?

Research

Suppose you conduct a study to investigate the relationship between self-esteem and anorexia nervosa. You have one hundred female and male students at your college or university complete an eating disorder questionnaire and a self-esteem questionnaire. You find that there is a moderately strong positive correlation ($r = 0.55$) between anorexia nervosa and self-esteem. What are the *three* possible explanations for this relationship? Why is it not possible to determine which explanation is correct on the basis of your findings?

THE MICROSCOPE

Annie Dillard

Psychological Concepts
intrinsic and extrinsic motivation, need for achievement

One Christmas Annie Dillard's parents give her what she has longed for: a microscope. By spring she is able to gather some warm puddle water that she hopes will yield an amoeba for her to see. Placing the drop of water on the slide under the lens, Dillard is elated: "I would have known him anywhere," she writes, "blobby and grainy as his picture." Excited, she runs to her parents. They must come and see her find. But they would rather sit on the porch smoking and drinking coffee! Why don't they go with her? How does their refusal affect Annie?

After I read *The Field Book of Ponds and Streams* several times, I longed for a microscope. Everybody needed a microscope. Detectives used microscopes, both for the FBI and at Scotland Yard. Although usually I had to save my tiny allowance for things I wanted, that year for Christmas my parents gave me a microscope kit.

In a dark basement corner, on a white enamel table, I set up the microscope kit. I supplied a chair, a lamp, a batch of jars, a candle, and a pile of library books. The microscope kit supplied a blunt black three-speed microscope, a booklet, a scalpel, a dropper, an ingenious device for cutting thin segments of fragile tissue, a pile of clean slides and cover slips, and a dandy array of corked test tubes.

One of the test tubes contained "hay infusion." Hay infusion was a wee brown chip of grass blade. You added water to it, and after a week it became a jungle in a drop, full of one-celled animals. This did not work for me. All I saw in the microscope after a week was a wet chip of dried grass, much enlarged.

Another test tube contained "diatomaceous earth." This was, I believed, an actual pinch of the white cliffs of Dover. On my palm it was an airy, friable chalk. The booklet said it was composed of the silicaceous bodies of diatoms—one-celled creatures that lived in, as it were, small glass jewelry boxes with fitted lids. Diatoms, I read, come in a variety of transparent geometrical shapes. Broken and dead and dug out of geological deposits, they made chalk, and a fine abrasive used in silver polish and toothpaste. What I saw in the microscope must have been the fine abrasive—grit enlarged. It was years before I saw a recognizable, whole diatom. The kit's diatomaceous earth was a bust.

All that winter I played with the microscope. I prepared slides from things at hand, as the books suggested. I looked at the transparent membrane inside an onion's skin and saw the cells. I looked at a section of cork and saw the cells, and at scrapings from the inside of my cheek, ditto. I looked at my blood and saw not much; I looked at my urine and saw long iridescent crystals, for the drop had dried.

All this was very well, but I wanted to see the wildlife I had read about. I wanted especially to see the famous amoeba, who had eluded me. He was supposed to live in the hay infusion, but I hadn't found him there. He lived outside in warm ponds and streams, too, but I lived in Pittsburgh, and it had been a cold winter.

Finally late that spring I saw an amoeba. The week before, I had gathered puddle water from Frick Park; it had been festering in a jar in the basement. This June night after dinner I figured I had waited long enough. In the basement at my microscope table I spread a scummy drop of Frick Park puddle water on a slide, peeked in, and lo, there was the famous amoeba. He was as blobby and grainy as his picture; I would have known him anywhere.

Before I had watched him at all, I ran upstairs. My parents were still at the table, drinking coffee. They, too, could see the famous amoeba. I told them, bursting, that he was all set up, that they should hurry before his water dried. It was the chance of a lifetime.

Father had stretched out his long legs and was tilting back in his chair. Mother sat with her knees crossed, in blue slacks, smoking a Chesterfield. The dessert dishes were still on the table. My sisters were nowhere in evidence. It was a warm evening; the big dining-room windows gave onto blooming rhododendrons.

Mother regarded me warmly. She gave me to understand that she was glad I had found what I had been looking for, but that she and Father were happy to sit with their coffee, and would not be coming down.

She did not say, but I understood at once, that they had their pursuits (coffee?) and I had mine. She did not say, but I began to understand then, that you do what you do out of your private passion for the thing itself.

I had essentially been handed my own life. In subsequent years my parents would praise my drawings and poems, and supply me with books, art supplies, and sports equipment, and listen to my troubles and enthusiasms, and supervise my hours, and discuss and inform, but they would not get involved with my detective work, nor hear about my reading, nor inquire about my homework or term papers or exams, nor visit the salamanders I caught, nor listen to me play the piano, nor attend my field hockey games, nor fuss over my insect collection with me, or my poetry collection or stamp collection or rock collection. My days and nights were my own to plan and fill.

When I left the dining room that evening and started down the dark basement stairs, I had a life. I sat to my wonderful amoeba, and there he was, rolling his grains more slowly now, extending an arc of his edge for a foot and drawing himself along by that foot, and absorbing it again and rolling on. I gave him some more pond water.

I had hit pay dirt. For all I knew, there were paramecia, too, in that pond water, or daphniae, or stentors, or any of the many other creatures I had read about and never seen: volvox, the spherical algal colony; euglena with its one red eye; the elusive, glassy diatom; hydra, rotifers, water bears, worms. Anything was possible. The sky was the limit.

Response and Analysis

1. Briefly describe Annie Dillard's delight in using the microscope. What are intrinsic and extrinsic motivation? Do you think Dillard is intrinsically or extrinsically motivated? Why?

2. How does Dillard respond to her parents' refusal to see the amoeba? What does Dillard mean when she writes, "I began to understand then, that you do what you do out of your private passion for the thing itself"? What are the characteristics of someone who has a strong need for achievement? Briefly describe a parenting style that may promote achievement motivation in children.

Personal Experience and Application

1. How was Annie "handed her own life"? Do you remember an incident with your parents, guardian, or a teacher in which you realized that you had been handed "your own life"? Briefly describe the incident.

2. Why are you seeking a college degree? To what extent were you influenced by your parents or guardians? Why do you believe a college education is important? What academic goals do you set for yourself? Do you believe they are easily attainable or that they require significant time and effort?

Research

Suppose you want to examine achievement motivation in children. You would like to know if children who score low in achievement motivation set different goals for themselves than children who score high in achievement motivation. After securing approval to conduct your study from the human subjects Institutional Review Board at your college or university and the children's parents, you administer a need for achievement test to forty children who are eight years old. Next, on the basis of the children's answers, you classify each child as being either low or high in achievement motivation.

You then take one child at a time and ask him or her to play a miniature bowling game. You tell the child that the object of the game is to knock down as many plastic bowling pins as possible with the plastic bowling ball during each throw. You allow the child to throw the ball ten times, and after each throw you reset the three bowling pins. You do not tell the child where he or she must stand. For each throw, you record where the child stands: (a) very close to the pins so that the game is very easy; (b) at an intermediate distance so that the game is challenging; or (c) far away so that the game is very difficult.

Where do you expect children high in achievement motivation and children low in achievement motivation will stand? Why? Might knowing the child's achievement motivation score influence how you record the location where the child stands? Why? How could you modify the procedure to guarantee that your observations would not be influenced by the child's score?

chapter 10

PERSONALITY

The child in the womb is already created as a
uniqueness to be developed, and this fact is
decisive: the origin of personality is the origin
of the potential personality: uniqueness.

MARTIN BUBER, in MAURICE FRIEDMAN,
Martin Buber's Life and Work: The Later Years

What shapes our personality? The concepts highlighted in this chapter reflect on possible answers by illustrating defense mechanisms; the struggle for self-identity; the relationship between self-concept and the social environment; and personality traits.

Isabel Huggan describes the plight of a child, Elizabeth, who is terrified at having other children cast her off with a classmate, Celia, who is awkward and unpopular. Elizabeth's feelings are so intense that even years later she blames Celia for what she, Elizabeth, fears about herself.

Born in America of Japanese immigrants, Kesaya Noda has so many conflicting images of who she should be that she struggles to understand who she is and who she would like to be. Noda confronts not only historical and cultural identities but also what it means to be a woman here and now.

Joyce Lee astutely points to the challenge many immigrant children face in elementary school. How does a child make herself understood when she doesn't know the language of her new land? One way is to demonstrate her skills at origami, a talent that impressed both her teacher and the children in her class. These early experiences of coming to America are powerful memories for Lee. How might these experiences influence personality?

Writing about the importance of reputation, tennis star Arthur Ashe reveals several of his personality traits. Honesty, fairness, and kindness are all qualities he tried to cultivate. Ashe saw a strong connection between the personal and the interpersonal. How he behaved affected others, and if he disappointed his father, his mother, or his community, they would let him know. Highly conscientious, he wants to be an honorable man.

CELIA BEHIND ME

Isabel Huggan

Psychological Concept
defense mechanisms

Why are children sometimes cruel to other children who wear glasses or are overweight, who may be awkward or who have certain restrictions because of health conditions? Are defense mechanisms at work?

In "Celia Behind Me," Elizabeth, a nine-year-old, is threatened by her mother, who says that if Elizabeth is not nice to Celia, who has diabetes, she will whip Elizabeth in front of all the other children. Celia, says Elizabeth, "was a little girl with large smooth cheeks and very thick glasses." Her name was "far too rare and grownup a name, so we always laughed at it."

Elizabeth has a problem, however. She suspects that she is next in line for being tormented by the other children. She too wears glasses, and she sucked her thumb in kindergarten, which earned her the name "Sucky." So Elizabeth calls Celia names and tries to distance herself from her. Elizabeth's hatred evolves into rage one day, and she physically attacks Celia. Who is at fault? Celia, says Elizabeth, because she evoked such feelings of hatred.

There was a little girl with large smooth cheeks and very thick glasses who lived up the street when I was in public school. Her name was Celia. It was far too rare and grownup a name, so we always laughed at it. And we laughed at her because she was a chubby, diabetic child, made peevish by our teasing.

My mother always said, "You must be nice to Celia, she won't live forever," and even as early as seven I could see the unfairness of that position. Everybody died sooner or later, I'd die too, but that didn't mean everybody was nice to me or to each other. I already knew about mortality and was prepared to go to heaven with my two aunts who had died together in a car crash with their heads smashed like overripe melons. I overheard the bit about the melons when my mother was on the telephone, repeating that phrase and sobbing. I used to think about it often, repeating the words to myself as I did other things so that I got a nice rhythm: "Their heads smashed like melons, like melons, like melons." I imagined the pulpy insides of muskmelons and watermelons all over the road.

I often thought about the melons when I saw Celia because her head was so round and she seemed so bland and stupid and fruitlike. All rosy and vulnerable at the same time as being the most *awful* pain. She'd follow us home from school, whining if we walked faster than she did. Everybody always walked faster than Celia because her short little legs wouldn't keep up. And she was bundled in long stockings and heavy underwear, summer and winter, so that even her clothes held her back from our sturdy, leaping pace over and under hedges and across backyards and, when it was dry, or when it was frozen, down the stream bed and through the drainage pipe beneath the bridge on Church Street.

Celia, by the year I turned nine in December, had failed once and was behind us in school, which was a relief because at least in class there wasn't someone telling you to be nice to Celia. But she'd always be in the playground at recess, her pleading eyes magnified behind those ugly lenses so that you couldn't look at her when you told her she couldn't play skipping unless she was an ender. "Because you can't skip worth a fart," we'd whisper in her ear. "Fart, fart, fart," and watch her round pink face crumple as she stood there, turning, turning, turning the rope over and over.

As the fall turned to winter, the five of us who lived on Brubacher Street and went back and forth to school together got meaner and meaner to Celia. And, after the brief diversions of Christmas, we returned with a vengeance to our running and hiding and scaring games that kept Celia in a state of terror all the way home.

My mother said, one day when I'd come into the kitchen and she'd just turned away from the window so I could see she'd been watching us coming down the street, "You'll be sorry, Elizabeth. I see how you're treating that poor child, and it makes me sick. You wait, young lady. Some day you'll see how it feels yourself. Now you be nice to her, d'you hear?"

"But it's not just me," I protested. "I'm nicer to her than anybody else, and I don't see why I have to be. She's nobody special, she's just a pain. She's really dumb and she can't do anything. Why can't I just play with the other kids like everybody else?"

"You just remember I'm watching," she said, ignoring every word I'd said. "And if I see one more snowball thrown in her direction, by you or by anybody else, I'm coming right out there and spanking you in front of them all. Now you remember that!"

I knew my mother, and knew this was no idle threat. The awesome responsibility of now making sure the other kids stopped snowballing Celia made me weep with rage and despair, and I was locked in my room after supper to "think things over."

I thought things over. I hated Celia with a dreadful and absolute passion. Her round guileless face floated in the air above me as I finally fell asleep, taunting me: "You have to be nice to me because I'm going to die."

I did as my mother bid me, out of fear and the thought of the shame that a public spanking would bring. I imagined my mother could see much farther up the street than she really could, and it prevented me from throwing snowballs or teasing Celia for the last four blocks of our homeward journey. And then came the stomach-wrenching task of making the others quit.

"You'd better stop," I'd say. "If my mother sees you she's going to thrash us all."

Terror of terrors that they wouldn't be sufficiently scared of her strapwielding hand; gut-knotting fear that they'd find out or guess what she'd really said and throw millions of snowballs just for the joy of seeing me whipped, pants down in the snowbank, screaming. I visualized that scene all winter, and felt a shock of relief when March brought such a cold spell that the snow was too crisp for packing. It meant a temporary safety for Celia, and respite for me. For I knew, deep in my wretched heart, that were it not for Celia I was next in line for humiliation. I was kind of chunky and wore glasses too, and had sucked my thumb so openly in kindergarten that "Sucky" had stuck with me all the way to Grade 3 where I now balanced at a hazardous point, nearly accepted by the amorphous Other Kids and always at the brink of being laughed at, ignored or teased. I cried very easily, and prayed during those years—not to become pretty or smart or popular, all aims too far out of my or God's reach, but simply to be strong enough not to cry when I got called Sucky.

During that cold snap, we were all bundled up by our mothers as much as poor Celia ever was. Our comings and goings were hampered by layers of flannel bloomers and undershirts and ribbed stockings and itchy wool against us no matter which way we turned; mitts, sweaters, scarves and hats, heavy and wet-smelling when the snot from our dripping noses mixed with the melting snow on our collars and we wiped, in frigid resignation, our sore red faces with rough sleeves knobbed over with icy pellets.

Trudging, turgid little beasts we were, making our way along slippery streets, breaking the crusts on those few front yards we'd not yet stepped all over in glee to hear the glorious snapping sound of boot through hard snow. Celia, her glasses steamed up even worse than mine, would scuffle and trip a few yards behind us, and I walked along wishing that some time I'd look back and she wouldn't be there. But she always was, and I was always conscious of the abiding hatred that had built up during the winter, in conflict with other emotions that gave me no peace at all. I felt pity, and a rising urge within me to cry as hard as I could so that Celia would cry too, and somehow realize how bad she made me feel, and ask my forgiveness.

It was the last day before the thaw when the tension broke, like northern lights exploding in the frozen air. We were all a little wingy after days of switching between the extremes of bitter cold outdoors and the heat of our homes and school. Thermostats had been turned up in a desperate attempt to combat the arctic air, so that we children suffered scratchy, tingly torment in our faces, hands and feet as the blood in our bodies roared in confusion, first freezing, then boiling. At school we had to go outside at recess—only an act of God would have ever prevented recess, the teachers had to have their cigarettes and tea—and in bad weather we huddled in a shed where the bicycles and the janitor's outdoor equipment were stored.

During the afternoon recess of the day I'm remembering, at the end of the shed where the girls stood, a sudden commotion broke out when Sandra, a rich big girl from Grade 4, brought forth a huge milk-chocolate bar from her pocket. It was brittle in the icy air, and snapped into little bits in its foil wrapper, to be divided among the chosen. I made my way cautiously to the fringe of her group, where many of my classmates were receiving their smidgens of sweet chocolate, letting it melt on their tongues like dark communion wafers. Behind me hung Celia, who had mistaken my earlier cries of "Stop throwing snowballs at Celia!" for kindness. She'd been mooning behind me for days, it seemed to me, as I stepped a little farther forward to see that there were only a few pieces left. Happily, though, most mouths were full and the air hummed with the murmuring sound of chocolate being pressed between tongue and palate.

Made bold by cold and desire, I spoke up. "Could I have a bit, Sandra?" She turned to where Celia and I stood, holding the precious foil in her mittened hand. Wrapping it in a ball, she pushed it over at Celia. Act of kindness, act of spite, vicious bitch or richness seeking expiation? She gave the chocolate to Celia and smiled at her. "This last bit is for Celia," she said to me.

"But I can't eat it," whispered Celia, her round red face aflame with the sensation of being singled out for a gift. "I've got di-a-beet-is." The word. Said so carefully. As if it were a talisman, a charm to protect her against our rough healthiness.

I knew it was a trick. I knew she was watching me out of the corner of her eye, that Sandra, but I was driven. "Then could I have it, eh?" The duress under which I acted prompted my chin to quiver and a tear to start down my cheek before I could wipe it away.

"No, no, no!" jeered Sandra then. "Suckybabies can't have sweets either. Di-a-beet-ics and Suck-y-ba-bies can't eat chocolate. Give it back, you little fart, Celia! That's the last time I ever give you anything!"

Wild, appreciative laughter from the chocolate-tongued mob, and they turned their backs on us, Celia and me, and waited while Sandra crushed the remaining bits into minuscule slivers. They had to take off their mitts and lick their fingers to pick up the last fragments from the foil. I stood there and prayed: "Dear God and Jesus, I would please like very much not to cry. Please help me. Amen." And with that the clanging recess bell clanked through the playground noise, and we all lined up, girls and boys in straight, straight rows, to go inside.

After school there was the usual bunch of us walking home and, of course, Celia trailing behind us. The cold of the past few days had been making us hurry, taking the shortest routes on our way to steaming cups of Ovaltine and cocoa. But this day we were all full of that peculiar energy that swells up before a turn in the weather and, as one body, we turned down the street that meant the long way home. Past the feed store where the Mennonites tied their horses, out the back of the town hall parking-lot and then down a ridge to the ice-covered stream and through the Church Street culvert to come out in the unused field behind the Front Street stores; the forbidden adventure we indulged in as a gesture of defiance against the parental "come right home."

We slid down the snowy slope at the mouth of the pipe that seemed immense then but was really only five feet in diameter. Part of its attraction was the tremendous racket you could make by scraping a stick along the corrugated sides as you went through. It was also long enough to echo very nicely if you made good booming noises, and we occasionally titillated each other by saying bad words at one end that grew as they bounced along the pipe and became wonderfully shocking in their magnitude . . . poopy, Poopy, POOpy, POOOOPy, POOOOPPYYY!

I was last because I had dropped my schoolbag in the snow and stopped to brush it off. And when I looked up, down at the far end, where the white plate of daylight lay stark in the darkness, the figures of my four friends were silhouetted as they emerged into the brightness. As I started making great sliding steps to catch up, I heard Celia behind me, and her plaintive, high voice: "Elizabeth! Wait for me, okay? I'm scared to go through alone. Elizabeth?"

And of course I slid faster and faster, unable to stand the thought of being the only one in the culvert with Celia. Then we would come out together and we'd really be paired up. What if they always ran on ahead and left us to walk together? What would I ever do? And behind me I heard the rising call of Celia, who had ventured as far as a few yards into the pipe, calling my name to come back and walk with her. I got right to the end, when I heard another noise and looked up. There they all were, on the bridge looking down, and as soon as they saw my face began to chant, "Better wait for Celia, Sucky. Better get Celia, Sucky."

The sky was very pale and lifeless, and I looked up in the air at my breath curling in spirals and felt, I remember this very well, an exhilarating, clear-headed instant of understanding. And with that, raced back into the tunnel where Celia stood whimpering half-way along.

"You little fart!" I screamed at her, my voice breaking and tearing at the words. "You little diabetic fart! I hate you! I hate you! Stop it, stop crying, I hate you! I could bash your head in I hate you so much, you fart, you fart! I'll smash your head like a melon! And it'll go in pieces all over and you'll die. You'll die you diabetic. You're going to die!" Shaking her, shaking her and banging her against the cold, ribbed metal, crying and sobbing for grief and gasping with the exertion of pure hatred. And then there were the others, pulling at me, yanking me away, and in the moral tones of those who don't actually take part, warning me that they were going to tell, that Celia probably was going to die now, that I was really evil, they would tell what I said.

And there, slumped in a little heap, was Celia, her round head in its furry bonnet all dirty at the back where it had hit against the pipe, and she was hiccupping with fear. And for a wild, terrible moment I thought I had killed her, that the movements and noises her body made were part of dying.

I ran.

I ran as fast as I could back out the way we had come, and all the way back to the schoolyard. I didn't think about where I was going, it simply seemed the only bulwark to turn to when I knew I couldn't go home. There were a few kids still in the yard but they were older and ignored me as I tried the handle of the side door and found it open. I'd never been in the school after hours, and was stricken with another kind of terror that it might be a strappable offence. But no one saw me, even the janitor was blessedly in another part of the building, so I was able to creep down to the girls' washroom and quickly hide in one of the cubicles. Furtive, criminal, condemned.

I was so filled with horror I couldn't even cry. I just sat on the toilet seat, reading all the things that were written in pencil on the green, wooden walls. *G.R. loves M.H.* and *Y.F. hates W.S. for double double sure. Mr. Becker wears ladies pants.* Thinking that I might die myself, die right here, and then it wouldn't matter if they told on me that I had killed Celia.

But the inevitable footsteps of retribution came down the stone steps before I had been there very long. I heard the janitor's voice explaining he hadn't seen any children come in and then my father's voice saying that the others were sure this is where Elizabeth would be. And they called my name, and then came in, and I guess saw my boots beneath the door because I suddenly thought it was too late to scrunch them up on the seat and my father was looking down at me and grabbed my arm, hurting it, pulling me, saying "Get in the car, Elizabeth."

Both my mother and my father spanked me that night. At first I tried not to cry, and tried to defend myself against their diatribe, tried to tell them when they asked, "But whatever possessed you to do such a terrible thing?" But whatever I said seemed to make them more angry and they became so soured by their own shame that they slapped my stinging buttocks for personal revenge as much as for any rehabilitative purposes.

"I'll never be able to lift my head on this street again!" my mother cried, and it struck me then, as it still does now, as a marvelous turn of phrase. I thought about her head on the street as she hit me, and wondered what Celia's head looked like, and if I had dented it at all.

Celia hadn't died, of course. She'd been half-carried, half-dragged home by the heroic others, and given pills and attention and love, and the doctor had come to look at her head but she didn't have so much as a bruise. She had a dirty hat, and a bad case of hiccups all night, but she survived.

Celia forgave me, all too soon. Within weeks her mother allowed her to walk back and forth to school with me again. But, in all the years before she finally died at seventeen, I was never able to forgive her. She made me discover a darkness far more frightening than the echoing culvert, far more enduring than her smooth, pink face.

Response and Analysis

1. Briefly describe how the children teased and mocked Celia. Why does Elizabeth say, "I knew, deep in my wretched heart, that were it not for Celia I was the next in line for humiliation"? Why does Elizabeth say she was unable to forgive Celia?

2. Is Elizabeth exhibiting a defense mechanism? If so, what behaviors demonstrate a defense mechanism at work? Which defense mechanism might Freud say Elizabeth shows?

Personal Experience and Application

1. Were you ever stigmatized because of your friendship with someone? Why? Did you remain with your friend or did the friendship dissolve? Why?

2. How might being stigmatized affect one's personality? What defenses might one use to lessen the pain of rejection and the subsequent isolation?

Research

Suppose you want to conduct a face-to-face interview with a student in your psychology class to find out about her or his academic interests, hobbies, and personality characteristics. Make a list of questions you would ask. How reliable and valid is the interview method in assessing personality? Why?

ASIAN IN AMERICA

Kesaya E. Noda

Psychological Concepts
self-concept, positive regard

What shapes our personality? How do we begin to understand who we are? Kesaya Noda struggled with the impact of her Asian heritage and the American world in which she lived. As a Japanese-American born in California and raised in New Hampshire, she faced cultural and gender issues that complicated her personal identity. In what way, she asked herself, was she Japanese? In what way was she Japanese-American? Was there any conflict between the ways these two cultures viewed women? Her search for answers to these questions helped confirm her identity.

Sometimes when I was growing up, my identity seemed to hurtle toward me and paste itself right to my face. I felt that way, encountering the stereotypes of my race perpetuated by non-Japanese people (primarily white) who may or may not have had contact with other Japanese in America. "You don't like cheese, do you?" someone would ask. "I know your people don't like cheese." Sometimes questions came making allusions to history. That was another aspect of the identity. Events that had happened quite apart from the me who stood silent in that moment connected my face with an incomprehensible past. "Your parents were in California? Were they in those camps during the war?" And sometimes there were phrases or nicknames: "Lotus Blossom." I was sometimes addressed or referred to as racially Japanese, sometimes as Japanese-American, and sometimes as an Asian woman. Confusions and distortions abounded.

How is one to know and define oneself? From the inside—within a context that is self-defined, from a grounding in community and a connection with culture and history that are comfortably accepted? Or from the outside—in terms of messages received from the media and people who are often ignorant? Even as an adult I can still see two sides of my face and past. I can see from the inside out, in freedom. And I can see from the outside in, driven by the old voices of childhood and lost in anger and fear.

I Am Racially Japanese

A voice from my childhood says: "You are other. You are less than. You are unalterably alien." This voice has its own history. We have indeed been seen as other and alien since the early years of our arrival in the United States. The very first immigrants were welcomed and sought as laborers to replace the dwindling numbers of Chinese, whose influx had been cut off by the Chinese Exclusion Act of 1882. The Japanese fell natural heir to the same anti-Asian prejudice that had arisen against the Chinese. As soon as they began striking for better wages, they were no longer welcomed.

I can see myself today as a person historically defined by law and custom as being forever alien. Being neither "free white" nor "African," our people in California were deemed "aliens, ineligible for citizenship," no matter how long they intended to stay here. Aliens ineligible for citizenship were prohibited from owning, buying, or leasing land. They did not and could not belong here. The voice in me remembers that I am always a *Japanese*-American in the eyes of many. A third-generation German-American is an American. A third-generation Japanese-American is a Japanese-American. Being Japanese means being a danger to the country during the war and knowing how to use chopsticks. I wear this history on my face.

I move to the other side. I see a different light and claim a different context. My race is a line that stretches across ocean and time to link me to the shrine where my grandmother was raised. Two high, white banners lift in the wind at the top of the stone steps leading to the shrine. It is time for the summer festival. Black characters are written against the sky as boldly as the clouds, as lightly as kites, as sharply as the big black crows I used to see above the fields in New Hampshire. At festival time there is liquor and food, ritual, discipline, and abandonment. There is music and drunkenness and invocation. There is hope. Another season has come. Another season has gone.

I am racially Japanese. I have a certain claim to this crazy place where the prayers intoned by a neighboring Shinto priest (standing in for my grandmother's nephew who is sick) are drowned out by the rehearsals for the pop singing contest in which most of the villagers will compete later that night. The village elders, the priest, and I stand respectfully upon the immaculate, shining wooden floor of the outer shrine, bowing our heads before the hidden powers. . . .

Our family has served this shrine for generations. The family's need to protect this claim to identity and place outweighs any individual claim to any individual hope. I am Japanese.

I Am a Japanese-American

"Weak." I hear the voice from my childhood years. "Passive," I hear. Our parents and grandparents were the ones who were put into those camps. They went without resistance; they offered cooperation as proof of loyalty to America. "Victim," I hear. And, "Silent."

Our parents are painted as hard workers who were socially uncomfortable and had difficulty expressing even the smallest opinion. Clean, quiet, motivated, and determined to match the American way; that is us, and that is the story of our time here.

"Why did you go into those camps?" I raged at my parents, frightened by my own inner silence and timidity. "Why didn't you do anything to resist? Why didn't you name it the injustice it was?" Couldn't our parents even think? Couldn't they? Why were we so passive?

During the several years that follow I learn about the people and the place, and much more about what has happened in this California village where my parents grew up. The *issei*, our grandparents, made this settlement in the desert. Their first crops were eaten by rabbits and ravaged by insects. The land was so barren that men walking from house to house sometimes got lost. Women came here too. They bore children in 114-degree heat, then carried the babies with them into the fields to nurse when they reached the end of each row of grapes or other truck-farm crops.

I had had no idea what it meant to buy this kind of land and make it grow green. Or how, when the war came, there was no space at all for the subtlety of being who we were—Japanese-Americans. Either/or was the way. I hadn't understood that people were literally afraid for their lives then, that their money had been frozen in banks; that there was a five-mile travel limit; that when the early evening curfew came and they were inside their houses, some of them watched helplessly as people they knew went into their barns to steal their belongings. The police were patrolling the road, interested only in violators of curfew. There was no help for them in the face of thievery. I had not been able to imagine before what it must have felt like to be an American—to know absolutely that one is an American—and yet to have almost everyone else deny it. Not only deny it, but challenge that identity with machine guns and troops of white American soldiers. In those circumstances it was difficult to say, "I'm a Japanese-American." "American" had to do.

But now I can say that I am a Japanese-American. It means I have a place here in this country, too. I have a place here on the East Coast, where our neighbor is so much a part of our family that my mother never passes her house at night without glancing at the lights to see if she is home and safe; where my parents have hauled hundreds of pounds of rocks from fields and arduously planted Christmas trees and blueberries, lilacs, asparagus, and crab apples; where my father still dreams of angling a stream to a new bed so that he can dig a pond in the field and fill it with water and fish. "The neighbors already came for their Christmas tree?" he asks in December. "Did they like it? Did they like it?"

I have a place on the West Coast where my relatives still farm, where I heard the stories of feuds and backbiting, and where I saw that people survived and flourished because fundamentally they trusted and relied upon one another. A death in the family is not just a death in a family; it is a death in the community. I saw people help each other with money, materials, labor, attention, and time. I saw men gather once a year, without fail, to clean the grounds of a ninety-year-old woman who had helped the community before, during, and after the war. I saw her remembering them with birthday cards sent to each of their children.

I come from a people with a long memory and a distinctive grace. We live our thanks. And we are Americans. Japanese-Americans.

I Am a Japanese-American Woman

Woman. The last piece of my identity. It has been easier by far for me to know myself in Japan and to see my place in America than it has been to accept my line of connection with my own mother. She was my dark self, a figure in whom I thought I saw all that I feared most in myself. Growing into womanhood and looking for some model of strength, I turned away from her. Of course, I could not find what I sought. I was looking for a black feminist or a white feminist. My mother is neither white nor black.

My mother is a woman who speaks with her life as much as with her tongue. I think of her with her own mother. Grandmother had Parkinson's disease and it had frozen her gait and set her fingers, tongue, and feet jerking and trembling in a terrible dance. My aunts and uncles wanted her to be able to live in her own home. They fed her, bathed her, dressed her, awoke at midnight to take her for one last trip to the bathroom. My aunts (her daughters-in-law) did most of the care, but my mother went from New Hampshire to California each summer to spend a month living with Grandmother, because she wanted to and because she wanted to give my aunts at least a small rest. During those hot summer days, mother lay on the couch watching the television or reading, cooking foods that Grandmother liked, and speaking little. Grandmother thrived under her care.

The time finally came when it was too dangerous for Grandmother to live alone. My relatives kept finding her on the floor beside her bed when they went to wake her in the mornings. My mother flew to California to help clean the house and make arrangements for Grandmother to enter a local nursing home. On her last day at home, while Grandmother was sitting in her big, overstuffed armchair, hair combed and wearing a green summer dress, my mother went to her and knelt at her feet. "Here, Mamma," she said. "I've polished your shoes." She lifted Grandmother's legs and helped her into the shiny black shoes. My Grandmother looked down and smiled slightly. She left her house walking, supported by her children, carrying her pocket book, and wearing her polished black shoes. "Look, Mamma," my mom had said, kneeling. "I've polished your shoes."

Just the other day, my mother came to Boston to visit. She had recently lost a lot of weight and was pleased with her new shape and her feeling of good health. "Look at me, Kes," she exclaimed, turning toward me, front and back, as naked as the day she was born. I saw her small breasts and the wide, brown scar, belly button to pubic hair, that marked her because my brother and I were both born by Caesarean section. Her hips were small. I was not a large baby, but there was so little room for me in her that when she was carrying me she could not even begin to bend over toward the floor. She hated it, she said.

"Don't I look good? Don't you think I look good?"

I looked at my mother, smiling and as happy as she, thinking of all the times I have seen her naked. I have seen both my parents naked throughout my life, as they have seen me.

I know this to be Japanese, this ease with the physical, and it makes me think of an old Japanese folk song. A young nursemaid, sent far from her home to be a servant, is singing a lullaby to a baby who is strapped to her back.

> If I should drop dead,
> bury me by the roadside!
> I'll give a flower
> to everyone who passes.

> What kind of flower?
> The cam-cam-camellia [tsun-tsun-tsubaki]
> watered by Heaven:
> alms water.

The nursemaid is the intersection of the human, the natural world, the body and the soul. In this song, she looks steadily at life, which is sometimes so terribly sad. I think of her while looking at my mother. . . .

I recently heard a man from West Africa share some memories of his childhood. He was raised Muslim, but when he was a young man, he found himself deeply drawn to Christianity. He struggled against his inner impulse for years, trying to avoid the church yet feeling pushed to return to it again and again. "I would have done *anything* to avoid the change," he said. At last he became Christian. Afterwards he was afraid to go home, fearing that he would not be accepted. The fear was groundless, he discovered, when at last he returned—he had separated himself, but his family and friends (all Muslim) had not separated themselves from him.

The man, who is now a professor of religion, said that in the Africa he knew as a child and a young man, pluralism was embraced rather than feared. There was "a kind of tolerance that did not deny your particularity," he said. He alluded to zestful, spontaneous debates that would sometimes loudly erupt between Muslims and

Christians in the village's public spaces. His memories of an atheist who harangued the villagers when he came to visit them once a week moved me deeply. Perhaps the man was an agricultural advisor or inspector. He harassed the women. He would say: "Don't go to the fields! Don't even bother to go to the fields. Let God take care of you. He'll send you the food. If you believe in God, why do you need to work? You don't need to work! Let God put the seeds in the ground. Stay home."

The professor said, "The women laughed, you know? They just laughed. Their attitude was, 'Here is a child of God. When will he come home?'"

The storyteller, the professor of religion, smiled a most fantastic tender smile as he told this story. "In my country, there is a deep affirmation of the oneness of God," he said. "The atheist and the women were having quite different experiences in their encounter, though the atheist did not know this. He saw himself as quite separate from the women. But the women did not see themselves as being separate from him. 'Here is a child of God,' they said. 'When will he come home?'"

Response and Analysis

1. Kesaya Noda asks, "How is one to know and define oneself?" Briefly describe Noda's three identities: racially Japanese, Japanese-American, and Japanese-American woman. What factors influenced each of these identities?

2. According to Carl Rogers, what is self-concept and positive regard? How might the evaluations by others, such as parents and teachers, and a child's need for approval influence the child's personality?

Personal Experience and Application

1. Write a brief essay in response to the following question: Who am I?

2. Do you believe that people are basically good? Why or why not?

Research

Suppose you want to examine how personality characteristics change over time. You decide to conduct a longitudinal study with 100 psychology students. Your plan is to administer the Minnesota Multiphasic Personality Inventory (MMPI) every year for ten years. However, because of scheduling difficulties, you are unable to administer the MMPI at the same time each year. During the first five years, the participants complete the MMPI in mid-December; during the second five years, they complete it in mid-June. How might the time of year influence your findings? Why?

RACISM DOESN'T GROW UP

Joyce Lee

Psychological Concepts
reciprocal influences, self-efficacy, self-esteem

Many children experience at some time feeling isolated from a group. To belong and to be like others is a powerful desire, especially for the young. Joyce Lee, who moved to Portland, Oregon, from Hong Kong when she was a child, faced the challenges that many newcomers face—learning to communicate, being accepted, and making friends. Here, Lee shares how her experiences brought forth certain qualities in her personality.

I came to Portland, Oregon in 1969 from Hong Kong. I came with my mother and my two brothers. I was placed at an elementary school in a working class neighborhood almost immediately after I arrived to America. I was five years old when I experienced, for the first time in my life, that being "different" was not something to strive for. Acting different could alienate you, looking different could make you feel inferior.

I remember in kindergarten standing next to the bathroom, in front of the children's coat rack, immobile, for one schoolyear. I had no friends, I didn't talk with anyone, including the teachers. After a few months, it seemed that teachers didn't talk to me either. We just co-existed in the room, me with the coat rack, the other children with the teachers. If a classmate gave me any attention, I stood as still as possible, wanting them to think I wasn't a real person. I pretended to be an inanimate object. Eventually the classmate would lose their interest. It got to be an understanding between myself and the class. They would treat me like a statue and I would behave like one. Actually, they treated me better than a statue; I didn't get vandalized. And, because I was a statue tucked away in the corner, I was never in anyone's way. I didn't make noise, I tried not to blink or move. I was actually content with the arrangement. I was even more content to stay home, but ended up in school everyday for no reason I could see.

I don't remember what happened at the end of the day. I think my mother must have come by to pick me up. When I saw her, I was human again.

If I had to use the bathroom, I waited until I thought no one was looking, used it as fast as I could, and returned to my corner.

It must have been frustrating for kindergarten teachers to have me in their class. They were probably at a loss as to what to do since I didn't respond or participate. They decided that I was mentally retarded.

My mother, who spoke no English, was told that I would be enrolled in a school for retarded children. She was horrified, but she couldn't convince my teachers that I was normal. My aunt, who did speak English, couldn't convince them either.

Out of ingenuity and desperation, my mother told me to fold lots of paper boats and birds in school. She taught me every paper boat she knew, every bird, frog, pig, and so on. (I already knew how to fold some boats, paper boat races are common among little children in Hong Kong.) When I displayed my origami skills at school, I was no longer categorized as a "special child." What happened after this time is a little fuzzy. I remember that the teachers had a different attitude toward me. The other kids didn't think I was dumb anymore. I still didn't talk, but eventually, a special effort was made to integrate me into activities, an effort to which I responded.

There was also a special effort to teach me English, which I had not understood before. When I understood some of the language, I started to excel.

Looking back, I try to understand why I refused to budge from my spot. I suspect that I distrusted everyone. With the exception of one American-born Chinese girl who spoke English, no one else looked like me. I also didn't understand the language and the interactions between teacher and student. In Hong Kong, corporal punishment and mental abuse were common methods of discipline at my school. To write the Chinese character "father" wrong meant a couple of slaps on the hand and face. If you persisted in writing the character wrong, you would lose bathroom privileges or lunch privileges. That was in nursery school. The Oregon kindergarten teachers, by contrast, didn't discipline the children. I didn't trust them.

Whoopi Goldberg has a standup routine in which she plays a little Black girl who wears a mop on her head and pretends to be White. As I was growing up, I wanted to be White, too. After third grade, the kids became meaner. When kids made fun of me in second or first grade, I didn't know enough of the language to be offended or hurt. After third grade, I knew a lot of English. The treatment seemed to get worse. "Chink," "slanty eyes," "jap," "Hong Kong phooey," were names I grew up with. When I wasn't called those names, I was sometimes beaten up after school by one or two kids waiting for me. Surprisingly, I was beaten up not just by White kids but also Black kids. In fact, the Black kids were worse than the White ones. The White ones would take me on singularly, but the Black kids were often in groups. When I reached high school, the name calling continued—although I didn't get beaten up anymore.

By high school, White kids and Black kids segregated, they had little to do with each other, except in school sports. The racial hatred I experienced was from the football jocks, not the jocks who were from educated middle class families, but primarily jocks from poor blue-collar families. There were quite a few of these guys. Some of the girls on the cheerleading team, girls from middle class families, also showed contempt for non-Whites.

My school had huge racial and economic class gaps. We had a program for Asian refugees from Cambodia, Vietnam, and Laos. We also had a program for juvenile delinquents, who had a choice of attending institutions or attending my high school. On the other side of the spectrum, we had programs for young scholars who were too advanced in certain subjects to continue high school and had the option of attending Reed College for a few courses on scholarship. With this ethnic, academic, and class diversity, one might have expected a little more sophistication, more tolerance from the students. Unfortunately, this was not the case.

The refugees were hated and often targets of racial violence. Sometimes, I would see other Chinese students get threatened and harassed. I felt sorry for them but at the same time, relieved that, for the moment, it wasn't me. I hated myself for a long time and was ashamed of being Chinese, was ashamed of being an immigrant with uneducated parents, was ashamed of being poor. For thirteen years, I endured the constant barrage of racial slurs.

I remember one incident that was particularly harrowing. During one of our annual picnics in the park, the varsity football rednecks decided that the picnic was being "invaded by gooks," and started bashing heads for recreation. The Asian refugees, probably tired of being picked on day after day, fought back for a change. The fight turned into a race riot involving 200 students. I avoided a pummeling that day by running out of the park as fast as I could.

Even though I was on the school paper and art staff, I was still regarded as a "gook." I had hoped that all the years I had endured of these rednecks had built me some kind of immunity. I was an active student, a student that had something to contribute on *their* terms. I was a senior at that time and had distinguished myself from the refugees, primarily to show that I wasn't like them. I was really "American."

My high school isn't too different from any other high school in America, nor my experiences particularly special. I know I had it better than many immigrants coming to this country.

What I found incredible after all these years is not so much the racism I encountered, or even the violence and hatred against my people, but the institutional blind eye to that racism. The educators, school administrators, and parents of those jocks did NOTHING about the racial problems at our school. Instead, the race riot in the park was hushed up. There was no discussion of what happened. After the riot, it was just another day. However, *I* will never forget that day. I will never forget how fast my heart raced, and the looks of hatred and fear around me. I still feel repercussions from those years in Oregon.

Today, in San Francisco, I run into an occasional racial slur—although not to the extent I did when I was younger. In the late 80's and early 90's, the phrase "Asian Invasion" was a label stamped on groups of Asians who accomplished the same goals as Euro-immigrants. I encountered a few paranoid and resentful Whites who feared our growing economic strength. However, most of the damage from my childhood manifests itself in more internal ways.

Feelings of insignificance, of low self-esteem, are qualities acquired from a childhood in the United States. Feelings of inadequacy creep up when I happen to date a White guy; guilt accompanies us to a movie or restaurant. I'm paranoid that White women secretly resent me; some have shown that they do. I feel inadequate around educated White middle class people in a social setting. I compensate by putting on a confidence mask. "Oh yes, I'm educated, too, and I grew up in a mainstream family. Oh, yes, we celebrate Christmas, of course—my family lives in the suburbs." I feel stupid when this happens because my conformity is transparent. The confidence mask is thin.

I would be kidding myself if I didn't acknowledge some Westernization and assimilation into American culture. My family calls me "banana," yellow outside, white inside. English is now my "first language" and I don't get to speak Cantonese that often. This doesn't mean that I'm not proud of my heritage and that I've embraced Western values 100 percent. I'm part of that culture that has rejected mainstream options like marriage, kids, house, security, suburbia—options available in both of my cultures: American and Chinese.

To totally embrace Chinese values is very similar to a total embrace of American values: marriage, kids, steady income, a house in suburbia, a set of "practical" goals. The obligation that is not part of the Western model is lifelong duty and allegiance to elders at the price of personal will and freedom. No thank you.

The greatest agony for me, even after those years in Oregon, is discovering how little things have changed. It's been approximately fifteen years since I was last enmeshed in the Portland Public School System. Five years ago, my little eleven-year-old cousin, who had arrived from China two years before, took me aside and revealed to me the shame she was facing in school. "There are things I don't tell my parents," she said. Reluctantly, she told me how the White kids at school picked on her, said mean racist things to her, pushed her around. Since she barely spoke English, she had a hard time making friends; she dreaded school.

What consoling words did I have for her? All I could say to her was: "It's not you, it's never you, it's their stupidity and ignorance. Unfortunately, there's a lot of them, and only one of you. Just remember, I'll be there if you need to talk to me anytime." I didn't have the heart to tell her what to expect in high school. I did tell her that I went through the same things she did. I felt helpless; I couldn't offer her anymore than those few scant sentences.

Response and Analysis

1. In what way was being an immigrant difficult for Joyce Lee? What makes a child feel isolated from his or her peers? How might that isolation affect personality?

2. How did the following factors influence one another when Lee was in kindergarten: Lee's personality, thinking patterns, and behavior, and the kindergarten classroom (including the other children and the teacher). How might Albert Bandura's concept of reciprocal influences (or reciprocal determinism) and self-efficacy explain Lee's experiences?

Personal Experience and Application

1. Were children ever mean to you or treat you badly when you were in elementary school? What did they do? How did you react? How did you feel? Were you ever mean to or treat badly another child when you were in grade school? What did you do? How did the child

react? How do you feel today about the way you treated the child?

2. Do you think that events in your childhood helped shape the kind of person you are today? Briefly describe a few of these events and the impact they have had on your personality.

Research

Suppose you want to design a correlational study to examine the relationship between self-efficacy and self-esteem. Write a hypothesis for your study. Whom might you ask to participate? Why?

A REPUTATION DESERVED

Arthur Ashe and Arnold Rampersad

Psychological Concepts
Eysenck's personality dimensions, five-factor model, honesty, integrity

What is the value of reputation? What personality traits make for a good reputation? Tennis champion Arthur Ashe writes that "if one's reputation is a possession, then of all my possessions, my reputation means most to me." By reputation, however, he does not mean behavior fabricated to impress others. Ashe wants to develop qualities that will be valued by others: kindness, calmness, and honesty. When he contracted the AIDS virus, it was especially painful for him to publicly acknowledge his condition because he feared that some people would think that he contracted the virus through drug use or sexual promiscuity—neither of which was true.

I f one's reputation is a possession, then of all my possessions, my reputation means most to me. Nothing comes even close to it in importance. Now and then, I have wondered whether my reputation matters too much to me; but I can no more easily renounce my concern with what other people think of me than I can will myself to stop breathing. No matter what I do, or where or when I do it, I feel the eyes of others on me, judging me.

Needless to say, I know that a fine line exists between caring about one's reputation and hypocrisy. When I speak of the importance to me of my reputation, I am referring to a reputation that is deserved, not an image cultivated for the public in spite of the facts. I know that I haven't always lived without error or sin, but I also know that I have tried hard to be honest and good at all times. When I fail, my conscience comes alive. I have never sinned or erred without knowing I was being watched.

Who is watching me? The living and the dead. My mother, Mattie Cordell Cunningham Ashe, watches me. She died when I was not quite seven. I remember little about her, except for two images. My last sight of her alive: I was finishing breakfast and she was standing in the side doorway looking lovingly at me. She was dressed in her blue corduroy dressing gown. The day was cool and cloudy, and when I went outside I heard birds singing in the small oak tree outside our house. And then I remember the last time I saw her, in a coffin at home. She was wearing her best dress, made of pink satin. In her right hand was a single red rose. Roses were her favorite flower, and my daddy had planted them all around the house; big, deep-hued red roses.

Every day since then I have thought about her. I would give anything to stand once again before her, to feel her arms about me, to touch and taste her skin. She is with me every day, watching me in everything I do. Whenever I speak to young persons about the morality of the decisions they make in life, I usually tell them, "Don't do anything you couldn't tell your mother about."

My father is watching me, too. My father, whose mouth dropped open when he first saw Jeanne, my wife. She looked so much like my mother, he said. He is still a force in my life. Some years ago, before he died of a stroke in 1989, I was being interviewed by the television journalist Charlayne Hunter-Gault in her home.

"Tell me, Arthur," she said, laughter in her voice, "how is it that I have never heard anyone say anything bad about you? How is it that you have never cursed an umpire, or punched an opponent, or gotten a little drunk and disorderly? Why are you such a goody-goody?"

I laughed in turn, and told the truth.

"I guess I have never misbehaved because I'm afraid that if I did anything like that, my father would come straight up from Virginia, find me wherever I happen to be, and kick my ass."

When I told that story not long ago on Men's Day at the Westwood Baptist Church in Richmond, Virginia, everyone smiled and some folks even laughed. They knew what I was talking about, even those few living in that little enclave of blacks surrounded by whites in Richmond who had never met my father. They knew fathers (and mothers) exactly like him, who in times past would come up and find you wherever you were and remind you exactly who you were and don't you forget it. You were their child, that's who.

My father was a strong, dutiful, providing man. He lived and died semi-literate, but he owned his own home and held jobs that were important to him and to people in the community where we lived. His love and his caring were real to me from that Sunday morning in 1950 when he sat on the bottom bunk bed between my brother Johnnie and me and told us between wrenching sobs that our mother had died during the night. From that time on he was father and mother to us. And the lesson he taught above all was about reputation.

"What people think of you, Arthur Junior, your reputation, is all that counts." Or, as I heard from so many older people as I grew up, "A good name is worth more than diamonds and gold."

What others think of me is important, and what I think of others is important. What else do I have to go by? Of course, I cannot make decisions based solely on what other people would think. There are moments when the individual must stand alone. Nevertheless, it is crucial to me that people think of me as honest and principled. In turn, to ensure that they do, I must always act in an honest and principled fashion, no matter the cost.

One day, in Dallas, Texas, in 1973, I was playing in the singles final of a World Championship Tennis (WCT) tournament. My opponent was Stan Smith, a brilliant tennis player but an even more impressive human being in his integrity. On one crucial point, I watched Smith storm forward, racing to intercept a ball about to bounce a second time on his side of the net. When the point was over, I was sure the ball had bounced twice before he hit it and that the point was mine. Smith said he had reached the ball in time. The umpire was baffled. The crowd was buzzing.

I called Smith up to the net.

"Stan, did you get to that ball?"

"I did. I got it."

I conceded the point. Later, after the match—which I lost—a reporter approached me. Was I so naïve? How could I have taken Smith's word on such an important point?

"Believe me," I assured him, "I am not a fool. I wouldn't take just anybody's word for it. But if Stan Smith says he got to the ball, he got to it. I trust his character."

When I was not quite eighteen years old, I played a tournament in Wheeling, West Virginia, the Middle Atlantic Junior Championships. As happened much of the time when I was growing up, I was the only black kid in the tournament, at least in the under-eighteen age section. One night, some of the other kids trashed a cabin; they absolutely destroyed it. And then they decided to say that I was responsible, although I had nothing to do with it. The incident even got into the papers. As much as I denied and protested, those white boys would not change their story.

I rode to Washington from West Virginia with the parents of Dickie Dell, another one of the players. They tried to reassure me, but it was an uncomfortable ride because I was silently worrying about what my father would do and say to me. When I reached Washington, where I was to play in another tournament, I telephoned him in Richmond. As I was aware, he already knew about the incident. When he spoke, he was grim. But he had one question only.

"Arthur Junior, all I want to know is, were you mixed up in that mess?"

"No, Daddy, I wasn't."

He never asked about it again. He trusted me. With my father, my reputation was solid.

I have tried to live so that people would trust my character, as I had trusted Stan Smith's. Sometimes I think it is almost a weakness in me, but I want to be seen as fair and honest, trustworthy, kind, calm, and polite. I want no stain on my character, no blemish on my reputation. And that was why what happened to me early in April 1992 hit me as hard as it did.

The night before I met Jimmy Connors in the men's singles final at Wimbledon in the summer of 1975, I went to bed and slept soundly. That match was the biggest of my life. It was also one that just about everybody was sure I would lose, because Connors was then the finest tennis player in the world, virtually invincible. In fact, the match was supposed to be a slaughter, and I was to be the sacrificial lamb. Before going to bed I had talked and talked with various friends about strategy and tactics, but when it was time to go to sleep, I shrugged off all the nervousness and the worrying, as I usually do, and slept peacefully—as peacefully as that proverbial lamb.

The night of Tuesday, April 7, 1992, was another matter altogether. Try as I could, I was not able to deliver myself to sleep. Once again I had talked and talked, this time mainly with my wife at home but also with friends on the telephone. Once again we discussed strategy and tactics as I tried to make myself ready for another ordeal, but one far more threatening to me than four sets in the final at Wimbledon against Connors. This time I could not bring myself to sleep, except in fits and starts. From my windows on the fourteenth floor of my apartment building in Manhattan I saw the lights of the city and watched for the sun to come up through the murk and mist of Brooklyn and Queens to the east. Before six o'clock, with the sky still dark, I was dressed and ready to go, ready to hunt for a newspaper, to discover if my secret was out, exposed to the world. I knew that once that happened, my life and the lives of my family would be changed forever, and almost certainly for the worse.

In a shop across the avenue I found the newspaper I was waiting for, *USA Today*. I scanned the front page, then flipped back to the sports section. There was not a word about me. I felt a great relief. And then I knew that the relief was only temporary, that it was now up to me to take the matter into my own hands and break the news to whatever part of the world wanted to hear it. And I would have to do it that day, Wednesday, because the days—maybe the hours—of my secret were definitely numbered. I had to announce to the world that I, Arthur Ashe, had AIDS.

Response and Analysis

1. Why did Arthur Ashe believe that he "must always act in an honest and principled fashion, no matter the cost"? Why were honesty, integrity, and reputation so important to Ashe? How did Ashe define reputation?

2. Briefly describe a few features of Ashe's personality using either Eysenck's major person-

ality dimensions or the five-factor model of personality. What are the similarities and differences of Eysenck's approach and the five-factor model approach?

Personal Experience and Application

1. What is your reaction to the value Ashe places on reputation? Do you believe that he is too concerned with how others view him? Why or why not?

2. Briefly describe a few of your personality traits using either Eysenck's major personality dimensions or the five-factor model of personality.

Research

Suppose you want to conduct a study examining how unconscious conflicts and motives influence personality. You decide to use a projective test and ask the participants what they see in a picture. How might you determine the test's reliability? Do you think the test would provide a valid measure of personality? Why or why not?

chapter *11*

PSYCHOLOGICAL
DISORDERS

A night flowing with birds, a ragged moon,
And in broad day the midnight come again!
A man goes far to find out what he is—
Death of the self in a long tearless night,
All natural shapes blazing unnatural light.

THEODORE ROETHKE, "In a Dark Time"

What is it like to feel the "death of the self"? What might people suffering from psychological disorders experience when "in broad day" they feel dark as midnight? Psychological disorders can bring great torment to those afflicted. This chapter presents narratives about people who suffer from schizophrenia; bipolar disorder; multiple personality disorder; obsessive-compulsive disorder; autism; and antisocial personality disorder.

Lori Schiller writes of her bout with schizophrenia. Schiller was able to deflect much of this illness's potential devastation. The Voices, which were Schiller's first indication that she was not well, are still with her. However, medication and support from family and professionals have enabled her to live a more normal life. She now teaches at the hospital where she was once a patient.

John Custance knows what it is to see a "ragged moon," to feel midnight in the bright light of day. Custance suffered from bipolar disorder. While he was hospitalized, he kept a journal detailing his experiences with his alternating states.

Quiet Storm is the pseudonym of a woman who writes about the anguish she endures from multiple personality disorder. A victim of child abuse, she adopted several personalities for protection from beatings, humiliation, and isolation. Speaking of herself in first-person plural, she recounts the torture "we" endured. In her "internal house" live several persons who struggle to heal their many wounds.

A woman suffering from obsessive-compulsive disorder tells in excruciating detail how she is compelled to do even the smallest daily tasks over and over before she can go on to the next chore. These ritualistic acts, she hopes, will allay her anxieties about harm that might come to herself or her family.

Few autistics are able to function in the world, and their silence leaves us with little understanding of their perceptions, feelings, and thoughts. Temple Grandin, Ph.D., is a high-functioning autistic woman who tells of her creative ways to live a less isolated existence. Grandin's fascinating story recounts her childhood experiences and the ways in which she has come to deal with her autism.

Geoffrey Wolff, who has no want of astonishment and love for his father, Duke, remembers him as a master of deception. Though Duke's father was a physician and his family was reasonably well-off, Duke invented a new biography for himself. He wanted others to believe that he had graduated from the best schools, had held the best jobs, and had served his country honorably. Though Duke knew how to charm and how to be a gentleman, he remained a "confidence man" through and through.

THE QUIET ROOM: A JOURNEY OUT OF THE TORMENT OF MADNESS

Lori Schiller and Amanda Bennett

Psychological Concept
schizophrenia

Lori Schiller came from a close-knit, upper-middle-class family. She knew she was well loved, and her childhood years were happy ones shared with close friends. Motivated to succeed, she earned grades that gained her admission to Tufts University.

By the time she was seventeen years old, however, Schiller had a secret life—one full of Voices that screamed at her. She received mysterious calls without a caller and even heard Walter Cronkite give her instructions on the evening news. She was certain she was possessed. Whom could she trust with her fears? How could she be helped? Now recovering, Schiller tells of her beginning bout with schizophrenia.

It was a hot night in August 1976, the summer of my seventeenth year, when, uninvited and unannounced, the Voices took over my life.

I was going into my senior year in high school, so this was to be my last time at summer camp. College, a job, adulthood, responsibility—they were all just around the corner. But for the moment I wasn't prepared for anything more than a summer of fun. I certainly wasn't prepared to have my life change forever.

I had been coming to Lincoln Farm for several years, first as a camper, later as a counselor. By day, I shepherded the nine- and ten-year-olds through sailing, canoeing and archery.

At night after the little kids were safely in bed, the counselors would hang out together in the long, low wooden bungalows we called "motels," playing cards, eating cookies and drinking a Kool-Aid type of concoction we called bug juice. Some nights the older counselors drove us into town to the Roscoe diner. We laughed, told jokes and fooled around.

It was just an ordinary summer, and I was just an ordinary girl. Except that sometime during that summer things began to change.

At first, the change was pleasant. Somehow, without my quite knowing why, everything seemed much nicer than it had been before. The lake seemed more blue, the paddlewheels bigger and the sailboats more graceful than ever before. The trees of the Catskill Mountains that ringed our camp took on a deeper green than I remembered, and all at once the whole camp seemed to be the most wonderful place in the world.

I was overwhelmed by what life had to offer. It seemed that I could not run fast enough, could not swim far enough, could not stay up late enough into the night to take in everything I wanted to experience. I was energetic and active, happy and bubbly, a friend to everyone. Everything around me was bright, clean and clear. And as for me, it seemed that I too was a part of this beauty. I was strong and attractive, powerful and exciting. It seemed that everyone around me had only to look at me to love me the way I loved them.

What's more, my memories became more vivid than ever before. It had been here at Lincoln Farm two years earlier that I had fallen in love. As I thought back to that summer, it too seemed wild and bright and wonderful. I had been in love as no one had been in love before. And the man I fell for was like no one I had ever met before.

He had been an exchange student that year, the summer I was fifteen. He was gorgeous, a real hunk, blond and lanky with bright blue eyes, and a cute little accent. Since I was short and dark, he seemed especially exotic. I really liked him, and could scarcely take my eyes off him. What's more, at twenty-three years old, he was my first older man. I admired him for his courage to come all the way over here alone for a summer, and I was charmed by his sense of humor.

We really enjoyed each other's company. My memories of those evenings became sweetly sad as I recalled talking about being in love, and how terrible it was going to be when he finally had to return home. We even made up an absurd little song to the tune of the Beatles' "Ticket to Ride":

> *He's got a ticket for home.*
> *He's got a ticket for home.*
> *He's got a ticket for home,*
> *And won't be back . . .*

But several weeks later, after camp was over and I had returned home to Scarsdale, he showed up at my house—with a pretty woman whom he introduced to my parents as his fiancée.

As the days went by, I found myself obsessing on that moment two years ago. Gradually, my mood began to shift, and the brightness of the world began to darken. As I remembered the past, the feelings began to blur the present. Then came the dreadful thoughts. Why had he left me that summer? Why hadn't I been good enough? Maybe it was because I really wasn't beautiful, exquisite and passionate. Maybe I was really ugly. Maybe more than ugly. Maybe I was fat and disgusting, an object not of romance but of ridicule. Yes, that was it. Maybe everyone around me, far from loving me, was instead laughing at me, mocking me to my face.

My mood began to turn black. A dark haze settled around me. The beautiful camp turned foul, a thing of evil, not of beauty. All around me were shadows, and I was wrapped in a dark haze.

My memories became so vivid that at night as I lay in my bunk wracked by unhappy thoughts and unable to sleep, it seemed as if I really were back in that summer. In my memory we were again down by the huge, dark, romantic lake. Over to the dockside we could hear the water lapping up against the sailboats and giant waterwheels the kids played on during the day. Late at night, the fireflies were gone, but we could still hear frogs croaking along the banks. The sky was heavy with stars I felt I had never seen before. We sat in the thick grass that ran right down to the water's edge and laughed and talked together.

In my memory, we snuggled and kissed. And then he became more insistent. We lay down together on the top of one of the picnic tables that ringed the lake. His hands began to roam, under my T-shirt, into my shorts. I was excited and worried, terrified and thrilled all at the same time. I wanted more, and I wanted him to stop. We were pushing the limits of my experience and I didn't know how to handle it. In my mind I was back there, rolling and caressing in the darkness, and I was washed over with complicated feelings from past and present—love, embarrassment, rejection, fear.

Then, in the middle of this chaos, a huge Voice boomed out through the darkness.

"You must die!" Other Voices joined in. "You must die! You will die!"

At first I didn't realize where I was. Was I at the lake? Was I asleep? Was I awake? Then I snapped back to the present. I was here at camp, alone. My summertime fling was long gone, two years gone. That long-ago scene was being played out in my mind, and in my mind alone. But as soon as I realized that I was in my bunk, and awake—and that my roommate was still sleeping peacefully— I knew I had to run. I had to get away from these terrible, evil Voices.

I leaped from my bed and ran barefoot out into the grass. I had to find someplace to hide. I thought if I ran fast enough and far enough, I could outrun the Voices. "You must die!" they chanted. "You will die."

Frantically, I ran out to the wide, open center lawn. The grass was wet under my feet. I raced for the huge trampoline where the kids practiced backflips and somersaults.

I climbed on. My head was filled with wild, strange thoughts. If I could jump fast enough and high enough, I thought, perhaps I could jump the Voices away. So I jumped and I jumped, all the while hearing the tormenting Voices ringing in my ears. "You must die. You will die." I jumped for hours, till I began to see the sun peeking over the hills. I jumped until I was out of breath, exhausted. I jumped until I really was ready to die.

Yet still they continued, commanding me, pounding into my head. They began to curse and revile me: "You whore bitch who isn't worth a piece of crap!" they yelled at me. I tried to answer them, to make them stop.

"It's not true," I pleaded. "Leave me alone. It's not true." Eventually, both I and the Voices collapsed in exhaustion.

In the nights that followed this torture continued. In the morning, I was exhausted, drawn and white from fear and lack of sleep. In the dead of night I jumped, pursued by the vicious Voices. Night after night I jumped, unable to sleep, either because of the screaming Voices, or my fear they would return.

As best I could during the day, I kept a calm but distant front. I spent as much time as I could in my bunk. But gradually people began to notice that something was wrong. My cheerful banter vanished, and I could sense that increasingly people were beginning to wonder what was the matter with me.

Finally at 9:30 A.M. on August 12 the camp owner, worried about my health, instructed a staff member to drive me home to Scarsdale.

Since that time, I have never been completely free of those Voices. At the beginning of that summer, I felt well, a happy healthy girl—I thought—with a normal head and heart. By summer's end, I was sick, without any clear idea of what was happening to me or why. And as the Voices evolved into a full-scale illness, one that I only later learned was called schizophrenia, it snatched from me my tranquillity, sometimes my self-possession, and very nearly my life.

Along the way I have lost many things: the career I might have pursued, the husband I might have married, the children I might have had. During the years when my friends were marrying, having their babies and moving into the houses I once dreamed of living in, I have been behind locked doors, battling the Voices who took over my life without even asking my permission.

Sometimes these Voices have been dormant. Sometimes they have been overwhelming. At times over the years they have nearly destroyed me. Many times over the years I was ready to give up, believing they had won.

Today this illness, these Voices, are still part of my life. But it is I who have won, not they. A wonderful new drug, caring therapists, the support and love of my family and my own fierce battle—that I know now will never end—have all combined in a nearly miraculous way to enable me to master the illness that once mastered me.

Today, nearly eighteen years after that terrifying summer, I have a job, a car, an apartment of my own. I am making friends and dating. I am teaching classes at the very hospital at which I was once a patient.

Response and Analysis

1. What does Lori Schiller say she lost while "battling the Voices who took over [her] life"? How is Schiller battling schizophrenia?

2. Describe Schiller's schizophrenic symptoms. Give examples of disorganized thinking, auditory hallucinations, emotional disturbances, and difficulties interacting with other people.

Personal Experience and Application

1. What do you believe are the possible causes of schizophrenia? Briefly discuss the following possible causes: biological factors, psychological factors, and a combination of both.

2. About one percent of Americans are diagnosed with schizophrenia. Many require hospitalization for weeks, months, or even years. Many are taking medication that may allow them to have more normal lives. However, about half of all patients in mental hospitals are diagnosed with schizophrenia. Three to four million Americans with schizophrenia are permanently unemployed, and many are unemployable. Considering these statistics, how should society care for victims of mental illness? Where should people suffering from mental illness live? Should society allow them to be homeless? Who should assist victims of mental illness when they cannot work and cannot pay for living expenses or for mental health treatment?

Research

Suppose you conduct a study to replicate research by Suddath et al. (1990) investigating whether structural defects in the brain are associated with schizophrenia. You use magnetic resonance imaging (MRI) to scan the brain. Your participants are fifteen sets of identical (monozygotic) twins who share the same genetic material, family, and socioeconomic background. Each set of twins is discordant for schizophrenia. That is, one is schizophrenic and the other shows no signs of schizophrenia. After obtaining the MRI images, you compare the MRI scans for enlarged ventricles. Assume that your results support Suddath et al. and show that the ventricles of the schizophrenic participants are larger than those of the nonschizophrenic participants.

What is the independent variable? What are the levels and conditions of the independent variable? What is the dependent variable? What is the hypothesis? Do the results support the hypothesis?

THE UNIVERSE OF BLISS
AND THE UNIVERSE
OF HORROR

John Custance

Psychological Concept
bipolar disorder

A victim of bipolar disorder, John Custance wrote the following selection while he was a patient in a mental hospital. For several months, he was held captive by real and imagined stimuli. When he was manic, he was exuberant. His senses were alive: lights were brighter; even grass tasted like a delicacy. He believed he was in communion with God. When he suffered from delusions of grandeur, he thought that all he asked would be granted.

Then depression would hit. Custance would be repulsed by excreta, by fears of being punished in Hell. Devils tormented him; hallucinations beguiled him. He was in danger of committing suicide.

Eventually, Custance's illness dissipated, and he apparently never suffered so severely again. Does Custance have any similar experiences in the manic and depressive states? Are manic and depressive states the opposite sides of the same coin?

All that follows in this chapter, describing the manic state, was actually written (subject to minor revisions) while in that state. I am at the moment in a typical state of hypo-mania, and am a patient in a Mental Hospital. One result of my condition is that I am writing with far greater ease than in normal circumstances. Usually I am a very slow-brained writer, whereas now my pen can scarcely keep up with the rapid flow of ideas. It is thus obviously a good opportunity to describe as it were at first hand the symptoms and sensations of the manic state. . . .

The first thing I note is the peculiar appearances of the lights—the ordinary electric lights in the ward. They are not exactly brighter, but deeper, more intense, perhaps a trifle more ruddy than usual. Moreover, if I relax the focusing of my eyes, which I can do very much more easily than in normal circumstances, a bright star-like phenomenon emanates from the lights, ultimately forming a maze of iridescent patterns of all colours of the rainbow, which remind me vaguely of the Aurora Borealis.

There are a good many people in the ward, and their faces make a peculiarly intense impression on me. I will not say that they have exactly a halo round them, though I have often had that impression in more acute phases of mania. At present it is rather that faces seem to glow with a sort of inner light which shows up the characteristic lines extremely vividly. Thus, although I am the most hopeless draughtsman as a rule, in this state I can draw quite recognisable likenesses. This phenomenon is not confined to faces; it applies to the human body as a whole, and to a rather lesser degree to other objects such as trees, clouds, flowers and so on. Coloured objects make a particularly vivid impression, possibly in view of the associations they arouse (see below) and, curiously enough, so do large vehicles, particularly steam-rollers, railway engines and trains. Perhaps the associations of childhood are involved here. Connected with these vivid impressions is a rather curious feeling behind the eyeballs, rather as though a vast electric motor were pulsing away there.

All my other senses seem more acute than usual. Certainly my sense of touch is heightened; my fingers are much more sensitive and neat. Although generally a clumsy person with an execrable handwriting I can write much more neatly than usual; I can print, draw, embellish and carry out all sorts of little manual operations, such as pasting up scrapbooks and the like, which would normally drive me to distraction. I also note a peculiar tingling in my fingertips.

My hearing appears to be more sensitive, and I am able to take in without disturbance or distraction many different sound-impressions at the same time. Thus, although busily engaged in writing this in a crowded ward with people walking up and down and the most diverse sounds all around me, from the cries of gulls outside to the laughter and chatter of my fellow-patients, I am fully alive to what is going on and yet find no difficulty in concentrating on my work. At times I have known sounds make a tremendous effect upon me, almost as though I were in a gallery with supernatural powers of resonance. At such times my own very ordinary bass voice appears to be as powerful as that of Chaliapin's at least; it is as though passages in my chest which are normally clogged were opened up, and my chest actually seems to set up abnormal vibrations.

At the moment my sense of smell seems more or less normal, and so does my sense of taste. In slightly more acute phases of mania, however, both these senses are well above par. Even now I have no doubt that if I were to be allowed to walk about freely in a flower garden I should appreciate the scent far more than usual; and I have often in manic states eaten ordinary cabbage leaves or new Brussels sprouts picked straight off the plants with such relish that they appeared to me the greatest delicacies—a kind of manna from Heaven. Even common grass tastes excellent, while real delicacies like strawberries or raspberries give ecstatic sensations appropriate to a veritable food for the gods. . . .

When in a depressive period I have an intense sense of repulsion to lavatories, excreta, urine, or anything associated with them. This repulsion extends to all kinds of dirt. I loathe going to the lavatory, using a chamber-pot, or touching anything in the least bit dirty. With this repulsion is associated extreme terror, in my case terror of eternal punishment in Hell. It is also associated with repulsion to fellow-creatures, repulsion to self, repulsion in fact to the whole universe. Finally it is associated with a sense of intense guilt.

In the manic phase repulsion gives place to attraction. I have no repulsion to excreta, urine and so on. I have no distaste for dirt. I do not care in the least whether I am washed or not, whereas I am terrified of the slightest speck of dirt and continually wash my hands like Lady Macbeth when in a state of depression. At the same time I feel a mystic sense of unity with all fellow-creatures and the Universe as a whole; I am at peace with myself; and I have no sense of guilt whatsoever. . . .

The best way to give an idea of what happens to the mind in the extremes of depression is to describe in some detail my last attack, which came early in 1939, shortly after the episode which took me to Brixton.

Twice before I had suffered from serious depression, with acute insomnia and impulses to suicide. Prolonged rest under drugs in an excellent nursing-home had effected a cure in each case. I could, however, no longer afford the fees at the nursing-home, and so had to go on this occasion to a private Mental Hospital. . . .

In my previous states of depression I had never really lost my grip of reality. I had begun to slip off the table-land down the slope to the left, but there was still as it were a ridge in front of me which might hold me up. I was utterly miserable and wanted to die, but my fears, troubles and worries were of normal human mischances which might happen to anybody. I feared poverty, failure in life, inability to educate my children, making my wife miserable, losing her, ending up in the gutter as the most revolting type of beggar and so on. My fears had in fact become so overpowering as to appear to me like certainties, but they were only earthly, human fears. Beyond the ridge bordering this ordinary universe of common human experience unending horrors awaited me. But I did not know; I had not crossed it, at any rate in that direction. . . .

I lay in my bed in the ward of the Hospital dominated above all by an overpowering sense of fear. At first I did not know exactly what it was that I feared, except of course that my mind, which I strove as hard as I could to keep blank, would insist on working about the ordinary, human fears I have outlined above. Wisely, no attempt was made to get me up, and I lay as motionless as I could, covering my head as a rule with the bedclothes, partly to shut out the sights and sounds of the ward, and partly as a sort of instinctive reaction.

. . . I had by now become quite convinced that I was finished for good and all. There was no possible chance of my coming out of the Hospital alive. In fact though not actually dead, I was as good as dead. For some inscrutable reason, perhaps because I had committed "the unforgivable sin" or just because I was such an appalling sinner, the worst man who had ever existed, I had been chosen to go alive through the portals of Hell, in an ordinary English lunatic-asylum. Therefore it was obviously too late for repentance. It was, I knew, quite unsound theology to imagine that people got another chance after they were dead. Obviously when they saw what they were in for they would repent; anybody would. But they would be cast into outer darkness and the Lord would not bother about them any more, however much they wept and gnashed their teeth. I knew what I was in for; I had been before the Bar (Bar————); I had been told there was no hope of a reprieve; and that was the end of it.

All this I kept to myself, of course; I did not argue with G.G. about it. Nor did I tell the doctors. They were not particularly sympathetic and did not invite confidences; moreover I was quite astute enough to realise that to talk on these lines would be regarded as further proof of insanity; I might even be certified. As long as I was voluntary, there was perhaps just the faintest chance that I might get out and succeed in making away with myself.

My wife, who visited me nobly at least twice a week for the whole eleven months of my confinement, never could understand the logic of this attitude. She was the only person to whom I dared confide my horrors, and I tried hard to show my train of reasoning. Roughly it was that I was a sort of opposite of Jesus Christ. Satan's job had been to catch a man, get him to sell his soul to him completely and utterly, like Faust, and then take him down alive into the pit. That was a sort of necessary counterweight to the resurrection of Jesus and the elect. I was the man. But if I could only kill myself, it might blow up the whole Universe, but at least I would get out of eternal torture and achieve the oblivion and nothingness for which my soul craved. I did in fact make three attempts at suicide, the most serious of which was when I tore myself from my attendant and threw myself in front of a car, with my poor wife, who was visiting me, looking on.

Although my attempts at suicide failed, they had one satisfactory effect; the doctors increased my drugs. As long as I was able to attain unconsciousness at night (with the aid of three or four doses of paraldehyde), and to maintain a fairly soporific state during the day (with anything up to four tablets of allonal), I could just keep the horrors at bay. My whole conscious effort was now directed towards the aim of putting off the moment when I would disappear finally into Hell. I visualised this process as happening quite naturally. Some day, at some moment, the iron control I kept on my terrors would break. I should start shrieking in agony. Naturally the attendants would then shut me up in a side-room, probably in one of the worst wards. After that the process of torturing a human soul in the living flesh would just go on. I should shriek, but so do many lunatics; nobody would do anything for me; they would naturally think my pains were imaginary. But they would be real pains; anyway I knew that the philosophical distinction between real and imaginary was very difficult to make. It did not matter much when I "died" in the body. I might spend days, months, or years shrieking in my side-room before they buried me. For me, it would all be the same process of eternal, progressively increasing torture.

Response and Analysis

1. Describe John Custance's emotional state, auditory and visual perceptions, and behavior when he was in a manic state and a depressive state.

2. What similarities does Custance show when he is in the manic and depressive states?

Personal Experience and Application

1. Most of us experience minor and temporary depression. Briefly discuss a time when you experienced minor depression. What factors influenced you to be depressed? How did you feel about yourself and the world? How did you relieve your depression?

2. Major depression is substantially different from minor and temporary depression. Many of the factors that are associated with major depression also are associated with suicide. List at least five warning signs of suicide. Although there is no simple formula for preventing suicide, the worst action is taking no action. List at least three recommendations to help prevent a suicide.

Research

Suppose you want to conduct a study to examine whether depressed people evaluate themselves and others more negatively than nondepressed people. The participants in your study will be twenty-five people who meet the DSM-IV criteria for major depression and twenty-five nondepressed people who are comparable to the depressed group in age and gender.

You are trying to choose a procedure that will best test your idea. One option is to ask participants to list ten traits and characteristics to describe themselves, their mother, their father, two other significant people, and two less significant people in their lives. This procedure will allow you to count the number of negatively evaluative versus positively evaluative statements listed by the depressed and nondepressed participants.

A second option is to give the participants a list of ten traits and characteristics and ask them to rate themselves, their mother, their father, two other significant people and two less significant people in their lives on each of the traits. For each trait and characteristic, the participants would indicate how well each trait or characteristic describes the person by using the following scale: not at all, a little bit, somewhat, very much, extremely.

What are the advantages and disadvantages of each option? Which option would you use? Why?

I HAVE MULTIPLE
PERSONALITY DISORDER

Quiet Storm

Psychological Concept
  multiple personality disorder (dissociative identity
  disorder)

Quiet Storm, a pseudonym the writer gave herself to symbolize the quiet surface that covers an inner storm, writes of the several "people" who she believes live within her. Each has a separate identity, career, and "memories, talents, dreams, and fears." She describes several of the women who are a part of her, and tells how they evolved as defenders against child abuse.

Her interior world is vast, filled with children, adolescents, and adults. People often notice great changes in her and remark that she often seems like a completely different person. All of her selves are gradually healing, but integration is not an issue she is ready to confront.

Some readers may find portions of Storm's article disturbing because of the abusive ordeals she presents as causes of her illness.

Elaina is a licensed clinical therapist. Connie is a nurse. Sydney is a delightful little girl who likes to collect bugs in an old mayonnaise jar. Lynn is shy and has trouble saying her l's, and Heather—Heather is a teenager trying hard to be grown-up. We are many different people, but we have one very important thing in common: We share a single body.

We have Multiple Personality Disorder (MPD). We have dozens of different people living inside us, each with our own memories, talents, dreams and fears. Some of us "come out" to work or play or cook or sleep. Some of us only watch from inside. Some of us are still lost in the past, a tortured past full of incest and abuse. And there are many who were so damaged by this past and who have fled so deep inside, we fear we may never reach them.

Imagine a little girl walking with her parents through a bookstore. She's only four, but she already knows how to read. She sees a book she really wants, and asks her parents if she can have it. They tell her no, and a single tear of disappointment rolls down her cheek. A single tear, but it is one tear too many.

The little girl's parents don't say anything in the store, but when they get home they take off her panties and beat her until her bottom is raw and bleeding.

The panties are replaced with a diaper that is fastened to her skin with silver duct tape. She is locked in a closet for three days. She is fed laxative mixed with milk in a baby bottle; her diaper is never changed. Her parents tell her again and again that she is a dirty little baby and will never grow up. They are right.

There is more, worse, but the little girl does not remember it. It's too painful to remember more. If she stays in that closet and refuses to acknowledge the passing of time, then maybe those awful things didn't really happen. Maybe there can be some other ending to her story.

In a way that little girl never left that closet. Another little girl did, one who shared the same body but whose existence began the moment the closet door opened. Where there was one, now there were two—one who understood that she must never ever cry to her parents for any reason and another who huddled forever in a dark inner closet, because to remember what happened next, when her parents finally came to get her, would be too much for a single young mind to bear.

Many of our Alter personalities were born of abuse. Some came because they were needed, others came to protect.

Leah came whenever she heard our father say "Come lay awhile with me." If she came, none of our other Alters would have to do those things he wanted. She could do them for us, and protect us from that part of our childhood.

Halfcup came when we were left at home for days on end with nothing to eat. She cooked meals for us. She cleaned up afterward so our parents wouldn't know we'd found a way to unlock our bedroom door. Halfcup still loves to cook. Last Christmas we bought her a new set of pots and pans.

Connie came when the body was beaten so badly that somebody had to come who didn't feel the pain, who could comfort the Alters who hurt, who could tell the doctor we'd fallen off our bike. We couldn't let anyone tell him what really happened. That would have made our parents even madder.

Unlike many of our Alters, Connie grew up into an adult as our body did. She was created to be a healer, so it was only natural that when she was old enough, she would enroll in nursing school.

Connie didn't know that at the same time she was in nursing school, Elaina was in grad school working on her social work degree. Nor did Elaina know about Connie. All they knew was that, even with only three hours of sleep each night, there never was enough time to get things done.

MPD is not a disease. It is not a sickness. It is a highly developed coping mechanism that allows the young mind to compartmentalize, or "dissociate," repeated and traumatic abuse. The six-year-old who smiles at her teacher at school cannot hold back the tears when her father enters her room in the middle of the night. Somebody else has to come, somebody who can do those things without crying because crying isn't ever allowed. And the little girl whose mother tucks her in at night and calls her Peaches will never understand why that same mother ties her to the bed when she has a fever and beats her and tells her only bad little girls get sick. Somebody else has to come—somebody whose nose isn't stuffy and who doesn't have a fever.

Being able to create Alter personalities to cope with the abuse is the only thing that allowed us to survive our childhood alive. MPD was never a disease—it was a gift, the gift of life we gave to ourselves.

Once we were grown up and had escaped from our abusive parents, the system that protected us for so many years became unnecessary. But still our internal system of multiple personalities survived, and the longer we went untreated the worse things became for us. We lost time, as Alters unknown to us took control of the body. Sometimes they went shopping. Sometimes they haunted libraries. Sometimes they cowered on the floor in the closet because one of our Alters saw a little girl walking hand in hand with her father and the very sight of it terrified her. Often an innocent remark from a friend would trigger old memories of abuse, and for the Alter who held those memories it was as if the abuse were still going on. We couldn't stand to be touched, or to have anyone tell us they cared for us. We felt worthless and alone.

It took five years and as many therapists before we found someone who recognized our MPD. It was another year before we fully accepted the diagnosis. Only then did we truly begin to know ourselves.

The more we learn about ourselves and the abuse that created us, the stronger our system becomes. We've become one another's friends. We form alliances, accept responsibilities. We take care of each other.

Elaina and Connie work for our living. Elaina is a respected therapist who is building an extensive private practice. Connie works weekends at one of the local emergency rooms. Heather drives the car, and watches out for all the children we still have inside of us. Sydney sits with the tiniest ones when they are crying, and Lynn holds the stuffed polar bear while we sleep and pesters Heather to make sure we have plenty of crayons on hand for when she and her inside friends want to color.

Like many Multiples, we have constructed a large internal house where we go to live when we are not occupying the body. It's several stories high, with crystal chandeliers and big picture windows, and there's an inner yard filled with rainbows where the little ones go to play while Elaina and Connie are busy at work. The little ones are never allowed out when the adults are at their jobs. We have enough trouble hiding our MPD from people as it is. We have to wear tinted contacts because our eye color changes every time a different Alter comes out, and if we had a dollar for every time somebody has said to us, "Jeez, it's like you're a completely different person," we wouldn't have to worry so much about paying the $7,000 a year we have to spend on therapy because our medical insurance doesn't cover MPD.

We each have our own rooms in our internal house. We can decorate them the way we want, and lock the door and be absolutely safe from harm. But it's sad to know there are many doors in this house of ours that have never been opened. Late at night we hear the sobs and screams of those who live behind these doors, Alters who are still imprisoned by their abusive pasts and for whom there is yet no peace.

One of our Alters named Molly recently told our therapist that the very first thing she can remember was being locked in a closet. There was someone in there with her, a little girl dressed only in a diaper that was taped to her skin. Molly remembered leaving the closet, but didn't know what became of that other little girl.

Our therapist tried hard to reach Molly's companion, but she wouldn't talk to him. She was too afraid to come out, terrified of the devastating memories that loomed just beyond her closet door.

That was the day of the tremendous thunderstorm. There were high winds, pelting sheets of rain, lightning, hail and thunder. We seem to gather a lot of internal energy from storms. We feel electric inside and sometimes seem to feel a part of the storm itself. We think of ourselves as a storm, a quiet storm where outside everything may appear calm and peaceful but inside violent tornadoes rage.

Anyway, as soon as the storm began, we went driving in Heather's car. All around us the storm was swirling and howling. We could see, we could practically feel, the rain pelting down on us through the glass T-top roof.

While Heather drove, Molly led many of us to the place deep inside where that little girl still cowered in her closet. She opened the door and went inside. She held the little girl in her arms, and told her about all of us and how we were waiting outside to love her and take care of her. All she had to do was remember the past and by remembering, free herself from it.

Bravely, the little girl took Molly's hand and walked with her out of that closet. Everything appeared misty to her at first, but then the memories coalesced and we all looked on as she remembered what happened more than a quarter of a century ago so vividly that it all seemed to be happening to her again, right then and there. She remembered the baths, the boiling hot water, the acrid lye soap, the wire brush with the rounded wooden handle. She remembered the pain, the blood, the searing violation of her private parts.

"You won't be a bad little girl anymore, will you?"

"No, Mama! No, Daddy!"

We remembered too. We wept, we screamed, we shared the pain while Heather drove us through streets full of water that sloshed against the wheel rims, through bolts of lightning that lit up the sky and through thunder that shook the car.

We named the little girl Misty, and when she was through remembering, Molly took her to her room where she removed her soiled diaper and bathed her ever so gently, and then helped her into a pink night dress and a pair of big-girl panties. The two curled up on fluffy pillows.

Outside, the storm was still raging, but inside, for a time, all was quiet in the eye of our storm.

Little by little we were healing ourselves and freeing ourselves from the tyranny of our past. Our therapist tells us that when we have remembered everything and worked through the pain associated with these memories, we will no longer need Alter personalities to protect us, and then and only then we can begin the process of integration into a single, cohesive personality. But that will be our decision—whether or not we will even want to turn from many back into one.

Integration isn't something we even think about right now. Right now we're far too busy working to heal all the wounded children inside us, the frightened adolescents and angry adults. Together we will continue to reclaim what was stolen from us by the perpetrators of our abuse. We cannot recapture the lost years, the shattered innocence, but we will not let our past destroy our future. We are survivors of our abuse, not its victims. We know that the loudest cries are often very, very quiet. We will listen to these cries, and we will honor each part of us that endured the pain in silence.

For us, the silence is broken.

Response and Analysis

1. What tragic events does the author suggest led to her developing multiple personality disorder? Why does she believe the personalities were needed? What does the author mean when she writes, "We think of ourselves as a storm, a quiet storm where outside everything may appear calm and peaceful but inside violent tornadoes rage"?

2. Briefly describe the alternate personality named Molly. What did Molly tell the therapist? When did the other personalities remember the terrible events that occurred when the author was a little girl? According to the psychodynamic perspective and the behavioral perspective, how do dissociative disorders like multiple personality disorder develop?

Personal Experience and Application

1. Suppose the office of psychological services at your college or university asks you to help create a public service announcement discussing the causes of child abuse. List three factors that are associated with child abuse. What recommendations might you offer to reduce its incidence?

Research

Suppose you want to conduct a study to examine whether adults suffering from multiple personality disorder have different physiological states (e.g., heart rate, blood pressure) associated with each personality. You want to determine whether the same physiological state always occurs with the same personality. You decide to interview five people suffering from multiple personality disorder. You interview each person for one hour each day on fourteen consecutive days. Assume that, during the first few interviews, half of the personalities show higher levels of physiological arousal than the other half. However, from the seventh to the fourteenth day, all personalities show the same low level of physiological arousal. On the basis of your results, would you conclude that different personalities show the same or different levels of physiological arousal? Why? What alternative explanations might account for your results?

WHEN ONCE IS NOT ENOUGH

Gail Steketee and Kerrin White

Psychological Concepts
obsessive-compulsive disorder, anxiety disorder

Drs. Steketee and White present a woman's account of her obsessive-compulsive disorder. She tells of feeling trapped by having to repeat many of her actions and chores. Getting dressed for the day often means performing each act more than once. When she walks by her stove and sees the reflection of her feet, for example, she feels compelled to walk by again so she "can see them twice."

Look for the patterns this woman has developed and the rituals she believes she must follow to manage her anxieties. What reasons does she give for her repetitive behavior? What frustrations might she and her family experience as a result of her illness?

"Why does it take you so long to do such simple things?" "If you're so aware of what you're doing, why can't you just stop?" These are questions people throw at me every week, and I don't have an answer for them. Why *can't* I stop? Why is my mind so full of fear and doubt from morning until evening, every day?

I fully realize the irrationality of my behavior. But the fear I have in my mind is so real that I must perform certain rituals every day to protect my family and myself from any wrongdoings. I guess I must believe these rituals help, or I wouldn't still be doing them. I hope that by my writing actual events that go on in my daily routine, people will begin to understand how difficult it is not only to do daily chores, but even to live each day.

I am an obsessive-compulsive disorder patient like millions of other people. I've suffered with this disorder for the past twenty years, and it has steadily grown worse with time. Some of the things in here are going to seem ridiculous and you will probably laugh, but that's OK. I laugh at them too, when I'm not doing them. It's time now to begin your journey into my mind: have fun!

Should I get up? It's 6:15. No, I better wait till 6:16, it's an even number. OK, 6:16, now I better get up, before it turns to 6:17, then I'd have to wait till 6:22.

OK, I'll get up, OK, I'm up, WAIT! I better do that again. One foot back in bed, one foot on the floor, now the other foot in bed and the opposite on the floor. OK. Let's take a shower, WAIT! That shoe on the floor is pointing in the wrong direction, better fix it. Oops, there's a piece of lint there, I better not set the shoe on top of it. Darn! There's another one over here, I can't put the shoe on top of them,

I shouldn't put it between them, maybe if I move this lint over to the right, the shoe can fit in here. OH, JUST TOUCH THE SHOE TWICE AND GET OUTTA HERE!

All right, I got to the bedroom door without touching anything else, but I better step through and out again, just to be sure nothing bad will happen. THERE, THAT WAS EASY! Now to the bathroom. I better turn that light on, NO, off, NO, on, NO, off, NO, on, KNOCK IT OFF! All right, I'm done using the toilet, better flush it. OK, now spin around, wait for the toilet to finish a flush, now touch the handle, now touch the seat, remember you have to look at every screw on the toilet seat before you turn around again. OK, now turn around and touch the seat again, look at all the screws again. OK, now close the cover.

OK, let's pick out some clothes in the bedroom. First I have to get out of the bathroom. Step in, step out, step in, step out, now look at all the hinges on the bathroom door. Do this on each step, both in and out of the bathroom. OK, I'm out of the bathroom. I wonder what time it is. NO! YOU CAN'T LOOK TILL YOU ARE DONE WITH YOUR SHOWER, IF YOU LOOK BEFORE, YOU WILL BE PUNISHED.

OK, let's get some underwear. I want to wear the green ones because they fit the best, but they're lying on top of the T-shirt my grandmother gave me, and her husband (my grandfather) died last year, so I better wash those again before I wear them. If I wear them, something bad might happen. I'll wear the pink ones, even though they are all stretched out and don't stay up. They're OK because they're lying on top of an orange towel. All right, but now I need a towel. I'm allowed to use this one with the green stripe. Good.

Now let's go to the bathroom. WHOOPS! I saw the reflection of my feet when I walked by the stove, better walk back so I can see them twice. Now to the bathroom. Put one foot in the bathroom, one foot in the hall. I wonder if it would be easier to use both feet at the same time and jump in and out of the bathroom. HMMMM! I WONDER? WOULD THAT WORK? YEAH, I GUESS SO, LET'S TRY IT! It's more work, but it saves time. OK, now put the towel on the floor so it's ready when I get out of the shower. NO! I CAN'T PUT IT THERE! THERE'S A BROWN SPOT ON THE FLOOR! If I put it on top of it, something bad might happen. OK, I'll put it over here. I'll put the underwear next to the towel, but not touching the towel, and not near the brown spot. PERFECT!

OK, now let's turn the water on. Should I put the cold water on first or the hot water on first? ALWAYS A BIG DECISION! Maybe I'll put them on at the same time, with both hands touching each of them. OK, now into the tub. One foot in, now step back out, now the other foot in, now out, now in, now out, NOW IN! OK, I'm in. Now wet my hair, pick up the shampoo, put it down, pick it up, now take the cap off, put it back on, take it off again, wash hair, rinse hair, now pick up soap, put it back down again, pick it up, soap body, now put soap down. Should I put it at the front of the tub or at the back of the tub? Well, I picked it up at the front so I better put it back there. Now touch it twice with both hands. NO, TWICE DIDN'T FEEL RIGHT, START OVER, ONE, TWO, THREE,

FOUR, FIVE, SIX, SEVENEIGHTNINE. Repeat once more and shut water off twice, using both hands. Step out of tub, step into tub, out, in, out, in. Now pick up towel, put back down, pick up again, dry off, now pick up underwear twice. BUT I CAN'T PUT THOSE ON IN THE BATHROOM, THAT MUST BE DONE IN THE BEDROOM, OR SOMETHING BAD MIGHT HAPPEN!

Now in and out of bathroom doorway twice, checking hinges along the way, repeat same steps into the bedroom. Now step right leg into underwear, step back out, check ALL seams on underwear and ALL tags twice, now step back in and pull on. Now let's attempt to pick out some clothes, first. Which leotard should I wear? I was thinking about wearing the orange one, so I better wear that one. OK, before I put it on I better check all seams and tags twice. Good! Now for my shorts. The gray ones are OK. Now let's put them on. Put right leg in shorts, take it back out, now put it back in, now pull up. Now pick out a shirt. Should I wear the black shirt? NO! My girlfriend said she likes shirts like that, and her father-in-law died last year, so I better wear something else. I'll wash the black one before I wear it again. I guess I'll wear the red one. YAY! That one's OK. Now first I must check all seams and tags before I put it on. OK, GOOD! OH BOY!

Now for socks. I guess I'll wear the blue ones. They're right up front, but there are the striped ones too and they match my outfit, but I already picked the blue ones first and they will feel bad if I change my mind, so I better stick with them. OK, now to put the socks on, right foot first. I have to put the sock on, now take it off, now put it back on again, check the seams on both sides of the heels, then put my foot into my shoe and then take it out and then put it back in. Now for the left foot, put the left sock halfway on, take it off and put it back on, then put the left foot halfway into the left shoe and take it back out. Oops! I forgot to check both sides of my heels before I put my foot in my shoe. START OVER! All done. Now let's tie the shoes once, untie, and redo. OK! I'M DRESSED!!!!

Response and Analysis

1. Why does this obsessive-compulsive disorder sufferer view her behavior as irrational? What does she fear? How has performing "rituals" affected her daily life? What frustrations might she and her family experience?

2. Briefly describe the reoccurring thoughts and behaviors of this obsessive-compulsive sufferer. What are obsessions and compulsions? What is an anxiety disorder?

Personal Experience and Application

1. Give a few examples of times when you repeated certain actions. For example, have you ever checked and rechecked that you locked the doors to your house before leaving on vacation? What prompted you to recheck? What feelings or thoughts contributed to your repetitious behavior?

2. What are the possible causes of an anxiety disorder like obsessive-compulsive disorder?

Briefly discuss the following possible causes: biological factors, cognitive factors, and learning.

Research

Suppose you want to identify the obsessive thoughts and compulsive behaviors that most fre-quently occur among people diagnosed with ob-sessive-compulsive disorder. You decide to inter-view one hundred people diagnosed with this disorder. Write five questions that you would ask the participants to determine the obsessive thought and compulsive behavior they experi-enced most frequently.

EMERGENCE LABELED AUTISTIC

Temple Grandin and Margaret M. Scariano

Psychological Concept
autism

Temple Grandin has a Ph.D. in animal science and teaches at Colorado State University. Although she is recognized for her contribution to the design of livestock equipment, she is equally well known for the information she provides on autism. A high-functioning autistic individual, Grandin tells about her experiences with sensitivity to sound and touch and her early frustrations communicating with others.

Although she credits early intervention beginning when she was two-and-a-half years old for her recovery, Grandin still retains some symptoms. For example, she developed a squeeze or hug machine that alleviates some of her anxiety about being touched. The machine has sides that exert various degrees of pressure depending on how the controls are set. After lying for twenty minutes in this machine, Grandin feels refreshed and relaxed. She demonstrated the machine for neurologist Oliver Sacks, who described it as leaving "a sweet, calming feeling—one that reminded me of my deep-diving days long ago, when I felt the pressure of the water on my diving suit as a whole-body embrace" (p. 265).

Here Grandin tells of her experiences as an autistic child. How does she react to various stimuli? What anxieties does she have? What seems to comfort her?

I was six months old when Mother noticed that I was no longer cuddly and that I stiffened up when she held me. When I was a few months older, Mother tried to gather me into her arms, and I clawed at her like a trapped animal. She has said she didn't understand my behavior and felt hurt by my hostile actions. She'd seen other babies cuddling and cooing in their mother's arms. What was *she* doing wrong? But she figured she was young and inexperienced. Having an autistic child was scary for her because she didn't know how to respond towards a baby who rejected her. Maybe my seeming rejection was not unusual so she shoved her apprehension aside. After all, my health was good. I was alert, intelligent, and well-coordinated. Since I was the first-born, Mother thought my withdrawal was probably normal, part of maturing and becoming independent.

This withdrawal from touch, so typical of autistic children, was followed in the next years by standard autistic behaviors: my fixation on spinning objects, my preference to be alone, destructive behavior, temper tantrums, inability to speak, sensitivity to sudden noises, appearance of deafness, and my intense interest in odors.

I was a destructive child. I drew all over the walls—not once or twice—but any time I got my hands on a pencil or crayon. I remember really "catching" it for peeing on the carpet. So the next time I had to go, instead of using the carpet, I put the long drape between my legs. I thought it would dry quickly and Mother wouldn't notice. Normal children use clay for modeling; I used my feces and then spread my creations all over the room. I chewed up puzzles and spit the cardboard mush out on the floor. I had a violent temper, and when thwarted, I'd throw anything handy—a museum quality vase or left over feces. I screamed continually, responded violently to noise and yet appeared deaf on some occasions.

At age three Mother took me to a neurologist to be examined because I did not act like the little girls next door. I was the first child in a family of four and none of my younger sisters or brothers behaved the way I did.

The EEG and hearing tests were normal. I was measured on the Rimland checklist where a score of +20 indicates classical autism (Kanner's syndrome). I scored +9. (Only about 10 percent of children described as autistic fit in the narrowly defined Kanner's syndrome because there are metabolic differences between Kanner's syndrome and other types of autism.) Although my behavior patterns were definitely autistic, the beginnings of basic, infantile but nonetheless meaningful sounds by age three and one half lowered my Rimland checklist score. But the frustration for both parent and child is evident in any degree of autism. After the evaluation, the doctor said there was no physical impairment. He suggested a speech therapist for my communication disability. . . .

Mother said at first I had a very limited vocabulary and stressed words heavily like "bah" for ball. I spoke in a one word pattern—"ice," "go," "mine," "no." My efforts must have sounded wonderful to Mother. What a step forward from humming, peeping, and squealing!

But it wasn't only my lack of speech that concerned Mother. My voice was flat with little inflection and no rhythm. That alone stamped me as different. Coupled with speech difficulty and lack of voice inflection, I was well into adulthood before

I could look people in the eye. As a child I remember Mother asking me time and again, "Temple, are you listening to me? Look at me." Sometimes I wanted to, but couldn't. Darting eyes—so characteristic of many autistic children—was another symptom of my autistic behavior. There were other tell-tale signs. I had little interest in other children, preferring my own inner world. I could sit on the beach for hours dribbling sand through my fingers and fashioning miniature mountains. Each particle of sand intrigued me as though I were a scientist looking through a microscope. Other times I scrutinized each line in my finger, following one as if it were a road on a map.

Spinning was another favorite activity. I'd sit on the floor and twirl around. The room spun with me. This self-stimulatory behavior made me feel powerful, in control of things. After all, I could make a whole room turn around. Sometimes I made the world spin by twisting the swing in our backyard so that the chains would wind up. Then I'd sit there as the swing unwound, watching the sky and earth whirl. I realize that non-autistic children enjoy twirling around in a swing, too. The difference is the autistic child is obsessed with the act of spinning.

There is a mechanism in the inner ear that controls the body's balance and integrates visual and vestibular input. Through a series of nerve connections, the eyes, after some amount of spinning, will start jumping about (become nystagmatic) and the stomach queasy. Then, the child will stop twirling or spinning. Autistic children often have reduced nystagmus.* It is as if their bodies were demanding more spinning as a kind of corrective factor in an immature nervous system.

Whatever the reason, I enjoyed twirling myself around or spinning coins or lids round and round and round. Intensely preoccupied with the movement of the spinning coin or lid, I saw nothing or heard nothing. People around me were transparent. And no sound intruded on my fixation. It was as if I were deaf. Even a sudden loud noise didn't startle me from my world. . . .

Deborah Fein and her colleagues in Boston have an interesting concept of the cause of autism. "In animals autistic-like behavior may result from a lack of input, whereas in autistic children, it may result from failure to attend to input. Because of the very early onset, these children may be deprived of the perceptual experience that normally forms the building blocks of higher percepts, concepts and language." This ties in with earlier studies concerning the inability of autistics to handle simultaneous stimuli and being able to attend to only one aspect of a compound visual or auditory stimulus. Today, even as an adult while waiting in a busy airport, I find I can block out all the outside stimuli and read, but I still find it nearly impossible to screen out the airport background noise and converse on the phone. So it is with autistic children. They have to make a choice of either self-stimulating like spinning, mutilating themselves, or escape into their inner world to screen out outside stimuli. Otherwise, they become overwhelmed with many simultaneous stimuli and react with temper tantrums, screaming, or other unacceptable behavior. Self-

---

*nystagmus: an involuntary, jerky movement of the eyes.

stimulating behaviors help calm an over aroused central nervous system. Some researchers believe that autistic children have a hyperactive nervous system, and some children with hyperactive behavior have a slow nervous system. The autistic child self-stimulates to calm himself and the hyperactive child is excessively active because he is trying to stimulate an under aroused nervous system.

Miss Cray, our governess, took advantage of my distress at noise. She used sound as a means of punishment. If I daydreamed, my spoon in mid-air, while eating lunch, Miss Cray would say, "Temple, eat. If you don't finish your soup right now, I'll pop a paper bag at you." She kept a supply of paper sacks on top of the refrigerator so that she could burst them in my face if I misbehaved or drifted away from the world of people. This sensitivity to noise is common among adult autistics. Even today, sudden loud noises such as a car backfiring, will make me jump and a panicky feeling overwhelms me. Loud, high-pitched noises such as a motorcycle's sound, are still painful to me.

But as a child, the "people world" was often too stimulating to my senses. Ordinary days with a change in schedule or unexpected events threw me into a frenzy, but Thanksgiving or Christmas was even worse. At those times our home bulged with relatives. The clamor of many voices, the different smells—perfume, cigars, damp wool caps or gloves—people moving about at different speeds, going in different directions, the constant noise and confusion, the constant touching, were overwhelming. One very, very overweight aunt, who was generous and caring, let me use her professional oil paints. I liked her. Still, when she hugged me, I was totally engulfed and I panicked. It was like being suffocated by a mountain of marshmallows. I withdrew because her abundant affection overwhelmed my nervous system.

But I survived those first five years—not always with grace, but invariably with gumption.

Response and Analysis

1. According to Temple Grandin, why do autistic children "have to make a choice of either self-stimulating like spinning, mutilating themselves, or escape into their inner world to screen out outside stimuli"? What did Temple Grandin do as a child to screen outside stimuli?

2. The DSM-IV identifies three key features of autism that must occur before the age of three: (a) impairment in social interaction; (b) severe impairments in communication; and (c) restricted, repetitive, and stereotyped patterns of behavior. List two behaviors reported by Temple Grandin that show evidence of impaired social interaction. List one behavior that shows evidence of impaired communication and one behavior that shows restricted, repetitive, and stereotyped patterns of behavior.

Personal Experience and Application

1. Briefly discuss the difficulties involved with teaching language to an autistic child. Can

you recommend an approach using the principles of learning?

2. Raising an autistic child can be extremely challenging. What factors might determine whether autistic children should be raised in their homes by their parents and taught in public schools or are better served in an institution?

Research

Suppose you develop a new technique that you believe may minimize the likelihood that autistic children will engage in self-injurious behavior, such as head banging, hair pulling, and self-biting.

You want to assess the effectiveness of your new technique. One of your first tasks is to identify participants for your study. Because autism is a rare disorder, it probably will be difficult to locate a large number of autistic children who engage in self-injurious behavior. As a result, you decide to use a single-subject design and evaluate the behavior of only one individual. The child will participate in your program three times a week for six months.

How will you determine if your program has effectively reduced self-injurious behavior? How can you be sure that your program will work with other autistic children?

THE DUKE OF DECEPTION

Geoffrey Wolff

Psychological Concept
antisocial personality disorder

Have you ever felt betrayed or deceived? Geoffrey Wolff was stunned when he discovered that the father he admired was not the person he said he was. "The Duke of Deception" is Wolff's account of the two histories of his father: the real and the fabricated.

Wolff's father, called Duke, said he was a Yale graduate, yet he wasn't. He said he wasn't Jewish, yet he was. He said he was a fighter pilot in World War II, and he wasn't. What he was was a con artist. What prompts Duke to create an imaginary world and to lead a dishonest life? Note the way Duke treats other people and the impressions he wants to make.

I listen for my father and I hear a stammer. This was explosive and unashamed, not a choking on words but a spray of words. His speech was headlong, edgy, breathless: there was neither room in his mouth nor time in the day to contain what he burned to utter. I have a remnant of that stammer, and I wish I did not; I stammer and blush, my father would stammer and grin. He depended on a listener's good will. My father depended excessively upon people's good will.

As he spoke straight at you, so did he look at you. He could stare down anyone, though this was a gift he rarely practiced. To me, everything about him seemed outsized. Doing a school report on the Easter Islanders I found in an encyclopedia pictures of their huge sculptures, and there he was, massive head and nose, nothing subtle or delicate. He was in fact (and how diminishing those words, *in fact*, look to me now) an inch or two above six feet, full bodied, a man who lumbered from here to there with deliberation. When I was a child I noticed that people were respectful of the cubic feet my father occupied; later I understood that I had confused respect with resentment.

I recollect things, a gentleman's accessories, deceptively simple fabrications of silver and burnished nickel, of brushed Swedish stainless, of silk and soft wool and brown leather. I remember his shoes, so meticulously selected and cared for and used, thin-soled, with cracked uppers, older than I was or could ever be, shining dully and from the depths. Just a pair of shoes? No: I knew before I knew any other complicated thing that for my father there was nothing he possessed that was "just" something. His pocket watch was not "just" a timepiece, it was a miraculous instrument with a hinged front and a representation on its back of porcelain ducks rising from a birch-girt porcelain pond. It struck the hour unassertively, musically, like a silver tine touched to a crystal glass, no hurry, you might like to know it's noon.

He despised black leather, said black shoes reminded him of black attaché cases, of bankers, lawyers, look-before-you-leapers anxious not to offend their clients. He owned nothing black except his dinner jacket and his umbrella. His umbrella doubled as a shooting-stick, and one afternoon at a polo match at Brandywine he was sitting on it when a man asked him what he would do if it rained, sit wet or stand dry? I laughed. My father laughed also, but tightly, and he did not reply; nor did he ever again use this quixotic contraption. He took things, *things*, seriously.

My father, called Duke, taught me skills and manners; he taught me to shoot and to drive fast and to read respectfully and to box and to handle a boat and to distinguish between good jazz music and bad jazz music. He was patient with me, led me to understand for myself why Billie Holiday's understatements were more interesting than Ella Fitzgerald's complications. His codes were not novel, but they were rigid, the rules of decorum that Hemingway prescribed. A gentleman kept his word, and favored simplicity of sentiment; a gentleman chose his words with care, as he chose his friends. A gentleman accepted responsibility for his acts, and welcomed the liberty to act unambiguously. A gentleman was a stickler for precision and punctilio; life was no more than an inventory of small choices that together formed a man's character, entire. A gentleman was this, and not that; a *man* did, did not, said, would not say.

My father could, however, be coaxed to reveal his bona fides. He had been schooled at Groton and passed along to Yale. He was just barely prepared to intimate that he had been tapped for "Bones," and I remember his pleasure when Levi Jackson, the black captain of Yale's 1948 football team, was similarly honored by that secret society. He was proud of Skull and Bones for its hospitality toward the exotic. He did sometimes wince, however, when he pronounced Jackson's Semitic Christian name, and I sensed that his tolerance for Jews was not inclusive; but I never heard him indulge express bigotry, and the first of half a dozen times he hit me was for having called a neighbor's kid a guinea.

There was much luxury in my father's affections, and he hated what was narrow, pinched, or mean. He understood exclusion, mind you, and lived his life believing the world to be divided between a few *us*'s and many *thems*, but I was to understand that aristocracy was a function of taste, courage, and generosity. About two other virtues—candor and reticence—I was confused, for my father would sometimes proselytize the one, sometimes the other.

If Duke's preoccupation with bloodlines was finite, this did not cause him to be unmindful of his ancestors. He knew whence he had come, and whither he meant me to go. I saw visible evidence of this, a gold signet ring which I wear today, a heavy bit of business inscribed arsy-turvy with lions and flora and a motto, *nulla vestigium retrorsit*. "Don't look back" I was told it meant.

After Yale—class of late nineteen-twenty something, or early nineteen-thirty something—my father batted around the country, living a high life in New York among school and college chums, flying as a test pilot, marrying my mother, the daughter of a rear admiral. I was born a year after the marriage, in 1937, and three years after that my father went to England as a fighter pilot with Eagle Squadron, a group of American volunteers in the Royal Air Force. Later he transferred to the OSS, and was in Yugoslavia with the partisans; just before the Invasion he was parachuted into Normandy, where he served as a sapper with the Resistance, which my father pronounced *ray-zee-staunce*.

His career following the war was for me mysterious in its particulars; in the service of his nation, it was understood, candor was not always possible. This much was clear: my father mattered in the world, and was satisfied that he mattered, whether or not the world understood precisely why he mattered.

A pretty history for an American clubman. Its fault is that it was not true. My father was a bullshit artist. True, there were many boarding schools, each less pleased with the little Duke than the last, but none of them was Groton. There was no Yale, and by the time he walked from a room at a mention of Skull and Bones I knew this, and he knew that I knew it. No military service would have him; his teeth were bad. So he had his teeth pulled and replaced, but the Air Corps and Navy and Army and Coast Guard still thought he was a bad idea. The ring I wear was made according to his instructions by a jeweler two blocks from Schwab's drugstore in Hollywood, and was never paid for. The motto, engraved backwards so that it would come right on a red wax seal, is dog Latin and means in fact "leave no trace behind," but my father did not believe me when I told him this.

My father was a Jew. This did not seem to him a good idea, and so it was his notion to disassemble his history, begin at zero, and re-create himself. His sustaining line of work till shortly before he died was as a confidence man. If I now find his authentic history more surprising, more interesting, than his counterfeit history, he did not. He would not make peace with his actualities, and so he was the author of his own circumstances, and indifferent to the consequences of this nervy program.

There were some awful consequences, for other people as well as for him. He was lavish with money, with others' money. He preferred to stiff institutions: jewelers, car dealers, banks, fancy hotels. He was, that is, a thoughtful buccaneer, when thoughtfulness was convenient. But people were hurt by him. Much of his mischief was casual enough: I lost a tooth when I was six, and the Tooth Fairy, "financially inconvenienced" or "temporarily out of pocket," whichever was then his locution, left under my pillow an IOU, a sight draft for two bits, or two million.

I wish he hadn't selected from among the world's possible disguises the costume and credentials of a yacht club commodore. Beginning at scratch he might have reached further, tried something a bit more bold and odd, a bit less inexorably conventional, a bit less calculated to please. But it is true, of course, that a confidence man who cannot inspire confidence in his marks is nothing at all, so perhaps his tuneup of his bloodline, educational *vita*, and war record was merely the price of doing business in a culture preoccupied with appearances.

I'm not even now certain what I wish he had made of himself: I once believed that he was most naturally a fictioneer. But for all his preoccupation with make-believe, he never tried seriously to write it. A confidence man learns early in his career that to commit himself to paper is to court trouble. The successful bunco artist does his game, and disappears himself: Who *was* that masked man? No one, no one at all, *nulla vestigium* [*sic*] *retrorsit* [*sic*], not a trace left behind.

Well, I'm left behind. One day, writing about my father with no want of astonishment and love, it came to me that I am his creature as well as his get. I cannot now shake this conviction, that I was trained as his instrument of perpetuation, put here to put him into the record. And that my father knew this, calculated it to a degree. How else explain his eruption of rage when I once gave up what he and I called "writing" for journalism? I had taken a job as the book critic of *The Washington Post*, was proud of myself; it seemed then like a wonderful job, honorable and enriching. My father saw it otherwise: "You have failed me," he wrote, "you have sold yourself at discount" he wrote to me, his prison number stamped below his name.

He was wrong then, but he was usually right about me. He would listen to anything I wished to tell him, but would not tell me only what I wished to hear. He retained such solicitude for his clients. With me he was strict and straight, except about himself. And so I want to be strict and straight with him, and with myself. Writing to a friend about this book, I said that I would not now for anything have had my father be other than what he was, except happier, and that most of the time he was happy enough, cheered on by imaginary successes. He gave me a great deal, and not merely life, and I didn't want to bellyache; I wanted, I told my friend, to thumb my nose on his behalf at everyone who had limited him. My friend was shrewd, though, and said that he didn't believe me, that I couldn't mean such a thing, that if I followed out its implications I would be led to a kind of ripe sentimentality, and to mere piety. Perhaps, he wrote me, you would not have wished him to lie to himself, to lie about being a Jew. Perhaps you would have him fool others but not so deeply trick himself. "In writing about a father," my friend wrote me about our fathers, "one clambers up a slippery mountain, carrying the balls of another in a bloody sack, and whether to eat them or worship them or bury them decently is never cleanly decided."

So I will try here to be exact. I wish my father had done more headlong, more elegant inventing. I believe he would respect my wish, be willing to speak with me seriously about it, find some nobility in it. But now he is dead, and he had been dead two weeks when they found him. And in his tiny fist at the edge of the Pacific they found no address book, no batch of letters held with a rubber band, no photograph. Not a thing to suggest that he had ever known another human being.

Response and Analysis

1. Did Geoffrey Wolff believe that Duke felt remorse or guilt about his actions? How were people hurt by Duke's actions?

2. What aspects of Duke's behavior reflect antisocial personality disorder? What are the possible causes of antisocial personality disorder?

Personal Experience and Application

1. Do you know someone like Duke who tries to impress others by exaggerating or fabricating facts? How does this make you feel? Why might it be difficult to have a relationship with someone who is not honest with you?

2. How do Duke's lies differ from white lies?

Research

Suppose you want to conduct a study to examine if people who are diagnosed with antisocial personality disorder show less concern for punishment and pain than other people. What is the null hypothesis? What is your research, or alternative, hypothesis?

chapter *12*

HEALTH, STRESS, AND COPING

*Humans cannot exist if everything that
is unpleasant is eliminated instead of
understood.*

Marlo Morgan, *Mutant Message Down Under*

Is our physical and mental health endangered when we suffer great stress? What
resources do we have to cope with misfortune? Health psychology looks at the
interrelationship between stress, health, and coping skills. This chapter presents
illustrations of several key concepts: coping and social support; posttraumatic stress
disorder; stress and the immune system; biofeedback; and stress management.

Tennis professional Arthur Ashe was at the peak of his life when he learned that
he had acquired immune deficiency syndrome (AIDS). He drew on personal
discipline and training to help sustain him. In the final years before his death, Ashe
began writing about his life and how he coped with AIDS. Ashe writes that he never
asked why it was he who had to suffer this tragic illness because then he would have
had to ask why it was he who had also been so fortunate.

Sometimes it may take a person a long time to overcome trauma. Vietnam
veteran John, who was diagnosed with posttraumatic stress disorder (PTSD), finds
it difficult to trust people. After devastating war experiences, John returned home
and found some Americans not proud of him for fighting for his country; instead
they called him "killer" and "rapist." John shows why certain forms of stress may be
difficult to overcome.

Psychologist James Pennebaker presents compelling evidence to show that
writing about stress may not only provide insights and understanding but may also
help our immune system. Pennebaker's research demonstrates that communication,
whether written or spoken, may help us face and possibly overcome significantly
disturbing events in our lives.

Psychologist Shelley Taylor shows how a positive attitude can help us when we
are ill or under stress. She became curious about why some people who suffered

crippling illnesses or extreme hardships did not become depressed and submissive. What Taylor discovered was that hope and "positive illusions" gave people energy that helped them cope with their misfortunes.

Biofeedback therapist Aleene Friedman describes how she helped "Joyce" relieve her almost constant headaches. Joyce was diagnosed as having migraine and tension headaches, and when she suffered an attack, she was unable to do more than stay in bed. Biofeedback therapy offered Joyce new strategies to deal with her pain, and she gained substantial relief.

DAYS OF GRACE

Arthur Ashe and Arnold Rampersad

Psychological Concepts
coping, social support, AIDS

Tennis champion Arthur Ashe was only thirty-eight years old when he suffered a heart attack. Four years later he had double-bypass heart surgery and received a blood transfusion to help him heal faster. That transfusion cost him his life: the blood was tainted with the HIV virus. In February 1993, at the age of forty-nine, Ashe died of AIDS.

In his autobiography, Ashe says that the qualities that helped him cope with his illnesses were those that had shaped his character: respect for reputation, honor, discipline, and dignity. These he learned from his parents. Later his tennis coaches taught him sportsmanship: to behave with grace, to keep anger in control, and to not let despair take over. He knew that to give in to anxiety or fear—even for a second—could lose a game.

Ashe had lived with hardship from birth. When he was asked by a reporter if having AIDS was the heaviest burden of his life, he hesitated but a second and then replied: "No, it isn't. It's a burden all right... but being black is the greatest burden I've had to bear" (p. 126).

No one in my hospital room that day had to ask the question I knew would be on many people's minds, perhaps on most people's minds. But the rest of the world would ask: How had Arthur Ashe become infected?

To almost all Americans, AIDS meant one of two conditions: intravenous drug use or homosexuality. They had good reason to think so. Of the 210,000 reported cases of Americans, male and female, afflicted with AIDS by February 1992, 60 percent were men who had been sexually active with another man; about 23 percent had been intravenous illicit drug users; at least 6 percent more had been both homosexual and drug abusers; another 6 percent or so had been heterosexual; 2 percent had contracted the disease from blood transfusions; and 1 percent were persons with hemophilia or other blood-coagulant disorders.

The link between individual behavior and infection is crucial to AIDS. Indeed, AIDS was "discovered" in North America in 1980, when doctors in New York and Los Angeles noticed that an unusually high number of young male homosexuals had contracted *Pneumocystis carinii* pneumonia without the usual precondition, an immune system depressed by prescribed medicine. At about the same time, a normally quite rare disease, Kaposi's sarcoma, also began to spread; and once more the victims were young male homosexuals. Later that year, Dr. Michael Gottlieb at UCLA, a federally funded clinical investigator, was the first to notify the Centers for Disease Control about the puzzling outbreak of infections.

By the middle of the following year, the evidence was conclusive and alarming that a new disease was with us, and that it was becoming a nationwide epidemic. The search then began for its cause. After much hard work, HIV was isolated and identified in 1983. An individual tested positive for HIV when a blood test determined the presence in the blood of antibodies fighting the attack by the human immunodeficiency virus, or HIV. Then AIDS was finally defined as a combination in any person of HIV and one or more of over two dozen opportunistic diseases. The search for a cure continued—and continues. . . .

So how, the public would want to know, did Arthur Ashe contract AIDS? Had I been quietly shooting up heroin over the years? Or was I a closet homosexual or bisexual, hiding behind a marriage but pursuing and bedding men on the sly? . . .

The facts of the case are simple. Recovering from double-bypass heart surgery in 1983, I felt miserable even though I had experienced post-operative pain before. I can remember a conversation I had with a doctor in which I complained about feeling unbelievably low, and he laid out my options for me.

"You can wait it out, Arthur, and you'll feel better after a while," he said. "Or we can give you a couple of units of blood. That would be no problem at all."

"I would like the blood," I replied. I don't think I hesitated for a moment. Why feel miserable when a palliative is at hand? Surely there was nothing to be feared from the blood bank of a major American hospital, one of the most respected medical facilities in New York City. In fact, less than a month later, in July 1983, Margaret Heckler, President Reagan's Secretary of Health and Human Services, confidently made an announcement to the people of the United States: "The nation's blood supply is safe." Her words are etched in my memory. . . .

The news that I had AIDS hit me hard but did not knock me down. I had read of people committing suicide because of despair caused by infection with HIV. Indeed, in the preceding year, 1987, men suffering from AIDS were 10.5 times more likely to commit suicide than non-HIV-infected people who were otherwise similar to them.

In 1988, the AIDS suicide rate fell, but only to 7.4 times the expected rate. In 1990, it was 6 times the expected rate. The drop continued, but the far greater likelihood of suicide among AIDS patients persists, according to a 1992 issue of the *Journal of the American Medical Association.* (Incidentally, most of the HIV-infected men who kill themselves use prescription drugs to do so, instead of the guns that most male suicides use.) The main reason for the decline in this suicide rate, according to the report, was the general improvement in treatment, including the development of drugs that gave AIDS patients more hope. By 1992, however, the suicide rate was starting to rise again, as many of the therapies for AIDS, including those I was dependent on, began to show their limitations.

For me, suicide is out of the question. Despair is a state of mind to which I refuse to surrender. I resist moods of despondency because I know how they feed upon themselves and upon the despondent. I fight vigorously at the first sign of depression. I know that some depression can be physically induced, generated by the body rather than the mind. Such depression is obviously hard to contain. But depression caused by brooding on circumstances, especially circumstances one cannot avoid or over which one has no control, is another matter. I refuse to surrender myself to such a depression and have never suffered from it in my life.

Here is an area in which there are very close parallels between ordinary life and world-class athletic competition. The most important factor determining success in athletic competition is often the ability to control mood swings that result from unfavorable changes in the score. A close look at any athletic competition, and especially at facial expressions and body language, reveals that many individuals or even entire teams go into momentary lapses of confidence that often prove disastrous within a game or match. The ever-threatening danger, which I know well from experience, is that a momentary lapse will begin to deepen almost of its own accord. Once it is set in motion, it seems to gather enough momentum on its own to run its course. A few falling pebbles build into an avalanche. The initiative goes to one's opponent, who seems to be impossibly "hot" or "on a roll"; soon, victory is utterly out of one's reach. I've seen it happen to others on the tennis court; it has sometimes happened to me. In life-threatening situations, such as the one in which I now found myself, I knew that I had to do everything possible to keep this avalanche of deadly emotion from starting. One simply must not despair, even for a moment.

I cannot say that even the news that I have AIDS devastated me, or drove me into bitter reflection and depression even for a short time. I do not remember any night, from that first moment until now, when the thought of my AIDS condition and its fatality kept me from sleeping soundly. The physical discomfort may keep me up now and then, but not the psychological or philosophical discomfort.

I have been able to stay calm in part because my heart condition is a sufficient source of danger, were I to be terrified by illness. My first heart attack, in 1979, could have ended my life in a few chest-ravaging seconds. Both of my heart operations were major surgeries, with the risks attendant on all major surgery. And surely no brain operation is routine. Mainly because I have been through these battles with death, I have lost much of my fear of it.

I was not always that way. I had been a sickly child, but for most of the first thirty-six years of my life, until 1979, I nurtured a sense of myself as indestructible, if not actually immortal. This feeling persisted even after my heel surgery in 1977. For nine years since my first heart attack, however, I had been living with a powerful sense of my own mortality. And I have had many other signs, in the deaths of others, that have led me to think of my own end as something that could be imminent. So AIDS did not devastate me. AIDS was little more than something new to deal with, something new to understand and respond to, something to accept as a challenge, as if I might defeat it.

One can ready oneself for death. I see death as more of a dynamic than a static event. The actual physical manifestation of the absence of life is simply the ultimate step of a process that leads inevitably to that stage. In the interim, before the absolute end, one can do much to make life as meaningful as possible.

What would have devastated me was to discover that I had infected my wife, Jeanne, and my daughter, Camera. I do not think it would make any difference, on this score, whether I had contracted AIDS "innocently" from a blood transfusion or in one of the ways that most of society disapproves of, such as homosexual contacts or drug addiction. The overwhelming sense of guilt and shame would be the same in either case, if I had infected another human being.

A friend of mine has ventured the opinion that much as I love Jeanne, I am truly crazy about Camera. Well, Jeanne loves me, but I think she, too, is truly crazy about Camera. The thought that this beautiful child, not yet two years old, who has brought more pure joy into our lives than we had ever known before we laid eyes on her, could be infected with this horrible disease, because of me, was almost too much even to think about.

Both Jeanne and Camera were quickly tested. Both, thank God, were found to be free of any trace of HIV. Their testing has continued, and they remain free of infection. . . .

With AIDS, I have good days and bad days. The good days, thank goodness, greatly outnumber the bad. And the bad days are not unendurable. Mainly my stomach lets me down and I suffer from diarrhea. I take my pills, and I am disciplined enough to stick to my schedule. Sometimes I become a little tired, but I have learned anew to pace myself, to take short rests that invigorate me. In this matter of AIDS, as in so many aspects of my life, I am a lucky man.

I believe that there are five essential pillars to support the health and well-being of every individual. The first is unhindered access to physicians who will render primary care, listen to and advise the patient, and follow up with treatments in a professional manner. The second is the availability of medicines, treatments, and other therapies. The third is the support of family and friends. The fourth is the determination of the patient to make himself or herself better, to take charge of his or her well-being in cooperation with others. The fifth essential pillar is health insurance, because few people can bear the cost of a serious illness without falling irretrievably into debt. Take away any of these five pillars, I believe, and the structure of individual health and welfare starts to collapse.

I have been fortunate to have all five pillars solidly in place: excellent physicians, perhaps the best that can be had; the most efficacious medicines, no matter what the cost; the loving support of a skilled, intelligent spouse and the most loyal and resourceful group of friends anyone could have; self-reliance taught from my boyhood by my father but reinforced by decades of rigorous training in a sport based on individualism; and no fewer than three generous health-insurance policies.

AIDS does not make me despair, but unquestionably it often makes me somber. For some time I have wrestled with certain of Susan Sontag's ideas or insights in her remarkable books *Illness as Metaphor* and *AIDS and Its Metaphors*. In the former, inspired by her battle against cancer, Sontag writes about "the punitive or sentimental fantasies concocted about" illness, especially illnesses such as leprosy, tuberculosis, and cancer. "My point is that illness is *not* a metaphor, and that the most truthful way of regarding illness—and the healthiest way of being ill—is one purified of, most resistant to, metaphoric thinking." AIDS is not a metaphor for me, but a fact; and yet I find it hard to avoid its metaphoric energy, which is almost irresistible. I reject the notion that it is God's retribution for the sins of homosexuals and drug abusers, as some people argue, but on occasion I find its elements and properties peculiarly appropriate to our age.

I live in undeniable comfort—some would say luxury—in a spacious, lovely apartment high above Manhattan. When I venture out to walk the streets below, I see how others live who have not been dealt as generous a hand. I see poverty, usually with a face as dark as mine or darker, sitting on a box in front of my bank with a cup in her hand; or trudging wearily along the sidewalks; or fallen down into foul gutters. Around the corner, huddled on chilly stoops near the Greek Orthodox church, I see loneliness gnawing at human beings who surely deserve a far better fate. I hear madness crying out in the indifferent streets.

Sometimes, gloomily, I wonder about a connection between AIDS and where we in the United States are headed as a people and a nation as this century moves to a close. Too many people seem determined to forget that although we are of different colors and beliefs, we are all members of the same human race, united by much more than the factors and forces that separate us. Sometimes I wonder what is becoming of our vaunted American society, or even Western civilization, as an unmistakable darkness seems to settle over our lives and our history, blocking out the sun. Our national destiny, which at times seems as bright as in the past, sometimes also appears tragically foreshortened, even doomed, as the fabric of our society is threatened by endless waves of crime, by the weakening of our family structures, by the deterioration of our schools, and by the decline of religion and spiritual values. AIDS then takes on a specially ominous cast, as if in its savagery and mystery it mirrors our fate.

Surely we need to resist surrendering to such a fatalistic analogy. Some people profess to see little purpose to the struggle for life. And yet that is precisely the task to which, in my fight against the ravages of AIDS, I devote myself every day: the struggle for life, aided by science in my fight with this disease. I know that we are all, as human beings, going to our death, and that I may be called, because of AIDS, to go faster than most others. Still, I resolutely do battle with this opponent, as I boldly did battle with my opponents on the tennis court. True, this fight is different. The biggest difference is that I now fight not so much to win as not to lose. This enemy is different, too—dark and mysterious, springing on civilization just when civilization was sure that it had almost rid itself of mysterious beasts forever. But it must be fought with science, and with calm, clear thinking.

I know that I must govern that part of my imagination that endows AIDS with properties it does not intrinsically possess. I must be as resolute and poised as I can be in the face of its threat. I tell myself that I must never surrender to its power to terrify, even under its constant threat of death.

Response and Analysis

1. Arthur Ashe applied lessons that he learned through his professional tennis career and through other illnesses to help him cope with AIDS. Briefly describe an emotion-focused and problem-focused coping strategy he used. Why was social support important to Ashe? How might social support reduce the effects of stress, emotional distress, and vulnerability to illness?

2. Arthur Ashe presented "five essential pillars to support the health and well-being of every individual." What are the five pillars? Does psychological research suggest that any of these "pillars" positively promote health and well-being?

Personal Experience and Application

1. Describe a lesson that you learned through one of your interests or hobbies that has helped you cope with a stressful situation. Why was this coping strategy effective?

2. Suppose you are invited to give a five-minute presentation on AIDS to a psychology class at your college or university. Write a speech in which you discuss (a) what causes AIDS; (b) four risk factors for being exposed to the HIV virus; (c) three common myths about how AIDS can be contracted; and (d) three ways to minimize exposure to the HIV virus.

Research

Arthur Ashe believed that the support of family and friends is important to our health and well-being. Suppose you want to design a study to test this idea. State Ashe's idea in the form of a hypothesis. Would you conduct your study in the lab or in the field? Why?

FROM VIETNAM TO HELL

Shirley Dicks

Psychological Concepts
posttraumatic stress disorder, general adaptation
syndrome model

The Vietnam War left in its wake many men who were unable to return to the life
they had known, and many veterans suffered from posttraumatic stress disorder
(PTSD). Some became abusive, alcoholic, and unable to find satisfying work. Many
of their marriages ended in divorce.

Shirley Dicks, whose former husband was a Vietnam veteran, interviewed
several men diagnosed with PTSD. These veterans speak of suffering from depression, emotional paralysis, headaches, isolation, and nightmares about Vietnam.
When young men become "screaming military fanatics" who are taught to kill, then
we can't, says one veteran, "bring them home unbriefed, untrained, and expect
them to be normal" (p. 57).

Here is the story of John, who reveals his anger and suffering as he speaks
about his experiences: "I became so unfeeling at nineteen years old that, after a
fight . . . I would pick up the dead and throw them in bags, and then we'd eat
lunch." What other experiences does John describe that may have contributed to
his developing PTSD? For a man so injured, what strengths does John appear to
have? Why is it important that he tell his story?

My name is John and I'd prefer not to use my last name. I don't trust many
people anymore, but the story of Vietnam needs to be told. I've been through
hell since the Vietnam War. My life was ruined and no one cared. I'm outraged at
the whole thing. I went to war at the age of nineteen to fight for this country, and
when I came home they were upset with me. I feel like a time bomb, that I could
go to jail at any time because I might do something stupid. I can't handle authority or someone telling me what to do. Right now I'm out in the woods by myself.

When I first went to Vietnam, I was scared like all the others. We were young
and knew we were going to war to be killed, wounded or whatever and it was scary.
When we landed in the country, we didn't know what to do. The people who had
been there awhile didn't want anything to do with us because we didn't know anything, and they felt their lives would be jeopardized. The jungle itself was beautiful,
green, blue vegetation, and the water in the mountain streams was crystal clear. I

was a rifleman during the Tet Offensive in nineteen sixty-eight. I stayed basically in the jungle, so my contact was mostly with the NVA* soldiers.

The NVA were trained soldiers, and we would fight face to face. They usually outnumbered us. The United States would tell the people back home how many we had killed. In reality they were hitting us hard, and that's where the Agent Orange came in. They decided that they would kill the foliage so we could see the NVA. They sprayed chemicals over the jungles, and it killed the foliage, but it also sprayed on the men and later caused cancer.

We never got much sleep in the jungles. Even the days we didn't see the NVA, at least three men would be shot in the head by snipers. You never knew if it would be you that day or if you were one of the lucky ones. I was eating lunch one day with my buddy, and we were talking about his girl back in the States. A round hit him in the head, and I had his brains in my lunch and all over me. He never felt a thing, but I did: I've never gotten over it and I don't think I ever will.

They would tell us that we had to stay up at night, that this was the night the NVA would come in and we needed to be ready. Can you imagine thinking that all night long? We were all so tired, but we didn't sleep. Nothing happened that night. I became so unfeeling at nineteen years old that, after a fight, I would pack up the wounded and send them off. I would pick up the dead and throw them in bags, and then we'd eat lunch. We'd sit down and eat lunch. We had to be hard; we were Marines and you couldn't let anyone see that it bothered you. You had to be a man and take it. I opened up my lima beans and ate them. Do you know why we ate the lima beans after a fight? We hated them but after seeing the death and destruction, you didn't taste them. That's why we ate them at that time.

I had been in the country about six weeks when we had to go out on patrol one night. I had dysentery and asked the sergeant if I could miss that one patrol. I was sick and didn't think I could make it, or be of help to anyone else. He said in no uncertain terms that I was going if I was dying. So I went down the trail with them. I was so sick, and it was uncomfortable. I wasn't trying to get out of going into the bush, I was just plain sick. My temperature was going up as the day wore on. The medic said that I should go back, that I was too sick to go on, but the sergeant said I would go on or die. They were not going to send a chopper in to take me out. I drank all of my water because I was so hot and feverish. Then I traded my fruit cocktail for a couple of swigs of water from the guy in front of me. I didn't have any more valuables on me, so I didn't get any more water. These guys didn't want to have anything to do with me because I was new in the country. They thought I couldn't take it, getting sick and all. We didn't make contact all day with the enemy. We reached our destination and got some water to drink. It was Thanksgiving Day, and they were cooking turkey and instant potatoes. I wanted to eat so badly, but I was so sick that I couldn't. The sergeant came over and asked me if I was going to

---

*NVA: North Vietnamese Army.

eat. I told him that I was too sick, so he just left me there and went down to eat. Finally I was put on a chopper and sent to the hospital. I woke up and the nurses were cleaning me. I smelled so bad and had sores all over my body. Two weeks later, I was back in the bush again.

One day on patrol three of our men disappeared. We didn't know what had happened to them until the second day. We came upon their bodies on the trail. The NVA had defaced them, cut off their penises and stuck them in their mouths. We were uptight now. We were scared because they might do this to us if they got a chance.

I remember it was Christmas, and I felt tears in my eyes. I said to myself that I was in some serious trouble. My nerves were getting bad, guys were dying like flies all around me, and it was kill or be killed. We were fighting in their backyards, and we stood out like sore thumbs, ready to be ambushed. They would use snakes to get us, put them about face height so we'd walk into them. They called them the five step snake. You couldn't go five steps after being bitten before you died. They had all kinds of booby traps. Sometimes they used poison gas, but the greatest fear we had was to be a POW.

When I came back to the United States, I couldn't believe the people would be mad at us. We thought we were heroes for laying our lives down for our country. We were warriors and had fought our war. They called me "baby killer" and "rapist," and I couldn't understand it. I hadn't done any of that over there, but the people here didn't understand the war. All they could do was place the blame.

I couldn't hold on to a job because of the PTSD. At first I thought it was normal for me to have hallucinations and dreams about Vietnam. I thought the flashbacks and the tiredness were normal, too, but they weren't. It was a symptom of post-traumatic stress disorder. I would take sleeping pills to get some sleep at night. The pills kept me drugged, but the VA wanted me to take them. I needed outside help since the VA wasn't doing anything but giving me sleeping pills. I went to a psychiatrist who treated me for the PTSD. I tried to get money from the government because of the PTSD, but the government refused. I think the veterans have a real problem and should be helped for their safety as well as for the safety of other people. We went to war to fight for our country. They send us out here with no money and some of us are unable to work because of the mental and physical stresses. If you can't work and support your family and it's because you fought for the government, then they should help us. They should have deprogrammed us as soon as we reached the US. I think it would have helped a lot of us if they had had some sort of programs for us.

For years after Vietnam, I lived out in the woods. I would wash in the stream, eat cold food, and go to the bathroom in the woods. Finally I got a little heater and would heat some of the canned food that I ate. I was getting modern then.

I've been diagnosed as having severe PTSD. I went to the veterans' centers and they helped. I couldn't hold a job for very long, and I couldn't sleep. I began to smoke a little marijuana; then I needed something to wake me up. It was a merry-go-round. I keep on having nightmares and flashbacks about Vietnam. I get into fights all the time because I can't stand somebody telling me what to do. I find myself on the edge of life all the time. Vietnam did that to me.

I used to sleep with a gun all the time until one night I was having a flashback and found myself shooting at some trees. I decided not to take a chance on that happening again. My wife could have come walking down the path and been killed.

I don't believe we belonged in Vietnam. They told us in training we were going over there because they didn't want the Vietnamese over here fighting on our backdoor and raping our women. They said it was necessary to go over and fight the war. I didn't see any necessity in it. We went over there with the good intentions of cleaning up these bad guys and coming home as heroes. That was a joke. The other wars were necessary, but not this one. My child isn't going to war for this country.

I can remember the happiest day in Vietnam. We were on the jet on our way back home, so high that the Vietnamese couldn't fire at us and that was a very happy feeling. We knew that now the only way we were going to die was if the jet were to crash. We were almost home with all our arms and legs. We weren't going home in a basket; we were going home in one piece. Little did we know, most of us were eaten up with Agent Orange, PTSD and traumas. We thought we were all set; we were going back. We got home and found out differently.

I've driven eighteen wheelers all over the country but can't seem to last very long at any one place. Vietnam haunts me today; I hear the groans of the dying. Everyone yells out to God when they know they're dying, and I used to wonder if I would do the same.

A man can't kill another man and be the same as he was when he was a child. You can cover it up and pretend, and try to forget it, but it never goes away. It poisons you, robs you, and changes you from what you once were. What I once was I can never be again because I fought for my country. A child went to war, and a crazy man came home. I don't know of any other way to put it.

Response and Analysis

1. What stressors and traumatic events did John experience during the Vietnam War? How did his behavioral, cognitive, and emotional reactions change during his tour of duty in Vietnam? What physical, behavioral, cognitive, and emotional problems did he experience upon returning to the United States?

2. According to the general adaptation syndrome stress model, what physical reactions occur at the alarm, resistance, and exhaustion stages? How did John cope with posttraumatic stress disorder?

Personal Experience and Application

1. Do you know someone who has experienced a traumatic event, such as a war, a violent crime, or a natural disaster? Briefly describe the event. What physical, behavioral, cognitive, and emotional reactions did the person experience in the weeks and months following the event? Did the person believe that he

or she had control over the situation? How might feelings of control affect the degree of stress a person experiences?

2. If you find yourself in an extremely stressful situation and are experiencing prolonged stress, what three actions might you take to minimize the likelihood that you will become ill?

Research

John and other Vietnam War veterans participated in an open interview in which they were asked similar questions and allowed to respond in whatever way they wished. List two advantages and two disadvantages of an open interview. Do the advantages outweigh the disadvantages, or vice versa? Why? Briefly describe another way to study how the Vietnam War affected veterans.

OPENING UP

James W. Pennebaker

Psychological Concepts
social support, coping, traumatic experiences, immune system

Could sharing our confidential or traumatic experiences activate our immune system and promote better health? Psychologist James Pennebaker investigated the relationship between people's health and their sharing of secret or upsetting thoughts or experiences with others. Because some people find it difficult to reveal private matters to others, Pennebaker also considered whether writing in a journal would offer the same health benefits as talking with another person. Pennebaker presents provocative results from his research.

The medical and science writer for the *Dallas Morning News*, Rita Rubin, had heard a rumor that we had found that writing about upsetting experiences was good for your health. She had recently moved from Ohio, where she had followed an up-and-coming research team that was investigating the links between psychological stress and immune-system function. Rita was the first to suggest that I contact them and, perhaps, join forces.

The research team was Janice K. Kiecolt-Glaser, a clinical psychologist, and her husband Ronald Glaser, an immunologist, both with the Ohio State University College of Medicine. Together, they were blazing a trail by showing that overwhelming experiences such as divorce, major exams in college, and even strong feelings of loneliness adversely affected immune function. Their most recent finding was that relaxation therapy among the elderly could improve the action of the immune system. The work by Jan and Ron was groundbreaking because it relied on precise state-of-the-art techniques to measure the action of t-lymphocytes, natural killer cells, and other immune markers in the blood. Further, unlike most researchers in immunology, Jan and Ron were sophisticated about psychology.

By a wonderful coincidence, Jan and I were invited to a small conference in New Orleans soon after Rita Rubin's introduction. The first night of the conference, before we had finished our first can of Dixie beer, Jan and I had outlined an experiment to see if writing about traumas could directly affect the action of the immune system. Three months later, the study was under way.

The experiment was similar to the first confession study.* Fifty students wrote for twenty minutes a day for four consecutive days about one of two topics. Half wrote about their deepest thoughts and feelings concerning a trauma. The remaining twenty-five students were expected to write about superficial topics. Unlike in the first confession study, however, the students consented to have their blood drawn the day before writing, after the last writing session, and again six weeks later.

The week of running the study was frenzied. I had a staff of almost a dozen people helping me with the experiment in Dallas. As before, the experimental volunteers poured out their hearts in their writing. The tragedies they disclosed were comparable to those in the first experiment. Instances of rape, child abuse, suicide attempts, death, and intense family conflict were common. Again, those who wrote about traumas reported feeling sadder and more upset each day relative to those who wrote about superficial topics.

Collecting the blood and measuring immune function was a novel experience that added to the frenzy. As soon as the blood was drawn, we'd pack it and drive like hell to get to the airport so we wouldn't miss the last plane for Columbus, Ohio. Once the blood samples arrived, the people in the immunology lab would work around the clock, in an assembly-line manner. The procedure involved separating the blood cells and placing a predetermined number of white cells in small dishes. Each dish contained differing amounts of various foreign substances, called mitogens. The dishes were then incubated for two days to allow the white blood cells time to divide and proliferate in the presence of the mitogens.

The logic of this procedure is fascinating. In the body, there are a number of different kinds of white cells, or lymphocytes, that control immune function.

---

*First confession study: one of Pennebaker's first studies on writing about trauma.

T-lymphocytes, for example, can stimulate other lymphocytes to make antibodies. Antibodies, along with parts of the body's defense system, can retard and kill bacteria and viruses foreign to the body. The immune measures that we used mimicked this bodily process in the dishes. Just as viruses and bacteria can stimulate the proliferation of t-lymphocytes in the body, the mitogens did the same in the laboratory dishes. If the lymphocytes divide at a fast rate in response to the mitogens, we can infer that at least part of the immune system is working quickly and efficiently.

So what did we find? People who wrote about their deepest thoughts and feelings surrounding traumatic experiences evidenced heightened immune function compared with those who wrote about superficial topics. Although this effect was most pronounced after the last day of writing, it tended to persist six weeks after the study. In addition, health-center visits for illness dropped for the people who wrote about traumas compared to those who wrote on the trivial topics.

There was another important finding as well. Every day, after writing, we asked people who had written about traumas to respond to the questionnaire item "To what degree did you write about something that you have previously held back from telling others?" As you can see, the question was intended to get at people's previous attempts at inhibition. That is, the more they had held back, the more they had inhibited talking about the topic. Overall, we found that those who showed the greatest improvement in immune function were the same ones who had held back in telling others about the things they had written. In other words, those who had been silently living with their upsetting experiences benefited the most from writing.

We had now completed two experiments that showed similar things. Taken together, the studies indicated that writing about traumatic experiences was beneficial depending on how people wrote about them. All indications suggested that the effects were not due to simple catharsis or the venting of pent-up emotions. Indeed, the first confession study demonstrated that writing only about emotions surrounding a trauma did not produce long-term health benefits. Further, both experiments indicated that writing about feelings associated with traumatic experiences was painful. Virtually no one felt excited, on top of the world, or even mildly cheerful immediately after writing about the worst experiences of his or her life.

In the surveys that we sent out several months after the experiments, we asked people to describe in their own words what long-term effects, if any, the writing experiment had on them. Everyone who wrote about traumas described the study in positive terms. More important, approximately 80 percent explained the value of the study in terms of insight. Rather than explaining that it felt good to get negative emotions off their chests, the respondents noted how they understood themselves better. Some examples:

> It helped me think about what I felt during those times. I never realized how it affected me before.

> I had to think and resolve past experiences. . . . One result of the experiment is peace of mind, and a method to relieve emotional experiences. To have to write emotions and feelings helped me understand how I felt and why.

Although I have not talked with anyone about what I wrote, I was finally able to deal with it, work through the pain instead of trying to block it out. Now it doesn't hurt to think about it.

The observations of these people, and everyone else who participated in these studies, are almost breathtaking. They are telling us that our thought processes can heal.

These studies were just the beginning of a research project that has been expanding in several directions. Several variations of the writing experiments have now been conducted by us and by researchers in other laboratories. I now trust the effects that we have gotten. In each study that has been conducted, we have discovered some limits to the writing technique as well as methods that boost its effectiveness. I will explore the meaning and applications of many of these findings throughout the book.

In the meantime, I want to share with you some of the main points about the writing method that I have found to be related to health. Keep in mind that I am speaking as a researcher and not a therapist. My recommendations about confronting upsetting events are based on experiments, occasional case studies, and my own experiences. It is very possible that your writing about your own traumas or upsetting feelings may not be helpful. If this happens, you should be your own researcher. Experiment with different topics and approaches. Something may work for you in resolving your own conflicts that may not work for anyone else. With these warnings in mind, here are some questions commonly asked about the writing method.

What should your writing topic be?   It is not necessary to write about the most traumatic experience of your life. It is more important to focus on the issues that you are currently living with. If you find yourself thinking or dreaming about an event or experience too much of the time, writing about it can help resolve it in your mind. By the same token, if there has been something you would like to tell others but you can't for fear of embarrassment or punishment, express it on paper.

Whatever your topic, it is critical to explore both the objective experience (i.e., what happened) and your feelings about it. Really let go and write about your very deepest emotions. *What* do you feel about it and *why* do you feel that way?

Write continuously. Don't worry about grammar, spelling, or sentence structure. If you run out of things to say or reach a mental block, just repeat what you have already written.

When and where should you write?   Write whenever you want or whenever you feel you need to. I am not convinced that writing about significant experiences needs to be done that frequently. Although many people write every day in diaries, most of the entries do not grapple with fundamental psychological issues. Also be attentive to too much writing. Don't use writing as a substitute for action or as some other type of avoidance strategy. Moderation in all things includes transcribing your thoughts and feelings.

Where you write depends on your circumstances. Our studies suggest that the more unique the setting, the better. Try to find a room where you will not be interrupted or bothered by unwanted sounds, sights, or smells.

What should you do with what you have written?   Anonymity is important in our experiments. In many cases, it is wise to keep what you have written to yourself. You might even destroy it when you're finished (although many people find this hard to do). Planning to show your writing to someone can affect your mind-set while writing. For example, if you would secretly like your lover to read your deepest thoughts and feelings, you will orient your writing to your lover rather than to yourself. From a health perspective, you will be better off making yourself the audience. In that way, you don't have to rationalize or justify yourself to suit the perspective of another person.

What if you hate to write—is there a substitute?   We have conducted several studies comparing writing with talking into a tape recorder. Among college students, writing appears to be slightly more efficient in getting people to let go and divulge their thoughts and feelings. This probably reflects, in part, the fact that college students are practiced at writing. Some of the people I work with who are not in school find writing to be quite aversive. For these people, I recommend their talking about their deepest thoughts and feelings into a tape recorder. As with writing, I urge them to talk continuously for fifteen minutes a day.

Whether writing or talking is a more comfortable medium for you, remember that letting go and disclosing intimate parts of yourself may take some practice. If you have never written or talked about your thoughts and feelings, you may find doing so particularly awkward at first. If so, just relax and practice. Write or talk continuously for a set amount of time. No one is evaluating you.

What can you expect to feel during and after writing?   As we have found in all of our studies, you may feel sad or depressed immediately after writing. These negative feelings usually dissipate within an hour or so. In rare cases, they may last for a day or two. The overwhelming majority of our volunteers, however, report feelings of relief, happiness, and contentment soon after the writing studies are concluded.

Exploring your deepest thoughts and feelings is not a panacea. If you are coping with death, divorce, or other tragedy, you will not feel instantly better after writing. You should, however, have a better understanding of your feelings and emotions as well as the objective situation that you are in. In other words, writing should give you a little distance and perspective on your life.

Response and Analysis

1. According to James Pennebaker, how might disclosing pent-up thoughts and emotions affect the immune system?

2. Pennebaker offers several recommendations for writing about traumatic experiences and upsetting events. Briefly discuss them. Why might these recommendations reduce stress?

Personal Experience and Application

1. Have you ever written about a traumatic experience or an upsetting event? How did you feel after writing about the experience? What are some of the similarities and differences between writing in a personal journal or diary and doing the type of writing described by Pennebaker?

2. How often do you talk with others about important problems or issues in your life? With whom do you talk? Do you believe talking with others about your problems is helpful? Why or why not?

Research

Suppose you wish to conduct an experiment that involves having students in introduction to psychology courses write about a distressing or traumatic event they have experienced. Before conducting the study, you must secure approval from the human subjects Institutional Review Board at your college or university. Two of the purposes of the Review Board are to ensure that your procedures are ethical and to protect the rights and dignity of the participants.

Most Review Boards require the researcher to submit a form describing, among other things, the activities in which the students will participate. Suppose the procedures for your experiment are as follows. When the participants arrive at your lab, you will escort them to individual cubicles where they cannot see the other participants or the experimenter. You then ask the participants to read and sign a consent form, and allow students who do not wish to participate to leave. Next, you will ask half of the participants to write for thirty minutes about a distressing or traumatic event that they have experienced. You will ask the other half to write for thirty minutes about their favorite summer vacation. You tell all participants that their essays are anonymous and that they should not put their names on their essay. At the end of the thirty-minute period, you ask the participants to place their essays in an unmarked envelope. Finally, you ask each participant to complete a brief survey indicating if they gained new insights about themselves by participating in the study.

In addition to a description of procedures, most Institutional Review Boards ask the researcher to list the potential benefits and risks of their study to the participants. Based on the above description, make a list of the potential benefits and risks to students who will participate in your study. Do you believe the risks outweigh the benefits, or vice versa? Why? Why is it important to allow those students to leave who do not want to participate? Why is it important to debrief participants about the experiment at the end of the session?

POSITIVE ILLUSIONS

Shelley E. Taylor

Psychological Concepts
coping (emotional, cognitive, behavioral), cognitive restructuring

Are we powerless when we suffer from severe illness or trauma, or can we react positively? What determines whether we respond with desperation and resignation or with hope and fortitude?

As a graduate student in psychology, Shelley Taylor became interested in how people confront unbearable burdens, such as the loss of a job and income, illness, or the death of a family member or friend. In looking for answers, Taylor discovered the value of what she calls "positive illusions." She found that people are more optimistic when they think they have control over their stress or illness. Why might believing in a "positive illusion" contribute to good health or a sense of well-being?

As a college student, I worked in a mental hospital for several months. When I took the job, I assumed that those who are confined to such institutions had been driven by the pain of life into madness. I expected to find people suffering intolerable stress—the death of a loved one, the destruction of home and property by a natural disaster, a divorce or other wrenching separation. This, I assumed, must be what leads to mental illness. I was quickly disabused of this belief. Indeed, as I soon learned, victims of disasters—personal ones such as assault or rape, or natural catastrophes such as a fire or flood—rarely develop the signs of mental illness. When interviewed some months after what would seem to be devastating losses, these people often report that their lives are at least as happy and satisfying as they were before these disastrous events.

These facts so intrigued me that, following my graduate training, I determined to study the processes whereby recovery from a tragic or near-tragic event takes place. Such problems are not to be studied lightly. Conducting interviews with rape victims, cancer patients, and men vulnerable to sudden death—the groups that would constitute our first investigations—is a wrenching way to make a living. People who are facing death or who have recently faced it have much to say and a lot of it is hard to hear. Yet there were also remarkable stories of recovery.

Originally, I had thought of adjustment to trauma and recovery from devastation as a homeostatic process, that is, as a mental regulatory system whose function it is to maintain psychological balance and stability. I suspected that there might be mechanisms within the mind that help restore people's emotional and cognitive balance to the levels experienced before a victimizing event. A homeostatic hypothesis is a logical choice, for it applies quite well to many biological problems. The gastric system, for example, has five different methods by which hydrochloric acid can be produced, and if one or more of them is disrupted, then the others can take over, maintaining gastric functioning at approximately its previous level. Homeostasis seemed on the surface to be an apt description of the recovery processes of the mind.

In fact, what we soon uncovered was a different process altogether. Rather than being restored to their previous level of functioning, many of the people we interviewed seemed actually to have achieved a higher level of functioning than they had experienced prior to the victimizing event. Many of these victims said that their lives prior to the victimizing events had simply rolled along as a life will when one makes no particular effort to intervene actively in its course. The threatening events to which they were exposed, however, forced them to rethink their priorities and values, and many victims indicated that their lives were now self-consciously lived a moment at a time, in order to extract as much enjoyment and meaning from life as possible. They thought about the reasons behind what they did as they had never before, put value on what truly mattered to them, and in some cases, undertook new activities that left them feeling more fulfilled. As one of the cancer patients we interviewed put it, "The trick, of course, is to do this without getting cancer."

My life was changed by contact with these people. After listening to hours of interviews in which victims thoughtfully appraised their lives and their accomplishments and explained how they had restructured their activities and thinking in order to make their lives more rewarding and meaningful, one feels almost embarrassed by the lack of similar attention to one's own life. Consequently, this work has the effect of forcing a rigorous scrutiny of one's own values and a questioning of the intrinsic merit of its activities, sometimes prompting as well an unwelcome contemplation of death. At these moments, my husband comments, "You and Woody Allen . . ." and sets off to find lighter diversions. Despite these risks, I have watched with pleasure as successive waves of students who have worked with me have also found their lives enriched by contact with people who have been forced to confront the meaning and value in their lives. After four or five interviews my students come back as changed people, and years later will write letters about how important the experiences were to their development as scientists and as mature adults.

A curious picture began to emerge in our research findings. Many of the psychological recoveries recounted by these victims seemed to depend on certain distortions of their situations, especially overly optimistic perceptions concerning chances of recovery from a disease, or the belief that they could actively control the likelihood of a repeat victimization in the future. It was surprising and disturbing to listen to a cancer patient recount the meaning that the experience had brought to her life, and to hear her state with confidence that she would never get cancer again, knowing from the chart records that she would almost certainly develop a recurrence and ultimately die of the disease. But what was more surprising was the discovery that those people who maintained these overly optimistic assessments of their situations and the beliefs that they could control the victimizing events were actually better adjusted to their circumstances and not more poorly adjusted. We came to call these adaptive fictions *illusions*, and although they did not exist in every account of recovery from victimization, they were nonetheless prevalent.

Puzzled by this unanticipated role of creative imagination in recovery, we looked for a context in which to explore it further. We turned first to the mental health literature, but although it was interesting in its own right, it was not especially helpful for understanding the illusions we observed among our victims of *life*-threatening events. We turned next to the research on cognition and social cognition, new and fast-growing subspecialties of psychology that have attracted many of the brightest scientists in the field. And it was here that we began to find clues. First, a brief digression is required.

At different points in their histories, most of the sciences have had frameworks that, once articulated, attracted the majority of scientists and advanced the field suddenly and abruptly in an all-new direction. Cognitive psychology has represented such a development for psychology. The cognitive perspective, which focuses on how the mind is organized and how it functions, has become a dominant framework for developmental psychologists, who study the lives of children and adults across the lifespan; social psychologists, who examine how people think about social activities and interact with others; and clinicians, who attempt to understand mental health and illness. These fields have been so overwhelmed by the cognitive perspective in recent years that, in many respects, social psychologists, clinicians, and developmental psychologists are often cognitive psychologists as well.

What is the cognitive perspective? It is an understanding of how people think about themselves and the world. The cognitive perspective focuses on the person's interpretations. It examines how ordinary people think about people and how they think they think about people and why they think that way. To a cognitive psychologist, for example, it is less important to know whether someone failed a test than to know whether he or she regards failure as a setback or as a learning experience. It is less important to know if a person is Protestant, Catholic, or Jewish than to understand what purpose religion serves in the person's life. It is less important to know if a person makes a lot of money and has an exciting job than it is to know if he or she is contented with those circumstances. Interpretation is the key element in the cognitive analysis.

Ironically, this literature helped us to understand better the kinds of adaptive fictions we saw in our victims, for cognitive research documents similar perceptions in normal, everyday thought. That is, rather than being firmly in touch with reality, the normal human mind distorts incoming information in a positive direction. In particular, people think of themselves, their future, and their ability to have an impact on what goes on around them in a more positive manner than reality can sustain. Just as victims of life-threatening events seem to be motivated to recover from victimization and actively restructure victimizing events in a positive manner, so people who are confronted with the normal rebuffs of everyday life seem to construe their experience so as to develop and maintain an exaggeratedly positive view of their own attributes, an unrealistic optimism about the future, and a distorted faith in their ability to control what goes on around them.

These labors and investigations have culminated in the perspective on mental health set forth in this book. I argue that the normal human mind is oriented toward mental health and that at every turn it construes events in a manner that promotes benign fictions about the self, the world, and the future. The mind is, with some significant exceptions, intrinsically adaptive, oriented toward overcoming rather than succumbing to the adverse events of life. In many ways, the healthy mind is a self-deceptive one, as I will attempt to show. At one level, it constructs beneficent interpretations of threatening events that raise self-esteem and promote motivation; yet at another level, it recognizes the threat or challenge that is posed by these events.

The viewpoint that people need to distort reality in order to adjust successfully to it would seem to be quite cynical on the surface. I hope to convey exactly the opposite sentiment. The ability of the mind to construe benefit from tragedy and to prevent a person from becoming overwhelmed by the stress and pain of life is a remarkable achievement. To a scientist, it makes the mind infinitely more interesting to study. If all our minds did was to take in information as it actually exists and represent it faithfully, the chief task of a psychologist would be to function as a historian of mundane mental activity. Exploring how the mind imposes structure and meaning on events and how it does so systematically in adaptive ways is truly an adventure. Moreover, one emerges from the exploration, not with cynical disdain for the petty ways in which people must cover up their faults and distort their tragedies, but with a huge respect for an organism that has evolved to the point that it can triumph over adversity through sheer mental effort. The mind's resources are exceptional and impressive, and their ability to help people overcome adversity is testimony to the resilience of the human spirit.

Response and Analysis

1. Why might believing in a "positive illusion" contribute to good health or a sense of well-being? Why would a cognitive psychologist be less interested in "whether someone failed a test than . . . whether he or she regards failure as a setback or as a learning experience"?

2. People may use one or more coping strategies to deal with stressful situations. Briefly describe and give an example of an emo-

tional, a cognitive, and a behavioral coping strategy.

Personal Experience and Application

1. Briefly describe a stressful situation in which either you or someone you know had optimistic perceptions or "positive illusions" about the outcome. What was the positive illusion? How did it help you or the person you know cope with the situation? In what

kind of situation might positive illusions not be an effective strategy?

2. List the stressors in your life, including daily pressures, life strains, and life changes. Which stressors create the most and the least stress? What can you do to reduce the amount of stress in your life?

Research

One of the first steps in the research process is developing an interesting idea to test. How did Shelley Taylor become interested in studying positive illusions? How did her interviews with victims of personal and natural disasters lead to new ideas and hypotheses to test? How has conducting research with victims of personal and natural disasters affected the lives of Taylor and her graduate students?

TREATING CHRONIC PAIN

Aleene Friedman

Psychological Concepts
biofeedback, stress management

How effective is biofeedback in helping patients find relief from their pain? What techniques do biofeedback therapists use to treat their patients?

Biofeedback therapist Aleene Friedman tells the story of Joyce, one of her patients who suffered from persistent headaches. She underwent extensive psychological and physiological diagnostic tests, none of which revealed any abnormalities. Since Joyce was a computer programmer, she and her physicians considered whether eye strain or poor posture could be causing her headaches. After determining that these were unlikely causes, Joyce and her physicians at Scripps Clinic decided that she would be an excellent candidate for the biofeedback program.

In the following selection, Dr. Friedman presents some of the biofeedback techniques she used to help Joyce. About a year after treatment, Joyce reported that she continued to monitor herself at home, and that she seldom suffered from headaches. What did biofeedback offer Joyce? What self-help procedures did Joyce learn to reduce her pain?

J oyce was self-referred for headaches. She had a mixed headache pattern of both muscle contraction and vascular (migraine) headaches. She had been medically treated without satisfactory results and stated that she had decided "to give biofeedback a try." When asked about her symptoms, she stated:

> I seldom have a day without a headache, but the symptoms vary in intensity. The migraines are the worst, and they generally occur about every four or five weeks, and really knock me out. The other headaches occur almost everyday, but there isn't an exact pattern. They do tend to occur more often in the late afternoon, but sometimes I wake up with a headache or get one in the evening. I seldom miss work because of a headache, but I am tired of having headaches and tired of trying to control them with medications.

During this first session I learned that Joyce's migraine headaches had started during her late teens but were not directly connected to her menses. She was now 32 years old, unmarried, lived alone, was not close to her family, and liked her work as a computer programmer. She earned an excellent income, enjoyed time with her friends, and liked the company of her dog and two cats. When asked how long she had been suffering from the muscle contraction headaches, she stated:

> Up until ten years ago I would sometimes have an occasional tension (muscle-contraction) headache, but I could take something like aspirin and decrease the symptoms within an hour. The headaches crept up on me over the past ten years, and I kept trying to ignore them, but now it is impossible. The funny thing is that the migraine headaches have remained about the same in frequency and intensity, and now I am more concerned about the tension headaches than the migraines—except, of course, when I have a migraine headache.

During our initial conversation I learned that Joyce often worked overtime, and did not exercise on a regular basis, but did like to camp and hike during her vacations. She was pleasant and did not appear to be in any distress during this first meeting. When asked about her condition, she stated that she had a very slight headache but did not have any other symptoms. She described herself as calm, energetic, perfectionistic, and sometimes driven. Joyce did not drink colas, she had one or two cups of coffee a day, did not smoke, and seldom drank alcohol. She was currently stressed by her parents (if they contacted her), her work (she tended to work long hours), her symptoms, and her finances (she was earning more money than she had ever expected to earn, and her affluence was a source of stress).

For several sessions I utilized the electromyograph (EMG) to help Joyce to reduce her upper-body tension levels. When the muscles exhibit elevated levels of tension during rest, it indicates a source of chronic tension. I monitored her upper-back muscles, neck and shoulder areas, forehead (frontalis), and the muscles of her jaw. We discussed ways to decrease eye tension and to utilize breathing techniques to reduce upper-body tension levels. On a scale of one to ten Joyce's highest levels of tension were over the frontalis and registered between 3.0 and 3.5. When she learned to reduce her jaw tension and to relax her eye tension, she brought this level down to a low of 1.5. I explained to her that it would not be normal to maintain a relaxed state throughout the day, but that the same is true of maintaining high levels of tension throughout the day. Ordinarily, a level of tension between 2.0 and 2.5 is considered a moderately low level of tension, and a tension level below 2.0 is considered a low level of tension. But this is not a standard that is accepted by all biofeedback therapists.

The EMG measures the electrical current that is produced by the muscle that is being monitored. During a time of rest the output should be low. But when a muscle or muscle group becomes chronically tense, the output is high, and the work load is inappropriate for the amount of work being done. This is a waste of one's resources, and it also contributes to chronic stress and chronic pain. The rhythm of the body is one of tense–relax, and when this rhythm is broken it exerts a stress that is communicated within the body as a whole.

Sometimes a patient will experience a dramatic reduction in his or her symptoms after only one or two sessions of biofeedback therapy. For a lasting effect the patient needs to incorporate what is being learned during the session into everyday life, and to generalize his or her ability to decrease the tension levels over one particular muscle group. EMG electrodes monitor surface muscle tension, and the ability to elicit a generalized relaxation response is important.

Joyce did not experience an immediate decrease in her symptoms, but she was becoming more aware of her habitual patterns of holding tension in the neck, shoulders, and facial area. When a pattern of tension becomes habitualized, it is not recognized and/or associated with the pain or discomfort that eventually surfaces. Then, too, some pain is referred pain, and it may be difficult to recognize the relationship between the pain itself and the actual source of the pain. This is especially true of back injuries, but temporomandibular joint (TMJ) disorders may also cause pain and/or discomfort that will appear to be unrelated to the primary source of the problem. Headaches, dizziness, ringing in the ears, facial pain, and other problems are often related to this common disorder.

I asked Joyce to practice "mini-exercises" off and on throughout the day so that she would begin to reduce her upper-body tension levels. These mini-exercises included using her breathing to reduce facial tension, short tense–relax exercises for the neck and shoulders, consciously relaxing the eyes and masseter muscles from time to time, and moving and stretching whenever she had the chance to do so. I encouraged her to take time for lunch and a short walk everyday. Joyce worked a 50- to 60-hour work week. It is difficult to reduce symptoms if a connection with nature and diversity is lacking. We discussed the fact that she had other options and that it would be possible for her to plan short weekend trips. This would provide an opportunity for hiking and a total break from her work.

Joyce was beginning to have a decrease in her muscle-contraction headaches, and she had not yet had a vascular headache. I continued to monitor her upper-body tension levels, but I also introduced the blood-flow (temperature) feedback.*

---

*Blood-flow (temperature) feedback: a type of feedback that measures peripheral blood flow, especially of the hands and feet.

This is a standard treatment modality for migraine headaches, but it is also a primary tool for general relaxation and to combat various other disorders. Except for the hands and feet, internal and external body temperatures remain about the same unless there is a traumatic injury or illness. The core temperature is usually about 99° F, and the external body temperature is slightly cooler. I have seen many patients who are chronically stressed, and their hand temperature is often in the low eighties. This is especially true of female patients. Migraine headaches are vascular headaches, and a drop in hand temperature is a warning sign that indicates the vascular tension that usually precipitates a migraine headache is occurring. I do not emphasize learning to warm the hands to abort a headache, but rather to utilize warming techniques to prevent migraine headaches.

It was not easy for Joyce to warm her hands so I covered her with a light blanket. She had become accustomed to her cool hands, and I wanted her to experience what it felt like to have warm extremities. Her pre-session finger temperature readings were in the low eighties and her post-session readings were in the low nineties. We worked on exercises that emphasized feelings of being heavy and warm, and I also introduced relaxing images. It takes time to relax the smooth muscles of the vascular system, but this is an excellent way to attain a deep state of relaxation.

Within 5 weeks Joyce's pre-session EMG levels were decreased, and she was able to maintain a low tension level throughout the session. She reported that she was having decreased tension headache symptoms but that she had suffered a migraine headache that had occurred over the weekend. It is not unusual for a vascular headache to occur after a week of hard work. Some patients feel punished for relaxing but it is often part of the "let down" phenomenon of the migraine headache pattern. With Joyce, as well as other patients, there is a need to explore one's own patterns. Diet, specific triggers, muscle tension, vascular tension, head injuries, extreme stress, and numerous other factors may contribute to an individual's headache pattern.

During the next month I continued to emphasize upper-body relaxation, temperature training, and the development of imagery skills. I gave Joyce some home practice tapes and some finger sensors that indicated changes in her hand temperature. This was still another way to help her to tune into the subtle body changes that contributed to her headache symptoms. Eventually, Joyce developed her own personal relaxation image. She was able to close her eyes, take a deep breath, exhale her chronic tension, and imagine her own personal relaxation image while she maintained relaxed breathing. This was a short exercise that provided a moment of deep relaxation. Joyce was beginning to understand her symptoms, and she was pleased by her progress. She was having fewer muscle-contraction headaches, and the intensity and duration of her migraine headaches had decreased. She had gone 6 weeks without having had a vascular headache, and she was now much more aware of the contributing factors. Joyce decided when it was time for her to continue working by herself, but we did schedule two follow-up sessions. She knew that she was not "cured," but she was aware of her own resources and her capacity for self-regulation. Joyce called me about a year after her final biofeedback session. She had purchased a house in a semi-rural area and she was able to do most of her work in her home computer center. She was taking daily walks, pacing herself, and enjoying her "almost headache-free existence."

Response and Analysis

1. What stressors did Joyce report to the biofeedback therapist? How did the therapist use the electromyograph (EMG) to help Joyce recognize muscle tension?

2. The therapist suggested several "mini-exercises" to reduce upper-body tension levels. Briefly describe a few of them. How did the therapist use temperature feedback to help Joyce reduce muscle tension?

Personal Experience and Application

1. How do you know when you are tense or stressed? In the past three months, when were you most tense and when were you most relaxed? What activities bring on tension? How do you relieve tension?

2. Which of the following stress management techniques would help you manage stress: a relaxation program, improved nutrition, increase in exercise. Why?

Research

Suppose you want to conduct a study to determine which biofeedback training technique most effectively reduces heart rate. Your study has one independent variable, training technique, with three levels or conditions: (a) present a tone and a light when heart rate decreases; (b) present a constant digital display of the heart rate; and (c) do not present any feedback about heart rate. Your study has one dependent variable: heart rate.

You must now choose whether the participants should participate in all three conditions or in only one condition. If they participate in all three conditions, in what order should you present the conditions? For example, should the participants first see the tone and light when their heart rate decreases, then see a constant digital display of their heart rate, and then receive no feedback about their heart rate? Or should you vary the order in which you present the stimuli? Why?

List one advantage and one disadvantage to having the participants participate in (a) all three conditions; and (b) only one condition. Which approach will you choose? Why?

chapter 13

SOCIAL THOUGHT AND SOCIAL BEHAVIOR

Let us now imagine two men, whose life is dominated by appearance, sitting and talking together. Call them Peter and Paul. Let us list the different configurations which are involved. First, there is Peter as he wishes to appear to Paul, and Paul as he wishes to appear to Peter. Then there is Peter as he really appears to Paul, that is, Paul's image of Peter, which in general does not in the least coincide with what Peter wishes Paul to see; and similarly there is the reverse situation. Further, there is Peter as he appears to himself, and Paul as he appears to himself. Lastly, there are the bodily Peter and the bodily Paul. Two living beings and six ghostly appearances, which mingle in many ways in the conversation between the two. Where is there room for any genuine interhuman life?

MARTIN BUBER, *Elements of the Interhuman*

Do we, as Martin Buber illustrates, try to create certain impressions of ourselves for others? How do our impressions of others affect how we respond to them? In addition to asking these questions, social psychologists also want to know how we form our opinions and attitudes and what makes interpersonal relations succeed or fail. This chapter illustrates several key concepts related to social thought and social behavior: attitude formation and change; self-identity; impression formation; stereotypes; prejudice; competition; and altruism.

C. P. Ellis, former member of the Ku Klux Klan, explains his long-standing attitude against African-Americans. Eventually, however, Ellis's experiences cause him to reverse his attitude, and he begins working with African-Americans in his community. Can his attitude change be permanent?

Edward Iwata finds the influence of culture so powerful that he attempts to distance himself from his Japanese heritage and to replace it with an American identity. The results of plastic surgery, which he hopes will alter his racial features and thereby uncomplicate his life, only force his search for another self-image. Is our self-identity contingent on the values of the culture in which we live?

If we act a little askew, a little lopsided, others may just leave us alone, or a police officer might arrest us. How much can we influence others by our behavior? D. Keith Mano shows how we might drive potential muggers away by leaving them with the impression that we are not someone they would want to confront.

What attitudes do we have toward people different from ourselves—different in race, citizenship, age, gender, or economic status? Fear is one reaction that Brent Staples evokes in many people who are not African-American like himself. To counter their fear, Staples finds that the only protection he has is to create a safer stereotype of himself for others to perceive.

Why are we sometimes kind, sometimes violent, sometimes competitive, sometimes cooperative? Alfie Kohn argues that "competition by its very nature is harmful." Too often one person ends up winning at the expense of another person who loses. Kohn believes that competition may foster destructive personality traits and injure human relationships.

When and why are we helpful toward strangers? The editors of *Random Acts of Kindness* asked people to describe when they had been the recipient of thoughtfulness or when they had helped strangers themselves. The altruistic acts these people experienced appear to have increased, at least temporarily, their sense of happiness and well-being.

C. P. ELLIS

Studs Terkel

Psychological Concepts
attitudes, attitude change, cognitive dissonance

Is it possible to change an attitude that we have held for nearly half a century? How do our attitudes influence behavior? Can our behavior influence our attitudes?

What follows is an interview that took place in 1978 between the well-known oral historian and writer Studs Terkel and former Ku Klux Klan member C. P. Ellis. Born into extreme poverty, Ellis and his father succumbed to bitterness as they struggled to survive. "I began to blame it on black people. I had to hate somebody," Ellis explains. Ellis became a leader in the Klan, a group his father considered "the savior of the white people." Yet Ellis accepted an invitation from the AFL/CIO union to work with African-Americans in the community. That decision dramatically changed his life and his attitudes toward African-Americans. In this interview, Ellis uses pejorative language toward African-Americans, though he asks Terkel to "pardon the expression" and says he doesn't speak that way often. What enables a man who held strong prejudicial attitudes toward people of another race to cooperate with, understand, and accept them?

My father worked in a textile mill in Durham. He died at forty-eight years old. It was probably from cotton dust. Back then, we never heard of brown lung. I was about seventeen years old and had a mother and sister depending on somebody to make a livin'. It was just barely enough insurance to cover his burial. I had to quit school and go to work. I was about eighth grade when I quit.

My father worked hard but never had enough money to buy decent clothes. When I went to school, I never seemed to have adequate clothes to wear. I always left school late afternoon with a sense of inferiority. The other kids had nice clothes, and I just had what Daddy could buy. I still got some of those inferiority feelin's now that I have to overcome once in a while.

I loved my father. He would go with me to ball games. We'd go fishin' together. I was really ashamed of the way he'd dress. He would take this money and give it to me instead of putting it on himself. I always had the feeling about somebody looking at him and makin' fun of him and makin' fun of me. I think it had to do somethin' with my life.

My father and I were very close, but we didn't talk about too many intimate things. He did have a drinking problem. During the week, he would work every day, but weekends he was ready to get plastered. I can understand when a guy looks at his paycheck and looks at his bills, and he's worked hard all the week, and his bills are larger than his paycheck. He'd done the best he could the entire week, and there seemed to be no hope. It's an illness thing. Finally you just say: "The heck with it. I'll just get drunk and forget it."

My father was out of work during the depression, and I remember going with him to the finance company uptown, and he was turned down. That's something that's always stuck.

My father never seemed to be happy. It was a constant struggle with him just like it was for me. It's very seldom I'd see him laugh. He was just tryin' to figure out what he could do from one day to the next.

After several years pumping gas at a service station, I got married. We had to have children. Four. One child was born blind and retarded, which was a real additional expense to us. He's never spoken a word. He doesn't know me when I go to see him. But I see him, I hug his neck. I talk to him, tell him I love him. I don't know whether he knows me or not, but I know he's well taken care of. All my life, I had work, never a day without work, worked all the overtime I could get and still could not survive financially. I began to say there's somethin' wrong with this country. I worked my butt off and just never seemed to break even.

I had some real great ideas about this great nation. (Laughs.) They say to abide by the law, go to church, do right and live for the Lord, and everything'll work out. But it didn't work out. It just kept gettin' worse and worse.

I was workin' a bread route. The highest I made one week was seventy-five dollars. The rent on our house was about twelve dollars a week. I will never forget: outside of this house was a 265-gallon oil drum, and I never did get enough money to fill up that oil drum. What I would do every night, I would run up to the store and buy five gallons of oil and climb up the ladder and pour it in that 265-gallon drum. I could hear that five gallons when it hits the bottom of that oil drum, splatters, and it sounds like it's nothin' in there. But it would keep the house warm for the night. Next day you'd have to do the same thing.

I left the bread route with fifty dollars in my pocket. I went to the bank and borrowed four thousand dollars to buy the service station. I worked seven days a week, open and close, and finally had a heart attack. Just about two months before the last payments of that loan. My wife had done the best she could to keep it runnin'. Tryin' to come out of that hole, I just couldn't do it.

I really began to get bitter. I didn't know who to blame. I tried to find somebody. I began to blame it on black people. I had to hate somebody. Hatin' America is hard to do because you can't see it to hate it. You gotta have somethin' to look at to hate. (Laughs.) The natural person for me to hate would be black people, because my father before me was a member of the Klan. As far as he was concerned, it was the savior of the white people. It was the only organization in the world that would take care of the white people. So I began to admire the Klan.

I got active in the Klan while I was at the service station. Every Monday night, a group of men would come by and buy a Coca-Cola, go back to the car, take a few drinks, and come back and stand around talkin'. I couldn't help but wonder: Why are these dudes comin' out every Monday? They said they were with the Klan and have meetings close-by. Would I be interested? Boy, that was an opportunity I really looked forward to! To be part of somethin'. I joined the Klan, went from member to chaplain, from chaplain to vice-president, from vice-president to president. The title is exalted cyclops.

The first night I went with the fellas, they knocked on the door and gave the signal. They sent some robed Klansmen to talk to me and give me some instructions. I was led into a large meeting room, and this was the time of my life! It was thrilling. Here's a guy who's worked all his life and struggled all his life to be something, and here's the moment to be something. I will never forget it. Four robed Klansmen led me into the hall. The lights were dim, and the only thing you could see was an illuminated cross. I knelt before the cross. I had to make certain vows and promises. We promised to uphold the purity of the white race, fight communism, and protect white womanhood.

After I had taken my oath, there was loud applause goin' throughout the building, musta been at least four hundred people. For this one little ol' person. It was a thrilling moment for C. P. Ellis.

It disturbs me when people who do not really know what it's all about are so very critical of individual Klansmen. The majority of 'em are low-income whites, people who really don't have a part in something. They have been shut out as well as the blacks. Some are not very well educated either. Just like myself. We had a lot of support from doctors and lawyers and police officers.

Maybe they've had bitter experiences in this life and they had to hate somebody. So the natural person to hate would be the black person. He's beginnin' to come up, he's beginnin' to learn to read and start votin' and run for political office. Here are white people who are supposed to be superior to them, and we're shut out.

I can understand why people join extreme right-wing or left-wing groups. They're in the same boat I was. Shut out. Deep down inside, we want to be part of this great society. Nobody listens, so we join these groups.

At one time, I was state organizer of the National Rights party. I organized a youth group for the Klan. I felt we were getting old and our generation's gonna die. So I contacted certain kids in schools. They were havin' racial problems. On the first night, we had a hundred high school students. When they came in the door, we had "Dixie" playin'. These kids were just thrilled to death. I begin to hold weekly meetin's with 'em, teachin' the principles of the Klan. At that time, I believed Martin Luther King had Communist connections. I began to teach that Andy Young was affiliated with the Communist party.

I had a call one night from one of our kids. He was about twelve. He said: "I just been robbed downtown by two niggers." I'd had a couple of drinks and that really teed me off. I go downtown and couldn't find the kid. I got worried. I saw two young black people. I had the .32 revolver with me. I said: "Nigger, you seen a little young white boy up here? I just got a call from him and was told that some niggers robbed him of fifteen cents." I pulled my pistol out and put it right at his head. I said: "I've always wanted to kill a nigger and I think I'll make you the first one." I nearly scared the kid to death, and he struck off.

This was the time when the civil rights movement was really beginnin' to peak. The blacks were beginnin' to demonstrate and picket downtown stores. I never will forget some black lady I hated with a purple passion. Ann Atwater. Every time I'd go downtown, she'd be leadin' a boycott. How I hated—pardon the expression, I don't use it much now—how I just hated the black nigger. (Laughs.) Big, fat, heavy woman. She'd pull about eight demonstrations, and first thing you know they had two, three blacks at the checkout counter. Her and I have had some pretty close confrontations.

I felt very big, yeah. (Laughs.) We're more or less a secret organization. We didn't want anybody to know who we were, and I began to do some thinkin'. What am I hidin' for? I've never been convicted of anything in my life. I don't have any court record. What am I, C. P. Ellis, as a citizen and a member of the United Klansmen of America? Why can't I go to the city council meeting and say: "This is the way we feel about the matter? We don't want you to purchase mobile units to set in our schoolyards. We don't want niggers in our schools."

We began to come out in the open. We would go to the meetings, and the blacks would be there and we'd be there. It was a confrontation every time. I didn't hold back anything. We began to make some inroads with the city councilmen and county commissioners. They began to call us friend. Call us at night on the telephone: "C. P., glad you came to that meeting last night." They didn't want integration either, but they did it secretively, in order to get elected. They couldn't stand up openly and say it, but they were glad somebody was sayin' it. We visited some of the city leaders in their home and talk to 'em privately. It wasn't long before councilmen would call me up: "The blacks are comin' up tonight and makin' outrageous demands. How about some of you people showin' up and have a little balance?" I'd get on the telephone. "The niggers is comin' to the council meeting tonight. Persons in the city's called me and asked us to be there."

We'd load up our cars and we'd fill up half the council chambers, and the blacks the other half. During these times, I carried weapons to the meetings, outside my belt. We'd go there armed. We would wind up just hollerin' and fussin' at each other. What happened? As a result of our fightin' one another, the city council still had their way. They didn't want to give up control to the blacks nor the Klan. They were usin' us.

I began to realize this later down the road. One day I was walkin' downtown and a certain city council member saw me comin'. I expected him to shake my hand because he was talkin' to me at night on the telephone. I had been in his home and visited with him. He crossed the street. Oh shit, I began to think, somethin's wrong here. Most of 'em are merchants or maybe an attorney, an insurance agent, people like that. As long as they kept low-income whites and low-income blacks fightin', they're gonna maintain control.

I began to get that feeling after I was ignored in public. I thought: Bullshit, you're not gonna use me any more. That's when I began to do some real serious thinkin'.

The same thing is happening in this country today. People are being used by those in control, those who have all the wealth. I'm not espousing communism. We got the greatest system of government in the world. But those who have it simply don't want those who don't have it to have any part of it. Black and white. When it comes to money, the green, the other colors make no difference. (Laughs.)

I spent a lot of sleepless nights. I still didn't like blacks. I didn't want to associate with 'em. Blacks, Jews, or Catholics. My father said: "don't have anything to do with 'em." I didn't until I met a black person and talked with him, eyeball to eyeball, and met a Jewish person and talked to him, eyeball to eyeball. I found out they're people just like me. They cried, they cussed, they prayed, they had desires. Just like myself. Thank God, I got to the point where I can look past labels. But at that time, my mind was closed. . . .

Then something happened. The state AFL–CIO received a grant from the Department of HEW, a $78,000 grant: how to solve racial problems in the school system. I got a telephone call from the president of the state AFL–CIO. "We'd like to get some people together from all walks of life." I said: "All walks of life? Who you talkin' about?" He said: "Blacks, whites, liberals, conservatives, Klansmen, NAACP people."

I said: "No way am I comin' with all those niggers. I'm not gonna be associated with those type of people." A White Citizens Council guy said: "Let's go up there and see what's goin' on. It's tax money bein' spent." I walk in the door, and there was a large number of blacks and white liberals. I knew most of 'em by face 'cause I seen 'em demonstratin' around town. Ann Atwater was there. (Laughs.) I just forced myself to go in and sit down.

The meeting was moderated by a great big black guy who was bushy-headed. (Laughs.) That turned me off. He acted very nice. He said: "I want you all to feel free to say anything you want to say." Some of the blacks stand up and say it's white racism. I took all I could take. I asked for the floor and cut loose. I said: "No, sir, it's black racism. If we didn't have niggers in the schools, we wouldn't have the problems we got today."

I will never forget. Howard Clements, a black guy, stood up. He said: "I'm certainly glad C. P. Ellis come because he's the most honest man here tonight." I said: "What's that nigger tryin' to do?" (Laughs.) At the end of that meeting, some blacks tried to come up shake my hand, but I wouldn't do it. I walked off.

Second night, same group was there. I felt a little more easy because I got some things off my chest. The third night, after they elected all the committees, they want to elect a chairman. Howard Clements stood up and said: "I suggest we elect two co-chairpersons." Joe Beckton, executive director of the Human Relations Commission, just as black as he can be, he nominated me. There was a reaction from some blacks. Nooo. And, of all things, they nominated Ann Atwater, that big old fat black gal that I had just hated with a purple passion, as co-chairman. I thought to myself: Hey, ain't no way I can work with that gal. Finally, I agreed to accept it, 'cause at this point, I was tired of fightin', either for survival or against black people or against Jews or against Catholics.

A Klansman and a militant black woman, co-chairmen of the school commit-tee. It was impossible. How could I work with her? But after about two or three days, it was in our hands. We had to make it a success. This give me another sense of belongin', a sense of pride. This helped this inferiority feelin' I had. A man who has stood up publicly and said he despised black people, all of a sudden he was willin' to work with 'em. Here's a chance for a low-income white man to be some-thin'. In spite of all my hatred for blacks and Jews and liberals, I accepted the job. Her and I began to reluctantly work together. (Laughs.) She had as many problems workin' with me as I had workin' with her.

One night, I called her: "Ann, you and I should have a lot of differences and we got 'em now. But there's somethin' laid out here before us, and if it's gonna be a success, you and I are gonna have to make it one. Can we lay aside some of these feelin's?" She said: "I'm willing if you are." I said: "Let's do it." . . .

I said: "If we're gonna make this thing a success, I've got to get to my kind of people." The low-income whites. We walked the streets of Durham, and we knocked on doors and invited people. Ann was goin' into the black community. They just wasn't respondin' to us when we made these house calls. Some of 'em were cussin' us out. "You're sellin' us out, Ellis, get out of my door. I don't want to talk to you." Ann was gettin' the same response from blacks. "What are you doin' messin' with that Klansman?"

One day, Ann and I went back to the school and we sat down. We began to talk and just reflect. Ann said: "My daughter came home cryin' every day. She said her teacher was makin' fun of me in front of the other kids." I said "Boy, the same thing happened to my kid. White liberal teacher was makin' fun of Tim Ellis's father, the Klansman. In front of other peoples. He came home cryin'." At this point—(he pauses, swallows hard, stifles a sob)—I begin to see, here we are, two people from the far ends of the fence, havin' identical problems, except hers bein' black and me bein' white. From that moment on, I tell ya, that gal and I worked to-gether good. I begin to love the girl, really. (He weeps.)

The amazing thing about it, her and I, up to that point, had cussed each other, bawled each other, we hated each other. Up to that point, we didn't know each other. We didn't know we had things in common.

We worked at it, with the people who came to these meetings. They talked about racism, sex education, about teachers not bein' qualified. After seven, eight nights of real intense discussion, these people, who'd never talked to each other be-fore, all of a sudden came up with resolutions. It was really somethin', you had to be there to get the tone and feelin' of it. . . .

I tell people there's a tremendous possibility in this country to stop wars, the battles, the struggles, the fights between people. People say: "That's an impossible dream. You sound like Martin Luther King." An ex-Klansman who sounds like Mar-tin Luther King. (Laughs.) I don't think it's an impossible dream. It's happened in my life. It's happened in other people's lives in America.

I don't know what's ahead of me. I have no desire to be a big union official. I want to be right out here in the field with the workers. I want to walk through their factory and shake hands with that man whose hands are dirty. I'm gonna do all that one little ol' man can do. I'm fifty-two years old, and I ain't got many years left, but I want to make the best of 'em.

When the news came over the radio that Martin Luther King was assassinated, I got on the telephone and begin to call other Klansmen. We just had a real party at the service station. Really rejoicin' 'cause that son of a bitch was dead. Our troubles are over with. They say the older you get, the harder it is for you to change. That's not necessarily true. Since I changed, I've set down and listened to tapes of Martin Luther King. I listen to it and tears come to my eyes 'cause I know what he's sayin' now. I know what's happenin'.

Response and Analysis

1. Briefly describe C. P. Ellis's feelings, thoughts, and behaviors toward African-Americans before and after he accepted the AFL/CIO's invitation to work with African-American groups. What factors contributed to his anti-African-American attitude?

2. Why do you think Ellis changed his attitude toward African-Americans? How might cognitive dissonance explain the change in Ellis's attitude after he accepted the AFL/CIO's invitation to work with African-Americans?

Personal Experience and Application

1. Have you ever acted in a way that was inconsistent with a strong attitude that you had? If so, what was the attitude and what was your behavior? How did you feel after acting in a way that was inconsistent with your attitude? Did your attitude or behavior change? If so, why?

2. Suppose a professor asks you to be a member of a task force whose mission is to improve the relations among students of all races at your college or university. Discuss two activities that you would propose. Why do you believe these activities would promote positive race relations?

Research

Suppose you want to investigate attitudes about race relations in America. You decide to randomly select Americans to participate in a telephone survey. First you need to write the questions for the survey. Write six questions that will allow you to measure the participants' feelings, thoughts, and actions concerning race relations. The participants should be able to answer the questions using the following scale: strongly disagree, disagree, neither disagree nor agree, agree, strongly agree. Some might provide socially desirable responses rather than honest responses to your questions. How might you construct the questionnaire to increase the likelihood that the participants will provide honest answers?

RACE WITHOUT FACE

Edward Iwata

Psychological Concepts
self-schema, self-identity

How does the social environment influence our self-schemas—the ways in which we think about ourselves? Self-schemas are cognitive representations of our physical characteristics, attitudes and preferences, and typical behaviors (Markus & Sentis, 1982). In this poignant essay, Edward Iwata, a Japanese-American, describes the desperation that can occur when one is caught between the actual self and society's representation of the ideal self. Iwata so despises his facial features that he undergoes plastic surgery. When he sees the result, he wants to "claw [his] new face." He writes, "I didn't realize at the time that my flaws were imagined, not real. I felt compelled to measure up to a cultural ideal in a culture that had never asked me what my ideal was." Even more difficult for Iwata was coming to terms with the cultural values of his Asian heritage as pitted against Western European values. What alternate images for Asian-American men does Iwata suggest? How does he resolve his issues of identity?

I would soon discover I was different from white people.

A cosmetic surgeon was about to cut into my face that gray winter morning. Hot lights glared as I lay on the operating table. Surgical tools clattered in containers, sharp metal against metal. I felt like a lamb awaiting a shearing of its wool.

Shivering from the air-conditioned chill, I wondered if I'd made a mistake. Had my hatred of Oriental facial features, fanned by my desire to do well in a white world, blinded me so easily?

An instant before the anesthetic numbed my brain cells, I felt the urge to cry out. I imagined ripping off my gown and sprinting to freedom. But at that point, even wetting my cracked lips was hard to do.

"I trust you implicitly," I said, as a supplicant might beseech a priest.

Oddly, I imagined seeing, as if peering through a bloody gauze, the contours of two faces rushing toward me. One face was twisted into sadness. The other glowed with a look akin to pride. One white, one yellow; one white, one yellow. I did not know which was which.

A month earlier in her Beverly Hills medical office, the surgeon said she planned to taper the thick, round tip of my nose. She also wanted to build up my flat bridge with strips of cartilage.

"Oriental noses have no definition," she said, waving a clipboard like an inspector on an auto assembly line.

While she was at it, she suggested, why not work on the eyes, also? They looked dark and tired, even though I was twenty years old then. A simple slash along my eyelids would remove the fat cells that kept my eyes from springing into full, double-lidded glory.

Why not? I had thought. Didn't I want to distance myself from the faceless, Asian masses? I hated the pale image in the mirror. I hated the slurs hurled at me that I couldn't shut out. I hated being a gook, a Nip.

It's a taboo subject, but true: many people of color have, at some point in their youths, imagined themselves as Caucasian, the Nordic or Western European ideal. Hop Sing meets Rock Hudson. Michael Jackson magically transformed into Robert Redford.

For myself, an eye and nose job—or *blepharoplasty* and *rhinoplasty* in surgeons' tongue—would bring me the gift of acceptance. The flick of a scalpel would buy me respect.

To make the decision easier, a close friend loaned me $1500. I didn't tell my parents or anyone else about it.

The surgery was quick and painless. My friend drove me at dawn to the medical clinic. At 7 A.M. sharp, the surgeon, a brusque Hispanic woman, swept into the office and rushed past us.

The next time I saw her, she was peering down at me and penciling lines on my face to guide her scalpel. A surgeon's mask and cap hid her own face; I saw only a large pair of eyes plotting the attack on my epidermis and cartilage. While I shivered, a nurse and an anesthesiologist laughed and gossiped.

"You have beautiful lashes, Edward," the surgeon said. It seemed like an odd thing to notice at that moment.

I tumbled into darkness. My last memory was a deep desire to yell or strike out, to stab the surgeon and her conspirators with their knives.

The surgeon went for my eyes first. Gently, she cut and scooped out the fat cells that lined my upper eyelid. That created a small furrow, which popped open my eyes a bit and created double lids, every Asian model's dream.

Ignoring the blood, she then slit the upper inside of my nostril. Like a short-order cook trimming a steak, she carved the cartilage and snipped off bits of bone and tissue. Soon she was done. After a coffee break or lunch, she would move on to the next patient.

Later that day, I was wheeled out of a bright recovery room. My head and limbs felt dull and heavy, as if buried in mud. A draft swept up my surgical gown and chilled my legs. Although my face was bound in bandages, I felt naked. Without warning, a sharp sense of loss engulfed me, a child away from home who is not sure why he aches so.

"Eddie, what did you do?" asked my mother when I next saw her. Then, her voice shaking, "Why did you do this? Were you ashamed of yourself?" As if struck by a lance, my legs weakened, my body cleaved. I was lost, flailing away in shadows, but I shrugged off her question and said something lame. I didn't sense at the time that whatever had compelled me to scar my face could also drive me farther from home.

One week passed before I was brave enough to take my first look in the mirror. I stood in the bathroom, staring at my reflection until my feet got sore.

Stitch marks scarred my face like tracks on a drug addict's arm. My haggard eyes were rounder; my nose smaller and puggy. In the glare of the bathroom light, my skin seemed pale and washed out, a claylike shade of light brown. I looked like a medical illustration from a century ago, when doctors would have measured my facial angle and cranium size for racial intelligence.

I wanted to claw my new face.

The image I pictured in the mirror was an idealized Anglo man, an abstraction. I didn't realize at the time that my flaws were imagined, not real. I felt compelled to measure up to a cultural ideal in a culture that had never asked me what my ideal was.

Indeed, to many Anglos, the males of our culture are a mystery. Most whites know us only through the neutered images: Japanese salarymen. Sumo wrestlers. Sushi chefs. We're judged by our slant of eye and color of skin. We're seen only as eunuchs, as timid dentists and engineers. Books and movies portray us as ugly and demonic. We're truly a race of Invisible Men.

Clearly, Asian-American men have been psychologically castrated in this country. Our history is one of emasculation and accommodation. Japanese Americans, for the most part, filed quietly into the internment camps. Proud Cantonese immigrants were trapped in their Chinatown ghettoes and bachelor societies by poverty and discrimination.

In the corporate arena, Asian-American men find their cultural values and strengths overshadowed by ego-driven, back-slapping, hypercompetitive whites. And, while socially we may be more "acceptable" than blacks and Hispanics, we are not acceptable enough to run legislatures, schools, corporations. Our women may be marriage material for whites, but our men are still seen as gooks. On the street, we're cursed or spat upon—even killed—because of our looks.

It cannot be denied, either, that we're regarded as kowtowing wimps not only by whites, but by a lot of Asian-American women—even those with racial and ethnic pride. Privately, they confess they see a lack of strong Asian-American men who fit an ideal of manhood: virile and sensitive, intelligent and intuitive, articulate and confident.

Of course, we must share part of the blame. Many of us grow up swallowing the stereotypes, accepting the role white society imposes on us. And aside from a handful of us in politics, law, the media, education, and the arts, the rest of us are too reserved and opinionless in the white world.

Simone de Beauvoir wrote that a woman "insinuates herself into a world that has doomed her to passivity." The same could have been said of too many Asian-American men, including myself. . . .

My bid for a cultural identity, a sense of manhood, quickened as my mother and father retired, and as Dad's health worsened. Clearly, a strong impulse pushed me to step up and fill their vacuum, to carry on a family legacy in some way.

My parents, Phillip and Midori, and sixteen relatives spent the years during World War II at Manzanar, the internment camp eight miles from the town of Independence in the Mojave Desert. When I was a kid, Mom never talked about Manzanar. Instead, she wove harmless tales for my brother, my sister, and me. The stories protected us from the truth.

Dad, a strong silent type, claimed he never cared about the political quest for redress—the twenty thousand dollars due each Japanese American interned during the war. Interviewing him for the first story I did on Manzanar was not easy. "You don't have to write about this, do you?" he asked. Speaking to him the next time was even harder. "I told you I'm not a good person to interview," he snapped. "Talk to Mom again."

His reticence was understandable. Conservative Japanese Americans hide their private faces in public. *Nomen no yo*, their ancestors said. *The face is like a Noh mask.* My mother and father calmly accepted their fates.

Like many Japanese Americans, my parents veiled the past and white-washed their memories. They believed the government line that Uncle Sam sent them to the concentration camps for their own good, for their safety. The camps also gave them postwar opportunities by spreading them across the great land, they were told.

In truth, the internment was a horror for families, a civil rights disaster, the death of the old Japanese-American culture. For the men, the sense of powerlessness must have been devastating.

In my parents' desire to hide the past, I sensed a reflection of my own self-hate. Like most *sansei* (third generation), I ignored or never sought out the tragic facts of that era. As a student, I never read about the camps. As a young journalist, I picked up shards of history, but never the whole dark tale.

But after much cajoling, I persuaded my folks to join me on a pilgrimage to Manzanar in 1988. Only tumbleweeds, stone ruins, and barbed wire remained at the windy, desolate site. Nonetheless, the pilgrimage was a glimpse into a forgotten world, a gateway to the past. The ghosts were powerful. But I found no neat, easy answers.

There was no stopping now. The next spring, we flew to Japan. While trade wars dominated the news in Tokyo, my parents and I journeyed into the rural heart of our ancestral homeland.

For the first time, we met the Iwata and Kunitomi clans, who still live on the rice farms in Wakayama and Okayama that our families have owned since the eighteenth century. Among other revelations, I learned that the head of the Iwata family, my father's cousin, shared my Japanese name, Masao ("righteous boy").

Seated on a *tatami* floor at the Iwata homestead, we enjoyed sukiyaki and country-style vegetables we hadn't eaten since my grandmothers died several years ago. The *gohan* (steamed rice) was the lightest and sweetest we had ever tasted. Masao smiled broadly as he served the hot food, its steam rising toward the small family altar in the corner of the dining room.

At one point, I noticed Masao staring at Dad. His steady gaze was rude by Japanese standards. But apparently struck by the family resemblance, Masao couldn't avert his eyes from Dad's face. With their wavy hair and thick eyebrows, their dark skin and rakish grins, they could have been brothers.

I'm not a misty-eyed romantic longing for an ancestral past. Peering for gods in mountain shrines and temple ruins is not my idea of good journalism. Still, this was my flesh and blood seated in an old farmhouse on that warm spring night. I thought of a line from *No-No Boy*, a novel of World War II by John Okada: "If he was to find his way back to that point of wholeness and belonging, he must do so in the place where he had begun to lose it." Here was my point of origin, where my family began. As we scooped bowlfuls of rice into our hungry selves, a light rain wet the furrows of black soil in the field outside.

For me, Japan brought to the surface cultural conflicts and competing values. Even though I was as American as teriyaki chicken, the old Buddhist and Confucian values reach me in southern California. *Giri* (obligation). *Omoiyari* (empathy). *Oyak-oko* (filial piety). The Japanese, in fact, have a phrase unique to them: "*Jibun ga nai,*" or "to have no self." They rarely use the first-person pronoun when they speak. Loyal samurai who followed their feudal barons to the grave had little over some Japanese-American kids.

Those values gave me strength—and also confused the hell out of me. The issue of personal independence and family ties was the most painful. How was I to pursue my goals, forge an identity, yet honor my parents without question? And if I chose filial piety, how was I to keep the bond strong without sacrificing my hard-won, American-style autonomy?

A Zen *koan* asks, "What was your face like before you were born?" I cannot know for sure how deeply the culture of my ancestors touches me, but I know I will never again see myself as a scarred, hollow man lost in the shadows, beating back death.

Japan freed my spirit and gave rise to an atavistic pride I had never known. The past, I realized, could be cradled like an heirloom found in an old trunk in the attic. I was a player in a family history that spanned the reigns of emperors, from feudal Japan to the modern Heisei Era, Year One—the year of my first visit to Japan. And my story would add a few scenes to that unfolding narrative.

After Manzanar and Japan, I began to see my surgery in a new slant of light. Like the victims of internment, I started coming to terms with my real and emotional scars.

Obviously, the surgery had been a rebellion against my "Japaneseness" and the traditional values of my parents. It was psychic surgery, an act of mutilation, a symbolic suicide. It was my self-hatred finding a stage.

Like many Asian Americans, I'm searching for a new cultural character and destiny. . . .

So where does this all lead me? Do I feel more whole in my newfound identity? Have I tossed the masks slapped on me by society, my family, myself? Do I know why I cut off my nose to spite my race?

Yes, to all of the above. Now I see my image and others in a less harsh light. I know one's slant of eye and color of skin are bogus issues. For beyond acculturation, beyond racial identity, is the larger question of *kokoro*—Japanese for heart and soul. Make no mistake: I've learned I *am* different from white people. Not better, not worse, but distinct. The faces rushing toward me in my presurgical daze were neither white nor yellow. They were mine.

Response and Analysis

1. Why did Edward Iwata feel that he needed to change his facial features? How did his actual self-schema—a schema about his current characteristics—differ from his ideal self-schema—a schema about the way he ideally wanted to be?

2. How can the social environment affect self-identity? How might stereotypes lead to self-hate?

Personal Experience and Application

1. Do you know someone who has experienced a conflict similar to Iwata's? Briefly describe it. What was the person's actual self-schema and ideal self-schema? Did the person resolve the conflict? How?

2. Has your self-identity changed during your life? If so, how?

Research

Suppose you want to conduct a laboratory study and a field study to examine how the social environment affects behavior. You want to know if people will conform more in ambiguous situations, in which the correct answer or behavior is not obvious, than in less ambiguous situations. How might you create an ambiguous situation in a laboratory at your college or university? "In the field" on your college campus? Will the findings of the lab study and the field study be similar? Why or why not?

HOW TO KEEP
FROM GETTING MUGGED

D. Keith Mano

Psychological Concepts
impression formation, schema, self-fulfilling prophecy

How do we judge the personal characteristics of people we have just met? Mano's half-serious, half-tongue-in-cheek essay describes ways we can influence how we are initially perceived. How might we want a potential mugger to see us? As too busy, too crazy, too shrewd? Muggers don't want to tackle people with strange behavior, Mano suggests, so we could "Sing aloud. Mutter a lot." When we are dressed in our finest clothes, we should turn our "tux jacket inside out and put a basketball kneepad around one trouser leg."

Why might first impressions be especially important to muggers? How do most people react to unusual or bizarre behavior?

Learn to walk gas-fast. Book it, baby: Lay a big batch behind. Not in panic, mind you: never run. A power-purposeful, elbow-out, crazy kind of stride. The way people moved in old silent films—you know, right before they fell into an open manhole. Wave one hand now and then as if you'd just seen three armed friends and were about to hail a cab. Your attitude should be: "Busy signal, dit-dit-dit. Can't fit you in today, fellas. Catch me tomorrow." In a real halfway-house neighborhood, walk dead street center: follow that white line; avoid ambush cover. Who's gonna mug you when he might get hit by a truck while doing it? Oh, you should see me squeeze out sneaker juice: I am Rapid City: I have no staying power, g'bye. A thug will get depressed by energy. He'd rather come down on someone wearing orthopedic pants. Also, if you can manage it, be tall.

Sing aloud. Mutter a lot. Preach Jesus. Interrogate yourself. Say things like: "Oh, the onion bagel won't come off. Oh, it hurts. Mmmmmm-huh. Mmmmm. Please, Ma, don't send me back to the nutria farm again. No. Oh, no. That three-foot roach is still swimming in my water bed. Ah. Oh. Ech." Muggers are superstitious. They don't like to attack loony people: Might be a cousin on the paternal side. Make sure your accent is very New York (or L. A. or Chicago or wherever). Tourists are considered table-grade meat: heck, who'd miss his super-saver flight to attend a three-month trial? Most of all, eschew eye contact. If your vision says, "Uh-oh, this creep is after my wallet," this creep may feel a *responsibility* to yank you off. Keep both pupils straight ahead, in close-order drill. Do not flash a bank-and-turn indicator. Sure, you may walk past the place you're headed for, but, *shees*, no system is perfect.

　　Dress way down. Mom-and-pop candy-store owners take their cash to deposit in an old brown Bohack[1] bag. Me, I *wear* the bag. I own two basic outfits: One has the *haute couture*[2] of some fourth-hand algebra-textbook cover; my second best was cut using three dish drainers as a pattern. If stagflation[3] were human, it'd look like me. No one messes with D.K.M.,[4] they figure I'm messed up enough now. But when you gotta go in finery, turn your tux jacket inside out and put a basketball kneepad around one trouser leg. Peg your collar. Stitch a white shoelace through your patent-leather pump. Recall what Jesus said about excessive glad-ragging (*Matthew*, chapter six): "Consider the lilies of the field . . . even Solomon in all his glory was not arrayed as one of these—so, *nu*,[5] what happens? They get picked, *Dummkopf.*"[6]

Response and Analysis

1. Why might first impressions be especially important to muggers? Why might people pay more attention to negative actions and weigh them more heavily than positive actions when forming first impressions?

2. Do our first impressions have a long-lasting influence over the way we perceive people? How might they change as we gain additional information? What is a self-fulfilling prophecy? How might self-fulfilling prophecies influence first impressions?

Personal Experience and Application

1. Think about someone who now is a good friend but to whom you were not attracted the first time you met him or her.

   A. The first time you met this person, what physical characteristics and behaviors influenced your impressions?

   B. The first time you met this person, did you have any expectations about the way this person would act? If so, what were your expectations and why did you have them? Did the person act in the way you expected?

   C. Did your impressions of the person change over time? Why?

2. Suppose the office of career services at your college or university asks you to help design a handout titled "How to Prepare for Your Job Interview." The handout will list recommendations on creating a good impression during a job interview. Write three recommendations.

---

[1] Supermarket chain in New York.
[2] French, high fashion.
[3] An economic condition combining relatively high unemployment with relatively high inflation.
[4] The author's initials.
[5] Yiddish, now.
[6] German, stupid (literally, dumbhead).

Research

Suppose you want to design an experiment to test Mano's suggestion that dressing "way down" creates negative impressions. You decide to have a group of psychology students meet a confederate dressed in either regular clothes or in a tux jacket turned inside out, with a basketball kneepad placed around one trouser leg and with a pegged collar.

What are the advantages and disadvantages of having participants meet a confederate dressed in one of the "costumes" versus having them watch a videotape of a confederate dressed in one of the costumes?

BLACK MEN AND PUBLIC SPACE

Brent Staples

Psychological Concepts
stereotypes, prejudice, discrimination, impression formation

Brent Staples, now on the editorial staff of the *New York Times,* writes about being prejudged because he is African-American. When he was a graduate student at the University of Chicago, he often took long walks at night because of his insomnia. He then became aware of the fear he instilled: women hurried across streets, running to get away from him; drivers quickly locked their car doors. One time as he rushed to a deadline at a magazine office, he was mistaken for a burglar and was pursued by the security officer. False charges against him were common. "Over the years," writes Staples, "I learned to smother the rage I felt at so often being taken for a criminal. Not to do so would surely have led to madness." What criteria did people use to assume the worst about Staples? How did other people's stereotypes affect his self-image?

My first victim was a woman—white, well dressed, probably in her early twenties. I came upon her late one evening on a deserted street in Hyde Park, a relatively affluent neighborhood in an otherwise mean, impoverished section of Chicago. As I swung onto the avenue behind her, there seemed to be a discreet, uninflammatory distance between us. Not so. She cast back a worried glance. To her, the youngish black man—a broad six feet two inches with a beard and billowing hair, both hands shoved into the pockets of a bulky military jacket— seemed menacingly close. After a few more quick glimpses, she picked up her pace and was soon running in earnest. Within seconds she disappeared into a cross street.

That was more than a decade ago, I was twenty-two years old, a graduate student newly arrived at the University of Chicago. It was in the echo of that terrified woman's footfalls that I first began to know the unwieldy inheritance I'd come into—the ability to alter public space in ugly ways. It was clear that she thought herself the quarry of a mugger, a rapist, or worse. Suffering a bout of insomnia, however, I was stalking sleep, not defenseless wayfarers. As a softy who is scarcely able to take a knife to a raw chicken—let alone hold one to a person's throat—I was surprised, embarrassed, and dismayed all at once. Her flight made me feel like an accomplice in tyranny. It also made it clear that I was indistinguishable from the muggers who occasionally seeped into the area from the surrounding ghetto. That first encounter, and those that followed, signified that a vast, unnerving gulf lay between nighttime pedestrians—particularly women—and me. And I soon gathered that being perceived as dangerous is a hazard in itself. I only needed to turn a corner into a dicey situation, or crowd some frightened, armed person in a foyer somewhere, or make an errant move after being pulled over by a policeman. Where fear and weapons meet—and they often do in urban America—there is always the possibility of death.

In that first year, my first away from my hometown, I was to become thoroughly familiar with the language of fear. At dark, shadowy intersections, I could cross in front of a car stopped at a traffic light and elicit the *thunk, thunk, thunk, thunk* of the driver—black, white, male, or female—hammering the door locks. On less traveled streets after dark, I grew accustomed to but never comfortable with people crossing to the other side of the street rather than pass me. Then there were the standard unpleasantries with policemen, doormen, bouncers, cabdrivers, and others whose business it is to screen out troublesome individuals *before* there is any nastiness.

I moved to New York nearly two years ago and I have remained an avid night walker. In central Manhattan, the near-constant crowd cover minimizes tense one-on-one street encounters. Elsewhere—in SoHo, for example, where sidewalks are narrow and tightly spaced buildings shut out the sky—things can get very taut indeed.

After dark, on the warrenlike streets of Brooklyn where I live, I often see women who fear the worst from me. They seem to have set their faces on neutral, and with their purse straps strung across their chests bandolier-style, they forge ahead as though bracing themselves against being tackled. I understand, of course, that the danger they perceive is not a hallucination. Women are particularly vulnerable to street violence, and young black males are drastically overrepresented among the perpetrators of that violence. Yet these truths are no solace against the kind of alienation that comes of being ever the suspect, a fearsome entity with whom pedestrians avoid making eye contact.

It is not altogether clear to me how I reached the ripe old age of twenty-two without being conscious of the lethality nighttime pedestrians attributed to me. Perhaps it was because in Chester, Pennsylvania, the small, angry industrial town where I came of age in the 1960s, I was scarcely noticeable against a backdrop of gang warfare, street knifings, and murders. I grew up one of the good boys, had perhaps a half-dozen fistfights. In retrospect, my shyness of combat has clear sources.

As a boy, I saw countless tough guys locked away; I have since buried several, too. They were babies, really—a teenage cousin, a brother of twenty-two, a childhood friend in his mid-twenties—all gone down in episodes of bravado played out in the streets. I came to doubt the virtues of intimidation early on. I chose, perhaps unconsciously, to remain a shadow—timid, but a survivor.

The fearsomeness mistakenly attributed to me in public places often has a perilous flavor. The most frightening of these confusions occurred in the late 1970s and early 1980s, when I worked as a journalist in Chicago. One day, rushing into the office of a magazine I was writing for with a deadline story in hand, I was mistaken for a burglar. The office manager called security and, with an ad hoc posse, pursued me through the labyrinthine halls, nearly to my editor's door. I had no way of proving who I was. I could only move briskly toward the company of someone who knew me.

Another time I was on assignment for a local paper and killing time before an interview. I entered a jewelry store on the city's affluent Near North Side. The proprietor excused herself and returned with an enormous red Doberman pinscher straining at the end of a leash. She stood, the dog extended toward me, silent to my questions, her eyes bulging nearly out of her head. I took a cursory look around, nodded, and bade her good night.

Relatively speaking, however, I never fared as badly as another black male journalist. He went to nearby Waukegan, Illinois, a couple of summers ago to work on a story about a murderer who was born there. Mistaking the reporter for the killer, police officers hauled him from his car at gunpoint and but for his press credentials would probably have tried to book him. Such episodes are not uncommon. Black men trade tales like this all the time.

Over the years, I learned to smother the rage I felt at so often being taken for a criminal. Not to do so would surely have led to madness. I now take precautions to make myself less threatening. I move about with care, particularly late in the evening. I give a wide berth to nervous people on subway platforms during the wee hours, particularly when I have exchanged business clothes for jeans. If I happen to be entering a building behind some people who appear skittish, I may walk by, letting them clear the lobby before I return, so as not to seem to be following them. I have been calm and extremely congenial on those rare occasions when I've been pulled over by the police.

And on late-evening constitutionals I employ what has proved to be an excellent tension-reducing measure: I whistle melodies from Beethoven and Vivaldi and the more popular classical composers. Even steely New Yorkers hunching toward nighttime destinations seem to relax, and occasionally they even join in the tune. Virtually everybody seems to sense that a mugger wouldn't be warbling bright, sunny selections from Vivaldi's *Four Seasons.* It is my equivalent of the cowbell that hikers wear when they know they are in bear country.

Response and Analysis

1. Give an example of prejudice and discrimination in Brent Staples's story. How did Staples use stereotypes to make others perceive him as less threatening? Why was this effective?

2. What criteria did people use to assume the worst about Brent Staples? How did other people's stereotypes affect his self-image?

Personal Experience and Application

1. Have you ever treated someone differently because of his or her ethnicity or age? What did you do? How did your actions make you feel? How do you think your actions made the other person feel?

2. Can people be prejudiced without being aware of it? Why or why not?

Research

Suppose you wish to conduct an experiment to examine first impressions. You decide to study whether a person's name influences how the person is perceived. You will have all participants read the same newspaper article. You will then tell one-third of the participants that the article was written by a person with an Irish surname, one-third that it was written by a person with an Asian surname, and one-third that it was written by a person with a Latin American surname. After reading the article, the participants will rate the quality of the writing and grammar using the following scale: poor, fair, good, very good, excellent. Do you believe that the participants will rate the article differently on the basis of the surname? If so, which author will receive the highest rating and which will receive the lowest? Is this an adequate way to study how stereotypes influence how people are perceived? Why or why not?

WHY COMPETITION?

Alfie Kohn

Psychological Concepts
competition, cooperation, interpersonal relations

Alfie Kohn challenges us to consider the ramifications of competition and cooperation. His points are thought-provoking: competition may be unhealthy because it
means that one person sets out to defeat another person (one has to be brighter
than, faster than, or prettier than the other); it injures community ("those on the
other side are excluded"); and it fosters deception (some may cheat and lie to win).
In short, one person's success and self-worth hinge on another person's defeat and
failure. Is competition unhealthy? Is it detrimental to individuals and groups?

"W-H-I-T-E! White Team is the team for me!" The cheer is repeated, becoming
increasingly frenzied as scores of campers, bedecked in the appropriate color, try to
outshout their Blue opponents. The rope stretched over the lake is taut now, as determined tuggers give it their all. It looks as if a few will be yanked into the cold
water, but a whistle pierces the air. "All right, we'll call this a draw." Sighs of disappointment follow, but children are soon scrambling off to the Marathon. Here,
competitors will try to win for their side by completing such tasks as standing up-
side-down in a bucket of shampoo or forcing down great quantities of food in a few
seconds before tagging a teammate.

As a counselor in this camp over a period of several years, I witnessed a number of Color Wars, and what constantly amazed me was the abrupt and total transformation that took place each time one began. As campers are read their
assignments, children who not ten minutes before were known as "David" or "Mar-
gie" suddenly have a new identity; they have been arbitrarily designated as members of a team. The unspoken command is understood by even the youngest among
them: Do everything possible to win for your side. Strain every muscle to prove
how superior *we* are to the hostile Blues.

And so they will. Children who had wandered aimlessly about the camp are
suddenly driven with a Purpose. Children who had tired of the regular routine are
instantly provided with Adventure. Children who had trouble making friends are
unexpectedly part of a new Crowd. In the dining hall, every camper sits with his or
her team. Strategy is planned for the next battle; troops are taught the next cheer.
There is a coldness bordering on suspicion when passing someone with a blue T-
shirt—irrespective of any friendship B.C. (Before Colors). If anyone has reserva-

tions about participating in an activity, he needs only to be reminded that the other team is just a few points behind.

"Why Sport?" asks Ed Cowan (*The Humanist,* November/December 1979). When the sports are competitive ones, I cannot find a single reason to answer his rhetorical query. Mr. Cowan's discussion of the pure—almost mystical—aesthetic pleasure that is derived from athletics only directs attention away from what is, in actuality, the primary impetus of any competitive activity: winning.

I would not make such a fuss over Color War, or even complain about the absurd spectacle of grown men shrieking and cursing on Sunday afternoons were it not for the significance of the role played by competition in our culture. It is bad enough that Americans actually regard fighting as a sport: it is worse that the outcome of even the gentlest of competitions—baseball—can induce fans to hysteria and outright violence. But sports is only the tip of the proverbial iceberg. Our entire society is affected by—even structured upon—the need to be "better than."

My thesis is admittedly extreme; it is, simply put, that *competition by its very nature is always unhealthy.* This is true, to begin with, because competition and cooperation are mutually exclusive orientations. I say this fully aware of the famed camaraderie that is supposed to develop among players—or soldiers—on the same side. First, I have doubts, based on personal experience, concerning the depth and fullness of relationships that result from the need to become more effective against a common enemy.

Second, the "realm of the interhuman," to use Martin Buber's phrase, is severely curtailed when those on the other side are excluded from any possible community. Worse, they are generally regarded with suspicion and contempt in any competitive enterprise. (This is not to say that we cannot remain on good terms with, say, tennis opponents, but that whatever cooperation and meaningful relationship is in evidence exists in spite of the competitiveness.) Finally, the sweaty fellowship of the lockerroom (or, to draw the inescapable parallel again, the trenches) simply does not compensate for the inherent evils of competition.

The desire to win has a not very surprising (but too rarely remarked upon) characteristic: it tends to edge out other goals and values in the context of any given competitive activity. When I was in high school, I was a very successful debater for a school that boasted one of the country's better teams. After hundreds and hundreds of rounds of competition over three years, I can assert in no uncertain terms that the purpose of debate is not to seek the truth or resolve an issue. No argument, however compelling, is ever conceded; veracity is never attributed to the other side. The only reason debaters sacrifice their free time collecting thousands of pieces of evidence, analyzing arguments, and practicing speeches, is to win. Truth thereby suffers in at least two ways.

In any debate, neither team is concerned with arriving at a fuller understanding of the topic. The debaters concentrate on "covering" arguments, tying logical knots, and, above all, sounding convincing. Beyond this, though, there exists a tremendous temptation to fabricate and distort evidence. Words are left out, phrases added, sources modified in order to lend credibility to the position. One extremely successful debater on my team used to invent names of magazines which ostensibly printed substantiation for crucial arguments he wanted to use.

With respect to this last phenomenon, it is fruitless—and a kind of self-deception, ultimately—to shake our heads and deplore this sort of thing. Similarly, we have no business condemning "overly rough" football players or the excesses of "overzealous" campaign aides or even, perhaps, violations of the Geneva Convention in time of war (which is essentially a treatise on How to Kill Human Beings Without Doing Anything *Really* Unethical). We are engaging in a massive (albeit implicit) exercise of hypocrisy to decry these activities while continuing to condone, and even encourage, the competitive orientation of which they are only the logical conclusion.

The cost of any kind of competition in human terms is incalculable. When my success depends on other people's failure, the prospects for a real human community are considerably diminished. This consequence speaks to the profoundly anti-humanistic quality of competitive activity, and it is abundantly evident in American society. Moreover, when my success depends on my being *better than*, I am caught on a treadmill, destined never to enjoy real satisfaction. Someone is always one step higher, and even the summit is a precarious position in light of the hordes waiting to occupy it in my stead. I am thus perpetually insecure and, as psychologist Rollo May points out, perpetually anxious.

> . . . Individual competitive success is both the dominant goal in our culture and the most pervasive occasion for anxiety . . . [This] anxiety arises out of the interpersonal isolation and alienation from others that inheres in a pattern in which self-validation depends on triumphing over others. (*The Meaning of Anxiety*, rev. ed.)

I begin to see my self-worth as conditional—that is to say, my goodness or value becomes contingent on how much better I am than so many others in so many activities. If you believe, as I do, that unconditional self-esteem is a singularly important requirement for (and indicator of) mental health, then the destructiveness of competition will clearly outweigh any putative benefit, whether it be a greater effort at tug-of-war or a higher gross national product.

From the time we are quite small, the ethic of competitiveness is drummed into us. The goal in school is not to grow as a human being or even, in practice, to reach a satisfactory level of intellectual competence. We are pushed instead to become brighter than, quicker than, better achievers than our classmates, and the endless array of scores and grades lets us know at any given instant how we stand on that ladder of academic success.

If our schools are failing at their explicit tasks, we may rest assured of their overwhelming success regarding this hidden agenda. We are well trained to enter the marketplace and compete frantically for more money, more prestige, more of all the "good things" in life. An economy such as ours, understand, does not merely permit competition: *it demands it.* Ever greater profits becomes the watchword of private enterprise, and an inequitable distribution of wealth (a polite codeword for human suffering) follows naturally from such an arrangement.

Moreover, one must be constantly vigilant lest one's competitors attract more customers or conceive some innovation that gives them the edge. To become outraged at deceptive and unethical business practices is folly; it is the competitiveness of the system that promotes these phenomena. Whenever people are defined as opponents, doing everything possible to triumph must be seen not as an aberration from the structure but as its very consummation. (I recognize, of course, that I have raised a plethora of difficult issues across many disciplines that cry out for a more detailed consideration. I hope, however, to at least have opened up some provocative, and largely neglected, lines of inquiry.)

This orientation finds its way into our personal relationships as well. We bring our yardstick along to judge potential candidates for lover, trying to determine who is most attractive, most intelligent, and . . . the best lover. At the same time, of course, *we* are being similarly reduced to the status of competitor. The human costs are immense.

"Why Sport?", then, is a good question to begin with. It leads us to inquire, "Why Miss Universe contests?" "Why the arms race?" and—dare we say it—"Why capitalism?" Whether a competition-free society can actually be constructed is another issue altogether, and I readily concede that this mentality has so permeated our lives that we find it difficult even to imagine alternatives in many settings. The first step, though, consists in understanding that rivalry of any kind is both psychologically disastrous and philosophically unjustifiable, that the phrase "healthy competition" is a contradiction in terms. Only then can we begin to develop saner, richer lifestyles for ourselves as individuals, and explore more humanistic possibilities for our society.

Response and Analysis

1. When Alfie Kohn worked as a camp counselor, he was surprised by how easily the campers formed group identities based solely on their arbitrary assignment to a team. The "children who not ten minutes before were known as 'David' or 'Maggie' suddenly [had] a new identity" and did everything possible to prove the superiority of their team. How might group identity promote competition? How might it promote cooperation?

2. Do you believe Americans have to compete with each other in order to learn? Why?

Why does Kohn believe that "competition by its very nature is always unhealthy"? List two situations in which competition may promote learning and two in which it may hinder learning.

Personal Experience and Application

1. Briefly discuss why you agree or disagree with Kohn's view of competition.

2. Suppose you are a counselor at a summer camp and are responsible for selecting a game every Friday afternoon in which

30 fourth-grade campers will participate. Would you select a game that requires the campers to cooperate or compete, or both? Why?

Research

Suppose you want to examine the effects of communication on how people compete and cooperate. Your study has two conditions. In the communication condition, you allow the participants to "talk" to each other using a computer. In the no-communication condition, you do not allow the participants to talk to each other. Before the participants arrive, you randomly decide who will be in the communication and no-communication conditions.

You have four psychology students participate in each session. When the participants arrive at your lab, you escort them to individual cubicles where they cannot see the other participants or the experimenter. Each cubicle is equipped with a computer, video monitor, and keyboard. You then ask the participants to read and sign a consent form and allow students who do not wish to participate to leave. You assign each cubicle a color code—red, blue, green, brown. During each session, the participants use only their color code to identify themselves; they never reveal their name or identity to the other participants.

Next, you ask the participants in half of the sessions to use the computer to "talk" with the other group members for fifteen minutes. You ask the participants in the other half of the sessions to write an essay describing themselves on the computer for fifteen minutes.

At the end of the fifteen-minute period, you ask each participant to play a game with the other three members in their session. During the game, each participant will have an opportunity to cooperate or compete with the other group members. Will the participants in the "talk" or "no-talk" group be more competitive? Why? Do you think your findings will generalize to adults who are not college students? Why or why not?

RANDOM ACTS OF KINDNESS

Editors

Psychological Concepts
helping behavior, altruism

When and why do we unselfishly help other people? Here are three charming stories from a small but remarkable book, *Random Acts of Kindness,* that tell about people who moved beyond their daily obligations and responsibilities and unselfishly helped other people. What might motivate people to commit random acts of kindness? What effects might helping others or bringing whimsical joy to others have on both giver and receiver?

My girlfriend and I are avid backpackers. I can't even describe the feeling I get after we lock up the car and hit the trail, and every step is one step farther into the hills and one step farther away from all the crazy stuff that goes on in the world. In my mind it is such a different reality once we are on the trail, and I guess that is why I always put all my "worldly" things in a small green zip-up bag and stuff it away in a corner of my backpack. I mean everything—wallet, with all my ID, credit cards, license, etc., all my money, my keys—everything you need to survive in the modern world and everything that is irrelevant back in the woods.

This particular trip was a five-day trek through some of the most beautiful parts of the Cascades. As we headed back down toward the parking area where we had left the car, I was really sad to be leaving what to me was such a simple and beautiful way of living. I could just feel the tension and anxiety beginning to creep back into my body as we got closer and closer to civilization. When we finally got to the car there was a small piece of paper tucked under the windshield-wiper blade that read, "left rear tire." I walked back and looked at the left rear tire but it was fine. The note made no sense to me at all—three seconds back into the world and already lunacy. Then I started fishing through my backpack for my green bag. It wasn't there. I look back at the left rear tire—there was the bag. I have no idea when I lost it, I have no idea who found it, or how they ever found my car amid all the possible parking places in that part of the Cascades. My keys, my wallet, nearly $100 in cash, all neatly tucked in my zip-up green bag sitting on top of my left rear tire. Thank you, whoever you are, you gave me back much more than you know.

*   *   *   *   *

I have been going to the same bagel/coffee shop every Sunday for years. One morning in the middle of a great dreary drizzly weekend, I trudged in dripping wet with my newspaper carefully tucked under my overcoat and ordered my usual bagel with lox and cream cheese and an espresso. I was casually informed that my coffee had already been paid for. I looked around expecting to see some friends sitting somewhere but didn't, and when I asked, the young woman at the register just smiled and said someone paid for twenty coffees and you are number eight. I sat there for almost an hour, reading my paper, and watching more surprised people come in to find their morning coffee pre-paid. There we all were, furtively at first and then with big funny smiles on our faces, looking at everyone else in the restaurant trying to figure out who had done this incredible thing, but mostly just enjoying the experience as a group. It was a beautiful blast of sunshine on an otherwise overcast winter day.

*   *   *   *   *

We were on vacation in Florida, with four kids all under the age of ten. The weather had been very hot and humid so this particular day we decided to pack a cooler full of sandwiches and soft drinks and drive out along the coast until we found a nice beach. It was sort of an adventure since we didn't really know where we were going, but after a while we found a really beautiful beach that was pretty isolated. We parked and unloaded ourselves onto the sand. It was really great, except that, after a few hours, it just got too hot for the kids and they were starting to whine and complain. So we decided to head back to the air-conditioned hotel. When we got back to the car, however, there were the keys, dangling from the ignition with all the windows rolled up and all the doors locked. In frustration, I screamed, "Who locked the doors?" to which Beth, my five-year-old, responded, "You tell us always to lock the doors." I felt totally defeated. At first I was just going to smash the window in, but after Beth's evenhanded comment, I thought that would be a bit too violent. So I walked up the road about a half mile to a house along the beach. When I got there, this elderly couple invited me in, let me use their telephone to call roadside service, then packed me into their car and drove back to pick up the rest of my family. They brought us all back to their home, and within a few minutes the kids were swimming in their pool while my wife and I sat on an air-conditioned veranda sipping a cool drink and swapping vacation stories. Roadside service came and went and three hours later we headed back to our motel, much refreshed and glowing from the surprising and wonderful experience.

Response and Analysis

1. What effects might helping others or bringing whimsical joy to others have on both giver and receiver? Summarize two theories that attempt to explain why people unselfishly help others.

2. Briefly discuss how the following characteristics influenced helping behavior in each

story: recognition of need for help, attractiveness of person in need, familiarity with surroundings, presence of others.

Personal Experience and Application

1. Make a list of five altruistic deeds that you could do. Make another list of five altruistic deeds that other people have performed to help you.

2. Briefly describe a situation in which you unselfishly helped someone. Now briefly describe a situation in which you knew someone needed assistance but you did not provide help. What features of each situation influenced your decision to provide assistance?

Research

Suppose you want to examine how physical proximity influences how much people like other people. You decide to have participants sit in a large 20-foot by 20-foot room and get acquainted for five minutes. You randomly assign participants to one of two conditions. In the close condition, you seat four subjects in a circle so that participants can touch one another with their arms extended. In the far condition, you seat one participant against each of the four walls. You tell the participants to talk and get acquainted for five minutes. Then you ask the participants to privately rate how much they like the other members in their group. Next you analyze the data. To your surprise, the participants in both the close and far conditions rated the members of their group as equally likable. List three reasons that may explain why there was no difference in likable ratings between the two groups. Although you thought that you manipulated proximity, is it possible that you did not manipulate it? Can you think of another way to experimentally manipulate proximity?

References

p. 123: Anderson, R. C., Reynolds, R. E., Schallert, D. L., & Goetz, E. T. (1977). Frameworks for comprehending discourse. *American Education Research Journal, 14,* 367–382.

p. 42: Brody, J. E. (1982, November 16). Noise poses a growing threat, affecting hearing and behavior. *New York Times.*

p. 155: Buber, M. (1952). *Eclipse of God: Studies in the relation between religion and philosophy.* New York: Harper.

p. 101: Loftus, E. F., & Palmer, J. C. (1974). Reconstruction of automobile destruction: An example of the interaction between language and memory. *Journal of Verbal Learning and Behavior, 13,* 585–589.

p. 286: Markus, H., & Sentis, K. P. (1982). The self in social information processing. In J. Suls (Ed.), *Psychological perspectives on the self* (Vol. 1, pp. 41–70). Hillsdale, NJ: Erlbaum.

p. 227: Suddath, R. L., Christinson, G. W., Torrey, E. F., Casanova, M. F., & Weinberger, D. L. (1990). Anatomical abnormalities in the brains of monozygotic twins discordant for schizophrenia. *New England Journal of Medicine, 322* (12), 789–794.2.

p. 56: Wiel, A. T. (1977). The marriage of sun and moon. In N. E. Zinberg (Ed.), *Alternate states of consciousness: Multiple perspectives on the study of consciousness.* New York: Free Press.

Credits

Chapter 1   Physiological Bases of Behavior

p. 3: Excerpt from *Carnal Acts* by Nancy Mairs. Copyright © 1990 by Nancy Mairs. Reprinted by permission of Beacon Press, Boston, MA, and Nancy Mairs. **p. 7:** Excerpts from *Journey with Grandpa: Our Family's Struggle with Alzheimer's Disease* by Rosalie Walsh Honel, pp. 1–3, 195–198. Copyright © 1988. Reprinted by permission of The Johns Hopkins University Press. **p. 12:** Excerpt from *Newton's Madness: Further Tales of Clinical Neurology* by Harold L. Klawans, M.D. Copyright © 1990 by Harold L. Klawans, M.D. Reprinted by permission of HarperCollins Publishers, Inc. **p. 18:** "I Refused to Be Sick . . . and It Almost Killed Me" by Katherine H. Lipsitz. This article originally appeared in *Mademoiselle*. **p. 23:** Excerpt from *Stroke Survivors* by William H. Bergquist, Rod McLean, and Barbara A. Kobylinski. Copyright © 1994 by Jossey-Bass Inc., Publishers. Reprinted by permission of Jossey-Bass Inc., Publishers.

Chapter 2   Sensation and Perception

p. 29: Excerpt from *A Natural History of the Senses* by Diane Ackerman. Copyright © 1990 by Diane Ackerman. Reprinted by permission of Random House, Inc. **p. 33:** Excerpt from *Moving Violations: War Zones, Wheelchairs, and Declarations of Independence* by John Hockenberry. Copyright © 1995 by John Hockenberry. Reprinted with permission of Hyperion. **p. 38:** Excerpt from *Deafness: An Autobiography* by David Wright. Copyright © 1993 by David Wright. Reprinted by permission of Sterling Lord Literistics, Inc. **p. 42:** Excerpt from *An Anthropologist on Mars* by Oliver Sacks. Copyright © 1995 by Oliver Sacks. Reprinted by permission of Alfred A. Knopf, Inc.

Chapter 3   Consciousness

p. 48: Excerpt from *Asleep in the Fast Lane: The Impact of Sleep on Work* by Lydia Dotto. Copyright © 1990 by Stoddart Publishing Co., Ltd. Reprinted by permission of Lydia Dotto. **p. 53:** Excerpt from *Lakota Woman*. Copyright © 1990 by Mary Crow Dog and Richard Erdoes. Used by permission of Grove/Atlantic, Inc. **p. 56:** Excerpt from *Always Running, La Vida Loca: Gang Days in L.A.* Copyright © 1993 by Luis J. Rodriguez. Used by permission of Curbstone Press. **p. 61:** Excerpt from *The Courage to Change* by Dennis Wholey. Copyright © 1984 by Dennis Wholey. Reprinted by permission of Houghton Mifflin Company. All rights reserved. **p. 66:** Excerpt from Robert G. Meyer, *Practical Clinical Hypnosis: Technique and Application.* Copyright © 1992 by Jossey-Bass Inc., Publishers. First published by Lexington Books. Reprinted by permission of Lexington Books. All rights reserved.

Chapter 4   Learning

p. 80: Excerpt from *Voices from the Future* by Susan Goodwillie (Editor). Copyright © 1993 by Susan Goodwillie. Reprinted by permission of Crown Publishers, Inc. **p. 85:** Excerpt from *The*

Jaime Escalante Math Program by Jaime Escalante and Jack Dirmann. Copyright © 1990 by Jaime Escalante and Jack Dirmann. Reprinted with permission of Jaime Escalante and Dusty Dragony.

Chapter 5 Memory

pp. 90 and 96: Excerpts from *Witness for the Defense* by Elizabeth Loftus and Katherine Ketcham. Copyright © 1991. Reprinted with permission of St. Martin's Press, Inc. **p. 102:** "The Lost 24 Hours" by Tony Dajer. Copyright © 1991 by The Walt Disney Co. This article originally appeared in *Discover.* Reprinted with permission of *Discover Magazine.* **p. 106:** Excerpt from *The Mind of a Mnemonist* by A. R. Luria. Copyright © 1968 by Basic Books. Reprinted by permission of Michael Cole.

Chapter 6 Thought and Language

p. 115: Five-page excerpt from *You Just Don't Understand* by Deborah Tannen, Ph.D. Copyright © 1990 by Deborah Tannen, Ph.D. Reprinted by permission of William Morrow & Company, Inc., and Deborah Tannen, Ph.D. **p. 119:** "Conversational Ballgames" by Nancy Masterson Sakamoto. Reprinted by permission of Nancy Masterson Sakamoto. **p. 123:** Excerpts from *Hunger of Memory* by Richard Rodriguez. Copyright © 1982 by Richard Rodriguez. Reprinted by permission of David R. Godine, Publisher, Inc. **p. 128:** Excerpt from *White Bears and Other Unwanted Thoughts: Suppression, Obsession, and the Psychology of Mental Control* by Daniel M. Wegner. Copyright © 1994 by Guilford Press. Reprinted by permission of Guilford Press. **p. 134:** "Fear" by Michele Mitchell. This article originally appeared in *Women's Sports and Fitness.* Reprinted by permission of Michele Mitchell.

Chapter 7 Human Development

p. 139: Excerpts from *Mollie Is Three* by Vivian Gussin Paley. Copyright © 1986 by The University of Chicago. Reprinted by permission of The University of Chicago Press and Vivian Gussin Paley. **p. 144:** "Shame," from *Nigger: An Autobiography* by Dick Gregory. Copyright © 1964 by Dick Gregory Enterprises, Inc. Used by permission of Dutton Signet, a division of Penguin Books USA Inc. **p. 148:** Excerpts from *An American Childhood* by Annie Dillard. Copyright © 1987 by Annie Dillard. Reprinted by permission of HarperCollins Publishers, Inc. **p. 150:** Excerpts from H. Michael Zal, "The Sandwich Generation: Caught Between Growing Children and Aging Parents," in *The Dilemma of Middle Age.* Copyright © 1992. Reprinted by permission of Plenum Publishing Corporation and H. Michael Zal. **p. 155:** Excerpt from *The View from 80* by Malcolm Cowley. Copyright © 1976, 1978, 1980 by Malcolm Cowley. Used by permission of Viking Penguin, a division of Penguin Books USA Inc. **p. 159:** "Celebrating Death—and Life" by Nsedu Onyile. This article originally appeared in the *International Herald Tribune.* Reprinted by permission of Nsedu Onyile.

Chapter 8 Mental Abilities

p. 164: Excerpt from *Talented Teenagers: The Roots of Success* by Mihaly Csikszentmihalyi, Kevin Rathunde, and Samuel Whalen. Copyright © 1993 by Cambridge University Press. Reprinted with the permission of Cambridge University Press and Mihaly Csikszentmihalyi. **p. 167:** Excerpt from *Through the Communication Barrier* by S. I. Hayakawa. Reprinted by permission of the Estate of S. I. Hayakawa. **p. 171:** Excerpt from *We Have Been There* by Terrell Dougan, Lyn Isbell, and Patricia Vyas. Copyright © 1979, 1983 by Dougan, Isbell, & Vyas Associates. Reprinted by permission of the publisher, Abingdon Press. **p. 173:** Excerpt from *The Spatial Child* by John Philo Dixon. Copyright © 1993 by Charles C. Thomas, Publisher. Reprinted courtesy of Charles C. Thomas, Publisher, Springfield, Illinois. **p. 177:** Excerpt from *Assessment of Children* by Jerome M. Sattler. Copyright © 1988 by Jerome M. Sattler. Reprinted by permission of Jerome M. Sattler, Publisher.

Chapter 9   Motivation and Emotion

p. 183: "Dying to Be Bigger" by D. H. This article originally appeared in *Seventeen.* D. H. wrote this essay while he was an undergraduate student. He is currently a graduate student studying counseling psychology. Reprinted by permission of the author. **p. 187:** "From Mexico, 1977." An interview with Miguel Torres. An excerpt from *American Mosaic* by Joan Morrison and Charlotte Fox Zabusky. Copyright © 1980 by Joan Morrison and Charlotte Fox Zabusky. Currently in paperback edition, from the University of Pittsburgh Press. Reprinted by permission of John A. Ware Literary Agency. **p. 190:** Excerpt from *New Hope for Binge Eaters* by Harrison G. Pope, Jr., M.D. and James I. Hudson, M.D., pp. 1–7. Copyright © 1984 by Harrison G. Pope, Jr., M.D. and James I. Hudson, M.D. Reprinted by permission of HarperCollins Publishers, Inc. **p. 196:** Excerpts from *An American Childhood* by Annie Dillard. Copyright © 1987 by Annie Dillard. Reprinted by permission of HarperCollins Publishers, Inc.

Chapter 10   Personality

p. 200: "Celia Behind Me" from *The Elizabeth Stories* by Isabel Huggan. Copyright © 1984 by Isabel Huggan. Used by permission of Viking Penguin, a division of Penguin Books USA Inc. **p. 206:** "Asian in America" by Kesaya E. Noda. Excerpt from *Making Waves* by Asian Women United. Copyright © 1989 by Asian Women United. Reprinted by permission of the author, Kesaya E. Noda. **p. 212:** "Racism Doesn't Grow Up" by Joyce Lee. In Elena Featherston (Ed.), *Skin Deep: Women Writing on Color, Culture, and Identity*, Crossing Press, 1994. Joyce Lee is an award-winning independent filmmaker who lives in the San Francisco bay area. Reprinted by permission of Joyce Lee. **p. 216:** Excerpt from *Days of Grace* by Arthur Ashe and Arnold Rampersad. Copyright © 1993 by Jeanne Moutoussamy-Ashe and Arnold Rampersad. Reprinted by permission of Alfred A. Knopf Inc.

Chapter 11   Psychological Disorders

p. 223: Excerpt from *The Quiet Room: A Journey Out of the Torment of Madness* by Lori Schiller and Amanda Bennett. Copyright © 1994 by Lori Schiller and Amanda Bennett. All rights reserved. Reprinted by permission of Warner Books, Inc. New York, New York, U.S.A. **p. 228:** Excerpts from *Wisdom, Madness, and Folly: The Philosophy of a Lunatic* by John Custance. Copyright © 1952 and renewed 1980 by John Custance. Reprinted by permission of Farrar, Straus & Giroux, Inc. **p. 233:** "I Have Multiple Personality Disorder" by Quiet Storm. This article originally appeared in *First for Women*, November 1, 1993. Reprinted by permission of the author. **p. 238:** Excerpt from *When Once Is not Enough: Help for Obsessive Compulsives* by Gail Steketee and Kerrin White. Copyright © 1990 by New Harbinger Publications, Inc. Reprinted by permission of New Harbinger Publications, Inc., Oakland, CA. **p. 241:** Excerpt from *Emergence Labeled Autistic* by Temple Grandin and Margaret M. Scariano. Copyright © 1986 by Arena Press. Reprinted by permission of Academic Therapy Publications, Arena Press. **p. 245:** Excerpt from *The Duke of Deception* by Geoffrey Wolff. Copyright © 1979 by Geoffrey Wolff. Reprinted by permission of Random House, Inc.

Chapter 12   Health, Stress, and Coping

p. 252: Excerpt from *Days of Grace* by Arthur Ashe and Arnold Rampersad. Copyright © 1993 by Jeanne Moutoussamy-Ashe and Arnold Rampersad. Reprinted by permission of Alfred A.

Subject Index

Create, Relate, & Pop @ the Library

SERVICES & PROGRAMS FOR TEENS & TWEENS

ERIN HELMRICH AND ELIZABETH SCHNEIDER

Neal-Schuman Publishers, Inc.
New York   London

Published by Neal-Schuman Publishers, Inc.
100 William St., Suite 2004
New York, NY 10038

Printed and bound in the United States of America.

The paper used in this publication meets the minimum requirements of American National Standard for Information Sciences—Permanence of Paper for Printed Library Materials, ANSI Z39.48-1992.

Library of Congress Cataloging-in-Publication Data

Helmrich, Erin, 1972-
    Create, relate & pop @ the library : services & programs for teens & tweens / Erin Helmrich, Elizabeth Schneider.
        p. cm.
    Includes bibliographical references and index.
    ISBN 978-1-55570-722-4 (alk. paper)
    1. Young adults' libraries—Activity programs—United States. 2. Young adults' libraries—United States. 3. Libraries and teenagers—United States. I. Schneider, Elizabeth, 1980- II. Title. III. Title: Create, relate, and pop at the library.

Z718.5.H45 2011
027.62'6—dc22

                                                                                2011004986

Contents

List of Figures

Inspirational? Excitable? Adaptable? Informational? Yes! Traditional? No. As two librarians who bonded as coworkers over a shared obsession with pop culture, the authors are well aware that not all young adult librarians share their over-the-top interest in this arena.

Thus, *Create, Relate, & Pop @ the Library: Services & Programs for Teens & Tweens* is intended to make it easier for the youth specialist and generalist to keep up with the fast-paced world of tween and teen pop culture. This book presents a framework of philosophy for providing creative, relatable, and pop culture–relevant services and programs with practical tips and ideas for keeping up with the world of tweens and teens. Awesomely, there are also 47 detailed program descriptions divided into 13 different topic-based chapters!

Create, Relate, & Pop @ the Library explores how infusing pop culture into teen services with a focus on programming and events can engage the teens in your community in new and exciting ways. Learn how to become a facilitator and innovator of programming on topics you may have little to no interest in or no knowledge of. Turn your own particular obsessions, interests, and talents into potential service or programming opportunities. Find practical and detailed examples, instructions, and resources for providing tween and teen programming that uses pop culture as a jumping-off point. This approach will excite interest from reluctant library users and potentially engage devoted users in new ways. Learn how many of your younger teens may be better served by programs for tweens, as well as how to engage the older and edgier teens in your community.

The title *Create, Relate, & Pop @ the Library* came from trying to find a fun and catchy way to encapsulate the authors' philosophy of service to tweens and teens. Create, Relate, & Pop is a framework with which to plan, conduct, and evaluate library services and collections.

- **Create:** Library collections and services, like free access to information and services, create opportunities for young people to explore and try new things. Librarians live to provide opportunities to create: art, movies, jewelry, rockets, science experiments, food, music, clothes, gifts, etc. The *Create* part of the equation is where libraries and librarians are already doing a top-notch job. Libraries are more often filling the recreational, explorational, and inspirational roles that schools used to provide with after-school clubs and more extensive elective class selections.

- **Relate:** In order to grab the interest of teens and hold it, you need to be relevant to their lives. This of course happens using pop culture and being in tune with their lives and what's important and current, but it also has to do with creating opportunities for teens and tweens to become healthy, caring, responsible, and well-rounded people. Staying relevant is often the hardest part because the job never ends—as tween and teen interests and obsessions change and flow, so must librarians keep up with this change and flow.

- **Pop:** The *Pop* is the easy part. *Pop* is fun; *pop* is current; *pop* is what they want. *Pop* is also flexible. *Pop* does not just mean what's popular with the majority. Thanks to the Internet and its ability to digitally unite people from across the globe or across the street, there are many niche and cultlike communities based on interests about which the average American has never heard. In a country with more than 300 million people, an interest that attracts 500,000 or even 2 million is tiny enough to be obscure, but large enough that it shouldn't be ignored.

Using *Create, Relate, & Pop*

This book can be easily consumed by the on-demand reader who skips to the chapter describing a program that is needed next week as well as by the reader who prefers a cover-to-cover approach. The initial six chapters describe the why and how teens became so powerful and an entity unto themselves between the world of child and adulthood; next, dive into philosophies and how best to Create, Relate, & Pop in your library; and finish with 13 chapters packed with programming ideas, instructions, and resources, plus a final concluding chapter.

Chapter 1, "From 'Dyn-o-*Mite*' to 'How *You* Doin'?': History of Teen/Tween Pop Culture," outlines a brief timeline of teen and tween pop culture in the twentieth and twenty-first centuries. Take a trip down memory lane using pop culture touchstones or use it as a reference for infusing retro popular culture experiences into programs for today's teens.

The philosophy at the heart of *Create, Relate, & Pop* is explored and defined in Chapter 2, "'Here It Is, Your Moment of Zen': Defining Create, Relate, & Pop." Moving away from the traditional library model of serving teens and tweens can breathe life into programming. Learn to capitalize on the latest consumer trends by programming around them.

Determining different interest groups in a teen population is discussed in Chapter 3, "'OMG!': Targeting Populations, Advertising, and Promotion." Knowing your audience is very helpful when defining services at your library or school. Survey your teens/ tweens and find out who is living in your community. This chapter will help you match programs to your kids, whether they are socs, greasers, outsiders, goths, hippies, burn-outs, freaks, geeks, mean girls, emos, indies, or whatever the particular teen tribes are in your community. Once you have identified your audience and their interests, we will teach you how to market your program to them.

Programming using popular celebrities and trendy hobbies must be supported by the library collection. Chapter 4, "Make It Work: Collections," gives tips on how to keep the collection current, healthy, and, most important, relevant to the teen and tween interests of the moment.

Chapter 5, "Keep 'Em Coming: Spaces," gives ideas on how to make a teen or tween area in the library pop culture friendly. The chapter describes easy and creative ways to keep current with the latest trends using input from the young adults being served, producing a space defined by the popular interests of the moment.

More than anything else, this book is about programming. Programs are the best way to engage your users, get them into the library, and keep them coming back. Chapter 6, "'I Want My MTV!': Programming," explains the foundations for a successful teen/ tween library program.

The heart of *Create, Relate, & Pop @ the Library* is the 13 programming chapters, which include detailed information featuring 47 different program ideas. Chapters 7 through 19 are divided by topic: art, celebrities and reality television, contests, cooking and food, do-it-yourself crafts, gaming, Japanese popular culture, beauty and body modification, magic and mystical worlds, music, physical activities, summer reading programs, and technology. Each program description includes the following:

- General description
- *Pop*—how and in what specific way it relates to pop culture
- *Relate*—what opportunities for learning and experience this provides for the young person and the assets it may potentially provide
- Instructors/talent
- Audience—who is the best or potential audience
- Planning and supplies
- *Create*—detailed instructions on how to run the program
- Food, technology, and other mandatory extras
- Analysis—thoughts on the success of the program and other ideas for similar programs or things to try when you do it again

- Marketing tips
- Resources

Learn how to freshen up tried-and-true craft programs or how to use reality television, fandom, movies, and teen obsessions with food to offer dynamic and fun programs. Programs described include Comic Book Academy, Pinhole Photography, *Top Chef* Winner Appearance, Graffiti Contests, Sushi Making, Shrinky-Dink Crafts, Pokémon Tournaments, Amigurumi Crochet, Nail Art, Pyschic Fair, Parkour and Freerunning, Filmmaking 101, and more.

It's a New World! Let's Jump In!

One of the greatest opportunities that libraries and librarians have is to expose young people to the world around them—from meeting neighbors and community members to the world at large and everything in between. From culture and the arts to hands-on opportunities to learn skills, sciences, crafts, trades, and arts from people working in those fields, libraries offer young people opportunities that often cannot be found elsewhere—and certainly not for the library's "free of charge" level. It's a post–"give them what they want" world. There is no longer time to debate whether what's popular is "okay" and whether catering to their interests is "dumbing down" what librarians do. As institutions of the people, librarians must be relevant to the lives of our taxpayers. Embrace the change! From introducing the power of well-honed information-seeking skills in the real world to providing opportunities to create their own information and express themselves with art or culture, librarians are in a unique position to empower young people with their neutral and open position in the world. *Create, Relate, & Pop @ the Library* will do just that, demonstrating how you can relate to your tweens and teens in new ways and harness the enthusiasm they have for their obsessions in constructive and fun ways to create engaging programs. This new participatory, user-created world is a perfect fit for creating programs that teens and tweens want.

Acknowledgments

This book is a collaboration by many fabulous people who allowed us to include their innovative programming which captures the attention of teens and tweens all over the United States. Their dedication to the profession of librarianship makes us proud to call ourselves librarians. The library services and programs described in this book are walking advertisements for the importance of the public library in their communities.

Thank you to Meaghan Battle, Vicki Browne, Sharon Iverson, Eli Neiburger, and the staff at the Ann Arbor District Library in Ann Arbor, Michigan, for your support and commitment to consistently pushing the envelope in creating original programming for young adults.

Many of the photographs and programming ideas illustrating best practices in the profession were added to this book in collaboration with the Sno-Isle Libraries in Washington State, Moorpark (CA) City Library, Monrovia (CA) Public Library, Darien (CT) Library, Kalamazoo (MI) Public Library, Steve Teeri from the Detroit Public Library, Stewart Fritz from the Kalamazoo (MI) Public Library, and Justin Hoenke of the Portland (ME) Public Library. We thank them for their assistance in providing excellent examples of library services and programs supporting teens and tweens throughout the country.

We extend a heartfelt thank-you to our editor, Sandy Wood, who had so much patience with two librarians trying to traverse the landscape of the writing world. Thank you for holding our hands throughout this process, giving us ample feedback, and being honest when we seemed confused. We cannot thank you enough for your help.

Finally, thank you to our friends and family for your support and encouragement. E.H. would like to thank her parents, and her close friends who lent listening ears and support during the "OMG" moments of this amazing writing process. E.S. would like to personally thank her husband Curtis Schneider (you are the best!), her parents, and the staff at the Monrovia Public Library for listening to her think through ideas and complain only a little, and for encouraging her to indulge her hobby of incessantly reading blogs and magazines to know up-to-the-minute information on movie stars and celebrities.

Chapter 1

From "Dyn-O-Mite!" to "How You Doin'?": History of Teen/Tween Pop Culture

Defined by the *Oxford English Dictionary* (2010) as the cultural traditions of the ordinary people of a particular community, using popular culture is a unique and innovative technique to reach the interests and needs of teens and tweens in the library setting. This chapter leads you through a brief history of the highlights of teen/tween pop culture from the 1950s, which is usually considered the modern-day birthplace of teenage popular culture, to present day. Use this chapter as a reminder that the more things change, the more they stay the same—and to illustrate how easy it can be to develop programming for teens and tweens based on pop culture icons of today and yesteryear. Anastasia Goodstein, founder of the *YPulse* (http://www.ypulse.com) website, clearly makes the point in her book, *Totally Wired: What Teens and Tweens Are* Really *Doing Online*, that current technology is the modern-day equivalent of passing notes and staying obsessively in touch with your friends. Nothing has changed except the tools that teens use to fulfill their adolescent destinies (Goodstein, 2007). Since part of adolescence is the tendency to rediscover the past, opportunities may arise to interest teens in the library in innovative ways using retro pop culture.

Popular culture has always been and will always be about music, entertainment, food, clothes, sports, games, and generally the way people live, have fun, socialize, and bond in their free time. Whether they are discovering The Beatles as their own or wearing retread 1980s' clothes, without realizing it, popular culture is constantly recycled and co-opted by youth culture. By mining retro popular culture in new ways with teens and tweens, libraries can learn how to use the fads of the past to connect to youth in the present. Travel down memory lane with us, and discover the possibilities of using pop culture in the library.

1950s

America was in a prosperous time after World War II, with an emphasis on family values and building a secure and happy future. U.S. soldiers home from war started families, which resulted in the baby boom and the eventual development of suburbs. At the same time, teenagers were breaking out of the role of children and starting to show society that they would very quickly become voters and consumers.

American Bandstand became the first national TV show devoted to pop and rock music, creating a huge teen fan club following. Teen heartthrobs "Elvis the Pelvis" Presley and Pat Boone topped the music charts, though they could not have been more different visually or stylistically. Presley won over swooning girls with his gyrating dance moves, shocking adults. Ed Sullivan refused Presley an appearance on his show, calling him "unfit for a family audience" (Duden, 1989: 32). Meanwhile, the more parent-friendly, clean-cut Boone crooned in his white buckskin shoes.

RCA announced its first color television on March 29, 1950, the same month newspapers reported that "children spent as much time watching TV as they did going to school" (Duden, 1989: 6). Entertainment through technology started to move away from the typical trip to the movie theater. Drive-in theaters were the cool place to hang out, with the number of theaters around the country climbing to 2,200 in 1950—twice the number of 1949. The public donned 3-D glasses to watch lions jump into their laps in *Bwana Devil* in 1952, the first 3-D color movie.

Eating out was reinvented when fast-food hamburgers and fries became available from McDonald's in 1955, revolutionizing what teens would eat for lunch in future years; by 1959, more than 100 McDonald's restaurants were open for business. Wham-O began marketing Hula-hoops, selling 30 million in a few months in 1958. At the end of the decade, college students took on the challenge of fitting as many people as possible into a telephone booth; 34 people stuffed themselves into a telephone booth at Modesto Junior College in California, though the feat was met with controversy because the booth was on its side. Twenty-two students from the College of Saint Mary's in Moraga, California, filled a phone booth, and they were considered the most efficient group to meet the challenge at the time.

1960s

No longer interested in cramming people in phone booths, the teens of the 1960s entered into a time of social change and experimentation. With a driving need for individuality, teens dealt with the pressures of a tumultuous time, seeking meaning while the war in Vietnam escalated and civil rights protests raged.

Almost half of the population of the United States was under age 18 in 1960 (PBS, 2005), so the wants and needs of this growing segment of society grew more visible as well. Teens continued to rebel against 1950s' moral values and explored an alternative counterculture. Happenings, a form of performance art, took center stage as a form of artistic expression influenced by the Eastern philosophy of valuing the act of being. Yoko Ono staged a happening in 1966, during which members of the audience cut away pieces of her clothing for an hour as she knelt silently. Experimental theater groups formed all over the country, as an innovative way to express political viewpoints and educate the public on current issues, instead of using pamphlets or speeches. In 1967, poet Allen Ginsberg toured college campuses, speaking to sold-out audiences about the Summer of Love, a national hippie celebration of life and love. Ginsberg spoke of imagination and expanded consciousness through the use of drugs, meditation, and anything else that "turned people on" to loving oneself and humanity (Holland, 1999: 98).

The sixties was a groundbreaking time for dance and music. "The Twist," a song by R&B artist Hank Ballard, gained popularity after Chubby Checker's performance on *American Bandstand* in 1960. The associated dance became an international fad among teens, considered "one of the first connections of international youth culture" (Holland, 1999: 104). British rock bands like The Rolling Stones and The Who became popular, combining the black roots of American music with a British twist. By 1961, The Beatles had unexpectedly created a sensation called Beatlemania, becoming one of the first boy bands in the international music scene and playing to more than 70 million viewers on *The Ed Sullivan Show*. Political folksingers like Bob Dylan and Joan Baez took the stage to express their opinions on war, justice, civil rights, and "The Establishment." In 1961, when teens were starting to question war for the first time, The Kingston Trio released "Where Have All the Flowers Gone?," a song penned by Pete Seeger and Joe Hickerson. Creating the first successful black-owned record company in the nation, Berry Gordy Jr. started the Motown Company in 1960 and launched the careers of many famous soul music legends. The Jackson 5, Stevie Wonder, Diana Ross & the Supremes, and Smokey Robinson kept teens dancing in the aisles. Half a million people showed up to the music finale of the sixties, Woodstock, in the summer of 1969, to show their support of peacefully living and the end to war and racial injustice. Celebrated singers Janis Joplin and Jimi Hendrix played to a peaceful crowd, with Hendrix giving a preview of the new music genre acid rock that would become popular in the early seventies. To document all of these great movements in music, *Rolling Stone* magazine debuted in 1967, with John Lennon on its cover, and has since played a principal role in pop culture through its in-depth reporting on current music and politics (Carlson, 2006).

1970s

The political turmoil of the sixties continued into the seventies; two of the most important U.S. political events that occurred in this new decade were President Richard

Nixon's resignation following the Watergate scandal in 1974 and, only eight months later, the end of the Vietnam War. Throughout the decade, teens searched for ways to define their generation. They flocked to stores to purchase hot pants in the earliest years of the 1970s. Such notables as Jackie Kennedy Onassis, David Bowie, and Sammy Davis Jr. were known to have worn this fashion item (Stewart, 1999). Other fad items included pet rocks (an ideal self-sufficient pet), and mood rings, which changed color to supposedly reflect the wearer's mood. In 1974, streaking became the craze. Teens ran naked through public events to shock and amuse the public; the most famous incident occurred in that year at the Academy Awards, while host David Niven was introducing presenter Elizabeth Taylor (Stewart, 1999).

As The Beatles as a group began to break apart, the influence of their musical breadth was evident on new performers taking the stage. Glam rock, whose musicians wore showy, glittery clothing and often conveyed androgynous images, became very popular, with David Bowie as its front singer in the United Kingdom. Folksingers like James Taylor and Carole King also maintained a solid presence in the music scene. Heavy metal came into existence in the late 1960s and early 1970s, showcasing such legendary bands as Black Sabbath and Led Zeppelin. As a rebellion against rock musicians for "'selling out' by creating music that was pure sentimentalism," the punk movement began in New York in the mid-seventies (Stewart, 1999). Disco had been on the rise in popularity and finally hit the mainstream in 1974 with the Hues Corporation's hit, "Rock the Boat." Platform shoes and glittery clothes were a staple of this cultural phenomenon, which was captured on film in the 1977 movie *Saturday Night Fever*. Disco has continued to renew its hold on the generations, such as through the musical *Mamma Mia!*, a play based on the music of ABBA which has been continuously in production on Broadway since 2001.

Television and movies were reinvented in the seventies. The film industry focused on drawing in urban black audiences by creating movies with black heroes, such as private detective John Shaft (*Shaft*, 1971) and reluctant hero Sweetback (*Sweet Sweetback's Baadasssss Song*, 1971).

The comedy sketch show *Saturday Night Live* debuted in 1975, satirizing current culture and becoming a cultural icon itself. Blockbuster cult classics that premiered during this decade included *The Godfather*, *Jaws*, and *Star Wars*.

1980s

Though the 1980s saw the collapse of communism and the end of the Cold War, much of the decade was dedicated to materialistic pursuit. The superficiality of the decade was noted in the popular teen-centered films of John Hughes, including *The Breakfast Club* and *Some Kind of Wonderful*, which deftly addressed the social separations of classes in high school: the jocks, the geeks, the popular kids, the punks, and the rebels. Money and materialism were of interest to teens in this time of prosperity. The preppy collegiate look was made popular in part by editor Lisa Birnbach's book, *The Official Preppy Handbook*. The punk kids rocked shoulder pads, big hairsprayed hairdos, ripped jeans, and stiletto heels.

Music history was made in 1981 when the first music television station, MTV, debuted with "Video Killed the Radio Star," a music video by The Buggles. New genres of music, such as new wave and synthpop, entered the scene. These bands sang out against large corporations, similar to the antiestablishment lyrics commonly found in punk rock. Rock and roll topped the charts with bands like Van Halen and Aerosmith. A form of harder rock called thrash metal appeared in this decade from bands like Metallica and Slayer. Michael Jackson and Madonna became both music and fashion icons. Their fame was enhanced by their individuality and penchant for pushing the boundaries, wearing such signature items of clothing as one sequined glove or a leather bustier and showing their timelessness by reinventing themselves to interest teens through the decades. Concert charity events were very popular in the 1980s. The most memorable event, occurring in 1985, was USA for Africa, in which a group of popular entertainers recorded a single, "We Are the World," to raise money to fight disease and hunger in Africa, especially concentrating on Ethiopia, which was experiencing a famine at that time.

The 1980s were also the start of the computer age. Personal computing, as we know it now, was initiated by IBM's development of the first personal computer in 1981 and the invention of the World Wide Web by an English physicist named Tim Berners-Lee in 1989. Video game technology soared with the creation of arcade games *Pac-Man* in 1980, followed by *Ms. Pac-Man* in 1981. In the late eighties, teens started to leave the arcade to stay at home with personal gaming systems, especially the Nintendo Entertainment System (NES), which was released in the United States in 1985; and to play *Tetris*, the second-best game on IGN's Top 100 Games of All Time, after the 1989 launch of the handheld Nintendo Game Boy (IGN Entertainment, 2009). Listening to music became more portable with the Sony Walkman, and audiocassette tapes lost ground to compact discs (CDs), which were the music industry's first foray into digital music recordings.

1990s

The 1990s began in political and social turmoil with the Persian Gulf War and the AIDS epidemic in Africa. As the decade progressed, teens began to focus on technological advancements that helped to shape the world today. Cellular phones, pagers, fax machines, the personal computer, and the Internet suddenly allowed people many more forms of instant communication, creating the Digital Age. Instead of using the television as the sole entryway for entertainment and information, people started using the World Wide Web, launched to the public in 1991. Companies turned to the Internet for advertising and product placement, targeting teens because they were estimated to spend $122 billion of their own and their parents' money each year on media-related products such as CDs and movie theater tickets (Kallen, 1999). Entertainment such as television, music, movies, and sports were the primary focus for these technology-connected teens.

More television programming was targeted toward teen viewers than ever before. Teens watched *Sabrina the Teenage Witch*, *Boy Meets World*, *Dawson's Creek*, *Buffy the Vampire Slayer*, and *The Simpsons*. Merchandise based on hot television shows blanketed the market. Animated programs geared toward adults became a fad and would sometimes create huge controversy. For example, *Beavis and Butt-head*, a cartoon on MTV, was considered responsible by some critics for a boy burning down his family's mobile home (The People History, 2009). The movie *Titanic* was the highest grossing movie worldwide, and the sixth highest grossing movie, adjusted for ticket price inflation (Box Office Mojo, 2009a,b). Professional baseball and football enjoyed huge audiences. One of the decade's most popular star athletes was professional basketball player Michael Jordan, who was paid $30 million by the Chicago Bulls in 1997.

MTV reached 50 million American homes by 1990; in 1989 it had debuted the show *Unplugged*, where artists played songs acoustically. In 1993, Nirvana made an appearance on the show, which was one of the last public performances by lead singer Kurt Cobain before his unexpected death in April 1994. Nirvana is considered one of the groups that put grunge, the 1990s' biggest new rock trend, on the map. Pearl Jam and Soundgarden continued the grunge trend, with teen fans dressing in Doc Martens and flannel shirts. From grunge came alternative rock, with Smashing Pumpkins as one of the lead bands of the genre. All-female musical groups showed their popularity at Lilith Fair from 1997 through 1999, and hip-hop and rap music reached the top of record charts. Among the most famous rappers of the decade were Tupac Shakur, Dr. Dre, and Snoop Doggy Dogg.

2000 to the Present

The advent of tween popular culture can be roughly pinned down to the end of the 1990s, when Britney Spears, Justin Timberlake, and Christina Aguilera hit headliner status. The three pop and rock artists were Disney Mouseketeers only a few years before they became pop icons. In 1999, Spears won the American Music Award for best pop artist, changing the music scene, as well as fashion, for girls ages eight to 13. Tween girls began dressing in schoolgirl-plaid skirts and halter tops to match her style, practicing hip-hop dance moves, and looking to emulate other youthful and bold female icons.

Rolling Stone magazine called this "teen pop" time the "all Britney, all the time" era (Carlson, 2006).

Fast forward to today, where Disney-made icons are still cornering the tween market. A recent endeavor by Disney was *High School Musical*, a made-for-television movie that aired on January 20, 2006. The *High School Musical* phenomenon, a musical trilogy with two made-for-television movies and one feature-length film, has reinforced the buying power of tweens. The original CD was the biggest selling disc in the United States in 2006, with 3.72 million copies sold (Brock, 2007). The soundtrack went into the Guinness World Records in 2007 for having nine songs on the Billboard Singles Chart, the most from a single CD ever (Walt Disney Television, 2006). William Strauss and Neil Howe (2006), coauthors of *Millennials and the Pop Culture*, observed the effect of *High School Musical*, including a rebirth in youth theater around the world. YouTube videos have popped up with kids reenacting the dances and dialogue from the movies. Disney Theatricals licensed more than 800 amateur productions around the country (Brock, 2007). Karaoke and acting have seen a resurgence in popularity with younger kids, creating a great avenue for program development at the library.

Other tween pop sensations like Miley Cyrus and Raven-Symoné, one of the Cheetah Girls, have sprung from the "Disney tween machine." "Disney has written the blueprint for the tween market," says Billy Johnson Jr., senior program director at Yahoo! Music. "What is so genius about what Disney does is that they have a machine that maximizes the full extent of the talent of their stars. They can showcase their acting on their television shows. They can exploit their singing abilities on their radio stations and record labels. The Jonas Brothers are an even better success story" (Ollison, 2008). The tween pop culture scene seems to have very high turnover, though, so it is key for librarians to stay up on which youthful stars are currently ruling the Disney roost.

To go along with these pop stars and teen idols, marketing companies have targeted tweens in a big way, with everything from pillows to stickers to board games branded with the names and images of tweens' favorite musical artists. Research in 2006 showed that tweens spend between $38 billion and $59 billion a year of their own and their parents' money on consumer goods (Booth, 2006). Recent research shows that even in these tough economic times, tweens are spending $43 billion a year and have influence on such purchases as cell phones, vacations, and even cars (Research and Markets, 2009). "What's happened is there's now media outlets oriented to kids, like Nickelodeon and Radio Disney. In the old days, we maybe had a couple cable channels, MTV and no Internet," says Cliff Chenfeld, co-owner of KidzBop (Booth, 2006). Radio Disney is one company that has taken advantage of the fact that parents are the ones driving their kids around. Jennifer Kobashi, Radio Disney director of brand marketing, said, "We know that for every three kids listening to us, we've got about one mom. We let advertisers know our station is for moms and kids in a car as they're driving. We're the last medium and the last message they hear before they step out to make that purchase" (Booth, 2006). So the radio station has advertisements for DVDs and games but also for minivans and pharmaceuticals because "10-year-olds don't drive" (Booth, 2006).

While much of tween popular culture is family friendly and even enjoyed by parents, teens, as usual, are more interested in edgier content. Teen and tween popular culture in the 2000s was dominated by reality television and interactive video gaming, giving the average teen or youth a chance at fame and fortune. The idea that the typical teen can rise to stardom by showing up on a television show has become commonplace in U.S. society. Shows like MTV's *MADE*, *The Real World*, *Laguna Beach: The Real Orange County*, and *The Hills* have propelled participants into national fame. The Nintendo Wii video gaming console introduced active gaming in 2006, where the wireless controller can be used as a tennis racket, a baseball bat, a steering wheel, and in a host of other functions. *Guitar Hero* and *Rock Band* also joined the electronic market, allowing teens to "rock out" on video gaming controllers.

Tweens are also watching the more skill-based reality television shows, such as *Dancing with the Stars*, *American Idol*, and *America's Got Talent*, which focus more on showcasing talent. The Ninetendo Wii, *Guitar Hero*, and *Rock Band* are also favorites of tweens, but Pokémon on the handheld Nintendo DS console has also become a big hit. Based on the show and graphic novels, *Pokémon Red and Blue* came out in the United States for the Game Boy in September 1998. The franchise has grown over the years to create further generations of Pokémon and many more games. Learning and partaking in aspects of Japanese culture has become a fad for both teens and tweens, making anime, manga, and Japanese candy and toys very popular.

Literature has also had a profound effect on teens and tweens, and in the adult communities centered around entertainment. The *Harry Potter* series of books by J.K. Rowling held the top three slots of the *New York Times* adult best-seller list for a year (Smith, 2000). Finally in 2000, the *New York Times* created a children's best-seller list to separate them from—and remove them from competition with— books on the adult list. This change is an example of how much impact teen and tween interests are having on adult popular culture, as adults are fans of the series as well. The *Twilight* saga, a collection of four novels by Stephenie Meyer, is another phenomenon that has created popular interest in vampire books, movies, and television for all age groups. *Twilight*, the first novel of the series, was published as young adult literature in 2005; yet it was the top-selling title in 2008, with its first two sequels as the number-two and number-three best-selling titles (*USA Today*, 2009). Teens and tweens, as well as adults, have latched onto the *Harry Potter* and *Twilight* phenomena, showing how much literature can impact a society, similar to the way Harper Lee's *To Kill a Mockingbird* and Joseph Heller's *Catch-22* did in the 1960s.

Technology has become a given for communication. Most Americans own or have access to cellular phones and personal computers. Music is listened to on MP3 players. Social networking has become a way to stay connected to people in all aspects of one's life, through Facebook, MySpace, and Twitter. Information is available in an instant with iPhones and laptops, creating a more informed teen society, many of whom get their news through two popular satirical programs on Comedy Central: *The Daily Show with Jon Stewart* and *The Colbert Report*, starring Stephen Colbert.

Library Services to Tweens

What can we learn from this research to help create services and programs for tweens? Well, it is true that ten-year-olds cannot get themselves to the library on their own unless they can walk or bike. Library services and programs targeted to this age group must cater to and attract the interests of parents as well as kids. Fads and icons are heavily based on the entertainment industry's marketing efforts, so it's crucial to keep abreast of upcoming and new trends. Staying current on the most popular entertainers is very important but can be difficult to do, as their popularity seems to come and go overnight.

Library Services to Teens

As always, library services will become applicable to a teenager's life if he or she feels the establishment has his or her interests in mind. Just as a program on performance art would have appealed to teens in the 1960s, librarians should be aware of teen interests right now, such as using technology to alter photographs, creating vampire-themed book groups, or holding a "Library Idol" to discover the hidden talent among community teens.

References

Booth, William. 2006. "In the Concert Hall, It Smells Like Tween Spirit: Radio Disney Nurtures, and Taps Into, Emerging Fan Base." *Washington Post*, August 6. http://www.washingtonpost.com/wp-dyn/content/article/2006/08/04/AR2006080400223.html.

Box Office Mojo. 2009a. "All Time Box Office: Adjusted for Ticket Price Inflation." Box Office Mojo/IMDb.com. Accessed August 14. http://boxofficemojo.com/alltime/adjusted.htm.

Box Office Mojo. 2009b. "All Time Box Office: Worldwide Grosses." Box Office Mojo/IMDb.com. Accessed August 14. http://boxofficemojo.com/alltime/world/.

Brock, Wendell. 2007. "Tween Appeal and Geeky Clean: Disney's Cultural Phenomenon Stage Production 'High School Musical' Opens This Weekend at the Fox." *The Atlanta Journal-Constitution*, January 13: A1.

Carlson, Peter. 2006. "How Does It Feel?" *Washington Post*. May 4. http://www
.washingtonpost.com/wp-dyn/content/article/2006/05/03/AR2006050302531
.html.

Duden, Jane. 1989. *1950s: Timelines*. New York: Crestwood House.

Goodstein, Anastasia. 2007. *Totally Wired: What Teens and Tweens Are* Really *Doing Online*. New York: St. Martin's Griffin.

Holland, Gini. 1999. *A Cultural History of the United States Through the Decades: The 1960s*. San Diego: Lucent Books.

IGN Entertainment. 2009. "IGN's Top 100 Games of All Time." IGN Entertainment. Accessed September 7. http://top100.ign.com/2007/ign_top_game_2.html.

Kallen, Stuart A. 1999. *A Cultural History of the United States Through the Decades: The 1990s*. San Diego: Lucent Books.

Ollison, Rashod D. 2008. "Disney Has Recipe for Tween Pop: As a Hot Act Cools, New One Warms Up." *Baltimore Sun*, July 20. http://articles.baltimoresun.com/2008-07-20/news/0807190096_1_jonas-brothers-hannah-montana-tween-pop.

Oxford English Dictionary. 2010. "Popular Culture." Oxford University Press, June. Accessed August 25. http://dictionary.oed.com.

PBS. 2005. "The Sixties: The Years That Shaped a Generation." Oregon Public Broadcasting. http://www.pbs.org/opb/thesixties/topics/culture/index.html.

The People History. 2009. "The People History: 1990s." The People History. Accessed September 7. http://www.thepeoplehistory.com/1990s.html.

Research and Markets. 2009. "Tween Spending and Influence." *Business Wire*. March 10. http://www.reuters.com/article/pressRelease/idUS145715+10-Mar-2009+BW20090310.

Smith, Dinitia. 2000. "The *Times* Plans a Children's Best-Seller List." *New York Times*, June 24. http://www.nytimes.com/2000/06/24/books/the-times-plans-a-children-s-best-seller-list.html.

Stewart, Gail B. 1999. *A Cultural History of the United States Through the Decades: The 1970s*. San Diego: Lucent Books.

Strauss, William and Neil Howe. 2006. *Millennials and the Pop Culture*. Great Falls, VA: LifeCourse Associates.

USA Today. 2009. "The Top 100 Books of 2008." USA Today, November 5. http://www.usatoday.com/life/books/news/2009-01-14-top-100-titles_N.htm.

Walt Disney Television. 2006. "*High School Musical* Receives Its European Premiere in London." Walt Disney Television, September 10. http://www.waltdisneytelevision.com/cms_res/pressoffice/pressreleases/HSM_premiere_10092006.pdf.

Chapter 2

"Here It Is, Your Moment of Zen": Defining Create, Relate, & Pop

It's hoped that this book will provide new ways to view the programs you already offer, as well as inspiration to try a new approach. You may already have a cadre of great programming that could simply use a more hands-on or participatory element to make it fresh. Let's explore the three aspects of this approach: *Create*, *Relate*, and *Pop*.

Create

Create is at the heart of what Web 2.0 and participatory culture are all about. Tweens and teens of today are comfortable with technology, using message boards to express their opinions; maintaining personal profiles of themselves and their world on MySpace, Facebook, and other equivalent social networking sites; posting videos of themselves on YouTube; reading their friends' LiveJournal accounts; posting their artwork on deviantART.com; and adding tags everywhere! Tags allow users to define how they search for things and help identify what is important to them. The invitation to express themselves has been extended to today's young people, and they have answered the call. Present-day tweens and teens are so enmeshed in this culture that most cannot imagine a time when putting everything about yourself online for the world to see was not always an option.

Create has many meanings and in a library setting can be manifested in countless ways. You may recognize that this is simply a different way to frame youth participation. Youth participation is the core of the "create" part of this philosophy. *Create* is about users creating content; therefore, since tweens and teens are the users, their participation in hands-on experiences—from helping to plan programs to assisting younger children at programs—will result in investment and buy-in from the users and ultimately lead to a more successful and supported program or service.

Create Access

Does your library make it easy for a teen to get a library card? Do you offer "fine for-giveness" opportunities or the chance to work off fines? Do you have open and easy Internet access policies? Do you allow nonresidents to attend programs or participate in contests? Thinking about access and the various ways it manifests itself in your li-brary is key.

Libraries as public places have many reasons to have policies in place, but when was the last time you took a look at those policies and thought about how they relate to open access for all users? Many teens may have gotten their first library card when they were very young, and over the years books were lost and fines mounted. Maybe a sibling or even a parent used the card and ran it up with lost materials. Now the cardholder is 13 and has $54 in fines and a parent that either cannot or will not help pay them off, creat-ing one big whopping obstacle for the teen who might still be interested in checking out materials.

Maybe a teen has lost his or her card. Does your library require individuals to show their cards to get online? Do they have to have a card to attend programs? How easy is it to get a replacement card? Often you will find that a reluctance to use the library, or even open hostility toward it, is based on these barriers enforced in library policies. Think about the various ways you can make access easier for teens and consider chang-ing access points like these.

- Allow young people to get a card without the signature of a parent or guardian. There are many fiscal reasons to require this step in a library registration pro-cess, but for many young people this is enough of an obstacle to prevent even the most basic entry into the library. The San Antonio Public Library has imple-mented this policy with great success and has consequently engaged many more youth by making it easier to use the library. The Moorpark City Library allows teens to acquire a library card with certain restrictions when a guardian is not present. Under Moorpark's policy, the teen can check out two books on a one-time-use card. The policy was put in place for teens that need research ma-terials for school and do not have a parent with them to sign for the card. Once the teen has the one-time-use card, his or her guardian needs only to stop by the library, show a picture ID, and sign the library card application so the teen can have full access to library privileges. The process should take only a few minutes, making it easy on busy parents and getting the teen's foot in the door for a library card. The official policy verbiage is shown in Figure 2.1.
- Offer opportunities for young people to volunteer and "work off" overdue fines. Offer "fine forgiveness" coupons as incentives for summer programs or at events. Get creative about amnesty days, and have teens bring in canned goods

> **Figure 2.1. Sample Policy: Restricted Temporary Library Cards for Teenagers without Parental Signature**
>
> Patrons 12 years of age through 17 years of age are classified as teenagers in this policy. Teenagers do not need a parent's or legal guardian's signature to get a restricted, temporary, one-time-use card; however, a parent or legal guardian must sign the application in person, in the presence of Library staff, for the teenager to obtain their permanent card, which allows continued checkout of material, use of the public computers, and the ability to check out videos or DVDs. In order to obtain a temporary, one-time-use card, the teenager must be a Moorpark resident or attend a Moorpark School. To obtain their temporary card, the teenager must present a picture ID verifying residency or attendance at a Moorpark School. The temporary, one-time-use card allows teenagers to check out two written material items only. Library staff will provide the teenager with a letter for their parent or guardian which explains the temporary card.
>
> *Source*: Moorpark City Council, 2010. City Council Policies Resolution 2010-1959.

for donation to local food banks in exchange for removing fines from their accounts. Whatever you end up doing, take the time to think about fines and how you can remove this barrier that keeps teens from coming through your doors.

- Remove the restriction of requiring a library card to use the computers, attend programs, or volunteer. Whatever the rationale for needing a library card for these activities, look at your policies and view them through the lens of providing open access to young people. Are the policies helping or hurting teen library patrons?

- Constantly and regularly advertise and remind teenagers that the library is a *free* service. Librarians know that libraries are free, but in the modern world this is a very difficult concept for people to grasp. When you hand out your program brochures or visit a school to promote summer reading, always be sure to emphasize the *free* aspect of the library. Culturally, some groups have no experience with free access in their home communities, so this message is an important part of educating users about what the library has to offer. Think about how often a teen runs home to describe all of the awesome stuff the library does—only to be met with parental skepticism about the hidden costs. Outreach is the only way to get the word out about the library's wealth of no-cost services.

Create Opportunities

Libraries are already very good at creating opportunities! Library missions revolve around providing education and recreational support. The fundamental role of libraries is usually to connect users with what they need; therefore, creating opportunities is the cornerstone of the library services model. That being said, take it a step further and think about how your programs and services can help expose young people to new ideas, cultures, philosophies, and experiences. Think about how to market or, if you already do, how to *continually* market your basic services to teens. Do you reinforce how much information they have access to and that it is free?

Whether you create an opportunity by providing programs on applying to college, getting a job, or obtaining financial aid for education, you must look at your programs as opportunities to expose teens to something new. Think about all of the different ways your programming exposes young people to ideas, careers, and ways of life that they never knew existed or considered exploring. Whether it is having a local chef discuss cooking and how to make it a career or a graphic novelist who opens the door for a teen to consider his or her art as a viable future, you are creating opportunities through education and validation. While you surely want to keep your community profile in mind, it is also good to consider exposing your community to something new.

Consider how video game tournaments can be used with this model. When a teen competes against other teens and wins a tournament due to his finely honed skills and obsession with, for example, an interactive game like *Rock Band*, you are creating an opportunity. You are creating an opportunity for that teen to feel good about himself and rewarded for something that is important to him. For some teens, this is a chance they may never before have encountered. School revolves around academics and sports, and there is rarely a year-end newsletter that will express how great Timmy is at *Rock Band*. However, *Rock Band* is important to Timmy, and the library video game tournament offers him something he's never had: an opportunity to feel good about a skill and enjoyable activity that is not necessarily "important" or noteworthy in the realm of real-world success.

Your collections create opportunities for teens to understand themselves better, as well as develop empathy for people whose lives are very different from their own. Your teen fiction collection creates the opportunity for teens to escape from their daily lives and peek into the lives of others. A nonfiction collection opens up the entire world to young people. They can learn how to repair a car, survive a shark attack, or plan a road trip. Audiovisual (AV) collections allow young people to see movies for free, listen to new music, or try out a new video game before spending their own hard-earned part-time job wages or allowance money.

Create Something

"*Create Something*" is the most basic and easy-to-apply aspect of *Create* in a library setting. Arts and crafts programs are often the cornerstone of library programs for young people, so this is an easy place to dive into the creation model.

Think about how structured most young people's lives are and how often their creativity is stifled or directed with such tight parameters that expression is rarely part of the goal. Libraries create access and opportunities for teens to create art, stories, videos, machines, fashion, and experiences in ways that are seldom encouraged in their day-to-day life.

Have you ever seen little kids who go nuts with glue and glitter because it is often the only time they are allowed to use these items with abandon? The same is often true for older kids. Programs that provide all of the supplies and allow the tweens or teens to make anything they want and take it home feeling good about the freedom of expression they experienced are one of the best gifts that libraries have to offer.

When a teen creates a Claymation puppet to take home or makes a gift for her mother or a pair of earrings for herself, it has value that cannot be measured. Think about teens who walk into the library and see 100 rolls of duct tape in 45 colors; come to a pizza-making program with tables covered in toppings; or attend a Halloween gingerbread event that has bowls filled with candy as far as the eye can see—and the only direction or expectation is that they can make anything they want. This is what *Create Something* is about: engaging curiosity, motivating self-expression, and building self-esteem.

Relate

Relate is often the hardest part of serving young people. Staying current on pop culture is the key to making relating easier. If you aren't familiar with the movies, TV, music, and websites that teens are into, it will make it impossible to plan relevant programs and harder to serve them as a whole.

Relate is when tweens come to the reference desk asking about Pokémon and, although you may not be able to spell it correctly, at least you know what they are talking about. Relating is when you are doing a book talk and can reference a currently popular movie or cartoon to make the connection for reluctant readers. Relating is when a cultural icon like Michael Jackson dies and you can talk to a tween who is asking for his music about how Jackson's music was a part of your own youth. Relating is about making connections and meeting young people where they are at, based on interests, maturity level, and location.

Relate Experiences

Whether it is an anecdote about your experience with Lego when you were a kid to kick off a Lego event or a conversation at the reference desk about soccer and how you used to play defense, relating experiences with young people should be a regular part of your job. Using pop culture as a reference point with young people makes it easier to meet their information needs and provide fun and relevant programs because you talk to your tweens and teens every day and know their interests.

Relating experiences is also one of the outcomes of offering diverse and experience-based programs. From the web-comic author to the martial arts enthusiast or the reality TV star, the presenters for these programs allow young people to learn about the experiences of other people and open them up to worlds that they may never have known existed. These real-life experiences teach teens empathy for others and also help form their views on lifestyle and freedom of choice. Some young people are not allowed much free choice in their lives, so learning about diverse experiences opens up options and opportunities that they may never have considered. By offering teens the opportunity to interact with your presenters and ask questions, you are empowering young people to be part of the world around them.

Make Connections

Look at using pop culture as an opportunity to connect with your tweens and teens in a meaningful way that will help you plan meaningful programs and services. At the reference desk, on the floor, or during a program, talk to young people and find out why Selena Gomez is so funny, why Pixar makes the best animated movies, or why Pokémon is so important to them. Chances are many tweens and teens have never been asked to explain their obsessions, and most will talk your ear off when given the chance.

Find out if the group of girls who sit and draw manga in your teen area all day would like to help teach a manga drawing class for younger kids. Ask the group of teens gathered around the Internet stations if there are any particular websites or software programs the library could teach classes about or have a program on that would be of interest to them.

The same tweens and teens you take the time to relate to may also end up being the ones who feel comfortable enough to ask for help finding books on GLBTQ (gay, lesbian, bisexual, transgender, questioning) topics or who have so enjoyed volunteering at the library that they feel comfortable enough to ask you to be a reference for their first job. Making connections is what youth services is all about.

Be Relevant

The relevance of libraries to young people, or lack thereof, is the most important issue facing youth services in libraries today. It is no longer acceptable to be passive about whether the library is relevant to users or continue to hold tried-and-true library programs without introducing new audiences to what the library has to offer. Are all members of your community being served by the library? If your library is quiet, you are doing it wrong. To be truly relevant to your community, the library should have permanent loud spaces, as well as regular, planned opportunities to be loud and involved. Silence is still a requirement in some areas of the library, but a library with 100 percent quiet at all times is an irrelevant library.

Some young people are lucky enough to have parents and families who embrace and participate in their interests. Some parents may want to engage on a topic but do not have enough information to get involved. The library can help both parents and children by offering collections and events to engage and educate both on different levels. Sometimes just having a conversation with parents about manga (or Justin Bieber, iCards, Silly Bandz, etc.) can help ease any worries they may have had about something foreign seeming or difficult to comprehend; sometimes that brief visit can give them perspective to allow them to talk to their children about their interests in new ways. The library is in a unique position to engage young people by providing collections and programs related to their recreational interests while also educating parents about the roles pop culture plays in their kids' lives from a neutral, nonprofit viewpoint. By using pop culture as an influence in different aspects of the library, the library can remain relevant to the young person and the parent at the same time.

Pop

Pop is the fun part of subscribing to this philosophy of programming and services. *Pop* is the flexible, the nimble, and the spontaneous approach to developing services, collections, and programs. *Pop* is now and what tweens and teens spend their lives obsessing about when they are not in school, involved in extracurriculars, or at home being a part of the family. "Popular" can mean "for the masses," but it can also apply to the underground, indie culture, fanzines, and more. "Popular" does not have to mean "for the majority." To truly engage the most teens in your community, you will need to go beyond the top 20 music video countdown. Look for the niche, fan, and cult interests in your community. Demonstrating relevance to more interests will keep teens coming back and looking for more of your offerings. With more than 300 million people in the United States, our "subgroups" are not small anymore and should not be ignored.

Be Current

Pop is what tweens and teens are interested in *now*. It means having books about the latest Pixar animated movie on the shelves before the movie hits theaters. *Pop* means that you weed your teen paperback series collection often enough that today's adult does not find their favorite TV shows among your collection. *Pop* means having a MySpace page for your library *before* teens start leaving in droves for a new social networking site. Your collections and your programs must reflect what your young people are into today, not yesterday, and not last year. It is true that trends can last over time and some things remain "in" for longer cycles. However, there should be a percentage of your collections and your programs that consistently reflect aspects of pop culture right now.

Staying current is either a chore or a delight, depending on your perspective, but staying current is a must. If you are a pop culture addict, you do not need any advice on how to keep up with what's hot. If you find it tough to keep up, track down the people in your life who consume pop culture (tweens, teens, co-workers, friends, etc.) and pick their brains! Getting the word from the fan's mouth is usually better than reading an article about it.

Some libraries have implemented "trend-spotting" committees that spend time identifying what the current hot topics and next best things may be, and then determining whether resources should be allocated in those directions. This system can be applied to collection development as well as programs and services. More important than the trend spotting itself is making sure that your policies and management allow for jumping on the bandwagon with certain interests. Bureaucracy may be your biggest obstacle to remaining current.

Be in Demand

With the recent economic downturn and the increased use of libraries in the past few years, libraries have not had to try hard to be in demand with patrons. With tighter budgets, many libraries are in demand without even trying because they have ordered only one copy of a new DVD instead of the ten copies they used to acquire. With tighter staffing levels, there may be fewer programs, which may cause you yourself to be in very high demand. We encourage you to think about your library services differently, and, ideally, by the time this book is in your hands libraries may be doing better budgetwise.

Think about being in demand as being the most popular kid in school. Be in demand because you are cool, your programs are fun, and you have a really popular graphic novel collection. Try to be in demand to the kids who think they are too cool for everything. To be in demand in this way is to anticipate the area where tweens and teens think you will get it wrong. Sometimes not having *Dance Dance Revolution* (*DDR*) is better than buying the cheapest pads around. If you are trying to get older teens involved, do not censor them at a poetry slam or have excessive rules about behavior at video game tournaments. Being in demand with teens means you are doing it right.

Having a low attendance at a certain program is to be expected in any library. Taking chances with your programs means that sometimes there will be a dud. Bad weather, a big school sports game at the same time, or a holiday you forgot about when you planned the event—all of these are reasons for occasional low attendance at a program. Nevertheless, working toward attracting a full group of kids should always be your goal. Sometimes this means not programming in certain areas if you consistently get low numbers. At the minimum you should be evaluating your low-attended events and thinking about what could be changed or how the marketing can be tweaked. Make it your goal to have at least a few events each season where you pack the house with lots of kids.

If you can get your tweens and teens to talk about your events and tell other kids about it, you know that you are in demand. Details on strategies for using word-of-mouth marketing and viral tricks are discussed in Chapter 3.

Have Fun

Being flexible and less rule oriented is at the heart of this attitude. Your staff should be having as much fun as the young people they serve. Staff at all levels should be on board with the idea of the library's need to serve tweens and teens.

Having fun means having a sense of humor about what you do and how you do it. Plan programs that are open-ended and can be adapted to the needs of all sorts of young people. Focus on providing structure and not creating obstacles. Do not worry about how the program turns out in the end, and ask yourself, *Did they have fun while they did it?* You often hear librarians trying to figure out how to get their teen advisory teens on task or struggle with the outcomes-based assessment of that type of program. As long as the teens are having fun and you are getting some useful feedback and involvement from them, that is usually all that should be expected.

Having fun means not worrying about whether the kids are reading everything they say they are during summer reading. The library is great at supporting the educational needs of its community, so having fun means focusing on recreation. Public libraries have the luxury of not being school. Use the freedom you have to embrace the full range of interests of your users.

Conclusion

Subscribing to the service model of using popular culture to create services and programs for teens and tweens allows librarians to relate more closely with their community and, therefore, make the library a more comfortable, relevant place to be. Be creative and bold with programming ideas, getting feedback from teens along the way. Trust your teens to tell you about their interests. Most of all, have fun while serving the informational and recreational needs of a community in this unique and fresh way.

Reference

Moorpark City Council. 2010. "Moorpark City Library Circulation Policy." Moorpark City Library, April 5. http://www.moorparklibrary.org/circulation.asp.

Chapter 3

"OMG!": Targeting Populations, Advertising, and Promotion

Introduction

Marketing is often the first term used to describe "getting the word out" about library events, but in actuality the correct term for this activity is *promotion*. Marketing in its purist form should happen at the highest levels of the library, from writing a mission statement to creating a strategic plan. True marketing involves a variety of facets, such as those explained in E. Jerome McCarthy's Product, Price, Promotion, and Place model (Perreault, Cannon, and McCarthy, 2010), which has become a standard for the marketing industry. In its simplest terms, this theory can be reduced to four questions:

- What product are we going to produce?
- What should we charge for the product?
- How will the product be distributed?
- How are we going to promote and sell this product?

This chapter does not include a formal description of marketing and promotion. Entire books have been written on marketing to libraries, such as Neal-Schuman's *Library Marketing That Works!* by Suzanne Walters (2004). Ideally, a true, robust marketing campaign will be initiated from the top of the organization and involve the entire library and all of its stakeholders, with marketing for young people one portion of the larger overall marketing plan. For this book's purposes, this chapter focuses solely on the "branding" of your tween or teen services (a small part of determining "what" your product is) and the promotion and advertising needed to let potential users know about your product (tween/teen collections, events at the library). The chapter explores various types of marketing: things that can be done very inexpensively or with some cash to spend. You may find that you are already doing some of these things but may need to tweak how you do them or find a more targeted approach. You will learn how to utilize the help of your teens to market your programs and techniques to market to specific niche populations.

Create: Branding Your Teen and Tween Services

It is not enough to just plan great programs and services for teens. Once you have done this work, it is imperative that you also work out how the services will be branded and promoted to the community. In its simplest form, a brand can be a name, a logo, a slogan, or a sign. A well-branded product makes it easy for users to refer to it by name and recommend it to others and also encourages users to become fans and followers of the brand. One of the biggest mistakes libraries make is assuming everyone knows how great the library is. Another mistake is thinking that simply advertising programs inside the library to those who already use it is enough to attract attendees. It is not. Being truly dedicated to changing the service model and reaching out to teens and tweens with these ideas means working to identify the population not being reached with current advertising and finding out how these potential users hear about things in the community and in the marketplace at large. The teen and tween audience is constantly targeted with advertising; therefore, promoting services to these age groups demands a more savvy and targeted plan. Using pop culture as your baseline means using mainstream for-profit tricks to promote your services. You want teens and tweens to align your programs within the framework in which they are used to consuming other cultural content. Part of any branding and promotion plan means meeting them where they are, using techniques and tricks with which they are familiar.

Let's get started! Start with branding your teen services first, and then think about how to separate your tween services from your regular children's services next. You are "selling" the library as a product, which is often difficult to stamp with any kind of "cool" factor. Coming up with a separate brand for teen services is a step toward changing the image of your services and creating the opportunity for your teens to feel a sense of ownership and investment in the library. A distinct and separate brand accomplishes several things:

- It lets the teens know that you are serious about serving them as a distinct and special group. Teens respond to things they perceive to be specifically designed for them. It lets them know that you recognize that they are not children, nor are they "stodgy" adults either.
- It acknowledges that your teens are different from other library patrons and should be treated differently and uniquely from others who use the library.

- Coming up with a brand separate from the general library brand makes it easier for teens to buy into it without feeling tainted with the potential uncool nature of being a "library teen."
- It creates a recognizable identity for your teens to look for once they know about the brand and want to start looking for the next program, event, or service that's designed just for them. Teens will be able to easily identify the events and services for them from within a webpage, a rack of brochures, or other marketing pieces that may contain multiple events and programs that target other members of your community. The brand allows them to cut through the clutter of your other services and quickly find the teen-centered items.
- Teens understand branding because it is modeled from the consumer culture that they know well. Teens are brand-conscious and therefore respond to direct marketing.
- It creates the opportunity to take the high-quality reputation that libraries have and combine it with a consumer-marketing model which teens respond to and which parents will be more likely to trust.

Once you are committed to creating a distinct teen brand it's important to *not* include the term *library* anywhere in the shorthand brand you're trying to create. Ask most any teen walking down the street or walking in the halls of school what the library means to them, and you will undoubtly hear responses like *uncool, frumpy, quiet, sshhh, mean librarians, no good books, I hate to read,* and surely some other choice comments. Consider the ways that movies, television shows, and the media in general portray libraries and librarians. In 2002's *Star Wars: Attack of the Clones*, future librarians have gray buns and a bad attitude. Sadly, even an episode of *Glee* featured an old lady librarian (even though she did have a sense of humor). Rare exceptions like Giles, the librarian on *Buffy the Vampire Slayer*, or the librarian cult favorite movie *Party Girl* can be found, but they are not necessarily geared toward teens, so the stereotypes remain.

A library that has worked hard to brand its teen services is the Ann Arbor District Library (AADL) in Ann Arbor, Michigan. AADL initially created AXIS as the name of its teen programming brochure, but it has become the shorthand reference to all teen services at the library. AXIS was chosen for several reasons:

- The alliteration of the name goes with Ann Arbor and AADL.
- It is short and evocative.
- It means the center of things or where things meet (like the library).
- AXIS sounds very similar to "access," and the ultimate goal of promoting to teens is to create more access.

The AXIS brochure does say "Stuff for Teens" and "Ann Arbor District Library" on the brochure itself, but the specially created marketing giveaways, like the popular rubber bracelets and custom containers of mints, have only "AXIS" with the axis.aadl.org website address printed on them. Teens knew that they received the item from the library, of course, but wearing the bracelet or otherwise referring to AXIS does not scream out "library teen!" If parents or others want to know what AXIS is and type in the website address, they would quickly realize it is part of the library.

In Washington, the Sno-Isle library system has branded their services as "Sno-Isle Teens: Infamous for Information" (see Figure 3.1). While this takes a slightly more traditional approach, it still does not include the word *library* in the branding and also has a great catch phrase attached to it for increased memorability. Hats and T-shirts have been made to promote the library in a covert way, without the word *library* stenciled on the item (see Figure 3.2).

Branding your services can be as simple as holding a contest and allowing teens to generate a name or even a logo for your brand. Then either pick one of their suggestions or vet the choices and then allow teens to vote. If there is funding, work with a graphic designer or graphic design firm to help brand your teen services. Coming up with an identifiable logo should be the minimum you do to create a brand. A logo can be used on print, digital, and ephemeral pieces, and even on signs within your teen space. If your logo is flexible enough it can be made to feel fresh with the use of different colors, themes, or seasons, depending on how you generally market the library. The AXIS logo incorporates spray paint designs which appear fresh and new, and can easily be redone with different colors each time a new brochure is created. This allows something relatively static to be dynamic in terms of the passage of time. Once your logo and brand are created, determine how you will use it on print materials (see Figure 3.3).

If you do not already do a program brochure or flyers for events, consider creating these pieces in order to showcase your services all in one place. Over time teens will begin to look for the brand and eagerly await the next brochure to find out about events.

Relate: Identifying Your Teens and Tweens

Before you embark on any new marketing campaign or services, you must identify who your teens are and what types of programs will be of interest to them. Determining audience is crucial in order to customize your promotion strategy. Pop culture is not "one size fits all," so determine the makeup of the teen crowds in your community and what slices of the cultural pie to focus on. The community may be full of country-music-loving NASCAR enthusiasts or hip-hop and R&B fans. Clearly, advertising and programs for these two audiences would be very different. Using teen input during the planning process of such a marketing campaign is crucial.

Figure 3.1. Sno-Isle Libraries Teen Logo

Source: © Sno-Isle Libraries.

Figure 3.2. Sno-Isle Teens Hat

Source: © Sno-Isle Libraries.

Figure 3.3. AXIS Logo from the Ann Arbor District Library

Maybe your library has already done community analysis, but did it include teens in the process? Seek out and use U.S. Census information and community data gathered by your local city hall or chamber of commerce. These numbers are a good starting point, but they will not give you everything you need to properly advertise and program for your teens. What you really want to determine is what your teens are interested in and what they like to do with their spare time. If your library has a Teen Advisory Board (TAB), that will also be a great help. But since most TAB teens are already "library teens" you will not necessarily gather the information you need to get the rest of your community's teens into the library. All librarians who serve teens know that on some level there are people on the library's staff who would not be upset if only quiet, studious library teens used the library. But we want the loud, jumping, excited teens too. We want all the teens!

The best and easiest way to get good information from teens about their interests is to create a comprehensive survey. Two example surveys can be found in this chapter (see Figure 3.4 and Figure 3.5). These surveys can easily be administered on paper as well as digitally. If you decide to create a digital version of your survey, there are many free survey services out there and reputable survey sites like SurveyMonkey (http://www.surveymonkey.com) that you can use to create it. These sites will do all of the software development for creating the survey and collecting the results. If you have programmers in your IT department, then a survey can be created in house to completely meet your needs. Digitally administered surveys can be added to your website for teens to fill out at their leisure or can be occasionally mailed to an e-mail list. Be sure you allow patrons to opt in to this list so you do not spam all your patrons. A digital survey will make compiling the results a bit easier if you are collecting lots of data.

Paper surveys are the easiest to use on the fly and are obviously the cheapest option available. Bring copies with you on routine school visits or ask teens at programs to fill them out. Also consider bringing them every time you visit outside the library where teens will be. With the cooperation of the schools, a larger-scale campaign could be conducted to survey as many of the teens as possible. Involving library media specialists (or library clerks or volunteers, where applicable) or English teachers are the most obvious choices, but you would certainly get more interesting and valuable information if you could ask art teachers or coaches to have their teens take the surveys, and therefore receive responses from different types of teens.

Surveys can be as long or short as you want them to be. If you want only to measure interest in one particular area, you might do a short survey targeted to teens interested in athletics. Ideally, with willing participants, it would be best to do a two-pronged questionnaire. The first portion would determine the teens' interests in movies, television, music, and recreation (see Figure 3.4). Be sure to ask about reading/watching/listening habits as well as questions about hair/style/identity. Use these results to establish the interests of your teens and inspire creative and unique programming ideas.

The second series of questions would measure the level of the teen interest in, involvement or lack thereof, and perceptions of the library (see Figure 3.5). This type of information is invaluable in determining what type of work you need to do in creating a advertising plan. Do you have a low number of teens with library cards? Do many of

Figure 3.4. Teen Patron Profile Survey

GRADE ___ 9 ___ 10 ___ 11 ___ 12   MALE ___   FEMALE ___
SCHOOL _____   TOWN where you live _____

Read for fun?   YES ___   NO ___
If you read magazines, please list your favorites: _____
Prefer fiction or nonfiction? _____
Name the most recent book you read for pleasure and enjoyed: _____

Watch TV? YES ___   List your five favorite shows:

_____
_____
_____
_____
_____

            NO ___   Why not? _____

Own a cell phone?   YES ___   NO ___   If yes, if you have a camera on your
phone, what do you do with the photos you take? _____

Listen to music?   YES ___   NO ___   If yes, name your five favorite bands/
performers:

_____
_____
_____
_____
_____

List up to five songs you recently downloaded or five CDs you are listening to right
now:

_____
_____
_____
_____
_____

Listen to radio?   YES ___   NO ___ If yes, then list your two favorite stations:

_____
_____

Have a job?   YES ___   If so, what do you do? _____
                   NO ___   If you don't have a job, what do you do for spending
                             money? _____

(Continued)

Figure 3.4 (Continued)

Other—if it's not listed above, tell us what you do in your free time!

Hang out with my friends	Spend time with family	Play paintball
Go to a movie	Volunteer	Go to the YMCA
Play a sport	Dance	Go to the Boys & Girls
Shop	Go to a museum	Club
Read a book of fiction	Read a nonfiction book	Go to a rec center
E-mail	Go to a club to see a live	Hang at a coffee shop
Listen to music	band/singer	Write fan fiction
Read online news	Sew/knit/needlepoint, etc.	Travel
Paint/draw/create	Dye/cut/braid my hair (or	Chat/IM
Go on a hike	someone else's hair)	Go to parties
Party	Talk on the phone	Collect things
Lift weights/work-out	Play video games	Text message
Read a magazine	Watch Japanese anime or	Watch TV
Play role-playing games	read manga	Read the newspaper
Eat in restaurants	Watch sports on TV	Do car-related activities

Describe your style:

punk	hip-hop	who cares
preppy	fashion-forward	black all the time, but not
sporty	retro	goth
goth	hippie	
clubber	T-shirt/jeans	

Other? _____

---

them have cards but also high fines? You might decide to do an amnesty day or offer "fine forgiveness" coupons at special events to get teens back into using the library. Maybe you will find out that most teens think the library does not offer anything for them. If this is the case, you will need to take a ground-up advertising approach to let parents and teens know that the library has special services for teens. In this case, consider asking the teens to get involved in more intense focus groups to gather information about how the library could better get the word out about teen services.

If you want more intensive results and have the staff time to devote to such an endeavor, you could do focus groups. Focus groups work best if you have the assistance of school counselors, local teen centers, or other youth-serving agencies to offer up the names of students who may be helpful and represent a diverse cross-section of the community of teens. Again, you want to find teens who are not already library users in order

Figure 3.5. Teen Patron Library Use Survey

GRADE   __ 9 __ 10 __ 11 __ 12   MALE __   FEMALE __
SCHOOL _____   TOWN where you live _____

Use your school library? YES __ How often? Daily Weekly Monthly Seasonally
                          NO __
Use the public library?   YES __ If yes, which location(s)?

                                    How often do you use the library?
                                        Daily   Weekly
                                        Monthly   Seasonally
                                    What do you use the library for?
                                        Homework __   Go online __
                                        Read magazines __   Hang out with friends__
                                        Attend a program __ Kill time __   Study __
                                        Other? _____
                          NO __   If you don't use the library, why not? _____
                                    No library card __   High overdue fines __
                                    I go online __   I buy books __
                                    I use another library __
                                    Other? _____

Ever attended a program or event at the library?   YES __   NO __
If yes, name the program(s): _____

How do you hear about events at the public library?

Friends   Parents   Flyer at store
Flyer at school   Teacher   I never hear about events
At the library   Newspaper ad   at AADL

Other: _____

Would you ever attend a program at the library? YES __   NO __

If you answered no, why not?
My friends won't come with me. __   I'm too cool for the library. __
I don't have any way to get to the library. __   My parents won't let me. __
I'm not interested in any of the programs offered. __
Other? _____

Do you know that all of the programs at the library are FREE?   YES __   NO __
Do you know that you usually don't have to sign up for a program (with a few
exceptions)? YES __   NO __

(Continued)

Figure 3.5 (Continued)

What kinds of programs would interest you? (Circle one.)

Arts and crafts	Dance	Hear an author talk
Music	How to get a job	Book discussion groups
Poetry	College help	See a TV personality or
Creative writing	Holiday-related events	other famous person
Video game events	Movies	talk about his or her
Comics/animation	Car repair/info	life/experiences
Food/cooking	Hair/makeup/fashion	Cultural events

Other? _____

Any ideas, questions, suggestions, or thoughts about the library?

_____

_____

_____

---

to accurately assess how your promotion is and is not penetrating the market. If you do only one or two focus groups, choose as broadly as possible in terms of gender, beliefs, culture, and socioeconomic levels of the participants. If you choose to facilitate several focus groups, you could gather together small groups of more like-minded teens to get a deeper picture of their interests. If you live in a community that is more homogeneous, you may find many teens who have similar interests. Dig deeper and find the secondary level that the teens might not necessarily self-identify with in a major way but, when pressed, admit to an interest in. For example, some teens may be fans of anime, manga, and Japanese culture, or role-playing games such as *Dungeons & Dragons*.

You may also find valuable demographic and interest information from other youth-serving agencies in the community. The local YMCA, Boys & Girls Club, and teen centers could share their program successes and failures to get you started in the right direction. Schools are also good places to gather this information. Teachers of physical education (PE), art, and theater could offer crucial information about teen interests in your community. Looking at what clubs, sports, and after-school activities are offered is a perfect way to determine what you can complement. For example, cup stacking, also known as sport stacking or speed stacking, has been popular in elementary schools for years, with more than 20,000 schools worldwide offering cup stacking as part of their PE program. Its popularity soared in the early 2000s and was featured on commercials by McDonald's, Firefox, and the American Egg Board. Schools are a ripe source for community interests. If you wanted to do a cup-stacking event at your library, PE teachers would be able to help you advertise the event to the cup stackers in their schools.

Pop: Types of Advertising and Promotion

In order to keep up with what teens are interested in and properly market to them, you must also constantly be plugged in to teen pop culture or have figured out ways to keep up. Pay attention to how marketing is done for television shows, movies, and websites geared toward teens. In the mid-1990s, advertisers saw the potential of the teen demographic as consumers, and many great books have since been written on the subject. Peter Zollo's (1999) *Wise Up to Teens: Insights into Marketing and Advertising to Teenagers* is a great place to start when you are framing your marketing campaign or gathering information to convince administrators of this unique approach.

Blogs like *Ypulse* (http://ypulse.com) are excellent places to use as ground zero for staying abreast on what is happening with tween and teen pop culture. *Ypulse* will help you keep up with what is new, and you can also use it as an idea generator for how to market to teens in new and exciting ways. *Ypulse* keeps close track of teen social networking, mobile devices, and viral trends. Look at how many libraries created MySpace pages long after the bloom fell off the rose. Reading blogs will help you keep up with which trends have more lasting power and educate you on the entire landscape of teen media.

In order for libraries to be successful, pieces from the private sector's advertising model must be tweaked for use in the nonprofit world. As librarians we are selling a product: the library. The library's strategies for getting the teens to buy in to the product will not look much different from corporate advertising in the end. One advertising method is utilizing well-known pop culture references to market a product. The Moorpark City Library in Moorpark, California, used a photo of Edward, a character from the movie *Twilight*, on flyers to promote a Vampire Wreath program, attracting both vampire enthusiasts and fans of the movie star (Figure 3.6).

Be aware of various types of advertising and promotion, and utilize the best approaches for your community. Different methods of advertising include print materials, social networking, word of mouth by teens, guerrilla and viral marketing, paid advertisements, and going out into the community.

Print Advertising

The cheapest and easiest way to market your library is with print materials. Whether you do a full-fledged brochure, telephone pole posters, or postcard-sized flyers, this is the quickest way to get started with your marketing campaign.

Figure 3.6. Vampire Wreath Program

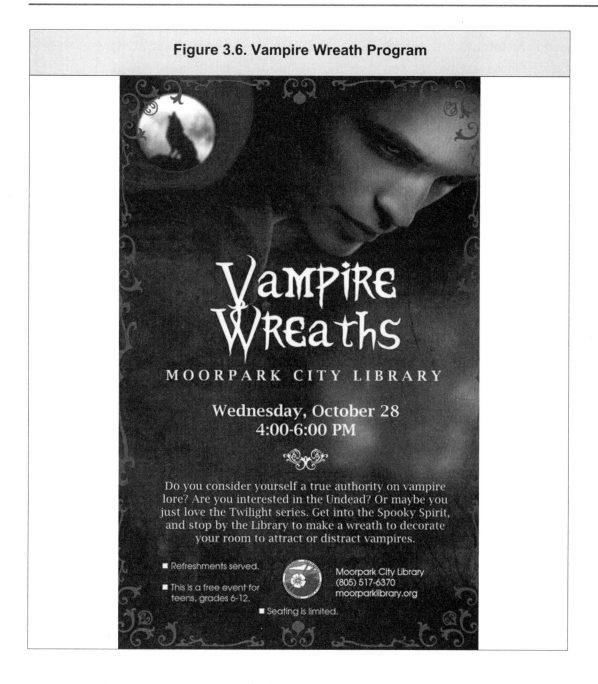

If you are looking to encourage hand selling of programs and want to take paper flyers to local businesses, schools, and hangouts, you must stick with a small size. Postcard size is standard; do not go any bigger if you expect people to take the flyers with them. In many cases, a business card–sized promo may be the perfect paper product. Multiple flyers can be made from a single sheet of paper, and more people are likely to take something small and portable that can easily go in a pocket. Also, if you plan to use teens to help hand out flyers, business card size is ideal. It is more discreet and easier for a teen to "sell" to the cool kids. If you look in any coffee shop, bookstore, or music store and find the freebies rack where music, art, and other events are advertised, everything is small and brightly colored. Small postcards can also be more easily used if you want to do stealth advertising in books or tucked into the book stacks. An example of this would be tucking a postcard with a list of local agencies and services for your lesbian/ gay/bisexual/transgender/questioning (LGBTQ) community into your teen fiction titles about LGBTQ teens.

Social Networking Promotion

Keeping up with social networking as a marketing tool is a dynamic task that can never be viewed as being "done." If you still have a MySpace page, it is definitely time to delete it. Conversely, if you are not on Facebook yet, you'd better hurry. Word on the street is that it is on its way out. However, what is in or replacing it has not yet been determined. One of the best things currently about Facebook, though it may change tomorrow, is its advertising power. It is highly likely that an outside performer/speaker/author that is presenting a program at the library has his or her own Facebook page. Harness the power of the fan base and increase the exposure of the event by linking to the Facebook fan page. A good example of this phenomenon was when John and Hank Green went on their Nerdfighters tour in 2008. The Green brothers started with a strong blog presence, then became a huge video blog (vlog) sensation on YouTube, which naturally led to a robust following on Facebook. Attendance at their events in libraries was phenomenal because they did much of their own advertising online.

Currently Twitter is very hot for adults, but teens do not use the service much at all yet. Of course, by the time I finish typing this sentence, this could change. Alas, this is the nature of the social networking beast. If you are nimble enough and ambitious enough, you can easily and cheaply dip your toe into all sorts of social networking.

Perhaps you are doing a program on creative bento boxes (Japanese lunchboxes that have taken decorative food to new heights). You will want to target the Flickr (http:// www.flickr.com) bento box group message boards. In addition to being a photo storage site, Flickr acts as a social site by allowing people to form groups based on common interests. This is one of the site's more popular features. There are several large bento box groups with hundreds and, in some cases, thousands of people as members. Obviously the members will not all be local. In fact, many will be from all over the world. Nevertheless, you will reach some new users, but in a place and a space that is unexpected and off the beaten path.

Targeted niche marketing is yet another way to utilize teen interests in creative ways. Other sites, such as the reviewing site Yelp (http://www.yelp.com) and the meet-new-people-around-common-interests site Meetup (http://www.meetup.com), are excellent choices for marketing your programs to 20- to 40-somethings. At the moment, these sites are not the best choices for targeting teens. Meetup is a great site to find instructors for programs and events that require some amount of "fandom," a cult-following fan base such as the passionate followers of *Harry Potter*. Do not forget to look to your staff for experts in specialized hobbies and interests to help with programs. It is necessary to note that websites may come and go very quickly, so keeping up is crucial.

Text messaging may not be the way to target new users, since libraries do not want to be in the spam text-messaging business, but it is a fantastic way to engage teens who have attended events and signed up to be on your text-messaging list. Send texts with reminders about events, teasers about upcoming events, and other select services you want to tell teens about. It is important that any text-messaging endeavor includes an "opt-in" feature from the user. Remember to consider the medium when crafting the message. Texting is by its nature short and concise so your messages should fit that model. For instance, "2nite@7 Downtown Library Mario Kart w/Prizes! Food! Free!" Cover the bases and keep it short. There are several software options for handling mass SMS text messaging. Companies like TextMarks (http://www.textmarks.com) or Club Texting (http://www.clubtexting.com) can be used to do this for the library, but they usually have advertisements attached to the messages. Any IT department worth its salt should be able to handle this type of service much more cheaply and without the ads. This can usually be done remotely and on a schedule so it does not actually require someone to type a text message into a phone.

Teens as Resource: Street Teams

Utilizing your teens as the library's street team is one of the best ways to encourage investment and ownership of your services by local teens and offer a level of credibility in marketing by having the message delivered by members of your audience. A street team by definition is a team of people that walks the streets, attends events, waits outside at movies or concerts for the crowds to emerge, and hands out promo bills for events that may be of interest to the targeted audience. For example, if Miley Cyrus is making an appearance at a mall or store near you, sending your team of teens to hand out flyers for programs would surely harness some new teen interest in the library. A street team could also help pass out flyers to local businesses and hangouts, and hang posters on telephone poles and in store windows, if local ordinances allow for this. Consider how unique it would be if one of your street-team teens handed out library postcards at a punk or metal show. This would surely change the perceptions that the attendees had about the library. The element of surprise cannot be underestimated as a marketing tool. Another way street teams can get the word out at their schools is putting flyers up in classrooms or hallways, or getting programs included in morning announcements. Again, teens tend to respond differently when they hear about events and programs from other teens.

Guerrilla, Viral, and Alternative Promotion

Guerrilla marketing is a term that was created by Jay Conrad Levinson (2010) in his now-popular series of books. Since his first use of the term in the mid-1980s, it has become mainstream and recognized as a distinct marketing tactic. Guerrilla marketing is defined as unconventional and potentially interactive, and often seeks to target its audience in surprising and unexpected places. The idea is to create a unique experience or concept to get the audience engaged and talking about whatever it is being advertised. Advertisers hope that this type of word-of-mouth approach will create buzz and then become viral.

Viral marketing is exactly what it sounds like: infecting consumers in quiet, intimate, face-to-face or computer-to-computer recommendations that pass from person to person, much like a virus spreads. The other benefit of these types of approaches is that they are often inexpensive to create and rely more on imagination than money.

The most infamous example of guerilla marketing was the 2007 Boston campaign for the *Aqua Teen Hunger Force* movie from the Cartoon Network Adult Swim animated TV show. Several lightboxes/machines were placed around the city and were intended to depict the characters in the movie. However, due to their flashing lights and other suspicious aspects of the devices, the campaign instead sparked a citywide bomb scare. Several freeways, subway stations, and bridges were closed while the devices were inspected. Clearly, the library does not want to model this scenario, but you get the idea. Think about how strategically placed billboards or a sign hanging from a tree with open-ended, vague, or even obtuse wording with a website listed could create interest and buzz about the library. The reality is that for teens, seeing the library running a tent at an outdoor street festival with *Dance Dance Revolution* or other video games is enough of a surprise to be considered guerrilla marketing and will very likely spark a viral word-of-mouth campaign.

Paid Advertising and Other Bells and Whistles

If you have a budget for more expensive advertising or perhaps have a Friends of the Library group who could put money toward promotion, there are many options. Paid ads in local papers, including school papers, can sometimes work depending on the topic. Paid ads on Facebook and other websites are also relatively inexpensive and can be targeted based on interest and location.

Movie theater advertising is another excellent option for grabbing teens' interest while they are a captive audience, waiting for a film to begin. Many theaters will offer a flat rate and show the ad before every showing of a particular movie. This is not cheap but certainly worth the bang you might get for a few select, high-profile events. Movie theaters are where many teens are, and choosing the right movie could provide maximum exposure for your event. Whether or not you have the ability to create an ad yourself, you surely could have teens themselves help with this process. You would be surprised at how easy it is to create a slick video with a very small budget—or even no budget at all.

Television advertising is also incredibly effective for reaching teens. It is possible to buy local airtime with the cable provider and then choose certain channels like MTV, Bravo, and Cartoon Network or other channels popular with teens. This is clearly an expensive proposition for many libraries, but even if it is something you only do once or twice a year the results may be dramatic. The market penetration would be quite deep using this medium.

Outreach Promotions

Taking your show on the road is the best and easiest way to meet teens where they are and advertise your programs and services in person. Classroom visits or having a table at open house or college/career nights that schools offer are obvious outreach marketing opportunities that you are most likely already doing in some form or another. Take a step further and think about all of the parades, street festivals, and fairs that the library could attend, and showcase programs or video game equipment by allowing teens to get hands on and learn more without ever having to enter the library. If your community has a teen center, consider holding events there once in a while. You will interest teens who probably would never respond to more traditional advertising models, as well as create connections between staff and teens. Your local YMCA or Boys & Girls Club may be interested in partnering with the library and allow you to bring your programs or services to them and share resources.

Price and Demand

Libraries often forget that for nonusers, it's not a well-known fact that library services are free or do not always require registration. The "freeness" of the library must be a constant part of all promotion the library does. For every person who asks, "What does it cost?" there are dozens more who assume the services are something they cannot afford and will never bother to ask. Teens are "sold" things so often that the *free* message is just as important for them to hear as well. Do not ever take for granted that the community knows how the library works.

Conclusion

More than anything else, be sure the advertising the library does for teens is fun, vibrant, and targeted. Start out with a plan and determine the most affordable option and what will get the most bang for the buck and the effort. Find out who the teens are, where they are, and what they are interested in. Stay on top of what kinds of advertising works in the for-profit sector, and copy what you can within your budget contraints. Use current social networking strategically and with discretion based on how the teens in the community use it and relate to it. Branding and advertising tween and teen services at the library is one of the most important ways to reach out to your teens with a pop culture focus and a mind toward being creative, relative, and popular.

All of these advertising, branding, and marketing tips will help you plan and promote the variety of programs we have laid out for you later in the book. Also, each of the programs listed in the book has specific tips for marketing that particular program in the most appropriate venues and to the right audience.

References

Levinson, Jay Conrad. 2010. *Guerrilla Marketing for Nonprofits*. New York: Entrepreneur Press.

Perreault Jr., William D., Joseph Cannon, and E. Jerome McCarthy. 2010. *Basic Marketing*. New York: McGraw-Hill Higher Education.

Walters, Suzanne. 2004. *Library Marketing That Works!* New York: Neal-Schuman.

Zollo, Peter. 1999. *Wise Up to Teens: Insights into Marketing and Advertising to Teenagers*. New York: New Strategist Publications.

Chapter 4

Make It Work: Collections

If you choose to follow the philosophy of using popular culture to create inventive programming for teens and tweens at your library, you should employ the same rules of thinking to your collection. Here are some tips on keeping your collection fresh and exciting, reflecting the current interests of teens.

Create

Maybe you are working on freshening up your teen collection to reflect the interests of your community, or maybe you are lucky enough to be creating an opening-day collection for a new building. Either way, it is important to keep your collection current with materials on popular trends and icons for teens and tweens to show that the library cares about their interests. Worried about knowing who is the popular teen idol of the month? You probably have a built-in focus group using your library every day. Let teens take part in creating your collection. Ask for feedback from teens at Teen Advisory Board meetings, put up a display in the teen section asking who or what is trendy and popular at the moment for teens, or post a survey on the library website asking teens their favorite singers, actors, television shows, and more.

In review journals, be on the lookout for biographies on musical groups and rappers, sports stars, movie celebrities, and reality show starlets. Fictionalized series and graphic novels based on popular television series are always being published, and teens and tweens love to read anything to do with their favorite show. The *Hannah Montana* and *High School Musical* book series for tweens were in high demand at the height of their popularity and enticed otherwise-reluctant readers to eat up these books like candy. Also, pay close attention to movie tie-in books, and try to have them in your collection while the movie is being marketed in time for the highest level of interest.

Create Access

Teens are a very diverse group with varied interests. Adding popular culture materials to your collection can be a way to attract many different types of teens to the library.

Make sure to search out materials that speak to the skateboarding population as well as reality television junkies. A biography on Paris Hilton will not likely appeal to a boy who is interested in the Woodstock music festival. Sometimes access to information on a pop culture reference can become educational, leading teens toward broader interests, such as how the advent of Japanese manga into mainstream U.S. society caused many teens to become interested in learning about Japanese culture through sushi making, learning to speak Japanese, and becoming involved with the fan culture of anime.

Create Opportunities

Adding popular culture materials to your collection is also a way to form opportunities for teens to find information on topics that they may be too shy or embarrassed to seek out on their own. For instance, adding biographies on prominent GLBTQ (gay, lesbian, bisexual, transgender, questioning) icons who have become successes in their own right is very important to share with those teens who are struggling with their own sexuality. This also goes for famous people of different races, cultures, and nationalities. While you may already make a conscious decision to include characters of different ethnicities in your fiction collection, make sure to carry over that philosophy into your nonfiction section. Teens need to read about people like themselves and be exposed to people that are not of their race or nationality to learn about other groups of people.

Create Something

Building a stellar popular culture collection does not just include books based on famous people and television shows. Materials on popular do-it-yourself activities and hobbies are also important in creating a well-rounded collection. Watch for hands-on books on fashionable crafts, sports, henna, jewelry, or cookbooks to support the latest crazes. For instance, the *Twilight* series has led to a teen obsession with vampires. There are tons of cookbooks and other kinds of books covering vampire culture that teens would enjoy; having those books in your collection encourages further reading on the topic.

Relate

Meet teens where they are at! A library collection should include materials to reflect the popular culture of the generation—or the collection will not be relevant to the community it is serving. A priority of a youth library collection is to have information for reports and projects, as well as materials to answer questions about life, health, and wellness. But another very important priority that sometimes gets overlooked is including materials that reflect the interests and famous people of the time. It is very important for that teen to find information on Greek mythology for his report, but we do not want him to walk away from the library thinking the only purpose of the library is to find factual information for school. One of the goals of a library is to serve the recreational needs of the community. If a teen sees that you have cookbooks based on the television show *Iron Chef*, then she may decide the library has her interests in mind and come back to check out materials for fun.

Relate Experiences

Trends do circle around to become popular again for different generations, but teens do not necessarily realize that trends recycle themselves. They are more in tune with the idea that they are the first to discover an exciting band or style of clothing. Use a short discussion about a book on how to repurpose a pair of old jeans into a purse as an opportunity to relate to teens that repurposing jeans into original creations to express your individuality was also very popular in the 1970s.

Make Connections

Being aware of the latest crazes is a great way to make connections with the teens that you serve. Owning materials on the topic acknowledges their interest, and being able to converse with them about it shows your intentional dedication to knowing about their passions. This does not mean spending every waking moment watching MTV. Flip through *J-14* magazine once in a while to discover the current heartthrobs for tweens. Pick up a *Rolling Stone* magazine to read the latest trends in music. If you cannot stomach some of the popular books series, at least read the first one so that you have some comprehension of who Bella and Edward are from the *Twilight* saga.

Making connections with teens now makes for future adult library users. Teens that feel comfortable at the library will eventually have families of their own. It is the hope of librarians everywhere that they bring their families to the library and passionately vote for the library in times of need.

Be Relevant

Include materials in your teen library collection that are of interest to the teen community. Introduce new teen audiences to your library through materials in your collection. Teens are using technology to gain and share information with friends. Instead of leaving their chair to look up the definition of a word while in a library, teens can text the services desk or a staff member who can then reply with the meaning of the word. Meet teens' needs by giving them access to audiobooks that can be downloaded to their iPods and other e-reading devices. Think about adding video games and Blu-ray movies to your collection. Highlight parts of the collection by blogging about the newest titles and allowing teens to leave comments. Instead of sending e-mails when books are due, send text messages. Be thinking of what new types of materials can be added to the collection that will better serve teens in the way they acquire information.

Pop

Staying up with trends in popular culture can become very expensive. If you have a small budget and can only purchase materials that will fill a need or receive the most use, you can still have a great collection that reflects current pop culture. At the very least, purchase books that go under the spotlight because movies and television shows come out based on them. Also spend a few dollars on books on popular hobbies and current kitschy trends. These materials can be highlighted at programs to increase visibility and circulation.

Be Current

Keep up with current popular culture materials in your collection. Teens will be your most honest customers, sometimes brutally so. Tweens may be more forgiving. While a television show or hobby can go out of style for fifth graders, the fourth graders coming up will discover this phenomenon like it is new. Therefore, there is less of a push to constantly weed the tween collection of outdated popular items.

Anticipate popularity. Publishers do this all the time. Look ahead to big events that are coming up, like the soccer World Cup or the Olympics. Purchase books on famous and well-known athletes in advance to be ready for the rush when the games begin.

Staying current means keeping up with books that are turned into movies; the release of the movie will spur interest in reading the original novel. Many times it is the reluctant readers that show the most interest in reading the books because they have such an interest in the movie. Making movies and television shows based on teen fiction and graphic novels is a huge trend in Hollywood right now. Take a look at the Youth Services Corner website and the GreenBeenTeenQueen blog for regular updates on the upcoming teen books being made into movies.

Be In Demand

Staying current with pop culture materials goes hand in hand with weeding your collection. Do not fall into the trap of keeping everything you purchase. A recent trip to a local library unearthed the find of a *Ghostwriter* book, based on the PBS children's series from the 1990s, prominently displayed on the endcap of a bookshelf. While tweens are more willing to overlook how out-of-date a book is, teens are not as forgiving! Regularly go through your biography section to weed out the fallen famous. Play close attention to entertainers and sports stars. While biographies on George Washington and Marie Curie will stand the test of time, a biography on 1990s' comedian Pauly Shore may not fly off your shelf any time soon.

Don't keep books for nostalgia's sake. Saving books because they may become popular again is a waste of shelf space. There is no point in keeping a book series on *Sabrina the Teenage Witch* in the hopes that it may become popular in the future. No one foresaw that the television shows *90210* and *Melrose Place* would be relaunched ten years later. At this point, teens are more interested in the actors in the new series than novelizations of the original characters of Brenda and Brandon Walsh. That said, beware of cult followings of what you feel is dated popular culture. If in doubt, check for fan sites or ask your teens to see what has fallen out of popularity.

Have Fun

So you have purchased the books, but how do you make sure teens know you have them in the collection? Most of the time, teens may not think to search out the Robert Pattinson biography in your collection. Create a display or face the books out in the shelving. Think about having programs to promote the new materials in your collection. The Ann Arbor District Library (AADL) had a Gundamfest, celebrating fandom for the Japanese anime series about giant robots called *Gundam*, which has franchised into video games, manga, and more. The AADL had purchased DVDs and manga, and to make the community aware of these materials the program included an anime showing, the opportunity to play *Gundam* video games, a craft component of making a *Gundam* model from a kit, and the opportunity to be the first to check out these new materials. Revive interest in cult classics to a new generation by holding trivia events on *Buffy the Vampire Slayer*, *Lord of the Rings*, and *Harry Potter*. These programs work best in conjunction with the release of a new movie, television show, or book—something that is getting attention in the media. Most of all, have fun showing off your great collection to teens and tweens.

Conclusion

There is a direct correlation between the library's collection and its programming. While this book focuses on using popular culture to create programs that will appeal to teens and tweens, there is little point in demonstrating to patrons the relevance of the library if the other services provided are not of high quality. The library is in a constant state of proving its worth to the community. If a teen comes in to participate in a comic-book-drawing event, there had better be materials in the collection to support the content of the workshop. Many times programs will pique teens' interests after they have attended a program, revealing to them that the library has further worth beyond homework and Internet access. High attendance to programs is great, but a large number of teens with library cards and high teen collection circulation is even better.

Alternatively, another purpose of the library is to serve the informational needs of the public. This is where staying up on the popular trends of youth is so important. The disappointment a teen feels when the librarian says the library does not have any Justin Bieber CDs and has no idea who that is can cause him or her to stop going to that library; that teen may never know about the programs that do interest him or her that are taking place at the library. From the teen's perspective, based on this one interaction, the library does not have his or her interests in mind, so why waste time going there? The bottom line is that the collection must support the programming that you do and the interests of the community.

Resources

GreenBeanTeenQueen [blog]. 2010. Accessed July 10. http://www.greenbeanteen queen.com/.

Youth Services Corner. 2010. Accessed July 10. http://www.youthservicescorner .com/.

Chapter 5

Keep 'Em Coming: Spaces

There have been many wonderful books, as well as regular columns in *VOYA*, dedicated to creating dynamic and wonderful teen spaces in libraries. Rather than replicate what these books have done or try to help plan the space of every teen's dreams, this chapter talks about simple ways to keep spaces responsive and related to pop culture without doing a complete makeover. Tween spaces are starting to crop up in some libraries and are definitely worth considering as an addition to a children's room. If money is no object or you are lucky enough to be getting ready to build a new library with a teen space, take the opportunity to expand "branding" teen services to the next level by branding the space. Signage with the logo on it is a simple and valuable way to expand the teen brand. It will remind the teens that said brand is all-encompassing. Taking branding to this next level of incorporating it into their own space completes the circle and connects all facets of teen services in the library.

Create

When planning to add or spruce up the presence of pop culture as part of a space in the library, think about it in terms of creating a space just for tweens or teens where their interests, obsessions, and passions are in the forefront, as well as engaging reluctant library users. From signage and furniture to displays and visuals, a space can be made more appealing with a big budget or even a small or nonexistent budget. The goal of spaces that incorporate pop culture materials is to let users know the library is up to the minute and responsive to what interests them.

Create Access

To hook a teen or tween visiting the library for the first time—or even for the hundredth time—having displays or posters that reflect what is happening now is an easy way to let the teen know that the library is not as out of it as he or she may have thought. The simplest way to have a constant visual presence of current pop culture is to maintain a robust magazine collection. A wall of current magazines on a variety of topics, including niche interests like skateboarding, manga, wrestling, music, and sports, is the cheapest and easiest way to keep a space looking new and current. Magazine subscriptions are one of the more inexpensive media types out there, so adding as many titles as possible is the way to go. If budgets are tight, consider asking your Friends of the Library group to pay for subscriptions, offer patrons the opportunity to "adopt" a subscription, or consider taking magazine donations. Teens who enjoy magazines are willing to overlook a missing issue since it is a recreational interest rather than a research need related to other, more studious periodical subscriptions in the library.

If the library has a graphic novel or a CliffsNotes collection, be sure the space and signage related to those collections is visible and prominent, since the goal is to alert even a casual visitor to your more unexpected collections. Teens visiting for the first time should be able to look around quickly and realize that the space is for them and identify the things that interest them most.

Create Opportunities

A teen space planned with pop culture in mind should also be responsive to teens with needs or interests that they may be too embarrassed or shy to ask for. Be sure that regular displays or posters reflect varied points of view, cultures, races, and ways of life. Prominently advertise programs that might be of interest to the GLBTQ (gay, lesbian, bisexual, transgender, questioning) community as well as those that discuss different cultures. Some users may never ask, so making it easy for them to stumble upon it should be part of the plan.

A well-planned space should also accommodate individual reading and study, as well as spaces for groups. A solo teen looking for a place to read should feel just as comfortable as a group that needs to find a place to hang out. Teens may also meet new people or be introduced to new things when given the room to explore.

Create Something

It is fairly commonplace to have manipulatives, art projects, or other hands-on activities for children in their spaces, but not as common in teen spaces. If the space is available, consider having constant hands-on crafts, puzzles, or brainteasers that encourage a teen who is killing time to want to hang out in the space. Some libraries have addressed this need by purchasing tables with chess, checkers, backgammon, or other game boards built into the tabletop. A magnetic tabletop or a whiteboard can encourage teens to hang out, leave messages, and be expressive. Of course, these "expressions" may also lead to profanity or gang tagging, but this is part of the teen landscape so learn to take the good with the bad and focus on the fact that some teens will appreciate the opportunity. Just remember to constantly monitor the space for inappropriate writing that needs to be taken down.

Relate

Offering teens a space that reflects the world they live in by acknowledging their interests is crucial. The quickest way to turn off a prospective user is to keep posters up that feature celebrities that are long past famous or irrelevant to the community. Encouraging reading is a large part of what libraries do, but clearly libraries also support other media and interests. Displays that focus only on reading for pleasure can easily turn off a new visitor who either does not know how or does not like to read. Posting images that portray music, sports, art, dance, or movies acknowledges the fact that not only does the library have collections that support these interests, but we're happy you're here! Yes, that potential user may eventually become a reader, but right now the goal is to make him or her feel welcome. Again, it is important to be mindful of whether displays or posters reflect diverse thoughts and life experiences.

Relate Experiences

One of the easiest ways to breathe life into your space with relevance in mind is to have displays that share reviews and opinions about books, movies, and magazines from the library staff, as well as other teens. It is important for teens to realize that the staff who work there are knowledgeable, interested in teen life, and able to offer recommendations. This can happen in the form of displays on a bulletin board or on the library's website, which is also a "space" for teens in the library. Give teens the opportunity to express themselves and relate their experiences with one another. Using a whiteboard or going "old school" with paper, consider having user polls on display in the teen area. Whether they are changed weekly, biweekly, or monthly, posting new polls (and the results of previous polls) keeps the space fresh and encourages teens to visit often. The poll questions could be anything, from asking teens about their favorite candy, food, drink, movie, or book to more involved questions about current events or "hot issues." Giving teens the opportunity to express themselves in the space encourages ownership of it and, therefore, of the library.

Make Connections

Having displays, signage, or activities in the space also creates the chance for staff to make connections with teens based on their interests. It also allows teens with similar interests to meet other teens or encourage connections among themselves. If there is a teen hanging out by the display of vampire-themed fiction, take the opportunity to talk to him or her and find out whether there is an interest in book recommendations and if he or she knows about the party the library is planning for the *Breaking Dawn* movie release. If the space is lively and inviting, these connections are that much easier to make.

Be Relevant

Having old series books in the collections is bad enough, but devoting a display to them is worse. This tells teens that the library does not know and does not care about what their interests are. Be sure that your most current items and displays are the first thing teens see when they enter the space. New books should be near the entrance, as should popular collections like graphic novels, music, and magazines.

Pop

Pop is where you can have fun and let the teens know that what they are into *now* is important! Having display cases in a teen room is a great way to accomplish a number of things. Perhaps local teens would enjoy putting their collections or artwork on display. Another idea for pop culture–oriented displays is to highlight interests like fairies, zombies, and unicorns, and include copies of book covers. Never take the most popular materials out of circulation! Include cool collectibles, toys, movies, or comics that are visually stimulating and get teens thinking about different ways to experience their interest. Also think about highlighting local events in the community that might interest teens. For example, include an advertisement for a local Renaissance festival in the fairy display, where teens are sure to pick up awesome glittery fairy wings and flower crowns. *Pop* is about visual appeal that works fast!

Be Current

Having collections that stay current is vital here, but continuously creating displays that feature the new materials or ongoing contests in the space takes it a step further. In anticipation of the next television show or movie being released based on a popular teen book or graphic novel, have a display highlighting what the library has related to that interest. Consider having "passive" contests, such as posters featuring the faces of celebrities with their eyes covered, and ask teens to guess their identities. This could be done with sports team logos, fonts from popular movies, or even lines of dialogue. These kinds of displays keep the space current and interesting and encourage teens to visit often.

Be In Demand

If budgets are tight, focus more money on what is most popular in the collections. The same is true for spaces. Consider displays or activities that highlight hidden gems that somehow relate to something currently popular. The passive displays and poll questions mentioned previously are a wonderful and simple way to make the teen space in demand. Teens are always looking for something new and interesting, and these types of efforts will make the teen space more popular and well used. Encouraging teens to create displays or help decorate the room will also create more demand and, again, increase the ownership that teens have of the space.

Have Fun

The goal of any changes or additions to a teen space should encourage fun. Let teens know that the library appreciates and encourages their recreational interests. Be sure that your purely recreational programming is prominently displayed and advertised in the space. Having teens involved in keeping the space current and popular is the best way to encourage fun!

Conclusion

Use popular culture as a muse for creating a teen-friendly environment in the library. Keep the space current using posters and displays that feature popular icons and trends of the moment. Enlist the help of teen advisory boards or teen library regulars to create displays based on topics they find interesting and appealing. But don't just think in two dimensions. The best bet in creating a teen-driven space is to have some sort of enclosed display space for teens to show off their collections. Some librarians that serve teens have collections of *Nightmare Before Christmas* figurines or Elvis memorabilia that teens may enjoy. Also, think of the teen space as a place to showcase events that may be happening in the library or elsewhere in the community, and create displays around these themes. Most important, think creatively!

Resources

Bernier, Anthony, ed. Forthcoming. *Making Space for Teens: Recognizing Young Adult Needs in Library Buildings*. Lanham, MD: The Scarecrow Press.

Bolan, Kimberly. 2008. "The Need for Teens Spaces in Public Libraries." Young Adult Library Services Association (YALSA) [white paper]. January. Accessed August 30. http://www.ala.org/ala/yalsa/profdev/whitepapers/teenspaces.cfm.

Bolan, Kimberly. 2009. *Teen Spaces: The Step-by-Step Library Makeover*. 2nd ed. Chicago: American Library Association.

"Teen Spaces 2nd Edition's Photostream." 2010. Flickr. Accessed August 30. http://www.flickr.com/ photos/kimbolan/. [Thousands of images of teen spaces are available through the Flickr website, including all of the images in Bolan's 2nd edition of Teen Spaces.]

Chapter 6

"I Want My MTV!": Programming

Foundations for Successful Teen/Tween Programming

The goals associated with offering programs at the library are many: attracting new patrons to use the library, enriching the lives of members of the community, and empowering the public by involving them in the creation and implementation of programming, to name only a few. Successful library programming is based on the interests of the community it serves. Many times, it can feel like you are programming in a vacuum, creatively coming up with fabulous ideas for programs that you believe teens and tweens will enjoy, only to have three people show up to the event. Many times, what is forgotten in the planning process is actually asking the members of your community what they want. More often than not, what happens instead is the event planners assume what teens will want to take part in based on successful programs at other libraries.

Involving your constituents is the first step in creating successful programs. This can be done through surveys either on the library website or on paper. If there is a teen advisory board, go to those teens for ideas on what they want to see happening at the library. Many times it works best to have a list of potential programming ideas for teens and tweens to pick from. Then, once the creative juices are flowing, ask them to come up with their own ideas for events. Empowering teens to help create programs will encourage higher attendance. Teens are being told what to do by many different adults, so the opportunity to make their own decisions is so important and satisfying that you may find you now have some very loyal library users.

Another important thing to keep in mind when programming with teens and tweens is to always follow through! If the teens come up with an idea, make it happen. If you offer up a suggestion that the teens take an interest in, make it happen. Trust can be lost very quickly. You want teens and tweens in your community to know that you will try very hard to not let them down. The library is a safe place to be, and honesty from and trust in the librarians and staff in the library is very important for building relationships with the youth community—for both creating lifelong library users and easing behavior problems. The teens that have the hardest time following the rules in the library but continually return consider the library a safe place whether or not they vocalize that feeling. Consider asking those teens to be involved with programming or helping around the library. They may be looking for an adult to pay attention to them. Plus, they may have great ideas for programs to engage reluctant readers.

Planning and Implementing Programs

Popular culture is a great muse for creating unique programming for teens and tweens. Teen and tween obsessions with singers, actors, video games, and toys can be very solitary activities. The library can design programs to make these obsessions social and introduce patrons to supporting resources available at the library about which they had been unaware.

Besides asking teens about their interests, keep up-to-date with what is popular and fresh by looking at magazines such as *J-14*, *Rolling Stone*, *US Weekly*, and *Game Informer*. Stay up on the trends by reading websites such as Ypulse.com (http://www.ypulse.com). Pay attention to which books are being checked out. Are they about vampires, werewolves, fairies, or dragons? Look to see what teens are doing at the library and what is on their clothes. Are teens playing chess? Is there a big group hanging out around the manga books? Do many tweens have *iCarly* on their backpacks? Is there a resurgence of Led Zeppelin T-shirts? All of these things can give you ideas for creating pop culture–centered library programs.

Once the idea for the program is in place, work on putting the program together based on the budgetary constraints of your library. Ask teens when is the best time to have the program, instead of assuming Saturdays are good days because they are not at school. Look throughout the community to make sure you are not duplicating a program. For instance, the teens may be keen on having a battle of the bands, but the local high school holds the event every spring. In that case, change the idea a little. Maybe the library battle of the bands is a warm-up to the big high school event, or maybe you can offer library teen volunteers to help with event or space at the library. Be creative with the idea. Be sure to advertise the event in places teens go, such as local coffee shops and arcades. But do not just stop with paper flyers. Advertise in electronic spaces, such as on the high school manga club website, Facebook, or community message boards. Again, ask teens where they get their information. You can ask tweens as well, but many times their parents are still finding out about events for them.

Conclusion

Chapters 7 through 19 contain ideas for teen and tween programs inspired by elements of popular culture. Each program write-up will include ideas on supplies, implementation, and advertising for the event. Take these ideas and make them work within the confines of your library's financial resources. These programs are meant to be suggestions to manipulate to work within your community. Strive to age-down the teen programs for your tween community as opposed to aging-up programs that were originally aimed at elementary school students. Many times, tweens are interested in the same things teens are, and they are also trying to pull away from being childish. It is hoped that the reader will find new ideas for programming in these chapters, as well as develop a mind-set for creating novel and unique programs created by and for teens and tweens, specific to your community using popular culture.

Chapter 7

Programs: Art

Various types of art and drawing go in and out of popularity with teens following media trends. The newest superhero movie creates interest in comic book art, and widespread interest in reading Japanese and Korean manga novels has piqued the interest of teens in drawing in that style. When a new Pixar movie hits theaters, cartooning as a hobby and profession become popular. The library can become the go-to place for learning the skills for creating these different forms of art through programs and resources. Learning the nuts and bolts of drawing is becoming harder for kids who cannot afford drawing classes, as art classes are often reduced in number and art electives are often the first to be cut from public school curricula during budget crunches.

Comic Book Academy

The Comic Book Academy program was written and contributed by Sharon Iverson, Teen Librarian at the Ann Arbor District Library.

General Description

The Comic Book Academy prepares teens interested in developing their graphic story-telling skills to create their own comic book or graphic novel. The class meets over a six-week period (two hours per class) to learn about the art of comic bookstorytelling, character design, writing dialogue, penciling the first draft, refining and completing the penciled pages, and inking or finishing the pages.

Pop

Movies based on superheroes, such as the *X-Men* and *Iron Man*, and cartoons like *Up* and *The Incredibles*, are very popular among the teen and tween crowd. Their box-office successes signal a heightened interest in comics and graphic novels. Likewise, Japanese manga and anime also continues to hold high interest. While many teens like to create fan art, other teens are interested in bringing their original stories to life on paper.

Relate

Becoming a successful comics and graphic novel creator involves much more than becoming a good artist. Many teens come to the academy thinking they will spend most of their time improving and refining their drawing techniques. Instead, they learn how to elevate their storytelling skills both as a writer and as an artist. Besides creating the opportunity for teens interested in art and comic books to learn more, it is also a way for the library to support writing stories as a different art form.

Instructors/Talent

A local comics artist instructs the program. Motivated teens who are knowledgeable in the creation of comic books can help with big groups.

Audience

Teens in grades 6 through 12.

Planning and Supplies

The program was created based on the guidance and suggestions of the instructor. He recommended the number and length of sessions, suggesting that teens could best learn the information in a relaxed, no-pressure setting. He also provided "homework" handouts that reviewed what had been learned that day, as well as outlines of skills for each teen to practice at home.

Supply List

- No. 2 pencils
- Erasers
- Unlined paper
- Rulers
- Fine-tipped markers
- Smooth Bristol board

Create

The instructor kicks off each session (20 to 30 minutes) reviewing the past week's instruction and presenting a new element. Teens then work on their stories and practice what they have learned while the instructor moves about the room and interacts with each participant. As the weeks progress, teens begin to develop their visual stories. The hosting librarian keeps the teens supplied with the basics (sharpened pencils, paper, etc.) and also retrieves reference material (photographs of settings, characters, etc.) from the library shelves.

Food, Technology, and Other Mandatory Extras

- Laptop with weekly PowerPoint presentation downloaded
- Access to the Internet
- Projector to show slide show or websites on a large screen
- An over-the-shoulder "comics" camera set up so participants can watch on a large screen as the presenter demonstrates drawing techniques
- Whiteboard and markers

Analysis

Attendance is usually consistent from week one through week six. The teens interact with one another as well as the instructor, often staying past the end time of the program. A few teens completed a minicomic by the end of the six-week session, while most teens had a good start on their graphic stories to finish off at home.

Marketing Tips

Because the program is time intensive, it was held during the summer. Promotion of the program occurred during school visits in May and in library advertising materials, such as the teen brochure and the library website. The local newspaper was alerted to write a piece promoting the unique and free program. Do not forget to let middle and high school art instructors know about the event so they can pass along the information to their students and potentially offer some type of extra credit.

Resources

Abel, Jessica, and Matt Madden. 2008. *Drawing Words and Writing Pictures: Making Comics, Manga, Graphic Novels, and Beyond*. New York: First Second.

Art & Story. 2010. [Weekly podcast by cartoonists Jerzy Drozd, Mark Rudolph, and Kevin Cross, who share their experiences making comics and try to wrap their brains around the larger ideas behind their chosen art form.] Accessed August 31. http://www.cvcomics.com/artandstory/.

Hogarth, Burne. 1995. *Dynamic Wrinkles and Drapery: Solutions for Drawing the Clothed Figure*. New York: Watson-Guptill.

Hogarth, Burne. 2003. *Dynamic Anatomy*. New York: Watson-Guptill.

Janson, Klaus. 2002. *The DC Comics Guide to Penciling Comics*. New York: Watson-Guptill.

Lee, Stan, and John Buscema. 1978. *How to Draw Comics the Marvel Way*. New York: Simon and Schuster.

McCloud, Scott. 1993. *Understanding Comics*. Amherst, MA: Kitchen Sink Press.

McCloud, Scott. 2006. *Making Comics: Storytelling Secrets of Comics, Manga, and Graphic Novels*. New York: HarperPerennial.

Comics Art Digital Coloring

Information on the Comics Art Digital Coloring program was provided by Sharon Iverson, Teen Librarian at the Ann Arbor District Library.

General Description

In the two-hour Comics Art Digital Coloring workshop, participants learn how to use Adobe Photoshop Elements to clean up their art, fill in line work with colors and half-tones, create cool lettering, prep the finished page for printing, and more.

Pop

In recent years, comics heroes like Spider-Man, Batman, and Iron Man, along with Japanese manga heroes and heroines, have thrived on the big and small screen. Their popularity has increased demand for more creative works. The use of Adobe Photoshop software has enabled artists to move graphic works more quickly into the hands of adoring fans and also allows artists to animate their work.

Relate

Becoming a successful comics and graphic novel creator involves learning how to become an accomplished visual storyteller. Teens who want to make a career as a comics artist benefit if they can do their own writing and artwork. They also benefit from using a tool like Adobe Photoshop to finish their work in a more technical and professional way. The ability to use Adobe Photoshop opens doors to careers in web design, TV, film, and much more, making this a great program to offer at the library for teens interested in the comic book industry and who may not have any other way of obtaining this professional information.

Instructors/Talent

A local comics artist, experienced in creating his own comics and offering comics art instruction to kids, teens, and adults, presented the program. Local artists may be interested in talking about how they can create comics for free to get their name out in the community.

Audience

Teens in grades 6 through 12.

Planning and Supplies

This workshop is offered the week after the conclusion of the six-week Comic Book Academy program presented at the library. Participants of the academy are encouraged to learn and try out Adobe Photoshop Elements. Because of the small Apple lab (14 stations) and large enrollment of the academy (25 to 30 teens), two sessions are offered.

Create

The instructor, using one of his own scanned comics pages, explains the basics of Adobe Photoshop Elements and has participants experiment with the various tools. This takes up to an hour. A library staff person with knowledge of Adobe Photoshop Elements is available to assist. Then the remaining time belongs to the teens as they work on their own scanned work brought in on a USB drive or scanned by the librarian hosting the event.

Food, Technology, and Other Mandatory Extras

If not already purchased, the Adobe Photoshop Elements software will need to be purchased. This software exists for both Mac and PC computers. The program will run more smoothly if there is access to a computer lab, where a presentation by an instructor will not bother any other library users and teens can be a little bit louder as they work on their projects. An additional computer connected to a projector for the instructor to use is a great tool for showing steps on a large screen for the group.

Analysis

Historically, most of the teens enrolled in the academy follow up with this additional workshop. It is impressive how quickly the teens learn to become proficient with Adobe Photoshop Elements. Consideration is being given to opening the lab periodically for teens to continue their finishing work once the program is over. Whether staff time or the computer space can be devoted for extra time to work on the projects must be well thought out.

Marketing Tips

Occurring in the summer so that teens have more time to devote to their projects, this program is promoted via school visits in May, in the teen brochure, on the library website, and in the local newspaper. It could also be promoted to middle and high school art instructors to pass along to their students.

Resource

Art & Story. 2010. [Weekly podcast by cartoonists Jerzy Drozd, Mark Rudolph, and Kevin Cross, who share their experiences making comics and try to wrap their brains around the larger ideas behind their chosen art form.] Accessed August 31. http://www.cvcomics.com/artandstory/.

Comics Artist Forum

Information on the Comics Artist Forum program was provided by Sharon Iverson, Teen Librarian at the Ann Arbor District Library.

General Description

The monthly Comic Artists Forum offers participants who have interest in comics or graphic novel creation an opportunity to share their work with others, gather fresh ideas, and listen to other comics/graphic novel artists discuss their favorite techniques or latest trends in comics publications. Each month a guest comic artist offers an art or publishing tip.

Pop

Japanese manga and superhero comic books have stimulated an interest in drawing for teens. On a larger scale, people can meet up at conventions, where groups who share similar interests in manga, graphic novels, anime, and various cult followings such as Star Wars can gather when these annual events are held.

Relate

Most comics/graphic novel artists work in isolation. The monthly forum offers teens as well as adults the chance to share and pick one another's minds for ideas. Teens wanting to make comics creation a career can talk with adults who are publishing their work and learn about the realities of making a living as a comics artist. This program further supports the notion of libraries becoming a meeting place for special interest groups in the community. Putting up displays of supporting materials offered by the library may attract additional library card users.

Instructors/Talent

Invite guest comics artists to speak at the program.

Audience

Teens in grades 6 through 12 and adults.

Planning and Supplies

Two hours was determined to be a good length for the program, given that time is needed for a guest artist presentation, along with casual time to work and interact.

Basic drawing supplies are required:

- No. 2 pencils
- Erasers
- Unlined paper
- Rulers

- Fine-tipped markers

Create

These two-hour sessions are informal. The guest artist usually kicks the program off with a short presentation of about 20 to 30 minutes, depending on what he or she chooses to cover. The remainder of the time, the guest artist mingles with participants as they work and discuss the process. After the presentation, participants can get up and move about the room to check out what others are doing and chat.

Food, Technology, and Other Mandatory Extras

- Laptop with weekly PowerPoint presentation downloaded
- Access to the Internet
- Projector to show slide show or websites on a large screen
- An over-the-shoulder "comics" camera set up so participants can watch on a large screen as the presenter demonstrates drawing techniques
- Whiteboard and markers

Analysis

Attendance is consistently strong as participants get to know one another. Each session has newcomers checking out what the forum is all about. Most of the time some participants hang around after the end of the session and talk, using the library as a social meeting spot.

Marketing Tips

A five-by-eight-inch colorful postcard is created to advertise the inaugural round of six forums. This is in addition to the series being promoted in the teen brochure, on the library website, as well as on the websites of area comics artists.

Resource

Art & Story. 2010. Accessed August 31. http://www.cvcomics.com/artandstory/. [Weekly podcast by cartoonists Jerzy Drozd, Mark Rudolph, and Kevin Cross, who share their experiences making comics and try to wrap their brains around the larger ideas behind their chosen art form.]

Pinhole Photography

Information on the Pinhole Photography program was provided by Sharon Iverson, Teen Librarian at the Ann Arbor District Library.

General Description

Participants learn how pinhole photography works and then create their own pinhole camera and shoot several pictures. Their pinhole photographs are then exhibited in the library.

Pop

Pinhole photography is an old technology, but it still fascinates people both young and old. Using this simple camera, photographers can create pictures with "special effects," like ghosts lurking in the background, super large monsters, or speed blurs.

Relate

Besides being a lot of fun, pinhole photography requires the photographer to take time to think about the shot he or she wants to take, carefully set it up, and then take the shot. For teens used to instant gratification, having to wait several weeks for the pictures to be developed is both agonizing and rewarding.

Instructors/Talent

A local community member interested in this hobby presented the program.

Audience

Teens in grades 6 through 12.

Planning and Supplies

The presenter suggested a three-hour program to allow time to explain pinhole photography history and function, pinhole camera construction, and taking pictures. Each camera could shoot one picture at a time. A closet was set up as a darkroom for participants to exchange paper film negatives. To keep track of which pictures belonged to which photographer, each teen was assigned a number. A list containing each teen's name and number was compiled. Each teen received several white round stickers with his or her number. As pictures were taken, teens placed their number stickers on the back of the paper negative. This helped the presenter keep the developed pictures organized later.

Supplies

- Quart-sized paint can (to be made into a camera)
- Magnet tape roll
- Sharps
- Paper photo negatives
- White round sticker dots
- Black photo boxes
- High-gloss paper
- Pie pans
- Foam board

Create

The presenter talked about the history of photography and how early pinhole-style cameras worked. He showed pictures taken with a pinhole camera. Teens then learned how to build a camera and take pictures. Their cameras could hold just one negative; the teens entered the darkroom to "load" their cameras. They then took their pictures on library grounds and returned to the darkroom to unload the exposed negative and reload with a fresh negative. They tried a variety of angles and shots. The exposed negatives were developed by the presenter and placed on foam board for display. Months later, the photos were exhibited in the library. Teens, families, and friends were invited to a special opening night reception complete with refreshments.

Food, Technology, and Other Mandatory Extras

A laptop connected to the projector was needed for the history portion of the program and to show examples of pinhole photographs.

Analysis

The program was a big success. However, executing it was a logistical challenge. Once photographing began, the presenter spent all the time in the darkroom helping small groups of teens unload and load their cameras. If this part were botched, no pictures would turn out, because any light exposure could ruin both exposed and unexposed film. One library staff person needed to be outside to keep the eager teens from opening the darkroom door prematurely. Having another pinhole camera expert managing the darkroom would have freed the presenter to advise teens as they set up their shots. In the end, about 50 percent of the photos turned out, which is average for this primitive style of photography. The teens were pleased with the results and particularly with seeing their photos on display at the opening-night reception. A project like this one is also a great way to spruce up a part of the library with free artwork, and the fact that it is created by patrons of the library is a plus.

Marketing Tips

This was a summer program, so it was promoted via May school visits, in the teen brochure, on the library website, and in the local newspaper. It could also be promoted to middle and high school art instructors to pass along to their students.

Resource

Matt Callow Photography. http://mattcallow.com/.

Chapter 8

Programs: Celebrity and Reality Television

Reality television has become increasingly popular in the past decade and has been instrumental in making fame more possible for everyday teens and tweens. As *Star Search* did in the 1970s, today's television shows, like *American Idol*, *Project Runway*, and *Jersey Shore*, create opportunities for regular teens with talent (or not) to become famous on television. Many of the skill-based reality shows have highly creative premises, which can easily be translated to a fun program at the library. Plus, the already-instilled audience for these shows allows teens to meet other teens with the same passion for them.

Popular movies and television shows are also helpful in creating programs. Superhero movies are insanely popular, so put together a superhero drawing program or a costume contest. For tweens, *Wizards of Waverly Place* on the Disney Channel is a well-loved fantasy show; you could host a program on making wizard wands to celebrate the premiere of the new season. Get imaginative with creating programs using ideas from popular television and movies.

Top Chef Season 4 Winner, Stephanie Izard, Appearance and Cooking Demo

General Description

Stephanie Izard, a participant of the hit television show *Top Chef*, spoke to teens and adults about her experiences on the reality television show. It was a large-scale event due to the cost associated with securing the speaker and the cooking demo supplies, the large attendance (400), and the sheer number of details involved in the planning of the event. It was also an incredibly fun event on all levels. No matter where your library is located, there is surely someone from a popular reality television show who grew up, attended college, got married, or is otherwise associated with your town, region, or state. Assess what is popular on television with your teens to determine what would be best for your community. Doing a simple poll with your teens is a great way to find out what they are watching and chances are they know that "so-and-so who went to high school in town x was on *American Idol*." Use their interest as your guide.

Pop

Top Chef has been a popular reality television show on the cable channel Bravo since its debut in 2006. Teens are just as much in love with cooking and food television shows as the rest of America, so anytime you can combine cooking and food with a teen event, you are in good shape. Competition shows are also an incredibly popular subgenre of the reality television landscape. *Top Chef* has several cookbooks out now, and the show's hosts Padma Lakshmi and Tom Colicchio are now celebrities in their own right. The show has now morphed into *Top Chef Masters*, where established chefs compete for charity, and will soon debut a teen version of the show.

Relate

Every teen and youth librarian knows that anything relating to food will be popular with teens. An event like this serves several populations and interests at once. Teens interested in reality television will be drawn to a program like this, as will those interested in cooking shows or becoming a chef. In addition to being a popular television show, there are also now several books based on *Top Chef* that serve as supportive materials to the event. Titles include *How to Cook Like a Top Chef* (Miller, 2010), *Top Chef: The Quickfire Cookbook* (Miller, 2009), and *Top Chef: The Cookbook* (Martin, Krissoff, and Scheintaub, 2008). There is also a *Top Chef* Quickfire Challenge board game. In addition to these "official" *Top Chef* publications, there are many books written by former contestants and the show's hosts. For teens without access to cable television at home or those who have missed the previous season, DVDs are other materials to add to the library collection and support this event. Lastly, any program relating to a celebrity, especially when combined with a local angle, will resonate with a certain segment of your teen population. The incredible popularity of *Top Chef* is an easy way to justify any event of this nature.

Instructors/Talent

Locating your local reality television star is easier than you think. Ask your local teens and do research in local papers or websites to determine if anyone in your city, region, or state has ever been on a reality television show. Depending on their level of popularity and how far removed from the show they are, you should be prepared to pay speakers fees in the range of $200 to $2,000.

Audience

Grades 6 through 12 and adults. Parents with younger children were also able to attend because often the intense interest in the topic will usually keep the attention span of a younger person.

Planning and Supplies

During the booking phase of this event it was determined that another library in the area had also asked Stephanie Izard to speak. Working with another library is always a great way to pull off a more expensive event. In this case, the travel costs and arrangements were split between two library systems. When it came time to transport Izard between the two cities, the drivers met halfway; that way neither librarian had to do the longer drive and the library did not have to pay for transportation.

The planning aspect of this event was extensive. To find Izard's contact information, the television network Bravo was contacted, which gave the number for the public relations firm handling her public appearances. Depending on your speaker, you may be able to nail down many of the supplies and details early, but the nuts and bolts do not usually come together for an event like this until only a month or so before the engagement. Speakers are usually traveling constantly and can only concentrate on most any event about a month ahead of time.

Supplies

- Electric cooktops—the number depends on needs of the presenter
- Bowls
- Pans
- Knives
- Spatulas
- Whisk, serving utensils, etc. (Be prepared to supply whatever your presenter requests.)
- Food based on the shopping list of the presenter (Library staff took Izard to the grocery store and she picked out her ingredients.)
- Paper plates, napkins, and plastic forks for tastings
- Sous chef assistance (A couple of local culinary students and enthusiasts were asked to help Izard prepare the food before and during her presentation. These people were not compensated, as the thrill of meeting Izard was payment enough for them.)

Many of the preparation and cooking supplies were borrowed from a local deli, but you may have staff members who are willing to lend all of these supplies. While the library paid for the food used to cook at this event, you might also find a store willing to donate the food in exchange for a mention at the program or in publicity.

Create

The event itself was a traditional lecture environment with Izard speaking and doing a cooking demo and the audience sitting in chairs listening. She did a casual talk and took questions while she cooked three different recipes that she had created. Library staff handed out the samples to the audience as she spoke. In this case, the "creation" happened with Izard and the magic of her talk and Q&A. The attendees got to hear about her experiences on the show, behind-the-scenes secrets about the other contestants, and, most important, about her journey from being an undergrad at the University of Michigan to being a Top Chef. Many teens asked questions about her cooking and professional experiences in restaurants.

Food, Technology, and Other Mandatory Extras

The library conducted a podcast interview with Stephanie Izard, asking behind-the-scenes questions about *Top Chef*. The podcast is now archived on the library website for future listeners (http://www.aadl.org/video/feed/audio). The event was also taped and is available on the library website as video on demand (http://www.aadl.org/video). In addition, the event was broadcast on the local cable access channel. The technical services department at the library is already set up for taping, as they do this for many events, and has support staff to tape the event, edit, and produce the video. If you do not have this setup, look into purchasing a small camcorder for recording YouTube videos.

Analysis

This is one of the most popular events the library has ever hosted. More than 400 people attended the event, and of that audience about 80 of the attendees were teens. For many of those in the audience, this was the first time they had ever been to the library, and for others the first time they attended an event at the library. It was a great opportunity to change perceptions of the library. For many attendees, meeting Izard was a major highlight, so the association with the library was quite popular. Izard noted that she had a fun time visiting Ann Arbor and had a very changed perception of libraries as well.

Even though *Top Chef* may not always be as popular with teens, there will always be another reality television show that is popular. You could also spin off the idea of this event by having a "*Top Chef*-Style Competition" event for teens. Similarly, you could have chefs from popular restaurants in your community do a cooking demo and tasting. The possibilities for taking off from this program idea are endless.

Marketing Tips

This was an event with many bells and whistles. The library occasionally runs ads on local television channels for high-profile events or events whose audience, like *Top Chef*, warrant a television campaign. When the library runs an ad, it usually runs on Bravo, MTV, Comedy Central, and Cartoon Network. The channels were selected based on the targeted audience. For this event, an ad was run in the local newspaper advertising Stephanie Izard's scheduled appearance, and the event was put on the front page of the teen event brochure.

Resources

Check out these resources to create displays supporting this program:

Bravo Media. 2010. "Top Chef." Accessed September 2. http://www.bravotv.com/top-chef.

Martin, Brett, Liana Krissoff, and Leda Scheintaub. 2008. *Top Chef: The Cookbook*. San Francisco: Chronicle Books.

Miller, Emily Wise. 2009. *Top Chef: The Quickfire Cookbook*. San Francisco: Chronicle Books.

Miller, Emily Wise. 2010. *How to Cook Like a Top Chef*. San Francisco: Chronicle Books.

MTV: *Made*

General Description

This event model is applicable to any popular reality television show that features real tweens, teens, or young adults from your community or state. If a local young person has participated on a show that has an interesting, controversial, educational, or just plain fun plot with a competition or talent showcase, invite him or her to speak at the library. Dylan, a teen in Ann Arbor who appeared on MTV's *Made*, was a "class clown" in high school who wanted to become a fashion designer. Dylan and his clothes were also featured in the library *Project Runway* Fashion Show program discussed in a later section of this chapter.

Pop

Made is a show on MTV that allows a teen to realize a dream or goal in life. The show is described on the MTV website as "An ugly duckling transforms into a beautiful prom queen. An overweight couch potato becomes a model. A sci-fi nerd morphs into a hardcore rapper" (MTV Network, 2010). MTV, while slightly faded over the years, is still a helpful barometer for what is popular and compelling to some teens in your community. Simply using it as a reference point is a great advantage to marketing and gives you much potential to build a fun and compelling event. Since MTV is one of the main media sources that feature teens and showcases their talents on shows, it is a nice fit with the library model of enrichment and broadening horizons. MTV brings a diversity of faces and lifestyles into the living rooms of many teens who have never met teens "like that" before. Use MTV's riskiness to your advantage.

Relate

The best thing about this event is that it showcased a local teen to other area teens going out on a limb and not necessarily (by his own admission) succeeding. Many young people feel like "success" or doing something "big" comes when you are an adult, and the library is in a great position to expose them to opportunities they may not have known about previously. Fashion design is a very popular and competitive career path and it is a great opportunity to expose young people to the real work required to achieve that goal. An event like this is an occasion to market the fashion materials in your collection and let the audience know about the other resources your library can offer to further their interest. While there are no official MTV publications about the television show *Made*, there are plenty of fashion, sewing, and design books to purchase or put on display to support the program. More teen-friendly titles such as *Generation T: 108 Ways to Transform a T-Shirt* (Nicolay, 2006) or *AlterNation: Transform. Embellish. Customize* (Okey, 2007) are excellent additions to the library collection. Books that deal generally with teen creativity would also support the program, such as *Creative Expression Activities for Teens: Exploring Identity Through Art, Craft, and Journaling* (Thomas, 2010).

Instructors/Talent

This event comes down to access. Ideally, a teen in the general area or your state at large has appeared on a reality television show. MTV, Bravo, and the basic networks have some of the most popular reality television shows, but do not forget to check out athletic competitions, game shows, or poker events for potential local talent to invite a teen to present an event like this for the library. Locals are often more willing to speak gratis or for a smaller fee and won't require travel expenses. Also, even if they do use an agent or agency, you can potentially get in touch through a community connection. Of course, if you have a generous programming budget you can always hire anyone from a reality television show, local or not, to come and do a talk. Ex-reality television stars often make a nice living doing appearances and talking about their experiences. You can expect to pay anywhere from $500 to $10,000 (or more, depending) for a speaker from out of state, plus travel expenses. Be prepared to book through an agent, agency, or public relations firm in most cases.

Audience

This type of event can be targeted generally to a middle and high school audience and to young adults in their twenties and thirties. Also, as long as the content (your local star may have been on a show with drinking or sex, for example) is age appropriate—which, in the case of fashion design, it is—tweens can enjoy the event as well.

Planning and Supplies

Other than the items Dylan brought with him and coordination of his technology and display needs, there was not much to plan other than venue details.

Create

The event was a basic casual lecture, plus question and answer for the audience members. Dylan showed video clips from his episode, which were fun to watch and definitely enhanced by his accompanying commentary. He had slides and brought the clothes he made for the show for display during the event. Dylan's parents were also there, since they and other family members were on the show, and they answered some questions as well.

The beauty of this event is that the *Create* came from the young person showcased. Seeing a person their own age talk about his experiences and demonstrating confidence and creativity is important for other young people to see. Creating opportunities to learn something new and see things from a different viewpoint are important experiences to explore.

Food, Technology, and Other Mandatory Extras

A projector is required that can be hooked up to technology to access DVDs or stream the Internet in order to show the visual portions. Having the clothes on display was an added component that enhanced the program.

Analysis

This event attracted an enthusiastic and engaged variety of families: tweens, teens, and adults of various ages. The chance to showcase local talent is a great opportunity to put a face on something based in the mainstream media and provide your community access to how reality television "really" works.

Marketing Tips

Use MTV (or other channels for a similar event) to your advantage and employ a light and modern tone when writing the press releases and program descriptions. Take flyers or promos to local businesses, teen centers, and gathering spaces for teens and young adults. Do direct marketing to sewing stores, local sewing or fashion-interest groups, which you may be able to locate via Meetup.com, for example. Make sure middle and high school art teachers and counselors know so they might target teens that they know have a particular interest in fashion. Put flyers in the fashion magazines in your collection. If your marketing budget is generous, run an ad on cable to reach your potential audience where their attention is likely already focused.

Resources

Check out these books as supporting materials for the collection:

Nicolay, Megan. 2006. *Generation T: 108 Ways to Transform a T-Shirt.* New York: Workman.

Okey, Shannon. 2007. *AlterNation: Transform. Embellish. Customize.* Cincinnati, OH: North Light Books.

Thomas, Bonnie. 2010. *Creative Expression Activities for Teens: Exploring Identity Through Art, Craft, and Journaling.* Philadelphia: Jessica Kingsley Publishers.

Check out these websites for more information:

MTV Network. 2010. "Dylan Is *Made* into a Fashion Designer: Ep. 705." Accessed September 2. http://www.mtv.com/shows/made/episode.jhtml?episodeID= 106703.

MTV Network. 2010. "Made." Accessed September 2. http://www.mtv.com/ shows/made/series.jhtml.

Project Runway Fashion Show or Challenge

General Description

Project Runway is a popular fashion design television show on the cable station Lifetime. This event can take a variety of forms based on how simple, complicated, or involved you want it to be. The basic idea is to have teens apply to be in the fashion show with a portfolio, sketches, samples, etc. The teens would have several months to create their outfits (two to six is realistic for most teens) and would then show their creations during a runway show with models. Depending on the community, expect anywhere from a handful to 20 teens to try out for the show. Other options for an event like this would be to have local boutiques or department stores showcase local fashions at the library. A local college or university might have a fashion program and their students could also show at the library, with the instructor talking about careers in fashion. As an alternative, hold a simple event (competitive or not, although the television show is a competition) where clothing that can be altered is provided, such as donated prom dresses, cloth scraps, old clothes teens bring themselves, or other creative materials. This idea is modeled after the unusual challenges on the television show *Project Runway*. Teens would have a time limit on how long they would have during the "challenge" to create a new look.

Pop

Project Runway has been one of the most popular competition reality television shows among young people of all ages. The show is a fashion design competition where a group of adults ranging in age from twenties to fifties compete in a series of difficult challenges to design outfits. Each week a panel of judges composed of models, designers, and fashion experts sends one designer home. A final group of three or four designers creates a 12-piece fashion collection and competes to win money and the support to create a full clothing line, among other prizes. The show debuted on Bravo in 2004, and moved to the Lifetime channel in 2009. The show's colorful contests and judges continue to fuel its popularity. Fashion is always a popular topic to use with tween and teen programming because that is often when they are their most creative and uninhibited. Showcasing creativity and artistic expression is an excellent cultural touchstone.

Relate

This event was teen-driven. A teen brought the idea to the library and helped plan it. The teen was given the opportunity to plan, organize, and lead the event, and because it was teen-driven it was easy to generate peer interest. An event about fashion that celebrates teen talent and creative expression is a character-building experience and an opportunity to showcase the fashion-design materials in your collections and other resources that can assist teens interested in pursuing fashion as a career.

Instructors/Talent

It is possible to host this event entirely without hiring someone, but the program would be better if talent, fashion instructors, fashion designers, or models spoke or were otherwise involved with the event.

Audience

If the event includes a runway show featuring teen designs, plan on an audience of all ages. Family and friends of the teen, the designers, and the models will want to attend. If doing a hands-on design event or challenge, teens are your primary audience. Tweens and adults in their twenties, thirties, and forties might also be interested, so either make sure the competition is broken up by age group or consider doing separate programs for these different age groups.

Planning and Supplies

Planning is crucial for a runway show event.

- If you have teens apply to participate, you must create an application, guidelines, or criteria (see Figure 8.1).
- Create submission session guidelines for interviewing teens interested in showing their work in a fashion show (see Figure 8.2).
- Regular communication with the teens about progress, finding models, etc., is crucial.
- Live or recorded music will have to be coordinated.
- Consider having a committee of teens help with the planning.
- If only a handful of teens show clothing, the show could be over in five to ten minutes, so having other speakers or activities is crucial. A local teacher, designer, business owner, or enthusiast could speak about the fashion industry or fashion design as a career. A boutique or department store could display dresses, provide the models and clothing, or participate in the runway show if not enough teens participate. A local model or someone who works at a modeling agency could talk about that side of the business. If there is a fashion design college program in your area, ask if its students could show their designs.
- Models are a very important consideration. If teens show their own work, then have it be part of the commitment that they provide their own models. If you work with a boutique or department store, they will usually supply the models.
- If the library does not have a suitable space with good lighting or a sound system, consider partnering with a local teen center, community center, or school to see if the event could be held there. If local teens are spotlighted, it is easier to get other agencies serving those same teens to volunteer their space.

When doing a hands-on event or competition, supplies make the program more extensive.

- Clothing or dress donations will have to be sought, resale clothing purchased, fabric scraps purchased, or participants must bring clothing themselves.
- Hand sewing or hot gluing are the easiest and most affordable options.
- Borrowing sewing machines from staff or a local business is an option, although it will involve a lot more work and coordination. Consider liability issues as well, since something may happen to a machine while in the library's care.
- Beads, sequins, and other embellishments can be sewn or glued on as well.
- Fabric markers will allow teens to write text or create patterns on their creations.

Figure 8.1. Project Design: High School Fashion Show

The first ever [*your city/library name here*] fashion design event is a juried design exhibition. If you design and sew your own clothes, you are invited to submit your work for the fashion show. This is not a competition. This is a juried event and submitting your work does not guarantee you a spot in the runway show to be held on [*x date*].

Submission Panel Sessions

List dates and locations.

Submission Guidelines and Details

1. Eligibility: Students in grades 9 through 12.
2. You must attend a Submission Panel Session to enter your work into the exhibition.
3. <u>You must bring the following to the submission panel sessions</u>: Sketches/drawings of your designs and a written description of your fashion philosophy (not to exceed 500 words).
4. You will complete an entry form when you arrive for the panel session. You must also bring copies (not originals) of your philosophy statement and your sketches. These will be used by the panel to make their decisions and will not be returned to you.
5. You may bring (but are not required to bring) any of the following: photos of your designs, letters of recommendation or any awards you may have won, samples of clothes you have created and any other visuals or hands-on materials. You will not leave any of the items with the panel.
6. You will have five minutes to present your work to the panel. Be prepared to answer questions from the panel about your work and your fashion philosophy.
7. You will be notified by [*x date*] whether your work has been selected for the runway fashion show on [*x date*].

What Else You Need to Know (rules, judging details, etc.):

1. Teens must design and sew their clothing themselves. However, some assistance with construction is permitted.
2. Once you have been notified of your acceptance in the fashion show, you will have six weeks to create a minimum of two complete outfits (maximum six outfits). An outfit must be a head-to-toe look. Store-bought accessories are allowable.
3. You will be required to preview your completed work two weeks prior to the fashion show.
4. You must provide your own models for your creations.

The Project Design Runway Show will be held on [*x date*].

Figure 8.2. Project Design: Submission Session Guidelines

Questions/Information for Entrants:

1. Welcome the teens and ask them if they have any questions before you begin.
2. In general, we want to be sure that the skin/cloth ratio of the designs favors the cloth. No see-through shirts, blouses, no halter tops, tank tops/tube tops, undershirts, muscle shirts, or other tops that expose the midriff. Shorts and skirts must be size appropriate (arm extended straight down at sides, shorts or skirt bottom reaches fingertips); excessively tight-fitting designs are prohibited.
3. What about this opportunity excited you enough to come today?
4. Can you tell us about your sketches and about your designs?
5. What were your inspirations?
6. Do you have any designers that you admire?
7. Do you read about fashion? If so, what do you read?
8. Are there any movies or TV shows that have inspired your love of fashion?
9. Do you plan to pursue fashion after high school as a career?
10. Please tell us about your fashion philosophy.
11. Why do you think we should choose your designs for the show?

Judging Criteria

Please use the following areas to judge the submitted work. Use a 10-point range to assign points in each of the areas, 1 being the lowest score and 10 being the highest. Circle the score you have assigned for each area. Space is provided to take notes as needed. These notes will help remind you of your likes/dislikes and specific details.

Creativity/Originality

(The ability to transcend traditional ideas, rules, patterns, relationships, or the like, and to create meaningful new forms, interpretations, etc.; progressiveness, or imagination. Does the teen's design fulfill these expectations?)

1   2   3   4   5   6   7   8   9   10

Overall Look/Styling
(Does the presentation look like a complete outfit, ready to leave the house? Is the styling consistent and well done from head to toe? Does it look like care was given to all aspects of the design, including clothing and accessories? Do the accessories complement the designs with use of color/shape, etc.?)

1   2   3   4   5   6   7   8   9   10

(Continued)

Figure 8.2 *(Continued)*

Shape/Form/Line
(Does the design look pleasing to the eye and to the contours of the body? Are the lines complementary to the body? Do the shapes appear as though they complement each other?)

1   2   3   4   5   6   7   8   9   10

Sketches
(Did the sketches give you a good impression of what the clothing might look like? Were they presented in a fairly neat and organized fashion?)

1   2   3   4   5   6   7   8   9   10

Fashion Philosophy
(Do you get a sense of how the teen feels about fashion? Was it well written and presented? Did the philosophy reveal knowledge of fashion?)

1   2   3   4   5   6   7   8   9   10

TOTAL POINTS:

If tie-breaking is needed when you compile totals later on, we will use these additional categories to break those ties. Assign each area a score from 1 to 10.

Enthusiasm/Fashion Passion

1   2   3   4   5   6   7   8   9   10

Color
(Is the use of color complementary? Is it pleasing to the eye? Does the use of color attract your eye? Does the use of color evoke an emotional response in you?)

1   2   3   4   5   6   7   8   9   10

Create

If planning a runway show, arrange for a 30- to 45-minute event. If teens show their own work, it is important that family and friends and the other audience members enjoy a robust event with the teens as the centerpiece. Determine what and how many other elements to include at the event. It is best to save the exhibition of the teens' work for last so it is the final presentation that the audience sees. Whether you have other speakers, show excerpts from *Project Runway,* or boutique or department store model popular designs, the event should conclude with the teen-designed runway show.

- Music is crucial, so consider having a live DJ (perhaps a local teen or young adult) or teen-selected recorded music.
- If models must change into their outfits, a private changing area will be necessary.

If you do a hands-on event, leave it as open and unrestricted as possible. Allow the teens the freedom to make whatever they want. If the event is a competition, then clear and simple guidelines must be presented. If prizes are given out, the rules must be fair to all. Prizes could include gift certificates for a fabric store, or for a class at a store or school.

Food, Technology, and Other Mandatory Extras

For a runway event that celebrates teen work, consider having light refreshments before the event starts to offer a more "art opening" vibe and also to make it more special for the teens. Music and audio are important. While a CD player or MP3 player with speakers will work, ideally a sound system would make the event more professional. Lowered lighting and spotlights on the runway would also lend an air of authenticity to the event. Whatever can be done to replicate a runway environment will help.

Analysis

The runway event held at the library featured a total of nine designs by three teen girl designers. The girls located their own models and handled hair and makeup. A professor from a local university spoke about fashion as a career, and three of her students also showcased their work. Dylan from MTV's *Made* series (a program discussed earlier in this section) also showed his clothing designs. A local model who has been doing runway shows for many years spoke about her experiences at shows and shared humorous anecdotes. Ultimately, the program was a success with more than 100 attendees, but detailed pre-planning was required.

Marketing Tips

For a teen-centered runway show, ask the teens to help promote the event at their schools, in their neighborhoods, and to their family and friends. Promote the event directly to local schools with a focus on art teachers and counselors. Put up flyers or take brochures to boutiques that sell fashion-forward clothes and to schools who have fashion programs.

Resource

Check out this website to learn more about the television show:

My Lifetime. 2010. "*Project Runway.*" Accessed September 2. http://www.mylifetime .com/shows/project-runway.

Silent Library

General Description

Shhhh! The goal is to stay silent in the library! Teens participate in challenges but must stay silent while doing them. The last person with his or her lips sealed receives a prize.

Pop

Silent Library is a segment on a popular Japanese variety show called *Downtown no Gaki no Tsukai ya Arahende!!* and has been developed into a game show aired on MTV. Six players are seated around a study table in a library. Each player flips a card. Five of the cards are "safe" cards, while the last card has a skull and crossbones. The unlucky player to flip this card must do a bizarre challenge. To win the challenge, the noise level must stay below the red zone on the on-screen gauge. The unusual challenges include drinking a glass of grape juice freshly stomped by a woman with dirty feet or chewing through a pair of meat suspenders until the pants they are holding up fall down.

Relate

Obesity is an important topic in our society today. According to the American Heart Association, the number of overweight children between ages 12 and 19 increased from 6.1 percent in a 1971–1974 study, to 17.6 percent in a 2003–2006 study. Promoting physical activities in the library is a way to promote healthy living in the community. This program will not necessarily break teens into a sweat (though it could, depending on your programming space), but it is a step in the right direction for getting kids active.

Instructors/Talent

None needed.

Audience

Choosing either teens or tweens for this program would work very well. It will be much harder for the tweens to stay quiet.

Planning and Supplies

Most of the challenges actually done on the show are too painful or humiliating to do in a library setting, such as having people eat hot soup over the participant. Use the stunts from another show, *Fear Factor*, as inspiration for your challenges—for example, eating bugs and strange foods. Check with your library to see if you should have release forms signed for those challenges for liability reasons.

Minute to Win It games were used in this program. All the instructions for each game are on the website listed in the Resources section. Most of the supplies needed are things found around the library, such as toilet paper, rubber bands, or empty soda cans. If you are using *Minute to Win It* challenges, you will need a stopwatch as well, because each stunt must be completed in 60 seconds. Prizes for the quietest teen could range from gift cards, copying the television show which gives out cash prizes, or something as cheap and simple as coupons to local restaurants. The prizes need not be spectacular because the fun of the program is participating in the strange and unusual challenges.

Create

It is important to have a large programming room or space to do this program. Some of the challenges need space, plus everyone wants to watch the competitor do something silly and not make a sound. Set up your room with a few tables for tabletop stunts and chairs for the teens waiting for their turn to do a challenge. For large groups, you may have teens do the stunts in groups so that each person does not have to wait too long to do a challenge (see Figure 8.3). Most teens will act irritated when they receive the unlucky card calling them out to participate in a challenge, but most of them secretly would like to do all of the challenges.

In this particular program, the large group was broken into groups of six. Each of the six stands around a table and receives a card. Everyone flips the card at the same time. The person with the joker has to complete a challenge. Challenges are chosen by picking a slip of paper out of a cup.

An example stunt that went over well is the "Face the Cookie" challenge listed on the *Minute to Win It* television show website. To complete the challenge, teens must move three Oreo cookies, one by one, from their foreheads to their mouths only using their faces. No hands are allowed. Those three cookies must be in their mouths in 60 seconds, and it is hysterical to watch! Only cookies are needed for this stunt.

The quiet component was self-monitored. Once a teen was out of the running for the prize, he or she stayed and laughed at the crazy stunts. The teens were also a great help with taking pictures while staff focused attention on setting up the stunts.

Food, Technology, and Other Mandatory Extras
None needed.

Analysis

An idea for keeping track of those who have not spoken is to have everyone wear a colored sticker. When a person talks or laughs, the sticker gets taken away. This gives you a way to visually see who is still in the game for the prize. This idea will probably not work if you have a very sensitive audience. Hurt feelings may be smoothed over by giv-

Figure 8.3. Teen Drinking from a Shoe during a *Silent Library* Challenge at the Monrovia (CA) Public Library

ing everyone a snack for participating and the silent winner a $5 gift certificate to a local store.

Marketing Tips

If it is possible to spend some money on commercial spots, it would be helpful to put up on ad on MTV to attract all those fans of the *Silent Library* game show. Also target anime clubs and fans of Japanese culture with flyers or post messages on their Facebook pages.

Resources

Check out these websites for ideas on challenges:

MTV Network. 2010. "*Silent Library.*" Accessed September 2. http://www.mtv .com/shows/silent_library/series.jhtml.

NBC. 2010. "*Minute to Win It.*" Accessed September 2. http://www.nbc.com/ minute-to-win-it/.

Superhero Smashup

General Description

In reaction to the superhero craze, a workshop was put together to teach patrons how to draw well-known superheroes and design their own superhero persona to create a comic strip.

Pop

Bringing superheroes to life from comic books to the big screen has become a popular trend in the 2000s. Fans are embroiled in the Marvel versus DC Comics battle, trying to choose who will win in a fight: Superman or Iron Man. The popular *X-Men* movie franchise has announced the *X-Men Origins* series, promising many movies to come, each focusing on a character from the popular superhero team. Remakes of such recognized characters as Batman, the Green Hornet, Wonder Woman, and the Green Lantern are also in the works, assuring the teen librarian profession many great years of material to utilize for programming.

Relate

Teens who enjoy superhero movies will enjoy this program, as will teens who like to draw. It is a great way for teens to show off their creative skills while creating their own characters and to highlight the library's graphic novel section, drawing books, and potentially the DVD collection.

Instructor/Talent

A local comic artist was asked to run a two-hour workshop, discussing how to develop a superhero character and how to effectively communicate story through a visual narrative. The program could be shortened and does not need to be so technical. It also does not necessarily need to be run by a professional if there is no local talent in your area or you need to save money. There are many books and websites to help you become a drawing expert.

Audience

Grades 6 through 12. The program could be done for younger tweens, but you must keep in mind the program involves a lot of sitting and listening to the instructor, so concentration skills and being able to sit still are needed.

Planning and Supplies

- White copy paper
- Pencils

- Colored pencils
- Rulers

Create

Strike a balance between teaching the skill of drawing and allowing time for drawing. Most teens do not want to sit and listen to a lecture, and you do not want your program to seem too much like school. It should be fun and enjoyable, keeping to the methodology that the library is for learning as well as for entertainment.

Start by asking the teens to brainstorm possible superhero powers and gadgets, and write the ideas where everyone can see them. This will help give them ideas for drawing their own superheroes later. Then lead the group in the basic drawing of one superhero of your choice, a popular character or one of your own creations.

Food, Technology, and Other Mandatory Extras

Having examples of superhero characters or ideas of potential superpowers and gadgets is always helpful for beginning drawers. Search your collection and the Internet for ideas.

Analysis

This program can be executed on many different levels. It can be an in-depth workshop on the technical aspects of cartooning, creating characters, and storyboarding; teaching how to create a comic from beginning to end. The program can also be as simple as explaining how to draw superheroes using examples from books and websites. Create the program according to how much your audience can handle. Another consideration that will help promote interest in the program is to plan to have the event near the premiere of a new superhero movie. Excitement will be in the air, and teens will be motivated to develop their own superheroes' personalities.

Marketing Tips

E-mail local middle school and high school art teachers about the program, and ask if they will give extra credit for participation. Also promote this program to anime and manga fans, as they are sometimes comic book and superhero enthusiasts as well. Make sure to let local comic book stores know about the program, and ask to leave small posters or flyers at the counter.

Resources

Use these books to help when designing the drawing program:

Amara, Philip. 2001. *So, You Wanna Be A Comic Book Artist?* Hillsboro, OR: Beyond Books.

Ames, Lee J. 1983. *Draw 50 Monsters, Creeps, Superheroes, Demons, Dragons, Nerds, Dirts, Ghouls, Giants, Vampires, Zombies, and Other Curiosa. . . .* New York: Random House Children's Books.

Chapter 9

Programs: Contests

Contests are healthy competition and a great way to freshen up a tried-and-true teen/tween programming model with elements of pop culture. Passive contests that include creation of materials outside the library can attract new users who may have been too shy to engage in library activities previously. Teens are probably creating their own YouTube videos, dabbling in photography, or recording their own beats and music using various types of technology. A contest would allow them to send in or drop off their creations for a chance at being validated with a big prize or at least recognition in the form of library display space or at a battle of the bands.

Graffiti Contest

The Graffiti Contest program was written and contributed by Vicki Browne, Teen Librarian at the Ann Arbor District Library.

General Description

During the Ann Arbor Art Fair, the library sponsors a Teen Graffiti Art Contest for area teens. Teens have 15 minutes to create a masterpiece using spray paint as their medium. Prizes are awarded at the end of the program to three winners, and the artwork is displayed in the library for a month.

Pop

The power of the spray can! A picture is displayed in minutes, empowering teens in their artistic creativity. Graffiti dates all the way back to when the Romans "tagged" their name on the buildings they conquered. New York City is where graffiti first became popular in the United States. It started on the sides of railway cars and quickly turned into a competition between artists to create works of self-expression. Starting as an underground art movement, it is found in many urban settings and became widespread in the 1980s as hip-hop culture extended across the country. While graffiti can be used to beautify otherwise grimy neighborhoods, it also has an association with gang activity, and the term has developed negative connotations over the years. Giving teens a productive place to develop their skills helps improve the perception of graffiti as an art form, as opposed to associating it with vandalism.

Relate

Rather than saying "Don't paint here" or Don't paint this," the library can encourage freedom of expression. This program may work very well in urban settings. Teens are also given a venue for showing their work if the library has room to create a display for the finished artwork. Many teens never have the opportunity to showcase their art, and it is another way to empower your local teen population.

Instructors/Talent

Often the contest's judge will talk about styles, techniques, and give feedback on the artists' works. Look into your community for local artists who specialize in graffiti as an art form, and ask them to serve as judges. Check with local art schools or art programs.

Audience

Grades 6 through 12.

Planning and Supplies

Supplies are purchased for the teens to use, which includes a variety of colored spray paint, nozzles, latex gloves, and paint masks. The tempered board, a thin, three-by-two-foot board, is purchased from a local lumber company and primed with white paint. The remaining supplies are all available from craft and art supply stores. The library was lucky enough to have talented staff in the facilities department make simple wooden easels to prop up the boards. The easels are reused every year.

Create

The program takes place in the library staff parking lot, and staff is asked to park elsewhere during the event (see Figure 9.1). Painter's plastic is put on any part of the library building that may get paint blown in its direction. Teens sign a registration form which allows us to exhibit their art at the library and also signifies that they understand that no "gang graffiti" artwork will be accepted. Volunteer staff members pass out supplies, and about a dozen teens can paint at once. While teens are waiting to paint, they can work on sketching out their ideas. Each teen has about 15 minutes to create his or her masterpiece. Allow two hours for the entire program.

Teens that finish their paintings early are encouraged to return at the end of the program and watch the judging. Finished boards are propped up around the library parking lot to dry and remain there so that they are available for judging. Prizes are gift

Figure 9.1. Graffiti Contest at the Ann Arbor District Library

certificates for art supplies at a local store. All canvases, labeled with the artist's name and grade, similar to a real art show, are displayed at the library for a month to share with the community. Then the teens can stop by and claim their works to keep.

Food, Technology, and Other Mandatory Extras

If this program happens during the summer, have a water cooler available for the teens.

Analysis

The program can be a stand-alone or a way for the library to contribute to a local festival or celebration. It is great outreach to show the community the caliber of program for teens that the library offers. Also, have big, old T-shirts available as smocks to protect the clothing of the teens participating in the event.

Marketing Tips

The library is able to schedule the contest during a citywide annual art fair so there is usually a sizable crowd, as it is advertised along with other art fair events. Advertise to local art programs and at art supply stores.

Resources

Check out these books to learn more about the history of graffiti and techniques:

Ganz, Nicholas. 2009. *Graffiti World: Street Art from Five Continents*. New York: Abrams.

Martinez, Scape. 2009. *GRAFF: The Art & Technique of Graffiti*. Cincinnati, OH: Impact.

Photography Contest

General Description

Pick a theme of some sort, like spring, summer, animals, or pets, and craft a basic photo contest for teens. Guidelines and rules will have to be formulated and a timeline planned. Then display the entries in the library and online if possible.

Pop

Teens see the world differently than adults and are always looking for ways to explore their point of view. Since it is increasingly popular for teens to have their own cell phones with cameras, you can use this angle in the photo contest. New cameras and apps with special effects are always coming out, and a photo contest is a way to play off that.

Relate

A photo contest is a great way to meet teens where they are at and showcase their talents and their points of view. Because entries for the photo contest are prepared at home, it just might reach some of the shyer or quiet teens who are looking for ways to be involved.

Instructors/Talent

No talent is required to run a photo contest, but you should consider finding photographers on the library staff or in the community to be judges for the contest.

Audience

A photo contest can be held for all ages, including teen categories such as grades 6 through 8 and 9 through 12, or it can be a contest just for teens.

Planning and Supplies

The planning for a photo contest will be all done up front. Come up with guidelines and rules for the contest, determine the date by which entries are due, and also the format in which those entries must be submitted. If the plan is to display the photos in the library, then it is best to require that entrants submit an actual photo and have it mounted on paper with their name. This way library staff will not have to spend time mounting photos and labeling the entries. Some photo contests are held online only to avoid dealing with the display of photos. Consider the following:

- How many entrants are allowed per person?
- What should the size of entries be?
- Will the photos be submitted in person at one location or by mail?
- Will there be an awards ceremony?
- What about prizes?

The contest can be as simple or as complicated as the planning allows for. In terms of supplies, they are minimal. If entrants are required to mount the entries, then staff will have only to locate a place to display them, provide pins for hanging the photos, and obtain prizes for the winners (if prizes are being given).

Create

This event is really all about the participants. The creation part happens with the teens and with the opportunity provided to them. Judging is an important component. Timing on judging can be difficult, so it is important to build in time between when entries are due, when judging happens, and when the display goes up. These dates and times should be stated into your contest guidelines. If the planning is done well, then the only "how" is perhaps an award ceremony. This can be very simple, with entrants gathering around the display and staff announcing the winners; or a reception atmosphere can work, with refreshments available, patterned after an art opening. Then, if there are winners to announce, this can be done at the end of the reception.

Food, Technology, and Other Mandatory Extras

Having photo entries available online on the library website is a nice addition to offer. These "galleries" can serve as publicity for future contests and are a lasting reminder to the teens about their participation. Having a reception with refreshments is also a nice touch.

Analysis

With any contest there will be a learning curve based on experience. There will always be a few things that come up due to participant questions or something that did not work that can be tweaked for the next year. Fairness and planning are the main things to focus on. As long as all involved feel that the judging was fair and enjoy seeing their photos on display, it is a successful event.

Marketing Tips

Market your theme well and get the word out to schools and art teachers. If the theme changes often to add freshness to the program, it will be something the teens look forward to year after year.

Resources

Check out these books for tips on photography:

Campbell, Mark. 2006. *Digital Photography for Teens*. Boston, MA: Course Technology.
Gaines, Thom. 2010. *Digital Photo Madness! 50 Weird and Wacky Things to Do with Your Digital Camera*. New York: Lark Books.
Wignall, Jeff. 2009. *Winning Digital Photo Contests*. New York: Lark Books.

LEGO Contest

General Description

This is a one-night-only LEGO contest that asks participants to create their projects at home and then bring them to the library for judging. The projects are available for viewing by the public on that day, and the contest ends with the awards ceremony. The event is in large part created by the users themselves. You will have to provide the venue, come up with rules, provide prizes, and then harness the enthusiasm. Summer is usually the best time to host an event like this since it is when kids and teens have the most free time on their hands to work on their projects. You will note that this contest does not include long-term display of the entries of winners. Without large, locking, and secure display cases it is not recommended to display the entries for longer periods of time when 100 percent staff presence cannot be guaranteed. Theft is an unfortunate reality considering how expensive LEGO sets are. Consider display issues carefully before making the decision.

Pop

LEGO has been a popular toy in the United States since its debut in its current form in the 1950s. Year after year, LEGO adds new themes and sets and now includes many popular TV and movie tie-ins, robots, and architecture sets. Aside from the toys, however, LEGO has further infiltrated popular culture with their popular video games, books, and of course the many stop-motion LEGO videos fans have uploaded to

YouTube. Further cementing their popularity have been their LEGO retail stores (over 30 in the United States alone) and their popular LEGO-Land theme parks.

Relate

Librarians often bemoan how difficult it is to get boys engaged in the library. LEGO is the single easiest way to engage and excite many boys in your community. While LEGO does appeal to both sexes, the most avid fans tend to be males, and holding a LEGO contest is a sure way to increase the number of boys your library reaches. LEGO enthusiasts are passionate about creating with LEGO and also enjoy looking at what others have created. A LEGO contest is an easy way to meet your users where they are at while rewarding their enthusiasm for LEGO with prizes!

Instructors/Talent

You surely have staff members or community members who are LEGO enthusiasts. Use these enthusiasts to conduct your judging. These people can help you determine the judging categories to use, guidelines, and other changes to the rules you might make for your community. (See Figure 9.2.) A local man who runs an annual educational LEGO event every year for families in the community was a judge for the event. Contacting local hobby and toy stores would also be another option for locating a LEGO hobbyist. However, in terms of conducting an event like thies, you do not need to be a LEGO fan yourself.

Audience

LEGO fans come in all ages and the library runs its contest for preschoolers through grade 12. While high school tends to be the smallest category in terms of the number of entrants, it is also the category that often has the most sophisticated entries, which everyone loves to look at. One high school entry included a replica of the family's ancestral castle in Europe.

Planning and Supplies

The bulk of the planning for an event like this is up front, when you create your rules and guidelines. Once your guidelines are released, you will need to work on getting prizes, getting medals (if you decide to give them out), and planning the details of the day of the event. Having a large enough space may be your biggest concern. The library's contest eventually outgrew its largest meeting room, so the event now uses an off-site location. Obviously, this is a budget consideration, if you go that route. In some communities it might work to trade with another organization or make other arrangements to have access to a larger space. If you do not have a large space then limit the maximum size that entries can be. However, the fewer limits the better, in order to fully encourage creativity.

Figure 9.2. LEGO Contest Rules and Guidelines

Your Library Presents: <u>Annual LEGO Contest Rules and Guidelines</u>
Awards Ceremony—When and Where: _____
Prizes will be awarded in five categories:
   Preschool, Grades K-2, Grades 3-5, Grades 6-8, and Grades 9-12

Prizes:
Within each category there will be three winners:
   1st Place, 1st Runner-Up, and 1st Honorable Mention

Winners will receive gift certificates for Toys 'R' Us in the amounts of $35.00, $25.00, and $15.00, respectively. Winners will also receive prize ribbons.

Prize ribbons will also be awarded in each category for the following:
   Best Motorized Project; Best Architectural/Engineering Project; Coolest Robot; Best Vehicle; Most Creative; Most Sophisticated, and [Your Library] LEGO Master Builder

Every entrant will receive a certificate of participation.

Rules:
1. Use your own LEGO, Duplo, Mega blocks, or other LEGO-compatible plastic bricks.
2. Entries must be your own creation, not a LEGO-designed kit, project found online, in a magazine, etc.
3. One entry per participant or team, where applicable.
4. Your creation must fit within a space of 24 inches by 24 inches. Your completed project may be no taller than four feet.
5. Team projects will be placed in the category of the oldest participant in the team. Individual entries will not be permitted for team participants. Please note that while all members of a team will receive a certificate and a prize ribbon (if applicable) for participation, a team will compete for a single prize.
6. Include a label/sign that explains the idea/inspiration for your creation to help the judges make their determinations.
7. Please provide a sign/label with your project with your name(s), grade(s), and phone number(s).
8. Completed projects must be delivered to _____ on _____ between 9 a.m. and 4 p.m.
9. Judging will be conducted the evening of _____ at _____ by a team of adult LEGO enthusiasts.
10. The doors will open at 7 p.m. to allow for the entries to be viewed by the public.
11. The awards ceremony will begin at _____.
12. Completed entries *must* be taken home on the evening of _____.

For more information, please contact _____.

PARENTS: If you authorize that your child's work or image may be considered for display and/or promotion of [Your Library] programming and services, please also complete the talent release form.

Disclaimer: LEGO is a trademark of the LEGO Group of companies which does not sponsor, authorize, or endorse this contest.

For the day of the event you will need the following:

- Tables, enough to cover the number of entrants you either anticipate or can estimate based on past events. With almost 100 entries, the library started with ten six-foot tables.
- Signage labeling each table and category
- Signs telling the public "do not touch" the entries
- Entry forms (this is helpful in keeping a tally of all attendees too)
- Amplification system to read out the winners

Create

On the day of the LEGO contest, the actual event takes four forms:

- Drop-off time: This is an excellent time for staff to meet and greet users as they drop off their projects, talk up other events, and have more one-on-one time with the young people than will be available later in the day. Have staff stationed during the entire drop-off period, and handle the intake of projects as they are dropped off. When you are planning your drop-off time, consider offering the evening before the event, say from 5 to 9 p.m. This allows daytime working families a chance to participate. Doing this will mean more staff time and that your room will be further occupied, so it might not always be possible, but it is something to consider.
- Judging/photography: Once the doors are closed, the judges can work together to make their decisions. Having your judges involved during the planning of the contest will help make the judging process go more smoothly. Allowing your judges the freedom to come up with their own method for determining the winners is the best thing you can do. Try not to micromanage your judges. The library allows three hours to conduct the judging. With well over 100 entries at this point, time is of the essence. During the judging, staff can take pictures of the entries. Two people will be needed to take pictures. Use the photographer's trick of holding up two white pieces of foam core to put around the entry as you take the photo to create a neutral background.
- Viewing: From 7 to 8 p.m. the library allows the public to come and view all of the entries. Many people who didn't enter the contest will come to view the entries, but the room is mostly filled with the families of the entrants. Be prepared for a large crowd! Take every entry and multiply it by at least three to guess how many people will attend the event (see Figure 9.3).
- Award ceremony: Starting at 8 p.m., library staff take to the microphone and welcome the attendees, announce other library events, and then begin the award

ceremony. Experience has taught us to ask the attendees to wait until the *end* of the ceremony to take their projects home with them, if possible. This will avoid the rudeness and disruption of winners trying to leave while you are still announcing winners in other categories. As winners are announced the medals and gift certificates are handed out. Consider how crowded the front of the room will get when planning the event and looking at your space. It is easy to lose control during this phase without enough planning.

In this case, again, it is the users themselves who get the opportunity to create. The library's role is mainly in creating the platform and the opportunity. When a tween or teen is awarded for excellence in LEGO building, it may often trump other more traditional awards because it acknowledges a love and interest that he or she is not often rewarded for. Any opportunity to reward a young person for creativity is a good thing. The library's role here is coming up with fun and exciting categories and great prizes.

Figure 9.3. LEGO Contest

Food, Technology, and Other Mandatory Extras

Taking photos of the entries is a wonderful added extra that your contest can offer. You can create a visual display of the event on a bulletin board or library website so patrons can continue to enjoy the event long after it is over for this year.

Analysis

LEGO events have continued to be popular in libraries year after year. At the library, the annual LEGO contest has grown in size every year and has become one of the most eagerly anticipated events. There is not much in libraries teens wait for with baited breath! You will find that the bang for the buck in engagement and new users that a successfully run LEGO event will garner is worth every penny. If you have a limited budget, hold a LEGO event.

Marketing Tips

The program is advertised in the summer reading program flyer, with directions to stop by the library or visit the library website for a copy of the rules and guidelines. The program is also promoted by a local LEGO enthusiast who runs another family LEGO event in town. Look for local groups or message boards online to post details about the event.

Resources

Check out these resources for help with a LEGO program:

Bedford, Allan. 2005. *The Unofficial LEGO Builders Guide.* San Francisco: No Starch Press.

Bulger, Aaron. 2010. "LEGO Contests." Accessed March 8. http://legocontests .blogspot.com/.

Lipkowitz, Daniel. 2009. *The LEGO Book.* London: DK Publishing.

Food is always popular with teens and tweens. Specific types of food go in and out of style and can be fun to highlight at library programs, where it might be the only place a teen has a chance to try that type of food. Pick an exotic type of food for your community such as sushi, vegetarian dishes, or a Tofurky Thanksgiving, and create a program where teens develop their cooking skills and try new dishes that they may enjoy.

Food Tastings

General Description

Tastings of any type of food are highly popular because the one thing most teens love to do is eat. Collectively, we have tried chocolate, cheese, gelato, bacon, soda, and pizza tastings. The tastings can be a game where participants guess the brand of a certain type of food, such as a chocolate candy bar tasting. Another angle for a tasting is to try different types of a certain category of food for the sake of awareness or just plain fun.

Pop

A *foodie* is defined as a person who is devoted to good food and drink. The term was coined in *New York Magazine* by food critic Gael Greene in the early 1980s. There are tons of websites dedicated to listing the best types of food in certain areas. Through Yelp (http://www.yelp.com), people can find others' opinions on restaurants and join meetups to tour cities for the best hot dogs in town.

Relate

The pizza-tasting program was used as a tool to make teens aware of the different local pizza places in the area. It helped the pizza restaurants out by giving them publicity, and it was a great day of eating pizza for the teens. We hoped it also opened the teens' eyes to other possibilities for ordering pizza besides the big chains.

Instructors/Talent

The cheese, gelato, and bacon tastings were coordinated by a local gourmet deli. The programs were run presentation style, where representatives from the deli gave a PowerPoint on the history of the food, while different types of cheese, for instance, were passed around the seated crowd. Adults also attended this speaker-audience program.

Audience

Both teens and tweens were invited to the pizza program. The teens took the tasting very seriously, but the tweens spent a lot of time giggling. It worked out fine to have the groups together, but it may be better to hold the program separately for each group. The teens seemed to appreciate the processes of choosing their favorite pizza. It was more of a party atmosphere for the tweens, which is great too, and more about just eating lots of pizza.

Planning and Supplies

Talk to area pizza restaurants for donations. You can offer promotion of their restaurant to the attendees and send out press releases to local newspapers for potential articles. Even one pizza from each place is fine because it can be cut it into small pieces. The event included pizza from six different places, so having small tastes of each was best to limit the upchuck possibilities. Create worksheets for the teens to write down notes as they try each pizza.

Create

As the teens taste each pizza, have them rate the pizzas for the best sauce, the best cheese, the best crust, and the best overall pizza. Everyone tries each pizza once while taking notes, then go through the pizzas again in order, asking if anyone needs a second tasting to make up their minds. Then take a group vote, discovering the best pizza in every category. Many of the pizza places gave coupons to pass onto the teens. The soda tasting was very similar, where bottles of colas from around the world were purchased from a local specialty soda shop. Small paper cups were used so that teens could have small tastes of ten different colas.

Food, Technology, and Other Mandatory Extras

Food is the point of the program, so food is definitely needed! A computer and projector are needed if you are doing a PowerPoint presentation.

Analysis

These are great programs because everyone loves to try different types of food. Choose a type of food that teens are into, like cookies or ice cream. Beware of feeding the teens too much food. There is potential for upchuck. If local businesses are kind enough to donate food, send a letter to each restaurant or business, thanking them with a picture of the teens enjoying the food.

Marketing Tips

If you are partnered with a local deli, ask them to promote the program at their establishment.

Resources

Check Yelp (http://www.yelp.com) for ideas on local establishments with interesting food that you want to showcase to your teens.

Sushi Making

General Description

Hire a local sushi restaurant to come and teach a hands-on sushi-making class or, if staff is feeling ambitious, try teaching the class without the experts. With a sushi chef the program can include some demonstrations of fancy knife work and show the teens the technique. Avoiding raw fish is easy as there are tons of vegetarian sushi rolls. Also consider making California rolls with imitation crab meat since that is a processed meat and not raw.

Pop

Anything having to do with the Japanese culture has been hot for teens for years, and sushi continues to be popular. Japanese culture and aesthetics are fascinating to American teens and exposing them to the how-to of sushi is a great way to engage teens who also like anime and manga.

Relate

This program has crossover appeal. Teens interested in anime, manga, and other aspects of Japanese culture will enjoy this event, as will teens who enjoy food programming and want to try something new. This is also a slightly exotic program and requires some special supplies, so it is a great way to expose teens to something they might not otherwise experience at home. Include this program in your repertoire to reach other cultures as well as for cultural awareness.

Instructors/Talent

Unless staff is feeling really ambitious and also feels versed in teaching some of the traditions of sushi, it is recommended to hire a restaurant to facilitate this program. A restaurant will already have all supplies and expertise on hand, and it is a great way for them to market their business to a new clientele. Depending on the restaurant, this event could be free to the library or an agreement can be made for a low-cost price.

Audience

This is definitely an event for teens and adults. Teens will love getting their hands dirty making sushi rolls and trying something new.

Planning and Supplies

Planning and supplies all depends on if the program is taught by a restaurant or library staff. If library staff conducts the program, this is just a sampling of the supplies that will be needed:

- Sushi rolling mats
- Saran wrap
- Rice cookers
- Sushi rice vinegar
- Gloves
- Nori (seaweed)
- A variety of Japanese vegetables
- Sharp knives for cutting
- Coverings to keep rice off the floor and tables

If a restaurant conducts the program, all of these supplies will be provided, and it is recommended that "kits" for each teen are created with nori and vegetables already portioned out. Since the rice needs to stay slightly warm so it does not stick together, the restaurant can handle this easily. Work closely with the restaurant and this will be a fun and smooth event.

Create

This event should start with a talk about the history or significance of sushi in Japanese culture, and this can be done while the sushi chef demonstrates and prepares some special rolls. Then the instructor will tell the teens what they will be making and how to make it. Ideally this event will go off better if the setup allows for a camera to be over the shoulder of the chef, then projected on a screen so the participants can follow along. If this is not possible, be sure to have several staff on hand (versed in the basics if they are not restaurant staff) that can walk around and assist the teens. After that, it is all about rolling and eating!

Food, Technology, and Other Mandatory Extras

As mentioned, a setup that allows for a cooking show atmosphere is ideal. If a camera can project what the chef is doing on a screen, then the participants can watch the chef demonstrate his or her impressive skills and follow along. If this is not possible, then having several staff on hand is important.

Analysis

This event must be hands on if the audience is primarily teens. If, however, it was more of a lecture-and-listen event with a sushi tasting, then this format is more ideal for older teens and adults. This has consistently been one of the most popular food events at the library and, depending on your community, you should be prepared for a large attendance. Running out of food is not an option.

Marketing Tips

Market this event in a way that will appeal to all teens, with a focus on teens interested in anime, manga, and Japanese culture. Be sure to emphasize that no raw fish will be used.

Resources

Check out these books for tips on sushi making:

Kariya, Tetsu. 2009. *Oishinbo: Fish, Sushi & Sashimi: A La Carte*. San Francisco: Viz Media.
Strada, Judi, and Mineko Takane Moreno. 2004. *Sushi for Dummies*. Hoboken, NJ: Wiley Publishing.

Vegetarian Cooking

General Description

Vegetarianism and all the various subsets, such as veganism, ovo, lacto, fruit vegetarianism and more, have been rising in popularity and commonality for more than 30 years now. It is often during the teen years that many people try it for the first time. Teens need good information about eating healthy while learning to make vegetarian food. This event can happen any time of the year and takes several forms, but consider offering it near Thanksgiving or Easter or any event that often centers around meat as the focus of a family meal.

Pop

Many people first explore vegetarianism during their teen years. Vegetarianism is trendy in certain circles of teens and is often the first time a teen takes control over something significant in his or her life. This can create challenges for the family in some cases. Many parents have concerns about proper nutrition for this diet, so information is important for teens. The various ethical, religious, environmental, and health reasons people become vegetarian is an important part of the movement. Millions of people around the world, the largest concentration in India, are vegetarians. Organizations like PETA are often in the news with their provocative and often controversial tactics and advertising.

Relate

Teaching vegetarian cooking to teens is an important educational life skill and will provide valuable information to teens looking to become vegetarians. Teens will not only learn new cooking techniques but may also meet other vegetarians.

Instructors/Talent

Hire a vegetarian chef, caterer, or talented local enthusiast to present a vegetarian cooking class. This event can be mostly demonstration wherein the chef cooks and talks about the food, cooking tips, and offers the audience samples (library staff or the chef's helpers will do this). Alternately, offer a hands-on cooking opportunity that allows participants to make items themselves. This can be done either with individuals making items like a single-serve salad or a group of teens cooking one recipe that allows everyone to try some when it is done. If you or other library staff are enthusiastic vegetarian cooks, it may not be necessary to hire someone to run this event.

Audience

Teens and also adults are the main audience for this type of event. Depending on the approach, it would also appeal to some tweens.

Planning and Supplies

If outside presenters are hired, they should ideally provide all of the supplies and materials. In that case, it will be necessary to determine electrical and setup needs for your space. Determine whether they will also provide plates, utensils, and napkins for sampling, or if the library will provide these. Participants will want copies of the recipes, so plan handouts for this part of the presentation.

Create

This event depends largely on the enthusiasm of the presenter. Determine if you want to stick with strictly vegetable products or if you want to introduce meat replacements as well. If you do the event near Thanksgiving, be sure to include a Tofurky since it is such an infamous meat replacement.

Food, Technology, and Other Mandatory Extras

If you are doing a cooking demo and have access to cameras or a projector, consider replicating the "over the shoulder" cooking camera seen on cooking shows so that participants can see the hands of the demonstrator.

Analysis

This is a popular event that can surely be offered every year to appeal to a new crop of teens each time. Since there are endless recipes out there, it is not possible to run out of new dishes to demonstrate. Some participants may be reluctant to try certain items. This is normal and a good reason not to focus exclusively on meat replacement options, since that is often what some people find odd to eat.

Marketing Tips

Take flyers and promos to health food stores, vegetarian restaurants, and other places where holistic services are offered. Promote the event to the schools, emphasizing the "hands-on" aspect of the program.

Resource

Check out this book for recipes:

Pierson, Stephanie. 1999. *Vegetables Rock! A Complete Guide for Teenage Vegetarians*. New York: Bantam Books.

Revolting Recipes

General Description

By blending cooking and the witty imagination of Roald Dahl, tweens can get creative with candy and re-create aspects from our favorite stories such as *Charlie and the Chocolate Factory* and *The Twits*. This program can be in honor of Roald Dahl Day, September 13, in celebration of another book turned to movie, or just because Dahl is one of the coolest authors ever.

Pop

One of children's literature's best-loved authors, Roald Dahl has captured the interest of everyone from book lovers to reluctant readers with his revolting humor. Many of his books have been made into movies, with *Charlie and the Chocolate Factory* made into two versions so far. Who cannot get a kick out of children smelling of dog droppings in *The Witches*, and a boy climbing into a giant peach and making friends with a bunch of insects in *James and the Giant Peach*? The most recent adaptation of a Dahl book to hit the big screen is *Fantastic Mr. Fox*.

Relate

Libraries are well-known for their book clubs and book-based programming. What better way to make a lasting impression than to make a book come alive with fun activities based on the magical elements of the stories?

Instructors/Talent

No instructors needed.

Audience

Tweens, grades 3 through 6.

Planning and Supplies

- Fruit Roll-Ups
- Frosting
- Candy
- Instant mashed potatoes
- Paper plates, plastic flatware, plastic wrap to take home creations
- Tarp

Create

The programming room was set up with three stations: Lickable Wallpaper, Mr. Twit's Beard, and a cookie frosting table. Staff members monitored the food tables throughout the room so that the candy was dispersed evenly.

Everyone has wondered what snozzberry wallpaper would really taste like because "Who ever heard of a snozzberry?" Well, you have, and you get to come up with your own lickable wallpaper. Each participant received a Fruit Roll-Up, frosting, and an assortment of candy and Pull-and-Peel Licorice to create sweet designs.

In honor of Mr. Twit and his scrumptious beard, kids were given their color choice of instant mashed potatoes dyed with food coloring. Using the mashed potatoes as their canvas, they added food pieces that would collect in Mr. Twit's beard as he ate, such as chow mein noodles, raisins, Maraschino cherries, and candy.

Finally, to use up the leftover candy, kids decorated cookies with frosting and candy. The program was topped off with fizzy lifting drinks: lemon-lime soda with a touch of sherbet to make it foamy.

Food, Technology, and Other Mandatory Extras

No extra food is needed for this event, as there will be enough candy to snack on while making delectable Dahl creations.

Analysis

This program is sure to cause a sugar rush and would be great paired with a book discussion, but the candy activities should probably happen at the end of the program to maintain concentration. It is also really important to put tarps on the floor because mashed potatoes and frosting will get everywhere. Another possible addition to this program could be to show one of the movies based on a Roald Dahl book. The kids can make their own snacks for the showing of the movie. Put up a display of Dahl books, so that those who are interested can pick out a new title to read.

Marketing Tips

Promote this program to fourth- and fifth-grade teachers, as well as homeschool groups, as a supplemental program to books they may be reading in class. Try some guerrilla advertising tactics by leaving flyers in the Roald Dahl books on the shelf or posting small posters in the shelving next to targeted books and the cookbook section.

Resources

Use these resources to add more activities to this program:

Dahl, Roald. 1997. *Roald Dahl's Revolting Recipes.* New York: Viking.
Roald Dahl Day. http://www.roalddahlday.info/.
Roald Dahl: The Official Web site. http://www.roalddahl.com/.

Smoothie Sensation

General Description

Smoothies are a blended, chilled, sometimes sweetened beverage made from fresh fruit or vegetables. The drink sometimes includes ice, frozen fruit, honey, yogurt, or ice cream, with 100 percent fruit as the healthiest option. This event could take many forms in terms of approach, but in its simplest terms you provide some recipes, some food, and blenders, and let the teens have a great time making smoothies! You could also hire a local smoothie store or stand to come and do this event if you have a budget to use.

Pop

With the increasing epidemic of childhood obesity, any opportunity to expose young people to healthy choices like fruit-based snacks is a good thing. Smoothies have been around in popular culture for years, going back to Orange Julius, which rose to popularity in the 1960s. The current smoothie house of choice for the popular sweet treat is Jamba Juice, which can be found at a mall near you.

Relate

Giving teens the chance to make their own snacks and explore their taste preferences is a great way to give teens a fun time at the library. Healthy eating is an important skill for teens to learn and this type of program lets them try new foods, find out how easy they are to make themselves, and leave with a variety of recipes to take home.

Instructors/Talent

This is an easy enough program for staff to conquer themselves, but hire an instructor if you have the budget to spend and do not want to fuss with the complications of collecting blenders and shopping for food. In addition to the franchises that serve smoothies, there are also many small neighborhood smoothie shops that may be interested in helping you with your event. Sometimes you may not need to pay them if they feel that they get enough marketing and publicity to offset the cost of the event.

Audience

Grades 6 through 12.

Planning and Supplies

It is very easy to track down a wide variety of smoothie recipes. Just using an Internet search engine will bring up a myriad of options. See the Resources section for more ideas.

- Kitchen
- Recipes: Laminate several copies of each recipe to keep them dry.
- Blenders
- Measuring cups and spoons, several sets
- Fruit
- Table covers

- Paper cups

Create

It is important to have several staff members on hand for an event like this. If you think you will get more than 20 teens, then two to three staff members are recommended. If you do not control the ingredients or have enough of everything, it is very easy for this to become a wild and insanely messy event. Too much planning is not possible. Ideally, you would like to have one staff member stationed in the kitchen or at a food station to hand out the supplies recipe by recipe, and to rinse out the blenders and measuring utensils in between uses. You will want to offer three to seven recipes for a more varied experience for the teens. Have the teens work in groups to make the recipes. This event is relatively fast moving so be prepared for the participants to prepare each recipe a minimum of four times.

Food, Technology, and Other Mandatory Extras

Use this event as an opportunity to expose the teens to some unusual fruits or textures. You do not have to go too weird in case they will not eat it, but be creative.

Analysis

Do this year after year with new recipes and it never gets old. The tweens and teens always have a blast when they are given permission to make a mess and do things themselves. Some teens never get the chance to explore or be inventive with food. Teens will have a great time at this event and leave with a variety of recipes to take home to their family to try again or adjust to their liking.

Marketing Tips

It is usually not difficult to attact tweens and teens to a program about food. In addition to the traditional library advertising, spread the word by putting flyers up in food establishments where teens hang out, such as coffee shops, pizza places, and fast-food joints. If the local schools have any type of home economics program, consider letting those teachers know and also ask if flyers can be posted in the cafeteria.

Resources

Check out these books for ideas for smoothie recipes:

Barber, Mary. 1997. *Smoothies: 50 Recipes for High-Energy Refreshment.* San Francisco: Chronicle Books.

Chace, Daniella. 1998. *Smoothies for Life! Yummy, Fun and Nutritious.* Rocklin, CA: Prima Publishing.

Constans, Gabriel. 1997. *Great American Smoothies: The Ultimate Blending Guide for Shakes, Slushes, Desserts, and Thirst Quenchers*. New York: Avery.

Bento Box Bonanza

General Description

The bento box event is a combination of fun, food, and cultural exposure. Bento boxes are a traditional Japanese way of holding lunch, but there is also an art to packing a nice bento. In recent years it has become an art form, making carrots look like anime characters or friendly animals. It is also a fun way to entice young people to try healthy foods in a new way. The library will provide the box, the food, and the inspiration, while the attendees will enjoy making their own decorative bento boxes. This event can also include inviting members of the Japanese culture to come and talk about bento.

The women who spoke at the library about bento took a video at a local Saturday Japanese school to show children eating their bento. They also did a cooking demonstration to show how a piece of hot dog can be cut and then cooked to look like an octopus. The cooking process makes the "tentacles" curl. Bento also usually includes molded rice that has nori (seaweed) or other things mixed in for color, texture, and details. Hard-boiled eggs at the right temperature can be molded in a special mold in the shape of a bunny or with other face details. Fruits, vegetables, processed meats, seeds, eggs, and more can be cut and arranged in decorative and clever ways.

Pop

Bento has a long history in Japan, but its popularity in the United States is just beginning. With the focus on getting young people to eat healthier, bento is a perfect Japanese tradition to become popular in the United States where obesity in children has become a concern. Like much in Japanese culture, the aesthetics and the *kawaii* (cute) aspect of bento are very aesthetically appealing. In Japan, there are bento contests, and parents often make bento lunches that look like Hello Kitty, Totoro, or video game characters. Over 400 photo groups on the popular photo-sharing website Flickr.com are devoted to bento boxes. Looking at photos of decorative bento boxes is an excellent way to get ideas. In September 2009, the *New York Times* published an article about the rise of bento boxes in United States homes (Storey, 2009).

Relate

Japanese pop culture has continued to be a popular interest for many tweens and teens. From Pokémon to Hello Kitty, sushi, and manga, in between there is a segment of every population with an interest in Japanese pop culture. This is a great way to engage your users who read manga or check out your anime collection. It is also an excellent educational event to explore the traditions and origins of bento culture in Japan. Involve teens who may want to share their culture with others and help out at the program. Many books can be added to your collection to complement the event as well. This is an excellent hands-on opportunity that gives tweens and teens a creative outlet while exposing them to another way to try healthy foods (see Figure 10.1).

Instructors/Talent

In order to fully conduct the program, you do not need to hire any experts, but it would be a far better event if you had volunteers from the Japanese community or staff from a local Japanese restaurant come to talk and do a demonstration of traditional bento boxes. This portion of the event could include a talk, a video, photo boards, bento samples, examples of rice molds, egg molds, food picks, and bento boxes.

Audience

Grades 4 through 8.

Planning and Supplies

You will have to locate boxes for each participant to use for their bento boxes. Whether you use real bento boxes which can be pricey, ranging from $1.50 to $3.00 each in bulk,

Figure 10.1. Healthy Bento Box Creation

Gladware, or even ask participants to bring their own containers, you can easily pull off this event. Locate any local Japanese cultural groups to find volunteers or contact Japanese restaurants in your area to see if they would be able to help do a bento box presentation.

Stick with the more traditional U.S. foods that are in bento boxes instead of Japanese specialty foods, unless you have a very large budget. Offering traditional ginger or pickled plums would be very costly but very cool. So use your budget to guide you. Use strawberries, grapes, tomatoes, leaf lettuce, processed cheeses and meats, broccoli, sunflower seeds, poppy seeds, sesame seeds, nori, asparagus, peppers, green beans, and snow peas, which are all easily acquired and make for a lovely bento box.

Supplies include:

- Kitchen
- Bento boxes or equivalent
- Plastic cookie cutters, e.g., letters, animals, foods, or shapes to cut shapes in the processed cheese and meat
- Food, including mostly fruits and vegetables like grapes, strawberries, lettuce, processed turkey (avoiding ham is good for dietary and religious reasons), processed cheeses, seeds, nori
- Scissors, sanitized, used to cut the nori
- Plastic knives to cut the food
- Napkins
- Trash bags, large quantity

Create

This is a very supply-and-setup-heavy event that will require several staff members. Ideally you will want someone in the kitchen or at a food station to hand out the food and be sure that the public does not touch the food. It is important for staff to wear gloves and use utensils to hand out the food. Scissors and the cookie cutters can be put out on the tables before the event. If you have a large crowd, it's best to release the participants to pick up their food table by table. It is a good idea to have paper and pencils or markers on hand, so that while participants are waiting to get their food, they can plan out how they want their bento box to look. Participants can think about characters or look at the display the volunteers or restaurant brought to give them ideas.

Food, Technology, and Other Mandatory Extras

One relatively easy way to add something extra to the program is to create an image slide show in PowerPoint of images of bento boxes from Flickr.com. Include a computer, projector, and screen to your list of supplies if this is feasible for you. A slide show was created with 40 images ranging from traditional aesthetic bento boxes to a variety of anime, manga, and character bentos in many colors. People looked to the images as inspiration for their drawings as they planned, and it also served as a pleasant diversion while the participants waited for food. Also, be sure to have a selection of books on hand for participants to check out after the event (see Figure 10.2).

Analysis

This event is one that seems to make everyone happy! Who doesn't enjoy using good ingredients to create cute characters in adorable little plastic boxes? Participants learn something new and are inspired to try new things. As an anecdote, at the end of the program a mother mentioned that her daughter started munching on a raw piece of asparagus for the first time ever! It is a great way to encourage healthy eating and smaller portion size.

Marketing Tips

Reaching out to Japanese nationals and to enthusiasts of Japanese culture is the best way to get the word out about this event. See if local sushi restaurants or Asian/Japanese markets will put up a flyer in their businesses. Many schools have anime/manga clubs, so seek out the teachers and students who run these groups and let them know about

Figure 10.2. Using Books to Inspire Bento Box Designs

the program. If there is a local comic book store or other business that sells manga and other Japanese pop culture items, be sure they get a stack of flyers too.

Resources

Check out these books for recipes and ideas:

Ishihara, Yoko. 2007. *The Manga Cookbook.* Japan: Manga University Culinary Institute.

Salyers, Christopher. 2008. *Face Food: The Visual Creativity of Japanese Bento Boxes.* New York: Mark Batty Publishers.

Staff, Joie. 2006. *Kawaii Bento Boxes: Cute and Convenient Japanese Meals on the Go.* New York: Kodansha.

Storey, Samantha. 2009. "Bento Boxes Win Lunch Fans." *New York Times.* September 8. http://www.nytimes.com/2009/09/09/dining/09bentohtml.

Chapter 11

Programs: Crafts

Libraries are very good at providing craft programs for everyone from preschool age through mature adulthood. Think about ways to add spice to your craft programs with the inspiration of pop culture. Bring back the pet rock from the 1970s. Use popular craft books to build programs that will teach a fun new skill as well as encourage use of the craft collection at the library.

Shrinky Dinks

General Description

This is a wonderfully versatile craft program that will appeal to boys and girls equally. Using Shrinky Dink plastic, the teens can make jewelry, key chains, pins, pet tags, and more. This is a workshop that is open-ended and does not have to be project based.

Pop

Shrinky Dinks appeal to the nostalgia factor for many adults and are still fun and weird enough for teens to get into it. The fact that it is something that many of their parents remember will be a fun aspect for teens to share.

Relate

Any teen who enjoys creating and making things will enjoy this workshop. The flexibility and open-ended nature of working with Shrinky Dinks is an appealing aspect for any teen. Also, Shrinky Dinks are incredibly easy to make, so the sense of success for the teen will be high.

Instructors/Talent

This is an easy program to conduct; no talent is needed.

Audience

Shrinky Dinks appeal to children, teens, and adults. Adults who recall Shrinky Dinks from their youth will love it, and it is easy enough for children as young as age five to participate. As long as the oven is an adult-only zone, this activity can safely appeal to many ages.

Planning and Supplies

This program involves providing all of the supplies and letting the teens do the rest. The shrinking plastic can be purchased at most craft stores and online. You will need to provide the following:

- Shrinky Dink plastic in a variety of colors (white, black, brown, etc.) but mostly the "rough and ready" clear plastic. Preroughened plastic allows for ink to stick to the plastic. Otherwise, it must first be sanded. Several other companies make this material, not just Shrinky Dink.
- Scissors
- Hole punches (any holes must be punched *before* the creation goes in the oven)
- Sharpie markers in a variety of colors
- Rubber stamps
- Stamp pads in a variety of colors
- Jewelry supplies like jump rings, hemp, string
- Key chains, pin backs, and jump rings to make pet tags
- Brown paper bags cut into pieces to put the Shrinky Dinks on when they go in the oven.
- An oven, preferably one with a glass door and light so you can see inside. Watching the plastic cook is the best part!

Create

Provide the supplies, then give the teens the basic rundown on how Shrinky Dinks work and what the various options are with the supplies available. Then let them go to it! Once teens have completed some projects, start putting the pieces in the oven. If it is possible, and there is enough adult supervision, teens will enjoy watching them shrink too.

Food, Technology, and Other Mandatory Extras

None needed.

Analysis

This is an event that will become part of your staple craft programs. Because the possibilities are endless and the teens can make whatever they want, they will not tire of the program. This event can be tailored to a specific project (for example, making pins for Mother's Day) and is as versatile as you make it.

Marketing Tips

When marketing to teens who may not know what Shrinky Dinks are, it might be necessary to briefly describe how it works. But be sure to mention the wide variety of things that can be made, particularly if an audience of both boys and girls is desired. Also, put up examples around the teen area to get teens interested.

Resources

Check out these books for ideas on how to be creative with Shrinky Dinks:

Phillips, Karen. 2007. *Shrink Art Jewelry*. Palo Alto, CA: Klutz.
Roulston, Jane. 2002. *Shrink Art 101*. Fort Worth, TX: Design Originals.

Jean Pocket Purses

General Description

Reworking and redesigning clothes is a popular hobby for teens and adults. Using the pockets of old jeans, teens can make tiny purses to accessorize their outfits, give as gifts, or use to put small gifts inside.

Pop

Personalizing jeans became very popular in the 1970s. Teens adorned their bellbottom jeans with bells, patchwork, embroidery, appliqués, and antiwar graffiti. Recycling jeans into cutoffs and miniskirts was a fashion commonly worn by flower children during the hippie revolution.

Relate

Creating a space for teens to make their own clothes to illustrate their original and unique fashion sense is very important. It is also great modeling to show teens you do not need to purchase new clothes all the time; instead, you can rework and repurpose what you already have in your closet to create a new look. It is "going green" for clothes. Highlight your clothing craft books and fashion materials, as well as your decade books, on a display near the project area. This program might prompt a teen to find out more about what the hippie culture was really like.

Instructors/Talent

No instructor is needed.

Audience

This is a great project for both tweens and teens. Crafty adults might want to sneak into this program too. Depending on how well your different-aged library groups get along, it might be best to have separate programs for tweens and teens. Tweens will need more attention and help with glue guns.

Planning and Supplies

What a great excuse to clean out your closet! Collect gently used jeans from staff or purchase jeans from a used clothing store as a last resort. Cut the pockets out of the jeans, but save the rest of the denim for another craft project later.

- Ribbons for handle
- Beads
- Fabric paint (if the audience can handle it)
- Fabric pens
- Jewels
- Buttons
- Craft glue
- Hot-glue guns
- Sharp scissors
- Needle and thread

Create

Make up a sample to inspire teens with ideas, and then throw all the supplies out on tables for teens to get creative. Craft glue worked very well to keep small embellishments attached to the pocket. The glue guns were broken out to secure the ribbon handles and kept in a corner for safety purposes, so staff could watch over them. Every teen was asked to take a pledge by putting the two "Scout's honor" fingers in the air and saying, "I will not burn myself." It was hokey, but it at least got everyone in the room remembering that the glue guns are hot.

Food, Technology, and Other Mandatory Extras

No treats are needed for the event.

Analysis

The program was scheduled for the week before Christmas. Teens came in to make last-minute gifts. Present this program before Mother's Day as well for all those kids who want to make their mothers a present. A lot of boys were attracted to this program, which was surprising, but they seemed to be in desperation mode for presents for loved ones.

Marketing Tips

Contact local home education classes and fashion clubs to spread the word about this program. Put flyers in the shelving next to the clothing craft books in the library.

Resource

Check out this book for other ideas of how to repurpose denim:

Blakeney Faith, Justina Blakeney, and Ellen Schultz. 2007. *99 Ways to Cut, Sew, & Deck Out Your Denim*. New York: Potter Craft.

Duct Tape Crafts

General Description

Duct tape events are fairly ubiquitous in libraries, but do not let that fool you into thinking it is not cool anymore. Duct tape craft events are a surefire way to bring in a consistently unisex audience. The library has been doing duct tape events for more than five years and there is still heavy attendance each time. Basically, all you need to do is provide tape, cutting surfaces, cutting implements, and some patterns. Voila! Instant program.

Pop

Duct tape has been a staple of library programming for years but not without good reason. Duct tape manages to be squeaky clean and tough at the same time, and it cuts across gender lines in a way few other hands-on projects do. Duct tape prom contests have been the rage for several years. Teens make the entire prom dress and suit from duct tape in schools across the country. Duck Brand tape sponsored its 10th Annual Stuck at the Prom Contest in 2010 with prizes of scholarships for the winners. Also in 2009 a teen whose home was rebuilt on *Extreme Makeover: Home Edition* got a bedroom decked out in duct tape creations and a work table and supply of duct tape to last him for years.

Relate

Offering duct tape seasonally or even monthly in some cases is a great way to engage a steady group of teens in library events. There will always be a group of teens who enjoy making things out of duct tape, and you want to be sure to offer a place in your library for their interests.

Instructors/Talent

The great thing about duct tape is that you do not need an expert. If you have a local teen who is really talented and enthusiastic, you might have him or her teach a workshop, but most teens can teach themselves how to make something out of duct tape using instructions and templates. You can also make an assortment of samples to keep on hand so that participants can have a tangible sample.

Audience

Grades 6 through 12.

Planning and Supplies

Purchase an inventory of a wide selection of duct tape, inexpensive scrap wood to make cutting boards that can be used again and again, a supply of X-Acto knives for cutting, and a wide assortment of project descriptions that you can laminate and keep on hand:

- Duct tape: primary colors, pastels, fluorescent, black, camouflage, caution, tie-dye, clear, plaid, glow-in-the-dark
- Cutting boards: 20 to 70 pieces, depending on attendance
- X-Acto knives: 20 to 70
- Instructions for duct tape projects like wallets, ties, flip-flops, purses, roses, etc., that have been laminated for repeated use
- Scissors
- Rulers
- Sharpie markers in a variety of colors
- Velcro in a variety of sizes and shapes

Create

This program is all about creating opportunities. How many teens would ever be able to have all of the colors of duct tape that the library can provide at a program? Give the teens the opportunity and the access, and the possibilities are endless. Provide all the supplies and the laminated directions, and other than being there to offer support, it is a self-running event (see Figure 11.1).

Figure 11.1. Creative Duct Tape Crafts

Food, Technology, and Other Mandatory Extras

As a frill-free event, if you felt so inclined you could create a slide show of duct tape prom images to show during the event for fun. PowerPoint, a laptop, projector, and screen would be required. As an alternative, you could have a laptop with a slide show set up for teens to take turns viewing during the event.

Analysis

The cost-benefit for this event is difficult to argue with. At how many events do you get equal numbers of boys and girls in high numbers? Not many. This is a solid creative event that will offer a continual positive perception of the library.

Marketing Tips

Promote this program to local Boys & Girls Clubs and teen centers looking for easy, entertaining events to refer their teens to during the summer. Put up displays of original and unique duct tape creations designed by staff or, even better, by teens to both showcase artwork and advertise the program.

Resources

Learn the art of creating things with duct tape and get some fun ideas of crafts to make:

Bonaddio, T.L. 2009. *Stick It!: 99 Duct Tape Projects*. Philadelphia, PA: Running Press Kids.

Duck. 2010. "Stuck at Prom Scholarship Contest." Accessed September 2. http://www.duckbrand.com/Promotions/stuck-at-prom.aspx.

Duct Tape Fashion. http://www.ducttapefashion.com/.

Schiedermayer, Ellie. 2002. *Got Tape? Roll Out the Fun with Duct Tape*. Lola, WI: Krause Publications.

Tape Brothers. http://www.tapebrothers.com/.

Wilson, Joe. 2006. *Ductigami: The Art of the Tape*. Ontario, Canada: Boston Mills Press.

T-shirt Remodel

General Description

In this project, teens rework old T-shirts to create funky and stylish new fashion designs.

Pop

Teens have their own sense of style, different from the clothing styles popular with adults, because teens use their clothes to express who they are and their own subculture within the hierarchy of high school. Clothing is a symbol for which clique or group they belong to: goth, preppy, sporty, nerd-chic?

Relate

If clothing is a great way for teens to express themselves, why not help them discover their style while at the library? It is a great way to showcase your DIY craft books.

Instructors/Talent

No instructor is needed.

Audience

Grades 6 through 12. The enormous decision of whether to use fabric paint might help you decide which audience to focus on.

Planning and Supplies

- T-shirts: Take donations from staff for the just-in-case scenario that a teen forgets to bring his or her own shirt.
- Ribbons
- Beads
- Fabric paint (if the audience can handle it)
- Jewels
- Hot-glue guns
- Sharp scissors
- Needle and thread

Create

Depending on the skills of the participants, this program can get as creative as you would like. As led by a scissors-and-hot-glue-gun kind of girl, the program was not heavy on sewing, though needles and thread were available for those more talented. If you can sew, you could even bring in a sewing machine for the teens to use. The *Generation T* books listed in the Resources section have good instructions for creating cool T-shirts with no sewing required (Nicolay, 2006).

Food, Technology, and Other Mandatory Extras

No extras are needed, but food is always appreciated by the participants.

Analysis

Boys also participated in this event, even though it seems more like a girl-centric program, because there were a lot of boy-friendly T-shirts available to remodel, including old shirts with name brands boys associate with, like Fear Street and Mossimo. Plus, having fabric paint allowed boys to add sayings to their shirts instead of ribbons and jewels, though they were more than welcome to use all supplies provided.

Marketing Tips

This program can be marketed as a T-shirt remodeling program or can be structured around a theme such as Valentine's Day or school spirit for football games.

Resources

Check out these books for ideas of how to rework T-shirts:

Marshall, Carmia. 2006. *T-Shirt Makeovers: 20 Transformations for Fabulous Fashions*. New York: Gliteratti Inc.

Nicolay, Megan. 2006. *Generation T: 108 Ways to Transform a T-Shirt*. New York: Workman Publishing Company.

Nicolay, Megan. 2009. *Generation T: Beyond Fashion, 110 T-Shirt Transformations for Pets, Babies, Friends, Your Home, Car, and You*. New York: Workman Publishing Company.

Chapter 12

Programs: Gaming

Video games have become increasing popular since their inception and have become a large part of our culture. The tough part now is staying up on the most trendy games of the moment. Take an extremely solitary activity and make it a social event where the library is the hangout. Look to different formats such as computer, handheld (PSP or Nintendo DS), or console games (Nintendo Wii, Sony Playstation 3, or Microsoft Xbox 360). Ask teens and tweens what their favorite titles are (see Figure 12.1).

Retro Octathlon

General Description

Showcase those older video games that you loved so much as a kid and introduce them to a newer generation. Go through that closet and pull out the Atari or your original Nintendo Entertainment System (NES), or play the new releases of older games on newer game consoles. (Note to whippersnappers: "retro" means pre-1990.)

Pop

Video games began their creation as hobbies for smart techies. The games were available only on large computers. In the 1970s, video games diversified into arcade, handheld, and home computers. *Pong*, based on table tennis, was a big hit for its revolutionary technology in 1972 and was played on the Atari, one of the first widely successful gaming consoles in the United States. Innovation in video gaming technology in the 1980s brought about such classic gems as *Street Fighter*, *Pac-Man*, and *Mario Bros.*, many of which could be played on the NES. These games are oldies but goodies; they have been reimaged again and again during the past 30 years.

Relate

This can be an intergenerational program, bringing together teens and twentysomethings in friendly competition. Young adults can introduce the teens to the enjoyment of these older video game titles.

Figure 12.1. *Dance Dance Revolution*

Instructors/Talent

No instructors are needed for this program.

Audience

Plan for teens, but expect young adults in their twenties and parents showing up and asking to play. Young adults are always the hardest age group to get into the library, and their interests usually straddle those of teens and older adults. If you are looking for a program to bring in young adults, especially men who stopped using the library after high school, this is the program to try out.

Planning and Supplies

Choose any older games that you enjoyed and want to share with others. If you decide on eight games, you have the "octathlon." And you can change the title of the program if you find fewer games to share; you can make it a "Retro Pentathlon." Some examples are original *Super Mario Bros.*, *Breakout*, *Marble Madness*, *Pole Position*, *Pac-Man*, and *Donkey Kong.* Several older games have been released on the newer consoles, including the Wii, Xbox 360, and Playstation 3. So do not worry about trying to dig up an old Nintendo. This program can be done very cheaply. Look to your staff to borrow older video games and consoles.

Decide whether you would like to run the program as a tournament or as an exhibition, where everyone cycles through the games and tries them out. An optimal situation would be to have multiple televisions, so people can play different games at one time, and cycle through the room. If that's not possible, using one television is also fine. In that situation, each person has a turn on a game and then the game is switched out for another.

Create

Depending on whether you are having a tournament or a retro video gaming petting zoo, have the teens write down their score for each game. Compare the scores on each game, having the high scorers on the most games win prizes. Give out gift cards to local video game stores, or dig up swag for retro games, such as *Mario Bros.* stuffed animals. These can be found most times at comic book stores.

Food, Technology, and Other Mandatory Extras

Food is a must! Especially if you have the teens play eight games. That means they will be playing for a couple of hours, and those teens do get hungry. Snacks like pretzels and Goldfish are great. Make sure there is water available too.

Analysis

This is a low-key program. It is a fun activity to do during school breaks when teens are looking for something to do and can spend the afternoon at the library. Also think about having the program in the evening to attract college students.

Marketing Tips

Promote this program in arcades, local video gaming centers, and comic book stores. Ask to put flyers next to the cash registers. Put up flyers in student unions of local colleges. Blog about this program on Facebook to get the word out to the gaming community.

Resource

Check out this book for the history of gaming:

Kent, Steven L. 2001. *The Ultimate History of Video Games.* New York: Three Rivers Press.

Pokémon Tournaments

General Description

Tweens and teens bring a Nintendo DS or other handheld console to battle their *Pokémon* characters against others.

Pop

Pokémon is a huge phenomenon that has branched out from manga graphic novels to anime, video games, card games, books, toys, and more. Parents to preschoolers know who Pikachu is, one of the best-known *Pokémon* characters. Created in Japan, *Pokémon* means "Pocket Monsters," which accurately explains the concept. The basic idea is that when a trainer comes upon a wild Pokémon, to capture it he or she must throw out the Poke Ball. If the trainer can catch the Pokémon in the ball, then it is his or hers to keep. Hence, the collection of the Pokémon.

Relate

Video gaming has become a major part of teen and tween culture for this current generation. Though at first glance, it does not seem educational, many reluctant readers are reading the text in the game, getting interested in the story line, and searching for books and graphic novels to read based on the characters from the game. This type of program can attract teens who are new to the library, so make sure you put out displays of materials that might interest them and show the value of using the library. Plus, these teens will be adults, having children in no time, and showing the library is interested in their interests now will help create future lifelong library users.

Instructors/Talent

Running gaming programs can be difficult if you have no interest or knowledge in this area. Check around with your staff for video game lovers who can help set up and facilitate the program. Members of the IT department are always good targets. Otherwise, the older kids who participate in the program can be very helpful with answering detailed questions about the game and manning the tournament. Plus, it is great to empower your participants, encouraging their input in the running of the program.

Audience

Plan for grades 3 through 6, but this program will attract younger kids and even middle schoolers.

Planning and Supplies

Based on your budget, this program can cost as little as the price of food. So starting small, the modern versions of the video game *Pokémon* are played on handheld video game systems such as the Nintendo DS, Nintendo DS Lite, and Nintendo DSi. If you have a Wii, buying the game *Pokémon Battle Revolution* for Wii will enable your players to link their DS systems up to the Wii and battle it out on the big screen.

Create

When teens enter the programming room, give them a piece of paper to keep track of their wins and losses during battles. Teens will play ten games with players around the programming room with their DS systems connecting to each other wirelessly. Everyone must have a character enter a certain room in the game ("The Union Room"), where they will pair off for battle. (This is a virtual room in the game, not a real room in your library, which causes confusion every time.) When all players have completed their battles, tally up the sheets, identifying the players with the most wins. Those players will go on to the next round. Everyone else is out of the tournament but can still hang out and keep playing for fun. Let the players in the tournament do battle, using a bracket system: one loss and you're out. The prize to the winner can be a gift certificate to a local video game store or the satisfaction of having the most awesome Pokémon that day and a paper crown with different Pokémon on it. Make the program work for your budget.

An option to consider is to ask that players do not use legendary Pokémon characters. Allowing players to use "Legendaries" gives advantage to the most experienced players and makes it harder for new players to have a chance. Also, if you have players that may have bought their copy of *Pokémon* in Europe or Asia, you can't guarantee that they'll be able to link up with players using the North American version of the DS or Wii games. Foreign copies might work, but they might not, and either way there's nothing you as a tournament organizer can do about it other than set the expectations at the beginning of the event to minimize disappointment.

Food, Technology, and Other Mandatory Extras

Snacks are very important. Make the program have a party atmosphere. Promote healthy eating by putting out fruits and carrots. Teens will pretty much eat anything put out on a table. Be sure to have treats too, like cookies or crackers. Some kids do not get to eat those things at home, so give those kids a little decadence with a root beer float.

Also think about putting the final battles on the big screen! Attach the Wii to a projector so that everyone in the room can watch the action.

Analysis

If you find some kids get finished with their ten games way before the rest of the group, you might have another activity available for them. Many times this program can turn into a family affair because older siblings bring younger ones. The younger kids tend to get bored quickly. There are quite a few craft projects centered around *Pokémon* characters on the Internet. Leave out craft foam, markers, and googly eyes for kids to make their favorite characters. Use all those leftover weeded CDs to create characters as well.

Marketing Tips

Be sure to target anime and manga groups, as well as any comic book or specialty manga stores, with flyers promoting the program. Also, stop by local arcades and check to see if you can leave flyers on a bulletin board or next to the register.

Resources

Check out these books to learn more about *Pokémon* and view the website for craft ideas:

DTLK's Crafts for Kids. 2010. "Chansey Pokémon Craft." Accessed September 6. http://www.dltk-kids .com/pokemon/mchansey.html.

Mylonas, Eric. 2006. *Pokémon: 10th Anniversary Pokédex.* Roseville, CA: Prima Games.

Ryan, Michael G. 2010. *Pokémon Heartgold Version, Soulsilver Version: The Official Pokemon Johto Guide & Pokédex.* Bellevue, WA: Pokémon Company International.

Chapter 13

Programs: Japanese Popular Culture

Japanese popular culture has moved to the United States. Teens and tweens heartily enjoy manga and anime and, because of this interest, have become very attracted to learning about Japanese culture. Teens want to learn the language and experience the food, the crafts, and various popular activities, such as Cosplay.

Cosplay Contest

General Description

Cosplay is short for "costume play" and is popular with enthusiasts of Japanese anime, manga, video games and pop culture. Cosplayers create highly detailed costumes and accessories to look like, and often act like, the character they are playing. A cosplay contest would appeal to teens and adults. Contestants will compete for prizes such as gift certificates for stores who sell Japanese merchandise or to fabric stores where they can buy the supplies they need for more costumes.

Pop

The term *cosplay* originated in Japan at a science fiction convention in the mid 1980s and is generally based around the comics and manga conventions in Japan and around the world. Cosplay is closely tied with *Otaku*, Japanese fan culture, and Tokyo's Harajuku district is the center of the scene in Japan. There are also "cosplay cafés" in Japan, where staff are dressed in cosplay. With the increased popularity of Japanese pop culture in the United States, cosplay has also risen in popularity and is mostly centered around anime and science fiction conventions. U.S. cosplay is varied and often includes more science fiction (*Star Wars*) and fantasy (*Lord of the Rings*) costumes, in addition to Japanese characters.

Relate

This event will appeal to a special portion of your community of teens. Depending on the community, this may be a small or large group of teens. Regardless of size, the enthusiasm that *Otaku* fans and cosplayers have will fill any room. If you have a popular manga and graphic novel collection, this event will appeal to some of those users. This event is a perfect opportunity to reach out to enthusiasts in the community who may not currently use the library. The contest celebrates creativity and individuality, and it also creates an opportunity for enthusiasts to meet new people. *Otaku* fans are passionate, dedicated, and once introduced to the library, may become some of its most dedicated users.

Instructors/Talent

There may be local adult fans willing to help plan this event or help judge the contest. There may be library staff that are manga and anime fans who could also help plan or judge. Perhaps someone at the local comic shop or Japanese market would be interested in helping as well. Knowledge of manga, anime, video games, science fiction, or fantasy is greatly beneficial and will make the contest better.

Audience

Teens and young adults are the main audience for cosplay. Due to the time and resources involved, the more intense enthusiasts are often older teens and adults. However, middle schoolers will enjoy themselves, so breaking the contest competition into age categories is important.

Planning and Supplies

This is an incredibly easy event to plan and set up.

- Rules and guidelines will need to be determined. For example: Judging will be based on a combination of enthusiasm for and knowledge of your character, costume quality, and execution.
- Determine what age categories are needed, such as grades 6 through 8, grades 9 through 12, and/or adult. Determine whether original characters are also allowed.
- Create a sign-in sheet.
- Set up the room to allow the participants to line up and walk in front of the judges' table.
- Make sure the judges have a table with chairs, tally sheets, and a laptop to look up images of characters to check authenticity of costume.

- Have something else for the teens to do, like *Dance Dance Revolution (DDR)*, screening anime, crafts, or all of the above.
- Display manga, graphic novels, and applicable magazines.
- Provide drinks and Japanese snacks like Pocky or gummy candies to add to a festive atmosphere.
- Purchase prizes such as gift certificates to Japanese stores, markets, or to a fabric store to support the cosplay habit. Provide prizes for all age categories.

Create

Having refreshments and video games set up, preferably *DDR* with Japanese pop playing loudly, is a great way to get participants in the mood for the contest. Have participants sign in when they arrive and let everyone know when judging will take place. Depending on how many entries there are, the judging could take 15 to 30 minutes or more if many people are participating. When it is time to start judging, have all participants line up. Each will approach the judges' table one at a time to tell the judges the character's name, why that character was chosen or created if it is original, and the process of creating the costume.

After everyone has had a turn, the judges will deliberate. During this process, the participants can take part in the other activities you have set up. Have fun awarding the prizes once the judges are done. Consider inviting other teens to come and watch and play *DDR* since that will help create more excitement with more attendees. Many teens may not create costumes themselves but will enjoy seeing what others have created.

Food, Technology, and Other Mandatory Extras

- Having something to drink and Japanese snacks makes the event more festive.
- Setting up *DDR* or other Japanese video games, screening anime, and putting out a selection of manga, graphic novels, magazines, and DVDs will expose new users to your materials and showcase what is new in the collection to current users.
- Having a laptop on hand to look up characters is very helpful in judging. Even someone who really knows manga, anime, and video games will come across an obscure character he or she has never seen. This resource will also help with judging costume quality and authenticity.

Analysis

Cosplay contests may not be popular in all communities, so use your collections, requests, and observation as guidelines for determining the desire for this event. Be prepared to start out slow and take time to build an audience. If the event is successful consider having contests several times a year.

Marketing Tips

Reaching out to the online cosplay community using message boards is the best way to get the word out about a cosplay contest. If there is a Japanese store or market in the area, take publicity there. Comic book stores, toy stores, and other places enthusiasts hang out are other places to advertise. Put flyers in manga, graphic novels, sci-fi, and fantasy materials in your collection. Costume and fabric stores are also places cosplayers might see an ad.

Resources

Check out these articles for more information on cosplay:

Brehm-Heeger, Paula, Ann Conway, and Carrie Vale. 2007. "Cosplay, Gaming and Conventions: Amazing Unexpected Places an Anime Club Can Lead Unsuspecting Librarians." *Young Adult Library Services* 5, no. 2 (Winter): 14–16.

Knight, Meribah. 2010. "A Thriving Business Built on Geeks' Backs." *Chicago News Cooperative.* May 14. http://www.chicagonewscoop.org/a-thriving-business-built-on-geeks%E2%80%99-backs/.

Amigurumi: Crochet Happy Fun

General Description

Patrons are invited to learn how to crochet small creatures, food items, and dolls inspired by the Japanese *amigurumi* tradition.

Pop

Amigurumi—literally translated as "knitted stuffed toy"—is the Japanese art of knitting or crocheting small stuffed animals and anthropomorphic creatures. *Amigurumi* are typically cute animals (such as bears, rabbits, cats, dogs) but can include inanimate objects endowed with anthropomorphism. *Amigurumi* can be either knitted or crocheted. In recent years, crocheted *amigurumi* are more popular and more commonly seen. This activity is another craze born from the Japanese obsession with "cute" things, commonly called *kawaii*.

Relate

Teens interested in *Otaku* of Japanese fan culture, manga, anime, or Japanese fashions, like those into the Gothic Lolita scene, will respond to a program like this. However, it also exposes teens who enjoy crafts and DIY culture to an interest they may not yet know about.

Instructors/Talent

When teaching a group of people something detailed, it is key to either have several people to assist or use technology to follow one person. Have a camera film a close-up of the instructor's hands while simultaneously projecting this image on a large screen. The instructor can talk the group through the techniques while demonstrating it in a way so that all can see. After this technique was utilized during a sushi instruction class, it was dubbed the "sushi cam" whenever this setup is requested for a program.

Audience

Teens in grades 6 through 12 and adults.

Planning and Supplies

Luckily, crochet is a relatively easy craft in terms of supplies. Supplies included a quantity of crochet hooks that ranged from G, H, I, to J sizes, based on the recommendation of the instructor, and an assortment of worsted weight 100 acrylic yarn in bright colors. The instructor came up with several designs of her own, but if you need patterns there are a multitude of *amigurumi* books to consult. The instructor also created visual handouts for the participants to take home.

Create

A local crochet instructor was located by posting on a local Meetup.com message board. In the message, the program was described, as were the skills the library was interested in. An instructor was hired who had experience working with young people and in teaching. Although she was not familiar with *amigurumi*, she was more than willing to learn. You may find an instructor in the opposite fashion—someone who is an *amigurumi* fan and took up crochet to fuel this interest. Some library staff who knit have helped with past programs, but in this case no staff was interested in learning the new craft. If you have in-house talent, use them.

Food, Technology, and Other Mandatory Extras

Food is not necessary for this program, and the technology mentioned under instructors/talent is very helpful but not mandatory if you have enough people to do hands-on instruction.

Analysis

This program can be very difficult for some people, so be prepared for some frustration and even some tears. Having an instructor who is patient and willing to show people the same thing over and over again is very important. Some people will be persistent enough to keep trying and others will not. Crochet is not easy to learn, but it is possible.

Marketing Tips

Advertise the program to anime and manga clubs at the local middle school and high schools. Consider introducing this new craft during a knitting program for creating scarves, mittens, and blankets. It might create some interest that could spread by word of mouth.

Resources

Take a look at these materials for techniques and patterns:

Haden, Christen. 2008. *Creepy Cute Crochet: Zombies, Ninjas, Robots, and More!* Philadelphia, PA: Quirk Books.

Obaachan, Annie. 2008. *Amigurumi Animals: 15 Patterns and Dozens of Techniques for Creating Cute Crochet Creatures.* New York: St. Martin's Griffin.

Rimoli, Ana Paula. 2008. *Amigurumi World: Seriously Cute Crochet.* Bothell, WA: Martingale & Co Inc.

Yee, Jou Ling. 2010. "Amigurumi Kingdom." Accessed September 2. http://www.amigurumikingdom.com/.

Chapter 14

Programs: Me—Beauty, Style, Body Modification, and Fashion

The tween and teen years are the time when youth start to become individuals, developing their own opinions and styles. Design programs to encourage self-discovery of beauty and fashion, as well as to provide good information about such big decisions as tattoos and piercings.

Nail Art

Information on the Nail Art program was provided by Meaghan Battle, Youth Services Librarian at the Ann Arbor District Library.

General Description
This project is a nail decoration extravaganza that encourages self-expression through the use of nail polishes, decals, and rhinestones.

Pop
This program takes advantage of the whole DIY craze and combines tween and teen creativity with fun!

Relate
Painting fingernails is a very solitary activity. Why not make it social and have a group of teens do it all together at the library?

Instructors/Talent
No instructors were used for this program, but it might be fun to invite a few airbrush technicians for an airbrushed nail station.

Audience

Grades 4 through 8.

Planning and Supplies

- Large selection of nail polish colors; nail rhinestones, which are much cheaper in large quantities when ordering online
- Nail decals
- Nail art brushes
- Emery boards
- Little plastic cups
- Palmolive (for soaking nails and cuticles)
- Paper towels
- Orangewood sticks
- Access to water

Create

Attendees are told where materials and design ideas are located and encouraged to ask questions for anything they need throughout the activity. Nail polishes, decals, and rhinestones can be distributed to each table before the program, or all such materials can be placed at a larger central table. A pitcher of water, small plastic cups, and Palmolive dishwashing liquid should be centrally located for those who want to soak their nails before they begin.

Each table should have a supply of emery boards, nail art brushes, cotton swabs, paper towels, nail polish remover, orangewood sticks, and top coat. This allows tweens to experiment with body art as a form of self-expression without the permanence of tattoos. Emery boards, orangewood sticks, and cotton swabs used by individuals become their property and should not be shared with others for hygienic reasons.

Food, Technology, and Other Mandatory Extras

No food is needed for this event, but fun, popular music playing in the background is a huge plus. It keeps the atmosphere lively.

Analysis

An hour is a great time frame for this program. Any longer and tweens may start to get bored. Be sure to put up a display showcasing books on sleepover activities. The Kitchen Cosmetics program in this chapter is also fun for tweens to try at home in a group.

Marketing Tips

Invite local Girl Scout groups. Put up flyers at nail and beauty salons.

Resource

Check out this helpful book for explicit instructions on trendy and simple nail designs:

Haab, Sherri. 2009. *Nail Art*. Palo Alto, CA: Klutz Publishing.

Kitchen Cosmetics

> *The Kitchen Cosmetics program was written and contributed by Meaghan Battle, Youth Services Librarian at the Ann Arbor District Library.*

General Description

Use food and other kitchen items to make skin care products. Create samples at the library and take some home with you. Example recipes are cucumber honey toner, refreshing orange scrub, and strawberry hand and foot exfoliant.

Pop

The movement toward green personal products fits perfectly with this environmentally conscious program. The ingredients for all of the products are natural and widely available at local markets.

Relate

All libraries are making a conscious effort to "go green" by using less paper in all aspects of operation. Some summer reading programs are only available online; fewer flyers are being distributed for promotion; amd websites and televisions placed throughout the physical library space instead does the promotion with electronic advertisements. Library programming should also model environmentally aware alternatives to common activities.

Instructors/Talent

If there is a spa or salon in town that specializes in all-natural treatments, consider inviting a technician. This is not a requirement. You can run this program very successfully if you have no training in making homemade beauty products. Miss Moorpark and Miss Simi Valley came to help in one iteration of this program (see Figure 14.1). Many times local beauty pageant winners are looking for opportunities to volunteer in their communities. Their presenace added an element of elegance to the program, and they even wore their crowns!

Figure 14.1. Miss Moorpark Helping to Prepare a Natural Face Mask at the Moorpark (CA) City Library

Audience

Grades 4 through 8.

Planning and Supplies

Simple recipes for making different beauty supplies can be found in many spa books or online. Favorite blogs include *Kitchen, Crafts, & More*, and the All Natural Beauty website. Below is a list of supplies needed for the program:

- Blenders
- Small tins or jars (Ziploc bags or small Tupperware containers will work too)
- Small labels
- Rubber spatulas
- Measuring spoons and cups
- Recipe sheets (with instructions for participants to re-create recipes at home)
- Necessary groceries
- Mixing bowls

- Mixing spoons
- Tablecloths

Create

- Set up a blender station or two at the front of the room. If a large crowd is expected, consider having more than one station to improved traffic flow. Make sure that you have enough staff to operate the blenders.
- The room can be arranged into stations, with ingredients for each recipe placed on tables around the room.
- Set up tables for seating with tablecloths, recipe sheets, mixing bowls and spoons, and storage tins. Encourage kids to choose recipes and go about mixing up their cosmetics. With a smaller crowd, it might be more convenient for everyone to work together to make each recipe and then divide it among the group to take home.

Food, Technology, and Other Mandatory Extras

Fun, popular music playing in the background is a huge plus. It keeps the atmosphere lively. Consider easy access to sinks for hand washing. Cosmetic creations can and will get messy.

Analysis

Remind participants that these ingredients are perishable, so any cosmetics taken home should be refrigerated and used within a few days of the program. Whatever supplies you purchase will be used up, so buy way more ingredients than you think you will need. Kids will want to make all of the recipes at least once and take home many of them. If you have a very limited number of tins or jars, set a limit from the beginning. This program is a messy proposition due to the mixing, so be ready to spend time cleaning up the room after the program.

Marketing Tips

Leave flyers at local beauty salons. Parents will pass along information about different and interesting programs to their teens.

Resources

Check out these books and websites for help with finding recipes:

All Natural Beauty. http://allnaturalbeauty.us/hbr_ingredients.htm.
Bonnell, Jennifer. 2003. *D.I.Y. Girl: The Real Girl's Guide to Making Everything from Lip Gloss to Lamps.* New York: Puffin Books.

Kitchen, Crafts & More (blog). http://www.kitchencraftsnmore.net/bath3.html.

Tattoo History, Culture, and Safety

General Description

While teens cannot get a tattoo until they are 18 in most states, the desire to get one often starts much earlier. This program should cover the historical and cultural significance of tattooing, as well as information about tattoo safety and health. For teens who may be tempted to have a friend do the tattoo, the health information is important.

Pop

Tattoos are now a very common and popular form of personal expression. At one time, only sailors or bikers had tattoos, but that has obviously changed considerably. In fact, a 2007 Pew Research Center poll found that one-third of "Generation Next," young adults ages 18 to 25, had tattoos (The Pew Research Center for the People & the Press, 2007). The popularity of reality television shows like *Miami Ink* and *LA Ink* have only made the art seem more appealing. Tattoos are now almost ubiquitous on sports players and celebrities—not to mention quite a few librarians.

Relate

Rather than taking a negative stand against tattoos or being precautionary about them, it is much wiser to give teens and their parents the information they need to make informed choices about whether getting a tattoo is something they might want to do. Tattoos are such a lightning rod of interest for many teens that it is a perfect way to show relevance to the teens in the community.

Instructors/Talent

This type of program should be conducted by a licensed and trained tattoo artist. Search around for tattoo artists that perhaps have experience teaching classes or otherwise have enough knowledge and enthusiasm for the topic. Ask library staff, family, or friends who have tattoos if they have a local shop or an artist that they really like. Ideally, the instructor would bring along some of the tattoo supplies to show to the group.

Audience

Teens, their parents, and adults are the best audience for this type of program. Younger children might also be interested, but in that case it would be best if their parents came along.

Planning and Supplies

The bulk of the planning for this event is up front in locating a tattoo artist who is up to the challenge. Beyond that, encouraging the artist to do a PowerPoint slide show or other visual presentation is recommended, since it is a visual art. Have the artist bring tattoo instruments and supplies so attendees can see them up close and ask questions. Be sure to have some books and magazines on tattooing available for checkout after the program.

Create

A knowledgeable and enthusiastic artist is all you need to create a unique and interesting program. Discuss the content of the presentation with the artist so you can anticipate questions from the audience. Be sure the artist emphasizes the lifelong commitment involved in getting a tattoo and encourages young people to think and plan long and hard before they make a decision (see Figure 14.2).

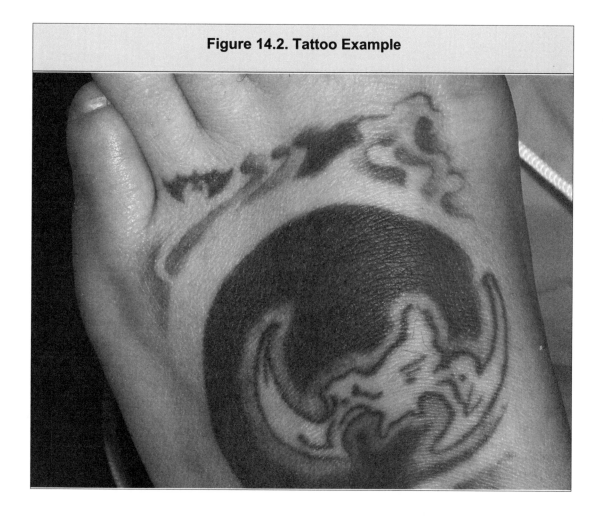

Figure 14.2. Tattoo Example

Food, Technology, and Other Mandatory Extras

If the instructor does a visual presentation, having a projector that can hook up to a laptop is key.

Analysis

Do not let fear of community outrage or potential bad apples keep this program from being planned. The intent is to educate and inform the public about tattooing and dispel myths and confusion. A well-planned program is the best strategy. Tattoo artists are in the business of staying in business, so they have an investment in making sure people are safe and responsible.

Marketing Tips

Target art teachers and coaches at the high schools to get the word out, since some teens who enjoy these activities may be the most inclined to be interested. Since tattoos are so prevalent in sports today, teens who play sports may be eager to learn more. If there are any tattooing interest groups on Flickr.com or Meetup.com postings, posting the activity on their message boards is also a good idea.

Resources

Check out these books for more information on tattoos:

Hesselt van Dinter, Maarten, 2007. *The World of Tattoo: An Illustrated History*. Amsterdam: KIT Publishers.

The Pew Research Center for the People & the Press. 2007. "How Young People View Their Lives, Futures and Politics: A Portrait of 'Generation Next.'" January 9. http://people-press.org/reports/pdf/ 300.pdf.

Von D, Kat. 2009. *High Voltage Tattoo*. New York: Collins Design.

Chapter 15

Programs: Magic, Fantasy, and the Mystical World

The mystical is always in style in one form or another. From *Dungeons & Dragons* role-playing games to fascination with vampires, teens are always interested in the mystical world. Create programs that engage teens with the most popular mystical creatures of the day: dragons, vampires, werewolves, fairies, or unicorns to name a few. The most popular books and movies are the best indicators to the current teen obsession. Think creatively about modifying typical craft programs to encompass these creatures simply by using different supplies. For example, what was once a house for a fairy last year is now a vampire shrine using bubble-gum eyeballs and red paint for blood.

Psychics, Astrology, and the Future Fair

General Description
Invite teens to get the chance to have readings from psychics, astrologers, palm readers, tarot card readers, aura readers, dream analyzers, runestone readers, and more. With a number of professional readers on hand, teens can get several readings.

Pop
Being fascinated with ghosts, astrology, past lives, the future, tarot cards, and palm reading are often part of adolescence. The recent popularity of television shows like *Psychic Kids: Children of the Paranormal* and *John Edward Cross Country*, and movies like *Paranormal Activity*, have only made teen fascination with the unknown more popular.

Relate
Giving teens the opportunity to explore their world and try out new things implies trust. This type of program is a great way to let teens try something new that normally is

143

fairly cost-prohibitive since using the services of psychics and other mediums can be expensive.

Instructors/Talent

Having a variety and quantity of six to eight readers is important to the success of this program. Depending on how popular the event is, some teens may need to wait, but with that many readers, teens should get several readings. Finding the readers will vary in difficulty depending on the location and size of the community. A fairly large metropolitan area should have some sort of guide or free weekly newspaper that features a directory of local practitioners. There are many national magazines that may be helpful in finding readers too. When contacting potential readers, be sure to ask if they have ever participated in an event like this for young people. Some may have been hired to work at birthday or high school graduation parties. Readers with that type of experience are what to look for. Negotiating the fees is very important, so be sure to look for someone who will charge for the block of time rather than the number of readings given. This way as many teens as possible can get a reading and the charge will not be based on the number of teens in attendance.

Audience

Teens and adults would be interested in such a program, but if space and resources are limited, then restricting the event to just teens is recommended. Adults looking for free readings could easily overwhelm the event and take chances away from the teens.

Planning and Supplies

The bulk of the planning will be up front and in organizing the space properly. When locating and booking readers, determine how much space each of them will need and ask about privacy considerations. During the readings, it is important that each teen has privacy. With an aura reader they will need space to set up a screen and possibly a printer if they are going to provide the teens with a printout of their aura. Most readers, other than aura, will not have much in the way of supplies, so setup is fairly easy.

Create

The most important thing to do is to be sure you have a system for determining how many readings each teen will get and getting them signed up in an orderly fashion. Depending on the number of attendees, this could get fairly complicated. Be sure to plan some alternate activities so that teens do not get bored waiting for their turn. Have a hands-on craft area available or set up some displays in the waiting area for teens who have time to kill.

Food, Technology, and Other Mandatory Extras

Some teens may want to record their readings so they can go back and listen to them later. Consider allowing teens to bring their own recording devices or, if you have access to several portable podcast devices, the files could be saved and sent to the teens via e-mail. This technology is constantly changing, but devices can usually be purchased for less than $100. In some cases, the readers may have these types of devices and could do the same thing for teens.

Analysis

This type of event is sure to be popular and will likely bring in some teens who have never before attended a library event. It is important to note that some people object to the notion of psychics and astrologers, usually due to religious reasons and sometimes because it is believed that there is something evil about the practice. As long as the library's mission statement is clear about serving people of all interests and beliefs, these types of complaints can be handled easily. Of course there are some communities and parts of the country where this may be a harder sell; nevertheless, it does not mean the program would not be popular or serve a need among the community's teens.

Marketing Tips

This type of event should be promoted at teen hangouts including coffee shops and other casual businesses where the hip teens hang out. It would also be a good idea to take flyers to places like the YMCA or Boys & Girls Clubs.

Resources

Check out these books for further information about the psychic realm:

Abadie, M.J. 2003. *Teen Dream Power: Unlock the Meaning of Your Dreams*. Rochester, VT: Bindu Books.
Abadie, M.J. 2003. *Teen Psychic: Exploring Your Intuitive Spiritual Powers*. Rochester, VT: Bindu Books.
Thompson, Alicia, Joost Elffers, and Gary Goldschneider. 2010. *Secret Language of Birthdays,* Teen Ed. New York: Razorbill.

Vampire Wreaths

General Description

Do you consider yourself a true authority on vampire lore? Are you interested in the undead? Or maybe you just love the *Twilight* series? Teens were invited to stop by the library and make wreaths to decorate their rooms to attract (or distract) vampires (see Figure 15.1).

Figure 15.1. Vampire Wreath to Attract Vampires

Pop

Stephenie Meyer's *Twilight* series is a teen phenomenon that began in 2005. A mix of vampires and forbidden loves, with an extra love interest thrown in for good measure, *Twilight* has become a favorite for girls, boys, and many adults. In current popular culture, everyone is forced to choose a side: Team Edward or Team Jacob. Vampire lovers are on the lookout for new books, television shows, graphic novels, and anything else they can sink their teeth into.

Relate

Teens are interested in reading anything with vampires. Spotlight other vampire materials in your collection, encouraging teens who are stuck on *Twilight* to branch out and potentially discover werewolves, ghosts, zombies, and other strange paranormals involved in love triangles.

Instructors/Talent

No instructors are needed.

Audience

Grades 6 through 12.

Planning and Supplies

To Keep Vampires Away
- Small wreaths (12-inch grapevine wreaths)
- Craft glue
- Hot-glue gun and glue sticks
- Red and black glass garden beads
- Red and black ribbon
- Craft wood to make wooden stakes and crosses
- Dried garlic
- Silver ribbon to simulate silver chains

To Attract Vampires
- Silver spray glitter
- Lavender
- Craft foam to create signs: "Welcome Vampires. Please come in."
- Red and black craft paint (for fake blood)
- Red ribbon roses
- Plastic eyeballs

Create

Place tables and chairs around the room; supply each station with glue, scissors, and wreaths. Fill another table with all of the craft supplies, separating the supplies into two areas: "Keeping Vampires Away" and "Attracting Vampires." Teens will be asked to choose which type of wreath they would like to make. Put the glue guns and glue sticks in one area so that use of the hot guns can be monitored.

Food, Technology, and Other Mandatory Extras

If the program is during Halloween, serve candy. Otherwise, serve vampire-inspired food such as Red Hots (for "red hot vampire love") or red velvet cupcakes with black chocolate frosting.

Analysis

This program works very well near Halloween. There are lots of great supplies to purchase, like plastic severed fingers, which would definitely attract vampires. The program would also be great paired with another activity, like watching a *Twilight* movie while doing the project or having a *Twilight* trivia tournament after the craft.

Marketing Tips

Make sure the librarians at the middle schools and high schools are aware of the program so they can promote it to the known *Twilight* fans.

Resources

Check out these books for fun facts about vampires:

Gray, Amy Tipton. *How to Be a Vampire: A Fangs-On Guide for the Newly Undead.* Somerville, MA: Candlewick Press.

Karg, Barb. *The Girl's Guide to Vampires: All You Need to Know about the Original Bad Boys.* Avon, MA: Adams Media.

Fairy Homes, Jewelry, Dolls, and More

General Description

Many different types of programs can be designed with fairies in mind: creating fairy homes out of natural materials, designing a mosaic fairy wand, making fairy clothes, sewing a fairy-attracting satchet or even making fairy food.

Pop

Fairies became part of the public consciousness with the popularization of Tinkerbell, the fairy from *Peter Pan*. Disney continues to keep Tinkerbell popular with her own books and movies. Mattel added to the craze by introducing Fairytopia dolls and all of their various incarnations. *Fairy Tale: A True Story*, a movie which came out in 1998, heralded the craze that has not abated since. Cicely Mary Barker's fairies have also been remade with a modern audience in mind, with books similar to the *Dragonology* titles. Of course, books for teens like *Wicked Lovely* by Melissa Marr have made fairies that much more popular too.

Relate

The fantasy and beauty associated with fairies is very magnetic to teens, and they enjoy the "darker" side of fairies with their mischievous tricks. Teens can indulge their love of fairies in a creative and hands-on manner with this activity.

Instructors/Talent

No instructors are required, but finding someone creative with a passion for fairies is a bonus. Florists or others who make their living creating fairy crafts or dolls would be good options to explore when looking for a potential instructor. However, many good fairy craft books are available now. An enthusiastic library staff person can easily conduct these workshops with a little planning and creativity.

Audience

Children, teens, and adults all love fairies, so it is up to the librarian and presenters to determine the audience's age range for any particular program.

Planning and Supplies

Fairy Houses or Gardens
- Shoebox to hold the house or garden
- A small dish for water
- Twigs, bark, small pine cones
- Flowers, real and silk
- Sand or gravel
- Moss (live or spanish)
- Hot-glue guns to attach twigs together to make structures

Fairy Sachet
- Loose dried lavender, chamomile, or other fragrant dried herbs
- Small pieces of colorful fabric to hold the herbs
- Ribbon to tie the sachet closed
- Silk cord to string it and wear as a necklace

Fairy Clothes
- Thick white paper to glue designs down to
- Dried flowers from potpourri or silk flowers cut up
- Dried leaves, grass, etc.
- Colored pencils
- Glue (See Figure 15.2.)

Create

The wonderful thing about a fairy program is that because it is fantasy, there are no rules. Having an abundance of supply options is always important, so that participants

Figure 15.2. Flower Fairy Clothes

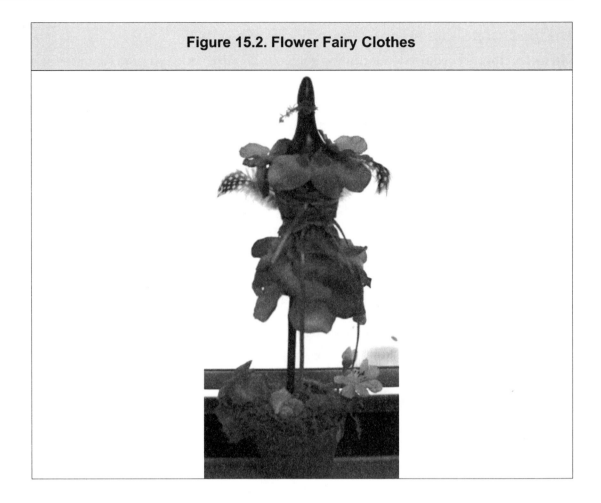

can be as free as they like. If the fairy house is going to be constructed out of twigs and less about the natural setting, then use hot glue to make something sturdier. Collecting things outside is ideal, but supplies can be purchased at craft stores too. For a fairy clothing or "fashion" event (see Figure 15.3), be sure to use the book *Fairie-ality: The Fashion Collection from the House of Ellwand* (Shields, 2002). The book has wonderful photos and ideas for inspiration.

Food, Technology, and Other Mandatory Extras

For a more festive fairy party vibe, considering offering special fairy cupcakes, fairy lavender punch, and fairy rings with mushrooms and fruit. Have fresh-cut flowers out to add to the ambiance.

Analysis

This type of program can go in any direction and lends itself to being altered and changed with new ideas. Supplies can easily be saved for another event or recycled in new ways.

Figure 15.3. Fairy Fashion in a Fairy Book

Marketing Tips

Advertise through craft stores, florist shops, English teachers at the schools, or to any businesses in the area that sell whimsical or fairy-related gift items.

Resources

Barker, Cicely Mary. 2004. *How to Host a Flower Fairy Tea-Party*. London: Frederick Warne.

Beery, Barbara. 2007. *Fairies Cookbook*. Layton, UT: Gibbs-Smith Publishers.

Kane, Barry. 2008. *Fairy House and Beyond!* Lee, NH: Light-Beams.

Mullaney, Colleen. 2010. *Fairy Parties: Recipes, Crafts, and Games for Enchanting Celebrations*. San Francisco: Chronicle Books.

Ross, Kathy. 2008. *Fairy World Crafts*. North Minneapolis, MN: First Avenue.

Shields, Genie. 2002. *Fairie-ality: The Fashion Collection from the House of Ellwand*. Somerville, MA: Candlewick.

Chapter 16

Programs: Music

Music is such a big part of teens' and tweens' lives. Musicals have become particularly popular lately, creating great fan bases and such movie and television phenomena as *High School Musical* and *Glee*. Think about modeling programs after popular musical-oriented television shows or movies, such as *American Idol* or *The Singing Bee*. But do not forget about using music teens listen to as inspiration for programs as well. Try a battle of the bands using video game technology or with actual band equipment. Let teens use the computer lab to create beats on GarageBand software or have a music video contest using YouTube.

High School Musical Karaoke

General Description

A twist on classic karaoke, *High School Musical* karaoke is a niche program, designed for fans of the movies and those interested in trying something new. Teens take turns going up to the laptop and picking their favorite songs to sing from the movies. While waiting their turn, other teens can design tote bags and picture frames with the *High School Musical* logos and pictures of the characters. Though a passing craze, this program can be used as a model for the next musical phenomenon, such as the Emmy award-winning television show *Glee*.

Pop

High School Musical (HSM) began as a made-for-television movie, which aired on the Disney Channel in 2006. Since then, two more movies have come out, including one in theaters. The movie phenomenon has created a resurgence in musicals for teens and tweens, and it has participated in the "tween marketing machine," with a diverse product line featuring everything from board games to books to bedspreads. Stage productions of the musical have popped up all over the country, and the Troy and Gabriella love story can even be enjoyed in video games and ice-skating shows.

Relate

Besides being a major entertainment interest for tweens and some teens, the movie also sends out a positive message about respecting your friends for having interests and skills that might not be considered popular. Many books about the movie and further adventures of the characters have been published, which can be promoted at your program. It would also be a great time to highlight your library's DVD and CD collections by introducing other musicals the kids might enjoy.

Instructors/Talent

No instructors needed.

Audience

Grades 4 through 8. *HSM* is hugely popular with grades 2 and 3 as well, so you could open the program up to younger kids.

Planning and Supplies

- Laptop
- *High School Musical* karaoke CD
- Craft supplies and decorations purchased from a party store

Create

Teens take turns picking their favorite *HSM* songs and singing them in the front of the room. Besides watching the others perform and singing along to the music, teens are engaged with crafts. Your local party store may have decorations and other items that sport the *HSM* characters and logo. Stickers of *HSM* characters, including the beloved Troy and Gabriella, can be used to decorate inexpensive acrylic picture frames, which can be purchased in bulk on the Internet. White cotton tote bags, also purchased in bulk, can be decorated with fabric markers, the school's mascot, the cougar; and basketballs, which are all aspects popular in the first movie.

Food, Technology, and Other Mandatory Extras

Your laptop can be plugged into the programming room's sound system, but using the laptop speakers in a small room may be sufficient. The laptop can be hooked into a projector so that the audience can sing along to the words. The preferred karaoke CD to purchase is a CD+G, which is an audio CD that contains embedded graphics, including the words to the songs that cross the screen as you sing. When purchasing a karaoke CD, check to see if it is only instrumental background music, or if you can sing along with the original movie's singers. Your tweens might be particular, so it is something to keep in mind. Decorate the room with posters from the movie and crepe paper to create a party ambiance. Place light snacks at each table.

Analysis

Though Troy and Gabriella have graduated from high school and moved on, there are many movie/musical acts from Disney and Nickelodeon to create karaoke programs around for tweens. Try a Jonas Brothers program or Justin Bieber karaoke. For an older audience, pick up the CD of songs performed on the television show *Glee* or the *Buffy the Vampire Slayer* musical episode. Even if a karaoke CD is not available, with a little extra legwork you can create a sing-along by printing off the words to the songs and passing them around. Another addition to the program could be a trivia component, quizzing the fans on the idiosyncrasies of the musicals.

Marketing Tips

Post the event on the library's Facebook page, and you might attract teens and tweens that do not normally attend library programs. Be sure to post details for the program in the teen and tween spaces of the library too.

Resource

Disney Channel. 2010. "*High School Musical* Official Website." Accessed September 2. http://tv.disney.go.com/disneychannel/originalmovies/highschoolmusical/index.html.

Chapter 17

Programs: Physical Activities

Popular physical activities can be inspired by musicians, movies, television, and famous sports stars. Also look to making programs hands-on involving science experiments, which have been promoted through television shows like *MythBusters* on the Discovery Channel. Reading is a stationary activity, so anything the library can do to promote activity is a plus.

Dance Programs

General Description

Teens are invited to attend one-time workshops on different types of dance, including a demonstration and instruction. Pick a type of dance that is popular at the moment: ballroom dancing, capoeira mandinga, breakdancing, bellydancing, krumping, and more.

Pop

Dancing is huge with teens, and dance sequences are currently big in movies marketed to teens and tweens. Popular reality television shows *So You Think You Can Dance* and *Dancing with the Stars* demonstrate that regular people can get their chance to become professional dancers. Dances like the tango are given a rebirth from movies such as *Mad Hot Ballroom*. Video games are created to teach the dance moves shown in such movies as *High School Musical*. Media interest in different types of dance creates fascination by teens to try out these dances.

Relate

Promoting health activity is always a plus for libraries, and dancing is a very energetic hobby. It is also a great way to highlight the library's music collection, whether it be CDs or music downloads.

Instructors/Talent

Unless you are an expert in a certain type of dance or feel comfortable learning a dance sequence and teaching it to a group, find a local instructor. Check with dance studios, dance groups at local colleges, or instructors for community recreation classes.

Audience

Grades 6 through 12.

Planning and Supplies

All that is needed is a large room. If the talent plans on doing a demonstration, make sure there is room for a stage or performance area. Use colored masking tape to designate the stage area so that participants will not sit in it if they are sitting on the floor. Collect CDs, dance instruction DVDs, and books, and create a display for participants who want to learn more about the dance. For ambiance, play appropriate music through a sound system or boombox as participants enter the room.

Create

Let the teens dance. The program should probably be 60 to 90 minutes at the most. Those that are dedicated will want to dance longer, but an hour and a half is probably long enough for teens to get a taste of the new dance.

Food, Technology, and Other Mandatory Extras

Water is a must because participants will be working up a sweat.

Analysis

Do not forget to look to musical groups who may have popular dance sequences or have made a certain type of music popular. Learning how to swing dance was a big deal in the late 1990s. The "swing revival" was supported by bands like the Squirrel Nut Zippers and Big Bad Voodoo Daddy. Plan to hold the event near school dances or proms. If a dance is particularly popular, partygoers will want to show off their dance skills in front of their classmates.

Marketing Tips

Ask to have the program promoted over the morning announcements at middle schools and high schools before a dance.

Resources

Resources are based on the type of dance chosen for the program.

Parkour and Freerunning

The Parkour and Freerunning program was written and contributed by Vicki Browne, Teen Librarian at the Ann Arbor District Library.

General Description

Parkour is the art of moving through your environment using only your body and whatever is in your surroundings to propel yourself along. It can include but is not limited to running, crawling, leaping, and climbing. Think the beginning chase scene in the movie *Casino Royale*. The local university's parkour running club members were asked to do a demo off-site at a local park and fitness center, and also talk about technique and training for parkour. A ready-made obstacle course right in your urban landscape is waiting to be explored!

Pop

Many films, like James Bond classics or *The Bourne Ultimatum*, have amazing free-running scenes. The hobby is highly appealing for teens: to try maneuvering pathways that are easy to reproduce wherever their urban landscape is. Parkour was highlighted in the television show *American Ninja Warrior* shown on G4, the video gaming television channel, where participants raced to complete obstacle courses with the fastest time.

Relate

Encouraging fitness and healthy living in programs for teens is a great goal. Holding events outside out of the library is also a beneficial form of outreach, to illustrate to community members who do not frequent the library what the library can offer them.

Instructors/Talent

One of our freerunning events was led by Levi Meeuwenberg, of *American Ninja Warrior* fame, who happened to be a local contact. The leader of the local college club did a live demo at a local county park as well.

Audience

Grades 6 to adult. This program may also appeal to the skateboarding crowd.

Planning and Supplies

Planning involves seeking out those in your area who are currently involved in the parkour and freerunning hobby. Look to local colleges to see if they have a club.

Create

Offer an informational meeting with discussion of background and the "how-to" of the activities; then hold a demo. At the demo, the leader and his guest performers were able to practice techniques of safe jumping and landing positions, talk about how to participate safely in the hobby, and how to work with the community to make this "sport" happen.

Food, Technology, and Other Mandatory Extras

The local county park facility had an indoor gym in which the informational discussion part of the program could take place, as well as an outdoor park with wooden play structures and benches perfect for an outdoor demonstration.

Analysis

This is a great program that highlights a little-known physical hobby and involves a partnership with a local organization. If an AV system is available, showing clips of parkour scenes from movies and television shows would be a great addition to the program.

Marketing Tips

Market this program at BMX, skateboarding, and snowboarding shops. Teens who are attracted to extreme lifestyle sports would be interesting in attending this program.

Resource

Check out this book to learn more about parkour:

Edwardes, Dan. 2009. *The Parkour and Freerunning Handbook*. New York: It Books.

Double Dutch Program

Information on the Double Dutch program was provided by Vicki Browne, Teen Librarian at the Ann Arbor District Library.

General Description

Incorporate physical activity into a fun and easy program for teens and tweens. Create a space for participants to jump rope and break a sweat while having a great time.

Pop

Double Dutch started on the sidewalks of New York City, and was brought over by Dutch settlers. It became particularly popular in urban areas, where kids and teens would sing along to rhymes while turning and jumping rope. The game became a sport when the first Double Dutch tournament was held in the 1970s and attracted almost 600 middle schoolers. Now a form of performance art, the combination of simple moves to music have become national and international pastimes, where people can join the International Double Dutch Federation, the National Double Dutch League, and the Dynamic Diplomats of Double Dutch team.

Relate

Jumping rope is healthy and fun. It is a sport where no one has to worry about being first string, nor does it take years of training. While being a physical activity, jumping rope does not take any special skill. Use this program to promote overall health in teens.

Instructors/Talent

A local jump rope team called the Heartbeats was invited to perform tricks and demos as a team for the program participants. The group stayed for the duration of the program and was available to instruct the finer points of Double Dutch. While enhancing the program and bringing something extra for the patrons, the group benefited from free advertisement to the community.

Audience

The program was offered to grades 4 through 12, but expect adults to attend the program. Lots of grown-ups are drawn in remembering when they jumped rope way back when.

Planning and Supplies

Purchase assorted jump ropes, including standard single-size ropes, Double Dutch ropes, and Chinese jump ropes. If purchasing jump ropes is not an option, try borrowing them from local schools or gyms like the YMCA. Block off a portion of your parking lot with orange cones. If the weather is very warm, set up a table with a water cooler, and you may even have on hand some spray bottles with water.

Create

If possible, have an experienced group perform for the first part of the program. Then throw the ropes out and let everyone have a good time. The participants will need to share the ropes.

Food, Technology, and Other Mandatory Extras

Nothing extra is needed for this event. If there is room in the budget, give the crowd a little summer treat like popsicles or small ice cream cups. No fancy sound system is needed. With a simple boombox you can add music to the mix, which is a great motivator.

Analysis

This is a simple, fun, low-budget program. The programming room of the library was reserved in case of rain. You may also request guest athletes from your local sports teams (university or high school) to join in and speak about the importance of incorporating physical activity into everyday life.

Marketing Tips

Some jump rope groups or organizations may exist in your community. Check with area schools and then make sure to invite them. Also, let physical education teachers know about the program. Maybe they can offer extra credit for attendance to the program.

Resources

For music, the *Jump In* soundtrack is a must:

Various Artists. 2007. *Jump In*. Walt Disney Records. CD.

Collect good jump rope rhymes:

Boardman, Bob. 1993. *Red Hot Peppers: The Skookum Book of Jump Rope Games, Rhymes, and Fancy Footwork*. Seattle, WA: Sasquatch Books.
Cole, Joanna. 1989. *Anna Banana: 101 Jump Rope Rhymes*. New York: HarperCollins.

EXPLODapalooza

General Description

Teens blow up things in the name of science! Different scientific concepts are illustrated in fun, hands-on experiments where liquids tend to erupt.

Pop

Most people, teens and tweens included, would love to be able to make things explode without hurting themselves or others or ruining anything. The hosts on the television show *MythBusters* allow the viewers at home to live vicariously through their large-scale science experiments, verifying and disproving myths while blowing stuff up. From rumors to myths, from classic movie scenes to news stories, the validity of each of these elements of popular culture is tested by professionals using the basic elements of the scientific method in hands-on experiments.

Relate

Library programming usually heavily supports reading and writing. Science and math are professions that not many kids are drawn to and, besides having resources for science fair projects and books on how things work, offering science programs in your library might spike the interest of some teens who never realized they might want to be chemists or other kinds of scientists someday.

Instructors/Talent

Do not be intimidated by science. All of the explanations of how things work can be found in books or on the Internet. If you do not feel comfortable explaining what happens chemically when baking soda mixes with vinegar to make a foamy, bubbly mixture, create a poster with the explanation or ask a local science teacher to come in and give some context to the experiments.

Audience

Grades 4 through 8.

Planning and Supplies

Alka-Seltzer Rockets

- Film canisters
- Soda water
- Alka-Seltzer
- Bowls
- Safety glasses
- Tarp

Volcanic Eruptions

- Baking soda
- Vinegar
- Food coloring
- Longnecked bottles

Air Cannons

- Plastic soda bottles
- Saran Wrap or Ziploc baggies
- Rubber bands
- Things to blow across the room, like pieces of paper, Ping-Pong balls, balloons

Balloon Station

- Long skinny balloons
- Balloon pumps

Mentos Fountains

- 2-liter Diet Coke
- Mentos

Create

The room was divided into stations, with one staff member or teen volunteer manning each table. The stations included Alka-Seltzer Rockets, Volcanic Eruptions, Balloons, and Air Cannons. A staff member talked for about five minutes showing the group each experiment, explaining a little of the science and asking them to hypothesize what might happen. The details of the science of how the experiments work should be posted at each station. The teens cycled through the stations at their own speed and then came together at the end for the finale: Mentos Fountains.

Alka-Seltzer Rockets

This is a wet station. If you have room, you can do it outside. This project was done inside, with a "splash zone" around the table created with a painter's tarp and masking tape. Only small amounts of soda water escaped from the experiments, and there was no element of danger, but the "splash zone" and the wearing of the goggles enforced the importance of safety when performing science experiments.

Four teens at a time put on safety goggles. They put about one-fourth of a tablet of Alka-Seltzer in a film canister filled with soda water, put the top on the canister and shook it as much as they could, putting the canister into a plastic bowl to minimize the amount of water flying around. Once the pressure is too great, the top of the canister flies off, along with the water, creating a wet explosion!

Volcanic Eruptions

Everyone has made the volcano before, but the most fun about this experiment is the teens got to mix food coloring to create great colors for the lava, plus try different sizes of bottles to see what would happen.

Two longneck, cleaned-out glass soda bottles were placed in a plastic tub to minimize mess and help with cleanup. Each teen received a paper cup of vinegar. They added any color of food coloring to the vinegar. A tablespoon of baking soda was put at the bottom of the bottle. When the vinegar was poured into the bottle, colorful lava flowed everywhere. Try using different sizes of bottles to compare the outcomes or race the bottles.

Balloons

Balloons will explode without too much effort. Long skinny balloons and plastic balloon pumps were set out, with different instructions for making dogs, flowers, and other balloon animals. The goal was not to explode the balloons on purpose, but it definitely happened.

Air Cannons

Make your own air cannon and see how powerful it can be. Cut the bottom off a plastic soda bottle, and fold Saran Wrap or a plastic Ziploc baggie over the end. Seal the end with a rubber band. Aim the open end (the end where the cap would go) at a pile of small pieces of paper, and then tap the plastic wrap with your finger. Paper should fly. Try moving Ping-Pong balls or air-filled balloons.

Mentos Fountains

For the last experiment, everyone went outside and circled around 2-liter bottles of Diet Coke. A few volunteers were picked to drop Mentos candies into the bottles and jump out of the way as the Diet Coke spurted up into a fountain.

Food, Technology, and Other Mandatory Extras

At the end of the program, everyone has a little exploding treat. One year the group enjoyed sparkling punch with lemon-lime soda and sherbet. Another year the treat was Fizzies drink tablets which when dropped into a glass of water create an instant sugary soda beverage. Eating Pop Rocks would also be a fun addition to this program.

Analysis

Beware! This can be a messy program. Take this time to try out different science experiments like making slime or acid-base chemistry. Choose experiments where teens can explore and guess what the outcome may be. Then try it out! If the experiment does not work the way you thought it would, allow the teens to try to figure it out. No matter what happens, it is a learning experience for everyone.

Marketing Tips

This might be a great program to have at the beginning of science fair season. It will get the kids in the mood for thinking about the scientific method. The program could be done in conjunction with a presentation on the resources the library can offer for creating science fair experiments. Promote the program to local science teachers.

Resources

Check out these websites for more details on the experiments:

Instructables. 2010. "Shockwave Air Cannon." Accessed September 3. http://www .instructables.com/id/Shockwave-Air-Cannon/.
Steve Spangler Science. 2010. "Alka-Seltzer Rocket." Accessed September 3. http:// www.stevespanglerscience.com/experiment/00000068.
Steve Spangler Science. 2010. "Mentos Diet Coke Geyser." Accessed September 3. http://www.stevespanglerscience.com/experiment/00000109.

Eggcellent Engineering

General Description

Teens have a half hour to design a container around an egg, which is then dropped off a ladder. The goal is for the egg to not break.

Pop

This is a classic science exercise performed in physics classics for upper elementary kids all the way through college.

Relate

Science does not show up in library programming that often, and it is a really important topic to expose teens to while they are thinking about career paths or hobbies. Create a dynamic display to highlight your science experiment and physics books.

Instructors/Talent

No instructor is needed, but inviting a teacher to talk about the physics of dropping an egg off a building might be interesting.

Audience

Grades 4 through 8.

Planning and Supplies

- Painter's tarps
- Tall ladder
- Eggs
- Recycled materials like rubber bands, toothpicks, small strips of windbreak material, straws
- Mini marshmallows: Limit marshmallows used per teen since they could be packed around the egg to make a sugary pillow

Create

At the beginning of the program, teens found a list of rules on each table. A staff member explained the rules too to make sure no one had any questions about how the program was going to work. (See Figure 17.1 for example rules and regulations.) Then the building began. Teens were able to build their creations from recycled materials collected around the library and at a local reuse supply center.

At the end of the allotted time, a staff member stood on an eight-foot ladder in the middle of the programming room and dropped the eggs. The entire room was covered in painter's tarps. Try to do this outside if you can. Another staff member stood at the bottom of the ladder and checked to see if the eggs had cracked.

The eggs that do not crack move on to the second round. The egg container and egg were weighed on a mail scale which could measure very small incremental differences in weight. The three lightest creations, meaning the egg-drop designs that used the least amount of materials to protect the egg, won. Prizes for this program were Eggcellent Engineer crowns.

Food, Technology, and Other Mandatory Extras

No food or extras are needed.

Analysis

This is a super-fun program for everyone involved. The teens get to be really creative, trying to use materials that are as far from pillows as they can be, and create a container that will keep an egg safe during an eight-foot fall. The best part is when the eggs splat all over. It is a good idea to create a splash zone so that only the staff members end up "egged," not the participants. Also, think about the amount of time to allow for building. Younger tweens may get done really quickly, but older middle schoolers will want more time to design. One of the best designs at a program so far was when a teen created a hang glider for his egg using straws and strips of windbreaker material!

Figure 17.1. Eggcellent Engineering Rules and Regulations

Rules:
- Kids must work individually.
- Each kid will get one egg. Eggs are supplied by the library (Grade A, Large).
- Containers for the egg must be made out of the materials provided.
- Only use eight marshmallows in the egg container.
- The egg must be easily placed into and removed from the container.
- Individuals are eliminated once the egg breaks.
- Balloons are not allowed.

Preliminaries:
All eggs are dropped during the preliminary trials. Eggs that survive (do not crack) will move on to the finals.

Finals:
Each egg within its container will be weighed. The lightest survivor is the winner, with the second and third lightest as runners-up.

Marketing Tips

This is a project commonly done in school science classes or in Boy Scouts. To increase the number of participants, it might be possible to coordinate your program with these other groups to have a major egg-drop event. Talk to local physics departments at universities to show off some really creative designs.

Resources

You can make up your own rules for the competition, but here are some examples where the winners can be based on nonbreakage and weight or dimensions of the container around the egg:

Columbia College. 2007. "Columbia University Egg Drop." Accessed September 3. http://www.columbiasc.edu/academics/math/Egg_Drop_Rules.pdf.

MMU Egg Drop. http://www.angelfire.com/vt2/eggdrop/.

Montshire Museum of Science. 2010. "Guidelines for the Montshire Egg Drop." Accessed September 3. http://www.montshire.org/eggdrop/rules.html.

Cup Stack Attack

General Description

How fast can you stack? Tweens and teens competed for the fastest time to stack cups in different configurations. The fastest three stackers in the beginner bracket and the advanced bracket received prizes.

Pop

Sport stacking, or cup stacking, is a sports phenomenon that started in the late 1980s and has become a competitive sport played all over the world. The sport involves individuals or teams stacking specialized plastic cups into prescribed sequences as fast as they possibly can. Rules are created and enforced by the WSSA (World Sport Stacking Association). Many schools have purchased the cups to help with development of hand-eye coordination and focus, as well as self-confidence and teamwork.

Relate

Sports programs can sometimes be difficult to create when having to stay within the library parameters. There usually is not enough in or near the library for a flag football event, plus there are liability issues to think about. Sport stacking is a great program to promote sporty activities and competition, and will fit right in your programming room.

Instructors/Talent

There is no need for an instructor. You can easily become the expert for this program, but find out if there are any schools in your area that have stacking teams. Empower older teens to teach younger ones how to stack and give demonstrations to get everyone excited to stack as fast as they can. It takes some of the pressure off you to get your skills up to speed before the big tournament. Speak with physical education teachers or school psychologists that implement speed stacking in their programs to identify teens/tweens that may want to help with the program and/or show off their skills.

Audience

Grades 3 through 8. Younger kids can have a tough time remembering the specific stacking sequences and learning the exact rules. It is nice to have a few extra sets for kids to mess around with and get a feel playing with the cups.

Planning and Supplies

- Speed Stacks Stackpack—12 plastic cups, one StackMat, and competitive timer
- Stopwatches

Sets of cups can be sold individually or with the mat and timer. Two stackpacks and extra sets of cups were purchased for this program. The sets are usually $39.99 and the cups on their own are $17.99. Two people could be competing and timing themselves on the mat, while others practiced with the cups around the room and had friends time them on the stopwatches.

This program can be as fancy or as laid-back as you and your budget would like it to be. The library can purchase the special cups as supplies to keep at the library, ask teens to bring their own if the cups are being used widely in the area, or ask a local school if you can borrow their sets for an afternoon.

Create

Teens chose an area in the room to practice stacking and took turns using the two StackMat and timer stations. As they practiced, they signed up for the tournament in either the beginner bracket or the advanced bracket for the competitive stackers.

First the teens were led in practice drills and activities in preparation for the tournament. Cups are stacked in pyramids with a certain amount of cups and can be stacked in patterns. For instance, the three-stack and the six-stack are commom formations and can be stacked in patterns like 3-6-3, 6-6, or 3-3-3. For the first activity, a staff member picked a stack like 3-3-3 and asked all participants to try to stack as fast as they could. When they were finished, they had to complete another task, such as raising their hands, do three jumping-jacks, or jogging in place until everyone completed the stack. Other warm-up activities included stacking certain patterns with their eyes closed, stacking to music and stopping only when the music stopped, or working in teams of two where one person stacks the cups on one side of the room and crabwalks back, and the partner crabwalks up to downstack the pyramid in the quickest amount of time.

Once everyone is warmed up, the tournament begins. A certain pattern of stacks must be picked so that everyone competes at the same thing. For beginners, choose the 3-6-3 stack; for the advanced teens, choose the cycle. The cycle stack is a pattern of a 3-6-3 stack, a 6-6 stack, and a 1-10-1 stack, ending in a downstacked 3-6-3. All participants get three tries to stack the formation as fast as they can, and the fastest time is selected. The winners from each bracket were given $5 gift certificates to a local bookstore, but a cheaper prize could be a Cup Stack Attack crown or ribbon.

Food, Technology, and Other Mandatory Extras

If possible, show an exciting clip from YouTube video on a television or projector to get the group ready for some stacking while watching some talented teens performing this activity.

Analysis

This is a great rainy-day program and fun for promoting healthy living. If sport stacking is not popular in your community, you might want to purchase one or two sets of cups and see if it catches on. In a pinch, regular party cups can be used, but they do not have the same weight as the special cups.

Resources

Check out these websites for more information on cup stacking:

Speed Stacks. http://www.speedstacks.com/.
World Sports Stacking Association. http://www.thewssa.com.

Chapter 18

Programs: Summer Reading

Summer reading programs for teens are not as rare as they used to be, but they are certainly not ubiquitous either. That being said, it is fairly common to have a summer program that focuses almost exclusively on reading and rarely offers opportunities to participate with other formats. Focusing solely on reading is a mistake and a lost opportunity for the library.

On the other hand, summer reading programs exclusively designed for tweens are few and far between. The normal model followed is to develop a program for toddlers and preschoolers all the way up to grade five. The needs and interests of fifth graders are extremely different from preschoolers. Start thinking about the graphics on the children's summer reading program materials. Are they targeted toward preschoolers? Are tweens that are trying to pull away from being treated as a child going to be excited to join that summer reading program?

Teen Summer Reading Program

General Description

Summertime is a school-free time for teens and should be flexible and relaxed. Libraries long ago started offering other formats and services in addition to books in their collections, so it does not make sense that a summer program should focus solely on books. While reading books should be a part of any summer program, it should not be the sole focus. A summer program should embrace the various formats available in the library as well as the variety of venues and media teens use to read, learn, listen, and otherwise spend their recreational time during the summer.

Pop

Teens who are avid readers rarely need encouragement to read, but teens who are not readers almost always need incentives. The main challenge for a teen librarian in the summer is figuring out ways to get teens into the library and engaged in the programs and services that the library offers. Offering a summer program that not only allows but encourages teens to listen to music, watch DVDs, read magazines, or better yet something unexpected, like teach an adult to play a video game, will change the way a teen views the library. An open and fun summer program demonstrates to teens that the library is not just an extension of learning and school but is also a place to have fun and try new things.

Relate

This type of open program, which does not focus only on reading books, is the simplest and best way to connect with the reluctant readers, the nonreaders, and the apathetic readers in your community. Teens who consume any content other than books will be able to join and feel active in the library in a different way. Relating to the multiformat world that teens live in is key to providing them with up-to-the-minute services. This type of program can also be tweaked and added to every year to reflect the newest interest or gadget.

Instructors/Talent

No instructors are needed for this program.

Audience

Teens in grades 6 through 12, with a focus on flexibility and fun for the full variety of teens in the community. This means that bookworms and reluctant readers are both welcome and invited to participate in the program.

Planning and Supplies

When planning the details and rules of a program, you should base it on what your library and your staff can support and what it cannot. If you are in a smaller library and you, as the teen librarian, are probably going to be the only one handling things, you might be able to get away with a more complicated and involved program. If you are in a larger system or depend on many other staff members to help teens with the program, then simple is best. Let's focus on the basic idea and leave it to you to decide how much further you want to take it.

Create

The Ann Arbor District Library (AADL) calls its summer program the Teen Game, and each year it has a different theme based on the overarching theme collectively picked for the youth, teen, and adult reading programs. The visuals of the larger theme are adapted to suit the teen audience. For example, in 2008 the overarching theme was "Under Construction." For the teens, this simply meant that the Teen Game visual was an image of an orange construction cone: evocative but not youthful or cluttered. Another year, the larger theme was "Figure It Out," so the Teen Game had a close-up photo of the locally infamous "gum wall," which is appropriately gross and cool at the same time. Think about using pop culture references that teens can relate to, such as "I Love DL," a teen summer reading program theme used by the Darien Library, that plays off the well-known slogan, "I Love NY" (see Figure 18.1).

In order to finish the Teen Game, teens must complete a minimum of ten activities listed on the game card. The library does not dictate which activities the teens choose or how many times they choose to do a certain activity. The activities are divided up into categories: Read, Watch, Listen, and Do. Each choice counts toward one of the ten activities the teens must do to complete the game.

Figure 18.1. 2009 Teen Summer Reading Program at Darien (CT) Library

Teen Summer Reading 2009

Source: Courtesy of Darien Library.

Options you might use underneath the main headings:

- READ options: a book of poetry; a collection of short stories; two magazines cover to cover; a newspaper online for one hour; a classic; a biography; a book from the teen collection; an old favorite; or anything you want for one hour.
- WATCH options: a documentary; an anime film; a movie based on a book; a how-to video; YouTube for one hour; streaming video online for one hour.
- LISTEN options: to your MP3 player for one hour; to your mom and dad's favorite CD; a podcast or podcasts for one hour; to a book on CD.
- DO options: attend a library event; post to the library blog; teach an adult how to play a video game; read to a child or senior citizen; spend an entire day without electronics or television; encourage a friend or family member to sign up for the summer game; volunteer your time for an hour.

You get the idea! Every year the options are tweaked a little bit by adding whatever may be the newest website, format, or media teens are using.

Food, Technology, and Other Mandatory Extras

In the case of a summer program, the extras that are most needed are prizes. Whether you offer a large grand prize like an iPod or a generous gift certificate to a popular store, prizes are the easiest way to encourage reluctant library users to join your program. It is always fun to announce the prizes to an auditorium full of teens during a promotional school visit. A loud response of happiness is usually heard. What prizes you offer is dependent on your budget, whether you have a Friends of the Library group who will fund prizes or whether you are savvy enough to solicit prizes from not just local businesses but also corporations who have locations in your neighborhood. Soliciting prizes is rarely fun, but asking for corporate donations is usually a more straightforward process, not as fraught with the often-uncomfortable action of begging a cash-strapped local business owner for something. Most corporations have a person or a department on staff whose job it is to field such requests.

AADL also offers smaller incentives that are just as important. Every teen who completes the program gets to choose a free book to keep from an assortment chosen by librarians and funded by the Friends of the Library. The past couple of years we have also offered every teen who completes the program a special two-sided coupon. Side one, and the most popular choice by far, is the "$5 Off Overdue Fines" choice. Anyone who works with teens knows that accumulated fines or losing one item can prevent a teen from being able to check out books in the future. Any opportunity to reduce these fines is crucial. For teens who do not have overdue fines, the other side of the coupon offers "One Free Zoom Lends DVD Rental." This allows the teen to check out one of the newer DVDs we own, from our special "Zoom" collection that normally costs $1 for a week. You surely have things in your collection that you can give as rewards without any real up-front cost to the library.

Another extra element to add to your program is a mechanism to give avid readers additional opportunities to win prizes for their efforts. You will find that sometimes your most avid readers forgo a summer program because it is not challenging enough. You may also find that the parents of avid readers are more open to the nonreading options and less resistant (certainly when you explain the goal of attracting all teens and not just some teens) when they see an opportunity for their overachiever to overachieve. The separate incentive program is called Bibliomaniacs, wherein teens can fill out slips that equal additional entries into the grand prize drawing for every 300 pages they read. Staff will not have to expend much energy on this incentive, aside from providing the slips and storing them as they come in. This is a self-directed way for prodigious readers to get credit for the reading without making the other teens feel like they are doing less.

Analysis
You will find that an entire new base of teens will be engaged in your library during the summer. When this model was first proposed at the library, a coworker commented, "Well, this will be the first time I can get my son to sign up!" Bingo! This is entirely the point.

Marketing Tips
May and June are good times to get the word out about the summer reading program. Ask school librarians, English teachers, and principals to give short presentations at the schools to get teens excited about participating in the program.

Tween Summer Reading Program

Expertise on creating a summer reading program for tweens was provided by the Kalamazoo Public Library in Kalamazoo, MI.

General Description
Tweens, grades 5 through 7, participate in a summer reading program designed just for them at the Kalamazoo Public Library (KPL) in Kalamazoo, Michigan.

Pop
Tweens have become a defined group by the consumer market and the media, which cannot be overlooked by the library.

Relate

Tweens are a consistently forgotten group when the summer reading program is created. The graphics on the reading log are usually geared toward preschoolers, even though upper elementary children are very active participants in the reading program. Attract even more participants with a program dedicated to this age group, with their interests in mind, including age-appropriate graphics.

Instructors/Talent

No instructor is needed.

Audience

For the specific program detailed in this section, the summer reading program was created for grades 5 through 7. How do you define your tween population?

Planning and Supplies

Using the developmental attributes of tweens, the program was developed into a game to foster interaction, instead of a reading log where only the titles of books read would be listed. The goal of the game is to complete all four corner boxes on the game board (see Figure 18.2). When each box is filled in, the tween receives a prize and a certain number of raffle tickets. Any type of material goes: books, magazines, and more. Reading extra pages earns the participant bonuses and rewards those who love to read. The page bonus square in the center of the board allows the tween to roll a die to earn extra raffle tickets.

In many summer reading programs, the participant can only participate once due to the amount of prizes available. In the KPL Tween Summer Reading Game, tweens are encouraged to ask for another game board when they complete their first one. They may not receive more prizes, but they can accrue more raffle tickets. This encourages more reading in the summer. Additional raffle tickets can also be earned by attending tween programs at the library.

Create

Prizes include small things like a wristband, a pen, a T-shirt, or a book. The raffle prizes are bigger ticket items either purchased by the library or donated by local businesses. The summer is divided into three reading periods, ending July 1, August 1, and September 1. The program goes all summer, right up to when school starts. A drawing is held at the end of each reading period and then the raffle tickets are discarded, so it is in the best interest of the tween to read all summer to continue adding his or her name to the next drawings.

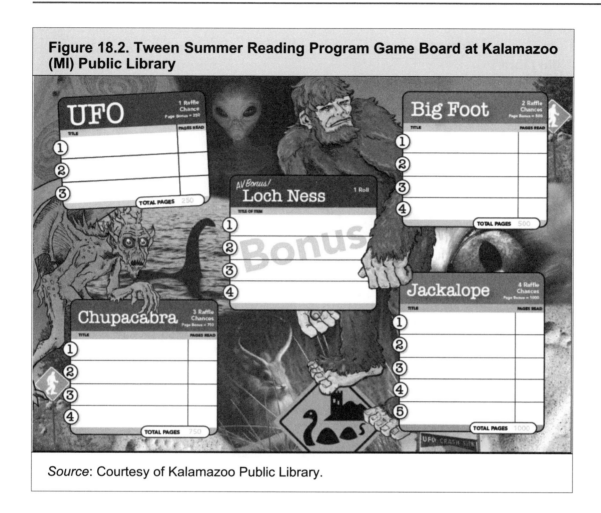

Figure 18.2. Tween Summer Reading Program Game Board at Kalamazoo (MI) Public Library

Source: Courtesy of Kalamazoo Public Library.

The graphics on the brochure and game piece are very important and should be age appropriate. In this case the theme, You Never Know!, integrated aliens, Big Foot, and other supernatural beings, an area of interest to tweens (see Figure 18.3).

Food, Technology, and Other Mandatory Extras

No food or technology is needed, but consider moving the program online. The participants are already technology savvy and can handle entering their completed books into a database. Another benefit of putting the summer reading program online is less money spent printing flyers, brochures, reading logs, and game boards. If you do not have a technology department that can build such a program, many companies have created templates that can be altered to fit what the library needs for such a summer reading program.

Analysis

Make this program as easy as possible. You probably already have a children's reading program, a teen program, and an adult program. Librarians tend to organize and cate-

Figure 18.3. 2007 Tween Summer Reading Program at Kalamazoo (MI) Public Library

Source: Courtesy of Kalamazoo Public Library.

gorize things to death, to the point of making their summer programs extremely confusing. Break down the programs in the best way possible so that they will not confuse staff and the participants.

Marketing Tips

Take the promotion of the summer reading program on the road. Promote the program at schools and summer camps, such as Boys & Girls Club, YMCA, and the city recreation camp. These large groups can participate but possibly in a modified version. Allow on-site sign-up for the program at city fairs, attracting participants that may never have entered the library. Create a YouTube video encouraging participation, and post it on your library website and Facebook. This video would be even better if tweens act in it, as well as create the video. Then it is tween approved!

Chapter 19

Programs: Technology

In just a few short years, technology has become a big part of young people's lives and has changed quite dramatically from days of the Rubik's Cube and the ghetto blaster. In some situations, kids are more tech-savvy than adults at downloading music to their iPods, creating videos for YouTube, and using Flash to create animations on their blogs or websites.

Though using technology can seem like a solo activity, you can create programs centered on these popular gadgets and turn a solo event to a social event. In some cases these programs can be a large expense to the organization because technology is expensive, but with a little creativity these programs can be put together for a low cost.

Social Networking Programs

General Description

Teens are given space in a computer lab or computer area to work on designing their own webpages, uploading pictures to their Facebook page, or editing videos to put on YouTube.

Pop

Using the Internet, people have discovered that they can find more than information; they can also find people. Websites like Classmates.com allow people to rekindle friendships with school friends they have not seen for many years. The concept of social networking websites has grown tenfold, allowing people to find long-lost girlfriends, boyfriends, and classmates; to link with business professionals on LinkedIn; to promote bands on MySpace; market businesses on Facebook; and catch up on the minute-to-minute activities of your friend of a friend on Twitter. Social networking sites bring complete strangers together to play games and are a major pastime for both teens and adults.

Relate

Connecting with friends on social networking websites like Facebook, MySpace, and YouTube is a common activity for teens. Teens go to the library to use the computers for homework but also to chat with friends, check out other people's photos and videos, and design their own virtual spaces. They want to comment to their friends about what they are looking at, and stand four around a computer. Most libraries do not have large enough computer areas to accommodate crowding around computers. If there is not a specific teen computing area, most of the time teens are sharing the space with adults, creating a war over quiet versus social space.

This program allows teens to have an environment where they can laugh and comment to one another while updating their Facebook pages. It also allows you, as the librarian, to talk a little about the security issues that come up with using social networking sites and point them in the right direction to find more information about using the technology, such as learning HTML to program graphics on a MySpace page.

Instructors/Talent

No instructor is needed for this program. It is helpful to have someone from IT on hand for complex computing questions, but you may already be well versed in all things computer. Make yourself a resource on using social technology for teens who may not otherwise have access to someone who can help them benefit the most from these popular websites. Especially in urban areas where the library is one of the only access points for teens to the Internet, there are not many opportunities for them to learn all of the technological ins and outs of the Internet, especially in situations where they do not have tech-savvy adults at home.

Audience

Grades 8 through 12. Policies from both Facebook and MySpace state that a child must be age 13 or older to register.

Planning and Supplies

- Computers (lab area or meeting room where laptops can be set up)
- Handouts with tips or suggestions for additions to MySpace/Facebook pages
- Video camera for making videos to upload to YouTube

Create

This program can range from being as simple as providing the space and time for teens to work on their MySpace/Facebook pages with the ability to socialize with their friends and keep the volume level a little higher than normal computer-area level. If you want to get a little more creative, teach teens how to write their own HTML code to design. Create a handout with fun tips on games and applications that can be added to a Facebook page. You can even lead the group in the creation of a short library promotional video and ask the teens to edit it to post on YouTube.

Creation of a YouTube video involves creating a script, for which the teens can brainstorm and help with the writing. Making a summer reading promotional video is a great project. Once the writing is completed and props have been prepared, have the teens film the video. Then show them how to edit the film on MovieMaker and upload it to YouTube. This project will probably take multiple times of meeting together. An alternative is to have a YouTube watching night, where you create a list of teen-appropriate videos to watch as a group. Each video is only about three to four minutes long, so choose 15 videos. It will likely be a fun time filled with laughter.

Food, Technology, and Other Mandatory Extras

Food is not needed, especially if your library does not allow food in the computer area.

Analysis

Make this program fun, not like school. Find passive ways to talk about privacy and security settings on these websites, such as telling anecdotes about the potential consequences of posting your phone number and address on your Facebook page. Some teens may not even realize what information they are putting out there for the world to see or even that the whole world can see it or that anything bad could happen to them.

Marketing Tips

Advertise this program to the teens that frequent your computer area. Word of mouth is the best approach to gaining interest in this program.

Resources

Check out these resources for ideas on how to put some more pizzazz into an online profile:

Facebook. 2010. "Facebook Application Directory." Accessed August 8. http://www.facebook.com/apps/directory.php.

Gunter, Sherry Kinkoph. 2010. *Sams Teach Yourself Facebook in 10 Minutes.* Indianapolis: Sams Publishing.

Hepner, Ryan. 2008. *MySpace for Dummies.* Hoboken, NJ: Wiley.

Windows Live. 2010. *Windows Live Movie Maker 2011.* [Software download for movies and slide shows from photos and videos.] Accessed August 8. http://explore.live.com/windows-live-movie-maker.

Library LEGO League

General Description

Library LEGO League is a program where kids design, build, and program a LEGO Mindstorms NXT robot that will complete in challenges against other teams. It was created as a joint effort by our Youth Department and Information Technology Department. Kids in grades four through eight form teams of two to four people, and spend one day, from 10 a.m. to 4 p.m., building their robots for the challenge held at the end of the program. The program was repeated for three days, with different challenges for each day, so that many kids could participate, as the supplies limited the participation in the program. Details on the winners of the challenge and discussion of challenge were posted on the L3 blog at http://www.aadl.org/l3. The challenges are designed for beginners, with minimal to no knowledge of using the equipment. The robot must complete a certain goal, such as going through a maze built of tables, circling around a garbage can and returning to a designated spot, or finding a ball using a motion sensor, picking it up, and taking it to a designated area.

Pop

Library LEGO League (L3) is a robotics program using a LEGO Mindstorms NXT robot, a commercial line from LEGO. This LEGO set combines electric motors, sensors, and LEGO bricks, as well as LEGO Technic pieces, which include gears, axles, and beams, to create motorized vehicles. Robots have received popular culture recognition through many avenues including the television show *BattleBots*. On that series, teams would design and build "combat robots" to be put in an arena to battle other robots, with the purpose of dominating or disabling other robots.

Relate

The L3 program was created to appeal to kids interested in robotics and computer programming, and to expose kids who may enjoy the concept of the television series *BattleBots* to the technical side of robots.

Instructors/Talent

This program can be run using staff within the library. Collaboration between youth/ teen staff and technology specialists works well, unless youth/teen staff are tech savvy. A nice touch to this program is to invite local robotics organizations to do demonstrations or help the kids with building and programming during the program. The program was loosely formatted after the FIRST LEGO League (FLL), a global program which utilizes theme-based challenges to excite kids in science and technology.

Audience

Grades 4 through 8. The program would obviously work for older teens as well. Third graders were invited the first year of the program, but the kids did not have the attention span to last the whole day. If you are defining your tween set as a little younger crowd, then it is advisable to shorten the program or have a different activity in the middle of the event to break up the day.

Planning and Supplies

- LEGO Mindstorms NXT set
- Computer
- Internet access
- Work space
- Prizes: For example, gift certificates can be given to the winning team of the competition.
- Participatory ribbons for all attendees of the program

Six LEGO Mindstorms NXT sets should be purchased so that six teams of four kids can build robots at the same time. Depending on the size of the expected audience and the computers available, fewer sets could be purchased, or more sessions could be planned so that more kids have a chance to use the sets. Another cost-saving alternative would be to borrow Mindstorm kits or ask kids to bring their kits from home. Currently, the LEGO Mindstorms NXT 2.0 set is out on the market for $279.99 each (see Figure 19.1).

Create

1. Each team has a workstation that includes a LEGO Mindstorms NXT set, a computer, and Internet access.
2. The challenge for the day, determined beforehand, is announced at the start of the session, so that no team has an advantage.
3. A quick tutorial is presented on the sensors and motors in the LEGO set and how to use the programming software.
4. Equipment is passed out to the teams, and they have until 3 p.m. to build and program a robot that will best complete the day's challenge. (See Figure 19.2 for rules.) Two to three staff members should stay in the room to help teams with any design or computer programming problems.
5. At 3 p.m., friends and family are invited to return and watch the robots compete in the challenge.

Figure 19.1. LEGO Mindstorms History

The LEGO MINDSTORMS NXT robotics toolkit comes with building instructions for 4 main models ranging in building complexity, going from the Quick Start model that you can assemble and program in 30 minutes, to the ultimate Humanoid—all models are designed for easy battery change.

6 building and programming challenges are included on the software CD, complete with step-by-step building instructions and programming guide for all models.

Shooterbot is a moving vehicle robot that can guard your room and will shoot balls at intruders!

Color Sorter is a robotic sorting machine that can sort different colored objects and dispense them as you please. It can easily be modified with a catapult mechanism that can precisely shoot the different colors where you like.

Alpha Rex is the ultimate robot. It is a humanoid robot, easy to assemble and with multiple functions; it walks and turns, dances, talks, can see and avoid obstacles, can grab and distinguish between different colored objects.

Robogator is the animal robot that moves like an alligator. It will protect its area and jump forward and snap at anything that comes too near. Watch out!

Source: http://mindstorms.lego.com/en-us/history/default.aspx.

6. When all teams have presented their robots, the fastest four teams at completing the challenge have 20 more minutes to fix up their robots. These teams have one more chance to show off their robots.

7. Prizes are given to the three teams to complete the challenge in the fastest time. Prizes are not mandatory for the program to be successful. The opportunity to build the robots and compete in the challenge can be reward enough. Knowing your audience and budget can help determine whether prizes are considered necessary.

Food, Technology, and Other Mandatory Extras

Lunch and snacks should be served because the program as presented is a full day long. Costs can be cut by asking kids to bring their own lunches.

Analysis

The Library LEGO League program is a marriage of technology, robotics, and physics, and fills the tween need for secure guidelines with room for creative expression. Each robot kit comes with specific instructions to make the basic robot. Each challenge is designed to be completed by the basic robot. If a team chooses to be more curious and cre-

---

Figure 19.2. Library LEGO League: The Rules

LEGO League Rules

1. No outside Lego is allowed. Robot must be built using only the Lego provided.
2. Teams may bring their own laptops, but programs can only be transferred to their robot from the teams' provided computer.
3. Teams may work elsewhere in the library, but Lego parts must remain in the multipurpose room.
4. Teams must be on time and should plan to stay through 4:00 p.m. This is not a walk-in event. Teams failing to appear by 10:30 a.m. on the day of the competition will be disqualified.

---

ative, they can experiment with the use of different sensors or design a completely new robot to complete the task more efficiently.

Marketing Tips

Let local science and physics teachers know about the event so they can encourage their students to attend. Look in your community for groups participating in engineering projects, such as children's science museums, that may be able to spread the word to interested parties. The video gaming community might enjoy this program as well.

Resources

Check out these books and websites on robotics, and specifically the NXT robot:

Ferrari, Mario, and Giulio Ferarri. 2002. *Building Robots with LEGO Mindstorms: The Ultimate Tool for Mindstorms Maniacs!* Burlington, MA: Syngress.

FIRST. 2010. "For Inspiration and Recognition of Science and Technology." Accessed August 8. http://www.usfirst.org/.

FLL. 2010. "FIRST LEGO League." Accessed August 8. http://www.firstLEGOleague.org/.

LEGO. 2010. "Mindstorms Official Web site." Accessed August 8. http://mindstorms.LEGO.com/en-us/Default.aspx.

Perdue, David J. 2008. *The Unofficial Lego Mindstorms NXT Inventor's Guide.* San Francisco: No Starch Press.

Perdue, David J. 2010. "The Unofficial LEGO Mindstorms NXT Inventor's Guide." Accessed August 8. http://nxtguide.davidjperdue.com/.

Technology Fashionistas

General Description

Crafts meet technology! Teens can jazz up their ear buds and flash drives, making them unique to their personalities and making accessories out of technology toys. They can also make bracelets that light up with LED (light-emitting diode) lights.

Pop

We live in a tech culture. While the Internet gave us anonymity, it also spurred on a great desire to carve out a unique space for ourselves on our websites, blogs, and Facebook pages so we could show the world who we are. This philosophy spilled over onto our tech toy culture, where teens and tweens own their own cell phones, iPods, laptops, and countless other toys, creating another avenue to proudly demonstrate individualism. We cover our laptops in designer stickers, coat our cell phone cases with jewels, and purchase iPods in many bright colors, all to show uniqueness in a technology-driven society.

Relate

This is a very involved program but worth it because physics is not often highlighted in youth and teen programming. Besides promoting your technical and crafty books, it might spur some interest in the physics and electrical books in your collection.

Instructors/Talent

Look into your staff and community to see if you can find someone who has experience working with LED lights. The books listed in the Resources section can teach you step by step how to build circuits, but if you do not feel comfortable building circuits with copper wire and batteries, try to find someone who is. Check with electrician or fashion programs at local community colleges for possible help with this program.

Audience

Grades 6 through 12. This is a very detail-oriented program, so it will appeal only to teens that can concentrate and not get frustrated easily. If the right decorative supplies are purchased, it is a great program for both girls and boys.

Planning and Supplies

Three activities were chosen: dressing up ear buds, accessorizing flash drives, and creating LED bracelets. If you are teaching yourself how to build the circuit for the bracelet, make sure you give yourself enough time for trial and error. Teens were asked to bring their own ear buds and flash drives, but the library could also provide them. They might be great giveaways for Teen Tech Week. Over-the-ear buds leave more room for adding decorations.

Ear Buds Activity

- Ear buds—over-the-ear or regular ear buds
- Craft felt
- Beads
- Glitter pens
- Thread
- Needles

Flash Drives Activity

- Flash drives
- Craft felt
- Army guys/action figures
- Ribbon
- Hot-glue gun, with glue sticks
- Scissors
- Permanent markers

LED Bracelets Activity

Most of the supplies for the bracelets were purchased at an electronics store. For information on specific types of batteries, LED lights, and the best materials to use for conductors, check out the books listed in the Resources section. The craft book *Fashioning Technology* has templates and instructions for the bracelet (see Figure 19.3).

Create

The supplies and decorations were laid out on the tables, along with example designs of ear buds and flash drives. The design of the LED bracelet was modified to be simpler than explained in the book because of my physics knowledge and sewing ability. The final product did not turn out as professional looking as the bracelet detailed in the book, so it is up to you how creative and high quality you want to be with the design. Instead of conductive wire, craft copper wire and electrical tape were used to connect the battery to the LED lights to create a circuit. The wire was scraped with a rough sponge to remove any oxidization on the copper and make it a better conductor of energy. A soldering iron would be a better, more permanent approach to connect the battery to the copper wire, instead of electrical tape, but the tool and solder may be tough to get your hands on. Black electrical tape was an easy and cheaper solution.

Figure 19.3. Technology Fashionista Program: Ear Buds, Flash Drive, LED Bracelet, and Lit-Up Figure

Food, Technology, and Other Mandatory Extras

The creations the teens can come up with are limitless. Make examples to give a starting point and to show some of the possibilities of mixing DIY crafts with technology. Be sure to create a display of the great technology craft books in the library collection to help the creative juices flow. Food is always appreciated, especially if it is an after-school event, but none is needed for this event to be a success.

Analysis

This can be a pricey program depending on the number of participants and if ear buds and flash drives are going to be given away. The cost for fabric, batteries, LED lights, copper wire, and decorations comes to around $100 for 40 participants.

Marketing Tips

This program was advertised during Teen Tech Week. It would be great to be publicized to any home economics classes, fashion clubs, or sewing groups. Because some boys aren't likely to attend a workshop that seems to be centered around crafts, you can play down the crafts aspect and put a technology slant on the flyer and blurb wordage; this is a good way to promote the program to computer and technology classes, which can often be male dominated.

Resources

Check out these books for templates and more techno-craft ideas:

Eng, Diana. 2007. *Fashion Geek: Clothing Accessories Tech*. Cincinnati, OH: North Light Books.

Lewis, Alison with Fang-Yu Lin. 2008. *Switch Craft: Battery-Powered Crafts to Make and Sew*. New York: Potter Craft.

Pakhchyan, Syuzi. 2008. *Fashioning Technology: A DIY Intro to Smart Crafting*. San Jose, CA: O'Reilly Media.

Library Makerspaces

The Library Makerspaces program was written and contributed by Steve Teeri of the Detroit Public Library.

General Description

Library makerspaces provides access for teens to design and fabrication technologies and the freedom to explore them. Through these interactions, teens can become more comfortable with concepts related to mathematics, engineering, and science. Of equal importance, the teens will feel a sense of accomplishment and an empowerment to create the world around them.

Teens today are technologically savvy. A library makerspace serves as a bridge to take their knowledge into the fields of design and manufacturing. By empowering teens with the ability to create and build their own objects and devices, a whole new world is opened to them. Instilling this Do-It-Yourself (DIY) attitude at a young age will pay dividends in the future of adults who are more knowledgeable and willing to explore.

Pop

The hackerspace or makerspace movement has caught on all over the world for people who are tired of paying to repair electronics and gadgets and have decided to create their own inventions incorporating technology and computers. The spaces are community labs where people can come together to share equipment and resources and create homemade technology (Saini, 2009). To showcase this ingenuity maker faires, which originated in San Francisco, are now taking place across the United States. These faires bring together makers from a wide variety of disciplines,and allow the public to see the innovation taking place within their communities. A trip to a maker faire, if feasible, would provide an excellent real-world demonstration of what can be accomplished through library makerspaces.

Relate

Work in a library makerspace is a collaborative process, allowing teens to learn together in mastering the technologies at their disposal. As cheap mass-produced goods have entered our markets, the concept of making your own things has dwindled. While it is easy to go to the store and buy something, you do not gain the same knowledge, enrichment, and satisfaction from making it yourself. Similarly, as the U.S. economy has evolved from a manufacturing-based economy to one based on service, fewer people in our society have the knowledge and ability to make things.

Instructors/Talent

Makerspaces have appeared throughout the United States and, indeed, throughout the world in recent years. These existing collectives offer a wealth of expertise into which libraries can tap, establishing their own makerspaces. Magazines such as *Make* offer articles on projects that can take place within libraries (*Make*, 2010). In addition, many websites offer current information on the maker movement at little or no cost. Library staff members and volunteers can be trained in the use of the equipment and technologies. As some of the maker equipment has the potential to cause physical damage if used improperly, it is imperative to have a disciplined and safe environment. Mitch Altman, inventor of the TV B Gone, is an expert in hosting a mobile soldering beginners' class (TV B Gone, 2010). Traveling around the United States and the world, Mitch is an evangelist for the maker spirit to young people.

Audience

Grades 8 through 12, with parental or guardian permission.

Planning and Supplies

1. Space where equipment will be set up (well ventilated, nonflammable)
2. Handouts with tips or suggestions on using equipment
3. Materials such as vinyl, plastic, wood, and metal that will be raw material for projects
4. Video camera for making videos to upload to a website, Twitter, YouTube, etc.

Create

Soldering irons are a good first step in learning the tools in a makerspace. Users can learn the basics of electricity while turning kits into useful electronic gadgets. A by-product of these programs will be teens gaining a greater familiarity with the multitude of electronics they come in contact with daily.

The Makerbot Cupcake CNC (Computer Numerical Controller) 3-D printer is another technology that would benefit a library makerspace. This printer allows users to design objects, from replacement machine parts to art sculptures, and transform them into real-life items made through the milling of plastic or other materials.

Shopbot offers a full-size CNC machine for creating life-sized objects, such as furniture. Once teens have mastered the art and science of creating small objects on the Cupcake CNC, they can then progress to larger and more complex projects.

Laser cutters, such as the Epilog Mini 24, allow precise cutting and engraving of materials. This ability makes them one of the most useful tools in a makerspace. High-tolerance parts engraving will allow teens to create things on level with professional goods in the market.

Vinyl cutters, such as the Roland CAMM-1 Servo GX-24, allow users to cut out detailed patterns, which can then be applied to clothing and objects. These devices allow users to express their artistic creativity on a computer and then receive a usable copy for application in the real world.

Food, Technology, and Other Mandatory Extras

Prizes and incentives can be offered in competitions to challenge young adults in building their skill sets as makers.

Analysis

Teens are smart, creative, and able people. Once the makerspace is assembled, give the teens required training and then let them explore the technology. Staff or volunteer experts should be made available to answer questions as the teens run across them. An environment fostering creativity and imagination should permeate the library makerspace.

Note that the term *makerspace* is interchangeable with *hackerspace*. The reason *makerspace* has been chosen for use in libraries is to avoid the unfortunate negative connotation the term *hacker* has become associated with over the years, and possible backlash from members of the community who do not understand its etymology.

Marketing Tips

Advertise this program to the teens that frequent your library locations. Word of mouth is the best approach to gaining interest in this program. Facebook, Twitter, and YouTube offer additional online avenues for marketing your library makerspace.

Resources

Check out these resources for more information on makerspaces:

A2 MechShop. http://www.a2mechshop.com.

Frauenfelder, Mark. 2010. *Made by Hand: Searching for Meaning in a Throwaway World*. New York: Portfolio Hardcover.

Hack Pittsburgh. http://www.hackpittsburgh.org.

I3 Detroit: Metro Detroit's Art & Technology Collective. http://www.i3detroit .com.

Make: Technology on Your Time. http://www.makezine.com.

Maker Faire. http://makerfaire.com.

Maker SHED: DIY Kits + Tools + Books + Fun. http://www.makershed.com.

Massachusetts Institute of Technology. 2010. "Mobile Fab Lab Hits the Road." Accessed October 25. http://web.mit.edu/spotlight/mobile-fablab.

Noise Bridge Makerspace. http://www.noisebridge.net.

Saini, Angela. 2009. "DIY Gadgetry." *BBC News*, June 19. Available: http://news .bbc.co.uk/2/hi/uk_news/magazine/8107803.stm.

The Hacktory. http://thehacktory.org.

TV B Gone. http://www.tvbgone.com.

Check out these supply websites:

Epilog Mini 24 Laser Cutter. http://www.epiloglaser.com.

MakerBot Store. 2010. "Cupcake CNC." Accessed October 25. http://store .makerbot.com/3d-printers/cupcake-cnc.html.

Roland CAMM-1 Servo GX-24 Vinyl Cutter. http://www.rolanddga.com.

Shopbot. http://www.shopbottools.com.

Filmmaking 101

Information on the Filmmaking 101 program was provided by Stewart Fritz, Kalamazoo Public Library.

General Description

Great filmmakers are not born, they're made. Filmmaking 101 teaches teens the basics of filmmaking, from drawing up storyboards and planning a shot list to operating a camera and digitally editing a short film masterpiece. Instructors brought cameras, tripods, and laptops with digital editing software, and teens and tweens brought their imaginations! No previous filmmaking experience necessary. Besides, as even the cheapest cell phones, laptops, and handheld gaming devices come standard with built-in video cameras these days, the number of tweens and teens who have never used a camera continues to shrink.

Pop

How many of your teen patrons come into the library and plop down in front of the computer, fire up YouTube, and spend the afternoon passively watching? Did you ever wonder if you could persuade them to actively create instead of just mindlessly consume? Now you can! Running a teen filmmaking program is not nearly as difficult as you might imagine, and the end results are well worth the effort.

Relate

If your library has a strong focus on reading, listening, and viewing for pleasure, especially with youth audiences, this is a great way to introduce them to your collection of DIY film books and materials. Also, budding filmmakers need inspiration and a well-stocked AV collection is a natural place for them to look.

If your city has a public access TV station or a college or university with film courses, it is definitely worth asking if they will partner with you to actually run the program. You get the expertise of a professional, and they get free exposure and the chance to do some outreach of their own. Plus, having someone else there to run the show gives you a chance to interact with your teen patrons in a new way. Library staff often get pulled in for supporting roles (with permission, of course) by teens shooting their magnum opus in the library.

Instructors/Talent

Obviously, pulling off a program like this requires at least a working knowledge of how to make movies. While a degree in film studies is not a prerequisite, at the very least if library staff members are going to run this program themselves they should know some filmmaking fundamentals. On the technical side, knowing how to set up and operate a variety of average consumer-grade video cameras is essential. If you cannot figure out how to turn it on or load a tape, you probably won't be able to teach someone else effectively.

Familiarity with editing software, even the free applications that come bundled with most computers, is also good to know. More important than just knowing hardware and software, however, are the fundamentals of good filmmaking: making a storyboard, planning a list of shots, and developing at least a bare-bones script so the director and actors are all on the same page before they begin shooting anything.

Audience

Any tween or teen with an interest in making their own movies should be able to handle this program. Chances are, they will catch on immediately and crank out a great film by the end of the program. Do not limit programs to camera geeks. A great film needs a script, and kids interested in comics can get involved with drawing up the storyboards as well.

Planning and Supplies

The one thing you absolutely cannot have too much of with this program is time. Even though the scripting and storyboarding phase of the film project can seem less exciting than breaking the camera out and filming away, it is an essential step in the process that can admittedly take a while. Shooting the footage for just a three-to-five-minute film can take at least an hour, and that's with no retakes. As much time as it takes to script and shoot the footage, plan to give your participants at least double that for editing and tweaking. If you can plan this program so that it takes place over two or even three days, it will be that much better. The final product will be well worth the time investment.

Aside from time, you will also need space to shoot scenes (if you don't want to let teens shoot in the stacks, that is), and you will need a meeting space to regroup and show rough footage. An ideal space is a computer lab or meeting room where videos can be played without disturbing other patrons; it's even better if the room is equipped with a projector or large monitor so everyone can see without having to crowd in.

Finally, and there is no way around it, you will need some equipment. This is filmmaking we're talking about here, and that means cameras. The good news is that you do not need to spend a bundle. You can get some fairly high-quality footage from digital video cameras that cost under $100 on the low end. You will also need a computer to edit the footage, but fortunately there is no need to spend money on editing software. Both Apple and Windows machines have free editing tools, and there are several open-source alternatives as well. The bad news is that you will need to take some time beforehand and learn how to use the software, but most of the packages are fairly easy to learn.

Create

The best part of the Filmmaking 101 program is that at the end of the day, your teens have something tangible they can take away with them and show off to the world. Beyond simply posting to YouTube or Facebook, the films the teens create can be the gateway into something even bigger. There are literally dozens of film festivals that promote works by young film directors, and local cable access stations are often willing to showcase student films. Teens interested in pursuing a film career can use the films they create in this program as part of their demo reels as well.

Food, Technology, and Other Mandatory Extras

Your teens will probably want to keep making films, and there are lots of resources available that can help put the polish on their productions. There are more books on low-budget filmmaking than you can possibly imagine, and tons of great DIY tips on the web for making movies on the cheap. Tons of tutorials can be found online, from how to make fake blood to making a camera crane out of PVC tubing. Instructables (http://www.instructables.com) and *Make* (http://www.makezine.com) are two great places to find all sorts of DIY tips and tricks. Other follow-up resources include the local cable access center (especially if they helped produce your program), community college, or high school film and video classes.

Analysis

When given direction and resources, the teens made highly creative films, way beyond what was imagined when this program was being put together. Hold a movie premiere night, complete with a red carpet and Hollywood stars on the floor, to show off the teens' finished products. Make the films available on the library website or teen space to highlight the fabulous works teens have done in your community.

Marketing Tips

Get the word out to schools, in particular any film or editing instructors, and also post advertisements at local movie theaters and places teens who pursue creative activities spend their time.

Resources

Check out these websites for DIY tips and tricks for creating films:

Instructables. http://www.instructables.com.
Make: Technology on Your Time. http://www.makezine.com.

Game On! Envisioning Your Own Video Game

The Game On! Envisioning Your Own Video Game program was written and contributed by Justin Hoenke of the Portland Public Library, Portland, Maine.

General Description

Have you ever had an idea for your own video game? In this workshop, teens will brainstorm, flesh out our ideas, create storyboards, and draft up a proposal to make their own video game.

Pop

Video games are now a staple in households with teens and tweens. Many families have more than one gaming console connected to their televisions. Young people are usually the consumers of video games instead of the creators. When given the opportunity to create their own video game, those passionate about the digital art form are sure to generate a unique creation.

Relate

When the Portland Public Library started lending out video games, the staff noticed new types of patrons coming to the library. The first was the avid video game player who before did not have much of a reason to come to the library. The other was the avid reader and casual video game fan that was mostly interested in video games for their story and characters. To best serve these two populations, the library partnered with a local writing organization in Portland, Maine, called The Telling Room (http://tellingroom.org), and together developed this program with the goal of showing just how important excellent writing, story, and characters are to successful video games.

Instructors/Talent

This program works best when done in collaboration with another organization, be it either a writing organization or a group related to video games.

Audience

The program was opened up to teens ages 12 to 18. A total of 12 teens signed up, all of whom were teenage boys between the ages of 12 and 16.

Planning and Supplies

- Laptop
- Projector
- Easel and paper
- Markers, crayons, and pens
- Cameras

Create

Scratch is a simple programming language that teens can use to actually build their ideas (http://scratch.mit.edu/). While they may not be able to create the exact game they are envisioning, using this program will show them how essential programming and planning is to game development. The program was broken up into six sessions, each lasting one hour, leading the participants step by step through the video game creation process.

Session One

- Ice breaker: Name, school, favorite video game character and why
- Introduction about the workshop
- Brainstorm characters lists: Name, place, etc.
- Share with the group
- Slide presentation: Classic video game characters
- 20 questions on your character (include special powers)
- Slides on supporting characters
- Create more characters

Session Two: World and Objective

- Discuss what a hero is and describe different types.
- Go out into the community with cameras and find images.
- Slide presentation: Different video game objectives and settings.

Session Three: Genre

- Brainstorm different genres of video games.
- Group work: Have teens combine their ideas to make one solid game; emphasize communication and collaboration as a way to accomplish goals.

Session Four: Continue Group Work

- Merging worlds, characters, objectives: Teens begin to collaborate on building their games.
- Storyboarding begins.

Session Five: Storyboarding

- Teens establish a beginning, middle, and end to their video game.

Session Six: Presentations and Ideas

- Teens pitch their ideas to staff as if they are looking to sell their title to a video game company.

Food, Technology, and Other Mandatory Extras

No other technology is needed unless demonstrations were held with various video games. If that is the case, have a Nintendo Wii or Xbox 360 and favorite games. Food is also a fun addition but not mandatory.

Analysis

This program is a surefire way to invite and engage teen boys in the library.

Marketing Tips

Marketing was handled mostly in house by the Portland Public Library and The Telling Room. The program was promoted through various local outlets (schools, workshops, homeschooling, and unschooling families) as well as media outlets. The program was also heavily advertised on the TV information boards at the Portland Public Library.

Resources

Check out these game development tools:

Game Star Mechanic. http://gamestarmechanic.com/.
Learn Scratch. http://learnscratch.org/.
Scratch: Imagine. Program. Share. http://scratch.mit.edu/.
YoYo Games. http://www.yoyogames.com/make.

Chapter 20

"Where Do We Go from Here?": Conclusion

Show your teen and tween communities that the library is in tune with pop culture. The original concept of a library was a quiet place to hold books, meant for studying and contemplation. However, libraries have had to change with the times and transform into something that can better serve the current communities. Libraries are now community centers, places for people to meet up and take part in common activities such as story time, lectures, and hands-on events. They are still a place for research and learning, but libraries have taken an active role in offering free opportunities for community members to discover new things through programs and events. For teens and tweens to be interested and take part in these experiences, the programs and services must be relevant. That is where popular culture plays an important part.

It is hoped that after reading this book, readers feel comfortable exploring the various aspects of popular culture and integrating it into their programming style. This integration takes something that teens and tweens are already interested in and shows them that the library can create opportunities for them to share in their passion or obsession. It also creates opportunities for teens and tweens to experience different aspects of pop culture that they might not have otherwise been exposed to because of where they live. If the library is about establishing access to information for all and creating recreational opportunities, then combining those two mission statements together will naturally generate popular culture–driven programs and services for teens and tweens.

Decisions made at the library to create spaces for teens and tweens, purchase teen-centered materials, and create appropriately themed events and programs should be driven by teen and tween interest. Ask them what they want to see and do instead of deciding for them. You will create lifelong users of the library who feel invested in what goes on there, further building community around the library.

Index

About the Authors

Erin Helmrich is a teen services librarian at the Ann Arbor District Library in Ann Arbor, Michigan. She has worked as a youth and teen librarian since 1996. She has been writing the popular Voice of Youth Advocates (VOYA) "Teen Pop-Culture Quizzes" since 1999. Erin is the chair of the 2012 Young Adult Library Services Association (YALSA) Printz Award Committee and served on the YALSA Board of Directors from 2006 to 2009. Erin is the recipient of two Michigan Library Association awards: she won the Loleta D. Fyan award (for imaginative and unique service) in 2002 and the Frances H. Pletz award (excellence in teen services) in 2008, both for providing excellent teen services. She has presented on teen collection development, programming and marketing for teens, video gaming, and teen popular culture around the country. Erin received her master's in library science at Wayne State University in Detroit, Michigan, and has an undergraduate degree in film studies. Originally from San Francisco, Erin lives to travel and try new things. A lover of animals, plants, and the outdoors, she is also a media junkie who loves news and gossip more than she should. Erin lives in Ann Arbor and is loving that the recent film incentives offered by the state of Michigan means regular celeb sightings are possible! Erin and Elizabeth became friends over a shared love of cats and pop culture, and they used to share a cubicle wall at the Ann Arbor District Library in Michigan.

Elizabeth Schneider is a youth services librarian at the Monrovia Public Library in Monrovia, California. She has been a librarian since 2006, focusing on services to teens and tweens. Elizabeth has also worked closely on video gaming events and special projects such as Library Lego League and podcasting at the Ann Arbor District Library in Ann Arbor, Michigan. She has been very active at the state level, presenting innovative tween programming at the Michigan Library Association Summer Reading Workshop in 2006 and serving on the 2008 Youth/Teen Spring Institute Conference planning committee. Elizabeth is currently serving on the Popular Paperbacks for Young Adults committee for YALSA. She received her master's in information at the University of

Michigan, Ann Arbor, and her bachelor's of science in chemistry from Washington State University. Elizabeth is a dedicated cat lover, constantly saving kittens from the wild, and enjoys hiking, college football, and looking out for movie star sightings in Los Angeles.